# principles *of*
# **services** marketing

# principles *of* services marketing

**THIRD EDITION**

A D R I A N   P A L M E R

Professor of Services Marketing at Gloucestershire Business School, Cheltenham, UK

**McGraw-Hill Companies**

London · New York · Burr Ridge IL · St Louis · San Francisco · Auckland · Bogotá · Caracas · Lisbon · Madrid
Mexico · Milan · Montreal · New Delhi · Panama · Paris · San Juan · Singapore · Sydney · Tokyo · Toronto

Published by

**McGraw-Hill Publishing Company**

Shoppenhangers Road, Maidenhead, Berkshire SL6 2QL, England
Telephone 01628 502500
Facsimile 01628 770224

**British Library Cataloguing in Publication Data**
A catalogue record for this book is available from the British Library

**Library of Congress Cataloging-in-Publication-Data**
The LOC data for this book has been applied for and may be obtained from
the Library of Congress, Washington, DC.

Further information on this and other McGraw-Hill titles is to be found at
http://www.mcgraw-hill.co.uk

*McGraw-Hill*

A Division of The McGraw-Hill Companies

| | |
|---|---|
| Publisher | Andy Goss |
| Sponsoring Editor | Tim Page |
| Senior Marketing Manager | Jackie Harbor |
| Production Editorial Manager | Penny Grose |

First Edition      1994
Second Edition    1998

ISBN 0 07 709748 3

Cover and text design: Barker/Hilsdon, Dorset, DT7 3TT.
Typeset by Steven Gardiner Ltd
Printed in Great Britain by Bell and Bain Ltd., Glasgow

# Brief contents

# Detailed contents

# Preface

Today, more people in the Western world earn a living from producing services than making manufactured goods. For consumers, increasing wealth has resulted in opportunities to consume services which were previously unattainable, or had to be produced within the household unit. For businesses, services are not a luxury, but have become essential inputs as firms concentrate on their core business activities and buy in specialist services from outside.

The growth of the services sector has presented many apparent paradoxes. Despite the efforts of service organizations to improve their quality standards, dissatisfaction has been seen to grow in many sectors, simply because firms haven't kept up with consumers' rising expectations. There is the paradox of many services companies developing relationship marketing programmes, but which result in relationships that are perceived by customers as being inferior to those which went before. The reason for such apparent paradoxes is that service benefits can only be defined in consumers' minds. With few tangible cues to go on, the same service can be perceived quite differently by two different consumers.

This book develops frameworks for understanding services and the effective marketing of them. The characteristics of intangibility, inseparability, perishability and variability have profound implications for the way that marketing managers in the services sector develop their service offer, promote it and then deliver it. Traditional marketing mix frameworks that apply to manufactured goods do not work well for services. Services are about processes as much as outcomes and these processes often involve considerable interaction between consumers and operations people. It follows therefore that marketing cannot be seen as an isolated function within an organization. Successful service companies make sure that their front-line people can competently deliver the promises which marketing people make to customers. Services marketing cannot be separated from services management.

This book begins by trying to define services and assessing the impacts of core service characteristics on marketing activities. In some aspects of marketing, for example pricing and promotion, the general principles of marketing can be adapted to meet the needs of services. In other aspects, new principles are called for. For this reason, a chapter is given to studying the service encounter where consumers become involved in the service production process. Another chapter is devoted to studying the interface between human resource management and marketing, something which is vital for the success of people-based services. Other themes which are emphasized in this book are the importance of information management and the development of relationship marketing policies. A chapter is devoted to the problems and opportunities open to firms expanding overseas in increasingly competitive global markets for services.

To illustrate the general principles of services marketing, each chapter contains contemporary examples of good practice drawn from successful services organizations around the world, and each concludes with a case study. The division of the material in this book into chapters is to some extent arbitrary and successful marketing must recognize the interrelatedness of all of the subjects covered. For this reason, the book concludes with an integrative case study. Each chapter also concludes with a summary of key linkages to other chapters. Suggestions are also made for further reading and useful websites.

## New to this edition

Coverage of the internet and e-marketing has been expanded and integrated throughout the text to highlight its growing importance to services marketing. The number of diagrams and illustrative examples have been increased to highlight the practical application of the key concepts in each chapter. To help bring together some of these key concepts, a new comprehensive integrated case study has been added to the end of the text. Finally, a new colour text has been added to make this text more visually appealing.

To assist you in working through this text, we have developed a number of distinctive study and design features. To familiarize yourself with these features, please turn to the Guided Tour on pages xix–xx.

## On-line resources

For this new edition we have provided an expanded and improved range of on-line resources to support lecturers in their teaching of Services Marketing, and students in their study. Please visit the text's website at www.mcgraw-hill.co.uk/palmer to gain access to these resources.

A selection of journal articles published by the author can be found at:
www.apalmer.com

Adrian Palmer
Gloucestershire Business School
Cheltenham, UK
e-mail: mail@apalmer.com

# Acknowledgements

Countless colleagues, reviewers and organizations, too numerous to mention here, helped to bring this book to fruition and their assistance is gratefully acknowledged. Many authors and organizations kindly granted permission to reproduce copyright material and this is specifically acknowledged throughout the text.

Tony Conway of the University of Salford contributed material for the chapters on the Service Offer and Promoting Services.

The following reviewers took the time and effort to take part in market research for this text and they have added enormously its development:

Alan Wilson – University of Strathclyde
Dr D. Pujari – University of Bradford
Deborah Rose – University of Derby
Sarah Dougan – University of Paisley
Jackie Clarke – Oxford Brookes University

# Guided tour

**Learning objectives** are clearly stated on the opening page of each chapter

**Figures** are rendered in colour to help you visualize and understand the key concepts

**Key information** is highlighted and indicated by a marginal icon for easy reference

---

1

## What is services marketing?

### Learning objectives

The services sector has come to dominate Western economies, and this chapter reviews their impact on national economies. But what do we mean by services? Most products we buy are made up of a combination of tangible goods and intangible services. This chapter explores the features of intangibility, perishability, inseparability and variability which distinguish services from manufactured goods. These features will be a recurring feature of this book and this chapter provides a foundation for further analysis in subsequent chapters.

Is the marketing of services different to the marketing of goods? This chapter reviews the argument that the marketing of services is just a special case of general marketing theory and the opposite view that services are so different from goods that new theories and frameworks for services marketing are required. Special requirements of not-for-profit marketing are considered.

1

---

**Figure 5.8**
The customer loyalty ladder (adapted from Christoper, M., A. Payne and M. Ballantyne, *Relationship Marketing*, Butterworth-Heinemann, 1991)

markets, some segments are likely to purchase repetitively out of inertia or lack of awareness of the alternatives available. The loyalty of customers who are influenced by such inertia is likely to be very different to that of a customer who strongly advocates a product and feels emotionally attached to it. Becoming an advocate of a company is the peak of a 'ladder of loyalty' (Figure 5.8).

Dick and Basu (1994) developed the notion of relative attitude as a theoretical grounding to the loyalty construct. Relative attitude refers to 'a favourable attitude that is high compared to potential alternatives' (Dick and Basu, 1994, p. 100). They suggest that loyalty is evidenced both by a more favourable attitude towards a brand (compared to other alternatives) and repeat buying behaviour. By their analysis, low relative attitude with low repeat purchase indicates an absence of loyalty, while low relative attitude with high repeat purchase indicates 'spurious' loyalty. Satisfaction with a service provider is seen as an antecedent of relative attitude because without satisfaction consumers will not hold a favourable attitude towards the service provider, compared to other alternatives available.

Just because customers repeatedly come back to a company does not necessarily mean that they are loyal to that company. This point was made, tongue-in-cheek, during the continuing war of words between British Airways and Virgin Atlantic Airways. The latter had objected to BA's use of the advertising slogan 'The world's favourite airline'. Statistically, it was true that more passengers travelled internationally with British Airways than with any other airline, but surveys of airline users has consistently put Virgin ahead of BA in terms of perceived quality of service. Virgin's Richard Branson claimed that on BA's logic, the M25, London's notorious orbital

---

### Relationship marketing and customer loyalty • 127

motorway, could be described as the world's favourite motorway. Despite coming back to the motorway day after day, few motorists could claim to be loyal to it – they simply have no other choice.

The spat between BA and Virgin serves to underline the point that loyalty is about more than repetitious buying. True loyalty involves customers becoming an enthusiastic advocate of a company.

Many loyalty schemes can be seen as classical sales promotion activities in that they offer a short-term incentive to disloyal brand switchers. It has been noted that much sales promotion activity is very short term in effect and can actually undermine the long-term task of developing a strong brand (O'Brien and Jones, 1995). There is evidence to suggest that sales promotion activity, by encouraging brand switching, can bring about a short-term increase in sales for a company. In the case of manufactured goods companies, this may simply bring forward consumers' purchases, resulting in a subsequent fall as stockpiles are used up. In the case of services, the problem of carrying forward stockpiles does not exist, but disloyal brand switchers who were attracted by one company's offer may be just as easily attracted away by another competitor's incentive.

A medium-term attempt to create loyalty from customers is sometimes made through the formation of structural bonds whereby buyers are tied to a seller. Structural bonds have been defined by Turnbull and Wilson (1989) in terms of investments that cannot be retrieved when a relationship ends, or when it is difficult to end the relationship due to the complexity and cost of changing relational partners. A structural bond between buyer and seller has the effect of tying one to the other, through the creation of barriers to exit, although such ties may be asymmetric. One way in which buyers can become tied to sellers is by designing services in such a way that transferring to another supplier involves significant switching costs (Jackson, 1985). Within the commercial banking sector, it has been noted that one means by which banks increase their retention rate is to increase switching costs by such means as long-term mortgages with penalties for early closure (Perrien, Filiatrault and Ricard, 1992). Airlines' frequent flyer programmes have a similar effect in seeking to make the cost of competitor airlines appear more expensive by virtue of the opportunity cost of forgoing loyalty rewards.

Where the process of tying-in is achieved through a process of mutually rewarding co-operation, mutual dependence and shared risk, the relationship is likely to show greater stability and endurance (Han, Wilson and Dant, 1993).

An important aim of relationship marketing is to encourage existing customers to spend a larger share of their total expenditure with the company. The mobile phone company One-2-One had large numbers of customers using their phones only during the low-price evening period and left them switched off during the day. How could it encourage its customers to switch on all day, thereby increasing potential use of its service and extending its relationship with them? The company developed

**Tables** are rendered in colour and highlight key statistical data

**Case studies** are clearly picked out at the end of each chapter

**Short questions** encourage you to review and discuss your understanding of the main topics

**Key terms** listed with page reference

The **Chapter summary** briefly reviews the main topics covered in each chapter

Useful **websites**

Suggestions for **further reading**

**Table 2.1** Standard industrial classifications used for the tourism sector

| SIC | Description |
| --- | --- |
| 661 | Restaurants, cafés, etc. |
| 6620 | Public houses and bars |
| 6630 | Night clubs and licensed clubs |
| 6650 | Hotels |
| 6670 | Other tourist or short-stay accommodation |
| 7100 | Railways |
| 7210 | Urban railways, buses, etc. |
| 7400 | Sea transport |
| 7500 | Air transport |
| 7700 | Travel agents |
| 8150 | Credit card companies |
| 8490 | Car hire firms |
| 9690 | Tourist offices, etc. |
| 9770 | Libraries, museums, etc. |
| 9791 | Sport and other recreational services |

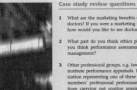

**Case Study**

### New line in marketing mobile phones

One of the oldest principles of marketing is that sellers may sell features, but buyers essentially buy benefits. This is a distinction sometimes lost on technology-led organizations, and the service sector is no exception. Recent experience of the UK's largest telecommunications company, Vodafone Airtouch, illustrates how crucial it is to see service offers in terms of the benefits they bring to customers.

By 1999, Vodafone had become the UK's largest mobile phone operator, with almost eight million customers, including 4.2 million 'Pay as you Talk' customers. It had opened the UK's first cellular network in January 1985 and had been the market leader since 1986. Vodafone's networks in the UK – analogue and digital – between them carried over 100 million calls each week. Such was the rate of growth that it took Vodafone more than 13 years to connect its first three million subscribers but only 12 months to connect the next three million. Vodafone had the largest share of the UK cellular market (33%) and had more international roaming agreements with 220 networks in 104 countries – more than any other UK mobile operator.

Extensive research had found high levels of confusion among purchasers of mobile phones, who faced a seemingly infinite permutation of features and prices. With four main networks to choose from, dozens of tariffs and hundreds of handsets, it is easy to see why buyers sought means of simplifying their choice process. Throughout the 1990s, Vodafone focused on high coverage rates, extensive roaming facilities and call reliability, among other things.

Vodafone was aware that although it was recognized as an extremely strong supplier in the market for corporate buyers, it was not so strong in the market for personal customers. Research indicated that personal buyers bought Vodafone for essentially rational reasons rather than having any emotional attachment to the brand. The success of the competing Orange network, which had developed a very strong brand image was a lesson to Vodafone that a significant proportion of personal buyers did not understand many of the product features on offer, but instead identified with a brand whose values they could share. Vodafone recognized that it needed to be perceived as contributing to a consumer's lifestyle. Given the increasing complexity of product features, positioning on technical features alone was likely to make life even more confusing for personal customers. An alternative approach was needed which focused on image and lifestyle benefits.

The company hired Identica – the consultancy that originally created the One 2 One brand – to revamp its brand communications and advertising strategy in an effort to make Vodafone more appealing to personal customers. Identica created a new 'visual language' for the Vodafone brand and the company embarked on the biggest TV, press, poster and radio advertising campaign in its 15-year history. Employing a completely new style, the advertising centred around the theme: 'You are now truly mobile. Let the world come to you' and featured a new end-line – 'Vodafone YOU ARE HERE'. The campaign demonstrated how Vodafone's products and services were designed to make life easier for its customers.

The campaign, created by BMP DDB, was worth £20 million over the first two months alone and ran through 2000. In an attempt to bring meaning to the Vodafone brand and what it represented, a series of advertisements showed how Vodafone let the world come to its customers, enabling them to be truly mobile. This portrayed how Vodafone always pioneered to make things possible for its customers in a wire-free world.

In press and poster executions, Vodafone used arrows photographed in various real-life situations to depict its flagship services, e.g. a weather vane was used to illustrate the Vodafone Interactive weather service, showing how weather information could be brought to customers through their mobile. Each advertisement again had the 'Vodafone YOU ARE HERE' end-line. The arrows indicated the directional approach of Vodafone, letting the world come to the customer. Other executions illustrated cinema listing information, sports updates, share price information, international roaming and the Vodafone Personal Roadwatch 1800 service.

The change in emphasis by Vodaphone seemed to be timely. The mobile phone industry was facing a new wave of confusing product features hitting consumers, with the development of Wireless Access Protocol (WAP) phones and the newer 'Third generation' phones due to be launched in 2001. It seemed inevitable that all of the competing networks would be offering confusing new permutations of features with their services, so Vodafone calculated that, given similar levels of reliability and sophistication by all networks, a favourable image and lifestyle association would be an important source of competitive advantage. Having developed a good image with existing technology, there would be a strong probability that consumers would migrate with the brand to the new technology when it arrived.

(Adapted from 'Vodafone Image Shift', Marketing, 4th May, 2000 and Vodafone Home Page, http ://www.vodafone.co.uk ##??)

---

### Case study review questions

1 What are the marketing benefits of attempting to measure the performance of doctors? If you were a marketing manager for an organization funding doctors, how would you like to see doctors appraised?

2 What part do you think ethics play in determining doctors' performance? Do you think performance assessment is really within the domain of marketing management?

3 Other professional groups, e.g. lawyers, engineers and architects, should perhaps institute performance appraisals. If you were a marketing manager of an organization representing one of these professional groups, how would you evaluate members' professional performance? What marketing benefits would you see from carrying out routine appraisals? What resistance would you expect to encounter in implementing an appraisal system?

### Chapter summary and linkages to other chapters

Human resource management is not something which should be considered as separate form marketing management. For services which involve a high level of contact between employees and customers, high levels of service quality may only be achieved with appropriate human resource management. There has been much debate about the nature of internal marketing and its relationship to human resource management theories. Control and empowerment are two important issues which have a long history of debate within the HRM literature.

The close relationship between this chapter and **Chapter 3** on the service encounter and **Chapter 8** on service quality should be evident. Issues of human resource management are central to many organizations' attempts to develop relationship marketing strategies (**Chapter 5**). Without appropriately trained staff, relationships can degenerate to little more than data stored on a computer. There is an important link between this chapter and **Chapter 14** on marketing management. At a strategic level, services organizations cannot afford to develop marketing plans in isolation from HRM plans, and much recent interest has gone into developing business processes and structures in a way that avoids these internal functional barriers.

www. linkages/URLs

**Key terms**

### Chapter review questions

1 What are the principal ways in which the management of personnel is likely to be different in a service organization, as compared with a manufacturer?
2 Discuss the ways in which a fast-food restaurant can increase the level of participation among its staff.
3 Using an industry with which you are familiar, identify methods by which the effects of variability of the personnel inputs can be minimized in order to produce a consistent standard of output.
4 What is the link between personnel and service quality?
5 What are the shortcomings of traditional personnel management for the effective marketing of services?
6 Using examples, show how human resource management policies can help to overcome the problems associated with peaked patterns of demand.

### Selected further reading

*This chapter has discussed very briefly some of the basic principles of human resource management as they apply to service organizations. For a fuller discussion of these principles, the following text is recommended:*

Beardwell, I. and L. Holden (1997) 'Human Resource Management: A Contemporary Perspective', 2nd edition, 1997, Pitman, London (new edition ■■)

*The following references provide a further insight into the role of internal marketing:*

Varey, R. J. and B. R. Lewis (1999) 'A Broadened Conception of Internal Marketing', European Journal of Marketing, Vol. 33, No. 9–10, pp ■■
Rafiq, M. and P. K. Ahmed (1993) 'The Scope of Internal Marketing: Defining the Boundary between Marketing and Human Resource Management', Journal of Marketing management, Vol. 9, No. 3, pp 219–32
Rafiq, M. and P. K. Ahmed (1998) 'A Customer-oriented Framework for Empowering Service Employees', Journal of services marketing, Vol. 12, No. 5, pp ■■
Forman, S. K. and A. H. Money (1995) 'Internal Marketing: Concepts, measurement and application', Journal of Marketing Management, Vol. 11, No. 8, pp 755–68

# What is services marketing?

**Learning objectives**

The services sector has come to dominate Western economies, and this chapter reviews their impact on national economies. But what do we mean by services? Most products we buy are made up of a combination of tangible goods and intangible services. This chapter explores the features of intangibility, perishability, inseparability and variability which distinguish services from manufactured goods. These features will be a recurring feature of this book and this chapter provides a foundation for further analysis in subsequent chapters.

Is the marketing of services different to the marketing of goods? This chapter reviews the argument that the marketing of services is just a special case of general marketing theory and the opposite view that services are so different from goods that new theories and frameworks for services marketing are required. Special requirements of not-for-profit marketing are considered.

## 1.1 Introduction

Citizens of the Western world are living in increasingly service-based economies. Services are no longer a minor or superficial part of economies, but go to the heart of value creation within the economy. Of course, the service sector is nothing new, as evidenced by biblical references to innkeepers and money lenders among others. But today most products that we buy include some element of service in them. We can readily identify activities such as accountancy, banking and hair-dressing as being service-based. In addition to these, a wide range of goods rely on service-based activities to give them a competitive advantage. A car buyer now buys a comprehensive bundle of service benefits, in addition to the tangible components of the car, as the case study at the end of this chapter illustrates. Even many apparently 'pure' goods such as television sets and washing machines usually come with service offers based on delivery, financing, insurance and maintenance benefits.

Although there has been a big growth in interest in the service sector in recent years, the academic literature has not always recognized their value. Early economists paid little attention to services, considering them to be totally unproductive, adding nothing of value to an economy. Adam Smith, writing in the mid-18th century, distinguished between production which had a tangible output – such as agriculture and manufacture – and production for which there was no tangible output. The latter, which included the efforts of intermediaries, doctors, lawyers and the armed forces he described as 'unproductive of any value' (Smith, 1977, p 430). This remained the dominant attitude towards services until the latter part of the 19th century when Alfred Marshall argued that a person providing a service was just as capable of giving utility to the recipient as a person producing a tangible product. Indeed, Marshall recognized that tangible products may not exist at all were it not for a series of services performed in order to produce them and to make them available to consumers. To Marshall, an agent distributing agricultural produce performed as valuable a task as the farmer himself – without the provision of transport and inter-mediary services, agricultural products produced in areas of surplus would be of no value. Today, despite some lingering beliefs that the service sector is an insubstantial and relatively inferior sector of the economy, considerable attention is paid to its direct and indirect economic consequences.

There are many definitions of what constitutes a service. Modern definitions of services focus on the fact that a service in itself produces no tangible output, although it may be instrumental in producing some tangible output. A contemporary definition is provided by Kotler, Armstrong, Saunders and Wong (1999):

> A service is any activity or benefit that one party can offer to another which is essentially intangible and does not result in the ownership of anything. Its production may or may not be tied to a physical product.

The *Economist* offered one of the simplest definitions when it described services as 'anything that cannot be dropped on your foot'.

The definition of **services** which will be used to show clearly the scope of this book is:

> The production of an essentially intangible benefit, either in its own right or as a significant element of a tangible product, which through some form of exchange, satisfies an identified need.

This definition recognizes that most products are in fact a combination of goods elements and services elements. In some cases, the service element will be the essential element of the service (e.g. hairdressing and management consultancy), while in other cases the service will simply support the provision of a tangible good (e.g. a loan facility provided to support the sale of a new car).

In the evolution of the services marketing literature, there has been argument about the extent to which services should be considered a distinctive area of study in marketing. On the one hand, some have argued that a service contains many important elements common to goods which makes services marketing as a separate discipline obsolete. Thus Levitt (1972) observed:

> ... there is no such thing as service industries. There are only industries where service components are greater or less than those of other industries.

On the other hand, many have pointed to the limitations of traditional marketing principles when applied to the marketing of services. Rathmell (1974), Shostack (1977), Gronroos (1978), Berry (1980) and Lovelock (1981) were among the early critics who argued that the differences which exist between goods and services mean that the marketing tools used for goods marketing cannot easily be translated to services marketing.

In reality, services marketing is about refining the basic philosophy of marketing to allow them to be operationalized more effectively in the services sector. Many of these principles will be familiar to those involved in the marketing of goods and can be applied to services with relatively little refinement. In some cases – such as the analysis of **service encounters** – a new area of marketing thought needs to be opened up.

In addition to the grey area between a pure good and a pure service, some marketing activities do not easily fit on this scale at all. The first of these which has attracted growing interest is the marketing of ideas, whether these be the ideas of a political party, a religious sect or an idea on a specific subject, such as road safety. The second – and related area – is the marketing of a cause, such as famine relief in Africa or a campaign to prevent the construction of a new road. Both of these types of activity are distinguished from normal goods and services marketing as there is no exchange of value between the producer and the individuals or organizations at whom the marketing effort is aimed. To take an example, the consumer of transport services enters into an exchange and pays for a transport service either directly and willingly – as in the case of a train fare, or indirectly – and possibly unwillingly – through general taxation, as is the case for the use of roads. By contrast, when a pressure group mounts a campaign to bring about the building of a new road, the concept of exchange of value becomes extremely tenuous, only really occurring where, for example, a member of the public subsequently contributes to a cause – either financially or by their actions. Generally though, the concept of services does not offer an appropriate framework for analysing the marketing of ideas and causes.

### 1.1.1 The growth of service-based economies

There is little doubt that the services sector has become a dominant force in many national economies. Between 1980 and 1992 the number of jobs in the UK services sector increased by 1.1 million, over twice the rate of growth for the economy as a whole (Labour Market Survey 1998). There appears to be a close correlation between the level of economic development in an economy (as expressed by its GDP per capita) and the strength of its service sector, although whether a strong service sector leads to economic growth or results from it is debatable.

The International Labour Office's Year Book of Labour Statistics (ILO, 1999) illustrates the magnitude of these differences. The more highly developed economies were associated with high percentages of workers employed in the service sector, for example the USA (75%), Canada (75%), Australia (74%) and the UK (73%). Western countries which are considered to be less developed have proportionately fewer employed in their services sector, for example Spain (59%), Portugal (53%), Ireland (53%) and Greece (49%). The lowest levels of services employment are found in the less developed countries, for example Mexico (30%), Bangladesh (28%) and Ethiopia (9%). Figure 1.1 indicates the close correlation between GDP per head and services sector employment.

Although it is conventional wisdom that the service sectors have grown strongly in recent years, we need to hedge this with a few caveats.

- The level of accuracy with which service sector statistics have been recorded is generally less than for manufacturing and primary sectors. The system of

**Figure 1.1**
Graph showing, for selected countries, the association between GDP per head and the percentage of employment which is in the services sector (compiled from OECD and ILO data)

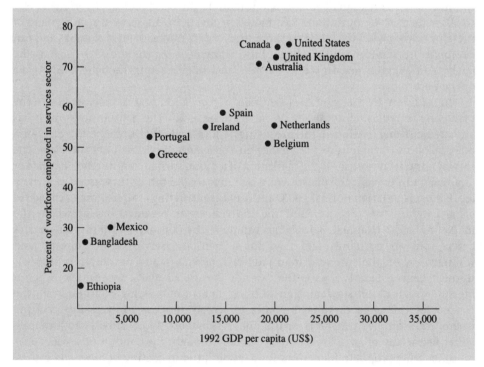

Standard Industrial Classifications (SICs) for a long while did not disaggregate the service sector in the same level of detail as manufacture or agriculture. Many service sectors do not fall neatly into one of the classifications, making it difficult to get an overall picture of that sector.

- The intangible nature of services can make them relatively difficult to measure, especially in the case of overseas trade. While flows of tangible goods through ports can usually be measured quite easily, trade flows associated with services are much more difficult to identify and measure. Furthermore, cutbacks in government statistical collection have increased the inaccuracy of many series. As an example, the UK trade figures relating to tourism and financial services frequently have to be revised after initial publication.

- Part of the apparent growth in the services sector may reflect the method by which statistics are collected, rather than indicating an increase in overall service level activity. Within many manufacturing organizations, people are employed producing service type activities, such as cleaning, catering, transport and distribution. Where a cook is employed by a manufacturing company, output and employment is attributed to the manufacturing sector. However, a common occurrence during the 1990s has been for manufacturing industry to contract out many of these service activities to external contractors. Where such contracts are performed by contract catering, office cleaning, or transport companies, the output becomes counted within the service sector, making the sector look larger, even though no additional services have been produced – they have merely been switched from internally produced to externally produced.

Nevertheless, services have had a major impact on national economies and many service industries have facilitated improved **productivity** in the manufacturing and agricultural sectors. As an example, transport and distribution services have often had the effect of stimulating economic development at local and national levels (e.g. following the improvement of rail or road services). One reason for Russian agriculture not having been fully exploited has been the ineffective distribution system available to food producers.

Services can have a **multiplier effect** on local and national economies in that initial spending with a service producer triggers further expenditure. The **services multiplier** works like this. The first producer spends money buying in supplies from outside (including labour) and these outside suppliers in turn purchase more inputs. The multiplier effect of this initial expenditure can result in the total increase in household incomes being much greater than the original expenditure. A good example of the multiplier effect was used to argue the case for the development of the Millennium Dome on a derelict site at Greenwich. Internationally, many governments have supported bids to host major sporting events such as the Olympic Games in order to gain the resulting multiplier benefits. While these events initially create direct employment within the events themselves, demand ripples out to other service sectors, such as hotels and transport. This in turn can generate additional demand for local manufacturing industry, for example visitors require food which may be produced locally, the producers of which may in turn require additional building materials to increase production facilities. The multiplier effects of additional service activity will depend on the proportion of the subsequent spending which is kept within the local area.

One approach to understanding the contribution of services to other aspects of economic activity is to analyse input–output tables of production and data on labour and capital inputs. Wood (1987) used these to estimate the effects which productivity improvements in all of the direct and indirect supply sectors had on the productivity levels of all other sectors. Some apparently high productivity sectors were shown to be held back by the low productivity of some of their inputs, including service inputs. On the other hand, efficiency improvements in some services such as transport and distribution were shown to have had widespread beneficial effects on the productivity contribution of other sectors.

Should Western developed economies focus on becoming service-based economies, even at the expense of the manufacturing sector? This may sound appealing, but the logic of this argument can be pushed too far, in particular:

1   A large part of the growth in the service sector during recent years has reflected the buoyancy of the manufacturing sector. As manufacturing industry increases its level of activity, the demand for producer services such as accountancy, legal services and business travel increases. The sudden decline of many UK financial services sectors in the early 1990s reflected the downturn in manufacturing activity, resulting in lower demand for business loans and export credits, etc.

2   In the UK, the assumption that the country has a comparative cost advantage in the production of services needs to be examined closely. In the same way that many sectors of UK manufacturing industry lost their **competitive advantage** to developing nations during the 1960s and 1970s, there is evidence that once unquestioned supremacy in certain service sectors is being challenged. Financial services markets which achieved prominence in London when Britain was the world's most important trading nation are increasingly following world trade to its new centres such as Tokyo and Frankfurt. High levels of training in competing nations have allowed those countries to firstly develop their own indigenous services and then to develop them for export. Banking services which were once a net import of Japan are now exported by the Japanese throughout the world.

3   Over reliance on the service sector could pose strategic problems for the UK. A diverse economic base allows a national economy to be more resilient to changes in world trading conditions.

The textbooks have traditionally described what happened in England during the early part of the 19th century as the 'Industrial Revolution'. Visions of new technologies involving steam power, factory systems and metal production have led to the dominant view that England advanced economically primarily as a result of progress in the manufacturing sector. But could the Industrial Revolution have happened without the services sector? The period saw the development of many services whose presence was vital to economic development. Without the

We deliver it. We plant it.

We email advice on it.

It's a wonder we don't come round

and tuck it in at night.

At Crocus, our trained gardeners will deliver* weekends, mornings or until 8 in the evening. We'll plant for you if you like. And after a fond farewell, we'll even send your plants a regular email to make sure they're alright.

## crocus.co.uk
**GARDENERS BY NATURE**

*Service only available in certain parts of the country.

**Figure 1.2**
Plant growing has traditionally been associated primarily with the agricultural sector. However, Crocus has shown how even such a basic agricultural activity can be transformed into a service. The company doesn't just grow and sell plants, but offers a complete service to the buyer which includes delivering and planting, as well as continuing to give advice about caring for the plant (reproduced with permission of Crocus)

development of railways, goods would not have been distributed from centralized factories to geographically dispersed consumers and many people would not have been able to get to work. Investment in new factories called for a banking system which could circulate funds at a national rather than a purely local level. A whole new service sector emerged to meet the needs of manufacturing, including inter-mediaries who were essential to get manufacturers' goods to increasingly dispersed markets. Today, we continue to rely on services to exploit developments in the manufacturing sector. Should we rewrite history and talk about the 'Service Revolution' rather than the Industrial Revolution of 19th century England?

## 1.2 Defining marketing in a services context

A traditional definition of **marketing** is provided by the Chartered Institute of Marketing:

> The management process which identifies, anticipates and supplies customer requirements efficiently and profitably.

Marketing orientation first emerged in the relatively affluent countries for goods where competition between suppliers had become the greatest. Adoption of marketing by the services sector generally came later, largely due to the effects of significant public sector monopolies and the existence of professional codes of practice which until recently have restrained many service organizations' marketing activities.

Many people have tried to define just what is meant by marketing orientation. Work by Narver and Slater (1990) has sought to define and measure the extent of marketing orientation and their analysis identified three important components:

- Customer orientation, meaning that an organization has a sufficient understand-ing of its target buyers that allows it to create superior value for them. This comes about through increasing the benefits to the buyer in relation to the buyer's costs or by decreasing the buyer's costs in relation to the buyer's benefits. A customer orientation requires that the organization understands value to the customer not only as it is today, but also as it will evolve over time.
- Competitor orientation, defined as an organization's understanding of the short-term strengths and weaknesses and long-term capabilities and strategies of current and potential competitors.
- Interfunctional co-ordination, referring to the manner in which an organization uses its resources in creating superior value for target customers. Many individ-uals within an organization have responsibility for creating value, not just marketing staff, and a marketing orientation requires that the organization draws upon and integrates its human and physical resources effectively and adapts them to meet **customer needs**. This aspect of marketing is crucial to the services sector where production and consumption are inseparable. Subsequent chapters will emphasize the importance to a company of satisfying

customer needs through the integration of marketing, human resource management and operations management.

Marketing orientation is used to describe both the basic philosophy of an organization as well as the techniques which it uses.

- As a business philosophy, marketing puts the customer at the centre of all the organization's considerations. Basic values such as the requirement to identify the changing needs of existing customers and the necessity to constantly search for new market opportunities are instilled in all members of a truly marketing-oriented organization, covering all aspects of the organization's activities. For a fast-food retailer, the training of serving staff would emphasize those items – such as the standard of dress and speed of service – which research had found to be particularly valued by existing and potential customers. The personnel manager would have a selection policy which sought to recruit staff who fulfilled the needs of customers rather than simply minimizing the wage bill. The accountant would investigate the effects on customers before deciding to save money by cutting stock-holding levels, thereby possibly reducing customer choice. It is not sufficient for an organization to merely appoint a marketing manager or set up a marketing department – viewed as a philosophy, marketing is an attitude of mind which pervades the whole organization.
- Marketing orientation is associated with a range of techniques. For example, market research is a technique for finding out about customer needs and advertising is a technique to communicate the service offer to potential customers. However, these techniques lose a lot of their value if they are conducted by an organization which has not fully embraced the philosophy of marketing. The techniques of marketing also include, among other things, pricing, the design of channels of distribution and new product development. Application of these techniques to the service sector is described in later chapters.

It is easy for a service organization to say that it is marketing oriented and puts customers first. But all too often it is very easy to spot tell-tale signs that marketing is only skin deep. Consider some of the following give-away signs:

- Opening hours which are designed to suit the interests of staff rather than customers (very common among many public sector services).
- Administrative procedures which make life easier for the company rather than its customers (e.g. expecting customers to contact several sections of the organization, rather than offering a 'one-stop' facility).
- Reserving prime car parking spaces for staff rather than customers.
- Advertising which is aimed at the egos of company managers rather than the needs and aspirations of potential buyers.

Can you think of any further giveaways?

### 1.2.1   The marketing mix for services

 The **marketing mix** is the set of tools available to an organization to shape the nature of its offer to customers. Goods marketers are familiar with the '4Ps' of Product, Price, Promotion and Place. Early analysis by Borden (1965) of marketing mix elements was based on a study of manufacturing industry at a time when the importance of services to the economy was considered to be relatively unimportant. More recently, the 4Ps of the marketing mix have been found to be too limited in their application to services. Particular problems which limit their usefulness to services are:

● The intangible nature of services is overlooked in most analyses of the mix. For example, the product mix is frequently analysed in terms of tangible design properties, which may not be relevant to a service. Likewise, physical distribution management may not be an important element of place mix decisions.
● The price element overlooks the fact that many services are produced by the public sector without a price being charged to the final consumer.
● The promotion mix of the traditional 4Ps fails to recognize the promotion of services which takes place at the point of consumption by the production personnel, unlike the situation with most fast-moving consumer goods which are normally produced away from the consumer and therefore the producer has no direct involvement in promoting the good to the final consumer. For a bank clerk, hairdresser or singer, the manner in which the service is produced is an essential element of the total promotion of the service.

As well as throwing up ambiguities about the meaning of some of these four elements of the marketing mix, this simple list also fails to recognize a number of key factors which marketing managers in the service sector use to design their service output. Particular problems focus on:

● Defining the concept of quality for intangible services, and identifying and measuring the mix elements which can be managed in order to create a quality service.
● The importance of people as an element of the service product, both as producers and co-consumers.
● The over-simplification of the elements of distribution which are of relevance to intangible services.

These weaknesses have resulted in a number of attempts to redefine the marketing mix in a manner which is more applicable to the service sector. While many have sought to refine the marketing mix for general application, the expansions by Booms and Bitner (1981) and Christopher, Payne and Ballantyne (1991) provide useful frameworks for analysis, although they are not empirically proven theories of services marketing. In addition to the four traditional elements of the marketing mix, both frameworks add the additional elements of People and Process. In addition, Booms and Bitner talk about Physical Evidence making up a seventh 'P' while the latter adds Customer Service as an additional element.

The principle of the **extended marketing mix** (as indeed with the traditional marketing mix) is to break a service offering down into a number of component parts and to arrange them into manageable subject areas for making strategic decisions. Decisions on one element of the mix can only be made by reference to other elements of the mix in order to give a sustainable product positioning (see Chapter 2). The importance attached to each element of the extended marketing mix will vary between services. In a highly automated service such as vending machine dispensing, the people element will be a less important element of the mix than a people intensive business such as a restaurant.

A brief overview of these marketing mix ingredients is given below with fuller discussion following in the subsequent chapters.

**Products** Products are the means by which organizations seek to satisfy consumer needs. A product in this sense is anything which the organization offers to potential customers, whether it be tangible or intangible. After initial hesitation, most marketing managers are now happy to talk about an intangible service as a product. Thus bank accounts, insurance policies and holidays are frequently referred to as products, sometimes to the amusement of nonmarketers, as where pop stars or even politicians are referred to as a product to be marketed.

**Product mix** decisions facing a services marketer can be very different from those dealing with goods. Most fundamentally, **pure services** can only be defined using process descriptions rather than tangible descriptions of outcomes. Quality becomes a key element defining a product. Other elements of the product mix such as design, reliability, brand image, and product range may sound familiar to a goods marketer, but assume different roles, as discussed in Chapter 2. There is also a significant difference with goods in that new service developments cannot be protected by patent.

**Pricing** Price mix decisions include strategic and tactical decisions about the average level of prices to be charged, discount structures, terms of payment and the extent to which price discrimination between different groups of customers is to take place. These are very similar to the issues facing a goods marketer. Differences do, however, occur where the intangible nature of a service can mean that price in itself can become a very significant indicator of quality. The personal and non-transferable nature of many services presents additional opportunities for price discrimination within service markets, while the fact that many services are marketed by the public sector at a subsidized or no price can complicate price setting.

**Promotion** The traditional promotion mix includes various methods of communicating the benefits of a service to potential consumers. The mix is traditionally broken down into four main elements – advertising, sales promotion, public relations and personal selling. The promotion of services often needs to place particular emphasis on increasing the apparent tangibility of a service. Also, in the case of services marketing, production personnel can themselves become an important element of the promotion mix.

**Place** Place decisions refer to the ease of access which potential customers have to a service. Place decisions can therefore involve physical location decisions (as in deciding where to place a hotel), decisions about which intermediaries to use in making a service accessible to a consumer (e.g. whether a tour operator uses travel agents or sells its holidays direct to customers) and nonlocational decisions which are used to make services available (e.g. the use of telephone delivery systems). For pure services, decisions about how to physically move a good are of little strategic relevance. However, most services involve movement of goods of some form. These can either be materials necessary to produce a service (e.g. travel brochures and fast-food packaging material) or the service can have as its whole purpose the movement of goods (e.g. road haulage, plant hire).

**People**   For most services, people are a vital element of the marketing mix. Where production can be separated from consumption – as is the case with most manu-factured goods – management can usually take measures to reduce the direct effect of people on the final output as received by customers. Therefore the buyer of a car is not concerned whether a production worker dresses untidily, uses bad language at work or turns up for work late, so long as there are quality control measures which reject the results of lax behaviour before they reach the buyer. In service industries, everybody is what Gummesson (1999) calls a 'part time marketer' in that their actions have a much more direct effect on the output received by customers.

While the importance attached to people management in improving quality within manufacturing companies is increasing – for example through the develop-ment of quality circles – people planning assumes much greater importance within the service sector. This is especially true in those services where staff have a high level of contact with customers. For this reason, it is therefore essential that services organiza-tions clearly specify what is expected from personnel in their interaction with customers. To achieve the specified standard, methods of recruiting, training, motivat-ing and rewarding staff cannot be regarded as purely personnel decisions – they are important marketing mix decisions.

People planning within the marketing mix also involves developing a pattern of interaction between customers themselves, which can be very important where service consumption takes place in public. An important way in which drinkers judge a pub might be the kind of people who frequent the pub. An empty pub may convey no atmosphere while a rowdy one may convey the wrong attitude to important segments. As well as planning the human input to its own production, marketing management must also develop strategies for producing favourable interaction between its customers – for example by excluding certain groups and developing a physical en-vironment which affects customers' behaviour.

**Physical evidence**   The intangible nature of a service means that potential customers are unable to judge a service before it is consumed, increasing the riskiness inherent in a purchase decision. An important element of marketing planning is therefore to reduce this level of risk by offering tangible evidence of the nature of the service. This evidence can take a number of forms. At its simplest, a brochure can describe and give pictures of important elements of the service product – a holiday brochure gives pictorial evidence of hotels and resorts for this purpose. The appearance of staff can give evidence about the nature of a service – a tidily dressed ticket clerk for an airline gives some evidence that the airline operation as a whole is run with care and attention. Buildings are frequently used to give evidence of service nature. Towards the end of the 19th century, railway companies outbid each other to produce the most elaborate station buildings. For people wishing to travel from London to Scotland, a comparison of the grandeur of the three terminals in London's Euston Road could give some clue about the ability of the railway to provide a substantial service. Today, a clean, bright environment used in a service outlet can help reassure potential customers at the point where they make a service purchase decision. For this reason, fast food and photo-processing outlets often use red and yellow colour schemes to convey an image of speedy service.

**Processes**   Production processes are usually of little concern to consumers of manufactured goods, but are often of critical concern to consumers of 'high-contact' services where the consumers can be seen as a co-producer of the service. A customer of a restaurant is deeply affected by the manner in which staff serve them and the amount of waiting which is involved during the production process. Issues arise as to the boundary between the producer and consumer in terms of the allocation of production functions – for example, a restaurant might require a customer to collect their meal from a counter, or to deposit their own rubbish. With services, a clear distinction cannot be made between marketing and operations management.

**Customer service**   The meaning of customer service varies from one organization to another. Within the service sector, it can best be described as the total quality of the service as perceived by the customer. As such, responsibility for this element of the marketing mix cannot be isolated within a narrowly defined customer services department, but becomes a concern of all production personnel, both those directly employed by the organization and those employed by suppliers. Managing the quality of the service offered to the customer becomes closely identified with policy on the related marketing mix elements of product design and personnel.

### 1.2.2   The use of metaphors in the services literature

The literature on services marketing evolved after the literature on goods marketing. In evolving, many metaphors have been used to describe services (Goodwin, 1996). Factory metaphors have frequently been used to describe services, using such terms as inputs, processing, outputs and productivity. The early phases of service research deliberately drew parallels between production of a tangible good and delivery of an intangible service. Early articles placed consumers in the factory, as contributors to production processes (Lovelock and Young, 1979) or as potential bottlenecks to be processed as quickly as possible (Chase, 1978). However, factory metaphors fail when marketers are forced to recognize the unique aspects of human as compared to inanimate inputs. The latter can be inventoried in a warehouse for months at a time, while the former can become dissatisfied after waiting for just a few minutes in a queue.

As we will explore in Chapter 3, discussion of services has drawn heavily on metaphors associated with the theatre. Services have been compared to theatrical productions, complete with script, actors, props, a stage, director and audience.

**Service processes** have been differentiated into front stage and back stage. The drama metaphor incorporates experiential, hedonistic elements of service consumption and, as in the theatre, there may be a desire of the audience (customers) to temporarily suspend their belief in the reality of the act.

## 1.3 Marketing in transition?

In recent years, marketing has matured as a discipline. One sign of this maturity is an increasing willingness of marketing academics and practitioners to look inwardly and become more self-critical of their discipline. An abundance of scholarly research and practitioner proclamations have suggested that marketing is undergoing a fundamental, epoch breaking change (Brady and Davis, 1993; Gronroos, 1997). Talk about new paradigms has been interspersed with gloomy predictions about the future of the marketing department and the triumph of chaos where previously there was order (Gummesson, 1997; Murray and O'Driscoll, 1997).

The scientific approach to marketing, based on the management of the marketing mix has been held by some to be too constraining in a world where consumers increasingly break 'rules' of consumption. Gronroos (1997) stated that 'the major problem with the marketing mix and its 4Ps has been their position as the major, and in many situations as the only acceptable marketing paradigm'. He asked why the marketing mix management paradigm and the 4Ps model have become such a straitjacket for marketers and suggested that the 'main reason is for pedagogical virtues'. The marketing mix is atheoretical and has formed the basis for the overwhelming majority of texts on marketing. A more creative, holistic approach to solving customers' problems has been called for, in place of company-focused marketing plans. **'Postmodern marketing'** and 'new marketing manifestos' typify recent debate (Brown, 1995; Grant, 1999). Wilson and Gilligan (1997, p 25) declared that 'there has been an increasing recognition over the past few years that marketing is, or may be facing what is loosely referred to as a mid life crisis', due to the widespread concern that 'something is amiss'. In addition, Brown (1995, p 42) proclaimed that the 'marketing concept is deeply, perhaps irredeemably flawed, that its seemingly solid theoretical foundations are by no means secure and that the specialism is teetering on the brink of serious intellectual crisis'.

It is possible that the domination of economies by services has led to the final breakdown of traditional marketing models which have been developed for goods-based economies. Trying to stretch goods-based models of buyer behaviour to fit services may not work, given the different search processes and credence qualities of services, for example. But despite talk of marketing being in 'crisis' and the need for new paradigms, the case for change is somewhat ambiguous. Consider the following anecdotal evidence from the services sector. In the UK grocery retail sector, 'new' marketing ideas stress the importance of individual one-to-one dialogue between a retailer and its customers, yet research has shown that the most profitable retailers are not those with personalized loyalty programmes, but those which offer standardized, low prices for all (Knox, 1998; Murphy, 1998). Similarly, in the airline sector, new marketing paradigms might have expected operators who finely tailor their operations to the needs of multiple small segments to win out over airlines which offer one standard of service to all. However, during one week in 1999, British Airways (which has made great efforts at customization of its services) reported a loss while the low fares, no frills, minimal segmentation airline Ryanair reported sharply increased sales and profits (*The Times*, 1999a).

## 1.4 Distinguishing features of services

Services have a number of distinctive characteristics which differentiate them from goods and have implications for the manner in which they are marketed. These characteristics are often described as intangibility, inseparability, variability, perishability and the inability to own a service. These characteristics will be a recurrent theme throughout this book, and their nature is introduced below.

### 1.4.1 Intangibility

A pure service cannot be assessed using any of the physical senses – it is an abstraction which cannot be directly examined before it is purchased. A prospective purchaser of most goods is able to examine the goods for physical integrity, aesthetic appearance, taste, smell, etc. Many advertising claims relating to these tangible properties can be verified by inspection prior to purchase. On the other hand, pure services have no tangible properties which can be used by consumers to verify advertising claims before the purchase is made. The intangible process characteristics which define services, such as reliability, personal care, attentiveness of staff, their friendliness, can only be verified once a service has been purchased and consumed.

The level of tangibility present in the service offer derives from three principal sources:

- Tangible goods which are included in the service offer and consumed by the user.
- The physical environment in which the service production/consumption process takes place.
- Tangible evidence of service performance.

Where goods form an important component of a service offer, many of the practices associated with conventional goods marketing can be applied to this part of the service offer. Restaurants represent a mix of tangibles and intangibles and in respect of the food element, few of the particular characteristics of services marketing are encountered. Therefore, production of the food can be separated from its consumption and the perishability of food is less significant than the perishability of an empty table. Furthermore, the presence of a tangible component gives customers a visible basis on which to judge quality.

The tangible elements of the service offer comprise not just those goods which are exchanged but also the physical environment in which a service encounter takes place. Within this environment, the design of buildings, their cleanliness and the appearance of staff present important tangible evidence which may be the only basis on which a buyer is able to differentiate one service provider from another.

While some services are rich in such tangible cues (e.g. restaurants, shops), other services provide relatively little tangible evidence (e.g. life insurance).

Tangibility is further provided by evidence of service production methods. Some services provide many opportunities for customers to see the process of production, indeed the whole purpose of the service may be to see the production process (e.g. a pop concert). Often this tangible evidence can be seen before a decision to purchase a service is made, either by direct observation of a service being performed on somebody else (e.g. watching the work of a builder) or indirectly through a description of the service production process (a role played by brochures which specify and illustrate the service production process). On the other hand, some services provide very few tangible clues about the nature of the service production process. Portfolio management services are not only produced largely out of sight of the consumer, it is also difficult to specify in advance in a brochure what the service outcomes will be.

**Intangibility** has a number of important marketing implications which will be examined in more detail in subsequent chapters. The lack of physical evidence which intangibility implies increases the level of uncertainty which a consumer faces when choosing between competing services. An important part of a services marketing programme will therefore involve reducing consumer uncertainty by such means as adding physical evidence and the development of strong brands. It is interesting to note that pure goods and pure services tend to move in opposite directions in terms of their general approach to the issue of tangibility. While service marketers seek to add tangible evidence to their product, pure goods marketers often seek to augment their products by adding intangible elements such as after-sales service and improved distribution.

### 1.4.2  Inseparability

The production and consumption of a tangible good are two discrete activities. Companies usually produce goods in one central location and then transport them to the place where customers most want to buy them. In this way, manufacturing companies can achieve economies of scale through centralized production and have centralized quality control checks. The manufacturer is also able to make goods at a time which is convenient to itself, then make them available to customers at times which are convenient to customers. Production and consumption are said to be separable. On the other hand, the consumption of a service is said to be inseparable from its means of production. Producer and consumer must interact in order for the benefits of the service to be realized – both must normally meet at a time and a place which is mutually convenient in order that the producer can directly pass on service benefits. This is termed the co-production of services. In the extreme case of personal care services, the customer must be present during the entire production process – a doctor cannot provide a service without the involvement of a patient. For services, marketing becomes a means of facilitating complex producer–consumer interaction, rather than being merely an exchange medium.

**Inseparability** occurs whether the producer is human – as in the case of health-care services – or a machine (e.g. a bank ATM machine). The service of the ATM machine can only be realized if the producer and consumer interact. In some cases,

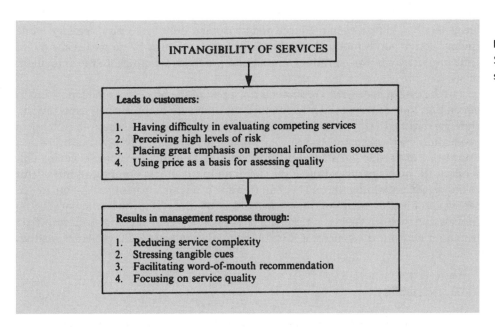

**Figure 1.3**
Some implications of service intangibility

it has been possible to separate service production and consumption, especially where there is a low level of personal contact.

Inseparability has a number of important marketing implications for services. Firstly, whereas goods are generally first produced, then offered for sale and finally sold and consumed, inseparability causes this process to be modified for services. They

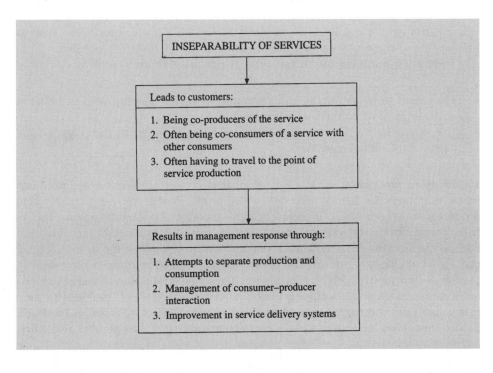

**Figure 1.4**
Some implications of service inseparability

are generally sold first, then produced and consumed simultaneously. Secondly, while the method of goods production is to a large extent (though by no means always) of little importance to the consumer, production processes are critical to the enjoyment of services.

In the case of goods, the consumer is not a part of the process of production and in general, so long as the product which they take delivery of meets their expectations, they are satisfied (although there are exceptions, for example where the ethics of production methods cause concern, or where quality can only be assessed with a knowledge of production stages which are hidden from the consumer's view). With services, the active participation of the customer in the production process makes this as important as defining the end benefit. In some cases, an apparently slight change in service production methods may totally destroy the value of the service being provided. A person buying a ticket for a concert by Cliff Richard may derive no benefit at all from the concert if it is subsequently produced by Boy George instead.

### 1.4.3 Variability

 For services, **variability** impacts upon customers not just in terms of outcomes but also in terms of processes of production. It is the latter point that causes variability to pose a much greater problem for services, compared to goods. Because the customer is usually involved in the production process for a service at the same time as they consume it, it can be difficult to carry out monitoring and control to ensure consistent standards. The opportunity for pre-delivery inspection and rejection which is open to the goods manufacturer is not normally possible with services – the service must normally be produced in the presence of the customer without the possibility of intervening quality control. Particular problems can occur where personnel are involved in providing services on a one-to-one basis – such as hairdressing – where no easy method of monitoring and control is possible.

There are two dimensions of variability which are relevant to services:

- The extent to which production standards vary from a norm, both in terms of outcomes and of production processes.
- The extent to which a service can be deliberately varied to meet the specific needs of individual customers.

Variability in production standards is of greatest concern to services organizations where customers are highly involved in the production process, especially where production methods make it impractical to monitor service production. This is true of many labour-intensive personal services provided in a one-to-one situation, such as personal healthcare. Some services allow greater scope for quality control checks to be undertaken during the production process, allowing an organization to provide a consistently high level of service. This is especially true of machine-based services. For example, telecommunication services can typically operate with very low failure rates (British Telecom claims that in over 99% of all attempts to obtain service, customers are able to make a connection to their dialled number at the first attempt).

The tendency today is for equipment-based services to be regarded as less variable than those which involve a high degree of personal intervention in the production process. Many services organizations have sought to reduce variability and hence to build strong brands – by adopting equipment-based production methods. Replacing human telephone operators with computerized voice systems and automating many banking services are typical of this trend. Sometimes reduced personnel variability has been achieved by passing on part of the production process to consumers, in the way that self-service petrol filling stations are no longer dependent on the variability of forecourt serving staff.

The second dimension of variability is the extent to which a service can be deliberately customized to meet the specific needs of individual customers. Because services are created as they are consumed, and because consumers are often a part of the production process, the potential for customization of services is generally greater than for manufactured goods. The extent to which a service can be customized is dependent upon production methods employed. Services which are produced for large numbers of customers simultaneously may offer little scope for individual customization. The production methods of a railway do not allow individual customers' needs to be met in the way that the simpler production methods of a taxi operator may be able to.

The extent to which services can be customized is partly a function of management decisions on the level of authority to be delegated to front-line service personnel. While some service operations seek to give more authority to front-line staff, the tendency is for service firms to 'industrialize' their encounter with customers. This implies following clearly specified standardized procedures in each encounter. While industrialization often reduces the flexibility of producers to meet customers' needs, it also has the effect of reducing variability of processes and outcomes.

The variability of service output can pose problems for brand building in services compared to tangible goods. For the latter it is usually relatively easy to incorporate monitoring and quality control procedures into production processes in order to ensure that a brand stands for a consistency of output. The service sector's attempts to reduce variability concentrate on methods used to select, train, motivate and control personnel, issues which are examined in Chapter 12. In some cases, service offers have been simplified, jobs have been 'deskilled' and personnel replaced with machines in order to reduce human variability.

**Figure 1.5**
Causes and consequences of service variability

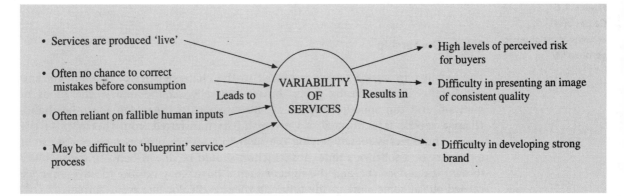

### 1.4.4 Perishability

Services differ from goods in that they cannot be stored. A producer of cars which is unable to sell all of its output in the current period can carry forward stocks to sell in a subsequent period. The only significant costs are storage costs, financing costs and the possibility of loss through obsolescence. By contrast, the producer of a service which cannot sell all of its output produced in the current period gets no chance to carry it forward for sale in a subsequent period. An airline which offers seats on a 9.00 am flight from London to Paris cannot sell any empty seats once the aircraft has left at 9.00 am. The service offer disappears and spare seats cannot be stored to meet a surge in demand which may occur at 10.00 am.

Very few services face a constant pattern of demand through time. Many show considerable variation, which could be a daily variation (city centre sandwich bars at lunchtime), weekly (the Friday evening peak in demand for railway travel), seasonal (hotels, stores at Christmas time), cyclical (mortgages) or an unpredictable pattern of demand (emergency building repair services following heavy storms).

 The **perishability** of services results in greater attention having to be paid to the management of demand by evening out peaks and troughs in demand and in scheduling service production to follow this pattern as far as possible. Pricing and promotion are two of the tools commonly adopted to tackle this problem and which are discussed in Chapter 13.

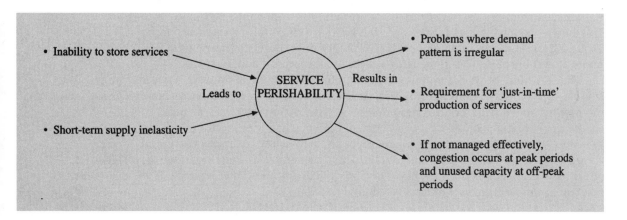

**Figure 1.6**
Causes and consequences of service perishability

### 1.4.5 Ownership

The inability to own a service is related to the characteristics of intangibility and perishability. In purchasing goods, buyers generally acquire title to the goods in question and can subsequently do as they wish with them. On the other hand, when a service is performed, no ownership is transferred from the seller to the buyer. The buyer is merely buying the right to a service process such as the use of a car park or a solicitor's time. A distinction should be drawn between the inability to own the service act, and the rights which a buyer may acquire to have a service carried out at some time in the future (a theatre gift voucher for example).

The inability to own a service has implications for the design of distribution channels, so a wholesaler or retailer cannot take title, as is the case with goods. Instead, direct distribution methods are more common and where intermediaries are used, they generally act as a co-producer with the service provider.

## 1.5  Analysis of the service offer

In practice, it can be very difficult to distinguish services from goods, for when a good is purchased, there is usually an element of service included. Similarly, a service is frequently augmented by a tangible product attached to the service. In this way, a car may be considered to be a good rather than a service, yet cars are usually sold with the benefit of considerable intangible service elements, such as a warranty or a financing facility. On the other hand, a seemingly intangible service such as a package holiday includes tangible elements in the purchase – use of an aeroplane, the hotel room and transfer coach, for example. In between is a wide range of products which are a combination of tangible good and intangible service. A meal in a restaurant is a combination of tangible goods (the food and physical surroundings) and intangible service (the preparation and delivery of the food, reservation service, etc.). Figure 1.7 shows schematically that considerable diversity exists within the service sector. In fact, rather than talking about the service sector as a homogeneous group of activities, it would be more appropriate to talk about degrees of service orientation. All productive activities can be placed on a scale somewhere between being a pure service (no tangible output) and a pure good (no intangible service added to the tangible good). In practice, most products fall between the two extremes by being a combination of goods and services.

The extent to which the five features of services described above can be used to distinguish between goods and services marketing has been questioned by many. For example, on the subject of variability, there are some non-service industries – such as tropical fruits – which have difficulty in achieving high levels of consistent output, whereas some service industries such as car parks can achieve a consistent standard of

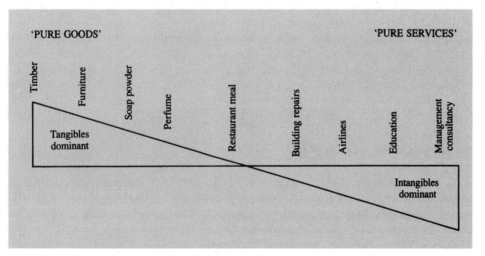

**Figure 1.7**
The goods and services continuum

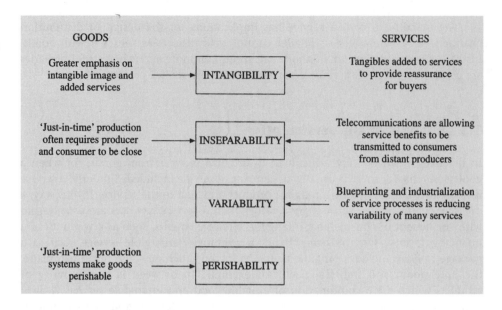

**Figure 1.8**
Points of convergence between goods and services marketing

service in terms of availability and cleanliness etc. Similarly, many tangible goods share the problem of intangible services in being incapable of full examination before consumption. It is not normally possible, for instance, to judge the taste of a bottle of wine in a supermarket before it has been purchased and (at least partially) consumed. Services marketers have learnt a lot from the marketing activities in the goods sectors and vice versa. Some of the points of convergence are illustrated in Figure 1.8.

Much of the usefulness of this list of distinguishing features comes back to understanding the nature of the service offer, in particular the extent to which it includes tangible goods elements. Shostack (1977) attempted to analyse the elements of a service in terms of a molecular model of interrelated services and goods components. Using this approach, an airline offers an essentially intangible service – transport. Yet the total service offer includes tangible elements such as the aeroplane as well as intangible elements such as the frequency of flights, their reliability and the quality of in-flight services. When many of these intangibles are broken down into their component parts, they too include tangible elements, so that inflight service includes tangible elements such as food and drink. The principles of services marketing have most relevance where the molecular structure is weighted towards intangible elements. A hypothetical application of the molecular model approach to the analysis of the complex output of a theatre is shown in Figure 1.9.

### 1.5.1 Goods as 'self services'

A distinction can be drawn between a service which is delivered directly by an organization to consumers, and services which are delivered by means of the goods which they have purchased. Conceptually, many goods purchases effectively result in a consumer buying a stream of internally produced services. In the evolution of the services marketing literature, Gershuny (1978) used the term

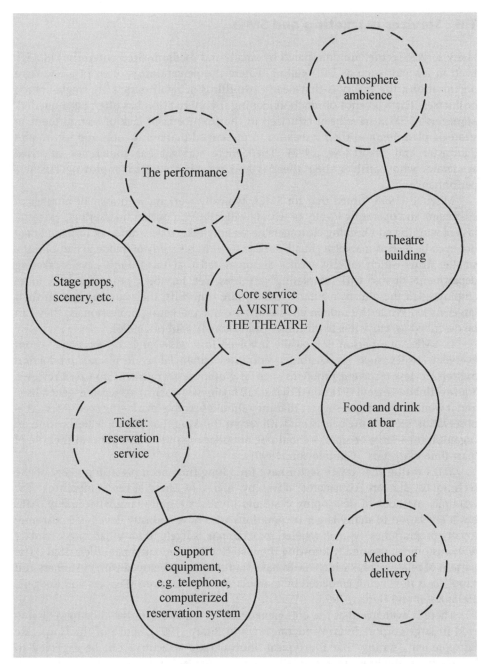

**Figure 1.9**
An application of Shostack's molecular model of service components to the output of a theatre. Unbroken circles = tangible elements; broken circles = intangible elements

'intermediate services' to describe complex manufactured equipment which private and industrial buyers purchase in order to provide services which may otherwise have been provided as a direct service activity. In this way, an automatic washing machine provides indirect service benefits which may otherwise have been provided directly by a launderette and a car provides benefits otherwise provided by taxis and public transport.

## 1.6 Services marketing and SMEs

Many service sectors are dominated by small- and medium-sized enterprises (SMEs). Even in a sector such as UK retailing, where the perception is often of a few large organizations, the reality is that nearly two-thirds of retail outlets are single-branch businesses. The relevance of much marketing theory to SMEs has often been queried. Managers of SMEs have been criticized in the past for their lack of commitment to strategic planning and their resistance to prescribed marketing tools and techniques (Lancaster and Waddelow, 1998). Their mere survival has sometimes surprised academics who consider their theories and practices vital to improving business performance.

Mitchell (1998) noted that for SMEs, typically working with a small number of customers and operating locally or with few distribution outlets, marketing's essential task of winning and keeping customers necessarily takes a very different form and may not even be seen as marketing at all. For example, in his study of 'hidden champions' – smaller firms which quietly excel – Simon noted that most don't have marketing departments or staff with 'marketing' job titles. Yet, he notes, proportionately more employees in these firms regularly spend more time with their customers than their larger rivals. While the hidden champions are not marketing professionals, they can be described as 'closeness-to-customer professionals' (Simon, 1996).

In SMEs, one person is typically involved in a wide range of decisions – from everyday issues such as customer enquiries, financial control and production matters, to less recurrent problems such as employee recruitment and rent reviews. Stanworth and Gray (1991) noted that small business owner-managers are 'generalists' and it would be wrong to suggest that they should become 'marketing specialists'. This observation seems quite consistent with recent thinking that all individuals within an organization – large or small – should be boundary-spanners and perform the role of 'part-time marketers' (Gummesson, 1999).

SMEs within the service sector have for a long time been practising many of the techniques that are considered novel by many of their larger competitors. For example, methods of developing customer loyalty are quite familiar to many SMEs but a revelation to many larger corporations who have recently developed customer loyalty programmes. A small retailer, for example, is likely to have had direct contact with customers, personally knowing them so that it could anticipate their needs. The pattern of relationships which SMEs have traditionally developed with customers and suppliers is now being emulated by many larger organizations (Peppers and Rodgers, 1995; Kahil and Harcar, 1995).

There is evidence that the entrepeneurship of small businesses is being rediscovered in large corporations. Vandermerwe and Birley (1997), spoke of the Corporate Entrepreneur, stating that the typical 'bureaucratic' executive can be expected to behave increasingly entrepreneurially. Corporations are transforming themselves 'so as to own customers' and to 'attack problems creatively', and entrepreneurs can today be expected to be able to manage a large corporation too. Goodwin stated that consumers today are being 'bombarded by confusion marketing' and that 'whereas we have all become accustomed to the sharpest, fastest-moving marketing ideas coming from small, entrepreneurial companies it is clear that the giants of UK industry have caught up and are rivalling their smaller companies' (Goodwin, 1998, p. 15).

## 1.7 Distinctive characteristics of public and not-for-profit sector marketing

The marketing of public and not-for-profit sector services is even further removed from goods marketing. The range of not-for-profit organizations covers local authorities, charities, and various 'QUANGO' type organizations that have been set up to run health services, schools and museums, among others. Here, marketing managers' financial objectives and the requirement to meet customers' needs must be further constrained by wider social objectives. In this way a public reference library may be set an objective of providing the public with a range of materials which help to develop the knowledge and skills of the population which it serves. Therefore the 'quality press' may be the only newspapers purchased, although popular customer request may call for the purchase of popular tabloids. This apparently centrally planned approach is not incompatible with a marketing philosophy the library may work within its objectives of developing knowledge and skills by seeking to maximize the number of people reading its quality newspapers. Marketing strategies which might be employed to achieve this could include a promotional campaign, the development of a friendly, welcoming attitude and accessible opening hours.

Many not-for-profit sector services such as museums and leisure services are increasingly being given clearly defined business objectives which makes it much more difficult for officers to continue doing what they like doing rather than what the public they serve wants. Marketing orientation has been most rapidly adopted by those public sector services which provide marketable goods and services such as swimming pools and municipal bus services. It is much more difficult to adopt marketing orientation where the public sector is a monopoly provider of a statutory service. In the provision of school places, the UK government has moved away from the traditional basis of centralized resource allocation to a quasi-market based system where funding – in principle – follows parents' choices. Those schools which are popular with parents and provide their service at a competitive cost to local and central government funding providers will grow, while those which don't will gradually lose resources. While developing a marketing framework for public services may sound fine in principle, new problems may be created. If consumers of services express their preferences for a provider, there is no guarantee that additional government funding will be provided to make available the additional capacity which consumers have demanded. And how able are government funding agencies to take a view of long-term capital commitments based on possibly short-term changes in consumer preferences?

In other public services, it may be even more difficult to introduce a marketing discipline. The core of the work carried out by the police force, fire brigades and the armed services cannot be easily subjected to the test of market forces. It is difficult for the consumer to exercise any choice over who polices their town and equally difficult in practice for local authorities to subcontract provision via a competitive tender.

The previous discussion indicates that it is difficult to generalize and talk about the not-for-profit and public sector services as though they comprised a homogeneous range of activities sharing similar marketing needs. There is in fact a range of activities from the pure public service to the pure private service and the marketing needs of 'pure' public services can differ quite markedly from those of the private sector. Some of the more important differences are summarized below.

1   Traditional definitions of marketing are based on an assumption that a market exists in which buyers and sellers are free to choose with whom they wish to do business. In effect, it is marketing without markets. In the public sector, choice is often neither available nor possible in practical terms. Consumers of social services cannot normally choose to receive their services from a provider other than that which has been designated. Similarly, many public sector service providers are constrained in the choice of clients which they are able to target. While government policy has aimed to create markets to replace central planning, there are limits to the extent to which this can be achieved in practice.

2   The aim of most private sector organizations is to earn profits for the owners of the organization. By contrast to these quantifiable objectives, many not-for-profit sector services operate with relatively diverse and unquantified objectives – for example a museum may have scholarly objectives in addition to a more quantifiable objective of maximizing revenue.

3   The private sector is usually able to monitor the results of its marketing activity as the benefits are usually internal to the organization. By contrast, many of the aims which not-for-profit organizations seek to achieve are external and a Profit and Loss statement or Balance Sheet cannot be produced in the way which is possible with a private sector organization operating to narrow internal financial goals.

4   The degree of discretion given to a public sector marketing manager is usually less than that given to a counterpart in the private sector. It could be argued that statutorily determined standards affect public sector organizations to a greater extent than the private sector – for example the marketing of educational facilities is constrained by the need to adhere to the national curriculum. Even where a local authority has a significant area of discretion, the checks and balances imposed on many public sector marketing managers reflects the fact that local authorities are accountable to a wider constituency of interests than the typical private sector organization.

5   Many of the marketing mix elements which private sector organizations can tailor to meet the needs of specific groups of users are often not open to the not-for-profit marketer. For non-traded public services, price – if it is used at all – is a reflection of centrally determined social values rather than the value placed on a service by the consumer.

6   It can be difficult in marketing nontraded public services to identify who the customer is. It could be argued that unlike most private sector services, the recipient is very often not the customer. In the case of publicly provided school education, the customer could be viewed either as the child undertaking the education, the parents of the children, or society as a whole which is investing in a trained workforce of tomorrow.

## 1.8   Services marketing and ethics

The intangibility of services and the fact that services cannot be examined before they are consumed implies that customers must trust a service provider to deliver the service that they promised. In some cases, the superior knowledge of the supplier relative to the customer may result in the customer not really being able to verbalize what they need (for example, a car owner may have no idea about the nature of a fault in their car and therefore what service needs to be carried out to repair it). Ethics therefore becomes an important element of services marketing.

Ethics is essentially about the definition of what is right and wrong. However, a difficulty occurs in trying to agree just what is right and wrong. It can also be difficult to distinguish between ethics and legality, for example it may not be strictly illegal to recommend unnecessary repairs to a car, but it may nevertheless be unethical. Ethics are very much culturally bound and what is considered unethical in one society may be considered perfectly acceptable in another.

In Western societies, ethical considerations confront services marketers on many occasions. Consider the following scenarios:

- The operator of a solarium may advertise its service and provide information which is technically correct, but omit to provide vital information about side effects associated with using the service. Should service suppliers be required to spell out the drawbacks of using their services, as well as the benefits?
- An estate agent may not disclose a favour which he is doing for a close friend in respect of a customer's property which he is selling. The agent may try to convince a seller of a house to accept a low price for the sale of their house, when the agent hasn't disclosed that his friend is interested in buying it. Should disclosure be required?
- A dentist is short of money and diagnoses unnecessary fillings. How does he reconcile his need to maximize his earning potential with the need to provide what is best for his patient?
- In order to secure a major new construction contract, a sales person must entertain the client's buying manager with a weekend all-expenses paid holiday. Should this be considered normal business practice in Britain? Or in South America?

Ethical judgements about services are made by consumers at a number of levels:

1 At an *instrumental* level, customers take a view of a service supplier's ethics and judge whether it will be a good organization to do business with. A patient of a dentist, for example, will form a view about whether the dentist will act in the patient's own best interest perhaps by not recommending unnecessary treatments for their teeth. A client of a financial services intermediary will judge whether they believe the adviser will give fair and impartial advice which does not put pressure on them to buy services which are not in their long-term best interest. The high credence qualities of many services makes this type of ethical evaluation very important for service providers. An individual is likely to be guided by the word-of-mouth recommendation of friends and by general media reports about the ethics of a service provider.

2 At a *product* level, buyers evaluate an individual product's acceptability to society at large. Initial interest in the social acceptability of products focused on the manufactured goods sector, with environmentalism emerging as a major factor affecting consumer purchases during the 1980s. Because of the intangible nature of services, social costs and benefits of services can be less easy to identify than

for goods. Nevertheless, there is evidence that some segments of the population are widening their evaluatory criteria to include the benefits which a service brings to society (or the social cost which they avoid). Within the financial services sector, there is now a wide range of fund management services available to investors who are concerned about the ethics of their investments. Within the travel and tourism sector, many tour operators now make claims about their fair treatment of host country populations. Some customers of package holidays – admittedly a small niche group – choose their package holiday destination on the basis of tourism's environmental impact at a resort and choose their service provider – the tour operator – on the basis of their policies towards environmentally benign development of resorts.

3   At a *corporate* level, buyers evaluate the overall ethics of a company. It is argued in later chapters that the promotion of service organizations' corporate brands is generally more important than the promotion of specific product brands. For this reason, many service organizations are keen to promote their ethical standards and to link themselves to good social causes. The Co-operative Bank, for example, has taken a distinctive position within the crowded financial services marketplace by agreeing to run its business in accordance with a set of ethical guidelines.

Are we all becoming more socially conscious, or just more aware of the short-comings of business organizations? While social commentators point to falling standards in many aspects of public morality, we are often only too keen to highlight the failures of businesses. Consumer programmes on television frequently attract large audiences and bad publicity for companies whose unethical practices have been exposed. More recently, the development of the Internet has allowed information about firms' bad practices to be rapidly gathered and disseminated. The fast-food restaurant McDonald's has its own website created by objectors who sought to monitor the company following its decision to prosecute two people in the UK for alleged libel against the company. However, some have argued that knocking large, profitable companies has become a popular pastime and one which television companies know will boost their ratings. How do we decide what is good, socially responsible business practice? Should issues of social responsibility be left to the interaction of consumer television programmes and companies' public relations departments, or left to a democratically elected government?

**Figure 1.10**
In a market which is dominated by basically similar service offers, an ethical positioning may give a service provider a competitive advantage in the eyes of some customers. Many people would regard the major UK supermarkets as being essentially similar in their service offer, but in this advertisement Sainsbury's is seeking to promote its ethical credentials (reproduced with permission of Sainsbury's Supermarkets Ltd)

## Ford cars go in for a service

This chapter has talked about a goods–services continuum, and to many people, cars come pretty close to the goods-dominant extreme of the continuum. They are produced in factories from the combination of thousands of components, and to most people the physical properties of a car can readily be assessed. But recent experience from the car sector suggests that car manufacturers may be rather more enthusiastic to describe themselves as service-oriented companies. Indeed, the modern car buyer is buying a bundle of service benefits, just as much as the tangible components of the product offer.

The days are long gone when a car manufacturer would sell a car on the strength of its design features, and then forget about the customer until the time came to replace the car three years later. Car manufacturers realized that car buyers sought more than the tangible offering – important though that was. Over time, they have moved increasingly into the services sector in an attempt to gain a larger share of car buyers' wallets.

In the UK, Ford has led the way in many aspects of this increasing service orientation. It saw an opportunity in the 1970s with the liberalization of consumer credit regulations to offer car buyers loan facilities with which to make their car purchase. Not only did this make it easier for middle income groups to buy its cars, it also allowed Ford to retain the margins which would otherwise have gone to banks who were the main alternative source of car loan finance. Ford Motor Credit has become a licensed credit broker and a major profit centre within the company.

The next significant attempt to gain a greater share of car buyers' wallets came through selling extended warranties on the cars it sold. Traditionally, new cars had come with just 12 months' warranty, but Ford realized that many buyers wanted to buy peace of mind that they were not going to face unexpected repair bills after their initial warranty had expired. Increased competition from Japanese importers, and the improving reliability of its new cars encouraged this development.

By the mid-1990s, Ford came round to the view that many of its customers were buying transport solutions, rather than a car *per se*. So it came up with schemes where customers paid a small deposit, followed by a fixed amount per month, in return for which they received comprehensive finance and warranty facilities. In addition, it promised that the company would take back the car after three years and replace it with a new one. Marketed under the 'Options' brand name, Ford was soon selling nearly half of its new cars to private buyers using this method. Over time the scheme was developed to include facilities for maintaining and insuring the car.

Repairs and maintenance have always been important in the car sector, but manufacturers tended to lose out on much of the benefits of this to a fragmented dealership network. Customer databases for maintenance and new car sales were often not co-ordinated and Ford found that it had very little direct communication with the people who bought its cars. By the 1990s, the dealership network was becoming more closely integrated with Ford's operations and new opportunities were seized for keeping new car buyers within the system. Recent buyers could be alerted to new services available at local dealers, using a database managed centrally by Ford. Numerous initiatives were launched, such as Ford's own mobile phone service. Ford sought to make it easy for customers to get back on the road when their own car was taken in for servicing, so the provision of car hire facilities contributed to the service ethos. In 1996, the company linked up with Barclaycard to offer a Ford branded credit card, so Ford found itself providing a service to its customers which was quite removed from the tangible cars that it sold (although points accrued using the card could be used to reduce the price of a new Ford car).

By 2000, volume car manufacturers had ceased to make big profits in the UK. Ford, with 18% of the market in 1998, lost money on its European operations. Falling profit margins on selling new cars were partly offset by profits made on service-based activities. For the future, Ford is increasingly positioning itself as a service provider offering transport solutions. In 1998, it sought to acquire the RAC's car breakdown service operation when it came up for sale. It lost out on that occasion to Lex, but later went on to acquire Kwik Fit, a leading UK car servicing and repair business, which had itself expanded into the car insurance market.

## Case study review questions

1   Given the evidence of Ford, is it still appropriate to talk about the goods and services sectors being quite distinctive?

2   What business is Ford in? What business should it be in?

3   Discuss the view that Ford should do what it is good at – designing cars – and leave services to other companies.

## Chapter summary and linkages to other chapters

Services are becoming an increasingly important element of developed economies, and this chapter has traced their development and the thinking which has been associated with their marketing. An important message of this chapter is that services are not a homogeneous group of activities, but rather we should see a continuum of products from pure goods to pure services. Intangibility, inseparability, perishability and variability have been introduced as key defining characteristics of a service. The effects on marketing activities of these characteristics have been noted. While the general principles of marketing may apply to all products, an extended marketing mix for services has been suggested which takes account of the staff interaction and intangible process characteristics of services. In the case of not-for-profit sector services, further constraints on marketing management have been noted.

This chapter has set the scene for subsequent chapters. Definitions of services introduced here will be elaborated later. For example **Chapter 2** defines what is meant by the service product offer and **Chapter 3** analyses services in terms of customer–provider encounters. Buyer behaviour and relationship development are considered further in **Chapters 4 and 5**. Information management (**Chapter 6**) is becoming increasingly crucial to achieving a marketing orientation and to develop sustainable competitive positions (**Chapter 7**). The concept of service quality in **Chapter 8** brings together various elements of marketing activity. The extended marketing mix of management tools is considered in **Chapters 8–11**. **Chapters 12–14** return to this first chapter by seeking to integrate the topics of the middle chapters within the marketing management framework. The final chapter (**Chapter 15**) offers an integrated perspective on how service firms might replicate their success in overseas markets.

## www linkages/URLs

Chartered Institute of Marketing:
http://www.cim.co.uk/

American Marketing Association:
http://www.ama.org/

Marketing magazine Online:
http://www.marketing.haynet.com

Marketing Week Online:
http://www.marketing-week.co.uk/      or      http://mad.co.uk/mw/

## Key terms

| | |
|---|---|
| Services 2 | Service encounters 3 |
| Productivity 5 | Multiplier effect 5 |
| Services multiplier 5 | Competitive advantage 6 |
| Marketing 8 | Customer needs 8 |
| Marketing mix 10 | Extended marketing mix 11 |
| Product mix 11 | Pure services 11 |
| Postmodern marketing 14 | Intangibility 16 |
| Inseparability 16 | Variability 18 |
| Perishability 20 | |

## Chapter review questions

1   To what extent do you consider that the principles of marketing which have been traditionally applied to the goods sector are appropriate for the services sector?

2   Of what use is the concept of a marketing mix for the development of marketing strategies for services?

3   What is meant by inseparability? Suggest why its existence might pose problems to service organizations and methods by which its impact may be reduced.

4   Analyse the nature of the needs which may be satisfied by a household mortgage.

5   What problems might be associated with an over-enthusiastic adoption of marketing within the public services sector?

6   To what extent do you consider that purchasers of services have concern for the ethics of how a service is produced? How would you assess firms' responses to such concerns?

## Selected further reading

*The first article is a classic which explores the idea of a continuum between pure goods and pure services marketing, and introduces a molecular model of all products as being composed of elements of goods and services.*

Shostack, G. L. (1977) 'Breaking Free from Product Marketing', *Journal of Marketing*, April, Vol. 41, pp 73–80

*The following paper article the issue of a lack of theory for services marketing and discusses marketing mix planning within the services sector.*

Gronroos, C. (1978) 'A Service Oriented Approach to Marketing of Services', *European Journal of Marketing*, Vol. 12, No. 8, pp 588–601

*The following five references are typical of the early debate about whether services marketing should be considered to be a separate subject in its own right. They are useful for identifying the key characteristics of services.*

Bateson, J. (1977) 'Do We Need Service Marketing?', in *Marketing Consumer Services: New Insights*, Report 77-115, Marketing Science Institute, Boston, MA

Berry, L. L. (1980) 'Services Marketing is Different', *Business*, May–June, Vol. 30, No. 3, pp 24–9

Levitt, T. (1981) 'Marketing Intangible Products and Product Tangibles', *Harvard Business Review*, May–June, Vol. 59, pp 95–102

Lovelock, C. (1981) 'Why Marketing Needs To Be Different for Services', in J. H. Donnelly and W. R. George (eds.), *Marketing of Services*, American Marketing Association, Chicago, IL

Rathmell, J. M. (1966) 'What is meant by services?', *Journal of Marketing*, October, Vol. 30, pp 32–6

*For a review of how the literature on services marketing has evolved, the following is a useful reference:*

Fisk, R. P., S. W. Brown and M. J. Bitner (1993) 'Tracking the Evolution of the Services Marketing Literature', *Journal of Retailing*, Vol. 69, No. 1, pp 61–103

*For a review of the distinctive aspects of the public sector and how they impact on marketing, the following article is useful. It examines relevant structural and process characteristics and their effects.*

Butler, P. and N. Collins, (1995) 'Marketing Public Sector Services: Concepts and Characteristics', *Journal of Marketing Management*, Vol. 11, No. 1, pp 83–96

*For a general introduction to the principles of marketing, numerous texts are available, including the following:*

Baker, M. (1999) *The Marketing Book*, 4th edition, Butterworth-Heinemann, Oxford
Kotler, P., G. Armstrong, J. Saunders and V. Wong (1999) *Principles of Marketing*, 2nd European edition, Prentice-Hall, London

*Limitations of the traditional marketing mix framework are discussed in the following:*

Brown, S. (1995) *Postmodern Marketing*, Routledge, London
Murray, J. A. and A. O'Driscoll, A. (1997) 'Messianic Eschatology: Some Redemptive Reflections on Marketing and the Benefits of a Process Approach', *European Journal of Marketing*, September–October, Vol. 31, No. 9–10, pp 706–20
O'Malley, L. and M. Patterson (1998) 'Vanishing Point: The Mix Management Paradigm Reviewed', *Journal of Marketing Management*, Vol. 14, No. 8, pp 829–52

# 2

# The service offer

## Learning objectives

Consumers buy products in the expectation that the benefits flowing from them will satisfy some underlying need. This is true for all products, whether goods-based or service-based. However, the nature of the features and benefits of a service can be much more difficult to identify than for goods. The absence of tangible evidence limits the extent to which services can be described using objective and verifiable criteria. This chapter begins by discussing the different levels at which a service offer can be defined. It will become clear from this analysis that services comprise a diverse range of activities, in which the descriptor of services may be considered too broad to be of any analytical value. Some time is therefore spent in classifying services on the basis of their characteristics. Finally, it should never be forgotten that services are essentially about processes, in which customers are not passive consumers of the product offer, but active participants in the creation of the service. This important point will be returned to in the following chapter when the nature of service encounters will be considered more fully.

## 2.1 Introduction

Products form the focal point for an organization's effort in satisfying its customers' needs. The features, design, styling and ranges of the product – among other things – help the organization to gain competitive advantage in meeting its customers' needs more effectively than its competitors. Product decisions form just one set of decisions which an organization makes in order to satisfy customers' needs. They must be related to decisions in respect of the other elements of the marketing mix in order to give a coherent market position for a service.

It was noted in Chapter 1 that the traditional marketing mix formulation which has been applied to goods may not be appropriate for the marketing of services. However, most reformulations of the marketing mix continue to place great emphasis on product decisions, although the concept of a product and the nature of product decisions for services can be quite different compared to goods. The purpose of this chapter is to consider conceptual frameworks for understanding the nature of service product offers.

## 2.2 The service offer

The term 'product' is used to describe both tangible goods offerings and relatively intangible service offerings. A starting point for understanding the nature of products is to take a generic definition provided by Dibb *et al.* (1994, p 194) who define a product as:

> '... a complexity of tangible and intangible attributes, including functional, social and psychological utilities or benefits. A product can be an idea, a service, a good or any combination of these three'.

While this definition is intended to be universal in its coverage, Kotler (1997) recognizes that significant differences occur between different product offerings and proposed four categories of product offers:

- Pure tangibles.
- Tangibles with accompanying services.
- Major services with accompanying minor goods and services.
- Pure services.

The fact that most products are usually a combination of goods and services has been highlighted in the evolution of the services marketing literature. Rathmell (1974) distinguished between support goods and facilitating goods in the service offer. The former are tangible aspects of a service that aid the service provision (a textbook in education for example), whereas facilitating goods must exist for the service to be provided in the first place (for example, a car is a prerequisite for the provision of a car hire service). In reality, customers do not buy products as such, but buy the benefits which a product offers. The most important element of any organization's marketing mix therefore can be considered to be its 'offer' and what is being considered in this chapter is the organization's 'service offer'.

An understanding of just what constitutes the service offer from both buyers' and sellers' points of view is imperative. Sasser, Olsen and Wyckoff (1978) defined purchase bundles, or the 'service concept' in terms of three elements:

- Firstly, physical items: these are the tangible/material elements which are the facilitating or support goods, for example the food or drink served in a restaurant.
- Secondly, there are sensual benefits, benefits that can be defined by one or more of the five senses, such as the taste and aroma of a restaurant meal or the ambience of a restaurant.
- Finally, Sasser *et al.* identify the psychological benefits of a service purchase bundle. These are benefits which cannot be clearly defined and are determined by the customer subjectively. The existence of this type of benefit makes the management of the service offer very difficult.

Service offers can be distinguished from goods offers by their inseparability. The fact that a service cannot usually be separated from the person who provides it, nor from the place where it is provided, results in services being 'consumed' as soon as they are produced and this therefore means a high degree of buyer/supplier interaction. The concept of value added in the product also takes on new meaning. In both production and marketing, the concept of value added is the difference between input and output at various levels on the supply side. Since services are not resold, Rathmell has argued that there can only be one level of value added, with the concept of input being redefined to mean only supplies consumed and the depreciation of capital goods used up in the production of a service.

## 2.2.1 Analysis of the service offer

A number of elements within the service offer can be identified, some of which are fundamental to the nature of the product, while others refine or differentiate it. For products in general, an analysis by Kotler *et al.* (1999) distinguishes between three different levels of an individual product.

- The first level is known as the *core* product. This is defined in terms of the underlying need which a product satisfies.
- The second level is known as the *tangible* product level. The core product is made available to consumers in some tangible form – this tangible form is expressed in terms of the product's features, styling, packaging, brand name and quality level.
- The third level of product defined by Kotler *et al.* (1999) is the *augmented* product. This is the tangible product plus additional services and benefits, included to satisfy additional needs of consumers and/or to further differentiate a product from its competitors. Many of these additional features tend to be services such as pre-sales and after-sales service, guarantees, etc.

An application of this multi-level approach to the analysis of the product offering of a car is shown in Figure 2.1. While this analysis is held to be true of products in

**Figure 2.1**

Analysis of the product offering of a car into core, tangible and augmented components

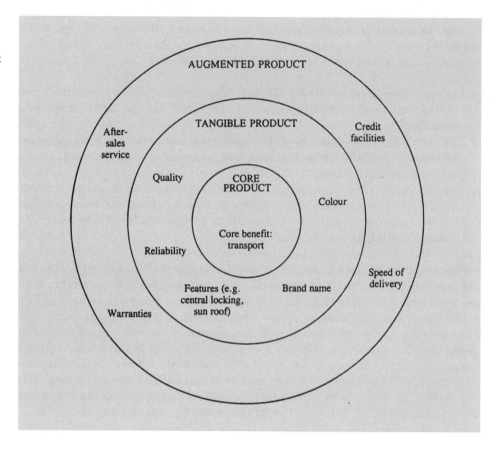

general, doubts have been expressed about whether it can be applied to the service offer. Is it possible to identify a **core service** representing the essence of a consumer's perceived need that requires satisfying? If such a core service exists, can it be made available in a form that is 'consumer friendly', and if so, what elements are included in this form? Finally, is there a level of service corresponding to the augmented product which allows a service provider to differentiate its service offer from its competitors in the same way as a car manufacturer differentiates its augmented product from its competitors?

A number of writers have sought to revise this basic framework to identify different levels of the service offer. Sasser *et al.* (1978) distinguished between the substantive service and peripheral services. Gronroos (1984) distinguished between the service concept and elements of what he calls the 'interactive marketing function'.

Most contemporary analyses of the service offer recognize that the problems of inseparability and intangibility make application of the three generic levels of product offer less meaningful to the service offer. Instead, the service offer is analysed here in terms of two components:

- The core service which represents the core benefit.
- The secondary service which represents both the tangible and augmented product levels.

## 2.3 The core service level

Sasser *et al.* (1978) called this the *substantive* service which is best understood as the essential function of a service. Gronroos (1984) used the term *service concept* to denote the core of a service offering. Gronroos stated that it could be general, such as offering a solution to transport problems, e.g. car hire, or it could be more specific such as offering Chinese cuisine in a restaurant.

In any event, there seems to be little difference between services and material goods when considering this fundamental level of a firm's offer. All customers' needs and wants are intangible – they cannot be seen or touched. The offer should be developed, produced and managed with consumers' benefit in mind in such a way that they perceive it as being successful in satisfying their needs and wants. The offer can be a tangible good, a service, or a combination of both.

It follows that an understanding of customers' needs and wants is vital if a service provider wishes to be successful, requiring a 'common view' or 'perceptual congruence' between itself and service users. This in turn requires 'soft' data of a behavioural nature which allows an understanding of what benefits the customer derives from a service. This highlights the importance of appropriate marketing research, in particular qualitative research and its attempts to measure consumers' perceptions, beliefs and attitudes. In formulating service design, market research should place great emphasis on customer perceptions of the service itself.

## 2.4 The secondary service level

It was noted above that the secondary level of a service offering can be seen as representing both the tangible level of a product and the augmented level. At the augmented level, service suppliers offer additional benefits to consumers that go beyond the tangible evidence. This is done either to meet additional consumer wants and/or to further differentiate the product from the competition.

As there is no 'tangible' level of a service in the manner that the term is understood in a goods context, it could be argued that it is not possible to define an augmented service. However, many of the elements normally considered to be part of the augmented product relate to how the product is distributed/delivered, e.g. installation, delivery, credit availability and after-sales service. The idea of intangibility implies that when a consumer decides to purchase a service there is no guarantee that he or she will be able to experience (feel, see, hear, taste or smell) the service before it is purchased. Rushton and Carson (1985) also noted that in many cases, services can also be mentally intangible in that they are concepts that are difficult to grasp.

Shostack (1977) looked into the issue of intangibility in more depth. She saw services as being more than just products which are intangible:

> ... it is wrong to imply that services are just like products except for intangibility. By such logic apples are just like oranges, except for their 'appleness'. Intangibility is not a modifier, it is a state.

Shostack's molecular model (discussed in Chapter 1) is merely her way of making the point that there is a product continuum. A service dominant offer concerned primarily with intangible elements is at one extreme, and a product dominant offer consisting predominantly of tangible elements is at the other. For Shostack, the greater the weight of intangible elements in an offer, the greater the divergence from the approach of goods marketing. Services knowledge and goods knowledge are not gained in the same way. Customers of physical products can 'know' their product through physical examination and/or quantitative measurement. Service reality must be defined experientially by the user and there are many versions of this reality.

For services, therefore, the secondary level of a service offer involves a combination of both tangible and intangible elements in order that the core benefit is realized by the customer. There are, however, a number of specific difficulties involved in determining the particular combination of these tangibles and intangibles. One major difficulty is the actual articulation of the elements, for it is far easier to articulate the tangible aspects than it is to produce and display the intangibles. In addition, the intangible elements are relatively difficult to control and therefore there is a tendency for service managers to emphasize the controllable, i.e. the tangible elements rather than the more difficult intangibles. Shostack (1977) believed that the more intangible the service, the greater the need for tangible evidence and the importance of managing tangible evidence.

Another major conceptual problem in defining the service offer is that because of inseparability of production and consumption, some elements of the secondary service level are not actually provided by the service provider but by customers themselves, for example the student who 'reads around' a subject before attending a seminar.

Notwithstanding the above difficulties, the secondary level of the service offer can be analysed in terms of a number of elements, some of which bear comparison with the elements used in analysing the offering of a tangible good. The principle elements are discussed below and some of these are illustrated in Figure 2.2 where an insurance product is used as an example.

### 2.4.1 Features

In the tangible product, features represent specific components of the product that could be added or subtracted without changing its essential characteristics. Features can be added or subtracted to the product so that an organization produces a range of products that appeal to a variety of different market segments, each with the same core needs but each segment requiring marginally different products to satisfy slightly differing secondary needs.

In much the same way, most service offers can be analysed in terms of differentiating features, for example banks usually offer different types of current accounts to appeal to segments of the population with slightly differing needs. Features may include ease of access (e.g. by telephone, Internet or through local branches); paying-in/withdrawal facilities; the use of an ATM card and overdraft facilities.

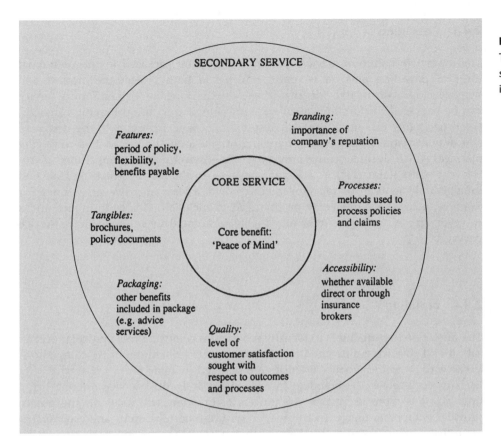

**Figure 2.2**

The core and secondary service elements of an insurance product

### 2.4.2 Styling

Styling means giving the product a distinctive feel or look. Is this a possibility with a service?

It would seem at first glance easier to do this in relation to the tangible elements of the service offer than for the intangible elements. However, if a broader definition of style is considered to comprise an external manner, mode or approach rather than merely a physical quality, there is little difficulty in applying this concept to the service offer. In this instance, the customer gains the 'sensual benefits' which were described earlier.

The inseparability of the service offer makes the relationship between customer and service provider of paramount importance and it is through this relationship that a service manager can develop a distinctive style. For example, there is a difference between the style of a McDonald's restaurant and that of a Little Chef, although they are both in the business of selling relatively low-value, high-speed food and drink. The style of a service is a result of the combination of features, including tangible decor and the intangible manner in which front-line staff interact with customers. The overall service style can be established either before or after the target market is identified.

### 2.4.3  Packaging

The intangible nature of services prevent them being packaged in the traditional sense of providing physical wrapping which can both protect the product and help develop a distinctive identity. However, the tangible elements of a service can be packaged, performing much the same function as the packaging of goods. Good packaging can make service consumption easier, for example the design of takeaway containers can ease the handling of take-away food as well as conveying messages which distinguish the provider of the service from its competitors.

In a wider sense, service packaging can refer to the way in which tangible and intangible elements are bundled together to provide a comprehensive service offer. For example, a mortgage offer may be packaged to include buildings insurance and a surveyor's report, or a restaurant may include a home delivery service in its service package.

### 2.4.4  Branding

The purpose of **branding** is to identify products as belonging to a particular organization and to enable differentiation of its products from those of its competitors. While most tangible product offerings are branded in some form, the service offer itself is less likely to be branded. Instead of the individual service offering being branded, it is more likely that the process of branding will focus on the service provider's corporate image. In this way, both fast-food restaurants and accountants are usually differentiated on the basis of their corporate name and reputation rather than the specific services which they offer.

There are, however, instances where the service itself is branded, or there is a hierarchy of brands and subbrands representing both corporate identity and service specific identity. Often, service specific branding has a tangible basis (e.g. a 'Big Mac' offered by McDonald's) although at other times the product brand is based largely on intangibles (e.g. where a bank applies specific brand names to types of account). The role of a brand in developing a market position for a service offer is considered further in Chapter 7.

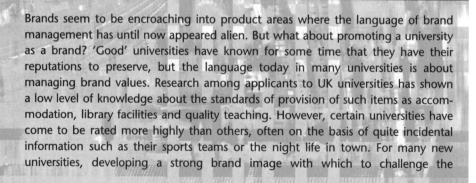

Brands seem to be encroaching into product areas where the language of brand management has until now appeared alien. But what about promoting a university as a brand? 'Good' universities have known for some time that they have their reputations to preserve, but the language today in many universities is about managing brand values. Research among applicants to UK universities has shown a low level of knowledge about the standards of provision of such items as accommodation, library facilities and quality teaching. However, certain universities have come to be rated more highly than others, often on the basis of quite incidental information such as their sports teams or the night life in town. For many new universities, developing a strong brand image with which to challenge the established ones has been seen as a priority. Even students felt it was important to belong to one which had a 'good' name, however irrational the basis for its standing. De Montfort University has been one of the pioneers in university brand building, supporting its efforts with television advertising. It undertook research among current students which showed, perhaps surprisingly, that many preferred limited university funds to be spent on a brand building advertising campaign, rather than improvements to the library facilities. Going to a known rather than an unknown university was seen as an important part of a university education. Cynics have been quick to criticize such efforts. How can a brand be sustained over the long term if the fabric of a university is crumbling all around?

### 2.4.5 Physical evidence

While manufacturers of goods tend to introduce additional services into their augmented product, service marketers are more likely to differentiate their services from the competition by adding tangible features, for example distinctive designs of brochures, staff uniforms and service outlets.

### 2.4.6 Service delivery

Just as delivery can be an important differentiator for goods, it can also be equally important for a service. According to Gronroos (1984b), service marketers should use the concept of accessibility rather than seeing service provision in terms of distribution/delivery as with goods. A number of resources affect this accessibility, e.g. human resources (especially contact personnel), machines, buildings and other physical infrastructure, as well as supplementary services. These resources can be managed by a service organization to enhance the accessibility of its service to consumers. The service itself may be intangible but these resources make the delivery of the service a reality.

### 2.4.7 Process

Most services are evaluated as much by their production process as by their final outcomes. Service design should therefore pay attention to processes and the manner in which service personnel interact with customers during this process. One approach to designing the process is to use Shostack's 'Blueprinting' approach (discussed in Chapter 3).

### 2.4.8 People

It was noted above that the people involved in the process of delivering a service can be crucial in defining that service and customers' perceptions of it. Personnel therefore become an important element of the service offer and management must define the role expectations of employees and support this with training where necessary. In addition to managing the interaction between customers and service producers' own personnel, other consumers who use or buy the service may influence the perception of the service where it is consumed in public. Many service industries therefore employ methods to control the behaviour of their customers where they are likely to influence other customers' enjoyment or image of a service.

### 2.4.9 Quality

The level of quality to which a service is designed is a crucial element in the total service offering. Quality is an important factor used by customers to evaluate the services of one organization in comparison to the offerings of other organizations. In fact, customers may judge not so much the quality of an individual service offer, but rather the quality of the service provider.

In goods marketing, quality can be understood as the level of performance of a product. In services marketing, quality is the perceived level of performance of a service, but with the major difficulty that measuring service quality can be much more difficult than measuring the quality of goods. Not only can it be difficult to measure quality parameters, it can also be difficult to identify which quality factors customers attach importance to. A service which may be seen by the producer as having high technical quality may in fact be perceived very differently by a consumer who has a different set of quality evaluation criteria.

The intangible nature of service quality standards is reflected in the difficulty which services companies have in designing quality standards which will be readily accepted by potential customers. Customer expectations form an important element of quality. A service which fails to meet the expectations of one customer may be considered by them to be of poor quality, while another customer receiving an identical service, but who did not hold such high expectations may consider the service to be of a high quality standard. In this way, an irregular traveller who has won a flight on Concorde may consider all aspects of the service experience to exceed their limited expectations. On the other hand, a regular business traveller with relatively exacting expectations may rate the service as being of low quality on account of niggling problems such as the speed of check-in facilities and the attentiveness of the cabin crew.

There is increasing interest in the concept of service quality, both among academics and practitioners who see superior quality levels as a way of gaining competitive advantage. For this reason, considerable research has been undertaken to understand the processes by which customers evaluate quality. A sound understanding of these processes can allow service companies to be clearer in their specification of quality levels which they incorporate in their offering, as well as allowing a clearer communication to potential customers of the service level on offer.

In general, tangible goods can be designed and produced to a pre-determined standard and because such standards can generally be quantified, it is relatively easy to monitor and maintain them. With intangible services, the difficulties associated with quantification of standards makes it much more difficult for an organization to monitor and maintain a consistently high standard of service. Furthermore, the intangibility and inseparability of most services results in a series of unique buyer/ seller exchanges with no two services being provided in exactly the same way. It is in an attempt to reduce the problems of uniqueness that many service providers have sought to 'industrialize' their output by offering a limited range of machine assisted services with lower variability in output.

Because of the importance of quality in the total service offer, the subject of defining, measuring, planning, implementing and monitoring quality standards is considered in more detail in Chapter 8.

### 2.4.10 Ongoing buyer–seller relationships

Finally, an increasingly important feature of many services is the level of support which is provided by a company to customers after the initial service process has been completed. A company offering a guarantee to rectify any results of faulty service delivery offers additional benefits compared to a company which leaves customers to sort out the results of failures by themselves. An ongoing relationship could be based on a contractual agreement or the reputation of the service provider. Companies also add an ongoing relationship to the service offer where this makes it easier for customers to request service. An ongoing maintenance contract and breakdown service for a central heating system offers benefits to customers compared to a series of one-off transactions for maintenance and repairs. The subject of ongoing relationships is discussed further in Chapter 5.

## 2.5 Customers' perception of service attributes

From the previous discussion it should become clear that it is much more difficult to objectively describe services than is the case for goods. Services, or at least the benefits from consuming them, can only really be described in the minds of their consumers. It is therefore important for services organizations to understand the processes by which customers evaluate the total service offer. In the early literature on services, Sasser *et al.* (1978) suggested that buyers initially assess the core service for its ability to satisfy their substantive need for a service, such as a basic need for transport. There are, however, a number of other secondary needs such as the need for a sense of control, trust, self-fulfilment and status which are translated into a number of sought service attributes. These are translated into desired attributes which Sasser *et al.* have labelled:

- *Security* (the consumer's desire for the safety of themselves and/or his/her property).
- *Consistency* (reducing mental anguish associated with unpredictable patterns of service delivery).
- *Attitude* (of the service provider, e.g. was service provided with a smile?).

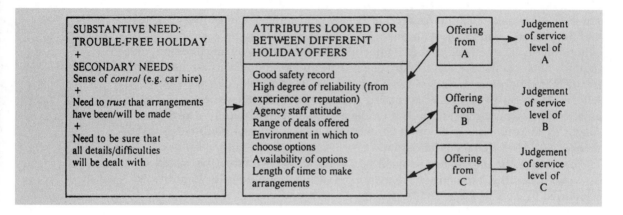

**Figure 2.3**

Consumer judgement
of the total service
offering

- *Completeness* (the comprehensiveness of the service range).
- *Condition* (the environment in which the service is provided).
- *Availability* (whether the service is available at the time and place that it is of most value).
- *Timing* (length of time required for and pace of performance of the service).

Service providers compete by producing service offers that contain a permutation of these attributes which meet customers' secondary needs better than their competitors.

An indication of the relationship between core and secondary service levels and their relationship to customer product evaluation processes is shown in Figure 2.3.

Faced with an array of service attributes, some understanding of the processes by which customers evaluate each bundle of attributes is desirable. Three basic approaches can be identified:

- Firstly, a consumer may make a judgement based on an overpowering attribute which for that particular individual is of great importance in a given situation.
- Secondly, judgement may be made on the basis of minimum levels of certain attributes but final judgement is based on the existence of a single specific attribute.
- Thirdly, the consumer may decide upon alternatives using a weighted average of attributes.

A major difficulty with this model, however, is that customers are often not consciously aware of what their needs are. Rathmell (1974) noted that in some respects, the service product is an idea, and as such, the need for a service is often unrecognized by the buyer until he or she becomes aware of its availability. Many people, for example, are not aware of their need for life insurance until advertising makes them aware of it. Even if consumers are aware of their needs, they often have difficulty in expressing their desires to service providers. In addition, customers' needs are unlikely to remain constant as individual customers and their marketing environment change.

A service offer cannot be defined without the consumer benefit concept being considered. Although the understanding of customer service requirements can be a difficult task, it is essential that service firms do not fall into the trap of being production oriented and is considered further in Chapter 4.

## 2.6 Classification of services

In the previous chapter, it was noted that most products lie on a continuum from a pure good to a pure service. This chapter has so far suggested that service offers can be very complex, satisfying a diverse range of consumers' needs. The contrast between a simple local window cleaning service and a complex international banking facility illustrates this diversity. Because of this diversity, any analysis of the service sector will prove to be very weak unless smaller categories of services can be identified and subjected to an analytical framework which is particularly appropriate to that category of service.

The most common basis for classifying services has been the type of activity which is performed. Statistics record service activities under headings such as banking, shipping and hotels, based largely on similarity of production methods. In this way, shipping is defined in terms of organizations who are largely engaged in movement by sea, even though freight movement between Dover and Calais is quite different from the operation of a cruise ship in the Caribbean.

Such simple classification systems are not particularly helpful to marketers. In the first place, a single production sector can cover a very diverse range of activities with quite different marketing needs. Small guest houses and international hotels may fall within the same sector, but their marketing needs are likely to be quite different. Secondly, most services are in fact a combination of services. Retail stores, for example, often go beyond their traditional sectoral boundaries by offering banking facilities. Thirdly, the marketing needs of a particular production-based subsector may share more in common with another unrelated subsector rather than other areas within its own sector.

Marketers should be more interested in identifying subsectors in terms of similarity of marketing requirements. In this way, the provision of hotel services may have quite a lot in common with some shipping operations in terms of the processes by which customers make purchase decisions: methods of pricing and promotional strategies, for example.

Defining categories of services is arguably more complex than for manufactured goods, where terms such as fast-moving consumer goods, shopping goods, speciality goods, white goods, brown goods are widely used and convey a lot of information about the marketing requirements of products within a category. The great diversity of services has made attempts to reduce services to a small number of categories difficult to achieve. Instead, many analysts have sought to classify services along a number of continua, reflecting the fact that products cannot be classified into dichotomous goods and services categories to begin with.

Many of the bases for classifying services derive from the five fundamental characteristics of services described in Section 1.4. Thus, groups of services as diverse as merchant banking and psychoanalysis show similar levels of intangibility which results in, among other things, high levels of uncertainty in the buying process. The following sections discuss further bases on which marketers can classify groups of services in order to identify common marketing needs.

### 2.6.1 Marketable versus unmarketable services

This first classification distinguishes between those services which are considered marketable and those where the social and economic environment of the time considers it desirable that benefits should be distributed by non-market-based mechanisms. Among the latter group, many government services are provided for the public benefit but no attempt made to charge users of the service. This can arise where it is impractical to exclude individuals or groups of individuals from benefiting from a service. For example, it is not possible in practice for a local authority to charge individuals for the use of local footpaths. The benefits are essentially external in that it is not possible to restrict the distribution of the benefit to those who have entered into some form of exchange relationship. Furthermore, many public services are said to result in no rivalries in consumption in that one person's enjoyment of a service does not prevent another person enjoying the same service. One person using a footpath does not generally prevent another person from using the same path.

A second major group of services which many cultures do not consider to be marketable are those commonly provided within household units, such as the bringing up of children, cooking and cleaning. While many of these services are now commonly marketed within Western societies (e.g. child-minding services), many societies – and segments within societies – would regard the internal provision of such services as central to the functioning of family units. Attempts by Western companies to launch family-based services in cultures with strong family traditions may result in failure because no market exists.

As with all service classifications, a whole range of services lie between these two extremes and the classification of any service is dynamic, reflecting changes in the political, economic, social and technological environments. Attempts are often made to internalize many of the **external benefits** of public services, turning them into marketable services. The provision of road facilities in the UK may have been considered until recently to be totally unmarketable, for the reasons described above. Since then, proposals for toll roads based on marketing principles of selling relatively uncongested road space to motorists have appeared. Similarly, attitudes towards which household produced services should be considered marketable have changed over time and government social policy has had the effect of forcing trade-offs between home produced services and bought-in services, for example in relation to the buying in of care services for elderly relatives.

### 2.6.2 Producer versus consumer services

**Consumer services** are provided for individuals who use up the service for their own enjoyment or benefit. No further economic benefit results from the consumption of the service. In this way, the services of a hairdresser can be defined as consumer services. On the other hand, **producer services** are those which are bought by a business in order that it can produce something else of economic benefit. A road haulage company sells services to its industrial customers in order that they can add value to the goods that they produce, by allowing their goods to be made available where customers want them.

Many services are provided simultaneously to both consumer and producer markets. Here, the challenge is to adapt the marketing programme to meet the differing needs of each group of users. In this way, airlines provide a basically similar service to both consumer and producer markets, but the marketing programme may emphasize low price for the former and quality and greater short-notice availability for the latter.

While this is a very common basis for classifying service sectors, it could be argued that a private household may act as a production unit in which services are bought not for their own intrinsic value, but in order to allow some other benefit to be produced. Thus a mortgage is not so much consumed, rather it is used to produce the benefit of homemaking. There is also evidence that industrial buyers of services do not simply judge a service on its ability to profitably add value to their own production process, but the personal, non-organizational goals of individuals within an organization may cause some decisions to be based on personal consumption criteria. A mobile telephone service may be judged for its personal status value as well as its productive value.

### 2.6.3 The status of the service in the product offering

It was stated above that most products are a combination of a goods and a service element. Services can be classified according to the role of the service in that total offering and three principal roles can be identified:

- A pure service exists where there is little if any evidence of tangible goods, for example an insurance policy or a management consultancy service. With this group, where tangible elements do exist, their primary function is to support an intangible service, in the way that a tangible aircraft supports the essentially intangible service of transport.
- A second group of services exist in order to add value to a tangible product. This can occur where a goods manufacturer augments its core tangible product with additional service benefits, such as after-sales warranties. In other cases, the service is sold as a discrete product which customers purchase to add value to their own goods – in this way, a car valeting service is purchased to add to the resale value of a used car.
- A third group of services may add value to a product more fundamentally by making it available in the first place. Such services can facilitate delivery of a tangible good from the point of production to the place where it is required by the consumer, or can provide the means through credit arrangements which allow tangible goods to be bought. In this way, mortgages facilitate house purchase and road haulage services facilitate delivery.

### 2.6.4 Extent of customer involvement

Some services can only be provided with the complete involvement of customers, whereas others require them to do little more than initiate the service process. In the first category, personal care services almost by definition require the complete in-volvement of customers during the service production and delivery process. This is often of an interactive nature, as where clients of a hairdresser answer a continuous series of questions about the emerging length and style of their hair. For such a customer, the quality of the service production process as well as of outcomes assume importance. For other services, it is not necessary for the customer to be so fully involved in the production process. Customers listening to music on a radio do not need to be involved for the service to be delivered – they can quite passively receive the service.

Customer involvement is generally lower where the service is carried out not on the mind or body directly, but on customers' possessions. The transport of goods, cleaning of a car or the operation of a bank account do not involve a service being carried out directly on the customer, whose main task is to initiate the service and to monitor performance of it. Monitoring can take the form of examining tangible evidence of service performance, such as examining whether a carpet has been cleaned to the required standard, or examining intangible evidence of performance, such as a statement about an investment which has been made on the customer's behalf.

Customer involvement has a psychological as well as a physical dimension. Services vary in the impact which they have on the consumer. Routinely purchased services may be forgotten about quickly and develop only minimal feelings in the consumer (e.g. a regular journey on a train). Others, however, have the potential to affect the state of mind of the recipient, as can be the case with many personal services, such as hairdressing. Because it is relatively difficult to maintain consistent production standards for services, many services organizations have sought to reduce the level of customer involvement in the production process. Simplification of the service production process and distant communication by mail or telephone have been used to achieve this.

### 2.6.5  The pattern of service delivery

Two aspects of service delivery are distinguished here:

- Whether a service is supplied on a continuous basis or as a series of discrete transactions.
- Whether it is supplied quite casually or within an ongoing relationship between buyer and seller.

With respect to the continuity of supply, a first group of services can be identified which are purchased only when they are needed as a series of one-off transactions. This is typical of low value, undifferentiated services which may be bought on impulse or with little conscious search activity (e.g. taxis and cafés). It can also be true of specialized, high-value services which are purchased only as required (e.g. funeral services are generally bought casually only when needed).

By contrast, other services can be identified where it is impractical to supply the service casually. This can occur where production methods make it difficult to supply a service only when it is needed (e.g. it is impractical to provide a telephone line to a house only when it is needed – the line itself is therefore supplied continuously) or where the benefits of a service are required continuously (e.g. insurance policies).

Continuous service supply is commonly – though not always – associated with a relationship existing between buyer and seller. A long-term relationship with a supplier can be important to customers in a number of situations; where the production/consumption process takes place over a long period of time (e.g. a programme of medical treatment); where the benefits will be received only after a long period of time (many financial services); and in cases where the purchaser faces a high level of perceived risk. Supply through an ongoing relationship rather than by discrete transactions can also reduce the transaction costs of having to search and order a service afresh on each occasion (e.g. an annual maintenance contract on domestic equipment avoids the need to find an engineer on each occasion that a failure occurs).

Sometimes, it is sensible to supply the central element of a service through an ongoing relationship, but to supply additional service benefits casually as and when required. In this way, a telephone line is supplied within an ongoing relationship, whereas individual calls are supplied casually as and when needed.

Services are classified according to the nature of their supply in Figure 2.4.

Service marketers generally try to move customers into the category where service is provided continuously rather than discretely and by an ongoing relationship rather than casually. The former can be achieved by offering incentives for the purchase of a continuous stream of service benefit (e.g. offering attractively priced annual travel insurance policies rather than selling individual short-term policies as and when required). The latter can be achieved by a number of strategies which are discussed more fully in Chapter 5. At its simplest, relationships could be developed through a communication programme to regularly inform existing customers of new service developments. It could develop into methods to tie customers to a single service provider by offering a long-term supply contract. In this way, a bus company may seek regular custom from individuals by offering season tickets which restrict the consumer's choice to one particular service provider.

### 2.6.6  People-based versus equipment-based services

Some services involve very labour intensive production methods. A fortune teller employs a production method which is almost wholly based on human actions.

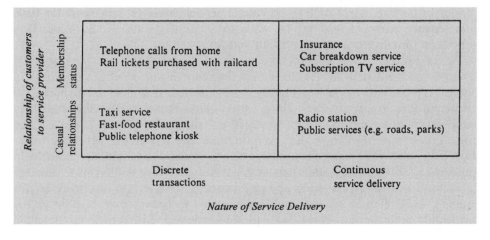

**Figure 2.4**
The nature of the relationship between producer and customer

At the other extreme, many services can be delivered with very little human involvement – a pay and display car park involves minimal human input in the form of checking tickets and keeping the car park clean.

The management of people-based services can be very different from those based on equipment. While equipment can generally be programmed to perform consistently, personnel need to be carefully recruited, trained and monitored. People-based services can usually allow greater customization of services to meet individual customers' needs. These issues are considered further in Chapters 3 and 12.

### 2.6.7 The significance of the service to the purchaser

Some services are purchased frequently, are of low value, are consumed very rapidly by the recipient and are likely to be purchased on impulse with little pre-purchase activity. Such services may represent a very small proportion of the purchaser's total expenditure and correspond to the goods marketer's definition of fast-moving consumer goods ('fmcgs'). A casual game on a slot machine would fit into this category. At the other end of the scale, long-lasting services may be purchased infrequently, and when they are the decision-making process takes longer and involves more people. Life insurance and package holidays fit into this category.

### 2.6.8 Multiple classification

A number of overlapping bases for classifying services have now been presented. In practice, services need to be classified by a number of criteria simultaneously in order that groups of similar service types can be identified. A number of researchers have sought to use a multi-dimensional approach to identify clusters of similar services. One example is provided by Solomon and Gould (1991) who researched consumers' perceptions of 16 different personal and household services. A cluster analysis revealed two statistically significant bases for grouping services. The first – called the service locus – was defined along a scale from personal (e.g. doctors' services) to environmental (services performed on a person's possessions rather than their body). The second – service instigation – referred to the underlying reason for a service being purchased. At one extreme, a service could be purchased for basic maintenance purposes (e.g. regular visits to a dentist) while at the other, it is purchased for enhancement (e.g. health and fitness clubs).

If the clustering of service types has been carried out in an appropriate manner, it could be deduced that all services within that cluster will benefit from a broadly similar approach to marketing strategy. In Figure 2.5, a simple and hypothetical clustering has placed services along three classificatory scales: the extent of customer involvement; the extent to which the pattern of demand is peaked; and the degree of variability in production from the norm. Within the sector defined by high customer involvement, a constant pattern of demand and middling variability in production, three service offers can be identified: language tuition in a language laboratory; eye testing services; and dry cleaning services. On the basis of this analysis, each of these services could be expected to benefit from broadly similar marketing programmes. These may include stressing the benefit to potential

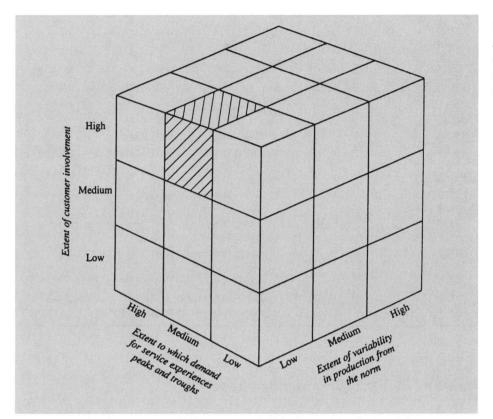

**Figure 2.5**
A three-dimensional classification of services showing points of convergence

customers of the service's equipment base for reducing variability, developing a strong brand and encouraging word-of-mouth recommendation. In fact, the marketing programmes of three large UK operators in each field – Linguaphone, Dollond and Aitchison and Sketchley – would appear to converge on these points.

Finally, it is worth noting that while classification of services on the basis of their underlying marketing needs is desirable, very little data is published on this basis. Where marketers seek to establish the size and characteristics of services markets, they must generally rely on data which is collected on the basis production-oriented measures. To give some indication of the nature of a published classification system, Table 2.1 shows the diversity of Standard Industrial Classifications (SICs) used for just one sector – tourism. While this system is widely used, marketers must question whether there is sometimes more similarity between the groups than within them.

**Table 2.1** Standard industrial classifications used for the tourism sector

| SIC | Description |
| --- | --- |
| 661 | Restaurants, cafés, etc. |
| 6620 | Public houses and bars |
| 6630 | Night clubs and licensed clubs |
| 6650 | Hotels |
| 6670 | Other tourist or short-stay accommodation |
| 7100 | Railways |
| 7210 | Urban railways, buses, etc. |
| 7400 | Sea transport |
| 7500 | Air transport |
| 7700 | Travel agents |
| 8150 | Credit card companies |
| 8490 | Car hire firms |
| 9690 | Tourist offices, etc. |
| 9770 | Libraries, museums, etc. |
| 9791 | Sport and other recreational services |

**Case Study**

## New line in marketing mobile phones

One of the oldest principles of marketing is that sellers may sell features, but buyers essentially buy benefits. This is a distinction sometimes lost on technology-led organizations, and the service sector is no exception. Recent experience of the UK's largest telecommunications company, Vodafone Airtouch, illustrates how crucial it is to see service offers in terms of the benefits they bring to customers.

By 1999, Vodafone had become the UK's largest mobile phone operator, with almost eight million customers, including 4.2 million 'Pay as you Talk' customers. It had opened the UK's first cellular network in January 1985 and had been the market leader since 1986. Vodafone's networks in the UK – analogue and digital – between them carried over 100 million calls each week. Such was the rate of growth that it took Vodafone more than 13 years to connect its first three million subscribers but only 12 months to connect the next three million. Vodafone had the largest share of the UK cellular market (33%) and had more international roaming agreements with 220 networks in 104 countries – more than any other UK mobile operator.

Extensive research had found high levels of confusion among purchasers of mobile phones, who faced a seemingly infinite permutation of features and prices. With four main networks to choose from, dozens of tariffs and hundreds of handsets, it is easy to see why buyers sought means of simplifying their choice process. Throughout the 1990s, Vodafone had positioned its UK network as superior technically to its competitors. Advertising focused on high coverage rates, extensive roaming facilities and call reliability, among other things.

Vodafone was aware that although it was recognized as an extremely strong supplier in the market for corporate buyers, it was not so strong in the market for personal customers. Research indicated that personal buyers bought Vodafone for essentially rational reasons rather than having any emotional attachment to the brand. The success of the competing Orange network, which had developed a very strong brand image was a lesson to Vodafone that a significant proportion of personal buyers did not understand many of the product features on offer, but instead identified with a brand whose values they could share. Vodafone recognized that it needed to be perceived as contributing to a consumer's lifestyle. Given the increasing complexity of product features, positioning on technical features alone was likely to make life even more confusing for personal customers. An alternative approach was needed which focused on image and lifestyle benefits.

The company hired Identica – the consultancy that originally created the One 2 One brand – to revamp its brand communications and advertising strategy in an effort to make Vodafone more appealing to personal customers. Identica created a new 'visual language' for the Vodafone brand and the company embarked on the biggest TV, press, poster and radio advertising campaign in its 15-year history. Employing a completely new style, the advertising centred around the theme: 'You are now truly mobile. Let the world come to you' and featured a new end-line – 'Vodafone YOU ARE HERE'. The campaign demonstrated how Vodafone's products and services were designed to make life easier for its customers.

The campaign, created by BMP DDB, was worth £20 million over the first two months alone and ran through 2000. In an attempt to bring meaning to the Vodafone brand and what it represented, a series of advertisements showed how Vodafone let the world come to its customers, enabling them to be truly mobile. This portrayed how Vodafone always pioneered to make things possible for its customers in a wire-free world.

In press and poster executions, Vodafone used arrows photographed in various real-life situations to depict its flagship services, e.g. a weather vane was used to illustrate the Vodafone Interactive weather service, showing how weather information could be brought to customers through their mobile. Each advertisement again had the 'Vodafone YOU ARE HERE' end-line. The arrows indicated the directional approach of Vodafone, letting the world come to the customer. Other executions illustrated cinema listing information, sports updates, share price information, international roaming and the Vodafone Personal Roadwatch 1800 service.

The change in emphasis by Vodafone seemed to be timely. The mobile phone industry was facing a new wave of confusing product features hitting consumers, with the development of Wireless Access Protocol (WAP) phones and the newer 'Third generation' phones due to be launched in 2001. It seemed inevitable that all of the competing networks would be offering confusing new permutations of features with their services, so Vodafone calculated that, given similar levels of reliability and sophistication by all networks, a favourable image and lifestyle association would be an important source of competitive advantage. Having developed a good image with existing technology, there would be a strong probability that consumers would migrate with the brand to the new technology when it arrived.

(Adapted from 'Vodafone Image Shift', *Marketing*, 4 May 2000 and Vodafone Home Page, http://www.vodafone.co.uk)

## Case study review questions

**1**  Identify the principal benefits to customers which derive from a mobile phone. What differences are likely to exist between market segments?

**2**  Is a strong brand identity on its own a source of sustainable competitive advantage? To what extent must this be backed up by real product features?

**3**  Are goods different to services in the way that a distinction is made between features and benefits?

## Chapter summary and linkages to other chapters

Services are intangible and can only be defined in the minds of consumers in terms of the benefits received. Services as a category of activities is very broad and some form of subdivision is useful to allow further analysis of the marketing needs of services. A number of bases for classifying services have been suggested. Above all, a service is a process rather than a tangible outcome and where the production process comes into contact with consumers, a service encounter occurs. The nature of service encounters is discussed in **Chapter 3**. How the components of a complex service offer influence the buying decision process is discussed further in **Chapter 4**. The idea of an ongoing relationship to provide support to customers is being seen as an increasingly important component of a service and this aspect is returned to in **Chapter 5**. Quality is an important attribute of a service which many people have sought to conceptualize and measure. The task is particularly difficult for intangible services and these issues are discussed further in **Chapter 8**. There are many approaches to the positioning of services relative to competition and the concept of competitive advantage, which positioning contributes to, is discussed further in **Chapter 7**. Finally, this chapter has emphasized service providers' employees as an integral part of the service coffer and this subject will be returned to in **Chapter 12**.

## Chapter review questions

1   Identify the key differences between the service product offering and the tangible goods offering.
2   Consider the various elements of a higher education course. Having identified the core service and the secondary service elements, could these be modified to be more customer oriented?
3   'Services can only be defined in the minds of consumers'. What is meant by this statement and to what extent is this a unique characteristic of services rather than goods?
4   What is the role of a brand name within the total service offer?
5   Outline the reasons why it is useful – from a marketing perspective – to classify services. Identify the most important bases for classification.
6   Is the process of classifying services a science or an art?

## Selected further reading

*A good starting point for studying the service product offer is the classic article by G Lyn Shostack, which sees all products as being made up of a combination of tangibles and intangibles:*

Shostack, G.L. (1977) 'Breaking Free From Product Marketing', *Journal of Marketing*, April, Vol. 41, pp 73–80

*One service sector can learn a lot about its marketing by looking to other sectors with similar marketing needs. The following paper discusses various bases for classifying services:*

Lovelock, C.H. (1983) 'Classifying Services to Gain Strategic Marketing Insights', *Journal of Marketing*, Summer, Vol. 47, pp 9–20

# The service encounter

## Learning objectives

Services are essentially about processes rather than about tangible outcomes, and for many services, consumers are very closely involved in the production process. The aim of this chapter is to review the issues and problems created for the services marketer which arise from having to produce a service 'live' in front of customers. The point of interaction is often called the service encounter and this chapter explores methods of classifying, designing and evaluating such encounters. Consumers are likely to regard some encounters as more critical than others and firms inevitably fail to meet all consumers' expectations at all times. Methods by which firms can recover from service failures will be discussed.

### 3.1 Introduction

Inseparability was introduced in Chapter 1 as a defining characteristic of services. The fact that the production of services cannot normally be separated from their consumption results in producer–consumer interaction assuming great importance within the service offer. The service process can itself define the benefit received by the customer, for example, the way in which customers are handled by a tour guide forms a very large part of the benefit which customers receive. By contrast, a company producing manufactured goods generally only comes into contact with its customers very briefly at the point where goods are exchanged for payment. In many cases, the manufacturer doesn't even make any direct contact with its customers, acting instead through intermediaries. Furthermore, the processes by which goods are manufactured are usually of little concern to the consumer.

This chapter begins by considering the basic nature of the interaction which occurs between producer and consumer, and some of the implications of this interaction which are reflected in marketing strategy.

### 3.2 The service encounter

Service encounters occur where it is necessary for consumer and producer to meet in order for the former to receive the benefits which the latter has the resources to provide. The concept has been defined broadly by Shostack (1985) as 'a period of time during which a consumer directly interacts with a service'. This definition includes all aspects of the service firm with which a consumer may interact, including its personnel and physical assets. In some cases, the entire service is produced and consumed during the course of this encounter. Such services can be described as 'high-contact' services and the encounter becomes the dominant means by which consumers assess service quality. At other times, the encounter is just one element of the total production and consumption process. For such 'low-contact' services, a part of the production process can be performed without the direct involvement of the consumer.

Some measure of the importance of the multiplicity of contacts between the organization and its customers can be found by counting the total number of interactions which customers have with a particular organization's employees – both marketing and non-marketing. These are sometimes referred to as 'moments of truth' and in a study of Scandinavian Airline Systems, Carlzon (1987) estimated these to be in the order of 50 million per annum.

From the consumer's perspective, interaction can take a number of forms, dependent upon two principal factors.

- Firstly, the importance of the encounter is influenced by whether it is the customer him- or herself who is the recipient of the service, or whether it is their possessions.
- Secondly, the nature of the encounter is influenced by the extent to which tangible elements are present within the service offer.

These two dimensions of the service encounter are shown diagrammatically in

**Figure 3.1**

A classification of service encounter types

|  | The consumer | Their possessions |
|---|---|---|
| **Tangible** | 1. HIGH-INVOLVEMENT PERSONAL SERVICES<br><br>e.g. Healthcare services,<br>   Hairdressing,<br>   Public transport | 2. GOODS MAINTENANCE SERVICES<br><br>e.g. Car servicing,<br>   Building renovation,<br>   Road haulage |
| **Intangible** | 3. SERVICES FOR THE MIND<br><br>e.g. Education,<br>   Television programme,<br>   Radio programme | 4. INTANGIBLE ASSET MAINTENANCE SERVICES<br><br>e.g. Litigation,<br>   Accountancy,<br>   Fund management |

How intangible is the service?

What is the service performed on?

matrix form in Figure 3.1 and some of the implications flowing from this categorization are discussed below.

1   *High-involvement personal services*   The most significant types of service encounters occur in the upper left quadrant of Figure 3.1 where the consumer is the direct recipient of a service and the service offer provides a high level of tangibility. These can be described as high-contact encounters. Examples are provided by most types of healthcare where the physical presence of a customer's body is a prerequisite for a series of quite tangible operations being carried out. Public transport offers further examples within this category. The benefits of a passenger train service are fundamentally to move customers and without their presence, the benefit cannot be received. Services in this quadrant represent the most intense type of service encounters. Customer and producer must physically meet in order for the service to be performed and this has a number of implications for the service delivery process:

- Quality control becomes a major issue, for the consumer is concerned with the processes of service production as much as with the end result. Furthermore, because many services in this category are produced in a one-on-one situation where judgement by the service provider is called for, it can be difficult to implement quality control checks before the service is consumed.
- Because the consumer must attend during the production process, the location of the service encounter assumes importance. An inconveniently located doctor, or one who refuses to make home visits, might fail to achieve any interaction at all.
- The problem of managing the pattern of demand is most critical with this group of services, as delays in service production have an adverse consequence not only for the service outcome, but for consumers' judgement of the service process.

2   *Goods maintenance services*   Here, services are performed on customers' objects rather than their person, an example being the repair of appliances or the transport of goods. A large part of the production process can go unseen without any involvement of the customer, who can be reduced to initiating the service process (e.g. delivering a car to a repair garage) and collecting the results (picking up the car once a repair has been completed). The process by which a car is repaired – the substantive service – may be of little concern to the customer, so long as the end result is satisfactory. However, the manner in which they are handled during the pre-service and after-service stages assumes great importance. It follows that while technical skills may be essential for staff engaged in the substantive service production process, skills in dealing with customers assume great importance for those involved in customer encounters. Because the consumer is not physically present during the substantive service production process, the timing and location of this part of the process allows the service organization a much greater degree of flexibility. In this way, the car repairer can collect a car at a customer's home (which is most convenient to the customer) and process it at its central workshops (which is most convenient to the service producer). As long as a service job is completed on time, delays during the substantive production process are of less importance to the consumer than would be the case if the customer was personally delayed during the production of the service.

3   *Services for the mind*   Here, the consumer is the direct recipient of a service, but does not need to be physically present in order to receive an essentially intangible benefit. The intangibility of the benefit means that the service production process can in many cases be separated spatially from the consumption of the service. In this way, viewers of an intangible television channel do not need to interact with staff from the television company in order to receive the benefits. Similarly, recipients of educational services often do not need to be physically present during an encounter with the education provider. Open University broadcasts and other distance learning schemes can include little direct contact.

4   *Intangible asset maintenance services*   The final category of service encounters is made up of intangible services performed on a customer's assets. For these services, there is little tangible evidence in the production process. It follows that the customer does not normally need to be physically present during the production process, as is the case with most services provided by fund managers and solicitors. Here, a large part of the substantive service production process (such as the preparation of house transfer deeds) can be undertaken with very little direct contact between customer and organization. The service encounter becomes less critical to the customer and can take place at a distance without any need to physically meet. Customers judge transactions not just on the quality of their encounter, but also to a much greater extent on outcomes (e.g. the performance of a financial portfolio).

### 3.2.1  Critical incidents

Incidents occur each time that producers and consumers come together in an encounter. While many incidents will be quite trivial in terms of their consequences to the consumer, some of these incidents will be so important that they become critical to a successful encounter. Bitner, Booms and Tetreault (1990) define **critical incidents** as specific interactions between customers and service firm employees that are especially satisfying or especially dissatisfying. While their definition focuses on the role of personnel in creating critical incidents, they can arise also as a result of interaction with the service provider's equipment.

At each critical incident, customers have an opportunity to evaluate the service provider and form an opinion of service quality. The processes involved in producing services can be quite complex, resulting in a large number of critical incidents, many of which involve non-front-line staff. The complexity of service encounters – and the resultant quality control problems – can be judged by examining how many critical incidents are present. A simple analysis of the interaction between an airline and its customers may reveal the following pattern of critical incidents:

| | |
|---|---|
| Pre-sales: | Initial telephone enquiry |
| | Making reservation |
| | Issue of ticket |
| Post-sales, | Check-in of baggage |
| pre-consumption | Inspection of ticket |
| | Issue of boarding pass |
| | Advice of departure gate |
| | Quality of airport announcements |
| | Quality of waiting conditions |
| Consumption | Welcome on boarding aircraft |
| | Assistance in finding seat |
| | Assistance in stowing baggage |
| | Reliability of departure time |
| | Attentiveness of in-flight service |
| | Quality of food service |
| | Quality of in-flight entertainment |
| | Quality of announcements |
| | Safe/comfortable operation of aircraft |
| | Fast transfer from aircraft to terminal |
| Post-consumption | Baggage reclaim |
| | Information available at arrival airport |
| | Queries regarding lost baggage, etc. |

This list of critical stages of interaction is by no means exhaustive. Indeed, the extent to which any point is critical should be determined by customers' judgements, rather than relying on a technical definition by the producer. Where there is a high level of involvement on the part of the consumer, an incident may be considered to be particularly critical. At each critical point in the service process, customers judge the quality of their service encounter.

Successful accomplishment of many of the critical incidents identified above can be dependent upon satisfactory performance by support staff who do not directly interact with customers – for example, the actions of unseen baggage handlers can be critical in ensuring that baggage is reclaimed in the right place, at the right time and intact. This emphasizes the need to treat everybody within a service organization as a 'part-time marketer' (Gummesson, 1999).

### 3.2.2 Identifying critical incidents

It can be quite easy to say that companies should pay attention to critical incidents, but much more difficult to identify just how a customer defines a critical incident. It can be even more difficult to determine when a company has failed in a critical incident. In the academic literature, critical incidents have most often been based on analyses of customers' spontaneous statements following a short interview (Edvardsson and Strandvik, 2000). Such an approach represents top-of-the-mind memories of service interactions that are socially acceptable to report to an unknown interviewer. Often, no probing has been done and respondents have not been asked to elaborate about how negative or positive such an incident has been. More importantly, within the context of buyer–seller relationships, it can be unrealistic to look at critical incidents in isolation from previous incidents and the whole context of the relationship. There is some evidence that the length of a customer relationship may moderate the effects of failure of a critical incident (Palmer, Beggs and McMullan, 2000). To overcome the problems of a series of critical incidents, Stauss and Weinlich (1995) have suggested the sequential incident technique (SIT). This technique considers the whole history of a relationship and the incidents which have occurred within it.

Many companies now facilitate complaining behaviour by customers in order that they can more precisely identify failed critical incidents. The increasing use of freefone helplines and customer comment cards is evidence of this. There is a suggestion that complaining may in itself lead to a feeling of satisfaction, simply because the complainant has managed to get the irritation off their chest. In one study of members of a fitness centre in the USA, it was found that the greater increase in satisfaction from customers who had been asked for their views came from the most dissatisfied customers (Nyer, 2000). Providing the opportunity to express feelings about a service can prove beneficial to satisfaction levels but must be seen in the context of the business's willingness to correct errors or offence. Against this, it must also be noted that many companies have experienced an increase in 'bogus complaints'. With such encouragement to complain, some customers may be tempted to push their luck in the hope of getting some form of compensation for quite spurious complaints.

Nipping complaints in the bud is an important part of **service recovery** strategy. But how far should companies go in actively encouraging customers to complain? There have been suggestions that Britain – well known for its traditional reserve – has developed a breed of professional complainers who abuse systems set up by

companies to invite complaints and feedback about their products. Restaurants, rail operators and hotels have handed out thousands of pounds in vouchers and compensation to bogus complainants who are exploiting firms' fears of losing their loyal customers. Companies seem to be victims of importing the American philosophy that once a customer has had a complaint successfully dealt with, they will stay loyal for life. It is commonly accepted that the cost of recruiting a new customer can be around five times the cost of keeping an existing one. But how do companies reconcile the need to satisfy complaining customers with the need to stem the tide of bogus complaints? One company, Sainsbury's, now logs all of its complaints centrally in order to try to identify frequent complainers.

### 3.2.3 The customer–producer boundary

The inseparability of services means that consumers will invariably be an important part of the production process, especially in the case of 'high-contact' services. Customers are not passive consumers of a service (as they may be in the case of goods), but are instead active co-producers of the service. But to what extent should they be 'designed into' this production process, rather than leaving the bulk of the inputs to the service provider? The customer–producer boundary is a moveable interface whose position can be central to the design and positioning of a service offer. Should the service provider position itself as a premium service in which it takes a lot of co-production responsibility away from the consumer (as in the case of home delivery of groceries), or should it offer a more basic service in which consumers are expected to put in more of their own effort, usually in return for a lower price?

Services are, in general, very labour intensive and have not witnessed the major productivity increases seen in many manufacturing industries. Sometimes, mechanization can be used to improve productivity (see below), but for many personal services, this remains a difficult possibility. An alternative way to increase the service provider's productivity is to involve the consumer more fully in the production process.

As real labour costs have increased and service markets become more competitive, many service organizations have sought to pass on a greater part of the production process to their customers in order to try to retain price competitiveness. At first, customers' expectations may hinder this process, but productivity savings often result from one segment taking on additional responsibilities in return for lower prices. This then becomes the norm for other follower segments. Examples where the boundary has been redefined to include greater production by the customer include:

- Petrol stations have replaced attendant service with self-service.
- The Royal Mail gives discounts to bulk mail users who do some pre-sorting of mail themselves.
- Train operators have replaced porters with self-service luggage trolleys.

- Television repair companies require equipment for repair to be taken to them, rather than collecting it themselves.
- Restaurants replace waiter service with a self-service buffet.

While service production boundaries have generally been pushed out to involve consumers more fully in the production process, some services organizations have identified segments who are prepared to pay higher prices in order to relieve themselves of parts of their co-production responsibilities. Examples include:

- Tour operators arrange a taxi service from customers' homes, avoiding the need for customers to get themselves to the airport.
- Car repairers collect and deliver cars to the owner's home.
- Fast-food firms avoid the need for customers to come to their outlet by offering a delivery service.

## 3.3 Conceptual frameworks for analysing the service encounter

Services are essentially about processes and cannot be as easily reduced to objective descriptions as in the case of most tangible goods. A fairly precise description of a confectionery bar is usually possible, so that it allows a buyer to judge it and a manufacturer to replicate it. Such a description is much more difficult in the case of a service encounter such as a restaurant meal where a large part of the outcome can only be subjectively judged by the consumer and it is difficult to define the service process in such a way that it can be easily replicated. This problem in defining the service encounter has given rise to a number of methodologies, which essentially 'map out' the service process. In this section we will begin with the basic process of 'blueprinting' a service, which has been elaborated into the development of 'servicescapes' and 'servuction' methodologies. We will also consider dramaturgical approaches to the service encounter which define the service encounter in terms of role playing.

### 3.3.1 Blueprinting

Where service production processes are complex, it is important for an organization to gain a holistic view of how the elements of the service relate to each other. **'Blueprinting'** is a graphical approach proposed by Shostack (1984) designed to overcome problems which occur where a new service is launched without adequate identification of the necessary support functions. The approach essentially attempts to draw a map of the service process

A customer blueprint has three main elements:

- All of the principal functions required to make and distribute a service are identified, along with the responsible company unit or personnel.
- Timing and sequencing relationships among the functions are depicted graphically.

| Stage in production process | Obtain seat | Take order | Make tea | Deliver tea | Pay for tea |
|---|---|---|---|---|---|
| | | | ↑⎯⎯⎯⎯⎯⎯⎯⎯⎯⎯⎯⎯⏋ Repeat if tea is unsatisfactory | | |
| Target time (minutes) | 1 | 1 | 3 | | 1 |
| Critical time | 5 | 5 | 8 | | 3 |
| Is incident critical? | Y | N | N | Y | N |
| Participants | Customer | Customer Waiter(ress) | Cook | Customer Waiter(ress) | Customer Cashier |
| Visible evidence | Furnishings | Appearance of staff | Tea, crockery, manner of service delivery | | Cash-collection procedures |
| 'Line of visibility' | | | | | |
| Invisible processes | Cleaning of tea room | | Preparation of tea Ordering of supplies | | Accounting procedures |

**Figure 3.2**

Customer service blueprint – a simplified application to the purchase of a cup of tea in a café

- For each function, acceptable tolerances are identified in terms of the variation from standard which can be tolerated without adversely affecting customers' perception of quality.

The essence of a blueprint is to show how customers, possessions and information are processed, an implication being that customers are inputs that can be viewed as sources of uncertainty. The principles of a service blueprint are illustrated in Figure 3.2 with a very simple application of the framework to the purchase of a cup of tea in a café.

A customer blueprint must clearly identify all steps in a service process, that is, all contacts or interactions with customers. These are shown in time sequential order from left to right. The blueprint is further divided into two 'zones': a zone of visibility (processes that are visible to the customer and in which the customer is likely to participate) and a zone of invisibility (processes and interactions that, although necessary to the proper servicing of a customer, may be hidden from their view).

The blueprint also identifies points of potential failure in the service production process – the critical incidents on which customers base their perception of quality. Identifying specific interaction points as potential failure points can help marketers focus their management and quality control attentions on those steps most likely to cause poor judgements of service quality.

Finally, the blueprint indicates the level of tolerance for each event in the service process and indicates action to be taken in the event of failure, such as repeating the event until a satisfactory outcome is obtained.

Blueprinting is not a new idea, with many precedents in methods of critical path analysis. What is important here is that marketing, operations management and human resource management focus on processes which deliver benefits that are effective to customers and efficient for the company. High involvement personal services can only be sensibly understood in terms of their production processes rather than outcomes, so blueprinting assumes particular significance.

The example of a blueprint shown in Figure 3.2 is of course very simplistic. In practice, firms with complex service processes produce lengthy manuals describing procedures for the different components of their processes. By way of example, a blueprint can be used to identify what employees should do in any of the following circumstances:

- When a dentist has to cancel appointments due to illness, who should inform his patients? When and by whom should alternative arrangements be made? Should some patients be regarded as higher priority than others for rescheduling of appointments?
- A restaurant customer complains of a badly cooked meal. Who should have the authority to decide whether any recompense should be given to the complainant? On what basis should compensation be assessed?
- A hotel overbooks its accommodation. Which alternative hotels should the duty manager approach first to try to obtain alternative accommodation for its guests? Should it actively try to buy-off intending guests with free vouchers for use on future occasions? If so, who will authorize them and how will their value be calculated?

It doesn't matter how a blueprint is expressed, whether it is in the form of a diagrammatic portrayal of processes or simply in words. The important point is that it should form a shared and agreed basis for action which is focused on meeting customers' needs effectively and efficiently. Of course, a blueprint cannot anticipate all contingencies for which a response will be required, for example a bomb explosion in a restaurant or the kidnapping of a bank clerk. Nevertheless, if the general nature of a process problem is identified, the outline of possible next steps can be developed.

### 3.3.2 Dramaturgical approaches

The concept of **role playing** has been used to apply the principles of social psychology to explain the interaction between service producer and service consumer (e.g. Solomon *et al.*, 1985). It sees people as actors who act out roles which can be distinguished from their own personality. In the sociological literature, roles are assumed as a result of conditioning by the society and **culture** of which a person is a member. Individuals typically play multiple roles in life, as family members, workers, members of football teams, etc., each of which comes with a set of socially conditioned role expectations. A person playing the role of worker is typically conditioned to act with reliability, loyalty and trustworthiness. An analysis of the expectations associated with each role becomes a central part of role analysis. The many roles which an individual plays may result in conflicting role expectations, as where the family role of a father leads to a series of role expectations which are incompatible with his role expectations as a business manager. Each role might be associated with competing expectations about the allocation of leisure time.

The service encounter can be seen as a theatrical drama. The stage is the location where the encounter takes place and can itself affect the role behaviour of both buyer and seller. A scruffy service outlet may result in lowered expectations by the customer and in turn a lower level of service delivery by service personnel (see Bitner, 1990). Both parties work to a script which is determined by their respective role expectations – an air stewardess is acting out a script in the manner in which she attends to passengers' needs. The script might include precise details about what actions should be performed, when and by whom, including the words to be used in verbal communication. In reality, there may be occasions when the stewardess would like to do anything but wish her awkward customers a nice day. The theatrical analogy extends to the costumes which service personnel wear. When a doctor wears a white coat or a bank manager a suit, they are emphasizing to customers the role which they are playing. Like the actor who uses costumes to convince his audience that he is in fact Henry VIII, the bank manager uses the suit to convince customers that he is capable of taking the types of decisions which a competent bank manager takes.

In a service encounter, both customers and service personnel are playing roles which can be separated from their underlying personality. Organizations normally employ staff not to act in accordance with this personality, but to act out a specified role (although of course personality characteristics can contribute to effective role performance). It follows that employees of banks are socialized to play the role of cautious and prudent adviser and to represent the values of the bank in their dealings with customers. Similarly, customers play roles when dealing with service providers. A customer of a bank may try to act the role of prudent borrower when approaching a bank manager for a small business loan, even though this might be in contrast to his fun-loving role as a family member.

Both buyers and sellers bring role expectations into their interaction. From an individual customer's point of view, there may be clear expectations of the role which a service provider should play. Most people would expect a bank manager to be dressed appropriately to play his or her role effectively, or a store assistant to be courteous and attentive. Of interest to marketers are the specific role expectations held by particular segments within society. As an example, a significant segment of young people might be happy to be given a train timetable by an enquiry office assistant and expect to read it themselves. On the other hand, the role expectations of many older people might be that the assistant should go through the timetable and read it out for them. Similarly, differences in role expectations can be identified between different countries. While a customer of a supermarket in the United States would expect the checkout operator to pack their bags for them, this is not normally part of the role expectation held by UK shoppers.

It is not just customers who bring role expectations to the interaction process. Service producers also have their idea of the role which their customers should perform within the co-production process. In the case of hairdressers, there may be an expectation of customers' roles which includes giving clear instructions at the outset, arriving for the appointment on time and (in some countries) giving an adequate tip. Failure of customers to perform their role expectations can have a demotivating effect on front-line personnel. Retail sales staff who have been well trained to act in their role may be able to withstand abusive customers who are acting out of role – others may resort to shouting back at their customers.

The service encounter can be seen as a process of simultaneous role playing in which a dynamic relationship is developed. In this process, both parties can adapt to the role expectations held by the other party. The **quality of the service** encounter is a reflection of the extent to which each party's role expectations are met. An airline which casts its cabin crew as the most caring crews in the business may raise customers' expectations of their role in a manner which the crews cannot deliver. The result would be that customers perceive a poor quality service. By contrast, the same standard of service may be perceived as high quality by a customer travelling on another airline which had made no attempt to try to project such a caring role on their crews. The quality of the service encounter can be seen as the difference between service expectations and perceived delivery. Where the service delivery surpasses these expectations, a high quality of service is perceived (although sometimes, exceeding role expectations can be perceived poorly, as where a waiter in a restaurant offers incessant gratuitous advice to clients who simply want to be left alone).

Over time, role expectations change on the part of both service staff and their customers. In some cases, customer expectations of service staff have been raised, as in the case of standards expected from many public services. In other instances, expectations have been progressively lowered, as where customers of petrol stations no longer expect staff to attend to their car, but are prepared to fill their tank and to clean their windscreens themselves. Change in customers' expectations usually begins with an innovative early adopter group and subsequently trickles through to other groups. It was mainly young people who were prepared to accept the simple, inflexible and impersonal role played by staff of fast-food restaurants which many older segments have subsequently accepted as a role model for restaurant staff.

Goodwin (1996) has described how a service encounter drama can involve game-based strategies to outwit an opponent. Service providers sometimes manipulate customers' perceptions of reality, for example by concealing queues to make them appear shorter than they actually are. Some customers also play games, by trying to obtain a higher level of service than the one to which they are entitled (e.g. airline customers seeking an upgrade). Customers may seek reward by abusing guarantees and complaint handling policies, complaining about non-existent problems and demanding refunds.

### 3.3.3 Servicescapes

The concept of a **servicescape** was developed by Booms and Bitner to emphasize the impact of the environment in which a service process takes place. Booms and Bitner (1981, p 36) defined a servicescape as

> The environment in which the service is assembled and in which seller and customer interact, combined with tangible commodities that facilitate performance or communication of the service.

In the service encounter the customer is in the 'factory' and is part of the process. Production and consumption of the service are simultaneous.

The design of a suitable service environment should explicitly consider the likely emotional states and expectations of target customers. Booms and Bitner distinguished between 'high-load' and 'low-load' environments, both of which can be used to suit particular emotional states and customer types. They noted (1981, p 39) that:

> A high-load signifies a high information rate; a low-load represents a low information rate. Uncertainty, novelty, and complexity are associated with high-load environments; conversely a low-load environment communicates assurance, homogeneity, and simplicity. Bright colours, bright lights, loud noises, crowds, and movement are typical elements of a high-load environment, while their opposites are characteristic of a low-load environment. People's emotional needs and reactions at a given time determine whether they will be attracted to a high- or a low-load environment.

The servicescape must encourage target customers to enter the service environment in the first place, and to retain them subsequently. Booms and Bitner discuss 'approach behaviour' as involving such responses as physically moving customers towards exploring an unfamiliar environment, affiliating with others in the environment through eye contact, and performing a large number of tasks within the environment. Avoidance behaviour includes an opposite set of responses. The likelihood of approach behaviour is directly linked to the two dimensions of pleasure and arousal, with a stimulating and pleasing environment being most likely to attract custom. Brightly lit window displays, a prominent and open front door and front-of-house greeting staff are typical actions designed to induce approach. A door which is difficult to find or difficult to open is more likely to achieve the opposite effect.

After entering the service production system, the servicescape must be efficient and effective for the service provider in securing customers' co-operation in the production system. Clearly explained roles for the customer, expressed in a friendly way will facilitate this process of compliance. The ambience of the environment, such as lighting, floor plan and signposting contribute to the servicescape. The physical aspects of the environment are brought to life by the actions of employees, for example staff could be on hand to help customers who find themselves lost in the service process. Ultimately, the servicescape should encourage customers to repeat their visit. The environment should leave no reminders of poor service (such as unpleasant queuing conditions) which will cause negative feelings about the service provider. The servicescape may include **tangible cues** to facilitate repeat business, for example a schedule of forthcoming events may be given to customers of a theatre.

### 3.3.4 Servuction

The **servuction** model, developed by Langeard *et al.* (1981), emphasizes experiential aspects of service consumption and is based on the idea of organizations providing consumers with complex bundles of benefits. The service features provided by an organization providing the service are divided into two parts – visible and invisible. The visible part consists of the physical environment within which the service experience occurs, and the service providers or contact personnel who interact with the consumer during the service experience. The visible part of the organization is supported by the invisible part, comprising the support infrastructure which enables the visible part of the organization to function. The model is completed by the introduction of other consumers, with whom the original consumer may interact within the system.

Everyone and everything that comes into contact with the consumer is effectively delivering the service. Bateson has noted that that identifying the Servuction system can be difficult because of the often large number of contacts between the service provider and the customers, which may be significantly underestimated (Bateson, 1989).

The servuction approach is particularly relevant to services which involve high levels of input from fellow consumers or third party producers. Consumers essentially create their own bundle of benefits from the contributory elements of the **service offer**. The servuction model has been applied to the marketing of towns as tourism and shopping destinations (Warnaby and Davies, 1997) in which consumers must essentially define their own bundle of benefits from the complexity of facilities provided by multiple organizations within the town.

## 3.4 The role of other customers in the service encounter

It is implicit from the above that many service offers can only sensibly be produced in large batches, while the consumers who use the service buy only individual units of the service. It follows therefore that a significant proportion of the service is consumed in public – train journeys, meals in a restaurant and visits to the theatre are consumed in the presence of other customers. In such circumstances, there is said to be an element of joint consumption of service benefits. A play cannot be produced just for one patron and a train cannot run for just one passenger – a number of customers jointly consume one unit of service output. An environment is created in which the behaviour pattern of any one customer during the service process can directly affect other customers' enjoyment of their service. In the theatre, the visitor who talks during the performance spoils the enjoyment of the performance for others.

The actions of fellow consumers are often therefore an important element of the service encounter and service companies seek to manage customer–customer interaction. By various methods, organizations seek to remove adverse elements of these encounters and to strengthen those elements which add to all customers' enjoyment. Some commonly used methods of managing encounters between customers include the following:

- *Selecting customers on the basis of their ability to interact positively with other customers* Where the enjoyment of a service is significantly influenced by the nature of other customers, formal or informal selection criteria can be used to try to ensure that only those customers who are likely to contribute positively to service encounters are accepted. Examples of formal selection criteria include tour companies who set age limits for certain holidays – people booking an 18–30 holiday can be assured that they will not be holidaying with children or elderly people whose attitudes towards loud music may have prevented enjoyment of their own lifestyle. Formal selection criteria can include inspecting the physical appearance of potential customers – many night clubs and restaurants set dress standards in order to preserve a high-quality environment in which service encounters take place. Informal selection criteria are aimed at encouraging some groups who add to customers' satisfaction with the service environment, while discouraging those who detract from it. Colour schemes, service ranges, advertising and pricing can be used to discourage certain types of customers. Bars which charge high prices for drinks and offer a comfortable environment will be informally excluding the segment of the population whose aim is to get drunk as cheaply as possible.

- *Determining rules of behaviour expected from customers* The behaviour of one customer can significantly affect other customers' enjoyment of a service. Examples include smoking in a restaurant, talking during a cinema show and playing loud music in public transport. The simplest strategy for influencing behaviour is to make known the standards of expected behaviour and to rely on customers' goodwill to act in accordance with these expectations. With increasing recognition by most people in society that smoking can be unpleasant for others, social pressures alone may result in most smokers observing no-smoking signs. Where rules are not obeyed, the intervention of service personnel may be called for. Failure to intervene can result in a negative service encounter continuing for the affected party, and moreover, the service organization may be perceived as not caring by its failure to enforce rules. Against this, intervention which is too heavy handed may alienate the offender, especially if the rule is perceived as one which has little popular support. The most positive service encounter results from intervention which is perceived as a gentle reminder by the offender and as valuable corrective action by other customers.
- *Facilitating positive customer–customer interaction* For many services, an important part of the overall benefit is derived from positive interaction with other customers. Holidaymakers, people attending a conference and students of a college can all derive significant benefit from the interaction with their peer group. A holiday group where nobody talks to each other may restrict the opportunities for shared enjoyment. The service providers can seek to develop bonds between customers by, for example, introducing customers to one another or arranging events where they can meet socially.

## 3.5 The role of third-party producers in the service encounter

Service personnel who are not employed by a service organization may nevertheless be responsible for many of the critical incidents which affect the quality of service encounters perceived by its customers. Three categories of such personnel can be identified:

- A service company's intermediaries can become involved in critical incidents before, during or after consumption of a service. The first contact which many people have with an organization is through its sales outlets. In the case of the airline above, the manner in which a customer is handled by a travel agent is a highly critical incident, the outcome of which can affect the enjoyment of the rest of the service, for example where the ticket agent gives incorrect information about departure times, or the ticket is ordered wrongly. The incidents in which intermediaries are involved can continue through the consumption and post-consumption phases. Where services are delivered through intermediaries, as is the case with franchisees, they can become the dominant source of critical incidents. In such cases, quality control becomes an issue of controlling intermediaries.

- Service providers themselves buy in services from other subcontracting organizations. Services organizations buying subcontracted services must ensure that quality control procedures apply to many of its subcontractors' processes, as well as to their outcomes. Airlines buy in many services from subcontractors. In some cases these generate very little potential for critical incidents with the airline's passengers. Where in-flight meals are bought in from an outside caterer, the subcontractor has few if any encounters with the airline's customers and quality can be assessed by the tangible evidence being delivered on time. On the other hand, some services involve a wide range of critical incidents. Airlines often subcontract their passenger checking-in procedures to a specialist handling company, for whom quality cannot simply be assessed by quantifiable factors such as length of queues or numbers of lost baggages. The manner in which the subcontractor's personnel handle customers and resolve such problems as over-booked aircraft, lost tickets and general enquiries assumes critical importance.

- Sometimes staff who are not employed by the service organization or its direct subcontractors can contribute towards critical incidents in the service encounter. This occurs, for example, at airports where airport employees, air traffic controllers and staff working in shops within the airport contribute to airline passengers' perception of the total service. In many cases, the airline might have little – if any – effective control over the actions of these personnel. Sometimes, it may be possible to relocate the environment of its service encounters – such as changing departure airports – but it may still be difficult to gain control over some critical publicly provided services, such as immigration and passport control. The best that a service organization can do in these circumstances is to show empathy with its customers. An airline may gain some sympathy for delays caused by air traffic controllers if it explains the reason for delays to customers and does everything within its power to overcome resulting problems.

## 3.6  Service failure and recovery

 Almost inevitably, service companies will fail at some critical incidents. The inseparable and intangible nature of services gives rise to the inevitability of failures occurring. From a customer's perspective, a **service failure** is any situation where something has gone wrong, irrespective of responsibility. The inseparability of high-contact services has a consequence that service failure usually cannot be disguised from the customer (Boshoff, 1997). Service failures may vary in gravity from being something serious, such as a food-poisoning incident, to something trivial, such as a short delay, and the service failure literature has produced many typologies characterizing the general nature of service failures (e.g. Kelley and Davis, 1994; Bitner,

Booms and Tetreault, 1990. It has been suggested by Halstead, Drogue and Cooper (1993) that a single service failure may have two effects. Firstly, a 'halo' effect may negatively colour a customer's perceptions (for example, if an airline loses a passenger's baggage, the passenger may subsequently associate any communication from the airline with failure). Secondly, a 'domino' effect may engender service failures in other attributes or areas of a service process. This can occur where a failure in an early stage of a service process puts a customer in a bad mood where they become more critical of minor failures in subsequent stages. A diner who has been unreasonably delayed in obtaining their pre-booked table may become more ready to complain about minor problems with the subsequent delivery of their food.

Service providers should have systems for identifying, tracking and analysing service failures. This allows management to identify common failure situations (Hoffman, Kelley and Rotalsky, 1995). More importantly, it allows management to develop strategies for preventing failures occurring in the first place, and for designing appropriate recovery strategies where failure is unavoidable. Firms with formal service recovery programmes supplement the bundle of benefits provided by the core product and enhance the service component of the firm's value chain (Hoffman and Kelley, 2000).

It is often suggested that a happy customer will go away and tell two or three people about the good service, but a dissatisfied customer will tell probably a dozen about a failure. Businesses commonly lose 15% to 20% of their customer base each year (Reichheld and Sasser, 1990). Although customers may defect to the competition for a number of reasons (e.g. better prices, better products, change of location), minimizing the number of customers who defect due to poor customer service, is largely controllable. However, there is plenty of evidence that firms do not take complaining customers seriously and that unresolved complaints actually strengthen the customer's negative feelings towards the company and its representatives (Hart, Sasser and Heskett, 1990). Organizations need to have in place a strategy by which they can seek to recover from failure.

There is a growing body of literature on the methods used by service organizations to recover from an adverse critical incident and to build up a strong relationship once again. **Service recovery** processes are those activities in which a company engages to address a customer complaint regarding a service failure (Spreng, Harrell and Mackoy, 1995). A good recovery can turn angry, frustrated customers into loyal ones and may create more goodwill than if things had gone smoothly in the first place (Hart, Sasser and Heskett, 1990).

IF YOU'RE **HAPPY** WITH YOUR MEAL
TELL A FRIEND!
IF YOU'RE **NOT**
TELL US!

*O'NEILL's RESTAURANT*

**Figure 3.3**
Like many service providers, this restaurant encourages dissatisfied customers to make their dissatisfaction known, rather than going away with an unresolved problem and passing on a negative word-of-mouth report

There have been many approaches to the study of service failure and recovery and their link with perceived levels of fairness (Woodruff, Cadotte and Jenkins, 1983; Spreng, Harrell and Mackoy, 1995). Equity theory, based on literature within social psychology, points to individuals' perceptions of the fairness of a situation or a decision. Oliver (1996) developed a notion of equity as the consumer's reward and investment proportion commensurate to some other proportion against which it is compared. The level of service recovery by a service provider should be commensurate with the consumer's effort and price paid. Bolton and Lemon (1999) used a measure of payment equity to examine how customers employ price and usage over time to update their evaluations of the fairness of an exchange.

The most important step in service recovery is to find out as soon as possible when a service has failed to meet customers' expectations. A customer who is dissatisfied and does not report this dissatisfaction to the service provider may never come back, and worse still, may tell friends about their bad experience. Service companies are therefore going to increasing lengths to facilitate feedback of customers' comments in the hope that they are given an opportunity to make amends. Service recovery after the event might include financial compensation which is considered by the recipient to be fair, or the offer of additional services without charge, giving the company the opportunity to show itself in a better light. If service recovery is to be achieved after the event, it is important that appropriate offers of compensation are made speedily and fairly. If a long dispute ensues, aggrieved customers could increasingly rationalize reasons for never using that service organization again and tell others not only of their bad service encounter, but also of the bad post-service behaviour encountered.

Rather than wait until long after a critical incident has failed, service companies should think more about service recovery during the production process. It can be possible for service organizations to turn a failed critical incident into a positive advantage with its customers. In the face of adverse circumstances, a service organization's ability to empathize with its customers can create stronger bonds than if no service failure had occurred. As an example, a coach tour operator could arrive at a hotel with a party of customers only to find that the hotel had overbooked, potentially resulting in great inconvenience to the former's customers. The failure to swiftly check its guests into their designated hotel could represent failure of a critical incident which results in long-term harm for the relationship between the coach tour operator and its customers. However, the situation may be recovered by a tour leader who shows determination to sort things out to their best advantage. This could involve the tour leader demonstrating to his or her customers that they are determined to get their way with the hotel manager and to get their room allocation restored. They could also negotiate with the hotel management to secure alternative hotel accommodation of a higher standard at no additional charge which customers would appreciate. If the process of rearranging accommodation looked like taking time, the tour leader could avoid the need for customers to be kept waiting in a coach by arranging an alternative enjoyable activity in the interim, such as a visit to a local tourist attraction.

The extent to which service recovery is possible depends upon two principal factors. Firstly, front-line service personnel must have the ability to empathize with customers. Empathy can be demonstrated initially in the ability to spot service failure as it is perceived by customers, rather than some technical, production-oriented definition of failure. Empathy can also be shown in the manner of front-line staffs' ability to take action which best meets the needs of customers. Secondly, service organizations should empower front-line staff to take remedial action at the time and place which is most critical. This may entail authorizing – and expecting – staff to deviate from the scheduled service programme and, where necessary, empower staff to use resources at their discretion in order to achieve service recovery. In the case of the tour leader facing an overbooked hotel, taking customers away for a complimentary drink may make the difference between service failure and service recovery. If the tour leader is not authorized to spend money in this way, or approval is so difficult that it comes too late to be useful, the chance of service recovery may be lost forever.

The role of blueprinting service processes can be emphasized again here. While it may not be possible to anticipate the precise nature of every service failure, a blueprint can indicate what to do in the event of certain general types of failure occurring.

Consider the case of the cancellation of an airline flight which causes great inconvenience to passengers. A blueprint should be able to immediately show:

- Who is responsible for informing intending passengers of the cancellation?
- Which passengers will have priority in being rescheduled to alternative services?
- What compensation choices will be offered to passengers?
- Who will handle unresolved claims for compensation?

In too many organizations, poor blueprinting of recovery processes merely compounds the problem of the original service failure, as customers gain further evidence that the company is not organized effectively and does not have their best interest at heart.

Train operators in the UK have a long tradition of giving excuses for service failures which have become stock-in-trade for stand-up comedians. 'Leaves on the line' is a problem which perplexes commuters each autumn, amazed that a few small leaves can halt a 100 tonne train. The greatest ridicule was given to British Rail in 1987 when 'the wrong kind of snow' grounded the latest Sprinter trains which had supposedly been tested in the Arctic.

There are signs that the newly privatized train operating companies have improved their standards of communication with passengers. Many companies have instructed their train crews that blaming delays on 'operating problems' or 'technical difficulties' is just not good enough for intelligent customers who, with a bit of careful thought, could be brought to empathize with the train company and its problems. Crews have also made greater efforts to keep passengers updated on progress towards resolving a problem, helped by improved two-way communication between trains and central control rooms.

At first sight, the strategy might appear to be paying off. During the first year of full privatization, total passengers carried by train companies increased by over 2%, despite a general worsening of reliability indicators (although, of course, other environmental factors could have explained the increase in passenger numbers). The media remains highly sceptical about train companies' excuses and running down the railways remains a national pastime. As an example, *The Times* in November 1997 ran a story about Connex South Central blaming delays on 'atmospheric conditions affecting adhesion of rolling stock'. Had the company gone back to insulting the intelligence of its customers with gobbledegook excuses? Rather than still having to make excuses, shouldn't it be addressing the underlying problems? One company which fully acknowledged the intelligence of its customers was Virgin Railways. Richard Branson wrote in the company's customer magazine that its service standards just weren't good enough, but pleaded with customers to be patient while the company invested money to reverse decades of government neglect.

## 3.7 Industrializing the service encounter

Service organizations face a dilemma, for while most seek to maximize the choice and flexibility of services available to customers, they need to reduce the variability of service outcomes in order that consistent brand values can be established. They also need to pursue methods for increasing productivity, and in particular reducing the amount and cost of skilled labour involved in production processes.

Complex and diverse service offers can result in personnel being required to use their judgement and to be knowledgeable about a wide range of services. In many service sectors, giving too much judgement to staff results in a level of variability which is incompatible with consistent brand development. The existence of multiple choices in the service offer can make training staff to become familiar with all the options very expensive, often matched by a minimal level of income which some services generate. For these reasons, service organizations often seek to simplify their service offerings and to 'deskill' many of the tasks performed by front-line service staff. By offering a limited range of services at a high standard of consistency, the process follows the pattern of the early development of factory production of goods. The process has sometimes been described as the **industrialization of services** and can take a number of forms:

- *Simplifying the range of services available* Organizations may find themselves offering services which are purchased by relatively few customers. The effort put into providing these services may not be justified by the financial return. Worse still, the lack of familiarity of many staff with little-used services could make them less than proficient at handling service requests, resulting in a poor service encounter which reflects badly on the organization as a whole. Where peripheral services do not produce significant net revenue, but offer a lot of scope for the organization to make mistakes, a case can often be made for dropping them. As an example, retailers have sometimes offered a delivery service at an additional charge, only to experience minimal demand from a small segment of customers. Moreover, the lack of training often given to sales staff (e.g. on details of delivery areas) and the general complexity of delivery operations (such as ensuring that there is somebody at home to receive the goods) could justify a company in dropping the service. Simplification of the service range to just offering basic retail services allows a wide range of negative service encounters to be avoided, while driving relatively few customers to competitors. It also allows service personnel to concentrate their activities on doing what they are best at – in this case, shop-floor encounters.

- *Providing 'scripts' for role performance* It was noted above that service personnel act out their role expectations in an informally scripted manner. More formal scripting allows service staff to follow the expectations of their role more precisely. Formal **scripting** can include a precise specification of the actions to be taken by service staff in particular situations, often with the help of machine-based systems. In this way, a telephone salesperson can be prompted what to say next by messages on a computer screen. Training in itself can help staff understand how they should handle a service encounter – for example, the manner in which cabin crew should greet passengers boarding an aircraft.

- *Tightly specifying operating procedures* In some instances, it may be difficult to set out operating procedures which specify in detail how service personnel should handle each encounter. Personal services such as hairdressing rely heavily on the creativity of individual staff and operating procedures can go no further than describing general conduct. However, many service operations can be specified with much greater detail. At a managerial level, many jobs have been deskilled by instituting formalized procedures which replace much of the judgement previously made by managers. In this way, bank managers use much less judgement in deciding whether to advance credit to a client – the task is decided by a computer-based credit scoring system. Similarly, local managers in sectors such as retailing and hotels are often given little discretion over such matters as the appearance of their outlets and the type of facilities provided – these are specified in detail from head office and the branch manager is expected to follow closely. In this way, organizations can ensure that many aspects of the service encounter will be identical, regardless of the time or place.

- *Replacing human inputs with machine-based inputs* Machines are generally more predictable in delivering services than humans. They also increasingly offer cost savings, which may give a company a competitive price advantage. Although machines may break down, when they are functioning they tend to be much less variable than humans who may suffer from tiredness, momentary inattentiveness or periodic boredom. In addition to reducing the variability of service outcomes, machine-based encounters offer a number of other advantages over human-based encounters:
  - the service provider may be able to offer a much wider range of encounter possibilities. For example, Internet banking and ATM machines allow many bank transactions to be undertaken at a time which is convenient to the customer, and also at a place which is convenient.
  - it is often possible to programme machinery to provide a range of services reliably in a manner which would not have been possible if the encounter was based on a human service producer. Many telephone companies now

offer a wide range of automated telephone services (e.g. call interception services) which can be delivered with high levels of reliability.

– studies have suggested that automated encounters give many customers a feeling of greater control over an encounter. A bank customer phoning his or her local branch to ask for the balance of their account may feel that they are having to work hard to get the information out of a bank employee and may feel intimidated by asking additional questions. By contrast, a caller to an automated banking information system or the user of an Internet banking service may feel greater control over their dealings with the bank.

A student visited her local branch of McDonald's in Northern Ireland. After she had received her burger and fries she asked the serving assistant for some mayonnaise to accompany her food. No sachets of mayonnaise were available, so the assistant obliged, with typical Irish hospitality, by taking some mayonnaise from a bulk container and putting it on a coffee cup lid for the student. This seemed a pragmatic solution which the customer was more than happy with. But for the serving assistant, it brought a sharp reprimand from her supervisor. This was evidently not allowed by the service blueprint. Perhaps handing over mayonnaise on a cup lid didn't present an image of consistently high professional standards. There may even have been food safety issues involved. But on this occasion at least the customer had been pleased that the server had thought for herself and resolved the problem. How does a company like McDonald's strike a balance between rigid procedures and the need for flexibility to meet individual customers' requirements?

### 3.7.1 Computer-mediated encounters

There has been a lot of recent excitement about how computer-based systems are likely to change the way consumers interact with service providers. The vision is presented of consumers sitting at home behind a computer terminal communicating with another computer at the other end, as a result of which services are provided. There is nothing new, of course, in the use of technology to intervene in a producer–consumer encounter. Banks, for example, have for some time reduced the amount of contact that their staff have with customers through the use of ATM machines, so Internet banking could be seen as an extension of this technological development.

The extent to which computers are able to intervene in service encounters is influenced by the type of service in question. Chapter 2 discussed bases for classification and it should become quite clear that the role of direct human encounters will always be crucial to some types of services. Where the services process requires direct contact with the customer's body (as in the case of many medical services), the possibilities for computer-based intervention is likely to be small (although it could nevertheless be used to provide support services such as advance booking facilities or a simplified diagnostic facility). Where services involve processes being carried out on the customer's physical assets (e.g. car repairs), there is still likely to be a point of contact where the assets are collected/delivered, although reservation and accounting

facilities may be undertaken without direct human encounters. It is in the area of pure services with few tangible manifestations that the development of the Internet has had greatest impact. Many 'pure' information services, such as the provision of bank savings accounts and share price information can be done with very little, if any, encounters between a customer and a company's employees.

By designing service processes around customers' needs and the opportunities provided by the new technology, more efficient and effective service processes can be designed. As an example, many airlines have developed web-based electronic ticketing systems which removes all need for intervention by the service provider's employees until the point where the customer is about to board the aircraft.

Of course, service encounters which are computer-mediated need to be designed with the same care and attention to detail as those which involve human encounters. It is not uncommon to find websites which are slow and confusing in their layout and operation or which fail to bring about the desired service. Just as in the failure of a human-based critical incident, failure during a web-based encounter may result in defection of the customer to a competitor. The study of **human-computer interaction (HCI)** is becoming an important area of study in its own right.

**Figure 3.4**
easyJet claims to be the 'Web's favourite airline' and has effectively used the Internet to simplify encounters between the company and its customers. During July 2000, 73% of the airline's customers used this medium for booking their tickets, saving administrative costs for the airline which are passed on in lower prices to customers.
(Reproduced with permission of EasyJet Airline Company Ltd.)

### 3.7.2 Services and productivity

Productivity can be defined as the efficiency with which an organization's inputs are turned into outputs. The Industrial Revolution of England in the 19th century was characterized by dramatic improvements in the productivity of human, equipment and financial resources. Many have pointed to a 'Service Revolution' during the past couple of decades when productivity in many service sectors has shown a significant improvement. This has been evident in sectors such as banking where large numbers of employees have been laid off and their jobs performed more cost-effectively by computer-based systems. Confirmation of the improvement in service sector labour productivity is provided by UK government statistics which show that during the period 1988–98 output at constant factor cost increased by 42.1%, but employment increased by only 14.2%.

The whole concept of productivity is much more complex for services than for goods. For goods, production can generally be separated from consumption, and consumers are not generally affected by the way in which a product is manufactured. Provided it performs to standard, a car buyer is not too concerned whether it has been produced with automated or manual methods of production. However, for the service consumer the nature of production methods can be crucial, because the inseparability of production and consumption means that the whole nature and benefit of the service can change when production methods change. A bank replacing its counter staff with ATMs and telephone banking may appear to be improving its productivity when assessed by such measures as customer transactions per employee or cost per transaction. However, the automated service may be perceived as something quite different from that which went before it. Because of the problem of inseparability, it can be difficult to gain a clear picture of what is happening to the true productivity of the service sector. More efficient does not necessarily mean more effective in meeting consumers' needs.

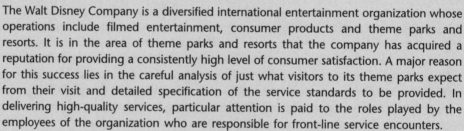

| **Case Study** | **Walt Disney makes everyone a star** |

The Walt Disney Company is a diversified international entertainment organization whose operations include filmed entertainment, consumer products and theme parks and resorts. It is in the area of theme parks and resorts that the company has acquired a reputation for providing a consistently high level of consumer satisfaction. A major reason for this success lies in the careful analysis of just what visitors to its theme parks expect from their visit and detailed specification of the service standards to be provided. In delivering high-quality services, particular attention is paid to the roles played by the employees of the organization who are responsible for front-line service encounters.

The company's business mission involves making guests happy, and this mission has embedded itself in the cultural values shared by all employees. Once employed, all new employees learn about the history of the Disney Company and gain an understanding of the original philosophy of Walt Disney himself and thus the whole corporate culture. One approach used by Walt Disney to achieve its mission is to treat its theme parks as giant entertainment stages in which a series of satisfying service encounters takes place. People paying to come into the park are considered not as customers, but as 'guests'. Similarly, employees are considered as 'cast members' in this encounter and wear 'costumes' appropriate to their task, rather than uniforms.

After being introduced to the basic cultural values of the organization, each 'cast member' is given clear, written instructions about their role expectations, where to report, what to wear, and how to handle typical encounters with guests. Role playing prepares cast members for a wide range of guest requests, for example meeting their requests for directions or guidance on the best places to eat.

New employees are assigned a particular role whose titles indicate the strength of the 'entertainment' culture:

- *Custodial hosts* – street cleaners
- *Food and beverage hosts* – restaurant workers
- *Transportation hosts* – drivers
- *Security hosts* – police

Walt Disney's role scripting is based on careful analysis of what guests particularly value in the actions of cast members and the interactions between cast members and guests are manipulated in such a positive way that the guests' expectations are exceeded. In order for roles to be performed effectively, Disney provides extensive training, including several days of training for each employee before they come into contact with guests. Regular training sessions and newsletters are used to keep employees informed of new developments. Should training have failed to prepare an employee to cope with a guest's problem on the spot, they can contact back-up support by telephone in order to satisfy the guest's request promptly.

In order to ensure that management is aware of the experiences of front-line staff, each member of the management team spends a week each year as a front-line member of the workforce. In addition, each member of management is also expected to bring his or her family for one day to experience the resort as a guest and thus perceive the experience from the guest's perspective.

Finally, employees themselves are used to monitor the quality of service encounters. Peer review by current cast members is used in the selection of new recruits, the primary criterion for selection being 'service', and all employees are expected to complete a questionnaire on their own perceptions of working for the organization. The results are then analysed and from this, employee satisfaction is measured. The Disney philosophy is that if employees are satisfied with their encounters, then so ultimately will be the customer.

## Case study review questions

1 Within the context of Disney World, what is meant by 'scripting'?

2 What is meant by a critical incident? How can Walt Disney identify what constitutes a critical incident and measure whether the company has achieved customer satisfaction?

3 Choose any encounter which is likely to occur within Disney's theme parks and apply a 'blueprinting' framework to an analysis of the service encounter.

## Chapter summary and linkages to other chapters

This chapter has built on the previous chapter by defining a service in terms of its processes. For **high-contact services**, consumers can be very closely involved in these processes, posing problems of quality control which are not present in the manufactured goods sector where goods can be produced out of sight and stockpiled during periods of low demand. Because they are produced 'live' in the presence of consumers, services have a high chance of failing to meet consumers' expectations, therefore firms must have a strategy for recovering from such failures.

Attempts to measure the quality of a service encounter are considered in more detail in **Chapter 8**. The quality of the service encounter contributes towards consumers' decisions on whether to repurchase from a particular supplier, to the extent that an ongoing relationship is developed (**Chapters 4 and 5**).

A critical factor in service encounters, which relies on staff inputs by the provider, is the quality and consistency of staff. This chapter has highlighted the preoccupation by many service providers with simplifying and deskilling staffs' tasks. There is a limit to which this can go and staff will usually need to be appropriately selected, trained and monitored for most service encounters. These issues are returned to in **Chapter 12**. Delays during a service process can impact directly upon consumers, therefore service providers aim to avoid bottlenecks by carefully matching their capacity with the level of demand. The issue of demand management is considered further in **Chapter 13**.

## Key terms

Critical incidents  63
Role playing  68
Quality of service  70
Tangible cues  70
Service offer  72
Service recovery  75
Scripting  79

Blueprinting  66
Culture  68
Servicescape  70
Servuction  71
Service failure  74
Industrialization of services  78
Human–computer interaction  81

## Chapter review questions

1  What distinguishes 'high-contact' services from 'low-contact' ones?
2  Choose one high-contact service sector with which you are familiar and identify the critical incidents which occur during the service production–consumption process.
3  What is meant by service failure? Suggest strategies which a fast-food restaurant can employ to recover from service failure most effectively.
4  What is meant by the industrialization of services? What are the limits to the industrialization process within the restaurant sector?
5  Many analyses of the service encounter have drawn analogies with the theatre. To what extent is this comparison valid?
6  The service encounter usually involves customers as active participants in the production process. To what extent is it desirable, or possible for a service provider to 'train' customers to be efficient co-producers of a service?

## Selected further reading

*The central role of the encounter between an organization's staff and its customer has led to a considerable literature in defining service encounters and prescribing methods for improving the quality of encounters. The following are important papers in the development of this stream of literature.*

Bitner, M. (1990) 'Evaluating Service Encounters: The Effects of Physical Surroundings and Employee Responses', *Journal of Marketing*, April, Vol. 51, 69–82

Bitner, M. J., B. H. Booms and M. S. Tetreault (1990) 'The Service Encounter: Diagnosing Favorable and Unfavorable Incidents', *Journal of Marketing*, January, Vol. 54, 71–84

Carlzon, J. (1987) *Moments of Truth*, Ballinger Books, Cambridge, MA

Shostack, G. L. (1984) 'Designing Services that Deliver', *Harvard Business Review*, January–February, pp 133–9

Shostack, G. L. (1985) 'Planning the Service Encounter', in J. A. Czepiel, M. R. Solomon and C. F. Suprenant (eds), Lexington Books, *The Service Encounter*, Lexington, MA, pp 243–54

*For an insight into the process of 'industrializing' the production of services, the following is useful.*

Levitt, T. (1972) 'Production Line Approach to Service', *Harvard Business Review*, September–October, pp 41–52

*The following papers offer a further discussion of role playing and scripting which is inherent in service industrialization.*

Gabbott, M. and G. Hogg (1996) 'The Glory of Stories: Using Critical Incidents to Understand Service Evaluation in the Primary Health Care Context', *Journal of Marketing Management*, Vol. 12, No. 6, pp 493–503

Goodwin, C. (1996) 'Moving the Drama into the Factory: The Contribution of Metaphors to Services Research', *European Journal of Marketing*, Vol. 30, No. 9, pp 13–36

Joby, J. (1996) 'A Dramaturgical View of the Health Care Service Encounter: Cultural Value-based Impression Management Guidelines for Medical Professional Behavior', *European Journal of Marketing*, Vol. 30, No. 9, pp 60–74

Parker, C. and P. Ward (2000) 'An Analysis of Role Adaptations and Scripts During Customer-to-Customer Encounters', *European Journal of Marketing*, Vol. 34, No. 3/4, pp 341–58

Solomon, M. R. and C. Suprenant, J. A. Czepiel and E. G. Gutman (1985) 'A Role Theory Perspective on Dyadic Interactions: The Service Encounter', *Journal of Marketing*, Winter, Vol. 49, pp 99–111

*The literature on failed service encounters and the ways in which companies recover from service failure has been growing in recent times. The following papers are relevant.*

Andreassen, T. W. (2000) 'Antecedents to Satisfaction with Service Recovery', *European Journal of Marketing*, Vol. 34, No. 1/2.

Boshoff, C. and J. Allen (2000) 'The Influence of Selected Antecedents on Front-line Staff's Perceptions of Service Recovery Performance', *International Journal of Service Industry Management*, Vol. 11, No. 1, pp 64–92

Edvardsson, B. (1992) 'Service Breakdowns: A Study of Critical Incidents in an Airline', *International Journal of Service Industry Management*, Vol. 3, No. 4, pp 17–29

Hart C. W. L., W. E. Sasser Jr and J. L. Heskett (1990) 'The Profitable Art of Service Recovery', *Harvard Business Review*, July–August, pp 148–56

Hoffman, K. D. and S. W. Kelley (2000) 'Perceived Justice Needs and Recovery Evaluation: A Contingency Approach', *European Journal of Marketing*, Vol. 34, No. 3/4, pp 296–304

# 4

# Services buying processes

**Learning objectives**

Companies undertake marketing activities in order to elicit some kind of response from buyers. The ultimate aim of that activity is to get customers to buy their product, and to come back again.

A company can put years of effort into developing a new service, but find it rejected by buyers in the few minutes, or sometimes even seconds, that it may take them to choose between the alternatives available. The company may have made false assumptions about the processes by which purchase decisions are made, for example, by under-estimating the role played by key influencers in the decision process. Much of this book breaks marketing activities down into distinct areas of decisions which have be made by management, for example, service design, pricing and promotion decisions. However, this chapter stresses that while companies may break their planning down into small manageable chunks, customers make an assessment based on a holistic view of the total service offer. How customers perceive the whole offer and react to it may be quite different to what the company had expected when it was developing its marketing plan.

This chapter explores the effects of intangibility on the service buying decision process and notes that choosing between competing services is often perceived as being more difficult and risky than is usually the case with goods. The lack of physical evidence means that sellers' claims about a product can often only be taken on trust and verified after consumption. The chapter will begin by discussing ways in which buyers make decisions and these will be integrated into models of buyer behaviour. An important theme of buying processes is the evident need of buyers to simplify their decision making when faced with sometimes seemingly endless choices.

Service providers seek to identify segments of the population who will react in similar ways to a given set of stimuli. This chapter will briefly review the bases for segmenting services markets. It is noted that the inseparability of services creates new opportunities for effectively segmenting markets.

## 4.1 Risk and services buying decisions

Consumers experience pre-purchase uncertainty during the purchase of most products. However, because the amount and quality of information available is generally less in the case of an intangible service, compared with goods, the amount of perceived risk would be expected to be higher. Intangibility often leads to a consumer's evaluation of a service being based on tangible evidence and price rather than the core service offer (Zeithaml, 1981).

A number of factors influence the level of risk experienced by a consumer when approaching a service purchase:

- *The level of tangible evidence which is available to support evidence of the service process and outcomes*  Service providers often go to great lengths to demonstrate service benefits using tangible cues, e.g. an airline which offers a premium price for its Club class seats may demonstrate the benefits of its seats with a replica seat in travel agents' offices.
- *The level of the buyer's involvement in the service*  Going back to our classification of services in Chapter 2, it will be recalled that services can be defined in terms of their level of involvement. Where involvement levels are high (as in the case of many personal healthcare services), the perceived risk of a decision is likely to be greater than a low involvement service such as the rental of a video.
- *The novelty of the purchase*  If this type of purchase is new to us, we are more likely to experience high levels of risk than if we are a repeat buyer. A first-time mortgage buyer will most likely perceive much higher levels of risk than somebody who has arranged many mortgages during their life.
- *The purchaser's individual risk threshold*  Just as some people are more prepared to take risks in the way they gamble money or drive their car, so some buyers will be more prepared to take risks. A cheap holiday with an unknown foreign airline may appeal to some, but be perceived as too risky by others.
- *Situational factors affect perceptions of risk*  If we are desperate to use a service, we may lower our risk threshold. If we have just missed the last bus home, we may be more prepared to risk a taxi ride in a 'dubious' car which is perceived as being risky than if we were choosing a taxi company in more relaxed conditions.
- *There may be a perception of safeguards available to consumers which reduces perceptions of risk*  In many cases, legislation protects consumers from non-delivery of a service where it would be possible to defraud consumers. Within the UK financial services sector, for example, there is an extensive protection mechanism which prevents small savers losing deposits paid to regulated banks. Most investors do not therefore perceive risk of losing their money when putting their savings in a domestic bank, but perceptions of risk would be much higher if the bank was 'offshore' and unregulated.

The whole subject of risk and its link to service expectations is relatively unexplored. One study has shown that uncertainty is negatively associated with pre-purchase expectations in industrial buying situations, in other words we expect better outcomes where risks are lowest (Paterson *et al.*, 1997). As expectations play a major role in determining consumers' post-consumption service quality evaluations (see Chapter 8), it follows that an understanding of perceived risk is important to understanding consumers' assessments of quality.

## 4.2 The buying process

It is important for services marketers to gain an insight into the processes and critical factors involved in an individual's purchase decision. Organizations must develop a thorough understanding of a number of aspects of their customers' buying processes, in particular:

- Who is involved in making the purchase decision?
- How long does the process of making a decision take?
- What is the set of competing services from which consumers make their choice?
- What is the relative importance attached by decision makers to each of the elements of the service offer?
- What sources of information are used in evaluating competing service offers?

The basic processes involved in purchase decisions are illustrated in Figure 4.1. Simple models of buyer behaviour usually see some underlying need triggering a search for need-satisfying solutions. When possible solutions have been identified, these are evaluated according to some criteria. The eventual purchase decision is a consequence of the interaction between the final decision maker and a range of influencers. Finally, after purchase and consumption, the consumer develops feelings about their purchase which influence future decisions. In reality, service purchase decision processes can be complex iterative processes involving large numbers of influencers and diverse decision criteria. Needs can themselves be difficult to understand and should be distinguished from expectations. The intangible nature of services and the general inability of buyers to check the quality or nature of a service until after it has been consumed adds to the importance of understanding the sources of information which are used in the process of evaluation.

**Figure 4.1**
Simplified stages in the
buyer-decision process

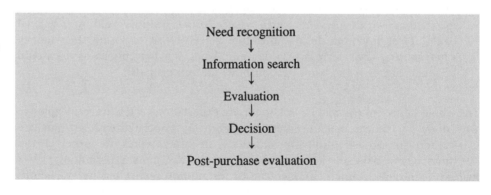

Need recognition
↓
Information search
↓
Evaluation
↓
Decision
↓
Post-purchase evaluation

### 4.2.1 Need recognition

The buying process is triggered by an underlying need. That need motivates us to seek a solution which will restore a sense of physiological and psychological balance which was previously absent. Needs can be extremely complex and are no longer dominated by basic physiological needs. The service industry sector has benefited from the tendency for societies to climb to higher levels of Maslow's 'Hierarchy of Needs' (Maslow, 1943). Among consumer services, a high proportion of new expanding sectors would appear to be catering for individuals' social and self-actualization needs. Mobile phones, flower delivery services and long-haul travel are all a long way from satisfying our basic needs but are typical of the sectors that have expanded rapidly in recent years by satisfying consumers' higher order needs. Figure 4.2 offers an illustration of how changing needs have influenced the type of food we buy. In less developed societies, consumers are driven primarily by the basic nutritional content of food in order to satisfy a basic need for body maintenance. In more developed societies, we are increasingly likely to base our search for food on the basis of a need for social togetherness or curiosity. Hence the great growth in social eating out, and in particular the variety of ethnic restaurants which can now be found in most towns.

In addition to our inherent physiological and psychological needs, our needs are influenced by the situation in which we currently find ourselves. The subjects of age and socioeconomic status can have profound effects on buying behaviour. The stage that an individual has reached in the 'family life cycle' also has a significant influence on needs.

It has been suggested that the basic need-stimulus-response model is too simplistic in the way that needs are portrayed as being something conscious. While this criticism may be true of products in general, it has particular relevance to services.

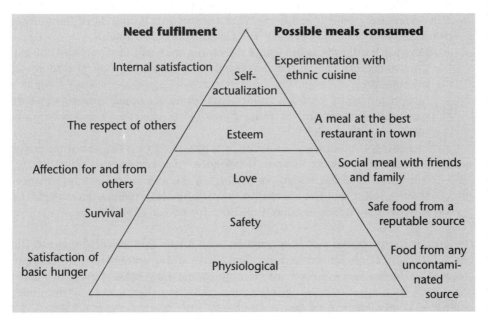

**Figure 4.2**

The food sector has developed from being primarily agriculturally-based to being increasingly service-based. Affluent societies no longer satisfy a basic need for food, but are motivated by higher order needs for sociality and self-actualization. This diagram, based on Maslow's 'Hierarchy of Needs' model, illustrates some of the effects of changing needs on the way in which we buy food-related services

As well as being physically intangible, many services may be mentally intangible. Few young people, for example recognize an underlying need for old-age security which a pension will provide. Such people may only purchase a pension policy if they become aware of the product. Prior to this, they may not have been aware of the underlying need which a pension policy seeks to satisfy.

### 4.2.2 Information sources

In the classic model of buyer behaviour, the next stage in the process is to collect information about services which are capable of satisfying the underlying need. These can be divided into two basic sources: those which are dominated by the service provider and those which derive from other sources.

Once a need has triggered the search for need-satisfying solutions, a search for information will begin. But where do buyers look for information when making purchases? In the case of the routine repurchase of a familiar service, probably very little information is sought about the product. But where there is a greater element of risk, buyers are likely to seek out more comprehensive information about the alternative ways in which they can satisfy their needs. The following information sources are likely to be used:

- Personal experience will be a starting point, so if a buyer has already used a company's products, the suitability of the proposed purchase may be assessed in the light of the previous purchases.
- Word-of-mouth recommendation from friends is important for many categories of services where an individual may have no previous need to make a purchase. When looking for a plumber or a solicitor, for example, many people will initially seek the advice of friends.
- Rather than referring to individuals on a face-to-face basis, we may use various other reference groups to guide us. What restaurant is it considered fashionable to eat in at the moment? What is the fashionable bar in town?
  - Newspaper editorial content and directories such as those published by the Consumers' Association may be consulted as a relatively objective source of information.
  - Advertising and promotion in all of its forms is studied, sometimes being specifically sought and at other times being casually seen without any search activity involved.
  - Increasingly, consumers are using the Internet to find information about alternatives available. There is evidence that within the travel sector, consumers undertake extensive 'surfing' of the web to establish information about a resort and the alternative means of getting there, even though the Internet may not be used as a medium for booking the holiday.

The greater the perceived risk of a purchase, the longer and more widespread the search for information. Of course, individuals differ in the extent to which they are prepared to methodically collect information. Some may make a purchase more impulsively than more calculating individuals, reflecting their lower risk threshold, lower level of involvement or greater familiarity with that type of purchase.

### 4.2.3 Evaluation of alternatives

A lot of effort has gone in to trying to understand the processes which consumers use to evaluate competing services. By the time that all possible competing alternatives have been reduced to a smaller shortlist (or 'choice set'), many possibilities will have been discarded on the way. This may be simply due to poor awareness of a product's existence, or an inability to acquire sufficient information about it. Even allowing for services which a consumer has not become aware of, they will probably be left with too many choices to evaluate each one individually in detail. It is therefore usual to base evaluation on a 'choice set' of a small number of alternatives, which will be subjected to a more detailed comparative analysis.

A private buyer seeking to buy a low-involvement service such as a car insurance policy may have narrowed down the set to a choice of four. Analysts of buyer behaviour have developed a number of frameworks for trying to understand how a consumer chooses between these competing alternatives. One approach is for the consumer to use a sense of intuition as to what feels best. Such non-systematic methods of evaluation may be quite appropriate where the service in question involves low levels of cost, risk and involvement.

Even apparently intuitive bases of evaluation can be reduced to a series of rules, implying some systematic basis. One framework is a multiple attribute matrix which holds that consumers refer to a number of component attributes of a product to evaluate the overall suitability of a product. Figure 4.3 shows a typical matrix where four competing car insurance policies are compared in terms of five important attributes. In this matrix, the four short-listed alternatives in the choice set are shown by the column headings A, B, C and D. The left-hand column shows five attributes on which buyers base their purchase decision. The second column shows the importance which the consumer attaches to each attribute of the service (with maximum importance being given a score of 10 and a completely unimportant attribute a score of zero). The following four columns show how each service scores against each of the five evaluation attributes. Consumers' perceptions of attributes and the importance they attach to them can only be found out through a programme of market research. Conjoint analysis has been widely used in the analysis of components of service offers.

| | Importance Weights | A | B | C | D |
|---|---|---|---|---|---|
| Location of branch | 10 | 10 | 7 | 8 | 10 |
| Friendliness of staff | 9 | 10 | 9 | 8 | 8 |
| Reputation | 8 | 10 | 10 | 9 | 9 |
| Overall cost | 7 | 10 | 10 | 10 | 5 |
| Short-term incentives | 6 | 4 | 10 | 10 | 4 |
| | | | | | |
| Overall rating | | 44 | 46 | 45 | 36 |
| Weighted rating | | 7.3 | 7.2 | 7.0 | 6.1 |

**Figure 4.3**
A hypothetical choice set for motor insurance: a multiple attribute matrix

If it is assumed that a consumer evaluates each service provider without weighting each attribute, service provider B will be the preferred supplier, as it has the highest overall rating. It is more realistic to expect that some factors will be weighted as being more important than others, therefore the alternative *linear compensatory* approach is based on consumers creating weighted scores for each service provider. The importance of each attribute is multiplied by the score for each attribute, so in this case, provider A is preferred as the attributes which consumers rank most highly are also those which are considered to be the most important. A third approach to evaluation is sometimes described as a *lexicographic approach*. This involves the buyer in starting their evaluation by looking at the most important attribute and ruling out those suppliers which do not meet a minimum standard. Evaluation is then based on the second most important attribute, with service providers being eliminated who do not meet their standard. This continues until only one option is left. In Figure 4.3, branch location is given as the most important attribute, so the initial evaluation may have reduced the choice set to A and D (these score highest on location). In the second round, friendliness of staff becomes the most important decision criterion. Only A and D remain in the choice set, and as A has the highest score for friendliness of staff, it will be chosen in preference to D.

Can we have too much choice? Making decisions involves effort and the psychological anxiety that we might have made the wrong decision. Limiting our choice is therefore a natural reaction. Ideally, we would like to be presented with just one choice that reflects our needs perfectly. Increasingly, with the use of databases, companies are able to limit the range of choice presented to each individual, so that only those options likely to appeal are presented. Summing up current developments in relationship marketing, Sheth and Parvatiyar have described firms' motivation to develop ongoing relationships as being based primarily on 'choice reduction' (Sheth and Parvatiyar, 1995).

The term 'Confusion marketing' has been used by some commentators to describe the practices of certain service providers. Even some companies have been heard to use the term, off the record. In an ideal world, we would all be able to evaluate the options open to us and make a rational choice from the available options. We might still appear to act irrationally by placing a high value on a service feature which somebody else would regard as being quite frivolous. But how do you go about the task of evaluation when there is enormous choice and service providers appear to go out of their way to confuse buyers? Many buyers of mobile phone services have been overwhelmed at the choices available to them – in the UK, four basic networks, dozens of different tariffs for each network and hundreds of different handsets. One professor of mathematics calculated that it would take a UK buyer over a year to evaluate the costs and benefits of all permutations of networks, tariffs and handsets. To many people, the tariff plans offered by the phone companies seem unbelievably complex, with an array of peak/off-peak price plans, 'free' inclusive minutes and discounts for loyalty. Is the approach of mobile phone companies an attempt to confuse buyers with low 'headline' prices, but a confusing range of supplementary prices? Or does the approach reflect a genuine concern to segment markets so finely that every buyer's preferences are catered for?

### 4.2.4 The decision-making unit (DMU)

Few service purchase decisions are made by an individual in total isolation from other people. Usually other people are involved in some role and have a bearing on the final decision. It is important to recognize who the key players in this process are, in order that the service format can be configured to meet these peoples' needs, and that promotional messages can be adapted and directed at the key individuals involved in the purchase decision. A number of roles can be identified among people involved in the decision process;

- *Influencers* are people or groups of people who the decision maker refers to in the process of making a decision. Reference groups can be primary (e.g. friends, acquaintances and work colleagues), or secondary in the form of remote personalities with whom there is no two-way interaction. Where research indicates that the primary reference group exerts major influence on purchase decisions, this could indicate the need to take measures which will facilitate word-of-mouth communication, perhaps by giving established customers rewards in return for the introduction of new customers. An analysis of secondary reference groups used by consumers in the decision process can be used in a number of ways. It will indicate possible personalities to be approached who may be used to endorse a product in the company's advertising. It will also indicate which opinion leaders an organization should target as part of its communication programme in order to achieve the maximum 'trickle-down' effect. The media can be included within this secondary reference group – what a newspaper writes in it columns can have an important influence on purchase decisions.

What role do children play in the purchase of services which they consume? There has been considerable debate about the extent of 'pester power' where parents give in to the demands of children. Increasingly, advertisers are aiming their promotional messages over the heads of adults and straight at children. The ethics of doing this have been questioned by many, and some countries have imposed restrictions on television advertising of children's products. However, even with advertising restrictions, companies have managed to get through to children in more subtle ways, for example by sponsoring educational materials used in schools and paying celebrities to endorse their products. For fast-food restaurants, gaining the mind of children is crucial to getting parents along. As a sign of its achievements, children's parties at McDonald's have become highly valued by the children themselves, no doubt helped by its internal décor which appeals to children by use of bright colours and play facilities. The food itself, and the presentation of it, is clearly aimed at the young consumer. Like many fast-food restaurants, McDonald's has developed a programme of educational support materials which it takes to schools. Its materials promote the identity of McDonald's in an apparently educational manner, while at the same time generating desire among pupils. Having access to these materials may help cash-strapped teachers by providing much needed resources, but is it ethical to target young children in this way? Does it make it harder for parents to encourage their children to eat a healthy diet?

- *Gatekeepers* are most commonly found among commercial buyers. Their main effect is to act as a filter on the range of services which enter the decision choice set. Gatekeepers can take a number of forms – a secretary barring calls from sales representatives to the decision maker has the effect of screening out a number of possible choices. In many organizations, it can be difficult to establish just who is acting as a gatekeeper. Identifying a marketing strategy which gains acceptance by the gatekeeper, or bypasses them completely is therefore made difficult. In larger organizations and the public sector in particular, a select list of suppliers who are invited to submit tenders for work may exist. Without being on this list, a provider of services is unable to enter the decision set. Although gatekeepers are most commonly associated with the purchase of services by business organizations, they can also have application to private consumer purchases. In the case of many household services, an early part of the decision process may be the collection of brochures or telephoning to invite quotations for a service. While the final decision may be the subject of joint discussion and action, the initial stage of collecting the decision set is more likely to be left to one person. In this way, a family member picking up holiday brochures acts as a gatekeeper for their family, restricting subsequent choice to the holidays of those companies whose brochures appealed to him or her.

- In some cases, ordering a service may be reduced to a routine task and delegated to a *buyer*. In the case of business-to-business services, low-budget items which are not novel may be left to the discretion of the buyer. In this way, casual window cleaning may be contracted by a buying clerk within the organization without immediate reference to anybody else. In the case of modified rebuys, or novel purchases, the decision-making unit is likely to be larger.

- The *users* of a service may not be the people responsible for making the actual purchase decision. This is particularly the case with many business-to-business service purchases. Nevertheless, research should be undertaken to reveal the extent to which users are important influencers in the decision process. In the case of the business air travel market, it is important to understand the pressure which the actual traveller can exert on their choice of airline, as opposed to the influence of a company buyer (who might have arranged a long-term contract with one particular airline), a gatekeeper (who may discard promotional material relating to new airlines) or other influencers within the organization (e.g. cost centre managers who might be more concerned with the cost of using a service, in contrast to the user's overriding concern with its quality).

- The *decision maker* is the person (or group of individuals) who makes the final decision to purchase, whether they execute the purchase themselves or instruct others to do so. With many family-based consumer services, it can be difficult to identify just who within the family carries most weight in making the final decision. Research into family service purchases which are purchased jointly has suggested that in the case of package holidays, wives dominate in making the final decision, whereas in the case of joint mortgages, it is the husband who dominates. Within any particular service sector, an analysis of how a decision is made can only realistically be achieved by means of qualitative indepth research. In the case of decisions made by commercial buyers, the task of

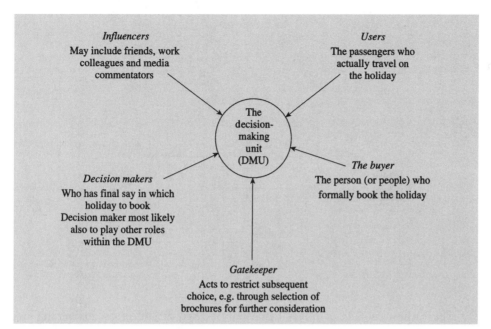

**Figure 4.4**
Typical members of the buying decision making unit for a family package holiday

identifying the individuals responsible for making a final decision – and their level within the organizational hierarchy becomes even more difficult.

In reality, people play multiple roles in this process, sometimes switching between roles. An illustration of the roles with reference to the purchase of a package holiday is shown in Figure 4.4.

## 4.3  Models of buyer behaviour

The very basic model of buyer behaviour which was described in Figure 4.1 provides a useful starting point and conceptual framework for analysing buying processes. If a model is to have value to marketing managers, it should be capable of use in predicting actual buying behaviour, given a set of conditions on which the model is based. For this reason, a number of researchers have sought to develop models which explain how buying decisions are made in specified situations, and from this to predict the likely consequences of changes to marketing strategy. Modelling buyer decision processes poses many problems. At one extreme, simple models such as that presented in Figure 4.1 may help in very general terms in developing marketing strategies, but are too general to be of use in any specific situation. At the other extreme, models of buyer behaviour based on narrowly defined sectors may lose much of their explanatory and predictive power if applied to another sector where assumptions on which the original model were calibrated no longer apply. In any event, most models of buyer behaviour provide normative rather than strictly quantitative explanations of buyer behaviour and there can be no guarantee that the assumptions on which the model was originally based continue to be valid.

**Figure 4.5**

A model of consumer buyer behaviour (based on Howard and Sheth, 1969)

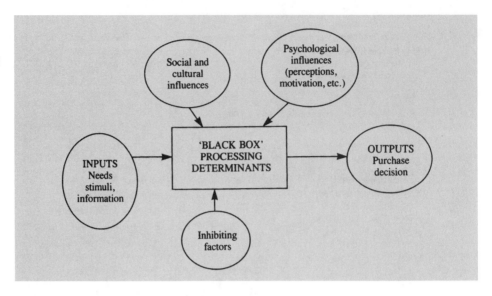

The earliest models of buyer behaviour focused attention on explaining the decision processes involved in goods purchases. One widely used framework which has been applied to consumer service purchase decisions is that developed by Howard and Sheth (1969), illustrated in Figure 4.5.

The framework incorporates a number of elements:

- *Inputs* This element comprises information about the range of competing services which may satisfy a consumer's need. Information may be obtained from personal or published sources.
- *Behavioural determinants* Individuals bring to the purchase decision a predisposition to act in a particular way. This predisposition is influenced by the culture they live in, family and personality factors, among others.
- *Perceptual reaction* Inputs are likely to be interpreted in different ways by different individuals, based on their unique personality make-up and conditioning which results from previous purchase experiences. While one person might readily accept the advertising messages of a holiday company, another might have been disappointed by that company in the past or by holiday companies' advertising in general. They are therefore less likely to perceive such inputs as credible.
- *Processing determinants* This part of the model focuses attention on the way in which a decision is made. Important determinants include the motivation of the individual to satisfy a particular need, the individual's past experience of a particular service or organization and the weight attached to each of the factors which are used in the evaluation. For some consumers for some services, critical product requirements may exist which must be present if a product is to be included in the decision set. At other times, consumers attach weights to each of its attributes and select the product with the highest weighted 'score' (see above).
- *Inhibitors* A number of factors might prevent an individual moving towards

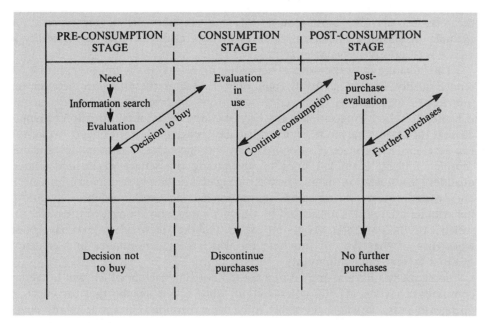

**Figure 4.6**
The consumption–evaluation process for services (based on Fisk, R. P., 'Toward a Consumption/Evaluation Process Model for Services', in J. H. Donnelly and W. R. George (eds), *Marketing of Services*, American Marketing Association, Chicago, IL, 1981, pp 191–95

making a decision to purchase a particular service, such as the difficulty of access to the service, the price of the service and the terms and conditions for service delivery.

● *Outputs* The outcome of the decision process may either be to go ahead and purchase or, alternatively, not to buy or to defer a decision to a later date.

The Howard–Sheth model was developed as a general framework to explain both goods and services decision processes. There has been more recent recognition that this type of model does not fully address the issue of producer–seller interaction which occurs during the evaluation process. The intangibility of services and the inability of consumers to evaluate a service before consumption can also result in a much more complex process of information collection and evaluation than is the case with goods.

An example of a model which is based specifically on the service sector was developed by Fisk (1981) and is shown diagrammatically in Figure 4.6. The model sees the purchase process as being divided into three stages – pre-consumption, consumption and post-consumption. The pre-consumption stage comprises the range of activities that commonly takes place before a purchase decision is made, beginning with the initial problem recognition, collection of information and identification of the choice set. At this stage, consumers identify what they *expect* to be the best solution. In the following consumption stage, the consumer actually decides through experience what they consider to be the best choice. During this phase, expectations raised during the pre-consumption phase are compared with actual service delivery. A gap between the two results in attempts to reduce dissonance, for example dissatisfaction resulting from failure to meet expectations may be resolved by complaining. In the post-consumption phase, the whole service encounter is evaluated and this determines whether the consumer will be motivated to purchase the service again. Like most models, this one simplifies the buying process, for example by showing evaluation as three distinct elements, whereas in reality a service is progressively evaluated.

The literature on services buyer behaviour models is closely linked with that on service quality. Service quality is commonly defined as the difference between an individual's expectations of a service and their perceptions of service delivery (Chapter 8). Where expectations have been met, the behavioural intention to repurchase is increased. One model which integrates service quality with buyer behaviour was developed by Davies *et al.* (1999). Their model encompasses measurable standards capable of being examined prior to undergoing the service experience (search qualities); consideration of experience during the service (performance qualities); and consideration of outcomes after service delivery (credence qualities). Behavioural intention is influenced by whether a purchase is novel to the buyer (in which case the emphasis will be on search qualities) or whether they have prior experience of that type of purchase (in which case performance and credence qualities become more important).

Some models have identified process and outcome factors which will influence consumer behaviour in only one direction, while others assume that the effect of changes in a variable will be reversible, influencing consumer behaviour in both directions. Yet other models suggest that certain threshold values must be exceeded before any effect will be apparent.

There has been discussion over the issue of whether some characteristics of a service generate satisfaction in customers while others generate dissatisfaction (Galloway, 1999). The general argument is that the achievement of some standard, or improvement in an element will generate satisfaction, but its absence, or reduction, will not generate dissatisfaction. Conversely, the failure to achieve a standard in another element may generate dissatisfaction in the customer, though its presence will not necessarily generate satisfaction and repeat purchase. Swan and Coombs noted that 'consumers judge products on a limited set of attributes, some of which are relatively important in determining satisfaction, while others are not critical to consumer satisfaction but are related to dissatisfaction when performance on them is unsatisfactory' (1976, pp 25–33). For a bank, increasing the number of branches may not be a satisfier which encourages a customer to spend more of their budget with that bank. However, a reduction in the number of branches may be a dissatisfier which reduces behavioural intention. In the retail banking sector, Johnston (1995) has shown that integrity and, to a lesser extent, reliability, are dissatisfiers. Consumers behaved as if these were assumed standards which all banks will achieve, and were dissatisfied when a bank failed to achieve them.

So far, models of services buying behaviour have been discussed at a general level. Marketers are particularly concerned with the factors that influence consumer behaviour in their own specific sector and therefore more specific models of buyer behaviour have been developed as a result of research into specific services sectors. Many of these have sought to rank in order of importance the factors which contribute towards the purchase decision and to identify critical factors, the absence of which will exclude a possibility from a choice set. As an example, research into restaurant choice decisions by Lewis (1981) identified five key factors which were used in the evaluation of a restaurant – food quality, menu variety, price, atmosphere and convenience. However, the research also found that the importance attached to each of these

**We'd try anything once. But now we're back with BT.**

**Figure 4.7**
The buying process does not end with a purchase. In this advertisement, BT encourages its UK phone customers who have recently switched to a rival company to reflect on their feelings towards their new supplier. As well as encouraging former customers to return, this advertisement makes current BT customers feel more comfortable with their current supplier, by reducing the temptation to search for alternatives (reproduced with the permission of British Telecommunications plc)

factors differed according to the implicit purpose of the visit to the restaurant. The factors influencing a choice of restaurant for a celebration were quite different from those used for a general social occasion. For most categories of use, image and atmosphere appeared to be critical factors which distinguished between restaurants within the choice set. In the case of some consumers who had no independent transport, location close to the town centre was found to be a necessary factor for further consideration.

## 4.4 Personal and organizational buyer behaviour compared

The processes by which private consumers purchase services can differ from the way in which organizations buy services. A number of reasons can be identified for this:

- Two sets of needs are being met when an organization buys services – the formal needs of the organization and the needs of the individuals who make up the organization. While the former might be thought of as being the more economically rational, the needs which individuals in an organization seek to satisfy are influenced by their own perceptual and behavioural environment, very much in the same way as would be the case with private consumer purchases.
- More people are typically involved in organizational purchases. High-value services purchases may require evaluation and approval at a number of levels of an organization's management hierarchy. An attempt should be made to find out where in an organization the final decision-making power lies. An analysis of the decision-making unit (see above) might also reveal a wide range of influencers who are present in the decision-making process.
- Organizational purchases are more likely to be made according to formalized routines. At its simplest, this may involve delegating to a junior buyer the task of making repeat orders for services which have previously been evaluated. At the other extreme, many high value service purchases may only be made after a formal process of bidding and evaluation has been undertaken.
- The greater number of people involved in organizational buying also often results in the whole process taking longer. A desire to minimize risk is inherent in many formal organizational motives and informally present in many individuals' motives, often resulting in lengthy feasibility studies being undertaken. In some new markets, especially overseas markets, trust in service suppliers might be an important factor used by purchasers when evaluating competing suppliers and it may take time to build up a trusting relationship before any purchase commitment is secured.
- The elements of the service offer which are considered critical in the evaluation process are likely to differ. For many services, the emphasis placed on price by many private buyers is replaced by reliability and performance characteristics by the organizational buyer. In many cases, poor performance of a service can have direct financial consequences for an organization – a poor parcel delivery service might merely cause annoyance to a private buyer, but might lead to lost production output or lost sales for an organizational buyer.
- The need for organizational buyers' risks to be reduced and their desire to seek the active cooperation of suppliers in tackling shared problems has resulted in greater attention being paid to the development of organizational buyer–seller relationships over time, rather than seeing individual purchases in isolation. The importance of mutual trust in the relationship between a service organization and its commercial buyers has been shown in a number of studies. It has been pointed out by Gronroos (1990) that as the complexity of service offerings increase, the organizational buying unit perceives a greater need for confidence and trust in its services suppliers. The subject of ongoing buyer–seller relationships is considered in more detail in the following chapter.

## 4.5 Market segmentation and buyer behaviour

The purpose of studying buyer behaviour is to develop a company's marketing mix so that a desired response is achieved from targeted buyers. Naturally, individuals differ in the way they respond to marketing stimuli, implying differences in individuals' processing determinants. Service providers need to understand these individual differences and fine-tune their marketing mix so that it achieves a desired response from each member of the target market. In a diverse society, it is unlikely that one formulation of the marketing mix will bring about a desired response from everybody. Just as a carpenter needs to adjust his hammers and drills to suit the job in hand, so too the marketer needs to adjust the marketing mix to the needs of individual buyers.

**Market segmentation** is a fundamental principle of marketing and its advantages are well documented, as are the conditions which are necessary for its successful implementation. In the service industries, there is a clear understanding of the benefits that may accrue from successful market segmentation and it is therefore used extensively throughout the sector. Many services organizations are at the forefront of the development of segmentation methods within the UK with banks, building societies, insurance companies, the travel and hospitality sectors, among others, having well-defined approaches to the segmentation of their markets.

Among the greatest exponents of segmentation are the high street retailers. As an example, the Arcadia Group covers the fashion clothing market with a range of highly segmented brands such as Top Shop, Principles and Dorothy Perkins. Similarly, grocery retailers have a very clear understanding of who their customers are and what needs they seek to satisfy, and position their stores in the marketplace accordingly (e.g. contrast the market position of Sainsbury's with that of Aldi).

The development of segmentation and target marketing reflects the movement away from production orientation towards marketing orientation. When the supply of services is scarce relative to supply, organizations may seek to minimize production costs by producing one homogeneous product which satisfies the needs of the whole population. Over time, increasing affluence has increased buyers' expectations. Affluent customers are no longer satisfied with the basic package holiday, but instead are able to demand one which satisfies an increasingly wide range of needs – not just for relaxation, but for activity, adventure and status associations. Furthermore, society has become much more fragmented. The 'average' consumer has become much more of a myth, as incomes, attitudes and lifestyles have diverged.

Alongside the greater fragmentation of society, technology is increasingly allowing highly specialized services to be tailored to ever smaller market segments. Using computerized databases, package holidays need no longer be aimed at broad market segments, but can cater for very small groups who have distinctive needs and buying processes.

Different buyers within a market can behave very differently when evaluating alternative services. To be fully marketing-oriented, a company would have to adapt its offer to meet the needs of each individual. In fact, very few firms can justify aiming to meet the needs of each specific individual – instead, they aim to meet the needs of small subgroups within the market. With developments in technology and the fragmentation of society, these segments have tended to become smaller over time.

The term 'one-to-one' marketing has been widely used recently, and while not many companies have managed to go this far, it certainly points the way to the future. Crude indicators of buying behaviour such as socioeconomic group and income have long been discredited as unsuitable indicators in their own right, as they hide considerable variation in buying behaviour within groups. Retail stores, fresh with their loyalty cards give some indications of the one-to-one future. Shortly after launching its Clubcard, Tesco sent all members an incentive in the form of shopping vouchers. However, only three different sets of incentives were produced, targeted at just three identified segments. By 1997, the company had refined its understanding of Clubcard members' buying behaviour and produced different incentives for each of 3000 identified segments. Retailers have been using loyalty card information to build up ever more detailed pictures of customers and their buying preferences. In one case, a retailer sought to increase sales of fresh fish. Focus group research had suggested that many people would have been happy to experiment, but simply did not know how to cook fresh fish. Based on their current shopping pattern, a number of hypothesized groups were identified who might be most likely to respond to an offer of a free fish recipe book and a discount voucher for fresh fish. After initial experimentation, the profile of the most likely respondent was identified by the combination of fresh ingredients which they purchased, and a shopping pattern which suggested that the buyer was not averse to innovation. Once the best profile had been identified, the incentive was sent to all individuals whose buying behaviour matched it. Sales of fresh fish rose significantly without the need to resort to across-the-board price discounting.

Although examples like this illustrate the value of marketing to very small segments, questions remain whether more traditional mass marketing may be more cost-effective in many situations. Within the retail grocery sector, two of Tesco's main competitors, Safeway and Asda, have stated their preference for an 'everyday low price' strategy, rather than one based on database-driven differentiation strategies and have withdrawn their loyalty club programmes. Does 'one-to-one' marketing have widespread potential? Or is it sufficient to treat buyers as a more homogeneous group in terms of their response to marketing stimuli?

### 4.5.1 Bases for market segmentation

If the segmentation methods used by services organizations are examined more closely, it becomes apparent that demographic variables tend to be the most widely used segmentation bases. In this respect service industries are no exception – the same tends to be true in goods marketing. Age, sex and socioeconomic analysis along with geographic location provide useful information for building up a profile of users of a service. This can be used for targeting purposes in media planning, assisting in new service development and can contribute to pricing policy and service outlet location. Some indication of the importance of demographic bases for segmentation can be seen in the choice of magazines in which American Express advertise, the range of accounts offered by NatWest Bank, the pricing practices of British Airways and the location of Lunn Poly Holiday Shops.

Demographic segmentation has an important role to play in the use of direct mail (an important element of the marketing mix of many financial services companies), although in this case, demographic analysis is usually employed in conjunction with a geographic database which enables an organization to identify and locate potential customers with the necessary characteristics. The combination of these two types of segmentation variables is often referred to as 'geodemographics'.

In all of these applications of segmentation methods there is a heavy reliance upon the availability of accurate and timely market data. Geodemographic methods of segmentation, for example, require sources of information which provide details of customers' demographics and their geographical location and can involve secondary data acquisition or primary investigations undertaken on behalf of an organization. The sophistication with which segmentation is being approached has moved forward immensely as advances in the capabilities of information technology have occurred. From the point of view of services organizations who are exponents of segmentation policies, two relatively recent developments should be mentioned:

- A number of firms offer a geodemographic segmentation analysis which allows the identification of small geographical pockets of households according to a combination of their demographic characteristics and their buying behaviour. These computerized data systems – such as MOSAIC – are of considerable value in the planning of direct mail campaigns, store location and merchandizing.
- The wealth of data provided by the operation of electronic point of sale systems (EPOS) means that services firms can study in detail the buying behaviour of individuals or groups of individuals. How often does an individual visit their store? What goods and services tend to be bought as complementary products to each other? How responsive are individuals to price reductions or coupon offers? EPOS offers new insights into buying behaviour.

**Figure 4.8**
MOSAIC is a widely used geodemographic classification system

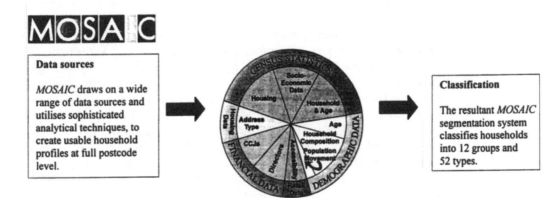

As further advances in information technology are made and competitive pressures among service marketers intensify, an even greater sophistication in the way that markets are segmented will be invoked.

For most practical marketing purposes, services organizations tend to rely upon demographic and geographic data. Yet there is a real conflict between the theoretical and practical aspects of market segmentation. In practice, the established bases are employed, at least in part, because the data is readily available in this format and targeting is therefore reasonably straightforward. However, although they do have this practical value they do not really explain *why* there are differences in the buying behaviour of consumers.

There are therefore a number of other approaches to segmentation which are seen to be more theoretically sound, such as psychographics (based upon personality, attitudes, opinions and interests) and self-concept (how customers perceive themselves). Such approaches rely on attitude measurement techniques including Likert scales and semantic differentials in order to elicit the necessary information from customers. These segmentation bases provide a useful supplementary set of tools for the subdivision of markets in practice, although they are generally used in conjunction with demographic profiles for targeting purposes.

An alternative qualitative approach to identifying clusters of customers is based around the analysis of the components of a particular service offering. This is effectively a benefit-based technique for distinguishing market segments. Cluster analysis of responses is commonly applied after the qualitative stage of a study. The segments derived from this type of investigation, based upon a combination of factors, may then be targeted by a service firm with specific product offers which have been designed in accordance with the observed buying processes of the segments.

## 4.6 Business ethics and the purchase decision

Finally in this chapter we will consider the role that ethical evaluations play in buyer behaviour.

Increasing numbers of services buyers are bringing ethical issues into their decision-making process. If two competing services are judged to be basically similar in all other respects, why not choose the service provider whose contribution to society's welfare is believed to be the greatest? Consider the following cases:

- Hundreds of thousands of customers of Shell throughout Europe boycotted the company's petrol service stations during 1995 in protest against the ethics of dumping an obsolete oil drilling platform in the North Sea. For most customers, visiting one petrol station rather than another incurred little, if any cost, yet allowed them to express their feelings about Shell's ethics.
- The UK retailer The Body Shop has attracted a loyal following of customers who share the company's attitudes towards human and animal welfare issues, and buy its products in preference to functionally similar competitors. Such is the importance of customers' perceptions of the company's ethics that its share price has fallen following allegations of poor ethical conduct.
- Many financial services companies now offer investment products which refuse to invest in companies whose business is considered to be unethical. In the UK,

the Co-operative Bank offers unit trusts which appeal to many market segments because of its refusal to invest in companies involved with animal experiments, tobacco manufacture and arms manufacture, among others.

Many have argued that when a consumer buys a product, he or she is inclined today to think not just of the benefit which it will bring to him or her directly, but also the benefit which it will bring to society more widely. Research undertaken in the UK by the organization Business in the Community during 1996 found that 83% of respondents had a more positive image about a company which supports a cause they care about. Moreover, 73% said they would switch brands and 61% said they would switch retailers to those which became associated with a good cause.

Ethical judgements involve the evaluation of an individual product's acceptability to society at large, and the overall **ethics** of a company. Initial interest in marketing ethics has focused on the manufactured goods sector, with environmentalism emerging as a major factor affecting consumer purchases during the 1980s. As with the development of a general marketing orientation, issues of marketing ethics have since found application within the services sector. Because of the intangible nature of services, social costs and benefits of services can be less easy to identify than for goods. Nevertheless, there is evidence that some segments of the population are widening their evaluatory criteria to include the benefits which they bring to society (or the social cost which they avoid). Within the financial services sector, there is now a wide range of fund management services available to investors who are concerned about the ethics of their investments. Within the travel and tourism sector, it is now recognized that intensive tourism development can create significant environmental problems. For example, the threat to the breeding habits of the loggerhead turtle on the Greek island of Zakynthos has resulted from the intensive development of beaches for recreational purposes. Some customers of package holidays – admittedly a small niche group at the moment – choose their package holiday destination on the basis of tourism's environmental impact at a resort, and choose their service provider – the tour operator – on the basis of its policies towards environmentally benign development of resorts.

It is argued in later chapters that the promotion of service organizations' corporate brands is generally more important than the promotion of specific product brands. For this reason, many service organizations are keen to link themselves to good social causes. The Tesco supermarket group's support for unleaded petrol and recycling schemes helped to give it a distinctive **positioning** as an environmentally friendly store during the late 1980s. The opposite – linking a corporate brand to a bad cause – can have long-term harmful effects on an organization, for example the Royal Bank of Scotland faced a boycott in 2000 when the bank became identified with anti-libertarian views publicly pronounced by one of its American shareholders.

It is suggested that society is becoming increasingly concerned about the ethical values adopted by its business organizations. With increasing levels of media availability and an increasingly intelligent audience, it is becoming easier to expose examples of unethical business practice. McDonald's Restaurants, for example, has been exposed on numerous occasions for alleged antisocial practices. Despite efforts made by the company to improve its ethical conduct, the availability of media to highlight minor violations has increased markedly.

**Case Study**

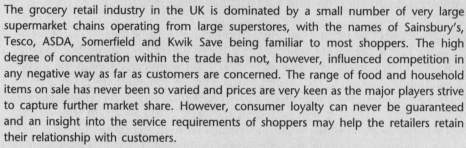

## Supermarkets get ready for a new generation of YABs

The grocery retail industry in the UK is dominated by a small number of very large supermarket chains operating from large superstores, with the names of Sainsbury's, Tesco, ASDA, Somerfield and Kwik Save being familiar to most shoppers. The high degree of concentration within the trade has not, however, influenced competition in any negative way as far as customers are concerned. The range of food and household items on sale has never been so varied and prices are very keen as the major players strive to capture further market share. However, consumer loyalty can never be guaranteed and an insight into the service requirements of shoppers may help the retailers retain their relationship with customers.

A study undertaken by the Henley Centre for Forecasting on behalf of one of the large multiples illustrates how research on the future of the market can form a basis for strategic change. In this instance the research was concerned with predicting patterns of shopping behaviour beyond the mid-1990s and particularly with establishing a set of market segments based on behaviour patterns.

The outcome of the Henley Centre's investigation was the identification of a number of different types of shopper based on a multivariable approach which took account of demographic factors such as age, sex and income as well as lifestyle, personality and, finally, attitude to the shopping experience. As with so many of these studies the resultant new breeds of shopper have been labelled with glib titles.

The Harried Hurrier was predicted to be the most important type of new shopper. These are typically burdened with squabbling children and crippled by a severe lack of time. Hurriers are averse to anything that eats into their precious minutes such as having too much choice, which makes them impatient. Another large group, but spending less money, were identified as the middle-aged Young-at-Heart who in contrast to the first group have time on their hands and like to try new products. An important and growing species of grocery shopper is the Young, Affluent and Busy (or 'YABs') for whom money is not a major constraint in their quest for convenience and more interesting products, but they do have a low boredom threshold. Two other types who were expected to grow in importance are the Fastidious who are attracted by instore hygiene and tidiness and the mainly male Begrudgers who only shop out of obligation to others. At the same time, the Perfect Wife and Mother who is concerned with the balanced diet would appear to be on her way out. She is likely to be more than compensated for by the Obsessive Fad-Followers whose choice of food tends to be dominated by brand image and current trends.

It was expected that the new breeds would act as a catalyst for a shopping revolution. Although the already established need for convenience will still predominate, retail analysts anticipate some significant changes, such as in-store traffic-routeing systems, one-way layouts, and themed food centres by nationality. There would appear to be a considerable amount to be gained from transforming the sometimes stressful encounter with the superstore into a pleasurable leisure activity.

However, balancing the needs of all these groups may prove to be a difficult task which may lead to greater specialization within the sector. For example, it is not imposs- ible to imagine chains of speciality food retailers that act as menu stores offering the YABs the alternative of buying different dinner party food on different days, switching the emphasis from French to Italian to Indian recipes.

(Adapted from 'Keeping 'em Rolling in the Aisles', *Marketing Week*, 11 August 1989)

## Case study review questions

1 To what extent are segment descriptions such as those used for YABs and Harried Hurriers useful to supermarkets in marketing planning?

2 Analyse some of the implications for a supermarket of the ageing of the population.

3 How can you explain differences between countries in grocery shoppers' behaviour?

## Chapter summary and linkages to other chapters

The intangibility of services and their perceived riskiness makes the buyer's task of choosing between competing products more complex than is the case for manufactured goods. Consumers cannot properly evaluate a service until after it has been consumed, therefore the bases for prior evaluation are limited. Tangible cues are vital to give some indication of subsequent service quality. Brands and ongoing relationships with a service provider can help to reduce the riskiness of a service purchase. Very often, the image of the service provider is more important in evaluation than the image of individual service offers, and this image is increasingly being influenced by its perceived ethical standards.

The development of ongoing buyer–seller relationships as a means of simplifying service purchase decisions is discussed further in **Chapter 5**. The role of brands in appealing to specific target markets is discussed further in **Chapter 7**. Methods of judging the quality of a service, and hence influencing repurchase intention, are discussed in **Chapter 8**. Attempts to influence buyer behaviour through promotional activities are discussed in **Chapter 11**. Finally, the importance of gathering information about customers' evaluation and purchasing processes is discussed in **Chapter 6** in the context of information management.

## www linkages/URLs

There are now many useful websites which seek to simplify the choice process for service buyers. For example:
www.buy.co.uk
www.shopsmart.com

A good example of a word-of-mouth recommendation site can be found at:
www.dooyoo.com

## Key terms

Market segmentation 103      Ethics 107
Positioning 107

## Chapter review questions

1   What are the causes and consequences of risk in the services purchasing process? What can service providers do to overcome problems of buyers' perceived risk?

2   Consider the case of a group of friends discussing which restaurant to go to for a social meal. Analyse the processes and information sources likely to be used in arriving at a decision.

3   In what ways do buying processes for airline travel typically differ between private buyers and business buyers? How should airlines respond to these differences?

4   With growing choice available to consumers of many types of services, to what extent do you consider that models of buyer behaviour are essentially about 'choice reduction'?

5   In what ways does the practice of market segmentation differ between a seller of prerecorded videos and the operator of a cinema?

6   To what extent are considerations of a service provider's ethics important in evaluating alternative service offers? Would you expect differences to exist between private and organizational buyers?

## Selected further reading

*For a general review of buyer behaviour, numerous books are available which deal with products in general, including:*

Bettman, J. R., M. F. Luce and J. W. Payne (1998) 'Constructive Consumer Choice Processes', *Journal of Consumer Research*, Vol. 25, No. 3, pp 187–198

Engel, J. F., R. D. Blackwell and P. W. Miniard (1997) *Consumer Behaviour*, 8th Edition, The Dryden Press Series in Marketing, Dryden Press, New York

Rice, C. (1997) *Understanding Customers*, 2nd edition, Butterworth-Heinemann, Oxford

Chisnall, P. (1994) *Consumer Behaviour*, 3rd edition, McGraw-Hill, Maidenhead

*For an early model of consumer behaviour which is specifically applied to the services sector, the following is useful.*

Fisk, R. P. (1981) 'Toward a Consumption/Evaluation Process Model for Services', in J. H. Donnelly and W. R. George (eds), *Marketing of Services*, American Marketing Association, Chicago, IL

*The following two papers review the general differences between goods and services in the way consumers make purchase decisions.*

Gabbott, M. and G.Hogg (1994) 'Consumer Behaviour and Services: A review', *Journal of Marketing Management*, Vol. 10, No. 4, pp 311–24

Zeithaml, V. A. (1981) 'How Consumers Evaluation Processes Differ Between Goods and Services', in J. H. Donnelly and W. R. George (eds), *Marketing of Services*, American Marketing Association, Chicago, IL, pp 186–90

*For an analysis of the specific role of perceived risk in the buying process for goods and services, the following provides an empirical study and extensive literature review.*

Murray, K. B and J. L. Schlacter (1990) 'The Impact of Services versus Goods on Consumers' Assessment of Perceived Risk and Variability', *Journal of the Academy of Marketing Science*, Vol. 18, No. 1, pp 51–65

# 5

# Relationship marketing and customer loyalty

## Learning objectives

A new paradigm or an old idea dressed in new clothes? To some, creating customer loyalty and ongoing buyer–seller relationships is superseding service as a framework for understanding competitive advantage. The elements of relationship marketing have been around for a long time, and this chapter offers a background to current discussion on the subject. The creation of ongoing relationships is very closely linked to buyer behaviour and helps to simplify buying decision processes. It is generally more profitable for a company to retain existing customers rather than constantly to recruit new ones. This chapter explores various methods used by companies to turn casual transactions into ongoing relationships and to create enduring customer loyalty. After you have read this chapter, you should be in a position to assess the contribution of relationship marketing to the marketing of services.

## 5.1  Defining relationship marketing

The term 'relationship marketing' has become very widely used in recent years. However, as with many new ideas in business which come along, confusion sets in as to just what the term means. There has been a lot of debate about what is meant by relationship marketing, with the strongest advocates claiming that it represents a paradigm shift in marketing, while some sceptics have argued that it is really all about well-established business practices dressed up as something new.

Conceptually, relationship marketing has been positioned variously between being a set of marketing tactics, in which any interaction between buyers and sellers is described as a relationship, regardless of the parties' affective commitment to each other, and a fundamental marketing philosophy which goes to the core of the marketing concept through its customer lifetime focus (Gummesson, 1999). To some, relationship marketing is seen as little more than database marketing (e.g. Bickert, 1992). Many have pointed to the central role played by the concepts of commitment, interdependence and trust (Boyle *et al.*, 1992; Crosby, Evans and Cowles, 1990).

Building on Berry's conceptualization of three levels of relationship marketing (Berry, 1995), the published literature on relationship marketing can be classified into three broad approaches.

1   At a *tactical* level, relationship marketing is used as a sales promotion tool. Developments in information technology have spawned many short-term loyalty schemes. However, the implementation of such schemes has often been opportunistic, leading to expensive loyalty schemes which create loyalty to the incentive rather than to the supplier (Barnes, 1994).

2   At a more *strategic* level, relationship marketing has been seen as a process by which suppliers seek to 'tie-in' customers through legal, economic, technological, geographical and time bonds (Liljander and Strandvik, 1995). Again, it has been pointed out that such bonds may lead to customer *detention* rather than *retention* (Dick and Basu, 1994) and that a company which has not achieved a more deep-seated affective relationship with its customers may be unable to sustain those relationships if the legal or technological environment changes. What often passes as a relationship, therefore, is an asymmetric association based on inequalities of knowledge, power and resources, rather than mutual trust and empathy. Where tying-in is achieved through mutually rewarding co-operation, mutual dependence and shared risk, the relationship is likely to show greater stability and endurance (Han, Wilson and Dant, 1993).

3   At a more *philosophical* level, relationship marketing goes to the heart of the marketing philosophy. Traditional definitions of marketing focus on the primacy of customer needs and relationship marketing as a philosophy refocuses marketing strategy away from products and their life cycles towards customer relationship life cycles. Recent conceptualizations of marketing as being the integration of a customer orientation, competitor orientation and interfunctional co-ordination (Narver and Slater, 1990) stress the key features of a relationship marketing philosophy; using all employees of an organization to profitably meet the lifetime needs of targeted customers better than competitors.

| Traditional transaction oriented marketing | Relationship marketing |
|---|---|
| Focus on a single sale | Focus on customer retention |
| Short-term orientation | Long-term orientation |
| Sales to anonymous buyers | Tracking of identifiable buyers |
| Salesperson is the main interface between buyer and seller | Multiple levels of relationships between buyer and seller |
| Limited customer commitment | High customer commitment |
| Quality is the responsibility of production department | Quality is the responsibility of all |

**Figure 5.1**
The components of transactional and relational exchange compared

The language of relationship marketing can be misleading. In the service sector, many organizations are simplifying and 'industrializing' their processes, usually in an attempt to improve their operational efficiency and consistency of performance. Such companies may talk about relationship development with customers, based on a dialogue which is driven by information technology. But such relationships can be qualitatively quite different from those based on social bonds and trust. While UK clearing banks have become vigorous in their development of customer databases and named personal banking advisers, many customers would feel that the relationship with their bank is qualitatively worse than when a branch manager was able to enter into a more holistic dialogue with customers.

Managers of firms seeking to develop relationships with their customers should avoid the arrogant belief that customers seek such relationships. Surveys have indicated that many categories of buyers are becoming increasingly confident in venturing outside a business relationship and reluctant to enter into an ongoing relationship. Relationship marketing strategies may fail where buyers' perception is of reduced choice and less freedom to act opportunistically rather than added value which can derive from a relationship. Added value must be defined by sellers in terms of buyers' needs, rather than focusing on customers as captives who can be cross-sold other products from a firm's portfolio.

## 5.2 Reasons for the development of relationship marketing

The simplest reason why firms seek to develop ongoing relationships with their customers is that it is generally much more profitable to retain existing customers than continually seeking to recruit new customers to replace lapsed ones. There have been many exercises to calculate the effects on a company's profits of even a modest improvement in the rate at which customers defect to competitors (e.g. Reichheld, 1993; Reichheld and Sasser, 1990). The example in Figure 5.2 illustrates the principles of profitable customer retention.

Of course, customers are not all equally profitable, and there may be some categories of customer with whom a company would not want to pursue a relationship. Being able to identify these segments is therefore also an important part of a relationship marketing strategy. Many companies use past records to develop a profile of the most promising groups to target and do less to encourage those inherently disloyal groups who are likely to leave the company as quickly as they were attracted to it. Sometimes, companies go through their customer list and actively seek to terminate their relationship with groups who are unprofitable. Many UK building societies have attracted media criticism when they have closed the accounts of customers who kept only minimal account balances and did not buy any other services offered by the society. Like many banks and financial services companies, they had recognized that relationship marketing needs to focus on profitable customers and that an exit strategy may be needed for unprofitable ones. Naturally, one bank's target customers for relationship development may be the same as its competitors' targets, so intense competition can occur for key types of customers. This competition can create a dynamic tension in which customers' loyalty is continually challenged by the efforts of competitors to undermine it.

**Figure 5.2**

Increasing the lifetime value of customers through relationship marketing

A worked example of profitable customer retention

- A credit card company has traditionally lost 10% of its customers each year, much of which is a preventable loss.
- This implies that the average lifespan of each customer with the company is 10 years
- On average, customers contribute £100 in profit to the company in a year
- It costs £75 to recruit a new customer (comprising advertising costs, application processing costs and special recruitment incentives)
- The company decides to initiate a relationship-based customer care programme which has the effect of reducing customer turnover from 10% pa to 5% pa. The cost of this programme is £20 per customer pa.
- This implies that the average lifespan of customers with the company is now 20 years.
- The lifetime profitability of customers can now be calculated.
- Previously, the company could expect to earn from each customer: 10 years × £100 pa = £1000, less £75 recruitment cost = £925
- With the customer care programme, the company could expect to earn from each customer 20 years × £100 pa, less £75 recruitment cost, less cost of care programme (20 years × £20 pa) = £1525
- By spending more on customer retention activity, the lifetime value of customers has increased by £600

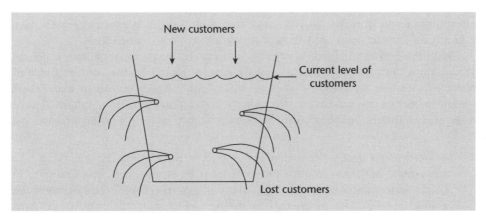

**Figure 5.3**
The 'leaky bucket' model of customer retention and defection

The mobile phone operator Orange has been much admired in the UK for its successful launch and rapid growth based on a strong brand. Key to its continuing success will be tackling the problem of 'churn' which affects all mobile phone operators. Some 20% of Orange customers defect each year, although this compares favourably to industry norms of 30%. On average, it cost Orange £256 in 1996 to recruit each new customer, reflecting the cost of introductory offers, subsidized phones and advertising. With a million customers, reducing the churn rate from 20% to 10% would bring about annual savings of over £25 million. But how does it stem its defections? Orange's research had suggested that the quality and range of services (especially the coverage area), not price were the main reason behind defections. Its response was to double the speed of its network expansion programme, with an investment of £800 million for the three-year period up to the end of 1999. As another approach, could the industry shake itself out of the habit of giving such big discounts to sign up customers for a year, then charging prices which, by European standards, are high? With the introduction of number portability (allowing customers to keep their telephone number, even if they change service providers), how else could mobile phone companies improve their ongoing relationships so that competitors were perceived as being inferior and a transfer would involve too much cost and disruption?

There is nothing new in the way that firms have sought to develop ongoing relationships with their customers. In simple economies, where production of goods and services took place on a small scale, it was possible for the owners of businesses to know each customer personally and to come to understand their individual characteristics. They could therefore adapt service delivery to the needs of individuals on the basis of knowledge gained during previous transactions, and could suggest appropriate new product offers. They would also be able to form an opinion about customers' credit worthiness. Networks of relationships between buyers and sellers are still the norm in many Far Eastern countries, and many Western exporters have found it difficult to break into these long-standing, closed networks.

With the growth in size of Western organizations, the personal contact which an organization can have with its customers has been diluted. Instead of being able to reassure customers on the basis of close relationships, organizations in many cases sought to provide this reassurance through the development of strong brands. Recent resurgence of interest in relationship marketing has occurred for a number of reasons:

- In increasingly competitive markets, good products alone are insufficient to differentiate an organization's products from its competitors. For example, in the car sector, manufacturers traditionally differentiated their cars on the basis of superior design features such as styling, speed and reliability. Once most companies had reached a common standard of design, attention switched to differentiation through superior added service facilities, such as warranties and finance. Once these service standards became the norm for the sector, many car manufacturers have sought to differentiate their cars on the basis of superior relationships. So most major car manufacturers now offer customers complete packages which keep a car financed, insured, maintained and renewed after a specified period. Instead of a three yearly one-off purchase of a new car, many customers enter an ongoing relationship with a car manufacturer and its dealers which gives the customer the support they need to keep their car on the road and to have it renewed when this falls due (Figure 5.4).
- Developments in information technology have had dramatic effects in developing relationship marketing activities. The development of powerful user-friendly databases has allowed organizations to recreate in a computer what the individual small business owner knew in his or her head. Large businesses are now able to tell very quickly the status of a particular customer, for example their previous ordering pattern, product preferences and profitability. Developments in information technology have also allowed companies to enter individual dialogues with their customers through direct mail and increasingly through

**Figure 5.4**

The changing focus of marketing from product emphasis to relationship emphasis – an illustration of the car sector

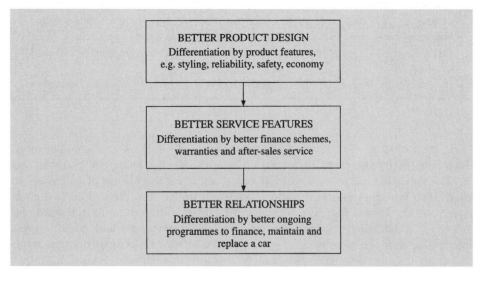

electronic means. Increased production flexibility based on improved technology allows many manufacturers and service organizations to design unique products which meet the needs of individual customers, rather than broad segments of customers.

● **Just-in-time (JIT)** production methods (JIT) have become very widespread in Western countries, thanks to the lead given by Japanese manufacturing companies. It often makes sense for a manufacturer to keep its holdings of component parts down to an absolute minimum. This way, it ties up less capital, needs less storage space and suffers less risk of stocks becoming obsolete. So instead of keeping large stocks of components, manufacturers arrange for them to be delivered 'just in time' for them to be used in their production process. It is not uncommon to find car manufacturers receiving batches of components which within an hour are incorporated into a car. Just-in-time systems demand a lot of co-operation between supplier and customer which cannot easily be achieved if each transaction is to be individually bargained. Some form of ongoing relationship between the two is essential. While JIT is essentially a concept of the manufacturing sector, its effects have been to draw the manufacturing and services sectors closer together. It implies a system of production in which manufacturing capacity becomes instantly perishable if component parts are not delivered at the right time. Service industries face a very similar problem of perishable output. Within the manufacturing sector JIT has also given many opportunities to services firms who organize the logistics of JIT delivery of materials.

● Finally, it has been commented that an emphasis on one-off transactions in which each transaction is bargained over is very much associated with masculine values of conquest and victory. There is an extensive body of literature on differences in personality traits which exist between males and females. One important area of difference is in the way that males and females develop relationships with others, with masculine gender traits being characterized as aggressive and instrumental, while feminine traits are more commonly associated with showing empathy and resolving conflicts through reconciliation (Barry, Bacon and Child, 1957; Meyers-Levy and Sternthal, 1991; Palmer and Bejou, 1995). Recent moves from warfare approaches to business exchange towards collaborative approaches may appear novel when judged by the stereotypical value systems of males, but may be considered normal by the value system of females. In recent years, females have taken on increasingly important roles in business, both as buyers and sellers of goods and services. Although there is the possibility of role conflict, women as buyers and sellers are likely to bring values to commercial exchanges which are more relational than transactional.

What is the lifetime value of a restaurant customer? A first-time customer may only be spending £20 on this occasion, but if they like what they get, how much are they likely to spend in the future? A typical diner eating out just once a month could be worth £1200 in just five years. If they are happy, they are likely to tell their friends. If they're not, they are likely to tell even more of their friends. It follows that customers should be seen as investments, to be carefully nurtured over time. When things go wrong (for example, through overbooking) it would probably be to the restaurant's advantage to spend heavily on putting things right for the customer (e.g. by offering money off a future meal). Judged on the basis of the current transaction, the restaurant may make a loss, but it has protected its investment in a future income stream. Like all investments, some customers are worth more than others. How should a company decide which customers are priority relationships to invest in? And what level of investment can be justified in terms of the expected future profitability from the relationship?

## 5.3 Theoretical paradigms underlying buyer–seller relationships

Before we look at the methods and practices of relationship marketing, we will briefly consider some of the theory which underlies the creation of buyer–seller relationships. Two streams of literature are particularly relevant here: transaction cost economics and resource dependence theory. This is not an exhaustive list of the theoretical roots of relationship marketing, but the ideas contained in these theories have made significant contributions to the subject.

Transaction cost economics, first given prominence by Williamson, is based on the notion that there are costs of doing business which are in addition to readily identifiable resource costs. These costs can cover administrative costs and the cost of insuring against contingencies when dealing with unknown customers and suppliers (Williamson, 1985).

Williamson noted that the primary objective of economic organizations is to 'economize in both transaction and neo-classical production costs' (Williamson, 1985, p. 28). Transaction costs are affected by information availability and uncertainty. Hybrid forms of organization, such as strategic alliances, networks and equity joint ventures, can be attributed to the search for efficiency in transaction costs (Williamson, 1993). In the theoretical model, all transactions lie somewhere on a continuum from being purely market-based to being internal to an organization. According to Williamson, firms exist as a means of reducing the risk (and hence transaction costs) of dealing with the uncertainties of a market, thereby reducing transaction costs. On the other hand, market forces can stimulate competition, and hence bring down production costs. Firms seek to reduce their total costs and in reality, 'hybrid' types of organization emerge. Networks of buyer–seller relationships represents a hybrid type of organization which reduces the uncertainty of pure market mediated exchanges, while overcoming the inefficiencies of internal (hierarchical) systems of exchange.

Co-operation between firms which creates value through lowering transaction costs and/or increasing benefits to each party may result in one or both parties giving preferential treatment to the other. Within a transaction cost framework, this could come about as a result of growing levels of trust, which reduces the need for contingencies against risk and uncertainty in transactions. It can also arise where scale benefits encourage preference being given to one partner who is capable of delivering increasing levels of benefits relative to costs.

*Resource dependency theory* approaches commercial relationships by conceptualizing them as a strategic response by firms to conditions of uncertainty (Pfeffer and Salanick, 1978). Firms have been conceptualized as bundles of competencies, such as tacit knowledge, skills, and so on, and this framework has been extended to the study of interorganizational relationships. Through co-operation, partners can exchange core competencies and thereby avoid the risk of tackling novel products or markets alone. In the discussion on strategic relationships between organizations, the ability of member organizations to exchange their technical and marketing competencies has been noted (Hamel, Doz and Prahalad, 1989; Day, 1995). As an example, many alliances between airlines and hotels are formed where individual companies calculate that there will be benefits in sharing access to each others' customers who are mutually exclusive in terms of their geographical representation and product preferences. The value of networks of relationships has been shown to be particularly valuable where 'strategic holes' exist in the connectivity between members, and the network can create social capital by bringing together disparate individuals and organizations (Burt, 1992; Baker, 1994).

## 5.4 Methods of developing buyer–seller relationships

A number of attempts have been made to analyse the development of relationships, often using the principles of life-cycle theories. A theoretical model proposed by Dwyer, Schurr and Oh (1987) identified five stages of relationship development: awareness, exploration, expansion, commitment and dissolution. Their model proposed that a relationship begins to develop significance in the exploration stage when it is characterized by attempts of the seller to attract the attention of the other party. The exploration stage includes attempts by each party to bargain and to understand the nature of the power, norms and expectations held by the other. If this stage is satisfactorily concluded, an expansion phase follows. Exchange outcomes in the exploratory stage provide evidence as to the suitability of long-term exchange relationships. The commitment phase of a relationship implies some degree of exclusivity between the parties and results in information search for alternatives – if it occurs at all – being much reduced. The dissolution stage marks the point where buyer and seller recognize that they would be better able to achieve their respective aims outside the relationship. Subsequent studies have validated the existence of a relationship life cycle (Palmer and Bejou, 1994).

Organizations use a number of strategies to move their customers through the stages of relationship development:

• The possibility of relationships developing can only occur where the parties are aware of each other and of their mutual desire to enter into exchange transactions. At this stage, the parties may have diverging views about the possibility of forming a long-term relationship. The supplier must be able to offer potential customers reasons why they should show disloyalty to their existing supplier. In some cases, low introductory prices are offered by organizations which provide a sufficient incentive for disloyal customers of other companies to switch supplier.

**Figure 5.5**

Stages in buyer and seller relationship development (based on Dwyer, F. R., P. H. Schurr and S. Oh (1987) 'Developing Buyer and Seller Relationships', *Journal of Marketing*, 51, April, pp 11–27)

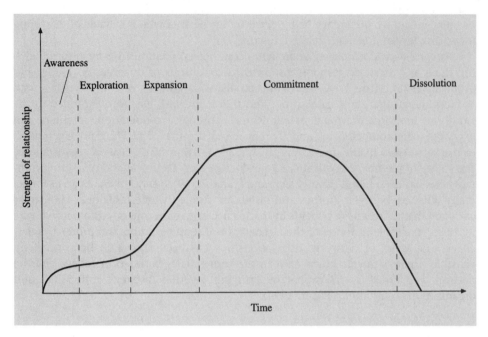

Non-price-related means of gaining attention include advertising and direct mail aimed at the market segments with whom relationships are sought. Over time, the supplier would seek to build value into the relationship so that customers would have little incentive for seeking lower price solutions elsewhere. Inevitably, sellers face risks in adopting this strategy. It may be difficult to identify and exclude from a relationship invitation those segments of the population who are likely to show most disloyalty by withdrawing from the relationship at the point when it is just beginning to become profitable to the supplier.

- On entering into a relationship, buyers and sellers make a series of promises to each other (Gronroos, 1989). In the early stages of a relationship, suppliers' promises result in expectations being held by buyers as to the standard of service that will actually be delivered. Many studies into service quality have highlighted the way in which the gap between expected performance and actual performance determines customers' perception of quality. Quality in perceived service delivery is a prerequisite for a quality relationship being developed.

- Many organizations record information about customers which will be useful in assessing their future needs. This can be used to build up a database from which customers are kept in touch with new product developments of specific interest to them.

- Financial incentives are often given to customers as a reward for maintaining their relationship. These can range from a simple money-off voucher valid for a reduction in the price of a future purchase, to a club-type scheme which allows a standard level of discount for club members. Incentives which are purely based on financial incentives have a problem in that they can defeat the service supplier's central objective of getting greater value out of a relationship. It is often expensive to initiate a relationship, and organizations therefore seek to

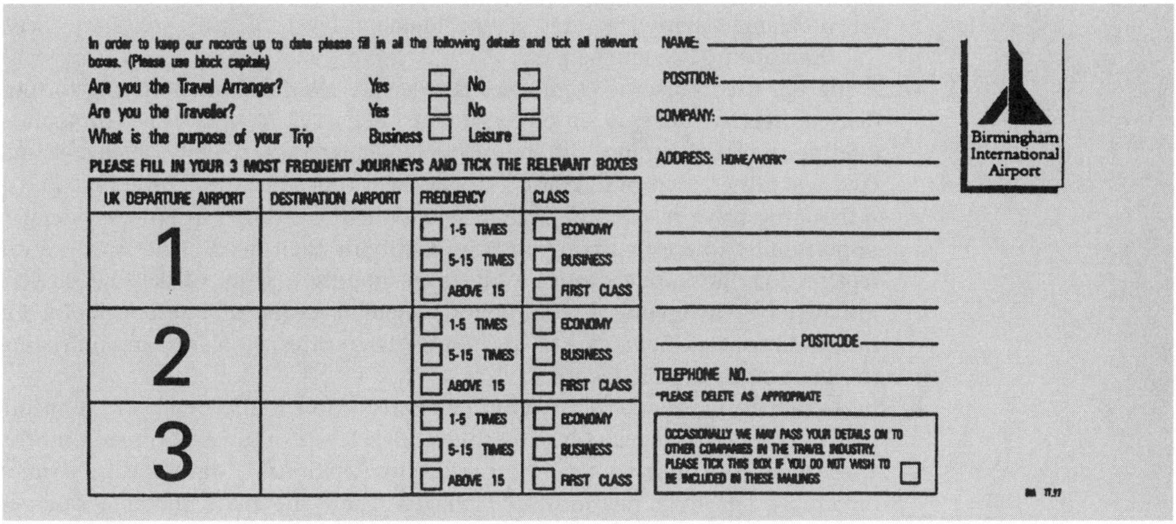

In order to keep our records up to date please fill in all the following details and tick all relevant boxes. (Please use block capitals)

Are you the Travel Arranger?      Yes ☐   No ☐
Are you the Traveller?      Yes ☐   No ☐
What is the purpose of your Trip      Business ☐   Leisure ☐

PLEASE FILL IN YOUR 3 MOST FREQUENT JOURNEYS AND TICK THE RELEVANT BOXES

| UK DEPARTURE AIRPORT | DESTINATION AIRPORT | FREQUENCY | CLASS |
|---|---|---|---|
| **1** | | ☐ 1-5 TIMES<br>☐ 5-15 TIMES<br>☐ ABOVE 15 | ☐ ECONOMY<br>☐ BUSINESS<br>☐ FIRST CLASS |
| **2** | | ☐ 1-5 TIMES<br>☐ 5-15 TIMES<br>☐ ABOVE 15 | ☐ ECONOMY<br>☐ BUSINESS<br>☐ FIRST CLASS |
| **3** | | ☐ 1-5 TIMES<br>☐ 5-15 TIMES<br>☐ ABOVE 15 | ☐ ECONOMY<br>☐ BUSINESS<br>☐ FIRST CLASS |

NAME: _____
POSITION: _____
COMPANY: _____
ADDRESS: HOME/WORK* _____

_____ POSTCODE _____
TELEPHONE NO. _____
*PLEASE DELETE AS APPROPRIATE

OCCASIONALLY WE MAY PASS YOUR DETAILS ON TO OTHER COMPANIES IN THE TRAVEL INDUSTRY. PLEASE TICK THIS BOX IF YOU DO NOT WISH TO BE INCLUDED IN THESE MAILINGS ☐

Birmingham International Airport

**Figure 5.6**
Birmingham International Airport uses the opportunity of an information request to build up a profile of its customers

achieve profits at later stages by raising price levels to reflect the value which customers attach to the relationship. There is a danger of buyers becoming loyal to the financial incentive, rather than the brand which it is designed to promote. Once the financial incentive comes to an end, loyalty may soon disappear. In some cases, greater bonding between customer and supplier can be achieved by selling membership plans to customers which allow subsequent discount, as is the case with a number of store discount cards. Having invested in a membership plan, customers are likely to rationalize their reasons for taking advantage of it, rather than taking their business elsewhere.

- Rather than offer price discounts, companies can add to the value of a relationship by offering other non-financial incentives. Companies must ask: 'Why should a customer want a relationship with us?' The answer is that a relationship, to be sustainable, must add value in the eyes of customers. This value can come about in a number of ways. They include the following:
  - To make re-ordering of services easier. Information about the preferences of individual customers can be retained in order that future requests for service can be closely tailored to their needs. In this way, a travel agent booking accommodation for a corporate client can select hotels on the basis of preferences expressed during previous transactions. By offering a more personalized service, the travel agent is adding value to the relationship, increasing the transaction costs of transferring to another travel agent. Similarly, many hotels record guests' details and preferences to speed up the checking-in process.
  - To offer privileges to customers who wish to enter into some type of formal relationship (for example, many retailers hold special preview events for card holders, and send a free copy of the store's magazine).
  - To develop an ability to jointly solve problems. For example, a car repair garage may undertake the identification of exactly what the problem is that a customer seeks to have fixed, rather than leaving it to the customer to have to specify the work that he or she requires to be carried out. Such joint

problem solving requires a considerable level of trust to have been developed between the parties.

- A strategy used by some companies is to create relationships by trying to turn discrete service delivery into continuous delivery. In this way, companies offering travel insurance often encourage customers to buy all-year-round coverage rather than purchasing a policy each time that they travel abroad.

- A more intensive relationship can develop where customers assign considerable responsibility to another company for identifying their needs. In this way, a car repairer may attempt to move away from offering a series of discrete services initiated by customers, to a situation where it takes total responsibility for maintaining a customer's car, including diagnosing problems and initiating routine service appointments.

- In a competitive marketplace, customer satisfaction is the best way to ensure that buyers return repeatedly. To achieve high levels of satisfaction requires the effort of all functions within an organization. Relationship development cannot be simply left to a relationship manager. There are many notable cases of companies that have not developed any explicit relationship marketing programme, but nevertheless achieve very high levels of customer advocacy.

- Even companies which have an apparently inferior standard of service can achieve high levels of repeat business by charging low prices. Airlines such as EasyJet and Ryanair have developed strong loyalty from price-sensitive customers who consider that the total service offer (ease of booking, flight times, range of destinations and friendliness, etc.) are acceptable in return for the price that they have paid. The danger here is that competitors may enter the market with similarly low prices, but offer higher levels of service. Would customers still remain loyal?

Although there has been much recent interest in relationship marketing – for goods as well as for services – this has tended to emphasize the producer's perspective on a relationship. It can be argued that with increasing knowledge and confidence, consumers are increasingly happy to venture outside a long-term relationship with a service provider. This is reflected, for example, in the observation by the Consumers Association that nearly 20% of the population had changed their bank account or credit card in a year, something which runs counter to earlier anecdotal observations that relationship which individuals have with their bank is more enduring than the relationship with their spouse. With increased knowledge of financial services, consumers are more willing today to venture to another bank which offers the best personal loan for them, or the most attractive credit card. Also, a long-term relationship often begins with attractive introductory discounts and a significant segment of many service markets is prepared to move its business regularly to the service provider which is offering the most attractive discount. The motorist who reviews his or her car insurance each year, for example, may not allow an insurance company to develop a long-term profitable relationship. In the case of many business-to-business services contracts, these may be reviewed regularly as a matter of course, as in the competitive tendering which is required for many government purchases of services. In such circumstances, it is often not possible to add value and higher prices to a long-term relationship.

## 5.5  Customer loyalty

Many services companies have developed customer loyalty programmes as part of their relationship development activities. As with the concept of relationship marketing itself, there is much debate and confusion about just what is meant by customer loyalty.

The *Oxford English Dictionary* defines loyalty as the state of 'being faithful ... true to allegiance'. However, too frequently, mere repetitive behaviour by customers has

**Figure 5.8**
The customer loyalty
ladder (adapted from
Christopher, M.,
A. Payne and
M. Ballantyne,
*Relationship Marketing,*
Butterworth-
Heinemann, 1991)

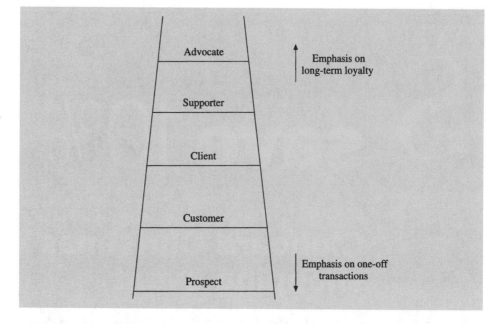

been confused with loyalty as defined above. It has been pointed out that repetitious purchasing behaviour may be a result of a market structure in which buyers find themselves with few alternatives, or where available alternatives can only be obtained at a high cost in terms of breaking current ties with a supplier. In many markets, some segments are likely to purchase repetitively out of inertia or lack of awareness of the alternatives available. The loyalty of customers who are influenced by such inertia is likely to be very different to that of a customer who strongly advocates a product and feels emotionally attached to it. Becoming an advocate of a company is the peak of a 'ladder of loyalty' (Figure 5.8).

Dick and Basu (1994) developed the notion of relative attitude as a theoretical grounding to the loyalty construct. Relative attitude refers to 'a favourable attitude that is high compared to potential alternatives' (Dick and Basu, 1994, p. 100). They suggest that loyalty is evidenced both by a more favourable attitude towards a brand (compared to other alternatives) and repeat buying behaviour. By their analysis, low relative attitude with low repeat purchase indicates an absence of loyalty, while low relative attitude with high repeat purchase indicates 'spurious' loyalty. Satisfaction with a service provider is seen as an antecedent of relative attitude because without satisfaction consumers will not hold a favourable attitude towards the service provider, compared to other alternatives available.

Just because customers repeatedly come back to a company does not necessarily mean that they are loyal to that company. This point was made, tongue-in-cheek, during the continuing war of words between British Airways and Virgin Atlantic Airways. The latter had objected to BA's use of the advertising slogan 'The world's favourite airline'. Statistically, it was true that more passengers travelled internationally with British Airways than with any other airline, but surveys of airline users has consistently put Virgin ahead of BA in terms of perceived quality of service. Virgin's Richard Branson claimed that on BA's logic, the M25, London's notorious orbital motorway, could be described as the world's favourite motorway. Despite coming back to the motorway day after day, few motorists could claim to be loyal to it – they simply have no other choice.

The spat between BA and Virgin serves to underline the point that loyalty is about more than repetitious buying. True loyalty involves customers becoming an enthusiastic advocate of a company.

Many loyalty schemes can be seen as classical sales promotion activities in that they offer a short-term incentive to disloyal brand switchers. It has been noted that much sales promotion activity is very short term in effect and can actually undermine the long-term task of developing a strong brand (O'Brien and Jones, 1995). There is evidence to suggest that sales promotion activity, by encouraging brand switching, can bring about a short-term increase in sales for a company. In the case of manufactured goods companies, this may simply bring forward consumers' purchases, resulting in a subsequent fall as stockpiles are used up. In the case of services, the problem of carrying forward stockpiles does not exist, but disloyal brand switchers who were attracted by one company's offer may be just as easily attracted away by another competitor's incentive.

A medium-term attempt to create loyalty from customers is sometimes made through the formation of structural bonds whereby buyers are tied to a seller. Structural bonds have been defined by Turnbull and Wilson (1989) in terms of investments that cannot be retrieved when a relationship ends, or when it is difficult to end the relationship due to the complexity and cost of changing relational partners. A structural bond between buyer and seller has the effect of tying one to the other, through the creation of barriers to exit, although such ties may be asymmetric. One way in which buyers can become tied to sellers is by designing services in such a way that transferring to another supplier involves significant switching costs (Jackson, 1985). Within the commercial banking sector, it has been noted that one means by which banks increase their retention rate is to increase switching costs by such means as long-term mortgages with penalties for early closure (Perrien, Filiatrault and Ricard, 1992). Airlines' frequent flyer programmes have a similar effect in seeking to make the cost of competitor airlines appear more expensive by virtue of the opportunity cost of forgoing loyalty rewards.

Where the process of tying-in is achieved through a process of mutually rewarding co-operation, mutual dependence and shared risk, the relationship is likely to show greater stability and endurance (Han, Wilson and Dant, 1993).

An important aim of relationship marketing is to encourage existing customers to spend a larger share of their total expenditure with the company. The mobile phone company One-2-One had large numbers of customers using their phones only during the low-price evening period and left them switched off during the

**Figure 5.9**
Following research into its readership, *The Australian* newspaper found large numbers of readers who read the newspaper only at weekends. Its challenge was to turn weekend-only readers into all-week readers. In this advertisement, it sells the benefits to readers of extending their relationship with the newspaper by taking out a regular subscription (reproduced with permission from News Ltd)

# WHY BE A WEEKEND AUSTRALIAN WHEN YOU COULD BE AN EVERYDAY AUSTRALIAN FOR JUST $2.30 MORE.

day. How could it encourage its customers to switch on all day, thereby increasing potential use of its service and extending its relationship with them? The company developed a promotional campaign that involved ringing a different customer every minute throughout the day. Those who answered were eligible for a range of prizes. One-2-One claimed that the promotion was a success, as 60% of phones were switched on during the promotion period, compared with just 50% immediately before. But were customers being loyal to this promotion or had the promotion itself brought about a profitable long-term change in their behaviour?

### 5.5.1 Loyalty programmes and profitability

The aim of loyalty programmes is to extend a customer's life with a company so that their lifetime profitability is increased. Unfortunately, it can be very difficult to measure the effectiveness of a loyalty programme. The conceptual difficulties in measuring the performance of loyalty programmes stem from the difficulty of comparing the performance of a marketing plan which includes a loyalty programme, with a plan which does not include one. Some companies have experimented with cross-sectional data by comparing sales performance at outlets which are similar, except for the existence of a loyalty programme. For companies operating in a competitive marketplace, the need to collect long-term data has to be balanced against the need to get a programme to the market ahead of its competitors. There are few published long-term studies of the effectiveness of loyalty programmes.

In any given industry sector, there are usually significant benefits of being the first company to offer a loyalty programme. However, while pioneers in a sector may introduce incentive schemes and gain additional profitable business from competitors, incentives can rapidly become a sector norm which buyers expect (Gilbert and Karabeyekian, 1995). For firms, the most rewarding relationships with customers result from continued investment to create affective loyalty, rather than financially-based incentives (Barnes, 1994; Kanter, 1994). The excessive use of financial incentives to create loyalty may put a firm at cost disadvantage in a market where cost leadership is important (Porter, 1985), while securing little underlying loyalty.

Loyalty schemes may fail to give a long-term strategic advantage to a company because they are easy for competitors to copy. There is evidence that once one innovator in a sector introduces a loyalty scheme, competitors soon follow.

During the mid-1990s, the UK grocery retail sector seemed to be going the way of the international airline industry in the way that it developed store loyalty cards. The 'card wars' were initiated by Tesco Stores which launched its Clubcard in 1993. The card was initially launched as a means of getting information about the shopping habits of its customers. Previously, the company had no way of routinely disaggregating its revenues between different groups of shoppers and was unable to track the spending habits of individuals. Information collected with each purchase allowed the company to target promotions at individuals whose spending pattern suggested that they would be particularly receptive to a particular promotion. To encourage use of the card, Tesco offered an effective rebate to customers of 1% of their bill which was forwarded in the form of vouchers. Tesco's Clubcard undoubtedly gave it a significant competitive advantage, helping it to beat Sainsbury's in the spot of largest UK grocery retailer. Meanwhile, Tesco's competitors had been researching their own loyalty cards and eventually joined the battle, and loyalty bonuses were to become part of customers' expectations. The pitch of the battle was upped when the supermarkets started adding financial services to their loyalty card, so that it became a debit/ credit card. From here, the way was open to developing a very broad relationship with customers – from baked beans to banking and potatoes to pensions.

Now that loyalty rewards had become the expectation of many customers, was the sector as a whole really any better off? If customer loyalty cards are here to stay, how can individual supermarkets position their card to give them a continuing competitive advantage? Had the supermarkets now got their hands on more customer information than they could realistically handle? Two UK supermarkets, Asda and Safeway, evidently thought so and withdrew their loyalty card pro- grammes in favour of an 'every day low price' policy.

## 5.6 Is relationship marketing universally applicable within the services sector?

Should relationship marketing be viewed as a blueprint which is of universal appli- cability to business, or a special case of limited applicability? The arguments in favour of pursuing strategies designed to obtain a greater share of customers' total expenditure have been well developed in terms of the effects on companies' profit- ability (e.g. Reichheld, 1993; Reichheld and Sasser, 1990). Initial interest in relational exchange focused on industrial marketing (e.g. Ford 1981; Cunningham and Turnbull, 1982) where transactions are typically large in value and limited in number. More recently, the concepts of relationship marketing have been applied to lower value consumer sales. In extending the application of relational exchange, proponents may be following a trend in circumstances where theory and practice suggest that one-off transactional exchanges may be a more appropriate method of securing profitability. Relational exchange may be an unrealistic pursuit in any of the following circumstances: where there is no reason why a buyer would ever wish to return to a seller; where buyers seek to avoid an asymmetric relationship in which they become dependent upon a seller; where buying processes become formalized in a way that prevents a seller developing relationships based on social bonds; where buyers' confidence lowers the need for risk reduction which is an outcome of rela- tionship development; and where the costs associated with relationship develop- ment put a firm at a cost disadvantage in a price sensitive market. Finally, from a social welfare perspective, relationships have been associated with anticompetitive practices which limit buyers' choice.

These limitations to the concept of relational exchange are considered below.

**1  Parties to an exchange may have no expectation of ongoing relationships**  One of the defining characteristics of relational exchange is a time orientation within which exchange takes place (Macneil 1980). However, it may be naive to assume that a longer time orientation implies a greater relational orientation. In the short to medium term, relational exchange may be seen by one or both parties as a means of gaining competencies which they can subsequently use to encroach on the other party's value adding activity (Hamel, 1991; Main, 1990). In this way, a small, developing airline may see a strategic alliance with a larger ailing airline as a means of gaining presence in a market. Once this is achieved, it may break off the relationship and pursue its own independent strategy. With hindsight, many have pointed to British Airway's involvement in US Air as a relationship of short-term expediency which was jettisoned when the opportunity for a more attractive relationship with American Airlines arose.

A second argument against time orientation being synonymous with relationship development is the observation that frequency of transactions between a buyer and seller does not necessarily imply any long-term loyalty from one to the other (O'Brien and Jones, 1995). The use of technological, economic and legal bonds between buyers and sellers may lead to a feeling of involuntary customer detention rather than willing customer retention. There is evidence that companies' loyalty schemes in fact have little effect on underlying affective commitment (e.g. Henley Centre, 1995).

Finally, many businesses serve market segments where customers have no underlying need to make further purchases of a category of product that a company is able to supply. In the extreme case, a small-scale company may appeal to the curiosity of buyers for whom a second-time purchase will have little of its original value – curiosity. This phenomenon is present in many tourism-related businesses in destinations of symbolic rather than aesthetic quality (for example, many people make a religious pilgrimage once in their lifetime with little incentive to return again). While firms with a diverse product and geographical coverage may be able to build on their initial curiosity contact, opportunities for relationship development by smaller companies in such circumstances is limited.

**2  Relationships may be created in an asymmetric manner leading to a desire by one party to reduce their dependence**  It was noted in Chapter 1 that the traditional marketing mix has been criticized for being production-orientated in the way in which the 4Ps provide a framework for things to be 'done' to buyers (Gronroos, 1994). Attempts to create ongoing relationships are similarly frequently initiated in a non-consensual manner. It has been suggested that buyers frequently have no wish to enter into a relationship with a company, despite the efforts of companies to use information from customers to build databases.

A non-consensual relationship where one superior party is able to exercise authority over a subordinate party has been seen as qualitatively inferior to a relationship based on bilateral governance mechanisms (Heide, 1994). In the absence of symmetrical dependence, an individual party will have little incentive to show flexibility, because no guarantee exists that such actions will be reciprocated. In fact, short-term disturbances might represent opportunities for individual parties to pursue opportunistically short-term advantages.

Recent conceptualizations of commercial exchange consider reciprocity to be a fundamental virtue which builds solidarity and contributes to the creation and maintenance of balance in social relations (Becker, 1990; Bagozzi, 1995). Equity theory has been used to argue that customers who feel that they are getting a better ratio of benefits to costs than their exchange partner will feel a greater sense of commitment to their exchange partner (Goodwin and Ross, 1992; Kelley and Davis, 1994) and are likely to show greater forbearance in the event of a failure by the supplier.

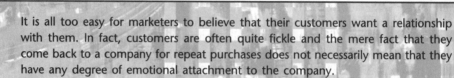

It is all too easy for marketers to believe that their customers want a relationship with them. In fact, customers are often quite fickle and the mere fact that they come back to a company for repeat purchases does not necessarily mean that they have any degree of emotional attachment to the company.

Research undertaken by the Henley Centre for Christian Brann indicated the fickleness of buyers. Respondents were asked about their feelings towards a brand which they had recently purchased. One question asked whether they felt they had a relationship with the company. Only 9% claimed to have a relationship with a tour operator, 11% with a travel agent and 44% with a personal loan provider. Very little loyalty was shown, with only 10% saying that they were loyal to a tour operator, 20% to a travel agent and 35% to a personal loan provider. As marketers increasingly focus on customer loyalty, is their excitement an illusion when customers in fact focus on much more short-term issues about a purchase?

**3 Formalized buying processes may prevent the development of ongoing relationships based on social bonds** Much of the literature on buyer–seller relationship development, especially in the business-to-business sector, has highlighted the importance of developing social bonds between buyers and sellers (Ford, 1981; Liljander and Strandvik, 1995). Social bonds have been observed to reduce buyers' perceived levels of risk and to simplify the reordering process.

An alternative view is that social bonds can become too pervasive to the point at which they allow economic inefficiencies to develop. In the extreme case, corrupt networks of buyers and sellers may acquire sufficient market power to result in an overall loss of economic welfare. Counter-balances are needed to offset such possible relationship-based inefficiencies.

Measures to suppress buyer–seller relationships based on social bonds have been most evident in the formalized ordering procedures for government contracts. In the UK, legislation requiring the compulsory competitive tendering of a wide range of services has transferred many services from being internally produced to being bought in from outside contractors. Previous deficiencies in accountability have been replaced by clearly specified contracts for which all parties are accountable. Where services continue to be provided by internal Direct Labour Organizations, the extent to which there has been a formal split between client and contractor roles has varied between local authorities. A relatively distinct client–contractor split is the norm (Shaw, Fenwick and Foreman, 1993).

Tightly specified supplier–buyer relationships, and a requirement for contracts to be resubmitted for tender after a specified period, reduces the scope for ongoing socially based relationships to be developed within a system of routine competitive tendering. It has been argued that the emphasis on obtaining value for money has stressed cost reduction at the expense of more qualitative measures of efficiency and effectiveness (Walsh, 1991).

**4 Buyers' increasing level of confidence reduces their need for an ongoing relationship** Much of the literature on relationship marketing has focused on *suppliers'* needs to develop relationships (e.g. Day and Wensley, 1983; Webster, 1992), overlooking the perspective of buyers' need, or lack of need to develop ongoing relationships. Commitment by a customer to one supplier relationship can imply forgoing alternative opportunities when they present themselves. Buyers may deliberately seek to minimize risk of dependency by developing a portfolio of suppliers.

In many consumer markets, buyers' need for ongoing trusting relationships has been reduced by legislation which has had the effect of reducing the risk associated with buying goods and services from previously unknown sources. In the UK, for example, statutory provision for investors' compensation funds has lessened the need for investors to rely on an intermediary who they have come to trust. Legislation has reduced the chances of a poor relationship being developed and provided means for compensating investors who suffer loss as a result of failure by an intermediary, thereby encouraging greater transactional orientation (Shrimp and Bearden, 1982).

Recent developments in information technology have emphasized the benefits to producers of being able to gain an asymmetrical position of power in private buyer–seller relationships (e.g. Copulsky and Wolf, 1990; Treacy and Wiersema, 1993). With further development, IT is strengthening the willingness and ability of private consumers to engage in multiple sourcing of purchases at the expense of ongoing relationships. For example, the Internet is increasingly allowing consumers to quickly and easily search for the cheapest quotation when their car insurance comes due for renewal, reducing the chances of renewal through inertia.

**5 Relationship marketing can add to costs, as well as to revenues** For firms, the most rewarding relationships with customers result from investment to create affective loyalty, rather than short-term financially based incentives. The excessive use of financial incentives to create loyalty may put a firm at a cost disadvantage in a market where cost leadership is important, while securing little underlying loyalty. While pioneers in a sector may introduce incentive schemes and gain additional profitable business from competitors, incentives for loyalty can rapidly become a sector norm which customers expect. In the case of airlines' frequent flyer programmes, a cycle of development has been described which began in the 1980s where the first companies to launch achieved revenue benefits. By the end of the 1980s, the use of frequent flyer programmes had become more widespread and their revenue benefits marginal. By the 1990s, most major airlines had developed programmes, yielding little advantage from this tool (Gilbert and Karabeyekian, 1995). Frequent flyer programmes had become part of travellers' expectations, resulting in heavy losses of revenue for airlines (Mowlana and Smith, 1993). It should also be noted that many service sectors are characterized by a range of firms which range from full service with a customer loyalty programme through to no frills and no loyalty programme. Within the airline sector, it has been noted that in 1999 British Airways, with its comprehensive customer loyalty programme made a loss, while the no-frills competitor Ryanair made substantial profits without a loyalty programme. At the same time, within the retail sector, the poorest performing stores were those such as Sainsbury's and Marks and Spencer which had invested in their customer relationships, while stores without a customer loyalty programme, including Asda, Matalan and Morrisons had out-performed the market.

6  **Networks of relationships can have anti-competitive implications**  Finally, the economic benefits of relationship marketing have been questioned because of the anticompetitive implications that can be present in close relationships between businesses. Karl Marx observed that capitalists were more concerned with *avoiding* risks rather than *taking* risks. The development of networks of buyer–seller relationships may be seen as a means of reducing entrepreneurs' exposure to risk, thereby reducing some of the presumed benefits of a competitive market environment.

More fundamentally, relationship marketing activities can be seen as a process by which a seller seeks to restrict the choice set of buyers. Restriction can come about consensually where buyers limit their choice set as a result of a history of satisfaction with their current supplier, or more non-consensually where bonds unwittingly lead to restricted access to alternative sources of need satisfying products. Summing up current developments in relationship marketing, Sheth has described firms' motivation to develop ongoing relationships as being based primarily on 'choice reduction' (Sheth, 1995).

Evidence of the abuse of preferential relationships by firms who are dominant in their markets has been seen in a number of cases. In July 1999, the European Commission fined British Airways €6.8 million for providing excessive loyalty rewards to its travel agents, thereby abusing its dominant position in the market (Mortished, 1999). British Airways had developed a loyalty programme for its travel agents which rewarded high volumes of business by granting loyalty bonuses to preferred agents. It was argued by the Commission that such action made it unacceptably difficult for smaller airline competitors to compete for distribution coverage within travel agents.

Regulatory bodies are increasingly recognizing that structural bonds can become anticompetitive. In 1996, British Telecom, which had a dominant position in the UK telephone market, sought to develop a strategic alliance with BskyB, the dominant player in the cable television sector. BT customers would gain preferential pricing for BskyB's services and would become committed to taking their telephone service from BT rather than one of its competitors. This relationship was held by the regulatory body OFTEL to be against the public interest, despite the benefits that it would appear to bring in the short-term to the parties involved.

It has been observed that the pattern of doing business in many countries may be based on a tightly knit network of relationships between buyers, sellers, suppliers and distributors, typified by Japan's manufacturing and distribution *keiretsu* (Ohmae, 1989; Cutts 1992). It may seem ironic that while companies in Western countries seek to develop closer relationships between businesses, many of those same companies have been applying pressure through their governments for such practices to be curtailed in Japan. Businesses in the latter country are characterized by networks of supply and distribution chains which have had the effect – intentional or not – of making it difficult for a new entrant to break into their market.

## 5.7 Relationship breakdown

Buyer–seller relationships may break down for a variety of reasons. It was noted earlier that in some cases the service supplier may actively seek to break off a relationship where a customer is judged to offer no long-term profit potential. At other times, it is the customer who drifts away. Sometimes there are good extraneous reasons for this defection. For example, a customer of an airline may break off their relationship if the airline ceases to serve their local airport, or if the customer moves their residence to an area not served by the airline. For some categories of product, relationships may end when a customer no longer needs that product and the supplier does not have any new service propositions which might satisfy the customer's changing needs. Many relationships fail when a customer dies or a company goes out of business.

Of more concern to marketers is where a breakdown in a buyer's commitment to a relationship is associated with greater competition and the availability of alternative suppliers. Competition tests the true loyalty of a customer. Defection may occur where the factors that helped to build a relationship go into reverse in terms of their evaluation by buyers. In view of the importance ascribed in the literature to the building of trust in the development of commitment, it would seem plausible that the undermining of trust is a significant factor leading to a decline in commitment. Maintaining and strengthening trust is essential to the long-term success of a relationship. Where trust is absent, the relationship will deteriorate. This area has been under-researched in the context of buyer–seller relationships. Similarly, apparent lapses in employees' knowledge base or their ethics may undermine buyers' commitment to a relationship.

Service failures test the commitment of an organization's customers. Service encounters can result in failure as perceived by customers in a number of ways, including the unavailability of a service, slow service and errors in delivery (Bitner, Booms and Tetrault, 1990). By failing to deliver on its promises, the trust which goes to the foundation of a relationship is undermined. Through a recovery process, service failure can be transformed into a positive act which creates increasingly strong attitudes of customers towards a supplier (Hart, Sasser and Heskett, 1990). A service failure can occur at any stage of a customer's relationship with a supplier. It has been argued that a failure occurring early in the customer's relationship with a supplier will be perceived more adversely than one which occurs later in a relationship because the customer has less experience of successful service experiences to counterbalance the failure (Boulding et al., 1993).

A further conceptual insight into the link between relationship development and commitment following service failure is provided by the stream of literature on conflict resolution between members of a distribution channel (Kaufmann and Stern, 1992). The existence of a relationship has been shown to moderate the effects of disputes on attitudes towards channel partners.

**Figure 5.10**

Relational exchange between organizations should occur between all of each organization's main functions. The traditional 'bow tie' approach, in which communications between firms was focused on firms' buyers and sellers is increasingly being replaced by the 'diamond' approach in which communication is dispersed through all of their main functions

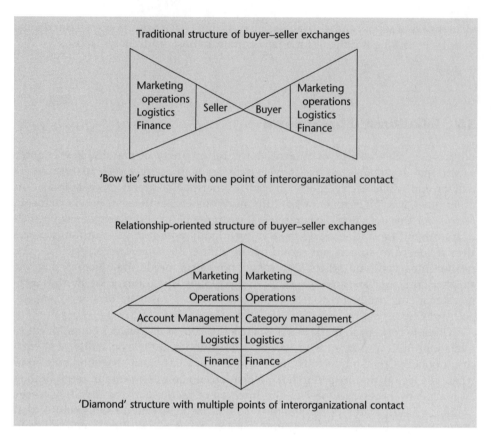

## 5.8 The multiple relationship markets of firms

Finally, it must be recognized that an organization's relationships can be very complex, especially in the case of business-to-business relationships. A company may see another organization as a co-operative relational partner in some aspects of its business, but competitive in others. An airline, for example, may compete fiercely with another airline for customers, yet have co-operative relationships in respect of aircraft maintenance. This has led to exchanges between organizations being seen increasingly as multi-faceted, rather than being based on contact solely through their respective buyers and sellers (Figure 5.10).

The question has often been raised whether there should be a consistency in an organization's pattern of relationships with the different groups with whom it does business. Can an organization pursue a strategy of relationship marketing with its customers while it pursues one of 'hire and fire' with its employees? A useful analytic framework for considering the consistency between an organization's multiple relationships is the 'Six Markets' model proposed by Christopher, Payne and Ballantyne (1991). The six markets comprise:

● Customers
● Suppliers

- Employees
- Other internal departments within the organization
- Referral markets, comprising advocates for the organization (e.g. intermediaries)
- Influence markets, comprising bodies such as regulatory agencies who can significantly affect the organization

Some organizations are notable for the way in which they have managed to create consistency in their dealings with each of their markets. The retailer Marks and Spencer has a long standing policy of creating long-term relationships with its suppliers and its employment practices have emphasized the development and retention of personnel (see Case Study). In recent years, the company has taken a number of measures to improve the quality of ongoing relationships with its customers. The quality of its goods and customer service has always encouraged buyers to return, and this has been supplemented in recent years by the development of its charge card and related financial services. At the opposite end of the retailing spectrum, some chains of discount shops position themselves as price leaders with little attempt to reward customer loyalty, other than continuing low prices. Negotiations with suppliers are likely to be based on bargaining of individual consignments. Staff may be paid little more than the minimum wage.

While consistency between the six markets may seem intuitively attractive, questions are asked where companies try to impose different patterns in each of their markets. British Airways has prided itself on the quality of its service and the benefits that customers receive from belonging to its Executive Club frequent flyer programme. During a cabin crew strike in the summer of 1997, many commentators expressed concern at the strong arm tactics used by the company to try to get its staff back to work. Could a company which prided itself on its customer loyalty expect loyalty from its staff when they had been treated in this way?

## Are relationships a help or hindrance for Marks and Spencer?                Case Study

The retailer Marks and Spencer has often been held out as an example of how to manage effective relationships – with suppliers, employees and customers. For many years the company was a favourite of the stock market, with regular and increasing levels of profitability. It seemed that loyalty from dedicated suppliers and its employees was feeding through into high levels of customer loyalty, with customers prepared to pay a price premium for the company's products. The company appeared to be following a 'textbook' approach in the long-term management of its relationships, and had success-fully built up a portfolio of services which satisfied customers were eager to buy. Then in 1998 things seemed to go badly wrong for the company, with its profits and share price falling sharply. Questions began to be asked about the value of M&S's relationship strategies.

An important reason for the high standing of M&S's products and perceived value for money has been that the company hasn't bought its products 'off the shelf' from suppliers. Instead, technologists, designers, buyers and merchandisers from both sides –

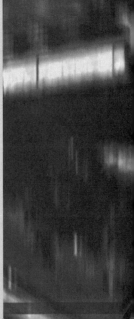

along with the raw material producers – have worked together to identify new products and designs. M&S doesn't have a specific research and development budget, but encourages its suppliers to invest to the mutual benefit of both companies. Competitive advantage has been gained for the supply chain as a whole, through sharing M&S's knowledge of its customers with its suppliers' knowledge of production, distribution, logistics and information technology. The result is that the sum of all companies' distinctive competence is more powerful than all companies acting alone. It can also allow greater flexibility to changing retail trends.

There are many more examples of M&S working closely with its producers to improve its profitability. Since ready-prepared Indian take-away meals were pioneered with supplier Northern Foods, the company claimed to have become the world's biggest Indian take-away retailer. Northern Foods has been supplying M&S for over 30 years and has eight factories committed to M&S production. It is the latter's largest food supplier. Despite the duration and breadth of their working relationship, there is no formal partnership between the two. Like relationships with all its suppliers, mutual trust is important to continued success. Some relationships with M&S have failed where suppliers have felt that the retailer pays too little to justify its continued investment, which is especially dangerous where a very high proportion of the supplier's business is with M&S. A small wallpaper manufacturer, for example, may put 80% of its business with M&S, but this would represent only a fraction of 1% of M&S's total business. Power imbalances have to be recognized and sensitively handled.

The idea of one integrated supply chain competing with another became crucial to gaining competitive advantage during the 1990s. Rivals such as Sainsbury's and Debenhams had been equally busy improving their supply chain, even if it did not always mean entering into such close understandings as obtained by M&S. By the end of the 1990s, however, observers were beginning to ask whether M&S's supply relationships would be sufficient to guide it through an economic downturn. During 1998, the company issued a profits warning and its share price fell sharply. The company had been accused of arrogance in the way it assumed the loyalty of its customers. Its selling prices had slowly crept up and had become significantly greater than those of its competitors, while the latter's services levels had matched M&S's. Faced with a downturn in its business, the company sought to lower its costs, and one obvious source of saving was to buy more of its goods overseas. Its competitors had been taking advantage of the high value of sterling to pass price savings on to customers, but M&S's trusted network of domestic suppliers seemed to be a millstone round its neck, preventing it being opportunistic and exploiting new opportunities as they arose.

With regard to its customer relationships, the company had annoyed many people by refusing to accept credit cards, other than its own M&S chargecard. The strategy may have been to develop closer relationships with customers and to try to cross-sell its growing range of financial services. It also had the direct effect of reducing the charges which the company paid to banks, by keeping transactions within the company. The company was accused of arrogance in its approach and had to climb down from this position, so from 2000 it accepted all major credit cards.

Does the experience of M&S raise serious doubts about the value of long-term supply chain relationships? Or had the company failed to develop relationships which were sufficiently flexible to a changing environment?

## Case study review questions

1   Critically assess whether close relationships with its suppliers have helped or hindered M&S's task of gaining competitive advantage.

2   What factors are crucial to the development and maintenance of long-term supplier–retailer relationships?

3   To what extent is it important for there to be consistency in the standards of relationships between a company and its employee, customer and supplier markets?

## Chapter summary and linkages to other chapters

An ongoing relationship between a service provider and its customers is very often a key feature of a firm's service offering. Indeed, many suppliers of manufactured goods have developed service-based relationships to differentiate themselves from their competitors. Developing ongoing relationships with customers is not a new idea, but has become popular as a result of changes in the business environment. By improving customer retention rates, the lifetime profitability of customers can be increased.

An ongoing relationship is one basis on which the service offer can be defined and distinguished from its competitors (**Chapter 2**). A relationship can improve the quality of the service encounter (**Chapter 3**), for example by configuring the service to meet the recorded preferences of each customer. The process of choosing between competing suppliers is facilitated by an ongoing relationship which can reduce perceived risk (**Chapter 4**). Service quality is a prerequisite for the development of an ongoing buyer–seller relationship (**Chapter 7**) and can often only be provided with appropriate selection, training and monitoring of employees (**Chapter 8**). To be effective, relationship marketing needs to embrace intermediaries (**Chapter 9**) and to be given a high priority by management (**Chapter 12**). The timely collection, analysis and dissemination of information is an important part of customer relationship development (**Chapter 6**).

## www linkages/URLs

The Association for the Advancement of Relationship Marketing provides a forum for the advancement and understanding of the disciplines of relationship marketing:
http://www.aarm.org/

## Key terms

Just-in-time 119

## Chapter review questions

1 Is relationship marketing a new business idea, or just traditional practices applied in a new context?
2 Critically assess methods used by banks to develop ongoing relationships with their personal customers.
3 To what extent should a services organization ensure that the style of exchange adopted with respect to its customers is similar to that adopted in relation to its employees?
4 If relationship marketing is a natural evolution from services marketing, what do you think may be the next basis on which firms develop a competitive advantage?
5 Critically define what is meant by customer loyalty in a services context.
6 Using a service company's loyalty scheme of your choice, critically assess its overall value to the company in developing profitable business.

## Selected further reading

*The literature on relationship marketing has grown considerably in recent years. Among the early publications on the subject are the following.*

Berry, L. L. (1983) 'Relationship Marketing', in L. L. Berry *et al.* (eds), *Emerging Perspectives of Services Marketing*, American Marketing Association, Chicago, IL

Christopher, M., A. Payne and M. Ballantyne (1991) *Relationship Marketing*, Heinemann, London

Jackson, B. B. (1985) 'Winning and Keeping Industrial Customers: The Dynamics of Customer Relations', Lexington Books, Lexington, MA

*For a more contemporary overview of relationship marketing, the following are comprehensive.*

Arias, J. T. G. (1998) 'A Relationship Marketing Approach to Guanxi', *European Journal of Marketing*, Vol. 32, No. 1–2, pp 145–55

Bagozzi, R. P. (1995) 'Reflections on Relationship Marketing in Consumer Markets', *Journal of the Academy of Marketing Science*, Vol. 23, No. 4, pp 272–77

Buttle, F. (ed) (1996) *Relationship Marketing: Theory and Practice*, Paul Chapman, London

Ford, D., L. Gadde, H. Hakansson, A. Lundgren, I. Snehota, P. Turnbull and D. Wilson (1998) *Managing Business Relationships*, Wiley, Chichester

Gummesson, E. (1999) *Total Relationship Marketing*, Butterworth-Heinemann, London

Payne, A., M. Christopher, H. Peck and M. Clark (1999) *Relationship Marketing, Strategy and Implementation*, Butterworth-Heinemann, London

For a more thorough understanding of the theoretical underpinnings of buyer–seller relationships, the following are frequently cited.

Duncan, T. and S. E. Moriarty (1998) 'A Communication-based Marketing Model for Managing Relationships', *Journal of Marketing*, Vol. 62, No. 2, pp 1–14

Gronroos, C. (1989) 'Defining Marketing: A Market-Oriented Approach', *European Journal of Marketing*, Vol. 23, No. 1, pp 52–60

Heide, J. B. (1994) 'Interorganizational Governance in Marketing Channels', *Journal of Marketing*, Vol. 58, pp 71–85

Liljander, V. and T. Strandvik (1995) 'The Nature of Customer Relationships in Services', in Advances in Services Marketing and Management, T. A. Swartz, D. E. Bowen and S. W. Brown (eds), Vol. 4, JAI Press, London

Morgan, R. M. and S. D. Hunt (1994) 'The Commitment-Trust Theory of Relationship Marketing', *Journal of Marketing*, July, Vol. 58, pp 20–38

Palmer, A. (2000) 'Relationship Marketing: A Darwinian Synthesis', *European Journal of Marketing*, Vol. 35, No. 6, pp 687–704

Sheth, J. N. and A. Parvatiyar (1995) 'Relationship Marketing in Consumer Markets: Antecedents and Consequences, *Journal of the Academy of Marketing Science*, Vol. 23, No. 4, pp 255–71

The processes of relationship development and dissolution have been explored in a number of papers, including:

Dwyer, F. R., P. H. Schurr and S. Oh (1987) 'Developing Buyer and Seller Relationships', *Journal of Marketing*, April, Vol. 51, pp 11–27

Palmer, A. and D. Bejou (1994) 'Buyer–Seller Relationships: A Conceptual Model and Empirical Investigation', *Journal of Marketing Management*, Summer, Vol. 6, No 10, pp 495–512

For discussion on how companies can maximize their profitability through improving customer retention, the following are useful references.

Hamilton, R. and B. J. Howcroft (1995) 'A Practical Approach to Maximising Customer Retention in the Credit Card Industry', *Journal of Marketing Management*, Vol. 11, No. 1, pp 151–63

Reichheld, F., W. Sasser and J. Earl (1990) 'Zero Defections', *Harvard Business Review*, Vol. 68, No. 5, pp 105–11

Reichheld, F. (1996), 'Learning from Customer Defections', *Harvard Business Review* (March–April), pp 56–69

The first reference develops an empirically tested model using linear discriminant analysis to predict which customers are most likely to close their bank accounts, based on various behavioural and socio-demographic variables.

A number of papers have sought to identify limits to the concepts of relationship marketing, highlighting the fact that it is often adopted cynically by many companies at the same time as the quality of relationships deteriorate.

Barnes, J. G. (1994) 'Close to the Customer: But Is It Really a Relationship?', *Journal of Marketing Management*, Vol. 10, No. 7, pp 561–70

Palmer, A. (1996) 'Relationship Marketing: A Universal Paradigm or Management Fad?' *The Learning Organisation*, Vol. 3, No. 3, pp 19–26

Tzokas, N. and M. J. Saren (1997) 'Some Dangerous Axioms Of Relationship Marketing', *Journal Of Strategic Marketing*, Vol. 6, No. 3, pp 187–96

*Finally, customer loyalty has emerged as a subset of the literature on relationship marketing and the following provide useful references, and a caution that loyalty to a service provider is about more than merely repetitious purchasing.*

Dick, A. S. and K. Basu (1994) 'Customer Loyalty: Toward an Integrated Conceptual Framework', *Journal of the Academy of Marketing Science*, Vol. 22, No. 2, pp 99–113

O'Brien, L. and C. Jones (1995) 'Do Rewards Really Create Loyalty?' *Harvard Business Review*, May–June, pp 75–82

O'Malley, L. (1998) 'Can Loyalty Schemes Really Build Loyalty?' *Marketing Intelligence and Planning*, Vol. 6, No. 1, pp 47–56

Palmer, A., U. McMahon-Beattie and R. Beggs, (2000) A Structural Analysis of Hotel Sector Loyalty Programmes, *Journal of Strategic Marketing*, Vol. 12, No. 1, pp 54–60

# 6

# Managing knowledge

### Learning objectives

Services organizations are increasingly surrounded by mountains of information. The best organizations make sure that they have the right information, collected at the right time, made available in the right place and given to the right people to act upon. Information processing is increasingly becoming a firm's source of competitive advantage. This chapter explores the role of information in allowing marketing managers to make better informed plans for the future, and to monitor the implementation of those plans. There are close links between this and other chapters, for example information is crucial to organizations' efforts to develop relationship marketing programmes. It is also vital for monitoring service quality levels and the effectiveness of pricing and promotion strategies.

## 6.1 What is meant by the knowledge based-organization?

Knowledge is one of the greatest assets of most services organizations and its contribution to sustainable competitive advantage has been noted by many (e.g. Quinn, 1992; Drucker, 1999). Information represents a bridge between the organization and its environment and is the means by which a picture of the changing environment is built up within the organization. Marketing management is responsible for turning information-based knowledge into specific marketing plans.

In 1991, Ikujiro Nonaka began an article in the *Harvard Business Review* with a simple statement: 'In an economy where the only certainty is uncertainty, the one sure source of lasting competitive advantage is knowledge' (Nonaka, 1991). A firm's knowledge base is likely to include, among other things, an understanding of the precise needs of customers; how those needs are likely to change over time; how those needs are satisfied in terms of efficient and effective production systems and an understanding of competitors' activities. We are probably all familiar with services organizations where knowledge seems to be very poor – the reservation which is mixed up, the delivery which does not happen as specified, or junk mail which is of no interest at all. On the other hand, customers may revel in a company which delivers the right service at the right time and clearly demonstrates that it is knowledgeable about all aspects of the transaction. The small business owner may have been able to achieve all of this in his or her head, but in large organizations, the task of managing knowledge becomes much more complex. Where it is done well, it can be a significant contributor to a firm's sustainable competitive advantage.

Let us begin by defining the terms 'knowledge' and 'information'. Even though in some senses they may be used interchangeably, many writers have suggested that the two concepts are quite distinct. In fact, knowledge is a much more all-encompassing term which incorporates the concept of beliefs that are based on information (Dretske, 1981). It also depends on the commitment and understanding of the individual holding these beliefs, which are affected by interaction and the development of judgement, behaviour and attitude (Berger and Luckmann, 1966). Knowledge only has meaning in the context of a process or capacity to act. Drucker noted that 'There is no such thing as **knowledge management**, there are only knowledgeable people. Information only becomes knowledge in the hands of someone who knows what to do with it' (Drucker, 1999). Knowledge, then, is evidenced by its association with actions and its source can be found in a combination of information, social interaction and contextual situations which affect the knowledge accumulation process at an individual level.

Here we need to distinguish between knowledge at the level of the individual, and at the level of the organization. Organizational knowledge comprises shared understandings and is created within the company by means of information and social interaction and provides potential for development. It is this form of knowledge that is at the heart of knowledge management. Organizational progress is made when knowledge moves from the domain of the individual to that of the organization.

Two different types of knowledge can be identified. First, there is knowledge which is easily definable and is accessible, often referred to as 'explicit' knowledge. This type of knowledge can be readily quantified and passed between individuals in the form of words and numbers. Because it is easily communicated it is relatively easy to manage. Knowledge management is concerned with ensuring that the explicit knowledge of individuals becomes a part of the organizational knowledge base and that it is used efficiently and contributes where necessary to changes in work practices, processes and products. This, however, is not the limit of knowledge management. The second type of knowledge comprises the accumulated knowledge of individuals which is not explicit, but which can still be important to the successful operation of an organization. This type of knowledge, often known as 'tacit' knowledge is not easy to see or express, it is highly personal and is rooted in an individual's experiences, attitudes, values and behaviour patterns. This type of 'tacit knowledge' can be much more difficult to formalize and disseminate within an organization. If tacit knowledge can be captured, mobilized and turned into explicit knowledge, it would be accessible to others in the organization and enable the organization to progress, rather than have individuals within it having to continually relearn from the same starting point. The owner of a small service business could have all this information readily available to him in his head. The challenge taken on by many large corporations is to emulate the knowledge management of the small business owner. One outcome of a knowledge-based organization has often been referred to as the 'learning organization' in which the challenge is to learn at the corporate level from what is known by individuals who make up the organization.

Information is often described as management's window on the world. But what happens if management work in a large corporate head office, far removed from customers and day-to-day operations? It is sadly all too familiar for senior management to become cut off from the service operations that they manage. A recent BBC television series *Back to the Floor* invited chief executives to spend a few days changing their role to that of a front-line employee. In one case, the chief executive of the grocery retailer Sainsbury's seemed to be oblivious of customers' annoyance with shopping trolley design and availability and in another the chief executive of Pickfords Removals couldn't understand why the company was so inflexible when minor changes in customers' requirements occurred. Of course, the managers of small businesses do not generally have such problems as they are in regular contact with their customers and do not need structured information management systems to give them a window on the world. Their success in keeping in touch with customers has led many larger businesses to emulate some of their practices. 'Management by walking about' has become a popular way in which senior executives try to gain information about their marketing environment which is not immediately apparent from structured reporting systems. Some companies have adopted a formal system of role exchanges where senior executives spend a period at the sharp end of their business.

### 6.1.1 The importance of knowledge management

Knowledge management permeates many activities of a service organization and should cut across departmental boundaries. These are some of the more common benefits which result from effective knowledge management:

- *Customer information management* Most companies need to assess what information they have on their customers and how individuals within the organization can use that information most effectively. For example, salespeople should know when they last talked with a customer and what issues that customer was facing and what he or she was thinking about buying six months from now. Without capturing that knowledge, a company can lose valuable information when this salesperson leaves. Even if he or she stays, there might be other people within the organization who could use this information, for example service support staff.
- *Demand forecasting* A company should have superior knowledge not just about demand conditions as they are today, but as they are likely to develop over the next few months or years. By being better informed, a company can downsize or expand capacity more effectively.
- *New service development* By looking at historical trends and retaining knowledge about competitors and changes in the marketing environment, a company can stay ahead in new service development. Very often, somebody within an organization would already have information relevant to a new service proposal, so an effective knowledge management system can prevent the company wasting time in 'reinventing the wheel'.
- *Performance monitoring* A company should have knowledge about which of its human and physical assets are performing effectively so that future procurement can reflect proven performance. Staff recruiters, for example, should have full knowledge about the performance patterns of different types of employees.

The transition from individuals' information to corporate knowledge which was mentioned earlier requires sharing of knowledge by all concerned. This raises problems where employees perceive that knowledge is a powerful asset which they can use in their negotiations with senior management or other functional departments. A knowledge management programme is needed to break down a *laissez-faire attitude*, and would typically include the following elements:

- A strong knowledge-sharing culture, which can only emerge over time with the development of trust.
- Measures to monitor that sharing, which may be reflected in individuals' performance reviews.
- Technology to facilitate knowledge transfer, which should be as user-friendly as possible.
- Established practices for the capture and sharing of knowledge – without clearly defined procedures, the technology is of only limited value.
- Leadership and senior management commitment to sharing information. If senior management doesn't share information, why should anybody else bother?

Marketing information cannot in itself produce decisions, it merely provides data which must be interpreted by marketing managers. As an interfunctional integrator, marketing information draws data from all functional areas of an organization, which in turn uses the data to focus on meeting customers' needs more effectively. Increasingly, information technology is allowing firms to deal with their customers on a one-to-one basis. Research involving employees, both as sources of information and recipients of research findings assumes importance as an integrating device.

As information collection, processing, transmission and storage technologies improve, information is becoming more accessible not just to one particular organization, but also to its competitors. Attention is therefore moving away from how information is collected, to who is best able to make use of it. It is too simple to say that marketing managers commission data collection by technical experts and make decisions on the basis of this data.

Recent technological innovations – for example electronic point of sale (EPOS) systems – have enabled service companies to greatly enhance the quality of their core services in terms of speed, accuracy and consistency. In turn, the resulting increase in operational efficiency, combined with the additional information which it is now possible to generate, has allowed services organizations to improve other areas of their service offering – such as the development of customer loyalty programmes – as a means of gaining competitive advantages. At the same time, the increasing ease with which data can be collected and disseminated has made it easier for services companies to manage service quality by setting quantifiable objectives that can be effectively monitored.

Organizations must also understand the effects of other environmental factors such as the state of the local or national economy. Without this broader environmental information, routine pieces of marketing research information – such as the market share held by a company's brands over the past year – cannot be interpreted meaningfully. Marketing information allows management to improve its strategic planning, tactical implementation of programmes and its monitoring and control. A practical problem is that information is typically much more difficult to obtain to meet strategic planning needs than it is to meet operational and control needs. There can be a danger of marketing managers focusing too heavily on information which is easily available at the expense of that which is needed.

## 6.2 Marketing information systems

Many analyses of organizations' information collection and dissemination activities take a systems perspective. The collection of marketing information can be seen as one subsystem of a much larger knowledge management system which was discussed earlier. Other component information systems typically include production, financial and human resource management systems. In a well-designed knowledge management system, the barriers between these component systems should be conceptual rather than real – for example sales information is of value to all of these subsystems to a greater or lesser extent (see Figure 6.1).

A **marketing information system** has been defined by Kotler as a system that:

> … consists of people, equipment and procedures to gather, sort, analyze, evaluate and distribute needed, timely and accurate information to marketing decision-makers (Kotler, 1999).

**Figure 6.1**

A systems approach to
managing information

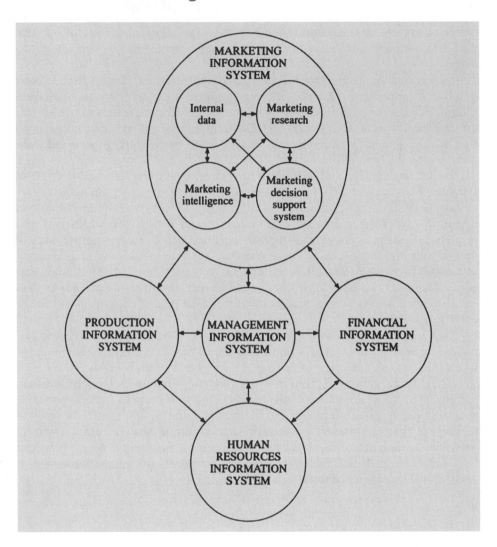

In so far as a marketing information subsystem can be identified, it can conceptually
be seen as comprising four principal components, although in practice, they are
operationally interrelated:

● Much information is generated internally within organizations, particularly in
respect of operational and control functions. By carefully arranging its collection
and dissemination, internal data can provide a constant and up-to-date flow of
information at relatively little cost, useful for both planning and control
functions.

● Marketing research is that part of the system concerned with the structured
collection of marketing information. This can provide both routine information
about marketing effectiveness – such as brand awareness levels or delivery
performance – and one-off studies, such as changing attitudes towards diet or
the pattern of income distribution.

- Marketing intelligence comprises the procedures and sources used by marketing management to obtain pertinent information about developments in their marketing environment. It complements the marketing research system, for whereas the latter tends to focus on structured and largely quantifiable data collection procedures, intelligence gathering concentrates on picking up relatively intangible ideas and trends. Marketing management can gather this intelligence from a number of sources, such as newspapers, specialized cutting services, employees who are in regular contact with market developments, intermediaries and suppliers to the company, as well as specialized consultants.

- Marketing decision support systems comprise a set of models that allow forecasts to be made. Information is both an input to such models – in that data is needed to calibrate a model – and an output, in that models provide information on which decisions can be based. Models are frequently used in service outlet location decisions (see Chapter 9), where historical data may have established a relationship between one variable (e.g. the level of sales achieved by a particular service outlet) and other variables (e.g. pedestrian traffic in a street). Predicting the sales level of a proposed new outlet then becomes a matter of measuring pedestrian traffic at a proposed site, feeding this information into the model and calculating the predicted sales level.

For those organizations that have set up marketing information systems, a number of factors will determine their effectiveness:

- *The accuracy with which the information needs of the organization have been defined* Needs can themselves be difficult to identify, and it can be very difficult to identify the boundaries of the firm's environments and to separate relevance from irrelevance. This is a particular problem for large multiservice firms. The **mission statement** of an organization may give some indication of the boundaries for its environmental search – for example, many banks have mission statements which talk about becoming a dominant provider of financial services in their domestic market. The information needs therefore include anything related to the broader environment of financial services rather than the narrower field of banking.

- *The extensiveness of the search for information* A balance has to be struck between the need for information and the cost of collecting it. The most critical elements of the marketing environment must be identified and the cost of collecting relevant information weighed against the cost which would result from an inaccurate forecast.

- *The appropriateness of the sources of information* Information for decision making can typically be obtained from numerous sources – for example quality perceptions can be measured using a variety of quantitative and qualitative techniques. Companies often rely on the former when only the latter can give a depth of understanding which makes for better management decisions. Successful services companies use a variety of appropriate sources of information.

- *The speed of communication* The marketing information system will only be effective if information is communicated quickly and to the people capable of acting on it. Deciding what information to withhold from an individual and the concise reporting of relevant information can be as important as deciding what information to include if information overload is to be avoided.

Research commissioned by the decision support software specialist Business Objects in 1997 painted a bleak picture of the way managers use information to make decisions. Of 100 senior managers from *The Times Top 1000 Companies*, more than three-quarters admitted to relying on gut instinct rather than hard facts when making decisions. Sixty per cent of managers claimed not to receive the right quality or quantity of information to make a decision, even though 99% had access to a computer. More worryingly, a majority of sales and marketing managers surveyed claimed that they relied on other people for information which they were dubious about, or which was out of date. The prospect emerged of an information underclass who relied on instinct-based decision-making processes.

Nevertheless, a question remains about the extent to which information can actually provide answers. In a changing environment, it is the quality of interpretation of data which gives a firm a competitive advantage in its use of information.

Will marketing management ever be reduced to a scientific study of data, or will there always be scope for intuition?

## 6.3  Managing customer information

During the 1990s a whole new industry based on managing customer information using databases has emerged. Direct response marketing (DRM) is a term which is now used to encompass marketing activities which are designed to induce a direct response from mail order, direct mail, direct response advertising, telemarketing and the Internet. These activities developed rapidly in the 1990s and have been reliant on the production of mailing lists. As the use of computers has expanded so has the production, sale and purchase of lists multiplied. The capture of personal data and its subsequent use, including the sale of the lists for mailing purposes has provoked a number of governments to introduce legislation to protect individuals' rights. In the UK, the Data Protection Act (1998) was introduced, which requires organizations holding personal data to register and abide by the Act.

It is useful to draw a distinction between direct response marketing (DRM) and database marketing (DBM), and the following explanation may be helpful. Think of database marketing as being the broader of the functions and having three subactivities of direct response marketing, computer-aided sales support and customer information and service (Figure 6.2). The term 'customer relationship management' is increasingly being used to describe the long-term dynamic integration of these elements.

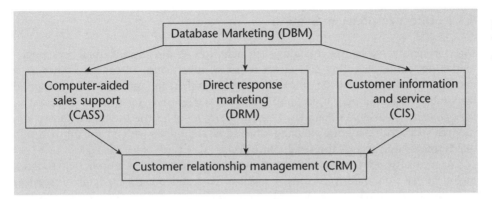

**Figure 6.2**
The components of
database marketing

Companies such as Direct Line continually set new standards for the use of IT in marketing management. But it seems that such companies are in a minority. According to a report in *Marketing* (26 February 1998), probably only 30% of marketing departments in UK companies are using IT effectively and a mere 2–3% operate strategic customer management systems.

It may be that many marketing directors in their 40s and 50s were not brought up on IT and simply do not understand it. Where companies do invest in IT, there is evidence that much of this investment is wasted. Unless a company installs the right systems to be used in the right way, it could be money down the drain. Another factor that emerges is the sometimes confused communications between marketing and IT departments within a company, with systems often failing to meet expectations because needs have not been defined accurately. As in other aspects of marketing, getting the interfunctional dynamics of a company right can be crucial in the quest for competitive advantage, and may explain the lead gained by Direct Line Insurance.

### 6.3.1 Computer-aided sales support

It is wrong to think of database marketing as being wholly about direct response marketing to consumers. When the database is made accessible to sales teams (through a modem), it has the potential to enhance their performance substantially. For companies involved in business-to-business services, the database may hold company information such as product listings, specifications, availability and pricing details. Customer and potential customer details may also be made available, including buyer details, contact details, quotations outstanding, order status, previous purchases, installed equipment and purchases from competitors. It is also possible to store information about competitors on the database, thereby making it directly available to the field salesforce where it is most needed, rather than being hidden away in inaccessible, centrally held files. As well as improving the productivity of sales personnel, a database can improve the quality of sales leads generated.

### 6.3.2 Direct response marketing

Direct response marketing includes such activities as direct mail, mail order, tele-marketing, e-mail targeting and direct response advertising. Direct mail relies on a database to identify specific market segments which are most likely to respond favourably to a mailing. Direct mail has been transformed by the development of very powerful relational databases. Telemarketing involves the use of a database and modern specialist telephone exchanges linked to computers which can automatically dial numbers and record the results of calls.

A company's database is likely to be constructed from a number of sources, including its own trading records, bought-in lists and bought-in database services from specialized service providers. The company can purge and merge these lists to form its own database. It is crucial for a company to maintain its list by removing duplicated names and the names of those who do not want to, or should not, be contacted. Numerous specialist companies offer database management services to client companies, including International Communications and Data plc which operates the National Consumer Database. This database is compiled from:

- The Electoral Roll, listing 42 million adults
- Investor data from 630 company share registers, comprising 8.5 million individuals
- Lifestyle data from the company's Facts of Living Survey Programme, which establishes lifestyle and product purchasing data and holds one million records
- Home data, including details on 350 000 properties such as value, location and size
- Telephone data, matching telephone numbers and addresses for 14 million individuals

A wide range of services is offered to clients from this database. For example, a client may require a mailing list to increase its penetration of a market. By supplying information about its current customers, the database company can establish the profile of the most profitable customers in terms of their location, lifestyle, media reading habits, etc. From this, it can select further names and addresses from its national database of people who could be expected to respond favourably to a mailing.

A growing number of companies now offer such database management facilities, indeed it has become a major service sector in its own right. Increasingly, firms are able to purchase data which can be input directly into their own computerized marketing information system.

### 6.3.3 Customer information and service (CIS)

There are many reasons why customers and potential customers may wish to contact a supplier of services direct. Companies may need to respond to enquiries about: the bill (public utilities), statements (banks), amount outstanding on a loan (finance company), adjusting monthly investment (pension company), technical questions (Internet service providers), availability (package holidays), or schedules (flights).

Provision of advice and information is now expected by customers immediately, either via the phone, fax, e-mail, or electronic data interchange. Increasingly, customers expect a supplier to have all of the information available at one contact point, without being passed around from department to department and from one nameless person to another only to be left with a vague promise of a call back.

Customer help lines are an important feature offered by a growing number of companies. The database and computerized telephone systems now provide the opportunity for companies to deal directly with their customers in a speedy and informed manner. Companies often use help lines to understand the causes of service failure and to enable them to put things right before a dissatisfied customer tells their friends about the failure.

Creation of call centres has become a major service activity in its own right, with banks, airlines, insurance companies and telephone companies, among others, establishing large centres which can handle all incoming calls efficiently using the latest technology. As an example, American Airlines decided to locate its new European reservation centre in Ireland which was predicted to result in savings of £20 million as it phased out five regional offices throughout Europe. The teleservicing centre was expected to handle 2.5 million calls a year, employing 220 multilingual staff.

### 6.3.4  Customer relationship management (CRM)

In too many organizations, numerous databases and customer service systems exist which are not linked to each other. A customer may make an initial enquiry to a freephone telephone line and make a subsequent order from another system within the company which is not connected to the initial enquiry line. The rapid growth of some companies, changes in corporate information technology policy and mergers and de-mergers have sadly resulted in disconnected information systems being a not uncommon phenomenon. CRM systems essentially seek to join up these systems and to track dealings with individual customers throughout the relationship life cycle. Many companies offer technological solutions which promise integrated information management. However, it was noted earlier that this is of little value if management does not give the leadership and create a culture which is conducive to integrated systems.

## 6.4  Forward planning with marketing research

Marketing research is an important source of a company's knowledge. As a planning tool, marketing research provides management with market and product-specific information, which allows it to minimize the degree of uncertainty in planning its marketing effort. This risk minimization function can apply to the whole of the marketing operation, or to any of its constituent parts, such as advertising.

It is difficult to define precisely the exact functions of marketing research within a marketing information system, as organizations differ widely in size and structure. However, in Figure 6.3, an attempt has been made to show by means of shaded boxes the areas inside which the marketing research function normally operates.

**Figure 6.3**

The role of marketing research within the sources and processes of a marketing information system [adapted from A. Parasuraman (1991) *Marketing Research*, Addison Wesley, Reading, MA]

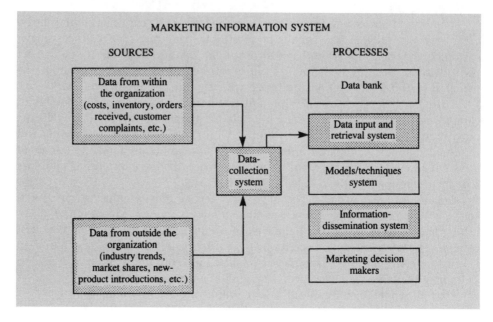

Information sources can be divided into those that are available internally within an organization and those collected from external data sources. It is in the area of internal data collection that the line between marketing research and other marketing information system functions is most difficult to define in a neat textbook fashion. Much depends on the size, scope and structure of the marketing information system itself. In many large organizations, the collation of regularly generated information, such as costs and sales figures, will not be central to the research activity. However, marketing research may well generate new information from within the organization, for example by collecting information on a more *ad hoc* basis from key groups such as management, the sales staff and front-line service personnel.

In practice, the main focus for marketing research activity within most service organizations is external data collection. Insofar as such data must be analysed and disseminated, market researchers become involved in data input and retrieval, and information dissemination systems. In smaller organizations, it is possible that the research function will also incorporate the setting up and operation of databases and the development of models and systems that incorporate information gathered by researchers.

### 6.4.1 Major uses of research in services marketing

There is little doubt about the importance of marketing research to service organizations. Christopher Lovelock identified a number of factors that tend to characterize successful service businesses (Lovelock, 1981). Among these, two are particularly relevant here:

- *Capturing and using customer data* The significance of information for the planning of marketing activities has already been stated. The implications for services marketers are therefore apparent and some of their specific needs in this area are outlined below.

- *Soliciting feedback from customers and employees* It has already been stated that the gathering of information from customers is vital to marketing success in general. However, in service industries it is particularly important as customers do not have a tangible product to assess according to some predetermined criteria that they have set out. A large number of predominantly intangible variables contribute to overall satisfaction and may influence the way that each experience is perceived. Therefore the constant or intermittent interaction between customers and the service provider, which occurs as a stream of service encounters, must be evaluated as an ongoing process in order to ascertain the degree of customer satisfaction, which may fluctuate from one encounter to another. Some aspects of the service may be perceived as good on one occasion and bad on another. For instance, a customer may be satisfied with the time spent waiting in a queue at a bank one week and dissatisfied the next. Loyalty comes from developing a good long-term relationship with customers and feedback should be solicited on a regular basis in order to determine the level of satisfaction that is being achieved. There should be some means by which the bank knows when a customer is dissatisfied and the reasons why.

The variability of services makes research into them very different compared to manufactured goods which may be used over and over again without any significant variance. In addition, goods marketing does not normally involve any face-to-face interaction with production staff, unlike services, where employees usually perform the service on, or in conjunction with, the customer. The crucial importance of staff in making the service offer a satisfactory one increases the necessity to examine their perceptions. Because employees contribute greatly to service quality in so many service industries it is important to consider their views about how well a service is being received by customers and how it may be improved. After all, it is the frontline staff within an organization who have regular and close contact with the users of a service, so the information that they provide can be of enormous value.

Organizations should also undertake employee research because they can be seen as internal recipients of marketing efforts. A successful services company should be just as proficient at managing the management–staff interface as it is at managing the staff–customer interface; feedback from these internal customers should be treated as an important aspect of services marketing research.

Current practice in services marketing research reflects the growing emphasis put upon the maintenance of quality standards of service. In very simple terms, the essence of service quality is understanding what customers want and ensuring that they are provided with it on a continuous basis. It is therefore important for services organizations to understand their customers' expectations. An appropriate programme of marketing research can identify the variance between what customers get as opposed to what they expect. This is a highly subjective matter and requires careful qualitative analysis of customers' expectations of the service and their perceptions of service delivery.

### 6.4.2 Major services research activities

The range of tasks which marketing research contributes to the services marketing planning process is growing. Some of the more important specific marketing research activities are listed below – many of these are in fact associated with service quality issues and covered in more detail in Chapter 8.

- *Research into customer needs*  Research is undertaken to learn what underlying needs individuals seek to satisfy when they buy services. Identifying needs which are currently unmet by service offerings spurs new service development.
- *Research into customer expectations*  Needs should be distinguished from expectations and a variety of qualitative techniques are used to study the standards of service that customers expect when consuming a service, for example with respect to delays and friendliness of staff.
- *Customer perception studies*  Perception studies can be undertaken during or after consumption to test the perceived level of quality delivery. Research can also be undertaken to test the extent to which external factors might have influenced the way an individual perceives an organization or its specific service offers.
- *Customer surveys  ad hoc* or regular programmes of survey research carried out among customers provide information about customers' behaviour, attitudes, perceptions and expectations. These can have the dual functions of providing the service organization with much needed information as well as providing a public relations tool by allowing customers to feel that they have made their feelings known in a way which may allow them to be acted upon.
- *Similar industry studies*  Many services industries can learn from research undertaken in what at first sight appear to be totally unrelated industries. By learning about operating practices and customer reactions to their service offering, marketing managers in one sector such as shipping can learn a lot from studies carried out within the hotel sector. Through a process often referred to as 'benchmarking', an organization can set itself targets based on best practice in its own, or a related, industry.
- *Research into service intermediaries*  Agents, dealers and other intermediaries are close to consumers and therefore form a valuable conduit for gathering marketing research. In addition, intermediaries are customers of service principals, therefore research is undertaken to establish – among other things – their perceptions of the standard of service that they are receiving from the service principal.
- *Key client studies*  Most organizations see some customers as being more important than others, on account of the volume and/or the profitability of the custom that they generate. Where a company derives the majority of its income from one customer, it may make particular effort to ensure that this customer is totally satisfied with its standards of service and prices. The loss of the business as a result of shortcomings of which it is unaware could otherwise be catastrophic. In some cases, the relationship with key customers may be of such mutual importance that each partner may spend considerable time jointly researching shared problems. For example, an airport operator with two or three key airline customers may jointly develop a programme of research to judge passengers' perception of the total experience that they perceive as they pass

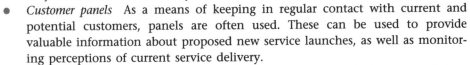

through the airport. Sometimes, **key clients** with whom a sound relationship has been built up can be used as a basis for researching new service ideas before they are released more widely.

● *Customer panels* As a means of keeping in regular contact with current and potential customers, panels are often used. These can be used to provide valuable information about proposed new service launches, as well as monitoring perceptions of current service delivery.

● *Employee research* As part of a programme of internal marketing, research into employees is often undertaken by service organizations. This can focus on employees as internal customers of services within an internal market as well as their thoughts on the methods of service delivery. Employee suggestion schemes can form an important part of research into employees.

### 6.4.3   Setting services research objectives

A market research problem almost always results from a gap in the market information already available to management. For example, a company may have comprehensive and up-to-date information on the market for its current products, but may wish to discover what – if any – market needs remain unsatisfied, in order to develop new products.

The marketing researcher could be given one of a number of types of briefs:

● Defining market characteristics (for example defining the services required from travel agents by people purchasing vacations).

● Describing market characteristics (e.g. a client may merely wish to have described to them the behaviour of families with children when purchasing overseas holidays).

● Measuring market characteristics (as where a client tour-operating company wishes to establish the market shares of major UK travel agents).

● Analysing market characteristics – a more thorough investigation of the above information (e.g. an analysis of holiday-buying behaviour according to the age, income or lifestyle of different segments of the population).

A problem in setting objectives lies in the difficulty of defining just what constitutes the market to be studied. For all products, it can be difficult to identify which near-competitors should be considered to be part of the market that is under analysis. With services, this becomes a problem where service availability is defined in geographical terms. Unlike goods, inseparable services often cannot be brought to where the consumer is located. But how far should the catchment area of a fixed location service extend, and therefore what is the achievable market? The market for a proposed new solicitor's office may look attractive when defined solely in terms of a small town that is being studied. However, if it is accepted that typically clients are prepared to travel some distance to see a solicitor, the market can only sensibly be assessed by including an analysis of the market for solicitors' services in the surrounding region, the boundaries of which are difficult to define.

**Figure 6.4**

The marketing research process

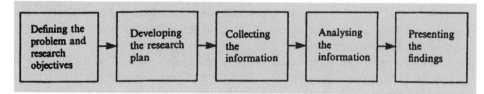

### 6.4.4 The marketing research process

Most definitions of marketing research activity focus on its role as a means by which those who provide goods and services keep themselves in touch with the needs and wants of those who consume their products. Within the context of services industries, this could be extended to include the means by which management keeps in touch with the motivation and behaviour of its staff. In either case, the key phrase, which encompasses all marketing research activity and differentiates it from the wider scope of marketing information systems, is *keeping in touch*. Data collected should be as up to date and relevant to a problem as time and cost constraints allow.

Kotler has described the stages of the marketing research process in a much simpler, linear format than that offered above. A simplified model of the research process, which begins with the definition of the research problem and ends with the presentation of the findings is shown in Figure 6.4.

It can be seen that this process follows the same basic pattern as for other forms of research activity, such as scientific or academic research. To be useful, keeping in touch needs to be conducted objectively and accurately. Casual, unstructured research is at best wasteful, and at worst misleading.

Market research is itself a service industry, with its own functions and specialists. In order to explain the way in which the process illustrated in Figure 6.4 works, it is useful to briefly describe the structure of the industry. Essentially, market researchers fall into two groups:

- Those employed by services companies themselves, for example banks, retailers and airlines (often referred to as 'client' companies). These researchers provide information for internal use and generally have specific product and market knowledge of their sector.
- A second group of researchers is employed by marketing research organizations whose specific purpose is the supply of information to other users. These supply companies are often referred to as 'agencies', something of a misnomer as they are paid on a fee rather than a commission basis. Staff employed by these companies can generally achieve a high level of expertise in particular research techniques, some of which were described above.

The research process allows for the expertise of both groups to be incorporated at different stages. Client company researchers define a research problem, after discussion with marketing and other management. This is usually communicated to potential suppliers in the form of a research brief. The objectives of the study are set by matching management information needs with what can realistically be obtained from the marketplace, particularly in the light of time and budgetary constraints, and may well be defined after initial discussions with possible suppliers.

The area in which marketing research agencies dominate is that of information collection. The degree to which the client company will be involved in developing the research plan and analysing and presenting the findings varies; to a large extent this depends on the size and expertise of its research department. Before deciding on the final plan, however, most client companies approach several possible suppliers and ask for their suggestions in the form of a research proposal.

### 6.4.5 Sources of information

Data sources are traditionally divided into two categories according to the methods by which they were collected. These are known as secondary and primary data sources – often referred to as 'desk' and 'field' research respectively. Most organizations would approach a research exercise by examining the available sources of secondary data.

Secondary data refers to information which in some sense is second-hand to the current research project. Data could be second-hand because it has already been collected internally by the organization, although for a different primary purpose. Alternatively, the information could be acquired second-hand from external sources.

Internal information, on products, costs, sales, etc. may be accessed through an organization's marketing information system. Where such a system does not exist formally, the information may still be available in relevant departmental records, though it would probably need to be reworked into a form that market researchers can use. Despite modern data processing technology, the task of going manually through stacks of back-invoices in order to quantify annual sales by product and customer is still not unknown.

There are numerous external sources of secondary data, in both document and electronic format. These cover government statistics, trade associations and specialist research reports. A good starting point for a review of these is still the business section of a good library. Some examples of secondary data sources are shown in Table 6.1.

---

**Table 6.1**  Some examples of secondary data used in services marketing research

- National media – e.g. *Financial Times* industry surveys
- Trade, technical and professional media – e.g. *Travel Trade Gazette, Marketing Week*
- Government departments and official publications – e.g. *General Household Survey, Transport Statistics*
- Local chambers of trade and commerce
- Professional and trade associations – e.g. Association of British Travel Agents, Law Society
- Yearbooks and directories – e.g. *Dataquest*
- Subscription services, providing periodic sector reports on market intelligence and financial analyses – e.g. Keynote, MEAL, Mintel
- Subscription electronic databases – e.g. Mintel OnLine, FT.com

Traditionally, it has been much easier to find external secondary information on goods than services. However, there has been a considerable increase in services marketing intelligence reports in recent years. Data is also often obtainable from special interest panels, for example information on attitudes towards airlines is obtainable from a regular airline users' panel. It is also worth checking on whether other organizations, possibly even competitors, have conducted similar studies to the one which is proposed. Although such information will not be as up to date or relevant as that obtained by commissioning a new survey, it will normally be available at a fraction of the cost.

While secondary, or desk research, as the name implies, is not the most exciting activity in the world, it is very worth while, although the research objectives may not be achieved by this method alone. It can, however, be conducted by company employees, and provides a useful starting point for further investigation. Undertaking unnecessary primary research which is available through secondary sources is an expensive and time-consuming exercise.

Primary, or 'field' research, is concerned with generating new information direct from the target population. The phrase *keeping in touch* was highlighted earlier, and marketing research professionals spend most of their time designing and implementing such studies, either on an *ad hoc* (one-off) or a continuous (monitoring) basis. Primary research in the services sector has expanded rapidly during the 1990s. Part of the reason for this may be the lack of previously published data.

### 6.4.6  Research methods

One important decision that needs to be made when developing a primary research plan is whether to conduct a qualitative or quantitative survey.

**Qualitative research**  Qualitative research is the exploration and interpretation of the perceptions and behaviour of small samples of target consumers, and the study of the motivators involved in purchasing choices. It is highly focused, exploring in depth, for example, the relationship between respondents' motives and their behaviour. The techniques used to encourage respondents to speak and behave honestly and unself-consciously are derived from the social sciences, in particular psychology.

When definitions and descriptions are needed – in other words, when no one knows exactly where to start – qualitative research is at its most useful. It can define the parameters for future studies, and identify key criteria among consumers that can then be measured by quantitative research. For example, if a bank observed that older consumers were not using automatic teller machines, they might conduct some focus groups with older consumers in order to develop hypotheses about why this particular group was reluctant to use this technology. It is important, however, that the consumers are asked in as objective and sympathetic a form as possible. Qualitative research plans generally incorporate a discussion outline for those collecting the information, but are essentially unstructured and respondent-led.

**Quantitative research**  Quantitative research is used to measure consumers' attitudes and choices where the nature of the research has been defined and described. These studies are designed to gather information from statistically representative samples of the target population. In order to achieve total accuracy it would be necessary to take a complete census of everyone in the target group. The scale and cost of the UK census, however, illustrates the impracticality of this in most cases. Therefore, samples of respondents are selected for interview, the sample size being related to the size of the total population and degree of statistical reliability required, balanced against time and cost constraints. In order to achieve margins of error small enough to make the final measurements useful, however, quantitative research is usually conducted among several hundred, sometimes thousands, of respondents. For this reason, information is generally obtained using standardized structured questionnaires.

### 6.4.7 Data collection

Data can be collected either indirectly by observation or through direct interaction with the person being researched.

Observational techniques claim objectivity, being relatively free of respondent bias, but are limited to descriptions of behaviour. They find a number of uses within the services sector for planning purposes, for example site location decisions which are often based on observation of pedestrian or vehicle flows past a site, as well as the routine monitoring of competitor price levels.

A survey, a direct interaction data collection method, would normally request some attitudinal, personal or historical information about respondents. Questions in a survey can be asked face to face, by telephone, or distributed for self-completion. While considerably cheaper than face-to-face interviews, the refusal rate for telephone surveys can be up to three times higher than for personal interviews. The increased used of computer-assisted information collection for telephone (CATI) and personal interviews (CAPI) has speeded up the whole survey process dramatically, with responses being processed as they are received. Immediately prior to the 1997 UK General Election these systems were used in the next-day publication of survey results from total sample sizes extending into thousands.

In the case of self-completion surveys, respondents obviously self-select, so no matter how carefully the original sample to be contacted is chosen, the possibility of bias is highest. Furthermore, the response rate may be as low as 10%, particularly where a postal survey is used. However, some service sector companies, in particular airlines and hotels, have used self-completion questionnaires for a number of years to obtain customer feedback.

In qualitative research, the open-ended nature of the questions, and the need to establish the confidence of respondents, precludes the use of telephone and self-completion interviews. Face-to-face (or personal) depth interviews are used particularly in business-to-business research, where confidentiality is especially important, and it is usually most convenient for respondents to be interviewed at their place of work.

In consumer markets, group discussions are frequently used. Groups normally consist of about eight people, plus a trained moderator – quite often a psychologist – who leads the discussion. Respondents are recruited by interviewers, who use recruitment questionnaires to ensure that those invited to attend reflect the demography of the target market, and to filter out unsuitable respondents. In national markets, groups are arranged at central points throughout the country, the number of groups in each region once more reflecting the regional breakdown of the target population.

It was noted earlier that the collection of market information is the part of the research process most dominated by research agencies rather than client companies. There are two main reasons for this. The first is that very few client companies, however large or diverse their range of services, can generate sufficient research to warrant the full-time employment of armies of interviewers throughout the country. The second is that respondents are more likely to give honest answers to third parties than when replying directly to representatives of the organization providing the service being discussed.

As more and more service organizations try to gather information about their customers, there is a danger of 'survey fatigue' setting in. Just how many times can you ask customers questions about what they think of their service encounter, before the whole process of carrying out a survey spoils the enjoyment of the service itself? Do customers think that their comments will ever be taken notice of by management? Careful organization of surveys can improve response rates. Stopping people when they are in a hurry to get away will not make an interviewer popular, but catching them when they are captive with nothing else to do (e.g. waiting at the baggage carousel in an airport) may be more successful. Some companies have tried to make the whole process of carrying out a survey enjoyable. The airline Virgin Atlantic uses its seat-back entertainment system to provide an interactive electronic questionnaire which passengers can complete at their leisure. Many companies offer prize incentives in return for completion, but does this encourage people to skip through the questions without much thought, simply in order to qualify for the prize incentive? If companies leave questionnaires for self-completion with no prize incentive and no intervention by an interviewer, how can they be sure that they get a representative sample of respondents? It has often been noted that customers who are very happy or very dissatisfied are the most likely to volunteer information. But what about the mass of people who hold average views about a service? These are likely to be under-represented and a challenge for marketers to learn about.

### 6.4.8 Effects on research methods of service inseparability

For manufactured goods, it is usually possible within the research process to separate the technical characteristics of a product from the identity and image of the company producing them. For example, in testing a drinks product, such as tea or beer, it is possible to isolate reactions to the core product by presenting it to respondents in blind format, i.e. in a plain (usually white) container with no clue as to the brand or manufacturing company. The respondent is then asked to rate the product along a number of dimensions, e.g. strength–weakness or light–dark colour. The extent to which perceptions are influenced by brand or company connotations can be measured by presenting an identically constructed sample with the same product, fully branded and packaged, and measuring the differences in response along the same dimensions.

It is not always possible to make this kind of neat separation when researching services – respondents cannot rate the level of satisfaction provided by a financial service, for example, unless they have actually experienced it, which may be difficult to achieve in a laboratory type of setting. Furthermore, interviewees' responses to proposed new services cannot be isolated from their perceptions of the service provider. An insurance policy cannot be seen in isolation from the reputation of the insurance company which will be responsible for delivering the service benefits at some time in the future. Indeed, some providers of services marketing research argue that attempting such a separation is undesirable and that it is essential to look at all aspects of the company–customer relationship – attitudinal and perceptual, as well as factual and transactional.

## 6.5 Demand forecasting

Forecasting the future is one of the most difficult aspects of knowledge management. It is often inadequate to assume that market conditions will continue on present trends, but what other knowledge can be used to predict the future? A stark indication of the rewards of looking forward rather than back is provided by an analyst who studied stock market performance. If a cumulative investment of $1 had been invested from 1900 on 1 January each year in the stock which had performed best in the previous year, and then reinvested the following year, the accumulated value in 2000 would be £250. However, if it had been invested each year in the stock which performed best in the year ahead, the accumulated value would be over $1 billion. Similarly for service provision, successful companies have often been those who correctly forecast the market and were able to satisfy customers' needs more cost effectively than competitors. Being first to market when trends are changing can be much more profitable than simply reacting to a market trend. However, predicting future trends can be very difficult and involve a lot of risk.

The amount of effort which an organization puts into refining its demand forecasting techniques will depend on a number of factors.

- The level of turbulence in the marketing environment will vary between firms operating in different markets. For example, the marketing environment of an undertaker has been – and will probably continue to be – less turbulent than that of a commercial radio station. An extrapolation of recent trends might be adequate for the former, but the latter must seek to understand a diverse range of changing forces if it is to accurately predict the likely future nature of its operating environment.
- The cost associated with an inaccurate forecast will reflect the capital commitment to a project. A window cleaner with only limited investment and transferable skills can afford to pay only limited attention to understanding their environment. On the other hand, the cost of developing a new rapid transit system will call for relatively sophisticated techniques if expensive failure is to be avoided.

- More sophisticated analytic techniques are needed for long-term projects where there is a long time lag between the planning of the project and the time when it begins to yield its stream of service output. The problem of inaccurate forecasting will be even more acute where an asset has a long lifespan with few alternative uses.
- Qualitative and quantitative techniques may be used as appropriate. In looking at the future, facts are hard to come by. What matters is that senior management is in a position to make better informed judgements about the future in order to aid strategic marketing planning.

A number of approaches to demand forecasting are considered below. While trend extrapolation should be possible with routine output from a marketing information system, expert opinion and scenario building are usually associated with more irregular activity by larger organizations operating in more turbulent markets.

### 6.5.1 Trend extrapolation

At its simplest, a firm identifies a historic and consistent long-term change in demand for a product and seeks to explain this in terms of change in some underlying variables. Marketing planning then seeks to predict changes in these underlying variables and therefore – on the basis of the long-term relationship between variables – the likely future size and nature of a market.

While correlation techniques can be used to identify the significance of historical relationships between a number of variables, extrapolation methods suffer from a number of shortcomings. Firstly, one variable is seldom adequate to predict future demand for a product, yet it can be difficult to identify the full set of variables which have an influence. Secondly, there can be no certainty that the trends identified from historic data are likely to continue in the future. Trend extrapolation takes no account of discontinuous environmental change, as was brought about by the sudden increase in oil prices in 1973 and the effects which this had on demand for air travel. Thirdly, trend extrapolation is of diminishing value as the length of time which it is used to forecast increases – the longer the time horizon, the more chance there is of historic relationships changing and new variables emerging. Fourthly, it can be difficult to gather information on which to base an analysis of trends – indeed, a large part of the problem in designing a marketing information system is in identifying the type of information which may be of relevance at some time in the future.

At best, trend extrapolation can be used where planning horizons are short, the number of dependent variables relatively limited and the risk level relatively low.

### 6.5.2 Expert opinion

Trend analysis is commonly used to predict demand where the state of the dependent variables is given. In practice, it can be very difficult to predict what will happen to these variables. One solution is to consult expert opinion to obtain the best possible forecast of what will happen to them.

In Diffenbach's (1983) study of US corporations, 86% of all firms said they used expert opinion as an input to their planning process. Expert opinion can vary in the level of its specialty, from an economist being consulted for a general forecast about the state of the national economy, to industry specific experts. Expert opinion may be unstructured and come from a few individuals either inside the organization, or from external advisers or consultants. The most senior managers in organizations of any significant size tend to keep in touch with developments by a number of means. Paid and unpaid advisers may be used to keep abreast of a whole range of issues such as technological developments, environmental issues, government thinking and intended legislation. Large companies may employ members of parliament as advisers as well as retired civil servants. Consultancy firms may be employed to brief the company on specific issues or monitor the environment on a more general basis.

Relying on individuals may give an incomplete or distorted picture of the future. There are, however, more structured methods of gaining expert opinion. One of the best known is probably the Delphi method. This involves a number of experts, usually from outside the organization, who preferably do not know each other and who do not meet or confer while the process is in play. A scenario or number of scenarios about the future are drawn up by the company. These are then posted out to the experts. Comments are returned and the scenario(s) modified according to the comments received. The process is run through a number of times with the scenario being amended on each occasion. Eventually a consensus of the most likely scenario is arrived at. It is believed that this is more accurate than relying on any one individual, because it involves the collected wisdom of a number of experts who have not been influenced by dominant personalities.

### 6.5.3 Scenario building

Scenario building is an attempt to paint a picture of the future by building a small number of alternative scenarios based on differing assumptions. This qualitative approach is a means of handling environmental issues which are hard to quantify because they are less structured, more uncertain and may involve very complex relationships.

In the real world, many unpredictable environmental factors can interact with each other, resulting in a seemingly endless permutation of scenarios. One method of analysing the relationship between environmental factors is a cross impact analysis that presents a framework within which the combined effects of changes in a number of factors can be assessed. A number of permutations are shown in Figure 6.5, where the interaction of the distinct possibility of oil prices rising to $50 per barrel with the 'wildcard' event of cancer being linked to flying can be noted. For an airline, a development option if this scenario came true might be to rapidly downsize its passenger carrying capacity and to concentrate on business and freight traffic.

The use of scenarios can allow a company to come to a view as to which is the most likely outcome, and plan accordingly, while still being able to develop contingency plans which could be rapidly implemented if any of the alternative foreseen scenarios came true.

## 6.6 Information and control systems

Many services organizations have developed elaborate planning systems but have failed because implementation of the plan was not appropriately monitored and

**Figure 6.5**

Cross impact analysis

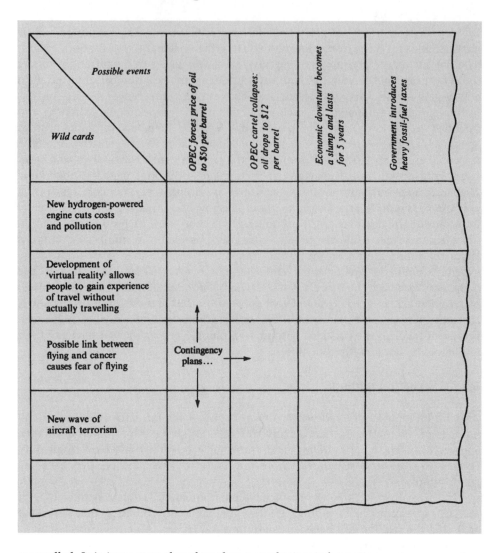

controlled. It is important therefore that a marketing information system recognizes the key elements of the plan which need to be monitored and provides information which will allow control action to be taken where a variance from the plan is observed. These are some of the things that most services organizations will need information on if they are to adequately monitor implementation:

- Financial targets – sales turnover/contribution/profit margin, disaggregated by product/business unit.
- Market analysis – e.g. market share.
- Effectiveness of communication – productivity of sales personnel, effectiveness of advertising, effectiveness of sales promotion.
- Pricing – level of discounts given, price position.
- Personnel – level of skills achieved by employees, survey of customer comments on staff performance.
- Quality levels achieved – e.g. reliability, complaint level.

Where performance is below target, the reasons may not be immediately obvious. A comprehensive marketing information system can allow an organization to analyse variance. A uniform fall in sales performance across the organization, combined with intelligence gained about the state of the market would suggest that remedial action aimed at improving the performance of individual sales personnel may not be as effective as a reassessment of targets or strategies in the light of the changed sales environment.

Successful control mechanisms require three underlying components to be in place:

- The setting of targets or standards of expected performance.
- The measurement and evaluation of actual performance.
- Taking corrective action where necessary.

### 6.6.1 Setting targets

A clear statement of objectives at the start of the planning process provides a vital foundation for comparing targets with actual performance. In general, the greater the level of disaggregation of targets, the greater the degree of control which will be possible. To be effective in a control process, targets should be specified and communicated:

- Give individual managers a clear indication of the standards of performance that are expected of them.
- Distinguish between controllable variables which can be managed by an individual manager and those that are uncontrollable and should therefore be excluded from their standards for performance.
- Allocate targets to the right person. Ultimately, all costs and revenues are somebody's responsibility and should be monitored and controlled at the appropriate point within an organization. Even a relatively fixed and uncontrollable element such as rent can become controllable over the longer term by senior management.
- Show which targets are to take priority. In any event, targets should not be mutually incompatible.
- Give sufficient flexibility to allow for changes in the organization's environment which were not foreseen at the time the targets were set.

For control purposes, quantitative targets are generally preferred to qualitative ones. Many apparently qualitative targets, such as customer satisfaction and attentiveness of front-line service personnel can often be reduced to quantifiable indices – for example by setting targets for the number of complaints received or the percentage of customers booking a repeat service, or by using an analytic technique such as **SERVQUAL** (see Chapter 8). There is a danger, however, in setting purely quantified targets that they may be represented by a series of relatively simple indicators. Staff seeking to achieve these targets may concentrate their attention on meeting these, possibly at the expense of other more important qualitative aspects of their performance. A telephone enquiry office set with a target of answering calls within a specified time may lose sight of the quality of information given during the call if its attention is primarily focused on responding within the target time. There is also an argument that marketing managers should not be assessed solely on the basis of their ability to meet quantifiable targets. A more realistic appraisal system might also examine the quality of the decisions which a manager made during the previous period, taking account of the fact that the operating environment posed numerous problems and opportunities which may not have been apparent at the time targets were initially set.

In its attempts to become more professionally managed, the UK National Health Service has increasingly set performance targets. By publishing many of these targets in the Patients' Charter, users of the NHS should be able to expect a minimum level of service as specified. The idea of introducing targets which mainly relate to customer handling rather than clinical issues has been dismissed by many as mere window dressing. But even the meaning of these non-clinical statistics is open to doubt, as hospitals find ways of making their performance look good on paper, if not in practice. Accident and emergency departments use triage nurses to assess new patients upon arrival, thereby keeping within their Patients' Charter target for the time taken to first see a new patient. However, accident and emergency departments may be slower to provide actual treatment. In order to keep the length of their waiting list below a specified target, hospitals have resorted to setting up a 'waiting list' to get on the main waiting list.

Even the whole value of publishing performance indicators for hospitals has been questioned by many. What does it mean if a consultant or a department has a long waiting time for appointments? Rather than being an indicator of inefficiency, could it be that a long waiting list is an indicator of a consultant who is very popular with patients?

### 6.6.2 Measuring performance

Information is needed to measure two aspects of performance: efficiency and effectiveness. Efficiency can be defined in terms of an organization's success in turning inputs into outputs, while effectiveness is the level of success in producing a desired result. An efficient business in a competitive market cannot succeed if it is efficient at doing the wrong things – that is, it is ineffective.

Where an organization competes in a market on the basis of its cost leadership, efficiency may be a key measure for evaluating management performance. Within the services sector, important efficiency measures can include the number of services performed per employee, value of sales achieved per sales person, the cost of advertising per 1000 valued impressions and the level of utilization of assets (e.g. load factors on aircraft).

In contrast to planning information, much of the information needed for control is derived from internal sources and can be collected routinely. Examples include:

- Technical measures of service quality, for example failure rates of ATM machines, percentage of flights delayed by more than 10 minutes, time taken to answer a telephone.
- Sales figures should be routinely analysed and actual values compared with budget under such headings as regional distribution, customer type, size of purchase. Invoicing should not be seen narrowly as an accounting function, but as an opportunity to collate marketing data.
- Routine analysis of invoices will indicate whether an organization has been able to maintain its price level.
- Expenditure budgets should give an up-to-date summary of actual against target expenditure under such headings as advertising, salesforce cost, intermediaries' expenses.
- Sales personnel's performance records are routinely maintained.

These regular sources of information may need to be supplemented with external sources of data and *ad hoc* studies. These are likely to include the following:

- Up-to-date information about the size of a market (collected through syndicated research, trade associations and government agencies) will allow an organization to monitor its market share.
- While technical quality can often be measured by an organization on a continuous basis, the measurement of functional quality frequently calls for marketing research to be commissioned. This can include periodic questionnaire surveys of customers, or less frequent and more in-depth diagnostic research sessions. For control purposes, a service organization may set its managers an objective that

**Figure 6.6**

Northern Ireland Railways employs Coopers and Lybrand to independently monitor the performance of its services. The findings, such as these for Spring 1997, are reported to customers under two headings. In the top half of the report, Coopers and Lybrand's observation of performance is compared against the railway's passenger charter commitments. After this, customers' own performance ratings report customers' opinions of the service provided (reproduced with permission of Translink Northern Ireland Railways) at least 90% of customers surveyed in such surveys should state that their service experience is 'good' or better.

- Observational research is becoming increasingly popular as a means of controlling the quality of the service delivery process. Trained '**mystery shoppers**' are now employed by many restaurants, banks and transport companies to check that the service format as specified is actually being delivered. Findings from this form of research are often linked to employees' pay.

- Transaction analysis issued by many organizations to track the progress of services provided to clients, both during and after delivery. This can provide valuable information about customers' perceptions of service quality compared to their expectations. It can also be used to internally monitor the attainment of performance targets.

- Analysis of complaints is often seen by services organizations as a positive source of information from customers. If complaints are communicated to management, it is in a better position to prevent future repeats of the factors which gave rise to the complaint, than would be the case if the aggrieved customer remained silent and quietly took their custom elsewhere. For this reason, many service organizations try to make it easy for their customers to communicate grievances to them, and carefully analyse their responses.

- Research is often commissioned to monitor the effectiveness of an organization's advertising, for example by monitoring awareness levels or enquiry response rates.

### 6.6.3 Using information for control

A good marketing information system can generate a lot of information. The key to effective control is to give the right information to the right people at the right time. Providing too much information can be costly in terms of the effort required to assemble and disseminate it and can also reduce effective control where the valuable information is hidden among information of secondary importance. Also, the level of reporting will be determined by the level of tolerance allowed for compliance to target. Analysis of variance from target should indicate if the variance is within or beyond the control of the person responsible for meeting the target. If it is beyond their control, the issue should become one of revising the target so that it becomes once more achievable. If the variance is the result of factors which are subject to an individual's control, a number of measures can be taken to try to revise behaviour and these are discussed in Chapter 12.

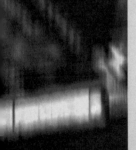

**Case Study**

## Information dries up in the knowledge society

The term 'knowledge society' is now widely used and this chapter has noted the competitive advantage which knowledge can give a firm. But the knowledge-based firm rests on an assumption that it is able to obtain a ready supply of information about customers, actual and potential, so what happens when those customers tire of giving information about themselves? After all, if information has value in the hands of firms, consumers might reasonably think that it has value if they retain the information about themselves.

Specialist data collection companies have come to play an important role in the task of collecting information about buyers. Organizations such as Experian, CACI and Claritas have developed a role in providing socioeconomic and lifestyle data which is sold on to client companies to make their targeting more effective. With the growth in direct marketing, it is important to many clients to have specific information about each individual customer, rather than a general aggregate for the whole market. This applies to information about new prospects, as well as new and additional information from people already on their databases, which is important because people's circumstances change. In contrast to client firms' need for this information, consumers by the end of the 1990s were showing increasing resistance to providing information for commercial purposes.

The market research industry has been concerned for a number of years about falling response rates to quantitative surveys. A Market Research Society report in 1997 pointed out that the public rarely distinguishes between anonymous research, database building, or telephone calls that start off asking for information but end up with a hard sell. A report prepared in 1998 by the Future Foundation found that only 50% of consumers were happy to provide personal information to firms with which they deal, down from over 60% in 1995. A core of people appear to be not interested in taking part in data collection exercises at all, and won't fill in questionnaires. For marketers, this is a worrying development. All marketing, and not just direct marketing, is based on what is known about customers – their needs, wants, attitudes and behaviour. If the public does not offer this information, it makes the life of the marketer more difficult.

There are a number of factors that may explain this trend. The first is that many more companies are now seeking to obtain information from buyers. The Market Research Society estimated that in 1998, more than £300 million was spent on quantitative studies and £150 million on continuous tracking studies and omnibus surveys. In addition, direct marketing companies have been building marketing databases of their own customers. Saturation appeared to be setting in.

Secondly, consumers are becoming increasingly aware that information which only they can reveal about themselves has commercial value. Research from the Future Foundation suggested that the majority of people were happy to provide personal details if the result was better products or services. However, the public's experience of how well this data is used often falls short of their expectations in terms of how it benefits them personally.

How can response rates to questionnaires be improved? Developing some form of meaningful relationship with a recipient prior to receiving a questionnaire seems to be important. At its simplest level, an individual would receive a very simple first form. If they complete and return this, it is followed a couple of months later with a reward pack of money-off vouchers and samples, plus a second, more detailed questionnaire. As an example, research by Air Miles concluded that the company gets much better, more robust data if it saves detailed questions until members have had some experience of its services, rather than asking detailed questions of new recruits.

Some service companies have tried to make the task of collecting information more engaging and enjoyable for participants. Virgin Atlantic is among a number of airlines that use seat-back video consoles to collect information from captive passengers on

long-haul flights. With the development of the Internet, many users have unwittingly been giving streams of information about the sites they visit and the items they purchase when 'cookies' embedded in their computer send back information to data collectors such as Doubleclick.com, who then use the data for targeting. So when a surfer who regularly views travel websites sees a banner headline on their home page for a travel company, its selective appearance is probably attributable to covert data collection methods rather than chance. There are clearly issues of privacy involved here.

Bigger bribes to encourage people to provide data are part of the researcher's armoury. This ploy has reached new heights in the US with reports of home-shopping companies offering free computers and Internet access in return for household data and the acceptance of advertising on their screen. But large bribes can lead to another problem of samples being biased towards a new breed of professional market research respondents. There have been reports that focus groups are increasingly being dominated by a small circle of individuals who can make a reasonable living off the fee paid to participants. For the research companies, such people may be readily available and need less training and instruction than a novice. But is the information that they yield of any great value?

(Adapted from 'Data firms react to survey fatigue', *Marketing*, 29 April 1999, pp 29–30)

## Case study review questions

1 Suggest additional methods which companies can use to improve the effectiveness of their consumer data collection. What examples have you encountered?

2 Discuss the limitations of statistically based consumer databases of the type discussed here. Do qualitative approaches based on small groups offer any advantages?

3 What effects do you expect the development of interactive electronic media will have on the collection of marketing research information from consumers?

## Chapter summary and linkages to other chapters

Information is becoming increasingly important as a means by which service organizations gain competitive advantage. With recent advances in firms' ability to collect data, greater attention is now placed on the effective integration of individual employees' information into corporate knowledge. This chapter has reviewed the planning and control uses of information. A number of effects of service intangibility and inseparability on research processes have been noted. It is often difficult to separate research into the characteristics of a service from the characteristics of the service provider. The interaction between employees and customers presents additional opportunities for data collection.

Information is vital for effective strategic management of a service organization (**Chapter 14**) and in managing capacity (**Chapter 12**). The importance of information has been noted in a number of other chapters, particularly in respect of quality (**Chapter 8**), segmentation and buyer decision processes (**Chapter 4**), targeting (**Chapter 7**), promotional effectiveness (**Chapter 11**) and pricing (**Chapter 10**). Current interest in relationship marketing programmes (**Chapter 5**) rests on the availability of information about customers.

## www linkages/URLs

Office for National Statistics:
**http://www.ons.gov.uk**

The library of online official EU and UK documentation:
**http://www.euro-emu.co.uk/atoz/indexmain.shtml**

The Market Research Society:
**http://www.thebiz.co.uk/markres.htm**

Market Research Directory (A Market Research Directory, Market Research Guide, and Index of Links related to Business Size):
**http://www.ahandyguide.com/catl/m/m25.htm**

Marketing Research Forum discussion group:
**http://www.marketresearch.info.com/forum/index.cfm**

## Key terms

Knowledge management 144
Mission statement 149
SERVQUAL 167

Marketing information system 147
Key clients 157
Mystery shopper 170

## Chapter review questions

1   Are there any major distinctions between the processes and practices of marketing research in services and goods markets?

**2** To what extent do you agree that the intangibility of services creates a researchability problem?

**3** How important is it to have a structured approach to marketing research?

**4** Identify the most likely marketing research objectives for a hotel chain.

**5** Explain how information on consumer buying processes may be important for a cinema chain seeking to enhance its service offer.

**6** Choosing a service industry of your choice, identify the ways in which information can be used for control purposes.

## Selected further reading

*For a general discussion of the principles of marketing research, the following texts are recommended:*

Birn, R. J. (1999) *Effective Use of Marketing Research*, Kogan Page, London

Chisnall, P. (1996) *Marketing Research*, 5th edition, McGraw-Hill, Maidenhead

Gofton, L. and N. Mitchell (1997) *Business Market Research*, Kogan Page, London

Proctor, T. (1997) *Essentials of Marketing Research*, Pitman, London

Quee, W. T. (1998) *Marketing Research*, 3rd edition, Butterworth-Heinemann, London

West, C. (1999) *Marketing Research*, Macmillan, Basingstoke

*The importance role played by information in marketing planning is discussed in the following articles:*

Collis, D. J. and C. A. Montgomery (1998) 'Creating Corporate Advantage', *Harvard Business Review*, Vol. 76, No. 3, pp 71–83

Czerniawska, F. and G. Potter (1998) *Business in a Virtual World: Exploiting Information for Competitive Advantage*, Macmillan, Basingstoke

Greco, J. (1999) 'Knowledge Is Power', *Journal of Business Strategy*, Vol. 20, March–April, pp 176–89

Nonaka, I. (1991) 'The Knowledge-Creating Company', *Harvard Business Review*, Vol. 69, No. 6, pp 96–104

Porter, M. and V. Millar (1985) 'How Information Gives You Competitive Advantage', *Harvard Business Review*, July–August, Vol. 85, pp 149–60

*The following references develop the above point by analysing the interpersonal dimension of information exchange within organizations.*

Moorman, C., G. Zaltman and R. Deshpande (1992) 'Relationships Between Providers and Users of Market Research: The Dynamics of Trust Within and Between Organizations', *Journal of Marketing Research*, August, Vol. 29, pp 314–28

Morten, T., M. T. Hansen, N. Nohria and T. Tierney (1999), 'What's Your Strategy for Managing Knowledge?', *Harvard Business Review*, March–April, Vol. 77, No. 2, p 106

Piercy, N. (1985) *Marketing Organisation: An Analysis of Information Processing, Power and Politics*, Allen and Unwin, London

*Finally, a structured approach to collecting information for a services marketing audit is discussed in the following article:*

Berry, L. L., J. S. Conant and A. Parasuraman (1991) 'A Framework for Conducting a Services Marketing Audit', *Journal of the Academy of Marketing Science*, Summer, pp 255–68

# 7

# Service positioning and targeting

### Learning objectives

So far we have considered two perspectives of services – the nature of the service offer supplied by the service provider and the needs of buyers who will consume those services. The conclusion until now may be that consumers are very varied in the way they buy services, matched by a great diversity in the types of services available. For an individual service provider, this diversity can be bewildering. Which groups of buyers should be targeted? What products should be offered to these groups? Firms seek to match their competencies to the opportunities available in the market, and it would be wrong to say that there is a logical starting point in the process of bringing services to consumers. Firms typically take an iterative approach until the most profitable combination of service offers and consumer groups are matched.

In this chapter we will begin by considering the issue of positioning. Within a crowded marketplace, firms take a view on how they wish their service offer to compare with those offered by competitors in terms of the benefits offered and the price charged. The variability of services makes the positioning of services more complex than is typically the case with goods.

An important aspect of developing a market position is the development of a brand image which concisely states and reinforces the adopted market position. This chapter will examine the problems and opportunities for developing brands where the service offer is highly variable and intangible.

Finally, service organizations, like all organizations, cannot afford to stand still with their existing service portfolio. As services approach the end of their life cycle, it is important to develop new services and to eliminate those which absorb more management effort than is justified by the contribution which they make. The chapter will conclude with a review of new service development processes and relate this back to the need to develop a clear position in the marketplace.

## 7.1 Service positioning

Imagine that you were considering starting a chain of restaurants in the UK. You look around at what is available to consumers already and you find a bewildering range from outlets offering low-cost, fast food, through to gourmet meals. You would probably find enormous variation in the size of restaurant, location, service formats and average price charged. What would be the distinguishing features and benefits of your proposed restaurant in relation to the existing competitors? This is the essence of positioning strategy.

Positioning strategy distinguishes a company's service offers from those of its competitors in order to give it a competitive advantage within the market. Positioning puts a firm in a subsegment of its chosen market, thus a firm which adopts a product positioning based on 'high reliability/high cost' will appeal to a subsegment which has a desire for reliability and a willingness to pay for it. For some marketers (e.g. Ries and Trout, 1981), positioning has been seen essentially as a communications issue where the nature of a service is given and the objective is to manipulate consumer perceptions of it. Others, such as Lovelock (1984) have pointed out that positioning is more than merely advertising and promotion, but involves considerations of pricing, distribution and the nature of the product offer itself, the core around which all positioning strategies revolve.

Organizations must examine their opportunities and take a position within a marketplace. A position can be defined by reference to a number of scales – service quality and price are two very basic dimensions of positioning strategy which are relevant to service industries. Figure 7.1 shows these two scales applied to UK super-market retailing in which both the price and quality scales are conceptualized as running from high to low. Quality in this case can be considered as a composite of range: speed of service, quality of personnel, quality of the shopping environment, etc. Price can be a general indication of price levels charged relative to competitors. The position of a number of UK retailers is shown on the grid. This shows clearly that most supermarkets lie on a diagonal line between the high-quality/high-price position adopted by Marks and Spencer and the low-price/low-quality position adopted by Kwik Save. Points along this diagonal represent feasible positioning strategies for supermarket operators. A strategy in the upper left quadrant (high price/low quality) can be described as a 'cowboy' strategy and generally is not sustainable, although it may be an attractive position in some instances – for example some tourism related activities where tourists are unlikely to return to the area. A position in the lower right strategy (high quality/low price) may indicate that an organization is failing to achieve a fair exchange of value for itself.

An analysis of competitors relative to market size can indicate the attractiveness of alternative positioning strategies. An analysis of UK clothing retailers towards the end of the 1990s indicated that while there was an abundance of stores in the upper right quadrant, there were relatively few in the lower left quadrant in relation to the numbers of people who sought this type of store. The result during the 1990s was the expansion of a number of low-cost/no-frills operators such as Matalan and Peacocks to take this position.

**Figure 7.1**
A simplified product
positioning map for UK
supermarkets

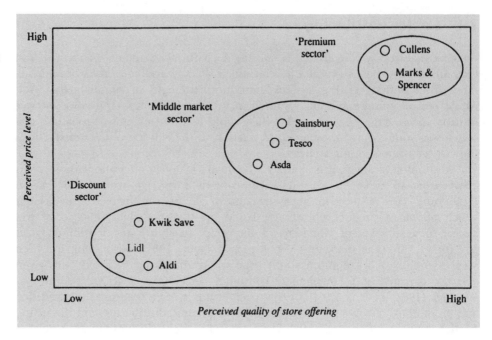

### 7.1.1 Competitor analysis

Any plan to develop a competitive advantage must be based on a sound analysis of just who a company's competitors are. At first, their identity may seem obvious, but as Theodore Levitt pointed out, a myopic view may focus on the immediate and direct competitors while overlooking the more serious threat posed by indirect and less obvious sources of competition. When railway companies in the 1930s saw their main competitors as other railway companies, they overlooked the fact that the most serious competition would derive from road-based transport operators. More recently, banks have been made to realize that their competitors are not just other banks, or even other financial services organizations, but any organization which has a strong brand reputation and customer base. Through these, supermarkets, airlines and car companies have all developed various forms of banking services which now compete with mainstream banks.

Even without considering the possibility of new market entrants appearing, it is possible to identify direct and indirect competitors. Direct competitors are generally similar in form and satisfy customers' needs in a similar way. Indirect competitors may appear different in form, but satisfy a fundamentally similar need. Consider the examples of services shown in Table 7.1. The table shows the underlying need which they satisfy and their direct and indirect competitors.

Taking this bigger picture to consider indirect competitors is important because consumers essentially seek to satisfy the underlying need which can be met in a number of ways. Many customers do not need a bank – they may simply need a cash withdrawal service which can be provided just as well by a supermarket or a petrol station. The precise form of a new competitor may appear quite unlike the

**Table 7.1** Examples of services, the needs they satisfy and the competition

| Product | Underlying need | Direct competitors | Indirect competitors |
| --- | --- | --- | --- |
| Overseas holiday | Relaxation | Rival tour operators | Garden conservatories |
| Restaurant meal | Social gathering | Other restaurants | Ready prepared gourmet meals for home consumption |
| Television programme | Entertainment | Other television programmes | Internet service provider |

established service format, but in terms of positioning within consumers' minds the new service could rank just as highly. If all that a customer needs a bank for is to withdraw cash, a petrol station may have a superior position in their mind in terms of accessibility and ease of use.

Michael Porter's (1980) model of industry competitiveness identified sources of turbulence in a market which can affect the positioning of a company's products in relation to the competition. Five forces require evaluation:

- The threat of new entrants.
- The threat of substitute products.
- The intensity of rivalry between competing firms.
- The power of suppliers.
- The power of buyers.

With many services being easy to copy, it is not surprising that positioning strategy has become much more complex in many markets. In recent years, the UK has seen the example of banks moving into car leasing; a gas supply company moving into car breakdown assistance; and retailers becoming Internet service providers.

### 7.1.2 Positioning criteria

Although price and quality were used in the example above, these are generally too simplistic in themselves as criteria for positioning. Wind (1982, pp. 79–81) suggested six generic scales along which all products can be positioned. These are examined below by reference to the possible positioning of a leisure centre:

- By specific product features – e.g. a leisure centre can promote the fact that it has the largest swimming pool in the area, or the most advanced solarium.
- By benefits or needs satisfied – the leisure centre could position itself somewhere between meeting pure physical recreation needs and pure social needs. In practice, positioning will combine the two sets of needs, for example by giving up gym space to allow the construction of a bar.

- By usage occasions – the centre could be positioned primarily for the occasional visitor, or the service offer could be adapted to aim at the more serious user who wishes to enter a long-term programme of leisure activities.
- By user categories – a choice could be made between a position aimed at satisfying the needs of individual users and one aimed at meeting the needs of institutional users such as sports clubs and schools.
- Positioning against another product – the leisure centre could promote the fact that it has more facilities than its neighbouring competition.
- Positioning by product class – management could position the centre as an educational facility rather than a centre of leisure, thus positioning it in a different product class.

Selecting a position for a service involves three basic steps:

- *Identifying the organization's strengths and the opportunities of the marketplace to be exploited* An organization which is already established in a particular product position will normally have the advantage of customer familiarity to support any new service launch. A holiday tour operator which has positioned itself as a high-quality/high-price operator can use this as a strength to persuade customers to pay relatively high prices for a new range of value added holidays. Sometimes a weakness can be turned into a strength for positioning purposes, for example, the Avis car rental chain stresses that by being the number two operator, it has to try harder. Against internal strengths must be considered the attractiveness of a subsegment. For the tour operator seeking to build upon its strong reputation for offering high-quality/high-cost holidays, an analysis of the market may reveal greater opportunities in a segment which seeks a basic budget range of holidays. Should the organization decide to enter this market, it must avoid tarnishing its established brand values by association with a lower quality product. One solution is to adopt a separate identity for a new service which assumes a different position.
- *Evaluating the position possibilities and selecting the most appropriate* An organization may discover a number of potential positions but many may have to be discarded if they result in uneconomically small market segments, or are too costly to develop. Other positions may be rejected as being inconsistent with an organization's image. Selection from the remaining possibilities should be on the basis of the organization's greatest differential advantage in areas which are most valued by target customers. When it entered the Indonesian market, the UK retailer Marks and Spencer realized that its UK positioning would be unsustainable against low-cost local competition. It therefore adopted a much more exclusive position with small shops, limited product ranges and relatively high prices.
- *Developing the marketing mix and establishing in the eyes of target customers the position which has been adopted* Organizations must develop programmes to implement and promote the position which they have adopted. In this way an airline such as British Airways, which positions itself as providing superior in-flight cabin crew services, must develop a programme for recruiting, training, motivating and retaining appropriate crews who can deliver the desired service.

## When you compare the local pizza restaurants, LaDolce takes some topping!

|  | LaDolce | Pizzaland | Deep Pan Pizza | Venito |
|---|---|---|---|---|
| Home delivery | Free on orders over £15 within 10 miles | ✕ | ✕ | £5 |
| Student discounts | ✓ | ✓ | ✕ | ✕ |
| Unlimited free car parking outside | ✓ | ✕ | ✓ | ✕ |
| E-mail your order to us | ✓ | ✕ | ✕ | ✕ |
| No quibble money back guarantee if not satisfied | ✓ | ✕ | ✕ | ✕ |

### LaDolce pizza restaurant
24 Noverton Road (opposite Curry's)
Telephone: 0845 4598012

**Figure 7.2**
This company clearly states its points of competitive advantage relative to other local pizza restaurants. While comparative advertising may often help, it also runs the danger of raising awareness of competitors' services

**Analysis**
Match firm's strengths and weaknesses with external opportunities and threats for position possibilities.
↓
**Planning**
Develop a strategic position which is sustainable and anticipates competitors' likely reactions.
↓
**Implementation**
Use marketing mix formulation to achieve chosen position.
↓
**Monitoring**
Has desired position been achieved? If not, why not?
↓
**Repositioning**
Reanalyse current marketing environment.

**Figure 7.3**
The process of positioning a service offer

It must also develop a creative platform for its promotional programme which makes clear in the minds of target customers just what a brand stands for. Positioning for a service industry differs from manufacturing industry in that the method of producing the service is an important element of the positioning process.

### 7.1.3  Positioning the service provider

Services can be positioned either on a stand-alone basis or as part of a service organization's total service range – in effect, the service organization adopts a position, rather than the individual service. The fact that consumers are likely to evaluate the service provider at least as much as a particular service makes this approach to position analysis attractive. Shostack (1987) suggested that within a range of services provided by an organization (or 'service family'), a marketer can consider positioning strategies based on structural complexity and structural diversity. Structural complexity comprises the number of steps which make up a service production process and diversity the extent to which service output is variable. In this way, a doctor's service is highly complex in terms of the number of processes involved in a consultation or operation. It is also highly variable, for service outcomes can be diverse in terms of both planned and unplanned deviations in outcomes. Some processes can be high in complexity but low in diversity. Hotels, for example offer a complete range of processes but are able to establish relatively low levels of diversity. An example of a service which is low in complexity but high in diversity is provided by a singer.

Positioning is seen by Shostack as a process of deciding how the service provider wishes to position its total range of services in relation to its customers – complexity and diversity are two key dimensions by which an organization can be positioned. Positioning decisions have implications for the overall image of the provider, and hence of individual services within its range. As an example, a dentist could take a more divergent position by adding general counselling on health matters or reduce it by undertaking only diagnostic work. Complexity could be increased by adding retailing of supplies, or reduced by offering only a limited range of dental treatments. These options are shown diagrammatically in Figure 7.4. The position adopted by an organization will be influenced by its strengths and weaknesses relative to the market which it seeks to address. A large dental practice may be better placed to position itself as a provider of complex services, but would need to ensure that diversity in outcomes was minimized in order not to adversely affect its image. A small dentist may find the most appropriate service position to be the provision of relatively simple services with divergent outcomes.

Many services organizations have found a low-complexity/low-diversity position to offer great opportunities for exploiting niche markets. In this way, solicitors have set up as specialist will writing businesses, offering one **product line** with little scope for variability. By developing expertise and reducing overheads, such companies can satisfy customers who do not have the need for the more complex, but also more divergent services of full service solicitors.

### 7.1.4  Repositioning

Over time, an organization may need to reposition its service offer. This could come about for a number of reasons:

- The original positioning strategy was inappropriate: over-estimation of an organization's competitive advantage or of the size of the subsegment who the posi-

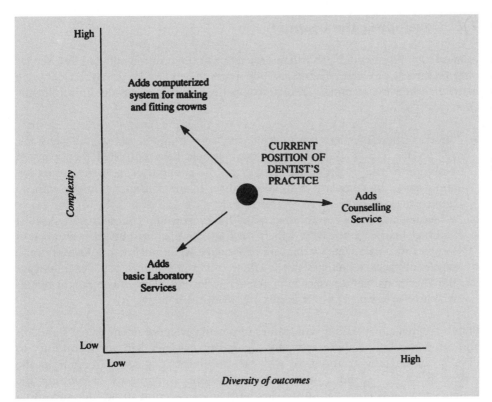

High

Complexity

Adds computerized
system for making
and fitting crowns

CURRENT
POSITION OF
DENTIST'S
PRACTICE

Adds
Counselling
Service

Adds
basic Laboratory
Services

Low

Low                                                              High

*Diversity of outcomes*

**Figure 7.4**
Service positioning
strategies based on
service structure (based
on Shostack, G. L.
(1987) 'Service
Positioning Through
Structural Change',
*Journal of Marketing,*
Vol. 51, pp 34–43)

tioning was intended to appeal to could force a re-evaluation of positioning strategy.

- Where the nature of customer demand has changed: for example it is argued that UK customers' attitudes towards package holidays have changed during the 1990s away from an emphasis on low price towards greater emphasis on high-quality standards. Many tour operators accordingly repositioned their offering to provide higher standards at higher prices.

- Service providers seek to build upon their growing strengths to reposition towards meeting the needs of more profitable subsegments. In many service industries, organizations start life as simple, no-frills, low-price operations, subsequently gaining a favourable image which they use to 'trade up' to relatively high-quality/high-price positions. This phenomenon is well established in the field of retailing in which McNair (1958) identified what has become known as the 'Wheel of Retailing'. This contends that retail businesses start life as cut-price, low-cost, narrow-margin operations which subsequently 'trade up' with improvements in display, more prestigious premises, increased advertising, delivery and the provision of many other customer services which serve to drive up expenses, prices and margins. Eventually, retailers mature as high-cost, conservative and 'top-heavy' institutions with a sales policy based on quality goods and services rather than price appeal. This in turn opens the way for the next generation of low-cost innovatory retailers to find a position which maturing firms have vacated.

## 7.2 Developing the brand

A brand identity provides a shorthand reference to the position adopted by a service offer or service provider. Brands are important in guiding buyers when choosing between otherwise seemingly similar competing services. Consider the following cases:

- Buyers of pension plans are typically not very knowledgeable about pensions, yet several tens of thousands of British people have entrusted their pension provision to the Virgin Group, largely on the strength of its brand reputation and despite the company being a newcomer to the pensions industry, with no proven track record.
- When booking an overseas hotel, many travellers would choose from a shortlist of hotel brand names with which they are familiar, despite the existence of locally run hotels which would probably offer better quality at a lower price.
- Buyers of package holidays in the UK are often prepared to pay a premium for the Thomsons brand name, in preference to less well-known competitor brands which offer lower prices for apparently identical holidays.

Brands are frequently used by companies to provide evidence of consistent standards and are particularly important where a company has not had an opportunity to develop an ongoing relationship with its customers. The use of brands in the service sector is becoming increasingly important as a means of limiting the search activities of potential buyers. Rather than considering all possible options, a brand encourages buyers not to consider other products which do not come with the statement of values which a brand stands for.

Historically, branding assumed significance when economies of scale meant that producers were no longer able to have a direct and individual relationship with their growing number of customers, and therefore could not provide personal reassurance of product quality. A brand acted as a substitute for a personal relationship in managing buyers' exposure to risk. Branding has been found to simplify the decision-making process by providing a sense of security and consistency which may be absent outside a relationship with a supplier (Barwise and Robertson, 1992). Risk levels are perceived as being higher for products that fulfil important needs and values, so in these situations the value of brands can be higher.

There have been many conceptualizations of the unique attributes of a brand and how these affect buying decision processes. These usually distinguish between elements which can be objectively measured (such as taste, shape and reliability) and the subjective values that can only be defined in the minds of consumers (such as the perceived personality of a brand). Gardner and Levy (1955) distinguished between the 'functional' dimensions of a brand and its 'personality', while other dimensions have been identified as utilitarianism versus value expressive (Munson and Spivey, 1981), need satisfaction versus impression management (Solomon 1983), and functional versus representational (de Chernatony and McWilliam, 1990). The functional dimensions of a brand serve to reassure buyers that important elements of a service offer will be delivered as promised, for example an airline can be trusted to operate safely, a tour operator not to overbook its hotels and a savings institution to return its investors' money promptly when required.

With increasing affluence, the non-functional expectations of brands have become more important. For services which offer very little tangible evidence, the emotional dimensions of a brand can be particularly important in guiding buyers' evaluations. A number of dimensions of a brand's emotional appeal have been identified, including trust, liking and sophistication. As consumers buy products, they learn to appreciate their added value and begin to form a relationship with them. For example, there are many companies selling petrol and credit cards, but individual companies such as Shell and American Express have created brands with which customers develop a relationship and guide their choice in a market dominated by otherwise generic products.

There is an extensive literature on the emotional relationship consumers develop between a brand and their own perceived or sought personality. Brands are chosen when the image that they create matches the needs, values and lifestyles of customers. Through socialization processes, individuals form perceptions of their self, which they attempt to reinforce or alter by relating with specific groups, products and brands (Solomon and Buchanan, 1991). There is evidence that branding plays a particularly important role in purchase decisions where the product is conspicuous in its use and purchase and in situations where group social acceptance is a strong motivator (Moschis, 1976; Miniard and Cohen, 1983). While conspicuous consumption is most commonly associated with manufactured goods (for example, brands of training shoes, designer clothes labels and makes of car), the concept of a conspicuous brand also has meaning in a services context. An individual may use their membership of an up-market gym or their possession of a 'gold' credit card to make statements about themselves in much the same way as they might use a Rolex watch or Nike trainers.

There has been a lot of recent discussion about the role of brands in influencing purchasing decisions. The growth in 'own-brand' products sold by many retailers has led some to suggest that we are becoming less conscious of brands in our buying decision process. With greater education, maybe consumers are 'seeing through' the efforts of brand-building marketers? Own brands first achieved prominence among low-value, low-involvement manufactured goods but have since become popular with many buyers of services. Retailers such as Tesco and Marks and Spencer have recently introduced own-brand bank accounts, savings schemes and personal loans to sell alongside their own-brand baked beans and underwear. Is this a challenge to the traditional role of branding, or merely a reorientation to meet changes in the business environment?

The traditional role of branding has been to differentiate products, but brands have been increasingly applied to **organizational image** too. This has occurred particularly with services where the intangibility of the product causes the credentials of the provider to be an important choice criterion. The notion of an emotional relationship to a product has been extended to develop an emotional relationship between an organization and its customers. In this way, Tesco and Marks and Spencer have become strong brands in their own right which command the respect and trust of buyers.

Service intermediaries such as Tesco and Marks and Spencer have developed strong functional attributes of their brand through consistent product quality, which has been supplemented with their portrayal as caring service organizations which develop strong preference at an emotional level. The brand position must be consistent throughout even when it is extended to diverse ranges of services. For example, the Virgin brand has traditionally been positioned as reliable, slightly offbeat and honest. This has been sufficient for customers to make the leap from trusting Virgin's CDs and cola to entrusting their savings and investments to the company. The brand needs to be carefully protected when it is extended to new products. Many came to question the Virgin position on reliability following the company's acquisition of the West Coast Main Line rail franchise. If the company's trains were consistently at the bottom of the league tables for performance, what did this say about the company's pension schemes?

It has been argued that a further challenge to the role of brands has emerged from the increasing importance of consumer legislation. Characteristics such as reliability and consistency may have traditionally added value to a brand, but these are increasingly enshrined in legislation and therefore less capable of being used to differentiate one organization's services from another. A good example of this is to be found in the financial services sector, where most countries have strict regulations which protect investors from being sold investment schemes which are of dubious security or inappropriate for their needs. There is less need to trust a financial services company with a strong brand name when legislation guarantees similar standards from all companies, and a compensation system if those standards are not met. Many financial services companies have recognized the limits on the development of functional aspects of branding by concentrating on the emotional aspects. The Virgin Group has been successful in this respect by appealing to groups who value its 'no-nonsense' approach to doing business, while Schroders has stressed its long-established history and comprehensive range of facilities.

How do people choose a taxi? An example of the effects of legislation on brand choice can be observed by contrasting buyer behaviour in areas with strict licensing (e.g. London) and areas where a relatively unregulated market exists (common in many UK provincial cities). In London, the famous black taxis are highly regulated in terms of the standards of drivers, the vehicle itself and prices charged. Drivers must pass a 'knowledge' test before being allowed to operate, and cannot refuse to carry a passenger, except in clearly specified cases. Few people would bother spending much effort in selecting one cab from another – they have been reduced to a commodity whose consistent standards are rigorously maintained by the licensing body, the Public Carriage Office.

Contrast this with the situation in towns where regulations are minimal and buyers may have little idea about the integrity of the car that they are getting into or the reliability of its driver. This is the classic opportunity for the development of brands by taxi operators to give them a distinctive position in the marketplace, and thereby simplifying buyers' choice processes. While many local authorities control the fares which all taxi operators must charge, it is open to individual operators to develop a brand which is associated with reliability, safety and courteousness. Next time a customer seeks a taxi, they may know which taxi companies to avoid and which to go for out of preference.

Debate has taken place between those who would like to see a free market in taxis and those who see regulation as vital to the public interest. What is the experience in your area? Of what value are brands in guiding the choices of taxi users?

### 7.2.1 Branding and buyer–seller relationships

There has been a lot of recent interest in the methods that companies use to develop ongoing relationships with their customers, including the use of databases, loyalty programmes and added value benefits for members. The subject of relationship marketing was considered in Chapter 5, and similarities between brand building and relationship development should be noted. Both seek to simplify buyers' decision processes by reducing the inherent riskiness of a purchase. Branding appeals to buyers' sense of trust in a product whose characteristics become familiar through reputation and promotion, such that the purchase of any other product is seen as highly risky. The presence of a brand simplifies buyers' decision processes, because it avoids the need to evaluate a wide range of competing sources of supply each time that a decision has to be made. Of course, a brand is only as good as its reputation, and a brand which fails to deliver its promises will not maintain its position in its marketplace.

Services have traditionally focused on relationship development and manufactured goods on brand development. Typical of the former are one-to-one relationships which buyers have developed with their bank managers, doctors, hairdressers and car repairers. In the goods sector, branding has been used extensively to position the functional and emotional attributes of a product. However, as the distinction between goods and services becomes blurred, so the roles of relationship and brand development have come to overlap. In the case of services, the industrialization and deskilling of many service processes renders the service provider relatively anonymous and incapable of having a personal relationship with its customers. Personal banking is a good example of a sector in which personal relationships have become much weaker as a result of the automation of bank branches and deskilling of bank managers' tasks. At the same time, all of the major UK banks have spent considerable effort in developing strong brand images in an attempt to develop an identifiable market position and to simplify the choice process of customers. By contrast, many manufactured goods have augmented their offering with services, for example cars are now frequently sold with the benefit of long-term service support. This implies an ongoing relationship which may exert very great influence on the next purchase decision (for example a car buyer may gain preferential treatment by trading in their car for a new one provided by their current provider).

In the 1990s the world airline industry underwent major changes as a result of deregulation, privatization and the creation of strategic alliances. In the early 1990s, British Airways – one of the first state-owned airlines to be privatized –

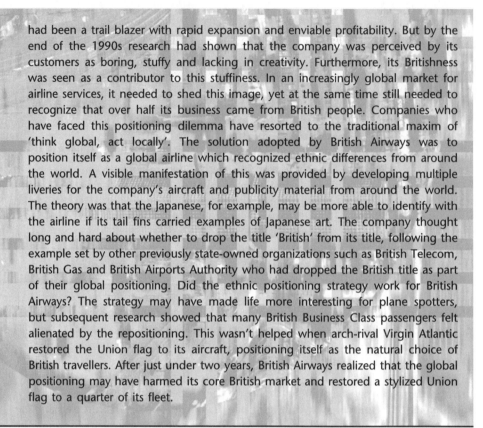

had been a trail blazer with rapid expansion and enviable profitability. But by the end of the 1990s research had shown that the company was perceived by its customers as boring, stuffy and lacking in creativity. Furthermore, its Britishness was seen as a contributor to this stuffiness. In an increasingly global market for airline services, it needed to shed this image, yet at the same time still needed to recognize that over half its business came from British people. Companies who have faced this positioning dilemma have resorted to the traditional maxim of 'think global, act locally'. The solution adopted by British Airways was to position itself as a global airline which recognized ethnic differences from around the world. A visible manifestation of this was provided by developing multiple liveries for the company's aircraft and publicity material from around the world. The theory was that the Japanese, for example, may be more able to identify with the airline if its tail fins carried examples of Japanese art. The company thought long and hard about whether to drop the title 'British' from its title, following the example set by other previously state-owned organizations such as British Telecom, British Gas and British Airports Authority who had dropped the British title as part of their global positioning. Did the ethnic positioning strategy work for British Airways? The strategy may have made life more interesting for plane spotters, but subsequent research showed that many British Business Class passengers felt alienated by the repositioning. This wasn't helped when arch-rival Virgin Atlantic restored the Union flag to its aircraft, positioning itself as the natural choice of British travellers. After just under two years, British Airways realized that the global positioning may have harmed its core British market and restored a stylized Union flag to a quarter of its fleet.

## 7.3 Developing the portfolio of services

Few service organizations can survive by offering just one specialized service. Instead, a mix of services is usually offered. This section considers the issues involved in managing a portfolio of services.

To begin, the service range offered by an organization can be disaggregated for analysis. The most basic unit of output is often referred to as an item – this is a specific version of a service. Such an item would normally be part of a service line which is a group of related service items. The service mix is the combination of services that an organization offers to customers. A distinction can be made between the depth of the service mix and its width. Product depth refers to the number of different services in a service line. Service width refers to the number of service lines offered by an organization.

An example of an individual service item offered by a bank is a young person's card-based savings account. This in turn will form part of a line of savings accounts. The depth of this line may be indicated by the presence of a wide range of savings accounts to meet the needs of customers who require services such as ease of access, high interest and flexibility. Savings accounts represent just one line of service offering for most banks – other lines would typically include personal loans, mortgages, credit cards, and so on.

Decisions about an organization's service mix are of strategic importance. In order to remain competitive in the face of declining demand for its principal service line, a service company may need to widen its product mix. For example, the increasing diversity in food tastes has forced many specialized fast-food outlets to widen their range. In the UK, for example, traditional fish and chip shops have often had to introduce new lines such as kebabs or home delivery services. On the other hand, decisions may need to be made to delete services from the mix in cases where consumer tastes have changed or competitive pressures have made the continuing provision of a service uneconomic. Service mix extension and deletion decisions are continually made in order that organizations can provide services more effectively (providing the right services in response to consumers' changing needs) and more efficiently (providing those services for which the organization is able to make most efficient use of its resources).

For any service organization, its service offering will be constrained by the capabilities, facilities and resources at its disposal. It is therefore important for service firms to constantly examine their capabilities and their objectives to ensure that the range of services provided meets the needs of the consumer as well as the organization. The process of ensuring that the right services are being provided in order to meet strategic objectives is often referred to as a service product audit. Key questions for an audit are:

- What benefits do customers seek from the service?
- What is the current and continuing availability of the resources required to provide the service?
- What skills and technical know-how are required?
- What benefits are offered over and above the competition?
- Are competitor advantages causing the organization to lose revenue?
- Does each service provided still earn sufficient financial return?
- Do services meet the targets which justify continued funding?

The answers to these questions form the basis of service mix development strategy.

Should a company 'stick to its knitting' and do what it is good at or search continually for new products and new markets? Countless companies have reported disastrous results after going into areas they knew very little about. The rapid growth of Next from its core of fashion retailing to newsagents and home furnishings contributed to its near collapse in the late 1980s. TSB Bank diversified into car leasing but regretted it later. WHSmith went through bad years in the mid-1990s when the newsagent's diversification into DIY retailing and television failed to work.

But isn't change essential for companies, especially those facing static or declining markets? One of the UK's leading grocery retailer's, Asda, would not be where it is today had not the Associated Dairy company taken a risk and set up a retailing operation. The security services company Securicor company knew that it was taking a risk when it invested in a joint venture with British Telecom to create the successful Cellnet mobile phone network. And a small company called

WPP (standing for Wire Plastic Products) took huge risks on its way to becoming the owner of the one of world's leading advertising agencies.

It is fine with hindsight to criticize a firm's decisions about which direction its product portfolio should take. But in an uncertain world, risks have to be taken. A sound analysis of a company's strengths and weaknesses and of its external environment certainly helps, but success also depends upon an element of luck.

## 7.4 Product/service life-cycle concept

It was noted earlier that the position adopted by a service offer needs to be continually reviewed. Repositioning may be needed because new competitors have entered a market, forcing a company to consider whether it wants to meet the new entrants head-on, or to find a position in the market which is less accessible to the new competitors. More importantly, most services go through some form of life cycle, necessitating changes in marketing strategy as the service passes from one stage in the cycle to the next. There is evidence that service life cycles are becoming shorter, especially where the service offer has a high technology base. Within the mobile phone sector, for example, analogue phone services were soon replaced by GSM and PCN services, which by 2000 were being challenged by new WAP and third generation phone services. The cyclical nature of many service offers calls for continued scanning of the environment for new service opportunities. These are discussed in the following section.

The product/service life cycle graphically depicts the changing fortunes of a service, or groups of services within an organization's portfolio. Services typically go through a number of stages between entering the portfolio and leaving, each calling for adjustments to marketing activities. Five stages are identified in Figure 7.5.

*Phase 1: Introduction*   New services are often costly to develop and launch and may have teething problems. People may be wary of trying something new, especially a new service whose intangibility prevents prior evaluation. Sales therefore tend to be slow and are restricted to those who like trying out new products or who believe they can gain status or benefit by having it.

*Phase 2: Growth*   By this time, the service has been tested and any problems have been resolved. The service is now more reliable and more readily available. Buyers now start to see the benefits that can be gained by using the service. Sales start to increase greatly and this is a signal for competitors to start entering the market.

*Phase 3: Maturity*   Almost everyone who wants to buy the service has now done so, which is a particular problem for services which are bought as a one-off rather than a recurrent purchase. The number of competitors in the market has risen.

*Phase 4: Saturation*   Here there are too many competitors and no further growth in the market. Competitors tend to compete with each other on the basis of price.

*Phase 5: Decline*   With falling demand and new substitute products appearing, organizations drop out of the market.

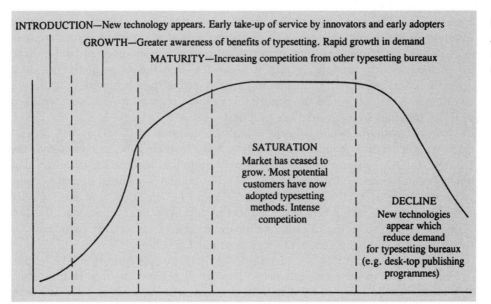

INTRODUCTION—New technology appears. Early take-up of service by innovators and early adopters

GROWTH—Greater awareness of benefits of typesetting. Rapid growth in demand

MATURITY—Increasing competition from other typesetting bureaux

SATURATION
Market has ceased to grow. Most potential customers have now adopted typesetting methods. Intense competition

DECLINE
New technologies appear which reduce demand for typesetting bureaux (e.g. desk-top publishing programmes)

**Figure 7.5**

A hypothetical product life cycle for typesetting bureaux

The usefulness of the life-cycle concept lies in the recognition that marketing activity for a service is closely related to the stage in the life cycle that a service has reached. In this way, promotional planning is closely related to the life cycle, with emphasis placed in the launch phase on raising awareness through public relations activity, building on this through the growth phase with advertising, resorting to sales promotion incentives as the market matures and becomes more competitive, and finally possibly allowing promotional activity to fall as the service is allowed to go into decline. The message used at each stage may position the service offer quite differently, beginning, for example, as a 'latest technology' message, through 'most reliable', and perhaps to 'lowest cost'. In a similar way, distribution and pricing decisions can also often be related to the stage which a service has reached in its life cycle.

Of course, the **product life cycle** presented above is a conceptual abstraction. Different products move through the life cycle at different paces. Some products have been in the maturity/saturation stage for many years (e.g. bank current accounts) whereas others disappear very soon after introduction (e.g. some trendy clothing retailers). Empirical evidence also seems to imply a variety of life cycle modifications and mutations.

### 7.4.1 Difficulties in applying the life-cycle concept

Although the idea of product life cycles is appealing and seems to be validated by research, it is important to be aware of the possible failings of this conceptual approach in terms of both goods and services. It can be argued that the product/service life-cycle concept is probably more useful for strategic planning and control purposes than for developing short-term forecasts and costed marketing programmes. In reality, life-cycle patterns are far too variable in both shape and duration for any realistic predictions to be made. A further difficulty in applying the life-cycle concept lies in the inability of marketers to accurately ascertain where in the life cycle a service actually is at any time. A stabilization of sales may be a movement into maturity or simply a temporary plateau due to external causes, for example. In fact, it is possible that the shape of the life cycle is a result of an organization's marketing activity rather than being an indication of environmental factors which the organization should respond to – in other words, it could in fact lead to a self-fulfilling prophesy.

Another criticism of the concept is that the duration of the stages will depend upon whether it is a product class, form or brand which is being considered. For example, the life cycle for holidays is probably quite flat, whereas life cycles for particular formulations of holidays and for specific holiday operators' brands become progressively more cyclical. Carman and Langeard (1979) noted that most service organizations have only a very small number of core services and consequently they suggest a degree of caution in using the life-cycle concept for services, particularly as the basis for portfolio approaches to service product planning.

Taking these points into consideration, the life-cycle concept may still be helpful in guiding a firm in its service mix decisions. Although life cycles may be unpredictable for services in terms of the length of time a service may remain at a particular stage, the understanding that services are likely to change in their sales and profit performance over a period of time implies a need for proactive service mix management.

## 7.5 New service development

As a result of analysis and evaluation of its product mix, an organization may consider the need to add to its service portfolio in response to the changing nature of its operating environment. The following are typical circumstances when **new services** may be necessary:

- If a major service has reached the maturity stage of its cycle and may be moving towards decline, new services may be sought to preserve sales levels.
- New services may be developed as a means of utilizing spare capacity, for example unoccupied rooms during off-peak periods may lead a hotel operator to develop new services designed to fill the empty rooms.
- New services can help to balance an organization's existing sales portfolio and thereby reduce risks of dependency on only a few services offered within a range.
- In order to retain and develop a relationship with its customers, an organization may be forced to introduce new products to allow it to cater for customers' diverse needs.
- An opportunity may arise for an organization to satisfy unmet needs with a new service as a result of a competitor leaving the market.

Putting the spoken word into print has seen a quickening pace in the technologies available to do the job as quickly and accurately as possible. The typewriter eventually gave way to the word processor and keyboard.

But what about the likely fortunes of a new speech recognition service launched in 1998?

A UK company called Speech Machines used computers to receive dictation over the telephone or as voice messages sent through the Internet by e-mail. The dictation is transcribed automatically by computer with a claimed 95% accuracy. Specially written software manages the incoming dictation and automatically sends the transcribed document to one of an army of contract typists the company uses for checking and correction of the final manuscript. It is then sent back to the customer through the Internet. In the USA, the service has found a useful niche with the legal and medical professions, offering a speedy and efficient alternative to employing a secretary in-house. But how long a life can this service expect before it is overtaken by increasingly sophisticated and user-friendly voice recognition software that allows users to complete the task in-house? If it is to maintain its business, how can the company offering this new service continue to develop its service offer so that it meets customers' changing needs better than any of the alternatives currently available?

### 7.5.1 What is meant by a 'new service'?

The intangible nature of services means that it is often quite easy to produce slight variants of an existing service, with the result that the term 'new service' can mean anything from a minor style change to a major innovation. Lovelock (1984) has identified five types of 'new' services:

- *Style changes* These include changes in decor or changes in logo or livery – the revised design of telephone kiosks introduced by BT in 1997, for example.
- *Service improvements* These involve an actual change to a feature of the service already on offer to an established market. An example is the computerization of travel agency information and booking procedures.
- *Service line extensions* These are additions to the existing service product range – new modes of study for an MBA course at a university, for example.
- *New services* These are new services that are offered by an organization to its existing customers, although they may be currently available from its competitors. Building societies offering current accounts, with cheque books, standing order facilities, etc. are an example.
- *Major innovations* These are entirely new services for new markets – the provision of diagnostic tele-medicine services, for example.

The distinctive features of services as compared to tangible goods would seem to imply that there are some special issues that need to be considered in new service development.

- The very intangibility of services has tended to lead to a proliferation of slightly different service products. Because of this intangibility, new services can be relatively easy to develop and the variety of different services can cause confusion.

As an example, banks frequently introduce 'new' mortgage offers which are only slightly differentiated from existing offers – e.g. by offering a lower rate for the first two years of the mortgage.

- The characteristic of inseparability between service production and consumption means that front-line operational staff have greater opportunity to identify new service ideas which are likely to be successful.
- As services are more likely than goods to be customized to the needs of individual customers, there could be greater opportunities for marginally different new services, each having its own unique selling proposition.

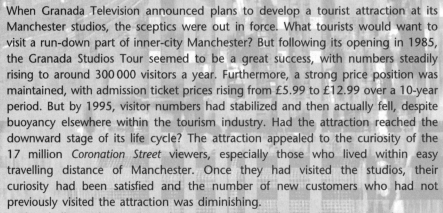

When Granada Television announced plans to develop a tourist attraction at its Manchester studios, the sceptics were out in force. What tourists would want to visit a run-down part of inner-city Manchester? But following its opening in 1985, the Granada Studios Tour seemed to be a great success, with numbers steadily rising to around 300 000 visitors a year. Furthermore, a strong price position was maintained, with admission ticket prices rising from £5.99 to £12.99 over a 10-year period. But by 1995, visitor numbers had stabilized and then actually fell, despite buoyancy elsewhere within the tourism industry. Had the attraction reached the downward stage of its life cycle? The attraction appealed to the curiosity of the 17 million *Coronation Street* viewers, especially those who lived within easy travelling distance of Manchester. Once they had visited the studios, their curiosity had been satisfied and the number of new customers who had not previously visited the attraction was diminishing.

The challenge facing Granada was to reinvent the product to appeal to new markets and to bring previous visitors back for repeat visits. A number of new markets were identified, including weekend breaks, linked with local hotels, which extended the market beyond the original local day-trip market. Corporate hospitality groups were identified as another important market segment. To get previous visitors back, investment was made in major new attractions including an interactive exhibition of futuristic technology and a footballing 'Hall of Fame'. An extensive programme of research among visitors and non-visitors was undertaken to try to understand the attraction's perceived image. One result was to drop the word 'Tour' from the title and just call it 'Granada Studios'. This reflected the high level of involvement which visitors felt during their visit.

### 7.5.2 New service development processes

Research has indicated that a systematic process of development helps to reduce the risk of failure when new products are launched. In reality, there is evidence that most firms do not have a formal NSD strategy. A study by Kelly and Storey (2000) showed that only half of a sample of firms in banking, telecommunications, insurance and transportation had a formal NSD strategy; that only a quarter had a culture in which ideas were continually generated; and only a third had an idea search methodology.

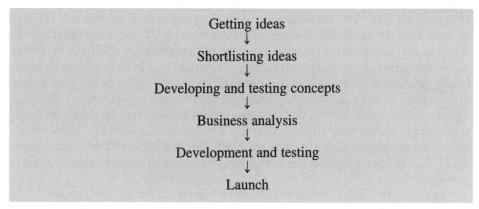

**Figure 7.6**
The new service
development process

Although a variety of different procedures have been proposed and implemented, they all tend to have the common themes of beginning with as many new ideas as possible and having the end objective of producing a tested service idea ready for launch. A common sequence is shown in Figure 7.6, although in practice, many of the sequential stages shown are compressed so their timing overlaps with other stages.

The question of whether such procedures are appropriate for services was posed by Easingwood (1986). He investigated how new service developments in services organizations reflected the major differences between goods and services – i.e. their intangibility, inseparability, variability and perishability – and found a number of differences between goods and services.

**Getting ideas**  Ideas can be generated from within an organization and also from outside, either formally or informally. Easingwood found that generating new ideas is not a problem for most service firms. Inseparability means that front-line staff have a closer understanding of both service operations and customer needs and therefore it would seem logical that a large number of new ideas would come from the operating staff. Perhaps surprisingly, Easingwood found that the most common internal source of new service ideas was the marketing function rather than the operational function. The marketing function had constant contact with both customers and competitors and thus had market information 'on-tap'. He found that a much smaller proportion of new ideas emanated from the operations function because 'new' services were perceived by them as a further burden which would complicate their operations. Cowell (1988) noted that although the generation of ideas is relatively easy for service organizations, the degree of novelty of idea tends to be slight. Many ideas tend to be conservative, focusing on minor modifications, geographical extensions or 'me too' ideas.

Customers can be an important source of ideas for new service and for this purpose, a study of the interaction between service provider and customer may be worth while. MacKay and Conway (1992) considered the variety of potential influences on new services idea generation within the corporate financial services sector and indicated that the application of a network perspective could be useful in identifying the various influences on the generation of new financial services ideas.

**Shortlisting ideas**   This stage involves evaluating the ideas generated and rejection of those that do not justify the organization's resources. Criteria are usually established so that comparisons between ideas can be made, but because each firm exists in its own particular environment, there is no standard set of evaluative criteria that fits all. Easingwood found a variety of screening practices, all with differing degrees of formality, noting that screening processes for financial services were particularly rigorous. Within this sector, each new idea would be evaluated by customer discussion groups, feedback on proposed features and advertising would be collected and financial projections calculated with some detail. It was suggested that this rigour is partly due to the difficulties in withdrawing a financial service once it is being provided.

Intangibility makes services difficult to assess and therefore 'image' is an important means by which customers reassure themselves about the credibility of a service provider. Easingwood found that enhancement or support of an organization's image was an important criteria used by firms in the screening process.

**Developing and testing concepts**   Ideas that survive the shortlisting stage need to be translated into service concepts. This then is tested by obtaining reactions from groups of target customers. Service positioning is important at this stage. This involves the development of a visual presentation of the image of an organization's service in relation either to competitive services or to other services in its own portfolio.

**Business analysis**   The proposed idea is now translated into a business proposal. The likelihood of success/failure is analysed including resource requirements in terms of manpower, extra physical resources etc. At this stage, many of the factors that will determine the financial success of the proposed new service remain speculative. The activities of competitors' new product development processes could have a crucial effect on the firm's eventual market share, as well as the price which it is able to sustain for its service.

**Developing and testing**   This is the translation of the idea into an actual service which is capable of delivery to customers. The tangible elements as well as the service delivery systems which make up the whole service offering all have to be designed and tested. Unfortunately, testing may not always be possible and evidence from Easingwood implies that test marketing generally among service firms is limited. One possible alternative is to introduce the new service with limited promotion just to test whether the new service operates effectively.

**Launch**   The organization now makes decisions on when to introduce the new service, where, to whom and how.

In 1997, the Virgin Group launched a new 'Virgin One' account which allowed customers to control their mortgage, banking, credit cards, loans and savings from a single account, with 24-hour telephone access. The service targeted busy people with neither the time, nor inclination to shop around for financial services.

But how many customers should the company have geared itself up to handle when it launched its new product? Launching a new product often involves a lot of guesswork. If the number is under-estimated and the company doesn't have the capacity to cope with large numbers, frustration and harm to the brand reputation can soon build up. Many new product launches have been victim of their own success as potential customers queue seemingly endlessly for a telephone to be answered and are then answered by an over-stretched operator. Prudential's Egg and Standard Life both seriously under-estimated the number of people who might respond to their newly launched banking services, leading to frustrated customers and over-stretched staff as call centres were swamped with calls.

Virgin undertook testing of its new banking service among a small group of customers before launching it to all its existing customers in November 1997. This allowed it to understand more about demand when it eventually went for a full public launch in January 1998. The company appeared to have managed an orderly launch of its new service and maintained the integrity of its brand, something that has been harmed by other companies in their rush to get to the market.

A successful new service development programme requires an organization which is aware of changing market conditions and has structures and processes which can respond quickly to such changes. Alternative forms of organization structures and their impact on new service development will be discussed in Chapter 14. Particular importance has been attached to the presence of product 'champions' who can oversee the development of a new service and help overcome potential problems of inter-functional co-ordination.

## 7.6 Service deletion

Good product management depends upon reliable marketing information to show when a product is failing to achieve its objectives. As well as maintaining successful services and investing in new ones, services organizations must also have the courage to eliminate services which are no longer likely to be of benefit to the organization as a whole. This implies a need for the following:

1   Establishment of targets for each service.
2   Periodic reviews of each service's performance.
3   Modification of existing services where necessary.
4   Elimination of services where necessary.
5   Development of new services.

In general, there is a tendency to 'add on' rather than subtract and thus many service offers do not die but merely fade away, consuming resources of an organization which could be better used elsewhere. 'Old' products may not even cover overheads. In addition, there are a number of 'hidden' costs of supporting dying products that need to be taken into consideration:

- A disproportionate amount of management time is spent on them.
- Short and relatively uneconomic 'production' runs may be required where a service has not been deleted and there is irregular demand for it.
- They often require frequent price adjustments (and stock adjustments where tangible goods are involved).
- The search for new products and services is delayed, as so much time is spent on existing products/services that the desired allocation of time to consider new ones is inadequate.

Firms should therefore have a marketing planning system that incorporates service deletion decisions. It would be naive, however, to assume that deletion is a simple process. In reality, there are a number of reasons why logical deletion procedures are not readily followed:

- Often firms do not have the information which they need to identify whether a service needs to be considered for elimination. Even if an organization is aware of a potential deletion candidate, the reasons for its failure may not be known and management may just leave things as they are and hope that the problem will go away by itself.
- Managers often become sentimental about services, hoping that sales will pick up when the market improves. Sometimes, particular elements of marketing strategy will be blamed for lack of success and there is the belief that a change in advertising or pricing, for example, will improve the situation.
- Within organizations, there may be political difficulties in seeking to delete a service. Some individuals will have vested interests in a service and may fight elimination efforts. In fact, some individuals may hide the true facts of a service's performance to ensure that deletion is not considered at all.
- Finally, there is sometimes the fear that the sales of other products and services are tied into the service being deleted. As an example, a car dealer which closes down its new car sales department may subsequently lose business in its servicing and repairs department. Furthermore, some candidates for elimination may be sold to a small number of important customers, leading to fears that deletion would cause all of their business to go elsewhere.

In fact, many companies tackle service elimination in a piecemeal fashion, only considering the matter once a service is seen to be losing money, or when there is some crisis leading to a cut-back. There is clearly, therefore, a need for a systematic approach. At regular intervals, every service should be reviewed in terms of its sales, profitability, average cost, market share, competitor share, competitor prices etc. Today, information technology allows firms to calculate important ratios that can indicate how a service is performing in its marketplace.

Having acquired the relevant information, an organization can identify 'weak' elements of its service portfolio using a number of warning signals. Some of these relate to poor sales performance, some to poor profit performance and others relate to more general danger signals such as new competitor introductions or increasing

| Factor (FWi) weighting | Factor | Product/service score (SRi) |
|---|---|---|
| 7 | Future market potential for product/service? | 4 |
| 7 | How much could be gained from modification? | 6 |
| 6 | How much could be gained from marketing strategy modification? | 5 |
| 6 | How much useful executive time could be released by abandoning product/service? | 8 |
| 5 | How good are the firm's alternative opportunities? | 7 |
| 4 | How much is the product/service contributing beyond its direct costs? | 3 |
| 4 | How much is the product/service contributing to the sale of other product/services? | 5 |

The product/service retention index SRI = the sum of FWi x SRi

**Figure 7.7**

Production retention index

amounts of executive time being spent on one service. The presence of these warning signals merely indicates a need for further consideration and the possibilities of either service modification or total elimination. Identification of a 'weak' service doesn't automatically mean that deletion is required.

One possible method of deciding which products to eliminate is the development and implementation of a product/service retention index. This can include a number of factors, each of these being individually weighted according to the importance attached to them by a particular firm. Each service is then ranked according to each factor, the product retention index thus being equal to the sum of the products of the weighted index. An illustration of a product retention index is shown in Figure 7.7.

Two of the product retention factors relate to potential modification approaches either in terms of the service itself or of the whole marketing strategy. A number of non-deletion alternatives for poorly performing services can be identified, that is, attempts can be made to reverse the decline stage of the product life cycle. In many cases, a potential deletion candidate can be saved by adjusting its marketing programme, including:

- Modifying the product or service.
- Increasing the price (may be a good idea if demand is fairly inelastic).
- Decreasing the price (may be useful if demand is elastic).
- Increasing promotional expenditure to stimulate sales.
- Decreasing promotional expenditure to cut costs.
- Revising the promotional mix.
- Increasing salesforce effort to boost sales.
- Decreasing salesforce effort to reduce costs.
- Changing the channels of distribution.
- Changing the physical distribution system (where there is a significant tangible element).
- Undertake additional marketing research to identify possible new markets for the service. Additionally, information relating to why success has declined may also be forthcoming.
- Licensing agreements to another firm.

If, on the other hand, deletion is the chosen alternative, decisions must be made as to how this is to be implemented. This is not always a simple task and a number of options can be identified:

- *Ruthlessly eliminate 'overnight'* The potential problem here is that there are still likely to be customers of the service. How will they respond? Will they take their business to other competitors? Will they take their business for other services in the mix with them?
- *Increase the price and let demand fade away* This could mean that the firm makes good profits on the service while demand lasts.
- *Reduce promotion or even stop it altogether* Again this could increase profitability while demand lasts.

Whichever decision is made, an organization has to consider the timing of such a decision. In determining a time for deletion, the following factors need to be taken into account:

- *Inventory level* Although pure services cannot be inventoried, the tangible elements of the service offer can be. Where these are an important element of a service offer, they should be taken into account in deciding when to delete the service.
- *Notification of consumers* It is generally better for firms to inform consumers that service deletion is imminent. Such a policy at least allows people time to make alternative arrangements and this may also have the added advantage of promoting the firm's 'caring' image. Some announcements of deletion have even had the effect of raising awareness of the service which has helped to build a long-term sustainable demand (e.g. announcement in 1997 of the proposed withdrawal of London–Scotland sleeper trains led to a surge in demand).
- *Resources* Management should move freed-up resources, particularly labour, to other appropriate services as soon as possible. This not only eliminates the

possibility of idle resources and layoffs of manpower but is also an important part of internal marketing which is important for services firms.

- *Legal implications* Service elimination may bring with it legal liabilities. In the case of suppliers, an organization may be committed to take supplies regardless of a deletion strategy (for example a holiday tour operator may be contractually committed to buying aircraft seats for the remainder of a season). In the case of customers, it may not be possible to delete services provided under a long-term contract until that contract comes to an end. This can be particularly important for the financial services sector where mortgages and pension plans usually allow no facility for a unilateral withdrawal of supply by the service producer, even though a pension policy may still have over 30 years to run.

The above implies that firms have a choice in deciding whether a service needs to be deleted from the mix. In fact, a study by Hart (1988) on product deletion in British companies found that deletion decisions were generally forced on management by circumstances beyond its control. Hart noted that by the time managers are contemplating deletion, the circumstances may well be outside management control. She doesn't, however, say that circumstances are unavoidable. In fact, by reading market climate, monitoring quality of their products and assessing the fit between their current offering, the market and future possibilities, managers are afforded greater time to consider, plan and execute the deletion for minimum disruption to revenue.

## Cordless phone service launch ends in a tangle

**Case Study**

In 2000, the UK government held an auction for five new 'third generation' mobile telephone licences. To the astonishment of observers, the auction raised a total of £22 billion, showing a huge act of faith by the phone companies in the new technology. To some observers, the price paid by the companies was excessive and would never be recouped, especially if another new technology came along which satisfied consumers' needs more cost effectively. Others saw the licence as the key to a whole new world of mobile telephony in which the mobile phone would be positioned not just as a device for voice communication, but a vital business and information tool. It may take some time to tell who was right, but lessons can be learnt from the launch of Telepoint services a decade earlier.

In the early stages of mobile phone development in the UK, mobile phones had been positioned as business tools, aimed at the self-employed, travelling sales personnel and business executives, among others who needed to be constantly contactable. The positioning initially adopted by Cellnet and Vodafone had been too expensive and over-specified for casual leisure users.

In January 1989, the government issued licences to four companies – Zonephone (owned by Ferranti); Callpoint (owned by a consortium of Mercury Telecommunications, Motorola and Shaye); Phonepoint (British Telecom, STC, France Telecom, Deutsche Bundespost and Nynex); and Hutchison Telecom – to operate a network of low-cost mobile phones aimed at the mass market. These would allow callers to use a compact

handset to make outgoing calls only, when they were within 150 metres of a base station, these being located in public places such as railway stations, shops and petrol stations.

As in the case of many new markets which suddenly emerge, operators saw advantages of having an early market share lead. Customers who perceived that one network was more readily available than any other would – all other things being equal – be more likely to subscribe to that network. Thus operators saw that a bandwagon effect could be set up – to gain entry to the market at a later stage could become a much more expensive market challenger exercise. With relatively low costs involved in setting up a Telepoint network, three of the four licensed operators rushed into the market, signing up outlets for terminals as well as new customers.

Such was the speed of development that the concept was not rigorously test-marketed. To many, the development was too much product led, with insufficient understanding of buyer behaviour and competitive pressures. Each of the four companies forced through their own technologies, with little inclination or time available to discuss industry standard handsets which could eventually have caused the market to grow at a faster rate and allowed the operators to cut their costs.

Rather than thoroughly testing out customer reaction to Telepoint in a small test market (as French Telecom had done with its Pointel system in Strasbourg prior to its full national launch), the operators sought to develop national coverage overnight. This inevitably led to very patchy coverage, with no outlets in some areas and heavy congestion in a few key sites. There were also the inevitable teething problems in getting the equipment to function correctly.

Worse still for the Telepoint operators, the nature of the competition had been poorly judged. Originally, a major positioning advantage of Telepoint was the removal of the need to find a working telephone kiosk from which to make an outgoing call. In fact, the unreliability of public kiosks on which demand was based receded as British Telecom dramatically improved reliability, as well as increasing their availability at a number of key sites. Competition from Mercury had itself increased the number of kiosks available to users. At the top end of the Telepoint target market, the two established cellular operators had revised their pricing structure which positioned them for a larger and more price-sensitive market.

The final straw for Telepoint operators came with the announcement by the government of its proposal to issue licences for a new generation of personal communications networks (PCNs) – these would have the additional benefit of allowing both incoming and outgoing calls, and would not be tied to a limited base station range. While this in itself might not have put people off buying new Telepoint equipment, it did have the effect of bringing new investment in Telepoint networks to a halt, leaving the existing networks in a state of limbo.

Faced with the apparent failure of their new service development strategies, the Telepoint operators looked for ways of relaunching their services by repositioning their benefits to new target markets. Now that the initial target of street-based outgoing callers had all but disappeared, new ideas were developed. Hutchison Telecom, for instance, combined an outgoing handset with a paging device which would allow business and self-employed people to keep in touch with base. The service was in effect being positioned as a cheap alternative to the two cellular networks, and was eventually superseded by its Orange PCN network. Similarly, the relaunch of

Phonepoint focused on meeting the needs of three key targets – small businesses, mobile professionals and commuters. Furthermore, the company aimed to achieve excellence within the London area – where a network of 2000 base stations was planned – rather than spreading its resources thinly throughout the country. Other targets had been identified for Telepoint technology – office networks, for example, offered the chance for employees within an organization to keep in touch, without the need to be near a wired phone.

Two years after its initial launch, it had been estimated that no more than 5000 subscribers in total had been signed up for Telepoint, or roughly one per base station, instead of the hundreds which were needed for viability. With hindsight, it could be argued that the launch might have been more successful had the service been more rigorously tested and developed before launch and if target markets had been more carefully selected. Moreover, many of the competitors might probably have wished that they had carried out a more rigorous environmental analysis, in which case they might have been less enthusiastic about launching in the first place.

## Case study review questions

**1**  How could the new service development process have been improved so that the costly failure described above was avoided?

**2**  Identify the factors in the marketing environment which affect the new service development process and assess these factors for their predictability.

**3**  How would the launch of Telepoint services differ in a less developed country with a less sophisticated telecommunications infrastructure?

## Chapter summary and linkages to other chapters

In competitive markets, service providers must select a position which builds on their strengths and profitably caters for identified needs of consumers. This chapter has argued that the task of positioning services is more complex than for goods. Positioning of the service provider can be just as important as positioning individual service offers. Most services go through some form of life cycle and service providers should have strategies for developing new services and deleting mature services which are no longer profitable.

An important element of service positioning is based on the configuration of the service offer and service encounter which were discussed in **Chapters 2 and 3**. Positioning must take account of differences in individuals' buying processes and their desire to seek ongoing relationships (**Chapters 4 and 5**). Positioning, new service development and deletion decisions call for adequate information has been covered in the present chapter. The perceived quality of the service offer can affect its position (**Chapter 8**). The marketing mix elements of accessibility, price and promotion (**Chapters 8–11**) help to define a position, while effective employees and management (**Chapters 12 and 14**) are essential for implementing and sustaining it.

## Key terms

Product line 182          Organizational image 185
Product life cycle 191    New service 192

## Chapter review questions

1   Critically discuss the idea that positioning is much more difficult for a services provider than a goods manufacturer.
2   Using examples, discuss the problems that are likely to result from a firm seeking to reposition its service offer.
3   To what extent can the various stages in the New Service Development process be distinguished? To what extent should they be integrated more fully?
4   What possible problems could be encountered by a service firm trying to develop new services?
5   What is the relationship between innovation and profitability? Can a service based firm succeed without being an innovator?
6   With reference to specific examples, examine the practical problems of deleting items from a company's service mix.

## Selected further reading

*The concept of service positioning is developed in the two following papers. The first paper argues that the inseparability of services leads to positioning being more relevant to service providers than individual service offers. The second examines positioning strategies in the retailing of financial services from the perspective of customers and suggests that despite the disappearance of the traditional distinction between UK banks and building societies, customers still tend to see the two as occupying distinct competitive positions.*

Shostack, G. L. (1987) 'Service Positioning Through Structural Change', *Journal of Marketing*, Vol. 51, pp 34–43

Devlin, J. F., C. T. Ennew and M. Mirza (1995) 'Organisational Positioning in Retail Financial Services', *Journal of Marketing Management*, Vol. 11, No. 1, pp 119–32

*For a more general insight into how positioning contributes to a firm's competitive advantage, refer to the following:*

Bharadwaj, S. G., P. Rajan and J. Fahy (1993) 'Sustainable Competitive Advantage in Service Industries: A Conceptual Model and Research Propositions', *Journal of Marketing*, Vol. 57, pp 83–99

Trout, J. and S. Rivkin (1996) *The New Positioning*, McGraw-Hill, New York

*For a general overview of brand development processes, refer to the following:*

Aaker, D. (1996) *Building Strong Brands*, Free Press, New York

De Chernatony, L. and M. McDonald (1998) *Creating Powerful Brands in Consumer, Service and Industrial Markets*, 2nd edition, Butterworth-Heinemann, Oxford

Kapferer, J.-N. (1997) *Strategic Brand Management: Creating and Sustaining Brand Equity Long Term*, 2nd edition, Kogan Page, London

*For an insight into new service development processes, the following articles are useful:*

Easingwood C. J. (1986) 'New Product Development For Service Companies', *Journal of Product Innovation Management*, No. 4

Ekdahl, F., A. Gustafsson and B. Edvardsson (1999) 'Customer-oriented Service Development at SAS', *Managing Service Quality*, Vol. 9, No. 6, pp 344–57

Kelly D. and C. Storey (2000) 'New Service Development: Initiation Strategies', *International Journal of Service Industry Management*, Vol. 11, No. 1, pp 45–65

Lovelock C. H. (1984) 'Developing and Implementing New Services', in *Developing New Services*, American Marketing Association, Chicago, IL

# 8

# Service quality

### Learning objectives

The subject of service quality has aroused considerable recent interest among business people and academics. Of course, buyers have always been concerned with quality, but the increasingly competitive market for many services has led consumers to become more selective in the services they choose. Conceptualizing the quality of services is more complex than for goods and the first aim of this chapter is to review conceptual frameworks for evaluating service quality. Because of the absence of tangible manifestations, measuring service quality can be difficult, and this chapter discusses possible research approaches. Comprehensive models of service quality are discussed and their limitations noted. Understanding just what dimensions of quality are of importance to customers in their evaluation process is not always easy. It is not sufficient for companies to set quality standards in accordance with misguided assumptions of customers' expectations. A further problem in defining service quality lies in the importance which customers often attach to the quality of the service provider as distinct from its service offers – the two cannot be separated as readily as in the case of goods. Finally, issues relating to the setting of quality standards and implementation of quality management are discussed.

## 8.1 Defining service quality

Quality is an extremely difficult concept to define in a few words. At its most basic, quality has been defined as 'conforming to requirements' (Crosby, 1984). This implies that organizations must establish requirements and specifications; once established, the quality goal of the various functions of an organization is to comply strictly with these specifications. However, the questions remain: whose requirements and whose specifications? A second series of definitions therefore state that quality is all about fitness for use (Juran, 1982), a definition based primarily on satisfying customers' needs. These two definitions can be united in the concept of customer perceived quality – quality can only be defined by customers and occurs where an organization supplies goods or services to a specification that satisfies their needs.

Many analyses of service quality have attempted to distinguish between objective measures of quality and measures which are based on the more subjective perceptions of customers. A definition of Swan and Combs (1976) identified two important dimensions of service quality – 'instrumental' quality describes the physical aspects of the service while the 'expressive' dimension relates to the intangible or psychological aspects. A development of this idea by Gronroos (1984) identified 'technical' and 'functional' quality as being the two principle components of quality. **Technical quality** refers to the relatively quantifiable aspects of a service which consumers receive in their interactions with a service firm. Because it can easily be measured by both customer and supplier, it forms an important basis for judging service quality. Examples of technical quality include the waiting time at a supermarket checkout and the reliability of train services. This, however, is not the only element that makes up perceived service quality. Because services involve direct consumer–producer interaction, consumers are also influenced by *how* the technical quality is delivered to them. This is what Gronroos describes as **functional quality** and cannot be measured as objectively as the elements of technical quality (see Mels, Boshoff and Deon, 1997). In the case of the queue at a supermarket checkout, functional quality is influenced by such factors as the environment in which queuing takes place and consumers' perceptions of the manner in which queues are handled by the supermarket's staff. Gronroos also sees an important role for a service firm's corporate image in defining customers' perceptions of quality, with corporate image being based on both technical and functional quality. Figure 8.1 illustrates diagrammatically Gronroos's conceptualization of service quality, as applied to an optician's practice.

If quality is defined as the extent to which a service meets customers' requirements, the problem remains of identifying just what those requirements are. The general absence of easily understood criteria for assessing quality makes articulation of customers' requirements and communication of the quality level on offer much more difficult than is the case for goods. Service quality is a highly abstract construct, in contrast to goods where technical aspects of quality predominate. Many conceptualizations of service quality therefore begin by addressing the abstract expectations that consumers hold in respect of quality. Consumers subsequently judge service quality as the extent to which perceived service delivery matches up to these initial expectations. In this way, a service which is perceived as being of mediocre standard may be considered of high quality when compared against low expectations, but of low quality when assessed against high expectations. Much research remains to be

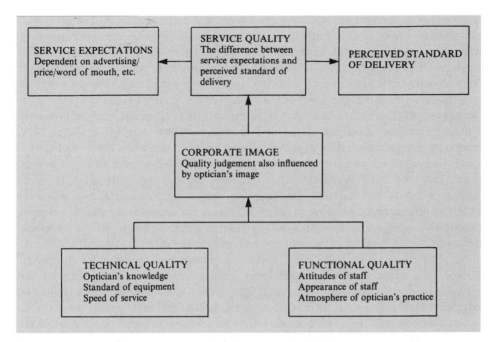

**Figure 8.1**
Consumer perception of technical and functional quality applied to an optician's practice (based on Gronroos, C. (1984) *Strategic Management and Marketing in the Service Sector*, Chartwell-Bratt Ltd)

done to understand the processes by which expectations of service quality are formed and is discussed later in this chapter.

Analysis of service quality is complicated by the fact that production and consumption of a service generally occur simultaneously, with the process of service production often being just as important as the service outcomes. Gronroos (1984) pointed out that a buyer of manufactured goods only encounters the traditional marketing mix variables of a manufacturer, i.e. the product, its price, its distribution and how these are communicated to him or her. Usually, production processes are unseen by consumers and therefore cannot be used as a basis for quality assessment. By contrast, service inseparability results in the production process being an important basis for assessing quality.

A further problem in understanding and managing service quality flows from the intangibility, variability and inseparability of most services which results in a series of unique buyer–seller exchanges with no two services being provided in exactly the same way. It has been noted that intangibility and perceived riskiness affects expectations, and in one study of a long-distance phone service, a bookstore and a pizza shop service, it was concluded that intangibility had some role in service quality expectations (Bebko, 2000 ). Managing customers' expectations can be facilitated by means of managing the risks a consumer perceives when buying a particular service.

### 8.1.1 Quality and satisfaction

A review of the literature will reveal that the terms 'quality' and 'satisfaction' are quite often used interchangeably. While both concepts are related and appear to be merging, there are still gaps in the understanding of the two constructs, their relationship to each other and their antecedents and consequences (Gwynne, Devlin and Ennew, 1998). A distinction has often been made between the two constructs. According to Cronin and Taylor (1992) 'this distinction is important to both managers and researchers alike, because service providers need to know whether their objective should be to have consumers who are satisfied with their performance or to deliver the maximum level of perceived service quality.'

Oliver (1997) takes the view that satisfaction is 'the emotional reaction following a disconfirmation experience'. Getty and Thompson (1994) defined satisfaction as a 'summary psychological state experienced by the consumer when confirmed or disconfirmed expectations exist with respect to a specific service transaction or experience'. Rust and Oliver suggested that customer satisfaction or dissatisfaction – a 'cognitive or affective reaction' – emerges as a response to a single or prolonged set of service encounters. Satisfaction is a 'post consumption' experience which compares perceived quality with expected quality, whereas service quality refers to a global evaluation of a firm's service delivery system (Parasuraman, Zeithaml and Berry, 1985; Anderson and Fornell, 1994). Perceived quality, on the other hand, may be viewed as a global attitudinal judgement associated with the superiority of the service experience over time (Getty and Thompson, 1994). As such, it is dynamic in nature and less transaction specific (Parasuraman, Zeithaml and Berry, 1988).

Not surprisingly there has been considerable debate concerning the nature of the relationship between the constructs of satisfaction and quality. While the majority of research suggests that service quality is a vital antecedent to customer satisfaction (Parasuraman, Zeithaml and Berry, 1985; Cronin and Taylor, 1992) there is now strong evidence to suggest that satisfaction may be a vital antecedent of service quality (Oliver, 1980; Bitner, 1990). Regardless of which view is taken, the relationship between satisfaction and service quality is strong when examined from either direction. Satisfaction affects assessments of service quality and assessments of service quality affects satisfaction (McAlexander, Kaldenberg and Koenig, 1994). In turn both are vital in helping buyers develop their future purchase intentions.

In one of the few empirical studies of the relationship between quality and satisfaction, Iacobucci, Ostrom and Grayson (1995) concluded that the key difference between the two constructs is that quality relates to managerial delivery of the service, while satisfaction reflects customers' experiences with that service. They argued that quality improvements that are not based on customer needs will not lead to improved customer satisfaction.

## 8.2 The service–profit chain

The increased emphasis on customer satisfaction begs the question whether improvements in customer satisfaction lead to improvements in the economic performance of firms (Anderson, Fornell and Lehmann, 1994). Heavy expenditures and importance attached to customer satisfaction measurement suggest that the link between customer satisfaction and economic performance is presumed by companies. Increasing levels of research is going into understanding the nature of the service-profit chain (Figure 8.2).

There is considerable support for a link between improvements in service quality and improvements in financial performance. Grant (1998) reports that the American

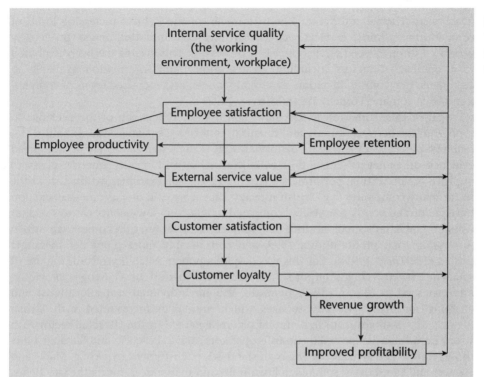

**Figure 8.2**
The service–profit chain (adapted from Heskett *et al.*, 1994)

Customer Satisfaction Index studies found a positive correlation between customer satisfaction and stock market returns. Much of the literature has sought to establish a link between satisfaction and loyalty. Dick and Basu (1994), in a conceptual paper on loyalty viewed satisfaction as an antecedent of relative attitude because, without satisfaction, consumers will not hold a favourable attitude towards a brand as compared to other alternatives available and will therefore not be predisposed to repurchase (Dick and Basu, 1994). The link between customer satisfaction and loyalty has been widely replicated (e.g. Anderson and Fornell, 1994; Fornell *et al.*, 1996). It was noted in Chapter 5 that it can be much more profitable for companies to retain loyal customers than to recruit new ones to replace lapsed customers.

The opposite of satisfaction – dissatisfaction – has been seen as a primary reason for customer defection or discontinuation of purchase (e.g. Anton, 1996). Zeithaml, Berry and Parasuraman (1996) suggested that a customer's relationship with a company is strengthened when a customer makes a favourable assessment about the company's service quality and weakened when a customer makes negative assessments about the company's service quality. They argued that favourable assessment of service quality will lead to favourable behavioural intentions like 'praise for the company' and expressions of preference for the company over other companies. In an earlier study Zeithaml *et al.* had reported a positive relationship between service quality and willingness to pay a premium price and to remain loyal even when prices go up (Zeithaml *et al.*, 1990.

Much of the research into the outcomes of satisfaction has measured behavioural intentions, for example the likelihood of recommending a service or repurchasing it

(Dabholkar, Thorpe and Rentz, 1996). However, in the light of increasing levels of competition in most services markets, behavioural intention based on loyalty generated through good service can easily be broken. This decline has been attributed to a number of factors including greater choice and information available to customers, the 'commoditization' of several services, and increased levels of competition (Anderson and Fornell, 1994; Schriver, 1997)

Against this, some researchers have pointed out that much of the evidence to support a link between quality and financial performance is anecdotal in nature and refuted by analysis of corporate performance. It is suggested that there is widespread evidence of managers' frustration with the inability of quality improvements to improve organizational performance (Grant, 1998). For example, within the airline sector many companies (e.g. British Airways) that score well on customer satisfaction have performed poorly financially, compared to relatively low-quality carriers such as Ryanair. The latter's small, no-frills operation earned over ten times more than British Airways in total profits during 1999, and considerably more profit per passenger carried (*The Times* 1999b). Yet this was despite a poorer reliability record, the use of smaller, less convenient airports (e.g. Prestwick instead of Glasgow), providing minimal services (e.g. no in-flight meals and no individual seat allocations) and charging for many ancillary services which are taken for granted with British Airways (e.g. in-flight drinks). A similar picture emerged in the UK retail sector with strong performance reported by no-frills operators such as Peacocks and Matalan while those retailers perceived as having high standards of customer service (e.g. Marks and Spencer and Sainsbury's) suffered falling profits and share prices during the late 1990s.

In a study by Cronin and Taylor (1992) service quality did not appear to have a significant positive effect on intentions to purchase again. Passikoff (1997) cites a Juran Institute study which indicates that less than a third of top managers of USA's largest corporations believed that their customer satisfaction programmes yield any economic benefit. Anderson, Fornell and Lehmann (1994) expressed the fear that if firms are not able to demonstrate a link between customer satisfaction and economic performance, then firms may abandon the focus on customer satisfaction measurement.

Situational variables determine to a large extent behavioural intentions in response to perceived levels of satisfaction. Customers may be 'captive' and therefore repeat purchasing behaviour is unlikely to be influenced in the short term by levels of satisfaction. Any observed loyalty may be what Dick and Basu have described as 'spurious' loyalty. For many buyers, the psychological cost of switching may be perceived as too high and they may therefore be prepared to tolerate high levels of dissatisfaction before a trigger point is reached and they switch. Individuals' perceptions of equity in service encounters has been shown to influence repeat service purchase (Bolton and Lemon, 1999).

Developments in information technology are offering new insights into the link between quality and financial performance. Large multiple outlet service organizations are increasingly able to experiment with elements of service quality in test sites and to judge economic performance over time. A fast-food restaurant, for example, may implement a new staff payment system or training programme in a number of 'experimental' sites and will be able to identify changes in performance relative to other 'control' branches. Some service providers have disaggregated their information even further by linking service quality questionnaires to features of the service which a respondent actually received. In this way, individual employees or groups of employees can be linked to measures of quality. While information technology is opening up new possibilities for correlating data about inputs and perceived outcomes, the problem of analysing cross-sectional data remains. It is very difficult within a research framework to isolate all of the contributors to customers' perceptions of quality except those which the researcher is interested in.

## 8.3 Researching service quality

The development of reliable, easy-to-use measures of service quality represents a key aspect of consumer behaviour and services marketing research. Indeed, an integral part of any organization's attempt to instil a 'quality culture' is a commitment to a process of 'continuous improvement' (Witt and Muhlemann, 1995). To support this a systematic approach to quality measurement is needed. This is especially true of 'pure' services organizations, as unlike their counterparts in the manufacturing sector they have fewer objective measures of quality by which to judge their production (Hudson and Sheppard, 1998). Cronin and Taylor (1992) concur with this viewpoint stating that managers need to know 'what aspects of a particular service best define its quality'. In turn, this should enable the organization to take up a competitive position based upon its ability to deliver what customers expect as opposed to what the organization thinks that customers expect. A clear, sustained and continuous quality improvement is not possible without some indication of quality performance. To know the real effect of changes over time, managers need measures to compare the quality performance of the service (Edvardsson, Thomasson and Ovretveit, 1994).

Ramaswamy (1996) identified three different sets of measures that a company must be concerned with:

1 Service performance measures that are primarily internally focused and evaluate the current performance of the service and ensure that it is continuing to reliably meet the design specifications.
2 Customer measures, on the other hand, which are both internally and externally focused aimed at assessing the impact of the service performance on customers.
3 Financial measures, which are indicators of the financial health of the organization.

Naturally the correlation between financial and customer measures will determine the revenue generating potential of the service, while the relationship between service performance measures and customer measures will give some indication as to how the service is performing in customers' eyes. In turn, this will have a direct bearing on a company's financial performance and overall market share.

There is clear evidence that the volume of research into service quality measurement is increasing markedly. *Inside Research*, a marketing research industry newsletter, estimated that the combined US and European customer satisfaction measurement expenditure was more than US$372 million in 1997 and expenditure has been growing at the rate of about 20% every year (*Inside Research*, 1998). These estimates exclude customer satisfaction measurement carried on in-house or those conducted by smaller firms.

The work of Zeithaml, Parasuraman and Berry (1990) suggests that one of the prime causes of poor performance by service firms is not knowing what their customers expect. Many organizations are keen to provide service quality but fall short simply because they do not have an accurate understanding of what customers expect from the company. The absence of well-defined tangible cues makes this understanding much more difficult than it would be in the case of goods. Marketing research is a means of eliciting information about customers' expectations and perceptions of services. In this respect, services organizations should ask the following key questions:

- What do customers consider the important features of the service to be?
- What level of these features do they expect?
- How is service delivery perceived by customers?

A number of methods for researching customers' expectations and perceptions are available which are examined below. However, as a set of general principles for the effective measurement of service quality, Zeithaml *et al.* stress the need for a marketing research programme to be:

1  *Varied*  Every research method has its limitations and in order to overcome this and to achieve a comprehensive insight into a problem, a combination of qualitative and quantitative research techniques should be used.
2  *Ongoing*  The expectations and perceptions of customers are constantly changing as is the nature of the service offer provided by companies and their competitors. It is therefore important that a service research process is administered on a continuous basis so that any changes can be picked up quickly and acted upon if necessary.
3  *Undertaken with employees*  The closeness of staff to customers within the services sector makes it important that they are asked about problems and possible improvements as well as their personal motivations and requirements.
4  *Shared with employees*  Employees' performance in delivering service quality may be improved if they are made aware of the results of studies of customer expectations, complaint analysis, etc.

### 8.3.1  Regular customer surveys

The incidence of surveys into the level of satisfaction that customers have experienced from service providers is increasing throughout the services sector. The increasing range of competing services available and customers' growing awareness of the fact that they are in receipt of a service for which they pay a price – whether directly or through taxation – has led them to expect to be consulted and to express an opinion about the level of satisfaction provided. Today, members of the public are in constant receipt of literature from a wide range of service providers asking for comments on the quality of service that they have received. It is probably true to say that most large service providers in both the private and public sectors have jumped on this quality bandwagon, although it is often questionable whether the most appropriate methods are employed to gather the information. Typical applications

**Please take a few seconds to rate your experience with us.
Just tick the appropriate oval. Either pen or pencil is fine.**

PURPOSE OF VISIT: ○ BUSINESS ○ PLEASURE ○ CONFERENCE/GROUP GENDER: M ○ F ○

HOW DID YOU HEAR ABOUT JURYS INNS?

○ COMPANY ○ COLLEAGUE ○ MEDIA ○ TRAVEL AGENT ○ OTHER

NATIONALITY: (PLEASE SPECIFY) _____

WHO MADE THE RESERVATION FOR YOU?

○ YOU ○ COMPANY ○ TRAVEL AGENT ○ OTHER

WITH WHOM DID YOU MAKE THE RESERVATION (If reservation was made personally)?

○ THE HOTEL DIRECTLY ○ JURYS CENTRAL RESERVATIONS

| HOW SATISFIED WERE YOU WITH THE RESERVATION SERVICE? | LOW | | MEDIUM | | HIGH |
|---|---|---|---|---|---|
| | ○ | ○ | ○ | ○ | ○ |

| LEVEL OF SATISFACTION | LOW | | MEDIUM | | HIGH |
|---|---|---|---|---|---|
| | 1 | 2 | 3 | 4 | 5 |
| Access to the car park/parking facilities | ○ | ○ | ○ | ○ | ○ |
| Overall quality of the hotel | ○ | ○ | ○ | ○ | ○ |
| Overall hotel value for money | ○ | ○ | ○ | ○ | ○ |
| Likelihood you would return | ○ | ○ | ○ | ○ | ○ |
| Hotel safety and security | ○ | ○ | ○ | ○ | ○ |

**Please share any additional comments**

_____
_____
_____

**Date of stay:** _____ **Room number:** _____

**Figure 8.3**
Jurys Inns uses this comment card to gather feedback from its guests effectively and efficiently. As well as providing data about customers' profiles, the card uses a combination of structured and unstructured approaches to assess guests' perceptions of service quality (reproduced with permission of Jurys Inns)

include filling in a questionnaire on the plane after a holiday or being asked by the local council to fill in a card headed Customer Service Enquiry. Such surveys usually ask recipients to relate any complaints that they may have about the services provided and any comments/suggestions for improving them. The assumption that most people make is that data from such surveys will be used to take corrective action where expectations are not reached. It must, however, be stated that many of these surveys are of dubious quality and therefore of limited value – many of them smack of a lip service approach to marketing, research and the issue of quality service. More rigorous and comprehensive expectation and perception studies are discussed later in this chapter.

### 8.3.2 Customer panels

These can provide a continuous source of information on customer expectations. Groups of customers, who are generally frequent users, are brought together by a company on a regular basis to study their opinions about the quality of service provided. On other occasions, they may be employed to monitor the introduction of a new or revised service – for example a panel could be brought together by a building society following the experimental introduction of a new branch design format.

The use of continuous panels can offer organizations a means of anticipating problems and may act as an early warning system for emerging issues of importance. Retailers have been involved in the operation of continuous panels to monitor their level of service provision as well as letting panels contribute to new product development research. User groups also have an important part to play in many of the UK's recently privatized industries such as gas, water, electricity and telecommunications. However, the validity of this research method is quite dependent on how well the panel represents consumers as a whole. Careful selection should therefore be undertaken to ensure that the panel possesses the same social/economic/demographic/frequency of use, etc., characteristics as the population of customers being analysed. There has been a suggestion that the number of people prepared to become members of panels is not rising as quickly as firms' appetite for information. The result has been the emergence of 'professional' panel members who may not be representative of service users as a whole.

### 8.3.3 Transaction analysis

An increasingly popular method of evaluative research involves tracking the satisfaction of individuals with particular transactions that they have recently been involved in. This type of research enables management to judge current performance, particularly customers' satisfaction with the contact personnel with whom they have interacted, as well as their overall satisfaction with the service.

The research effort normally involves a mail-out questionnaire survey to individual customers immediately after a transaction has been completed. A wide range of UK services organizations are now using this approach. For example, the Automobile Association surveys customers who have recently been served by its breakdown service and many building societies invite customers who have just used their mortgage services to express their views on the service received via a structured questionnaire. An additional benefit of this research is its capability to associate service quality performance with individual contact personnel and link it to reward systems.

### 8.3.4 Perception surveys

These investigations use a combination of qualitative and quantitative research methods. Many professional services organizations have employed such studies in order to develop future marketing strategies. Their aim is to achieve a better understanding of how customers view an organization, in other words, to help the firm see itself as clients see it. The initial qualitative stages of a study involve researchers in identifying the attitudes of clients (past, present and future) towards the firm as well as how the firm is perceived by the community at large (this may involve eliciting information from journalists, intermediaries and even competitors). Group discussions and/or in-depth interviews are the vehicles used for assessing the perceptions of people at this stage. In the quantitative phase of a survey, clients are asked to judge the company's performance using a battery of attitude statements. Perception studies often include an analysis of the perceptions of a firm's employees.

### 8.3.5 Mystery customers

The use of 'mystery customers' is a method of auditing the standard of service provision, particularly the staff involvement in such provision. A major difficulty in ensuring service quality is overcoming the non-conformance of staff with performance guidelines. This so called service-performance gap is the result of employees being unable and/or unwilling to perform the service at the desired level. An important function of mystery customer surveys is therefore to monitor the extent to which specified quality standards are actually being met by staff.

This method of researching actual service provision involves the use of trained assessors who visit service organizations and report back their observations. Audits tend to be tailored to the specific needs of a company and focus on an issue that it wishes to evaluate. The format of the enquiry is therefore something which is determined jointly by the client and research organization.

The constructive nature of this research technique has to be stressed, as the mystery customer can quite easily be mistaken by staff as an undercover agent spying on them on behalf of the management. In particular, if the techniques are applied correctly, they can allow management to know what is really happening at the sharp end of their business. To be effective, mystery shopping surveys need to be undertaken independently, should be objective and must be consistent. The training of assessors is critical to the effective use of this research method and should include, for example, training in observation techniques which allow them to distinguish between a greeting and an acknowledgement.

Would you want a 'mystery shopper' trying to measure your performance while you are working? They're not spies, but assessors, insists the market research industry. In fact, mystery shoppers are now highly trained, professional assessors. In the early days of mystery shopping, subjective questions were the norm. Today,

80–90% of mystery shopping questionnaires are objective, for example questions for a mystery shopper survey of a pub include: 'How long was it before I was served?; Was I served in turn?; Was I offered a clean glass when re-ordering?' Rather than being seen as sneaky spying, companies should place a lot of importance on involving staff in the whole measurement process. Not only do staff provide useful insights into the service, if handled correctly they can feel a sense of ownership of the programme.

### 8.3.6 Analysis of complaints

Dissatisfaction of customers is most clearly voiced through the complaints that they make about service provision. For many companies, this may be the sole method of keeping in touch with customers. Complaints can be made directly to the provider or perhaps indirectly through an intermediary or a watchdog body. Complaints by customers, referring to instances of what they consider poor-quality service may, if treated constructively, provide a rich source of data on which to base policies for improving service quality. However, customer complaints are at best an inadequate source of information. Most customers don't bother to complain, remain dissatisfied and tell others about their dissatisfaction. Others simply change to another supplier and do not offer potentially valuable information to the service provider about what factors were wrong which caused them to leave (although this could, of course, be researched by the service provider).

In truly market-oriented organizations, complaints analysis can form a useful pointer to where the process of service delivery is breaking down. As part of an overall programme for keeping in touch with customers, the analysis of complaints can have an important role to play. The continuous tracking of complaints is a relatively inexpensive source of data which enables a company to review the major concerns of customers on an ongoing basis and hopefully rectify any evident problems. In addition, the receipt of complaints by the firm enables staff to enter into direct contact with customers and provides an opportunity to interact with them over their matters of concern. As well as eliciting customers' views on these issues in particular, complainants can also contribute views about customer service in general. Many companies have gone to great lengths to make it easy for customers to complain, for example by creating Freephone telephone lines and making comment cards readily available.

How far should a company go in encouraging its customers to complain? Of course, cultures differ greatly in their willingness to complain about bad service. The traditional reserve of the British may seem like a gift to the average duty manager of a restaurant who doesn't have to put up with the rough ride which more demanding

Australian or American customers may give. In principle, the idea of collecting feedback from customers is good because of the opportunities which it gives to put things right, both immediately in terms of the complainant's satisfaction and strategically in terms of designing more effective processes. But could this lead to a culture among some clients of always complaining, just to see what they can get back? Many tour operators can recount stories of customers who routinely submit complaints about trivial matters, in an effort to get some compensation which will be put towards the cost of their next holiday. How does a company strike a balance between listening to customer complaints and keeping its costs of compensation down, especially when it is positioning itself as a low-cost supplier and operating in an environment where things are quite likely to go wrong?

### 8.3.7 Employee research

Research undertaken among employees can enable their views about the way that services are provided and their perceptions of how they are received by customers to be taken into account. Data gathered from staff training seminars and development exercises, feedback from **Quality circles**, job appraisal and performance evaluation reports, etc., can all provide valuable information for planning quality service provision. One way in which formal feedback from staff can be built into a systematic research programme is the operation of a staff suggestion scheme. The proposals which staff may make about how services could be provided more efficiently and/or effectively certainly do have an important role to play in improving service quality.

Research into employees' needs can also allow identification of policies which improve their motivation to deliver a high quality of service. Many of the techniques employed to elicit the views of employees as internal customers are in principle the same as those used in studies of external customers. Interviews and focus groups may be used in the collection of qualitative data on employee needs, wants, motivations and attitudes towards working conditions, benefits and policies. This can be followed up with appropriate quantitative analysis, such as the SERVQUAL methodology (see below) which it is suggested can be equally applied to internal employee studies.

In Chapter 12, the issue of obtaining involvement and participation of the workforce is considered in some detail. In this respect, involving employees in the research process and its findings, for example by using them to gather data, showing them videotapes of group discussions and interviews with customers and circulating them with the findings of research reports, can do a lot for improving their understanding of service quality issues throughout their organization. In high-contact, people-intensive service sectors, the importance of employees as sources of information about customers' perceptions of service quality cannot be over-emphasized. There are many barriers to the flow of information from employees to managers, especially in organizations where there is no culture of listening to staff. Where there are clearly identified means of listening, and for acting on the results, a shared commitment to improving quality can greatly improve customers' perceptions.

### 8.3.8  Benchmarking studies

The nature of customers' quality expectations in other similar service industries can be a useful source of information for managers. It is often apparent that customer needs may be similar between different industries, even though the service product on offer is ostensibly quite different. Many common dimensions cut across the boundaries of industries and apply to services in general – for example courteous and competent staff, a pleasant environment, and helpfulness, to name but a few. It can therefore be beneficial to investigate the nature of service provision in closely related service areas, and draw upon the findings of any research that has been made available. In particular, it is worth while investigating what is known in those services sectors that have a good track record of analysing and responding to customers' needs and identifying whether it is applicable to an industry that has only recently adopted a customer-led approach. For example, it is possible to learn a lot about certain aspects of hospital service from what hotel and catering establishments have been researching and practising for some considerable time. Continuing with this theme, many services organizations that have been operating outside the private marketplace for many years can benefit from an understanding of the operations of their counterparts in other countries that have openly marketed their services in a freely competitive market. In this way, managers within the UK National Health Service may learn a lot about customer care by examining health services in the USA.

The term **benchmarking** is frequently used to describe the process by which companies set standards for themselves, based on a study of best practice elsewhere. Best practice could be defined in terms of firms within the same sector, or completely different sectors which share similar processes (e.g. benchmarks for waiting time in a bank could be based on benchmarks established within the convenience retail sector).

Benchmarking can be undertaken at a number of levels, based on what is compared and what the comparison is being made against:

- *Performance benchmarking*  This is essentially based on outcome measures (e.g. throughput per hour, profit per customer).
- *Process benchmarking*  For example, the efficiency and effectiveness of customer handling procedures.
- *Strategic benchmarking*  For example, comparing the integrity of a company's strategic plan with best practice in the industry.
- *Internal benchmarking*  This involves comparing internal processes and structures.
- *Competitive benchmarking*  This may be with respect to market share, selling price, etc.
- *Functional benchmarking*  Sometimes the task will be to compare the performance of a company's functions (e.g. advertising or sales) with best practice.

Benchmarking involves a five-step continuous process: plan the study; form the benchmarking team; identify potential benchmarking partners; collect and analyse the information; and adapt and improve. While benchmarking produces a standard against which improvement can be made, these improvements are continuous and benchmarks can go out of date very quickly.

### 8.3.9  Intermediary research

It has already been noted that services intermediaries often perform a valuable function in the process of service delivery, performing their role in quite a different manner to goods intermediaries. Research into intermediaries focuses on two principal concerns:

- Firstly, where intermediaries form an important part of a service delivery process, the quality perceived by customers is to a large extent determined by the performance of intermediaries. In this way, the perceived quality of an airline may be tarnished if its ticket agents are perceived as being slow or unhelpful to customers. Research through such techniques as mystery customer surveys can be used to monitor the standard of quality delivered by intermediaries.
- Secondly, intermediaries as co-producers of a service are further down the channel of distribution and hence closer to customers. They are therefore in a position to provide valuable feedback to the **service principal** about consumers' expectations and perceptions. As well as conducting structured research investigations of intermediaries, many services principals find it possible to learn more about the needs and expectations of their final customers during the process of providing intermediary support services such as training.

## 8.4  Comprehensive expectation and perception studies

Quality is clearly a complex concept which cannot satisfactorily be measured by a series of isolated *ad hoc* studies. This, and the increasing importance of quality as a means of gaining competitive advantage, has seen the emergence of comprehensive programmes to research **customers' expectations** and perceptions of service quality. Pre-eminent among these comprehensive studies is the work of Berry, Parasuraman and Zeithaml, who have been strong advocates of the need for services organizations to learn more about their customers through a rigorous marketing research oriented approach which focuses on the expectations and perceptions of customers. Their research offers a number of insights into the marketing of services which should benefit practitioners throughout the services sector. Their research concentrates on the belief that service quality is measurable, although due to intangibility it may be more difficult to measure than goods quality. It tackles two basic dimensions of service provision – outcomes and processes – and supplements this with a number of additional dimensions of service quality which transcend these two basic dimensions. Furthermore, they make the point that the only factors that are relevant in determining service quality are those that customers perceive as being important. Only customers judge quality – all other judgements are considered to be essentially irrelevant. They set out to determine what customers expect from services and what the characteristics are which define these services. (Effectively, that is to determine what is the service in the mind of the customer?) A service is deemed to be of high quality when consumers' expectations are confirmed by subsequent service delivery. Because of the emphasis on differences between

expectations and perceptions, this type of model is often referred to as a disconfirmation model. Berry, Parasuraman and Zeithaml developed an instrument for
measuring customers' perceptions of service quality compared to their expectations.
Their findings have evolved from a set of qualitative marketing research procedures
culminating in the quantitative technique for measuring service quality which is
known as SERVQUAL.

### 8.4.1  The SERVQUAL methodology

The SERVQUAL technique can be used by companies to better understand the
expectations and perceptions of their customers. It is applicable across a broad
range of services industries and can be easily modified to take account of the
specific requirements of a company. In effect it provides a skeleton for an investiga-
tory instrument which can be adapted or added to as needed.

SERVQUAL is based upon a generic 22-item questionnaire designed to cover five
broad dimensions of service quality which the research team consolidated from its
original qualitative investigations. The five dimensions covered, with some description of each and the respective numbers of statements associated with them are as
follows:

| *Dimension* | *Statements* |
|---|---|
| • Tangibles (appearance of physical elements) | 1 to 4 |
| • Reliability (dependability, accurate performance) | 5 to 9 |
| • Responsiveness (promptness and helpfulness) | 10 to 13 |
| • Assurance (competence, courtesy, credibility, and security) | 14 to 17 |
| • Empathy (easy access, good communications, and customer understanding) | 18 to 22 |

Customers are asked to self-complete the 22 statements relating to their expectations
and a perceptions section consisting of a matching set of company-specific statements about service delivery. They are asked to score in each instance, on a Likert
scale from 1 (strongly agree) to 7 (strongly disagree), whether or not they agree with
each statement. In addition, the survey asks for respondents' evaluation of the
relative importance they attach to each of the dimensions of quality, any
comments that they wish to make about their experiences of the service, and their
overall impression of it. Customers are also asked for supplementary demographic
data. The contents of a typical questionnaire are shown in Figure 8.4.

To measure the level of customer satisfaction for a service provided by a particular
company, the results for perceptions and expectations need to be calculated for each
customer. From this, measures of service quality can be derived quite simply by sub-
tracting expectation scores from perception scores, either unweighted, or weighted to
take into consideration the relative importance of each dimension of quality, or the
relative importance of different customer groups. The outcome from a one-off study is
a measure that tells the company whether its customers' expectations are exceeded or
not.

Beyond this simple analysis, SERVQUAL results can be used to identify which
components or facets of a service the company is particularly good or bad at. It can
be used to monitor service quality over time, to compare performance with that of

**Please complete Part A by indicating your expectations of hotels in general. Then complete Part B indicating your perceptions of this hotel in particular. Please answer on a scale from 1 (strongly disagree with the statement) to 7 (strongly agree).**

**[PART A]**

|  | Strongly Disagree | | Strongly Agree |
|---|---|---|---|

(1) An excellent hotel will have modern looking equipment e.g. dining facility; bar facility, crockery, cutlery, etc.　　1...2...3...4...5...6...7

(2) The physical facilities, e.g. buildings, signs, dining room decor, lighting, carpet etc., at an excellent hotel will be visually appealing　　1...2...3...4...5...6...7

(3) Staff at an excellent hotel will appear neat, e.g. uniform, grooming etc.　　1...2...3...4...5...6...7

(4) Materials associated with the service, e.g. pamphlets, statements, table wine, serviettes will be visually appealing in an excellent hotel　　1...2...3...4...5...6...7

(5) When an excellent hotel promises to do something by a certain time, it will do so　　1...2...3...4...5...6...7

(6) When patrons have a problem, an excellent hotel will show genuine interest in solving it, e.g. an error in a bill　　1...2...3...4...5...6...7

(7) An excellent hotel will perform service right the first time　　1...2...3...4...5...6...7

(8) An excellent hotel will provide its services at the time it promises to do so　　1...2...3...4...5...6...7

(9) An excellent hotel will insist on error-free service　　1...2...3...4...5...6...7

(10) Staff at an excellent hotel will tell patrons exactly when services will be performed　　1...2...3...4...5...6...7

(11) Staff at an excellent hotel will give prompt service to patrons　　1...2...3...4...5...6...7

(12) Staff at an excellent hotel will always be willing to help patrons　　1...2...3...4...5...6...7

(13) Staff at an excellent hotel will never be too busy to respond　　1...2...3...4...5...6...7

(14) The behaviour of staff at an excellent hotel will instil confidence in patrons　　1...2...3...4...5...6...7

(15) Patrons of an excellent hotel will feel safe in their transactions　　1...2...3...4...5...6...7

(16) Staff at an excellent hotel will be consistently courteous with patrons　　1...2...3...4...5...6...7

(17) Staff at an excellent hotel will have the knowledge to answer patrons' requests　　1...2...3...4...5...6...7

(18) Staff at an excellent hotel will give patrons individualized attention　　1...2...3...4...5...6...7

(19) An excellent hotel will have opening hours convenient to all of its patrons　　1...2...3...4...5...6...7

**Figure 8.4**

A typical application of the SERVQUAL survey questionnaire, applied here to the hotel sector (based on Gabbie, O. and M. O'Neill (1997) 'SERVQUAL and the Northern Ireland Hotel Sector: A Comparative Study', *Managing Service Quality*, Vol. 7, No. 1, pp 43–9)

**Figure 8.4**
(*contd*)

| | Strongly Disagree | | | | | | Strongly Agree |
|---|---|---|---|---|---|---|---|

(20) An excellent hotel will have staff who give its patrons personal attention — 1...2...3...4...5...6...7

(21) An excellent hotel will have the patrons' best interests at heart — 1...2...3...4...5...6...7

(22) The staff of an excellent hotel will understand the specific needs of their patrons — 1...2...3...4...5...6...7

**[PART B]**

| | Strongly Disagree | | | | | | Strongly Agree |
|---|---|---|---|---|---|---|---|

(1) The hotel has modern looking equipment — 1...2...3...4...5...6...7

(2) The physical facilities at the local hotel are visually appealing — 1...2...3...4...5...6...7

(3) Staff at the hotel appear neat — 1...2...3...4...5...6...7

(4) Materials associated with the service are visually appealing — 1...2...3...4...5...6...7

(5) When the hotel promised to do something by a certain time, it did it — 1...2...3...4...5...6...7

(6) When patrons have problems, the hotel shows a genuine interest in solving them — 1...2...3...4...5...6...7

(7) The hotel performs the service right the first time — 1...2...3...4...5...6...7

(8) The hotel provides its services at the time it promises to do so — 1...2...3...4...5...6...7

(9) The hotel insists on error-free service — 1...2...3...4...5...6...7

(10) Staff at the hotel were able to tell patrons exactly when services would be performed — 1...2...3...4...5...6...7

(11) Staff at the hotel give prompt service to the patrons — 1...2...3...4...5...6...7

(12) Staff at the hotel are always willing to help patrons — 1...2...3...4...5...6...7

(13) Staff of the hotel are never too busy to respond to patrons — 1...2...3...4...5...6...7

(14) Behaviour of staff at the hotel instil patrons with confidence — 1...2...3...4...5...6...7

(15) Patrons of the hotel feel safe in their transactions — 1...2...3...4...5...6...7

(16) Staff of the hotel are consistently courteous with patrons — 1...2...3...4...5...6...7

(17) Staff of the hotel have the knowledge to answer patrons — 1...2...3...4...5...6...7

(18) The hotel gives patrons individualized attention — 1...2...3...4...5...6...7

(19) The hotel has opening hours convenient to all of its patrons — 1...2...3...4...5...6...7

(20) The hotel has staff who give its patrons personalized attention — 1...2...3...4...5...6...7

(21) The hotel has the patrons' best interests at heart — 1...2...3...4...5...6...7

(22) The staff of the hotel understand the specific needs of their patrons — 1...2...3...4...5...6...7

competitors, or to measure customer satisfaction with a particular service industry generally.

An organization or industry group can use the information collected in this way to improve its position by acting upon the results and seeking to surpass customers' expectations on a continuous basis. Additionally, the expectations–perceptions results, along with the demographic data, may facilitate effective customer segmentation.

It is important that service providers decide upon a target quality of service level and then communicate the level of service on offer to both consumers and employees. This allows employees to know what is expected of them and customers will have an idea of the level of service they can expect to find.

The SERVQUAL methodology highlights the difficulties in ensuring high quality of service for all customers in all situations. More specifically, it identifies five gaps where there may be a shortfall between expectation of service level and perception of actual service delivery.

*Gap 1: Gap between consumer expectations and management perception*  Management may think that it knows what consumers expect and proceed to deliver this when in fact consumers may expect something quite different.

*Gap 2: Gap between management perception and service quality specification*  Management may not set quality specifications or may not set them clearly. Alternatively, management may set clear quality specifications but these may not be achievable.

*Gap 3: Gap between service quality specifications and service delivery*  Unforeseen problems or poor management can lead to a service provider failing to meet service quality specifications. This may be due to human error but also mechanical breakdown of facilitating or support goods.

*Gap 4: Gap between service delivery and external communications*  There may be dissatisfaction with a service due to the excessively heightened expectations developed through the service provider's communications efforts. Dissatisfaction tends to occur where actual delivery does not meet up to expectations held out in a company's communications.

*Gap 5: Gap between perceived service and expected service*  This gap occurs as a result of one or more of the previous gaps. The way in which customers perceive actual service delivery does not match up with their initial expectations.

The five gaps are illustrated in Figure 8.5 where a hypothetical application to a restaurant is shown.

The gaps model is useful as it allows management to make an analytical assessment of the causes of poor service quality. If the first gaps are great, the task of bridging the subsequent gaps becomes greater, and indeed it could be said that in such circumstances quality service can only be achieved by good luck rather than good management.

Much attention has been given to the processes by which customers' expectations of service quality are formed. Two main standards of expectations emerge. One standard represents the expectation as a *prediction* of future events (Asubonteng,

**Figure 8.5**
Sources of divergence between service quality expectation and delivery (modified from Parasuraman, A., V.A. Zeithaml and L.L. Berry (1985) 'A Conceptual Model of Service Quality and its Implications for Future Research', *Journal of Marketing*, Fall.

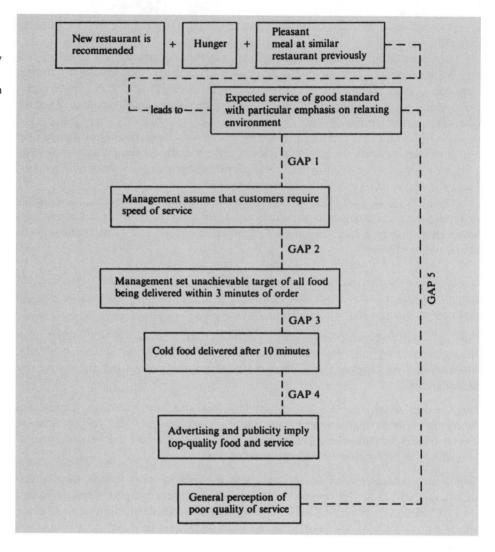

McCleary and Swan, 1996). This is the standard typically used in the satisfaction literature. The other standard is a normative expectation of future events, operationalized as either desired or ideal expectations. This is the standard typically used in the service quality literature (Parasuraman, Zeithaml and Berry, 1988).

Zeithaml, Berry and Parasuraman (1993) have proposed that three levels of expectations can be defined against which quality is assessed:

- The *desired* level of service, reflecting what the customer wants.
- The *adequate* service level, defined as the standard that customers are willing to accept.
- The *predicted* service level – that which they believe is most likely to actually occur.

This has led to the idea that *zones of tolerance* may exist in consumers' perceptions of

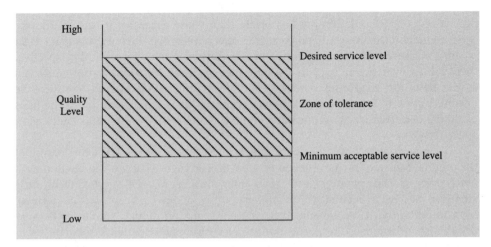

**Figure 8.6**
Consumers' zones of
tolerance for service
quality

service quality. If perceptions fall below the desired level of service, this may still be acceptable as long as it does not fall below expectations based on a minimum acceptable level of service. In other words, rather than a service either meeting or failing a consumers' quality expectations, there is an intermediate zone of tolerance (Figure 8.6).

## 8.4.2 Limitations of the SERVQUAL methodology

Disconfirmation models of service quality have been challenged on a number of grounds. One stream of objections holds that absolute measures of attitudes provide a more appropriate measure of quality than explanations based on disconfirmation models (Cronin and Taylor, 1992). Researchers have asked whether the calculated difference scores (the difference between expectations and evaluation) are appropriate from a measurement and theoretical perspective. Invariably, customers' expectations are measured after consumption of a service, at the same time as they are asked about their perceptions of a service. Shouldn't expectations be based on a respondent's state of mind before consumption, free of influence from actual consumption? There has been debate about whether it is practical to ask consumers about their expectations of a service immediately before consumption and their perceptions of performance immediately after. It has also been suggested that expectations may not exist or be clear enough in respondents' minds to act as a benchmark against which perceptions are assessed (Iacobucci, Grayson and Omstrom, 1994). Furthermore, expectations are only formed as a result of previous service encounters, that is, perceptions feed directly into expectations (Kahneman and Miller, 1986).

From a measurement perspective, there are three psychometric problems associated with the use of difference scores: reliability, discriminant validity and variance restriction problems. A study by Brown, Churchill and Peter (1993) found evidence that these psychometric problems indeed arise with the use of SERVQUAL; they recommend instead use of non-difference score measures which display better discriminant and nomological validity. However, Parasuraman, Zeithaml and Berry (1993) respond by arguing that the alleged psychometric deficiencies of the difference-score formulation are less severe than those suggested by critics. Despite their argument that the difference scores offer researchers better diagnostics than separate measurement of perceptions and expectations, from a theoretical perspective, there is little evidence to support the relevance of the expectations–performance gap as the basis for measuring service quality (Carman, 1990). Instead, considerable research supports a more straightforward approach of assessing quality on the basis of simple performance-based measures (Bolton and Drew, 1991; Cronin and Taylor, 1992, 1994).

There have been numerous criticisms of SERVQUAL for the inductive nature of the original research in that it failed to draw on the theory base in the disciplines of psychology, social sciences and economics (Anderson, 1982). Relatively little attention has been devoted to an understanding of how perceptions are formed. Most importantly, it can be argued that disconfirmation models are flawed because *when* a respondent gives a response to their perception of service delivery can be just as important as the actual recorded score, or the level of expectations against which perceptions are compared. For example, a person may have a very negative attitude towards a haircut immediately after leaving a hairdresser, but their perceptions of the haircut may become more favourable over time as they get used to it (O'Neill, Palmer and Beggs, 1998). It could be argued that in terms of understanding behavioural intention, it is the later measure of perceptions which is most useful to management.

### 8.4.3  SERVPERF

Problems with disconfirmation models have led to the development and application of a more direct form of measurement technique in the form of SERVPERF. Like SERVQUAL this approach requires the customer to rate a provider's performance extending from (1) strongly disagree to (5) strongly agree. Unlike SERVQUAL, however, it does not seek to estimate difference scores and is a one-off set of questions addressing post-consumption perceptions only. The instrument requires the consumer to rate only the performance of a particular service encounter. This eliminates the need to measure expectations on the grounds that customer expectations change when they experience a service and the inclusion of an expectations measure reduces the content and discriminant validity of the measures (Cronin and Taylor, 1992; McAlexander, Kaldenburg and Koenig, 1994). The model argues against the use of expectations because an accurate expectations measure can only be obtained prior to the service encounter. As such it is an absolute rating of customer attitudes towards service quality. A further study by the Boulding Group (Boulding *et al.*, 1993) of which Zeithaml herself is a member concluded that service quality should only be measured via a 'perceptions-statements instrument'.

Studies conducted using this performance-based measure found that SERVPERF explained more of the variance in an overall measure of service quality than did SERVQUAL. Cronin and Taylor (1994) acknowledge that it is possible for researchers to infer consumers' disconfirmation through arithmetic means (the P – E gap) but that 'consumer perceptions, not calculations, govern behaviour'. This approach also overcomes some of the problems raised regarding SERVQUAL, namely: raising expectations, administration of the two parts of the questionnaire and the statistical properties of difference scores (Hope and Muhlemann, 1997). Taking a single measure of service performance is seen to circumvent all of these issues.

## 8.5 Setting quality standards

A precise specification of service standards serves a valuable function in communicating the standard of quality which consumers can expect to receive. It also serves to communicate the standards which are expected of employees. While the general manner in which an organization goes about promoting itself may give a general impression as to what level of quality it seeks to deliver, more specific standards can be stated in a number of ways which are considered below.

- At its most basic, an organization can rely on its terms of business as a basis for determining the level of service to be delivered to customers. These generally act to protect customers against excessively poor service rather than being used to proactively promote high standards of excellence. The booking conditions of tour operators, for example, make very few promises about service quality, other than offers of compensation if delays exceed a specified standard or if accommodation arrangements are changed at short notice.

- Generally worded **customer charters** go beyond the minimum levels of business terms by stating in a general manner the standards of performance which the organization aims to achieve in its dealings with customers. In this way, banks publish charters which specify in general terms the manner in which accounts will be conducted and complaints handled. NatWest Bank's Code of Practice for Business Banking, for example, includes general promises to inform customers in writing of any special conditions attached to loans, to discuss the price to be charged for any special services and to investigate any dissatisfaction with service through a formalized complaints procedure.

- Specific guarantees of service performance are sometimes offered, especially in respect of service outcomes. As an example, parcel delivery companies often guarantee to deliver a parcel within a specified time and agree to pay compensation if they fall below this standard. Many of the public utilities now offer compensation payments if certain specified services are not delivered correctly. For example, Southern Electricity aims to restore any loss of power within 24 hours of failure – if it fails in this aim, it pays compensation of £40 plus £20 for each subsequent 12-hour period of power failure. Increasingly, service organizations set their service guarantees with reference to benchmarks established by best-practice companies within their sector, or in a completely different sector. Sometimes, guarantees concentrate on the manner in which a service is produced rather than specifically on final outcomes. In this way, Building Societies set standards for the time which it will take to give a decision on a mortgage application and to subsequently process it. While there can be great benefits from publicizing specific guaranteed performance standards to customers, failure to perform could result in heavy compensation claims, or claims for misleading advertising. Many highly specific targets are therefore restricted to internal use where their function is to motivate and control staff rather than to provide guarantees to potential customers. While the major banks give their branch managers targets for such quality standards as queuing time for counter staff and availability of working ATM machines, it does not guarantee a specified level of service to its customers.

- Many services companies belong to a trade or professional association and incorporate the association's code of conduct into their own service offering. Codes of conduct adopted by members of professional associations as diverse as car repairers, undertakers and solicitors specify minimum standards below which service provision should not fall. The code of conduct provides both a reassurance to potential customers and a statement to employees about the minimum standards which are expected of them.
- Of more general applicability is the adoption of British Standard 5750 (or its international equivalent ISO 9000 series). Contrary to popular belief, a company operating to ISO 9002 does not guarantee a high level of quality for its service. Instead, ISO accreditation is granted to organizations who can show that they have in place management systems for ensuring a consistent standard of quality – whether this itself is high or low is largely a subjective judgement. Although this standard was initially adopted by manufacturing industries, it has subsequently found significant use among service companies, including education (see case study), leisure centres and building contractors. Increasingly, industrial purchasers of services are seeking the reassurance that its suppliers are ISO registered.
- In the case of some public sector services which operate in a monopolistic environment, quality standards are sometimes imposed from outside. In the case of privately owned utilities in the UK, the relevant regulating authority has the power to set specific service targets – for example the telephone regulatory body, Oftel, sets limits on what proportion of public telephone kiosks should be out of service at any one time. In the case of UK publicly owned services, the government has issued a series of customer charters setting out the standards of service which users of the service can expect – for example the period of time which a hospital patient has to wait for an operation. Critics of such charters would argue that they provide little – if any – practical compensation for users of a service who suffer from poor standards of quality. Worse still, they may raise users' expectations unrealistically without providing resources which would allow the organization to meet them.

## 8.6 Managing the marketing mix for quality

Service quality management is the process of attempting to ensure that the gap between consumer expectations and the perceived service delivery is as small as possible. There are a number of important dimensions to this task.

Firstly, the marketing mix formulation and its communication to potential customers must be as realistic as possible. Exaggerated claims merely lead to high expectations which an organization may not be able to deliver and thus the service is likely to be perceived as being of a poor quality.

Secondly, non-marketer dominated factors such as word-of-mouth information,

**Figure 8.7**
Southern Electric distinguishes between general standards of service which it seeks to maintain, and specific guarantees of service delivery. If it fails in the latter, predetermined compensation payments are offered to customers. As an example, if the company fails to honour an appointment to visit a customer, it will pay compensation of £20 (subject to a few exclusions). During 1996–97, out of 674 958 appointments, the company claimed that it was only required to make compensation payments for 18 missed appointments (reproduced with permission of Southern Electric plc)

traditions also need to be considered as once again their presence may have the effect of increasing expectations.

Finally, service companies must recognize that the relationship between customers' perceptions and expectations is dynamic. Merely maintaining customers' level of perceived quality is insufficient if their expectations have been raised over time. Marketing mix management is therefore concerned with closing the quality gap over time, either by improving the service offer, or restraining customers' expectations (see Figure 8.8).

Quality affects all aspects of the marketing mix – decisions about service specification cannot be taken in isolation from decisions concerning other elements of the mix. All can affect the level of customer expectations and the perceived standard of service delivery.

● *Promotion* decisions have the effect of developing consumers' expectations of service quality. Where marketer dominated sources of promotion are the main basis for evaluating and selecting competing services, the message as well as the

**Figure 8.8**

The changing quality gap

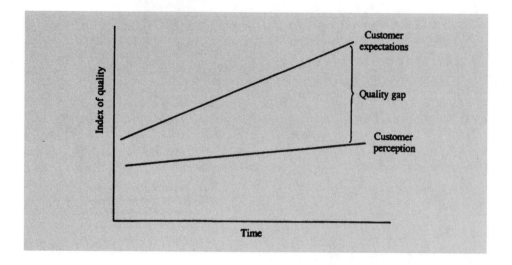

medium of communication can contribute in a significant way towards customers' quality expectations. Invariably, promotion sets expectations which organizations struggle to meet.

On some occasions, however, the image created by promotion may actually add to the perceived quality of the service. This is quite common for goods of conspicuous consumption, where the intangible image added to products such as beer can actually lead to consumers believing that the beer is of higher quality than another beer of identical technical quality which has been promoted in a different way. The possibility for achieving this with services is generally less, on account of the greater involvement of customers in the production/consumption process and the many opportunities which occur for judging quality. It is, however, possible in the case of some publicly consumed services, where high-profile advertising may actually add to the perceived quality of the service. In this way, promotion of a gold credit card may add to a customer's feeling that they have an exclusive and prestigious facility. Without the advertising, the prestigious value of the card would not be recognized by others.

- *Price* decisions affect both customers' expectations and perceptions of service quality, as well as the service organization's ability to produce quality services. In cases where all other factors are equal, price can be used by potential customers as a basis for judging service quality. If two outwardly similar restaurants charge different prices for a similar meal, the presumption may be made that the higher priced restaurant must offer a higher standard of service, which the customer will subsequently expect to be delivered. It will be against this benchmark that service delivery will be assessed.

The price charged can influence the level of quality which a service organization can build into its offering. The concept of price positioning was raised in Chapter 7 where it was noted that while any position along a line from high price/high quality to low price/low quality may be feasible, high price/low quality and low price/high quality positions are not generally sustainable over the long term. As an example, the low prices which many UK tour operators have offered relative to the levels charged in many overseas markets has resulted in insufficient margins to provide a high quality of service. Delays and inconvenience due to over-scheduled aircraft or over-booked flights have been among the consequences.

- *Place* or accessibility decisions can affect customers' expectations of quality as well as actual performance. A poor quality service sold through a high-quality agent may give heightened expectations of quality. Poor delivery may subsequently harm the image of the agent itself, which partly explains why many travel agents are reluctant to continue to act as intermediaries for tour operators with poor service-quality records. The manner in which an intermediary initiates, processes and follows up the service delivery process can often affect perceived quality received by the customer – an agent who incorrectly fills out the departure time for a coach ticket harms the quality of the service which the customer receives. For these reasons, an important element of quality management involves the recruitment and monitoring of a network of intermediaries who are able to share the service principal's commitment to quality standards.
- *Personnel*, especially front-line contact personnel, are important elements of consumers' perceptions of functional quality, and therefore the nature of the buyer–seller interaction becomes crucial in the management of service quality. Recruitment, training, motivation and control of personnel are therefore important elements of the marketing mix which impacts on quality standards. Front-line employees have the best possible vantage point for observing quality standards and are the most able to identify any impediments. Whether these contact personnel have the ability to articulate these failings can be another matter.

## 8.7 Organizing and implementing service quality

Service quality doesn't come about by chance – organizations need to develop strategies for ensuring that they deliver consistent and high-quality services. A number of people have sought to identify the organizational factors which are most commonly associated with successful quality management. Kotler (1991), as a result of research involving successful service firms in the USA proposed the following requirements:

1  A strategic concept which is customer-focused.
2  A history of top-management commitment to quality, i.e. seeing quality indicators as being just as important as financial indicators.
3  The setting of high standards and communicating these expected standards to employees.
4  Systems for monitoring performance. Top service firms regularly evaluate their own and their competitors' performance.
5  Systems for satisfying complaining customers. It is important to respond quickly and appropriately to customers' complaints.
6  Satisfying employees as well as customers. Successful organizations understand the importance of contact personnel and see an important role for 'internal marketing', i.e. 'applying the philosophies and practices of marketing to people who serve the external customers so that (1) the best possible people

can be employed and retained and (2) they will do the best possible work' (Berry, 1980). The subject of 'internal marketing' is discussed in more detail in Chapter 12.

Service personnel have emerged as a key element in the process of quality management. Maintaining a consistent standard of quality in labour-based services becomes very difficult on account of the inherent variability of personnel, as compared to machines. Furthermore, it has already been noted that the inseparability of most services does not generally allow an organization to undertake quality control checks between the points of production and consumption. Many services organizations link employees' salaries to customer satisfaction scores achieved by the team that they work in. It is reported that at the fast-food chain KFC about 35% of a manager's annual bonus is tied to the customer satisfaction scores they achieve (McNerney, 1996).

In this section, strategies to reduce the variability of the human input are examined.

### 8.7.1 Total Quality Management (TQM)

Total Quality Management (TQM) is an approach to improving the effectiveness and efficiency of an organization as a whole. It is a multi-disciplinary approach, in that marketing inputs to TQM processes cannot be seen in isolation from issues of operations management and human resource management. TQM is essentially a means of organizing and involving everybody employed in an organization, in all activities, in all functions and at all levels. The approach recognizes that the activities of every staff member have an impact on the quality received by customers, including non-contact personnel, whose actions in activities such as processing invoices or orders could nevertheless have implications for customer satisfaction. It follows that an important aim of TQM is the generation of a widespread awareness of customer needs among employees, and in particular the standards of quality which are expected by customers.

In addition to focusing on meeting customer requirements effectively, TQM is concerned with the efficiency with which these requirements are met. An important element of TQM therefore comprises strategies to reduce waste – defined as anything that neither adds value, nor contributes towards meeting customer requirements. One target for cost reductions are 'transaction' costs. These are distinguished from production costs and represent the costs of 'governing' production systems, referring to the costs of monitoring and negotiating work contracts and their level of performance (see Williamson, 1975). In this way, many services organizations have budgeting procedures which can be slow and cumbersome in responding to changes in customer expectations, resulting in greater cost or loss to the organization. For example, a local-authority-owned leisure centre may consider it necessary to upgrade the standards of its squash courts in the face of competition from a newly opened, privately operated leisure centre. Permission to spend the necessary money to improve standards might require prolonged negotiations with senior managers and possibly a committee of the authority. By the time that approval is given for the quality improvement, the competition may have taken away a significant share of its market, representing a transaction cost of not having in place an effective system for TQM.

Total Quality Management may be introduced as part of a package of other quality initiatives such as just-in-time (JIT) production methods to control stock levels – widely employed now by the retail sector. Within the services sector, the concept of JIT can be extended to the deployment of staff, whereby extra staff are brought in at short notice to meet peak demands.

Total Quality Management has many points of congruence with marketing in its internal and external manifestations. It rests upon the generation of an organizational mission or philosophy which encourages all employees and functional areas to regard themselves as providers and customers of other departments. Human resource management policies play a key role in facilitating TQM, for example in the way that total quality training and quality appraisals are taken on board by line areas in their efforts to contribute to overall corporate goals.

The principles of TQM sound fine in theory, but many organizations have experienced difficulty in their implementation. Some estimates have suggested that over three-quarters of all attempts by organizations to introduce TQM fail. Too often, TQM consists of a lot of rhetoric but little management commitment to develop an organization-wide culture in which quality initiatives are actively initiated, supported and followed through. An inability of individuals to act outside of their narrowly defined role, preoccupation with organizational processes rather than customer perceptions of value and a focus by management on short-term cost saving rather than long-term customer value frequently undermine efforts to implement TQM. The language of TQM may have been ridiculed in the eyes of many, but many of the principles have been embraced by newer variants of TQM, such as Business Improvement Programmes.

It is widely suggested that most attempts to introduce TQM systems fail. Some estimates have put the failure rate as high as 80%. But why should this be? A report in 1997 by the consultancy IRS concluded that poor management is the most commonly cited reason for the failure of efforts to improve service quality. The study found that more than half of those firms surveyed had run into problems getting senior and middle management committed to the quality process, with evidence of managers paying little more than lip service to the ideas of improving quality. A particular problem occurred where managers who previously had autonomy over a specific department found themselves now having to listen to ideas from other people on how to improve their quality. This was especially difficult where these people were lower down the management hierarchy. Many managers also failed to generate sufficient enthusiasm from members of their staff to carry out improvements. In short, the research emphasized the problem of creating a management culture of quality improvement. If the leaders of an organization are not committed to improving service quality, how can employees be expected to follow?

### 8.7.2 Quality Circles (QCs)

Quality Circles (QCs) often work within a TQM framework and consist of small groups of employees who meet together with a supervisor or group leader to discuss their work in terms of production and delivery standards. If QCs are to be used in the delivery of services, the marketing aims of the service organization must be incorporated into the TQM package and the agenda of the QCs. Quality Circles are especially suited to high-contact services where there is considerable interaction between employees and consumers. Front-line service staff who are in a position to identify quality shortcomings as they impact on customers are brought together with operational staff who may not interact directly with customers but can significantly affect service quality. By sitting down and talking together, employees have an opportunity to jointly recognize and suggest solutions to problems. In this way, a QC run by a car repair garage would bring together reception staff who interact with the public and mechanics who produce the **substantive service**. By analysing a quality problem identified by the receptionists (e.g. delays in collecting completed jobs), the mechanics might be able to suggest solutions (e.g. rescheduling some work procedures).

To be successful, the QC leader has to be willing to listen to and act upon issues raised by QC members. This is essential if the QC is to be sustained. Circle members must feel that their participation is real and effective, thus the communication process within the QC must be two-way. Consent can be real or perfunctory. In the latter case, if the QC appears to become only a routinized listening session, circle members may consider it to be just another form of managerial control. While circle members might consent to such control, their active participation in processes to improve service quality may be absent.

Quality Circle members need speedy and real feedback on ideas they might come up with to solve operational problems. Where a QC has successfully identified reasons why marketing objectives are not being attained, its suggestions should be commented on in a constructive manner. The effectiveness of QCs can be improved if staff reward mechanisms are linked to performance.

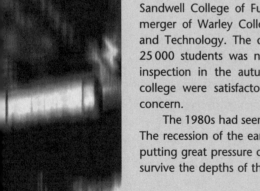

**Case Study**

## College sets standards for quality

Sandwell College of Further and Higher Education was created in 1986 through the merger of Warley College of Technology and West Bromwich College of Commerce and Technology. The quality of the training provided by its 520 teaching staff to its 25 000 students was not at the time a major item on the college agenda. A major inspection in the autumn of 1988 indicated that the general standards within the college were satisfactory to good, although there were one or two small areas of concern.

The 1980s had seen significant change in Sandwell College's operating environment. The recession of the early 1980s had hit local manufacturing industry particularly badly, putting great pressure on local employers' training budgets. Those companies which did survive the depths of the recession realized that if they were to survive and prosper, the quality of their own output would have to be raised to meet that of their overseas competitors. The attention given to the quality of these firms' output was matched only by their concern with the quality of their inputs.

Manufacturing firms sought to obtain British Standards Institution approval BS 5750 as a means of reassuring their customers of consistency of production processes. Firms working to this standard are expected to pass similar standards back through their supply chains. It was the college's involvement with local manufacturing industry that led it to look at the possibilities of obtaining a recognized quality standard. Obtaining BS 5750 would have the advantage of showing local industry on its own terms what the college was capable of achieving. Moreover, training managers of local employers were being increasingly selective about where they placed their training budgets and the college needed every marketing tool possible to preserve and build its business.

A Quality Assurance Unit was established within the college in November 1989 to consider the applicability of BS 5750 Part II (and its international equivalent ISO 9002) to education and training.

From the outset, the unit recognized that the language and concepts of the Standard would require radical translation and interpretation from their original manufacturing context into terms and ideas that are current within further and higher education. Among the early tasks was to define just what the 'product' was which the college was seeking to promote. Initially, there was some ambivalence as to whether this was the course or package of training, or the value added to the student who underwent the process of education or training. After some debate, it was decided that the 'product' was in fact the value added or enhancement of the student in terms of skills developed, knowledge acquired, experience gained or increased self-confidence and personal development. The 'process' was considered to be curriculum delivery.

The process of managing quality focused on course teams, which became responsible for the planning, development, review and evaluation of the educational process. Quality procedures grew out of existing good practice and allowed for the possibility of considerable diversity of procedures to meet a diverse range of courses. For example, all course teams had to obtain feedback on their course from students, but could choose how they did so, using one of four models presented by the Quality Assurance Unit, or their own approved method.

In December 1990, the quality system developing within Sandwell College was audited by a team of internal auditors, in preparation for an external audit by three auditors from the British Standards Institution in April 1991. The audit involved a rigorous inspection of the quality system, looking at the procedures followed by course teams across the college's six campuses.

Sandwell College was granted BSI registration with effect from May 1991. The immediate benefit of registration was to generate a quality assurance ethos where all of the issues that affect the quality of service provided by the college are constantly on its agenda. This in turn has benefited the college by attracting quality sensitive education and training work away from other private and public sector institutions in an increasingly competitive market for education and training services.

The value of the pioneering steps taken by Sandwell College were soon recognized by other colleges and universities. Within a year of its registration, over 100 colleges in the UK had begun working towards obtaining registration under the standard. However,

questions remained to be answered. Could higher education be reduced to systematic processes which might be fine for a fast-food restaurant, but not appropriate in an environment characterized by individuality and creativity? While the concept of total quality management systems seemed to spread rapidly through the UK higher education sector, spurred on by the government's Quality Assurance Agency, some universities were notable for their opposition to this process. Some of the strongest criticism for TQM principles came from Oxford and Cambridge Universities, the two universities which regularly topped league tables of academic performance. Was this superiority achieved in spite of, or because of, a less formalized approach to quality management?

## Case study review questions

1 Identify the various stakeholders' perspectives from which quality in higher education may be viewed.

2 How does quality affect students' choice of educational establishment?

3 Has quality in universities got better or worse in recent years?

## Chapter summary and linkages to other chapters

Quality is a complex concept when applied to services and this chapter has reviewed some of the difficulties in seeking to measure a concept which can only be defined in consumers' minds. Much of what passes for service quality measurement is *ad hoc* and misleading. However, there is disagreement over more comprehensive approaches to service quality measurement and the role of expectations in influencing quality evaluations. Quality measurement alone is of little value if management does nothing to set standards for quality and to successfully implement these standards. This chapter has reviewed issues involved in the management of quality which will be returned to in **Chapter 12** in the context of human resource management and in **Chapter 14** on marketing management processes.

A large part of this chapter's discussion on quality can be related back to **Chapter 3** which discussed service encounters – blueprinting can be a valuable tool for designing services processes that consistently meet customers' expectations

(**Chapter 3**). Quality delivery of service is a prerequisite to the development of stable long-term buyer–seller relationships (**Chapter 5**) and is an issue which should be shared between a company and its intermediaries (**Chapter 9**) to create quality through a value chain. The need for a constant flow of information to monitor quality standards was underlined in **Chapter 6**.

## www linkages/URLs

Lis-qual – a discussion group for quality systems, assurance service, and measurement:
**http://www.mailbase.ac.uk/lists/lis-qual**

American Society for Quality—resources and search engine:
**http://www.asq.org**

## Key terms

Technical quality 208
Quality circles  219
Services principal 221
Customer charters 229

Functional quality  208
Benchmarking 220
Customer's expectations 221
Substantive service 236

## Chapter review questions

1   Discuss the reasons why quality has become an increasingly important issue in services marketing.
2   In what ways can an airline attempt to measure the quality of its services?
3   Using a public sector organization of your choice, give examples of the methods by which the organization can seek to manage quality.
4   Giving examples, distinguish between the concepts of 'functional' and 'technical' quality.
5   Critically assess the usefulness of the SERVQUAL technique for measuring quality in an industry of your choice.
6   In what ways can the personnel input to services be managed in order to achieve more consistent quality standards?

## Selected further reading

*In recent years, debate about service quality has tended to be dominated by discussion of the SERVQUAL methodology. The following reference is an early publication from the research group that developed the SERVQUAL. It sets out the theoretical framework and the factor analysis on which the five dimensions of service quality were defined.*

Parasuraman, A., V. A. Zeithaml and L. L. Berry (1988) 'SERVQUAL: A Multiple-Item Scale for Measuring Consumer Perceptions of Service Quality', *Journal of Retailing*, Vol. 64, No. 1, pp 12–40

*The following reference offers a comprehensive literature-based review of the SERVQUAL methodology, summarizing nearly a decade of debate and offering suggestions for important and under-researched aspects of service quality:*

Buttle, F. (1996) 'SERVQUAL: Review, Critique, Research Agenda', *European Journal of Marketing*, Vol. 30, No. 1, pp 8–32

*For a discussion on the subject of how different levels of expectations are formed, the following articles by the developers of the SERVQUAL methodology are useful:*

Bebko, C. P. (2000) 'Service Intangibility and Its Impact on Consumer Expectations of Service Quality' *Journal of Services Marketing*, Vol. 14, No. 1, pp 10–26

Boulding, W., A. Kalra, R. Staelin and V. A. Zeithaml (1993) 'A Dynamic Process Model of Service Quality: From Expectations to Behavioural Intentions', *Journal of Marketing Research*, Vol. 30, No. 1, pp 7–27

Zeithaml, V. A., L. L. Berry and A. Parasuraman (1993) 'The Nature and Determinants of Customer Expectations of Service', *Journal of the Academy of Marketing Science*, Vol. 21, No. 1, pp 1–12

*Numerous subsequent articles have challenged the principles of SERVQUAL, on theoretical and empirical grounds, including:*

Bolton, R. and J. Drew (1991) 'A Multistage Model of Customers' Assessments of Service Quality and Value', *Journal of Consumer Research*, March, Vol. 17, pp 375–84

Bolton, R. N. and K. N. Lemon (1999) 'A dynamic model of customers' usage of services: usage as an antecedent and consequence of satisfaction', *Journal of Marketing Research*, Vol. 36, No 2, pp 171–86

Carman, J. M. (1990) 'Consumer Perceptions of Service Quality: An Assessment of the SERVQUAL Dimensions', *Journal of Retailing*, Vol. 66, No. 1, pp 33–55

Cronin, J. J. and S. A. Taylor (1992) 'Measuring Service Quality: A Re-examination and Extension', *Journal of Marketing*, July, Vol. 56, pp 55–68

O'Neill, M., A. Palmer and R. Beggs (1998) 'The Effects of Survey Timing on Perception of Service Quality', *Managing Service Quality*, Vol. 8, No. 2, pp 126–32

*While much of the service quality literature has focused on private consumers, the following article puts forward the case for analysing service business clients' expectations of quality. It argues that ongoing surveys of clients' expectations can play a beneficial role in the development of client–supplier relationships.*

Szmigin, I. T. D. (1993) 'Managing Quality in Business-to-Business Services', *European Journal of Marketing*, Vol. 27, No. 1, pp 5–21

*The following contain discussions of the link between service quality and organizational performance:*

Bloemer, J., K. de Ruyter and M. Wetzels (1999) 'Linking Perceived Service Quality and Service Loyalty: A Multi-dimensional Perspective, *European Journal of Marketing*, Vol. 33

Gilbert, G. R., and A. M. Parhizgari (2000) 'Organizational Effectiveness Indicators to Support Service Quality', *Managing Service Quality*, Vol. 10, No. 1, pp 46–51

Sivadas, E. and J. L. Baker-Prewitt (2000) 'An Examination of the Relationship between Service Quality, Customer Satisfaction, and Store Loyalty, *International Journal of Retail & Distribution Management*, Vol. 28, Issue 2, pp 55–68

# 9

# Making services accessible to consumers

## Learning objectives

Given that producers and consumers must usually meet in order for the benefits of a service to be created, strategies to make services accessible to consumers become a key part of marketing planning. The first aim of this chapter is to explore the factors which affect firms' choice of service outlet sites, and the extent to which service production and consumption are spatially flexible. Services organizations use a variety of methods to reduce the effects of inseparability on service production and delivery and these are discussed. The development of the Internet in achieving this is discussed. A diverse range of intermediaries exist to facilitate the task of making services accessible, but unlike most goods intermediaries, they become a co-producer of a service. This chapter explores the diversity of service intermediaries, their roles and the factors that influence their selection. Finally, most services involve some tangible elements and a brief review is made of the methods by which services firms make these elements available to consumers.

## 9.1  Introduction

Consider the following recent successful service innovations:

- First Direct telephone banking from home.
- McDonald's out-of-town 'drive-through' restaurants.
- Domino's Pizzas home-delivery service.

In each case, success has been based on making an existing service more readily accessible to customers. So the bank customer no longer needs to visit their local branch to carry out many types of transactions; somebody looking for a Big Mac need no longer leave their car; and a pizza eater need not even leave their home.

Actually achieving these high levels of accessibility calls for a strategy which is capable of achieving desired levels within a specified time period. For the pizza company to be able to put a pizza in anybody's home requires an effort which is probably not achievable by the company acting alone. It may therefore seek a variety of arrangements, such as franchising, with local companies who are able to implement its strategy better than it could itself.

The inseparability of services makes the task of passing on service benefits much more complex than is the case with manufactured goods. Inseparability implies that services are consumed at the point of production, in other words, a service cannot be produced by one person in one place and handled by other people to make it available to customers in other places. A service cannot therefore be produced where costs are lowest and sold where demand is greatest – customer accessibility must be designed into the service production system.

In this chapter, strategies to make services accessible to customers will be analysed by focusing on four important, but related issues:

- Where and when is the service to be made available to the consumer?
- What is the role of intermediaries in the process of service delivery?
- How are intermediaries selected, motivated and monitored?
- How are tangible goods which form a part of many service offers to be made available to final consumers?

## 9.2  Service location decisions

In this section, choices facing service providers about the place and time at which a service is to be provided are considered. First, it should be repeated that because consumers of services are usually involved as co-producers of the service, the time and place at which they are expected to take part in this process becomes an important criterion for evaluation. Production location decisions therefore cannot be taken in isolation from an analysis of customers' needs. While services organizations often have a desire to centralize production in order to achieve economies of scale, consumers usually seek local access to services, often at a time which may not be economic for the producer to cater for. Service location decisions therefore involve a trade-off between the needs of the producer and the needs of the consumer. This is in contrast to goods manufacturers who can manufacture goods in one location where production is most economic, then ship the goods to where they are most needed.

For some services, production is very inflexible with respect to location, resulting in relatively production-led location decisions. In other cases, production techniques may by their nature allow much greater flexibility, but location decisions are constrained by the inflexibility of consumers to travel to a service outlet, either because of their physical inability or merely their unwillingness. In the case of some intangible, low contact services, it is possible to separate production from consumption, using some of the methods described later in this chapter. In such cases, services can be produced in the most economic location and made available wherever customers are located.

### 9.2.1 Flexibility in production

The extreme case of inflexibility in production is provided by services where the whole purpose of the service is to be at one unique location – for example tourism related services based on a unique historic site by their very nature cannot be moved. A further group of services are locationally inflexible because they can only sensibly be produced in large-scale centralized production facilities. This can be the case where the necessary supporting equipment is expensive and offers opportunities for significant economies of scale. Where this equipment is also highly immobile, customers must come to a limited number of central service points to receive service. This is true with much of the specialized and expensive equipment needed for complex medical care, such as trauma care which tends to be provided at a small number of central locations. In cases where the equipment offers less scope for economies of scale and is more easily transported, service production can be distributed more widely. This explains why breast screening services are frequently taken to users, while users must travel to trauma centres.

Some service organizations operate a 'hub and spoke' system where the benefits of large-scale, centralized production of specialized services is combined with locally accessible outlets. In the banking sector, specialized business and investment services can often only be competitive if they are produced in units which have a high enough critical mass to support the payment of an expert in that field of activity and to cover associated overheads. The major British banks have accordingly developed specialized business advisory centres located in a few key locations. Their services are subsequently made available through local branches by a combination of telephone, mail, computer link or a personal visit from the centrally based expert. Similarly, much of the processing work involved in producing a service can be transferred to an efficient regional centre, leaving local outlets to act as an interface with customers. In this way, many banks and building societies have transferred mortgage processing from high street branches, leaving the latter to act as little more than sales outlets. The principal components of a hub and spoke system are illustrated in Figure 9.1.

As well as internal economies of scale, external economies of scale are sometimes an important influence on a firm's location decisions. The first kind of external economies occur where a location close to other service producers reduces a firm's input costs. For this reason, many diverse financial services companies have

**Figure 9.1**

A hub and spoke
system of service
production and delivery

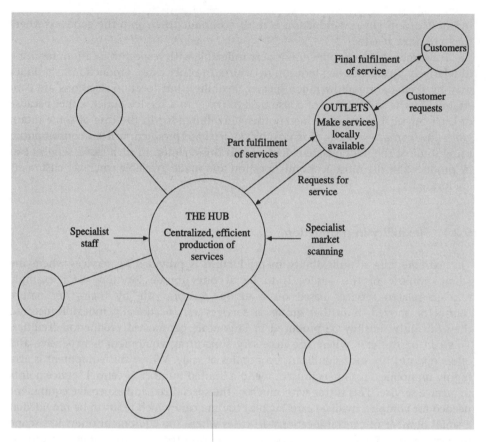

congregated in the City of London. A ship-broking agency may find significant
benefits from being located within walking distance of Lloyds insurance market and
banks for sources of finance. Similarly, clusters of advertising agencies, graphic
designers, typographers and typesetters can be found to maximize benefits from
internal trading, to the benefit of suppliers and customers alike. However, the importance of such external economies of scale to location decisions is declining due to
technological developments which allow production to be separated from consumption. In both of the above examples, service benefits can now be delivered elec-
tronically, reducing the need for direct interaction.

A second source of external economies of scale can result from locating in a
recognized local marketplace, as occurs where jewellers or estate agents locate in
one neighbourhood of a town. Because the existence of the marketplace is widely
recognized, any firm locating within it will need to spend less on promotion to
attract potential customers to its location.

Production economies are likely to be a less important influence on location
decisions where economies of scale are insignificant. In a market environment, competitive advantage will be gained by maximizing availability through more widespread
distribution outlets, rather than cost saving through centralization. To illustrate this,
hairdressing offers fairly limited scope for economies of scale, and competitive
advantage is gained by providing small outlets which are easily accessible to
customers.

Finally, the competitiveness of the market environment can affect the locational flexibility of service producers. A service producer which is able to be flexible in its location decisions may nevertheless be unwilling to be flexible if its customers have little choice of supplier. For this reason, many government provided services (e.g. housing administration) are provided through centralized administrative offices which may be inconveniently located for most users.

### 9.2.2 Flexibility in consumption

Decisions on service location are also influenced by the extent to which consumers are willing or able to be flexible in where they consume a service. Inflexibility on the part of consumers can arise for a number of reasons:

- Where a service is to be performed on a customer's possessions, those possessions may themselves be immovable, requiring the supplier to come to the customer (e.g. building repairs).
- Sometimes, the customer may also be physically immobile (e.g. physically disabled users of healthcare services).
- For impulse purchases, or services where there are many competitive alternatives, customers are unlikely to be willing to travel far to seek out a service.
- For specialist services, customers may show more willingness to be flexible in where they are prepared to receive the service, compared to routine purchases for which they would be unwilling to travel.

In reality, most service consumers' decisions involve a trade-off between the price of a service, the quality of delivery at a particular location, the amount of choice available and the cost to the consumer in terms of time and money involved in gaining access to a service. For the buyer of a few odd items of groceries, price and choice are likely to be relatively unimportant compared to ease of access – hence the continued existence of many small corner shops. For a consumer seeking to purchase the week's groceries, price and selection may become much more important relative to ease of access. For more specialized services, such as the purchase of expensive hi-fi equipment, consumers may be willing to travel longer distances to a retailer which offers competitive prices and/or a wide selection of equipment.

It follows therefore that access strategies should be based on an identification of market segments made up of users with similar accessibility needs. Access strategies can then be developed which meet the needs of each segment.

- Age frequently defines segments in terms of the level of access sought. For many elderly users of personal care services, there is sometimes an unwillingness or inability to leave the home, making home availability of a service a sought attribute. For other groups, such as older teenagers, the very act of getting away from home to receive a service may be attractive. This could explain continuing interest in going out to see a film at a cinema in the face of the competing alternatives provided by local video rental shops and satellite television services.

- Segmentation on the basis of an individual's economic status can be seen in the willingness of more affluent segments to pay premium prices in order to consume a service at a point and time which is convenient to themselves rather than the service provider. Evidence of this is provided by home-delivery food services which target groups with high disposable incomes.
- Psychographic segmentation can be seen in the way groups of people seek out services which satisfy their lifestyle needs. As an example, some segments of the population are prepared to travel long distances to a restaurant whose design and ambience appeals to them.
- The cultural background of some individuals can predispose them to seek a particular kind of accessibility. This can be seen in the reluctance of some groups to become involved in service delivery methods which remove regular personal contact with the service provider. Insurance companies that collect premiums from the homes of customers may give reassurance to some segments who have been brought up to distrust impersonal organizations, whereas a periodic visit to a bank or annual payment by post may satisfy the needs of other segments.
- Access strategies can be based on the type of benefit which users seek from a service. As an example, customers are often prepared to travel a considerable distance to a restaurant for a celebration meal, but would expect it to be easily accessible for a business lunch.
- High-frequency users of a service may place a higher premium on easy accessibility than casual users.
- In the case of business-to-business services, the level of access to a service can directly affect the customer's operating costs. A computer repair company which makes its services available at buyers' offices avoids the costs which the latter would incur if it had to perform part of the service – delivery and collection – itself.

For some services, the location of the service delivery point is the most important means of attracting new business. This can be true for low-value services for which consumers show little willingness to pre-plan their purchase or to go out of their way to find. Location is also very important in the case of impulse purchases. Petrol-filling stations, tea shops in tourist areas and guest houses are typically chosen as a result of a customer encountering the service outlet with no prior planning. It is unlikely for instance that many motorists would follow media advertisements and seek out a petrol station which is located in a back street – a visible location is a vital factor influencing consumers' choice.

The perishability of service offers results in their time accessibility being important as well as their spatial location. Again, customers can be segmented according to their flexibility with respect to the time at which they are prepared to consume a service. At one extreme, some segments for some services may be prepared to wait until a specified time to receive the service – as an example, ardent fans of a pop group would probably buy a ticket for a concert regardless of the time and date that it takes place. In other cases, no purchase would be made if a service is not instantly available – for example a taxi operator that makes its service available only at specified times will probably lose all custom outside these times to other operators.

Service accessibility by time can be used to give an organization competitive advantage in much the same way as spatial accessibility. When building societies started offering banking services from the mid-1980s, their longer opening hours gave them a competitive advantage over banks and attracted many traditional bank customers who found banking hours of 9.30 am to 3.30 pm too restrictive. Having lost significant elements of their core business to building societies, banks were forced to respond by opening certain branches on Saturdays and extending their opening hours in the afternoon.

### 9.2.3 A typology of service location influences

An attempt to develop a typology of service location decisions is shown in Figure 9.2 where inseparable services are classified in a matrix according to their degree of flexibility in production and consumption.

Services in the upper left quadrant often have little locational flexibility because they are associated with a unique site, for example outstanding scenery or a historical association. Nevertheless, attempts have sometimes been made to replicate the original site at a point which is closer to consumers, for example the creation of Disneyworld Paris was an attempt to bring the unique features of the American Disneyland to a European audience.

Services in the bottom right quadrant may have little locational flexibility because consumers are unable to move themselves or their possessions. In the case of some fixed assets such as buildings, this inflexibility may be absolute and the service provider must come to the consumer. However, consumers may merely be unwilling to be flexible or it may be part of their expectations that a service should come to them.

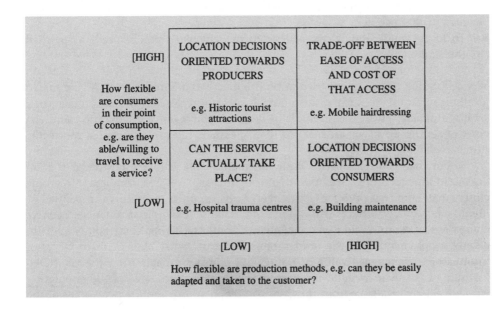

**Figure 9.2**

Locational flexibility in production and consumption of inseparable services

It is in the upper right quadrant where trade-offs between convenience for the consumer and for the producer are greatest. Here, markets can often be segmented by accessibility preferences and producers adapt their production methods to the price/convenience preferences of each segment. The retailing sector shows a wide variation from large hypermarkets, which are efficient for the producer but relatively inaccessible to most consumers, through to corner shops which are more accessible but less efficient. Many consumers are prepared to pay a premium for ease of access, even to have goods delivered to their door.

Where both producer and consumer are inflexible, it may be difficult for any service to take place at all, and where it does it may be under distress conditions (e.g. hospital emergency admissions). With developments in technology, it is sometimes possible to increase the production flexibility (e.g. through mobile operating theatres and tele-medicine).

### 9.2.4   Service location models

Before a network of service outlets can be designed, an organization must clearly define its accessibility objectives. In particular, it must have a clear idea of the volume of business, market share and customer segments that it seeks to attract. Accessibility objectives derive from the positioning strategy for a service. A high level of accessibility may only be compatible with business objectives if it is also associated with a premium price position. A high level of accessibility may also reduce and change the role played by promotion within the marketing mix. By contrast, a strategy which involves a low level of accessibility may need to rely heavily on promotion to make potential customers aware of the location of service outlets.

Examples of accessibility objectives include:

- To provide a hotel location in all towns with a population of 200 000 or more
- To develop supermarket sites which are within 10 minutes driving time of at least 50 000 people.
- To locate retail sites where pedestrian or vehicular traffic exceeds a specified threshold.

Service-location decisions are used at both a macro and a micro level. At the macro level, organizations seek the most profitable areas or regions in which to make their service available, given the strength of demand, the level of competition and the costs of setting up in an area. Micro-level decisions refer to the choice of specific sites.

Macro analysis begins with a clear statement of the profile of customers that an organization is targeting. Areas are then sought that have a geodemographic profile closely matching that of the target market. At its simplest, indicators can be used to identify potentially attractive locations. As a simple example, a financial services company seeking to set up a national chain of outlets offering home equity loans to elderly people may select the most promising areas on the basis of three pieces of information: the average value of houses in an area (available from the Chartered Institute of Surveyors' regular monitoring report); the percentage of the population who are elderly (available from the Census of Population); and the percentage of the population who are owner-occupiers (available from *Regional Trends*). The attractiveness of a market could be indicated by a weighted index of these factors and subjected to a more detailed analysis of competitor activity in each area. A number of more specialized segmentation methods have been developed which allow organizations to evaluate the profile of an area. An example is MOSAIC developed by Experian Systems, which is based on an analysis of postcodes.

Methods used by an organization to select service outlet locations tend to become more complex as the organization grows. In the early stages of growth, simple rule-of-thumb methods may be acceptable. With further growth, simple indexes and ratios are commonly used. With more service outlets established, an organization can begin to gather sufficient data to analyse the performance of its existing outlets, and from this to develop models which can be used to predict the likely performance of proposed new locations. Regression techniques are used to identify relationships between variables and the level of significance of each variable in explaining the performance of a location. The development of regression models requires considerable initial investment in creating an information base and calibrating the model, but once calibrated they can help to reduce the risk inherent in new service location decisions. It should be noted, however, that models cannot be extrapolated to cover types of decisions which were not envisaged in the model as originally calibrated – for example a model calibrated for UK site location decisions may be inappropriate for making site location decisions in France.

The level of risk associated with opening a new supermarket in a fiercely competitive environment can be considerable, yet large retailers claim that they can predict the turnover of a new store opening to within a few percentage points. While a small general retailer may be able to rent shop space on low-risk short-term leases, modern supermarkets requires considerable investment in purpose-built facilities which meet customers' ever-increasing needs and expectations. A study by Jones and Mock (1984) of a small American supermarket chain illustrates the value of regression-modelling techniques. The supermarket chain being studied had previously relied on rule-of-thumb methods for store location, but as the size of its new stores increased, so too had the level of risk. As its business grew, it was also able to gather more data to understand the factors that are associated with the success of a particular store.

The regression modelling started by grouping sites according to similarities in their environments. On the basis of socioeconomic data, five distinctive environments were identified – city centre, suburbs, old-established shopping streets, the urban fringe and non-metropolitan locations. To find out which of the many variables available were the most relevant for each retailing environment, a series of cross-tabulations between individual key variables was carried out. The relevant variables were then put into a series of stepwise regression models, one for each environment, allowing the identification of the variables which were most effective in explaining sales performance. In the case of suburban stores, variation in store sales was best explained by three measures – the percentage of the neighbourhood which had recently been developed, accessibility of the site by car and the number of competitors located within three blocks. Each increase of 1% in the share of new houses resulted in an additional weekly sales turnover of $120, whereas each nearby competitor reduced sales by $656.

Such models tend to give good results when the business environment is stable. But how useful are they when it is possible for operators to set up rival facilities quickly, changing the assumptions on which the model is based? After all, if one supermarket is running such a model, its competitors are probably doing the same and coming up with similar results. Should they be concentrating on flexibility so that the start-up and close-down costs are reduced?

A number of additional problems in the application of regression modelling techniques can be noted. Because such techniques require large amounts of data for calibration, they are only really suited to high-volume services. It can also be difficult to identify the key variables that cause variation in sales turnover, or to exclude interaction among the variables. Finally, regression is essentially an incremental planning technique which is less appropriate for designing networks of service outlets, such as may occur following the merger of two service organizations resulting in a need to rationalize outlets. For the latter, an alternative approach is to use a spatial-location model.

Spatial-location models measure the geographical dispersion of demand and seek to allocate this demand to service outlets on the basis that the probability of a consumer using a particular outlet will be:

- positively related to the attractiveness of that outlet, and
- negatively related to its distance from the points where demand is located.

These principles are developed in the following model (Huff, 1966) which has frequently been used as a basis for retail location models, but also has applications in locating leisure facilities and health services etc.

$$P_{ij} = \frac{\dfrac{A_j^a}{d_{ij}^b}}{\displaystyle\sum_{n=1}^{i} \dfrac{A_j^a}{d_{ij}^b}}$$

where $P_{ij}$ = the probability of a trip from origin $i$ to destination $j$

$A_j$ = the attractiveness of destination $j$

$d_{ij}$ = the distance between origin $i$ and destination $j$

$a$ and $b$ = parameters to be empirically determined

The intuitive appeal and simplicity of such a model can hide a number of conceptual and practical problems in their application and this has triggered considerable research in an attempt to operationalize the basic model. The concept of attractiveness can be difficult to measure. Fishbein (1967) has pointed out that although an individual may have a belief that a location is attractive, this attractiveness may not be of importance to that particular individual. Distance itself can be difficult to measure and can be measured objectively (e.g. mileage or average travelling times), or subjectively according to users' perceptions of distance. As an example of research into the distance components of such models, Mayo and Jarvis (1981) showed that subjectively perceived distances increase proportionately less than the objective measured distance.

Spatial location-allocation models are powerful tools which emphasize long-term marketing strategies rather than short-term decisions about opening or closing a specific location. They can be used to evaluate all possible combinations of location possibilities in relation to the geographical pattern of demand. The criteria for selecting the most efficient network of outlets usually involves balancing the need to maximize its attractiveness to customers against the service provider's need to minimize the cost of operating the network. Sophisticated computer models allow assumptions about consumer behaviour to be varied – for example the maximum distance which people are prepared to walk to an outlet. Such models are expensive to develop in view of the data requirements and the need to use specialized staff to develop them. Where the risks associated with a bad location decision are low, it may be more cost effective to use rule-of-thumb methods than to commission such a model. In the UK, the high cost of acquiring and refurbishing property in the mid-1980s led to spatial-location models becoming very popular as risk reducers. However, the fall in property-related costs – and associated risk levels – in the early 1990s saw many companies (such as Sketchley's Dry Cleaners) dropping their use and reverting to more cost-effective rule-of-thumb methods or regression models. Spatial allocation models do, however, continue to be used extensively in both the private and public sectors (e.g. in planning a network of clinics which minimizes patients' travel distances).

### 9.2.5 The Internet as a means of reducing locational dependency

The traditional idea that service production and consumption are inseparable would appear at first sight to pose problems in achieving both maximum productive efficiency and maximum accessibility to a service. One method of resolving this apparent problem is to try to make production and consumption separable – that is, to design a service which can be produced where it is most efficient and consumed where it is most needed.

Telecommunications can be used to allow the substantive element of a service to be produced at a central processing unit and made available at any point of consumers' choice. Information databases used by businesses and prerecorded telephone information used by personal consumers are typical of the type of service where this separation has been possible. Banks have recognized the distribution implications of improved telephone and Internet technology and most of the large banks in the UK have developed telephone-based banking services. These allow customers to receive statements and to transfer funds from one account to another, or to pay bills to outside organizations, direct from customers' home or office. Internet banking and TV banking have extended the possibilities for spatial separation of customer and provider. The locational implications of such delivery systems are quite significant. Banks have been steadily reducing their costly branch networks and seeking to channel more of their business through electronic media. As well as cutting costs through the use of an efficient centralized administration centre, Internet banking makes the banks' services available to customers at any location and at any time of day.

Nevertheless, problems remain with excessive reliance on the Internet, as most services usually involve a tangible benefit which must be transferred from producer to consumer at some point. Bank customers usually require cash, necessitating physical locations to supplement the Internet-based service delivery. In February 2000, UK banks discussed levying charges for other banks' customers withdrawing cash from their cash machines. This was seen by many as an attack on the new generation of Internet-based banks (e.g. Egg and First E) which had gained competitive advantage through a low-cost structure, but did not have their own cash machines with which they could fulfil customers' requests for cash.

In the early stages of Internet development, the technology has been used to provide a modest incremental improvement on what was previously possible using voice telephone or postal services. With increasing sophistication, possibilities arise for the Internet to provide additional benefits which are not possible using more traditional distribution methods. Personalization of websites can facilitate re-ordering of routinely purchased services (e.g. an airline site which opens with previously recorded preferences). Many websites are now linked with other complementary value-adding services (e.g. a travel informediary's website which has links to national and regional tourist board websites).

Banks have been at the forefront of efforts to tackle the problems of service inseparability. The big four UK banks run large and expensive branch networks and have faced increased competition from new low-cost telephone and postal banking services. Many non-bank competitors have appeared, especially supermarkets who have developed banking to complement their customer relationship building activities. A study by Ernst and Young in 1997 indicated some of the reasons why banks are keen to reduce their dependence on a large branch network. The study found that each transaction in a bank branch cost an average of 64p. By contrast, the average cost of transactions by telephone was 32p; 27p through an ATM and just 0.5p through the banks' Internet services. But how do banks exploit the opportunities made available by new means of separating production and consumption? Closing local branches is never popular with customers and may lead to the defection of profitable ones to competitors. Some banks have tried differential pricing by charging a fee for users of counter facilities. When Abbey National began charging its 'Instant Access' account customers £1 each time they cashed a cheque within a branch, there was understandable bad publicity. The company was clearly trying to encourage its customers to use its ATMs and telephone-banking facility. But how large and fast growing is the market segment which is prepared to sacrifice personal face-to-face contact for a cheaper and more efficient machine-based method of distribution?

## 9.3 The role of intermediaries in distributing services

Having now discussed issues of *where* services should be made available to consumers, this chapter now considers *how* they should be made available. More specifically, *who* should be involved in the process of delivering the benefit of a service to consumers? Should a company seek to perform the whole service process itself? If not, who should it involve, and at what stages of the production process?

In the context of goods marketing, the concept of an **intermediary** can be understood as being a person who handles goods as they pass from the organization that manufactured them to the individual or business which finally consumes them. The intermediary may physically handle the goods, splitting them into progressively smaller volumes as they pass through channels of distribution, or may simply buy and sell the rights to goods in the role of a commodity dealer.

Any discussion of service intermediaries immediately raises a number of conceptual issues:

- Services cannot be owned, therefore it is difficult to talk about rights to service ownership being transferred through channels of distribution.
- Pure services are intangible and perishable, therefore stocks cannot exist.
- The inseparability of most services should logically require an intermediary to become a co-producer of a service.

A distinction should be made between intermediaries as co-producers and their role as mere sales agents. While the former is an active part of the production process, the latter doesn't actually deliver a service itself, only the right to a service. As an example, a shop selling postage stamps is not significantly involved as a co-producer of postal services. It can be difficult to distinguish between these two situations – a theatre ticket agency, in addition to merely selling the right to a service may provide a valuable service for consumers in procuring specific seats.

Service intermediaries perform a number of important functions on behalf of service producers (the latter are often referred to as 'service principals'). The role expectations of intermediaries vary according to the nature of the service in question and some of the most important are described below:

- As a **co-producer** of a service, an intermediary assists in making a service available locally to consumers at a place and time that is convenient to them. An estate agent providing a cheque cashing facility for a building society is assisting in the process of producing and making financial services available to consumers. In other cases, an intermediary may become the dominant partner involved in co-production. A national key cutting or shoe heeling service may leave almost the entire service production process in the hands of intermediaries, leaving the principal to provide administrative and advertising support and to monitor standards.
- Intermediaries usually provide sales support at the point of sale. For some customers of personal services, a two-way personal dialogue with a local intermediary may be more effective at securing a sale than advertising messages derived centrally from a service principal.

- Consumers may prefer to buy services from an intermediary who offers a wide choice, including the services offered by competing service principals. A holiday tour company seeking to sell its holidays direct to the public might encounter resistance from segments of the population who prefer to have choices presented to them at one location.

- Consumers may enjoy trusting relationships with intermediaries and prefer to choose between competing alternatives on the basis of the intermediaries' advice. In the financial services sector, intermediaries develop trust with their clients in guiding them through often complex choices. To be successful with such segments of buyers, a financial services company must establish its credentials with the intermediary if its products are to enter the final consumer's shortlisted choice set.

- An intermediary as co-producer of a service often shares some of the risk of providing a service. This can come about where a service principal requires intermediaries to contribute some of their own capital to the cost of acquiring equipment and both share any subsequent operating profit or loss.

- The use of independent intermediaries can free-up capital which a service principal can reinvest in its core service production facilities. An airline which closes its own ticket shops and directs potential customers to travel agents is able to reinvest the proceeds in updating its aircraft or reservation systems which may give it greater competitive advantage than having its own ticket outlets.

- Once the initial service act is completed, there may be a requirement for after-sales services to be provided. Intermediaries can make this support more accessible to the consumer and assist the service principal as co-producer of the after-sales support. Insurance is a good example where many segments of the insurance-buying public feel happier with easy local access to a local agent who can give advice about making a claim. The agent in turn simplifies the task of the insurance company by handling much of the paperwork involved in making a claim, thereby reducing the latter's workload.

### 9.3.1 Push and pull relationships with intermediaries

'Push' and 'pull' channels of distribution are familiar concepts in the marketing of goods, but they also have application within the services sector. A traditional 'push' channel of distribution involves a service principal aggressively promoting its service to intermediaries by means of personal selling, trade advertising and the use of trade incentives. The intermediary in turn aggressively sells the service to final consumers, often having to strike a balance between maximizing the customer's benefit and maximizing the incentives offered to the intermediary by the service principal. This approach sees the service as essentially a commodity – the consumer starts with no preference of service principal and seeks the best value available from an intermediary. A push channel is typical of the way in which basic motor insurance is made available to customers. For many buyers, insurance is a 'distress' purchase where the only perceived difference between policies is the price. Many people

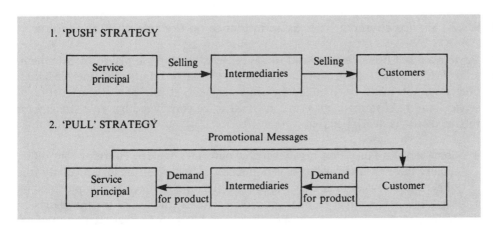

**Figure 9.3**
Push and pull strategies
for making services
available to consumers

rely on their intermediary to suggest the lowest cost insurance available to them. Intermediaries will be most aggressive in the sale of policies which meet buyers' criteria and on which they receive the most attractive commission payments.

For service principals, push strategies can be quite risky, as any product differentiation policy can only be effective if the intermediary effectively communicates the unique benefits to potential customers, rather than relying on price alone as the point of differentiation. To try to reduce this risk, service principals can aim messages directly at consumers, seeking to establish at an early stage in the buying process the values which their brand stands for. Having developed an attitude towards a brand, consumers are more likely to specifically ask for that brand from an intermediary or to express a preference for it when offered a choice by the intermediary. For a pull strategy, the intermediary's role is reduced to one of dispensing pre-sold branded services. The UK pensions industry has seen considerable activity by companies such as Prudential, Legal and General and Standard Life seeking to build up favourable images of their services so that potential customers enter discussions with intermediaries with a favourable predisposition towards the insurance company. Buyers may know very little about the merits of one pension policy over another, but they approach an intermediary with attitudes about their preferred principal. Push and pull strategies are compared in Figure 9.3.

It can sometimes be difficult to distinguish between pure push and pull strategies. A company may act as an intermediary for some services, but as a service principal for other similar services. As well as selling a service for a principal as an intermediary, the latter could buy in rights to services as though the principal was in fact a subcontractor. In this way, small local travel agents sometimes put together package holidays aimed at segments of their own market. An agent which acts as intermediary for the sale of other tour operators' coach holidays may buy in hotel, coach and sightseeing services direct from the principals and sell the entire tour under its own brand name. The travel agent effectively becomes a principal. While there is potential benefit from being able to earn both the retail agent's and the tour operator's profit margin, this strategy poses potential risk for the intermediary who must cover all the fixed costs of the principal, rather than just earning a commission on every service sold.

### 9.3.2 Service characteristics as an influence on the role of intermediaries

Services are not homogeneous and this is reflected in the role played by intermediaries. While some services can be handled by a large number of intermediaries, others cannot easily be handled by intermediaries at all. The characteristics of services and of customers' expectations need to be considered before a strategy for intermediaries is developed.

- Some services experience highly variable outcomes, making efforts at controlling quality through intermediaries very difficult to achieve. This is particularly true of personal services such as hairdressing which are most commonly provided by small businesses direct to final consumers without the use of intermediaries.
- Some services may be highly specialized and likely to be neglected by intermediaries with inadequate training or knowledge. A service principal may gain no competitive advantage if intermediaries are incapable of giving appropriate sales and co-production support. Where a service is complex, the service principal must pay careful attention to the selection of intermediaries, or alternatively deal directly with consumers. Within the package holiday industry, skiing and activity holidays are quite specialized services for which most travel agents have inadequate knowledge to handle effectively. Some operators of these holidays have chosen to operate through intermediaries such as specialist outdoor pursuit agencies, while many more prefer to deal directly with their target markets.
- Margins available on a service may be insufficient to support many intermediaries, if any at all. Domestic and industrial cleaning services often operate on very low margins, resulting in most services being provided direct to consumers.
- Legislation or voluntary codes of conduct may limit the choice of intermediary available to a service principal, or make it impossible to act through them at all. In the UK, the Financial Services Act 1986 is a good example of legislation which directly constrains the distribution opportunities available for certain services. The Act requires that specified financial services may only be handled by authorized intermediaries. Also, voluntary codes provide an additional constraint for some services. An example is that operated by the Association of British Travel Agents (ABTA) governing the manner in which package holidays can be sold. ABTA does not generally allow its retail agent members to sell any overseas holidays of tour operators who are not themselves members of the association.

## 9.4 Direct sale

Should a service principal involve intermediaries at all? Direct sale is a particularly attractive option for service providers where the service offer is complex and variable and where legal constraints make the involvement of intermediaries difficult. With increasing use of centralized electronic databases and the development of the Internet, direct sale is becoming more important for many organizations. The attractions of direct sale are numerous:

- The service provider is in regular direct contact with consumers of its service, making faster feedback of customer comments a possibility. This can facilitate the process of improving existing services or developing new ones.

- It can be easier for service principals to develop relationships with customers if they are in regular contact. Databases can be built up to provide a profile of individual customers, allowing for more effective targeting of new service offers.

- Intermediaries may jealously guard their customers from the service principal, in the fear that any initial contact between the service principal and consumer could result in the role of the intermediary being diminished. Having spent time and effort attracting their customer, they do not wish to see the service principal picking up the long-term benefits of repeat business without the revenue earning involvement of the intermediary. The service principal therefore loses a lot of valuable feedback. In the travel industry, agents deliberately do not pass on the addresses of customers to the tour operating company with whom they are booked, disclosing only a telephone number for emergency use.

- In the public sector, political considerations or fears over confidentiality may prevent services being provided by private sector intermediaries. Definitions of what is politically acceptable change over time. In the UK, many have considered that school catering, refuse collection and leisure centre services are vital public services which could only be supplied directly by public sector bodies. It is now widely accepted that all of these can be provided through service intermediaries of one form or another, although debate continues about whether more contentious services such as prisons and security services should be provided through private sector intermediaries. From the opposite approach, the use of public sector organizations as intermediaries has been increasingly accepted. As an example, hospitals are being used to make a widening range of private sector, health-related services available, including financial and legal services.

- The service principal can retain for itself the profit margin which would have been paid to an intermediary. This could be beneficial where its own distribution costs are lower than the commission that it would have paid to an intermediary.

Quite often, service principals choose to make their services available both directly and through intermediaries. This can be an attractive option as it allows the principal to target segments which may have very different buying behaviour. As an example, one segment of the holiday-buying public may seek the reassurance provided by being able to walk into and talk to a travel agent, while another segment might be more confident, price sensitive and short of time, for whom direct booking with a tour operator by telephone or Internet is attractive. Against the advantages of segmenting the market in this way can come significant problems. Intermediaries can become demotivated if they see a principal for whom they are working as agent selling the same services direct to the public. To make matters worse, direct sale promotional material often emphasizes the benefits of not using an intermediary, typically lower prices and faster service. Occasionally, agents' trade associations have threatened to boycott the products of principals who act in this way – Eagle Star Insurance, for example, encountered initial hostility when it launched Eagle Star Direct in apparent competition with its agents. One solution

**Figure 9.4**

NIG Skandia has built a successful insurance business by working closely with insurance brokers. This advertisement from a 1997 campaign sought to redress the drift of customers to direct sales companies which had occurred, by stressing an advantage of using an intermediary (reproduced with permission of NIG Skandia)

# DIRECT LINE CUSTOMERS COULD SAVE 20% BY TALKING TO AN INTERMEDIARY.

A recent survey of ex Direct Line car insurance customers now insuring with NIG Skandia, on the advice of their BROKERS & INDEPENDENT INTERMEDIARIES, showed on average they saved over 20% of the Direct Line price. If you are a Direct Line customer we suggest you call a broker or intermediary today to see how much money you could save.

is to split an organization into two distinct operating units with their own brand identity, one to operate through intermediaries and the other to sell direct to the final consumer. This was the solution adopted by the Thomson Travel Group, who in addition to selling holidays through travel agents under the Thomson and Horizon brand names (among others) also sell basically similar holidays direct to the public under the Portland brand name.

## 9.4.1 The Internet and disintermediation

With the early development of the Internet, it was widely predicted that service principals would be able to dispense with intermediaries and distribute their services directly to each customer. The growth of direct selling intermediaries such as Direct Line Insurance appeared to confirm the ability to cut out intermediaries, who were often portrayed as parasitic and delaying middlemen. The inelegant term '**disintermediation**' has been used to describe the process of removing intermediaries from a distribution channel and developing direct communications.

The Internet does not change the basic principles of the role of intermediaries who exist to simplify buyers' choice processes. When several companies seek to develop direct relationships with their customers, buyers are faced with a confusing array of messages. Faced with dozens of insurance companies seeking to sell insurance directly, consumers are likely to simplify their choice process by using an intermediary who can carry out some of the buyer's search activity on their behalf. The result has therefore been the emergence of a new generation of Internet intermediaries, or '**informediaries**'. In the travel sector, numerous informediaries such as Expedia and Travelocity have emerged to simplify consumers' buying process, fulfilling very much the same type of role as the traditional high street travel agent. Many service principals have realized that gaining the attention of the final consumer is becoming increasingly difficult in a congested cyberspace. 'Electronic shelf space' may be almost infinite, but service principals need to be sure that target customers will come past their site. So instead of heavily promoting their own site, many companies have resorted to using informediaries. Disintermediation has turned into '**reintermediation**' and the basic principles of channel design are little changed.

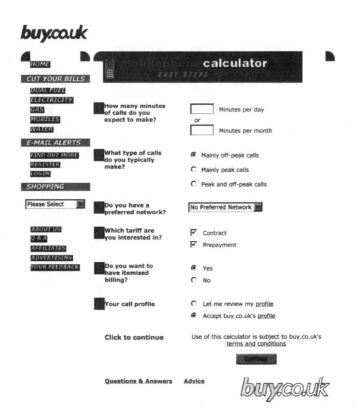

**Figure 9.5**

Many Internet-based companies have emerged to make the buying process easier. At the click of a mouse, buy.com allows visitors to its site to compare prices of such services as electricity and gas supply and mobile phones. For the consumer, it makes for an easier search process. For an informediary such as buy.com a good site brings revenue as visitors 'click through' to service suppliers who pay a commission in respect of each sale that is generated (reproduced with permission of buy.com)

## 9.5 Selection of intermediaries

Service principals often decide that the most efficient and effective means of delivering their service is in collaboration with intermediaries of various types. Service intermediaries take many forms in terms of their size, structure, legal status and relationship to the service principal. Because of this diversity, attempts at classification can become confused by the level of overlap present. In this section, attention is focused on the characteristics of four important types of intermediary – agents, retailers, wholesalers and franchisees.

### 9.5.1 Service agents

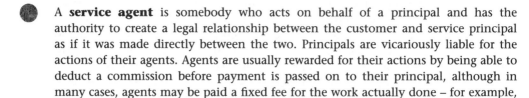

A **service agent** is somebody who acts on behalf of a principal and has the authority to create a legal relationship between the customer and service principal as if it was made directly between the two. Principals are vicariously liable for the actions of their agents. Agents are usually rewarded for their actions by being able to deduct a commission before payment is passed on to their principal, although in many cases, agents may be paid a fixed fee for the work actually done – for example, in preparing a new market prior to the launch of a new service.

For service principals, the use of agents offers many advantages:

- Capital requirements for creating a chain of distribution outlets are minimized, allowing reinvestment in core service production.
- Consumers may expect choice at the point of service purchase, and it is usually easier for an independent agent to do this rather than the service principal to set up distribution outlets which sell competing products. (In the case of many financial services, the UK Financial Services Act 1986 makes it difficult for service principals to both sell their own products and those of competitors – for example banks and building societies must choose between becoming a 'tied' agent of one service principal, or offering a genuine choice to customers.
- Where a service principal is entering a new market, it may lack the knowledge which allows it to understand buyer behaviour and the nature of competition in that market. Many overseas financial institutions with a poor understanding of the UK mortgage market chose to make mortgage services available by means of independent mortgage brokers and, in some cases, established UK building societies.
- In the case of overseas markets, it may be illegal for a service principal to deal directly with the public, a problem which can be remedied by acting through a local licensed agent.
- In some cases, special skills are required by a service principal which would be very costly to develop in-house. A shipping company may not have the need for a full-time employee to be based at the Baltic Exchange charter market and it would therefore be more sensible to employ an agent who is a member of the Exchange to sell shipping capacity as and when required, either on a commission or fixed charge basis.

In an age when direct sales of car and household insurance have been rising markedly, should we be writing the epitaphs for the traditional insurance broker?

Increasing segments of customers have been prepared to trade in the impersonality of telephone sales for the lower cost and greater convenience which 'direct sell' insurance companies tend to offer. From the viewpoint of the insurance companies themselves, there has been a growing desire to enter into a dialogue with customers directly, cutting out the inefficiencies which could occur by acting through intermediaries. This can also eliminate the variability inherent in insurance brokers' efforts at selling policies and in acting as co-producers of companies' policies.

However, a large segment of insurance buyers remained unmoved by the efforts of the direct sell companies. For this segment, the reassurance of face-to-face contact and the ability of a broker to shop around on behalf of the customer were undoubtedly attractions. So, while many insurance companies sought to reduce the role of intermediaries in distributing their policies, others, such as Independent Insurance, sought to develop sales through them. A key part of Independent's strategy to gain competitive advantage rested on the quality of service which customers received at its network of agencies. The company found itself with an expensive and lumbering network of over 10 000 agents, the majority of which had very little detailed knowledge of the services offered by Independent and produced insignificant levels of business. The company decided to cut the size of its distribution network to the 4000 agents who were most effective at generating business and to support this focused network with a higher standard of service.

A key part of Independent's efforts revolved around collaboration with agents by offering free staff training, regular newsletters, the services of Independent's marketing department (for example to develop local advertising campaigns), a profit sharing scheme and priority attention from the company to its selected agents.

Independent also used its agents to do something which the direct sell companies were getting better at – listening to customers. Feedback and brainstorming sessions were held during which Independent could pick up information about customer needs and discuss with agents ways of improving the service which between them they offered.

Independent's strategy towards distribution appeared to have contributed to its financial success during the 1990s. Its actions illustrate the need to segment markets between groups who have differing needs in terms of accessibility to a service. But as more people become familiar with buying financial services direct from a centralized provider, will Independent's market diminish? Or has it taught us a lesson that intermediaries – as co-producers of a service – can add significant value in selling sometimes complex financial services to buyers for whom a direct sale service lacks the benefits of perceived local access and personal contact?

### 9.5.2  Retail outlets

The notion of a retailer in the service sector poses conceptual problems, for it has already been established that a retailer cannot carry a stock of services, one of the important functions of a retailer of goods. The distinction between a retailer and an agent or franchisee (see below) can be a fine one. In general, a retailer operates in a manner which does not create legal relations between the service principal and the final customer – the customer's relationship is only with the retailer.

Many services which pass through retailers have a significant goods element. As an example, many film-processing companies sell their services through retail chemists under the brand name of the chemist. The latter takes a profit margin while allowing the film-processing company to make its service available locally. Many services, such as key cutting and fast-food catering are often retailed in the form of a franchise agreement which is discussed below.

Sometimes, service retailers undertake another of the traditional goods retailer's function in taking risk. A retailer can buy the right to a block of service transactions and if these rights are not sold by the time the service is performed, the value of these rights disappears. This can happen where a ticket agent buys a block of tickets on a no-return basis from an event organizer.

### 9.5.3  Service wholesalers

Similar conceptual problems apply to the role of the wholesaler. For services, the term is most sensibly understood where an intermediary buys the right to a large volume of service transactions and then proceeds to break these down into smaller units of rights to a service for handling by retailers or other intermediaries. Hotel booking agencies who buy large blocks of hotel accommodation earn their margin by buying in volume at low prices and adding a mark-up as a block booking is broken down into smaller units for sale to retailers or agents. As with retailers, it can be difficult to distinguish a wholesaler from an agent. A hotel wholesaler may have some rights to return unsold accommodation to the hotels concerned and may include in their dealings with customers a statement that the transaction is to be governed by conditions specified by the service principal.

## 9.6  Franchised service distribution

 The term '**franchising**' refers to a relationship where one party – the franchisor – provides the development work on a service format and monitors standards of delivery, while coming to an arrangement with a second party – the franchisee – who is licensed to deliver the service, taking some share of the financial risk and reward in return. Vertical franchising occurs where a manufacturer allows a franchisee an exclusive right to sell its goods within a specified area. The more recent business format franchising occurs where an organization allows others to copy the format of its own operations.

The International Franchise Association has defined a franchise operation as:

> ... a contractual relationship between the franchisor and franchisee in which the franchisor offers or is obliged to maintain a continuing interest in the business of the franchisee in such areas as know-how and training; wherein the franchise operates under a common trade name, format or procedure owned by or controlled by the franchisor, and in which the franchisee has made or will make a substantial capital investment in his business from his own resources.

The services sector has seen considerable recent growth in franchising. According to the annual NatWest Bank/British Franchise Association survey, the total turnover of UK business format franchises in 1998 was £7bn, and it has been estimated that this figure has been growing at a rate of about 5 % per annum. Franchising offers particular opportunities for service industries which are people intensive by combining the motivation of self-employed franchisees with the quality control and brand values of the franchisor.

Franchise agreements cover a diverse range of services, from car hire to fast food, kitchen design services, veterinary services and hotels. Of the top 10 UK business franchise operations (in terms of turnover), all are involved in essentially service-based activities, ranging from fast food to car hire and car servicing. Although most franchisees are self-employed individuals or small companies, they can also be very large organizations. To illustrate this, it is quite common to find corporate franchisees who operate a large number of hotels for a franchisor, making the franchisee a very large organization. Franchising also has applications within the public sector (see below).

Once franchising has taken hold within an organization, it tends to expand rather than contract. If a franchisor has built up a successful brand format coupled with successful management, it can usually achieve greater returns on its capital by selling the right to use its name rather than operating its own outlets. The British School of Motoring, for example, has steadily increased the proportion of its outlets which are franchised from 24% in 1980 to over 80% in 1998. Other strongly managed brands which have followed this route include Prontaprint, Wendy's Restaurants and Swinton Insurance.

There is a limit to which operations can be franchised and most franchisors choose not to franchise their operations entirely. There are two important reasons for this. Firstly, new product development is usually easier to carry out in-house rather than at a distance through a franchise. In this way it avoids alienating franchisees should experimental new services fail. Secondly, some operations may be too specialized to expect a franchisee to have the standard of training to ensure a consistent standard of delivery and the franchisor may choose to retain responsibility for providing these.

Maintaining and motivating franchisees is a constant challenge for franchisors. Franchisees can become only too aware of the payments which the franchisor takes from them on an ongoing basis in return for dubious support. During 1997, the UK franchisees of the restaurant chain Pierre Victoire collectively protested at the franchisor's management abilities. In the USA, some franchisee associations have brought legal actions against their franchisor for granting excessive numbers of franchises which have adversely affected existing franchisees. In such situations, many franchisees may be tempted not to renew their franchise at the end of their agreement and to either go it alone or sign up with another franchise operation. Where brands are strong, the former route can be very risky – for example Benetton retail franchisees who have used their premises to provide their own competing service format have lost customers when the franchisor creates a new outlet in the locality. Payment of franchise fees represents good value to a franchisee for as long as it receives good back-up from the franchisor and a steady supply of customers who are attracted by the reputation of the franchise brand.

### 9.6.1 The nature of a franchise agreement

A franchise agreement sets out the rights and obligations of the franchisor and franchisee and typically includes the following main clauses:

- The nature of the service which is to be supplied by the franchisee is specified. This can refer to particular categories of service which are to be offered – for example a car repair franchise would probably indicate which specific service operations (such as brake replacement, engine tuning) are covered by the franchise agreement.
- The territory in which the franchisee is given the right to offer a service is usually specified. The premium which a franchisee is prepared to pay for a franchisee usually reflects the exclusivity of its territory.
- The length of a franchise agreement is specified – most franchises run for a period of 5–10 years with options to renew at the end of the period.
- The franchisee usually agrees to buy the franchise for an initial fee and agrees the basis on which future payments are to be made to the franchisor. The level of the initial fee reflects the strength of an established brand – a high initial fee for a strong established brand can be much less risky for a franchisee than a low price for a relatively new franchise. Payment of ongoing fees to the franchisee is usually calculated as a percentage of turnover. The agreement also usually requires the franchisee to buy certain supplies from the franchisor. Agreements vary widely – for example the British School of Motoring makes no initial charge to franchisees but subsequently charges a fixed weekly fee which includes much of the equipment which the franchisee uses.
- The franchisee agrees to follow instructions from the franchisor concerning the manner of service delivery. Franchisees are typically required to charge according to an agreed scale of prices, maintain standards of reliability, availability and performance in the delivery of the service and to ensure that any advertising follows the franchisor's guidelines.
- The franchisee usually agrees not to act as an intermediary for any other service principal, insisting that their franchised outlets show the same loyalty to the organization as if they were actually owned by it. Thus the operator of a Pizza Express franchise cannot use a franchised outlet to sell the services or goods of a competing organization such as Burger King. Franchising implies a degree of control which the franchisor has over the franchisee, unlike a retail agent who usually has considerable discretion over the manner in which they conduct their business. For the franchisor, considerable harm could result

from its promotion being used to draw potential customers into the franchisee's outlets, only for them to be cross-sold a service over which the franchisor has no control nor is likely to receive any financial benefit. However, in many cases, service franchises are sold on the understanding that they will form just one small part of the franchisee's operations – for example a franchise to operate a courier service's collection point may be compatible with the business of a service station or newsagent franchisee.

- The franchisor agrees to provide promotional support for the franchisee. The aim of such support is to establish the values of the franchisor's brand in the minds of potential customers, thereby reducing the promotion which the franchisee is required to undertake. The franchise agreement usually requires certain promotional activity of the franchisee to be approved by the franchisor.
- The franchisor usually agrees to provide some level of administrative and technical support for the franchisee. This can include the provision of equipment (e.g. printing machines for a fast-print franchise) and administrative support such as accounting.
- Franchise agreements usually give either party the right to terminate the franchise and for the franchisee to sell their franchise. The right to terminate can act as a control mechanism should either party fail to perform in accordance with the conditions of the franchise. A successful franchisee would want a clause in an agreement allowing him or her to sell the goodwill of a franchise which they have developed over time.

### 9.6.2 Public sector franchising

Public services are increasingly being delivered by franchise agreements in order to capitalize on the motivation of smaller scale franchisees which was described above. Franchising can take a number of forms:

- The right to operate a vital public service can be sold to a franchisee who in turn has the right to charge users of the facility. The franchisee will normally be required to maintain the facility to a required standard and to obtain government approval of prices to be charged. In the UK, the government has offered private organizations franchises to operate vital road links, including the Dartford river crossing and Severn Bridge. In the case of the latter, an Anglo-French consortium acquired the right to collect tolls from users of the bridge and in return paid to develop a second river crossing and agreed to carry out routine maintenance work.
- Government can sell the exclusive right for private organizations to operate a private service which is of public importance. Private sector radio and television broadcasting is operated on a franchise basis where the government invites bids from private companies for exclusive rights to broadcast in specified areas and/or times.
- Where a socially necessary but economically unviable service is provided in a market-mediated environment, government can subsidize provision of the service by means of a franchise. In the UK, rail passenger services are now provided by private train operators who have a franchise to operate a route,

typically for about seven years. As most rail services are loss making, this has entailed government paying franchisees to operate a service, with franchisees being selected on the basis of, among other things, the amount of subsidy they would need to operate a service. Successful bidders keep the revenue which they generate from passengers, subject to meeting the minimum requirements of the rail regulator in terms of timetables, reliability, fares, etc.

- Even though a public service is not market-mediated at the point of delivery, production methods may nevertheless be market-mediated and part of the production function provided through a franchise agreement. Such an arrangement can have benefits for customers where the franchisee is rewarded partly on the basis of feedback from users. A recent application of this type of franchise can be found in the field of higher education where many universities have franchised their courses to colleges of further education.

- In the UK, possibly the longest established public sector franchise is seen in the Post Office. In addition to government owned 'Crown' post offices, 'Sub' post offices have traditionally been operated on a franchise basis in smaller towns. Franchises have been taken up by a variety of small shops and newsagents and generally offer a more limited range of postal services compared to Crown offices.

The past 20 years have seen many major changes in the way higher education is managed in the UK, with marketing playing a much greater role. Underlying this has been a growth in numbers entering higher education, rising from under 10% to about 30% of all 18-year-olds in a couple of decades. Making additional capacity available to the enlarged number of students has been a challenge for universities, whose facilities have become increasingly stretched. One solution adopted by many of them has been franchising, using principles borrowed from the private business sector.

Franchising offered benefits to universities and to franchisee colleges of further education who would deliver part of the former's programmes. For universities, local accessibility to courses and expansion in numbers was allowed using staff and facilities of another organization. It could allow the universities to concentrate on higher level teaching and research, while colleges undertook foundation courses. For colleges, a franchise would allow a broader portfolio of courses to be marketed, which was especially important, given the rising levels of competition from schools for its traditional students.

Both the university and the local college become involved in the marketing of franchised courses. The franchisee college can appeal to its local population on the basis of being a caring local community facility, while the university can add to this at both a local and national level. If the reputation of the university is itself weak, the task of recruiting students for franchised colleges will be more difficult.

At the heart of an educational franchise is the requirement to maintain consistent standards so that a student studying at a franchised college receives substantially the same education as one studying at the franchising university. Vetting of colleges at the outset is crucial to ensure that they have the staff, accommodation and technical resources capable of delivering the specified course. Once a scheme is running, close monitoring is required from the university on such matters as assessment standards and the quality of teaching materials delivered.

Quality control of franchise colleges has been highlighted in numerous reports by the government's Quality Assurance Agency (QAA). These have often pointed to a failure of quality control from the beginning of many franchise operations, for example through poor specification of requirements at the outset and through some of the essential quality requirements not having been met. Subsequent reports have shown the difficulties which some universities have got into, especially when franchising their courses to overseas colleges where quality control is much more difficult.

What is the future of higher education franchising? If the experience of most other service sectors is anything to go by, it will continue to grow. A franchise relationship between university and college will last for as long as it is in both organizations' interests for it to do so. A college could in some cases run a course on its own without reference to a university, but against the saving in franchise fees must be set the greater cost and difficulty of recruiting students who may be unaware of the qualities of the college. Students may perceive a franchised course which is validated by a university as being much more valuable than one validated by a local college in its own name. But given that quality control is crucial to maintaining the good brand image of the franchising university, will many come to think that maintaining such controls over culturally different and geographically dispersed colleges is too much effort? Could they overcome their capacity problems or exploit new accessibility possibilities opened up by the Internet?

## 9.7 Accessibility through co-production

Some services organizations choose to make their services available to consumers in combination with other goods and services with the collaboration of another producer. The outputs of the two organizations can be quite diverse – for example a finance company could offer loan facilities in conjunction with customers buying hi-fi equipment. Other examples include a combined train fare and museum admission ticket and a combined hotel and travel offer.

On other occasions, a service can be made available in combination with similar services provided by potential competitors. The basis for doing this is that the combined value of the enlarged service offer will generate more business and ultimately be of benefit to all service providers involved. In this way, many regional travel tickets allow passengers to travel on the trains and buses of potentially competing operators, thereby making public transport as a whole a relatively attractive option. Similarly, banks benefit by sharing cash dispenser networks – those sharing gain a competitive advantage over a bank which chooses to go it alone with its own dedicated but smaller network. In Britain, as in most Western countries, legislation exists to restrict such collaborative activities where they are deemed to be anti-competitive and therefore against the public interest. Banks, for example, were accused of collusion in 2000 when they collectively agreed a scale of charges for using each others' ATM machines which was deemed by many to be far in excess of the banks' actual costs.

Technology has had significant effects on the way service organizations deal with their customers, and whether they have to rely on delivering their service through intermediaries rather than directly to customers. The use by insurance companies of databases which can maintain a one-to-one dialogue with each customer is evidence of this. But what are we to make of current developments in the Internet? Could this be one more step down the road towards direct delivery by a service principal and the elimination of intermediaries?

The idea of service principals all dealing with each of their customers on a one-to-one basis may sound initially appealing, but reality needs to be separated from the hope and the hype. Consider the following factors which all suggest a continuing role for service intermediaries:

- Will there remain significant segments of buyers who prefer face-to-face contact with a locally appointed intermediary?
- Will Internet facilities be able to offer buyers an effective and easily found choice? In fact we are seeing the emergence of new Internet intermediaries whose function is to create easily assessable choices for customers.
- Where services involve the delivery of tangibles (e.g. home delivery/fast food), how can a centrally located Internet service provider manage without local distribution agents?

## 9.8 Making the tangible components of the service offer available to consumers

For some services, tangible goods are a vital element of the overall offering and a strategy is needed for making them available to consumers. Managing the availability of tangibles assumes importance for a number of reasons:

- Tangibles may be vital in giving pre-sales evidence of a service offer in the form of printed brochures and order forms, etc. An indication of the logistical problems in making brochures available to potential customers is provided by the task facing Thomson Holidays. If the company was to distribute 50 copies of its main summer holiday brochure to each of over 7000 ABTA travel agents in Britain, it would need to move over 350 000 brochures. The fact that Thomson produces multiple brochures aimed at different segments of the holiday market makes the logistical task even greater.
- Tangibles often form an important component of a service offer and failure to deliver tangibles reduces the quality of a service or makes it impossible to

perform at all. This is true of fast-food restaurant chains for whom perishable raw materials have to be moved regularly and rapidly.

- Sometimes the fundamental purpose of a service process is to make goods available. Retailers and equipment rental companies provide a service, but without a strategy to move the associated goods effectively, their service becomes of little value.
- The freight transport service sector exists solely to move goods.

Where tangibles form an important part of a service offer, their efficient and effective distribution can give an organization a competitive advantage. An inefficient and unreliable distribution system can negate a restaurant chain's efforts at improving service quality if it is unable to deliver advertised meal offers. There are many texts covering the subject of physical distribution management in detail (refer to Selected Further Reading at the end of this chapter). Here, a brief overview of the key elements of a physical distribution system is offered.

### 9.8.1  Physical distribution management

The design of a physical distribution system begins by setting objectives. Ideally, a system should make the right goods available in the right place at the right time. Against this must be balanced the need to minimize the cost of distribution, so objectives are stated in a form which involves a trade-off – for example a holiday tour operator might realistically aim to deliver 80% of brochure requests to travel agents within three working days at the minimum possible cost. Distribution objectives in turn are based on an assessment of customers' needs. While a fast-food restaurant chain might be happy to live with a three-day delivery objective for orders for packaging materials, 24-hour delivery may be required for perishable foods. The importance of rapid and reliable delivery of fresh food would be reflected in a greater willingness to pay premium prices for a service which is capable of meeting objectives – failure to deliver could have a harmful effect on sales and reputation.

Physical distribution systems can be seen as comprising six basic elements which can be manipulated to design an optimum system. They are shown in Figure 9.6 and the management decisions which need to be made in respect of each of these are considered below.

**Suppliers**  A marketing-oriented services organization must balance the need to have supply sources close to customers against economies of scale which may be obtained from having one central point of supply. Where markets are turbulent, the distribution system may favour suppliers who are closest to the customer rather than necessarily the cheapest sources of production. During a period of market turbulence, a domestic tour operator may source brochures at home rather than wait for them to be delivered from a possibly cheaper source overseas.

**Outlets**  These can range from the individual household through to the largest hypermarket. If the unique offer of a service is home delivery, strategy must

**Figure 9.6**

Elements of a physical distribution system

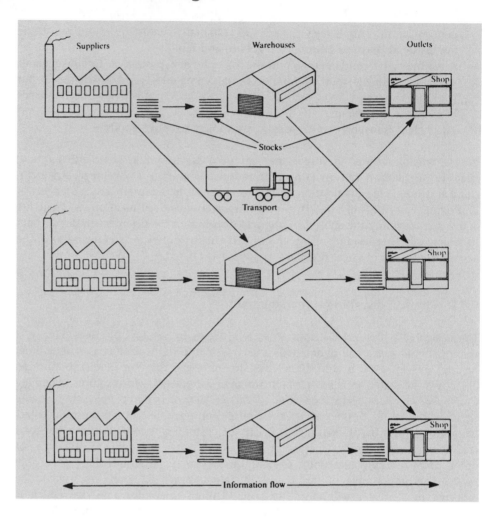

identify the most efficient and effective means of moving associated tangibles to customers' homes.

**Stocks**   These need to be held in order to provide rapid availability of goods and to provide contingencies against disruptions in production. Stocks also occur because of the need to achieve economies of scale in production, resulting in initially large stockholdings which are gradually reduced until the next production run. Seasonal patterns of production and consumption may also contribute towards fluctuating stock levels. The need to make stock readily available has to be offset against the need to minimize the cost of stockholding which can result from capital charges, storage charges and the risk of obsolescence.

**Warehouses**   These are incorporated into a system to provide a break of bulk point, and to hold stocks. A company must decide on the number and nature of the warehouses which are incorporated into its system, in particular the balance between the need for local and accessible warehouses against the need for efficiency

**FREE***
**home delivery**
SOMERFIELD

**Figure 9.7**
Somerfield Stores competes on the strength of its home-delivery service, which it developed in 1998 and has led the major supermarket chains. This calls for a reconsideration of physical distribution strategy if customers' expectations are to be met efficiently and effectively. From the start, Somerfield made deliveries from its existing stores, but greater efficiencies could be obtained by using centralized and automated warehouses. Problems still remain of delivering goods at a time when busy households are at home to receive them (reproduced with permission of Somerfield Stores plc)

savings which favour large warehouses. Automation of warehouses with the development of computerized picking systems is increasingly favouring larger warehouses – a typical national supermarket in the UK would now include just half a dozen strategically located warehouses in its distribution system to serve a national chain of outlets.

**Transport**   This moves stocks from manufacturers to retail outlets and sometimes – as in the case of mail order or home delivery of milk – to final consumers. Transport is becoming an increasingly important element of distribution systems, with goods tending to travel for longer average distances within the system. UK government statistics indicate that in 1998 over 60% of all tonnage was carried by road (Transport Statistics, 2000).

**Information flow**   The need to respond to customers' requirements rapidly, while at the same time keeping down stockholding levels, demands a rapid flow of information. The development of just-in-time (JIT) systems has only been possible with the improvement of data-processing techniques. The introduction of bar codes has achieved notable results in this respect. A supermarket can now know minute by minute the state of stocks for all its products and can order replacement stocks – by an electronic data link – for delivery from a regional distribution centre the following day. The regional distribution centres can similarly rapidly reorder stocks from their suppliers. The development of JIT systems has not only allowed a more reliable level of availability of goods to the final consumer, but it has also allowed retailers to reduce warehouse space provided within shops. Because it is no longer necessary to hold large stocks locally, warehouse space can be turned over to more valuable sales floor space.

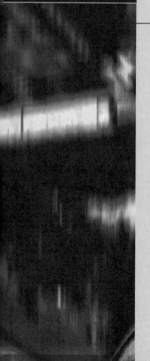

**Case Study**

## Shell chooses franchisees to put the service back into service stations

Petrol is a commodity which cannot easily be differentiated. During the 1980s and 1990s, oil companies had sought to increase their share of retail petrol sales by attempting to differentiate their corporate image and occasionally the product itself. The Shell oil company had tried both corporate and product differentiation strategies to boost its market share but remained subject to severe price competition in an overcrowded petrol station market. One attempt to differentiate its tangible product – the introduction of 'Formula Shell' – had gone badly wrong with reports of additives in petrol burning out customers' engines. The idea of a service station offering a comprehensive range of services appeared to have been lost in the rush to sell more petrol.

From the late 1980s, the strategy of Shell focused increasingly on the manner in which petrol was retailed. Instead of simply being a point at which a commodity was dispensed, Shell sought to position its outlets as places where customers could enjoy a wide range of services in a pleasant environment. The blueprint for the proposed service mix of its service stations included the provision of minimarkets, facilities for obtaining hot snacks as well as the more traditional petrol station services such as car washes.

Research had shown that a significant segment of the petrol buying population was not very price sensitive. This included individuals buying petrol which is later reimbursed by their employers and those who only infrequently need to purchase petrol. For these segments, the quality of service received at an outlet was more important than price alone. Shell needed a strategy for managing its sites which would put the service back into its service stations and to ensure that customers could be sure of the same high standards of service whichever Shell station they visited. Shell aimed to be the Marks and Spencer of the forecourt world with not only good products on sale, but also high-quality customer service.

Like most other oil companies, Shell had traditionally granted licences to operators to run its company-owned sites. The licence focused on the agreement to supply petrol with little stipulation about the manner in which it was to be sold, other than basic operational and safety rules. In the early 1990s, Shell introduced a franchise scheme called SHARE (Standards, High Quality and Retailer Excellence) which allowed individuals to buy a 10-year franchise to operate a site. The franchisee pays a sum of money for a franchise which he or she is free to develop within limits specified by Shell, and subject to meeting minimum standards of service. In return, Shell provides business and marketing support to the franchisee.

Forecourt shops are an area which Shell has seen as a growth area and has given valuable support to franchisees in their operation. This support has included the development of store designs which are based on customer research, negotiation with suppliers to get advantageous deals for franchisees, promotional and merchandising support and assistance with bookkeeping and administrative duties.

One person who saw the advantages of the SHARE scheme was Andrew Brown who had run a Shell company-owned site on the outskirts of Alcester, Warwickshire for a number of years. A proposed bypass would have had the effect of drastically reducing traffic flows past the site. Out of this apparent problem, Brown saw a possible opportunity, for land was available for development at an important new junction of the bypass where traffic flows were expected to reach 40 000 vehicles per day by 1995. He therefore set about buying the site and obtaining planning permission for a new service station ahead of the opening of the new bypass. Unlike the existing station, the new site is operated on a franchise basis with a 10-year fuel supply agreement running in tandem with the franchise. It opened after Brown had undergone a mandatory franchisee training programme at the Shell Management Training Centre in Coventry which gave him the foundations for running a successful SHARE service station and the ability and motivation to maintain the constant high standards required. The programme covered new ideas in multi-tasking, the setting up of rotas and sticking to them, and methods of ensuring standards of cleanliness and staff selection which were very different to what most company-owned site managers had been previously been practising.

He has successfully developed a wide range of services on the new site, including a shop and car wash. The franchise arrangement had worked to the mutual benefit of both partners, prompting them to begin negotiations to convert a second company-owned site at nearby Stratford-on-Avon into a similar franchise operation.

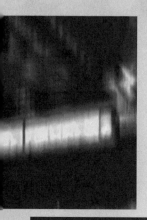

## Case study review questions

1  What business is Shell in, with respect to its filling stations?

2  Discuss the relative merits of franchising and direct management for service stations owned by Shell.

3  How and in what ways can services help to differentiate a commodity product such as petrol?

## Chapter summary and linkages to other chapters

Making services accessible to consumers involves some different principles compared to goods, largely arising out of the inseparability and intangibility of services. In particular, intermediaries become co-producers of a service. Services vary in the extent to which producers and consumers are able or willing to travel to each other in order for an inseparable service to be performed. Services firms in many sectors have sought to reduce the effects of inseparability through mail, telephone and internet access systems.

Intermediaries are often the main contact a customer has with an organization, therefore they can be critical to successful service encounters (**Chapter 3**) and contribute to the overall quality of a service (**Chapter 8**). Increasingly, intermediaries are being used to promote service firms' relationship marketing strategies, although problems still remain where intermediaries are suspicious of service principals who they fear are trying to reduce or eliminate their role (**Chapter 5**). The level of accessibility to a service is often reflected in the price charged for a service at a particular time and location (**Chapter 10**). When firms seek to expand overseas, new problems in developing accessibility are raised and these are discussed in **Chapter 13**.

## www linkages/URLs

British Franchise Association:
**http://www.british-franchise.org.uk/**

Southern Center for Logistics and Intermodal Transportation Georgia:
**http://www2.gasou.edu/coba/centers/lit**

Vanderbilt University eLab – contains useful discussion about electronic intermediaries:
**http://ecommerce.vanderbilt.edu**

## Key terms

Intermediary 255
Disintermediation 261
Reintermediation 261
Franchising 264

Co-producer 255
Informediaries 261
Service agent 262

## Chapter review questions

1   What are the most important factors influencing the location decision for a proposed new gymnasium?
2   Of what value are modelling techniques in deciding on retail store location?
3   In what ways does a travel agent assist tour operators in the process of making holidays available to its customers?
4   In what situations is a service principal likely to prefer dealing directly with its customers, rather than through intermediaries?
5   Using examples, contrast the role of 'push' and 'pull' methods of making services available within the services sector.
6   Analyse the potential problems and opportunities for a dry cleaning company seeking to expand through franchising.

## Selected further reading

*For a general discussion of the principles of distribution and the use of intermediaries, the following is useful:*

Rosenbloom, B. B. and G. Behrens Urich (1998) *Marketing Channels*, 6th edition, Dryden Press, New York

*The following paper investigates the relationship between distribution structure, consumer involvement and perceived service quality in the context of services marketing. Research found that perceived service quality is significantly affected by the type of channel structure (direct versus indirect) as well as consumers' level of involvement.*

Csipak, J. J., C. Chebat and V. Venkatesan (1995) 'Channel Structure, Consumer Involvement and Perceived Service Quality: An Empirical Study of the Distribution of a Service', *Journal of Marketing Management*, Vol. 11, No. 1, pp 227–41

*Much of the literature on relationship marketing is relevant to the analysis of relationships between service principals and their intermediaries. The following are useful:*

Ford, D., L. Gadde, H. Hakansson, A. Lundgren, I. Snehota, P. Turnbull and D. Wilson, (1998) *Managing Business Relationships*, Wiley, Chichester

Gummesson, E. (1999) *Total Relationship Marketing*, Butterworth Heinemann, London

Payne, A., M. Christopher, H. Peck and M. Clark (1999) *Relationship Marketing, Strategy and Implementation*, Butterworth-Heinemann, London

*For more detailed coverage of retailing issues, the following is useful:*

Fernie, J. (1997) 'Retail Change and Retail Logistics in the UK: Past Trends and Future Prospects', *The Service Industries Journal*, Vol. 17, No. 3, pp 383–396

*Finally, this chapter has considered only briefly the principles of physical distribution management, as they affect the tangible elements of a service offer. The following references offer further discussion of the principles:*

Bowersox, D. J. and D. J. Closs (1996) *Logistical Management: The Integrated Supply Chain Process*, McGraw-Hill, New York

Christopher, M. (1992) *'Logistics and Supply Chain Management'*, Pitman, London

Handfield, R. B. and E. L. Nichols (1999) *Introduction to Supply Chain Management*, Prentice-Hall, Englewood Cliffs, NJ

# 10

# The pricing of services

## Learning objectives

Getting pricing right is a crucial element of the marketing of most products, but can be particularly important for services. For service providers, calculating the cost of supplying a service can be very difficult where fixed costs are high and the service is highly perishable. Because of the inseparability of the service offer, new opportunities for price discrimination arise because service benefits cannot generally be transferred from one beneficiary to another. For highly intangible services, buyers often have few other bases for evaluating one service from another.

This chapter begins by reviewing the factors influencing an organization's price decisions, including organizational objectives, cost levels, strength of demand, level of competition and external price regulations. On the basis of these factors, pricing strategy is developed and implemented. Pricing strategy must be linked to other elements of service development strategy, so that customers perceive a price as representing value to themselves, while also being profitable for the supplier. Finally, specific issues raised in the pricing of public services and internally traded services are reviewed.

## 10.1 Introduction

Within the services sector, the term 'price' often passes under a number of names, sometimes reflecting the nature of the relationship between customer and provider in which exchange takes place. Professional services companies therefore talk about fees, while other organizations use terms such as fares, tolls, rates, charges and subscriptions. The art of successful pricing is to establish a price level which is sufficiently low that an exchange represents good value to buyers, yet is high enough to allow a service provider to achieve its financial objectives.

The importance of pricing to the development of marketing strategy is reflected in the diverse range of strategic uses to which it is put:

- At the beginning of the life of a new service, pricing is often used to gain entry to a new market. As an example, a firm of estate agents seeking to extend its operations to a new region may offer initially very low commission rates in order to build volume in a new market.
- Price is used as a means of maintaining the market share of a service during its life and is used tactically to defend its position against competitors.
- Ultimately, for organizations working to financial objectives, prices must be set at a level which allows them to meet their financial objectives.

Services are more likely than goods to be made available to consumers by methods where price is not the focal point of the exchange. Many public sector services are provided to the end consumer at either no charge or at a charge which bears little relation to the value of a service to the consumer or producer. Public services such as museums and schools which have sought to adopt marketing principles often do not have any control over the price element of the marketing mix. The reward for attracting more visitors to a museum or pupils to a school may be additional centrally derived grants, rather than income received directly from the users of the service.

## 10.2 Organisational influences on pricing decisions

Organizations show a wide variation in the objectives which they seek to achieve. An analysis of corporate objectives is a useful starting point for understanding the factors which underlie price decisions. Some commonly found organizational objectives and their implications for price decisions are analysed below.

- *Profit Maximisation*  It is often assumed that all private sector organizations exist primarily to maximize their profits and that this will therefore influence their pricing policies. In fact, the notion of profit maximization needs to be qualified with a time dimension, for marketing strategies which maximize profits over the short run may be detrimental to achieving long-term profits. An organization charging high prices in a new market may make that market seem very attractive to new entrants, thereby having the effect of increasing the level of competition in subsequent years, and so reducing long-term profitability. Also, the time frame over which profitability is sought can affect pricing decisions. If an innovative service is given an objective to break even after just one year, prices may be set at a low level in order to capture as large a share of the market as quickly as possible, whereas a longer term profit objective may have allowed the organization to tap relatively small but high-value segments of its markets in the first year and save the exploitation of lower value segments until subsequent years. The notion of profit maximization has a further weakness in the service sector where it can be difficult to establish clear relationships between costs, revenue and profits (see below).

- *Market share maximization* It has been frequently argued (e.g. Cyert and March, 1963) that it is unrealistic to expect the managers of a business to put all their efforts into maximizing profits. To begin with, there can be practical difficulties in establishing relationships between marketing strategy decisions and the resulting change in profitability. Secondly, management often does not directly receive any reward for increasing its organization's profits – its main concern is to achieve a satisfactory level of profits rather than the maximum possible. Managers may be more likely to benefit from decisions which increase the market share of their organization (e.g. through improved career opportunities and job security). An objective to maximize market share may be very important to service industries where it is necessary to achieve a critical mass in order to achieve economies of scale, and therefore a competitive advantage. The price competition which accompanied the emerging market for Internet Service Providers in the late 1990s was based on the desire of the main competitors to achieve a critical size which made them consumers' first choice for Internet-related activities.

- *Survival* Sometimes, the idea of maximizing profits or market share is a luxury to a service provider whose main objective is simply to survive and to avoid the possibility of going into receivership. Most businesses fail when they run out of cash flow at a critical moment when debts become due for payment. In these circumstances, prices may be set at a very low level simply to get sufficient cash into the organization to tide it over its short-term problems. During the Gulf War in 1991, demand for air travel fell significantly, putting severe pressure on the resources of many airlines who suffered doubly from the increase in aviation fuel prices. In a bid to stay afloat, many airlines were forced to lower fares dramatically simply in order to keep cash flowing into the business over what they thought would be the last hurdle before regaining a long-term growth path.

- *Social considerations* Profit-related objectives still have little meaning to many public sector services. At one extreme, the price of many public services represents a tax levied by government based on wider considerations of the ability of users to pay for the service and the public benefits of providing that service (e.g. fixed charges for National Health Service dental work in the UK with exemptions for disadvantaged groups). Where public services are provided in a more market mediated environment, pricing decisions may nevertheless be influenced by wider social considerations (e.g. non-vocational educational classes run by local authorities may charge a nominal fee for an adult literacy class, but a much higher fee for a golf tuition class). Although social objectives are normally associated with public sector services, they can sometimes be found within the private sector. Services provided by employers for their staff are often provided at a price which does not reflect their true value, but instead contribute towards staffs' total benefit package – examples include staff restaurants and sports clubs which are often priced at much lower levels than their normal market value.

In practice, organizations work to a number of objectives simultaneously – for example a market share objective over the short term may be seen as a means towards achieving a long-term profit maximizing objective.

## 10.3  Factors influencing pricing decisions

An organization's objectives determine the desired results of pricing policies. Strategies are the means by which these objectives are achieved. Before discussing pricing strategy, it is useful to lay the groundwork by analysing the underlying factors that influence price decisions. Four important bases for price determination can be identified:

1  What it costs to produce a service.
2  The amount that consumers are prepared to pay for it.
3  The price that competitors are charging.
4  The constraints on pricing that are imposed by regulatory bodies.

The cost of producing a service represents the minimum price that a commercial organization would be prepared to accept over the long term for providing the service. The maximum price achievable is that which customers are prepared to pay for the service. This will itself be influenced by the level of competition available to customers to satisfy their needs elsewhere. Government regulation may intervene to prevent organizations charging the maximum price that consumers would theoretically be prepared to pay. These principles are illustrated in Figure 10.1.

## 10.4  Costs as a basis for pricing

Many empirical studies have shown the importance of costs as a basis for determining prices within the service sector. For example, Zeithaml, Parasuraman and Berry (1985) in their study of service firms in the USA found that it was the dominant basis for price determination.

At its most simple, a 'cost-plus' pricing system works by using historical cost information to calculate a unit cost for each type of input used in a service production process. Subsequent price decisions for specific service outcomes are based on the number of units of inputs used, multiplied by the cost per unit, plus a profit margin. This method of setting prices is widely used in service industries as diverse as catering, building, accountancy and vehicle servicing. An example of how of a coach hire operator might calculate its prices on this basis is shown in Figure 10.2.

There are many reasons why 'cost-plus' type pricing methods are so widely used in the services sector:

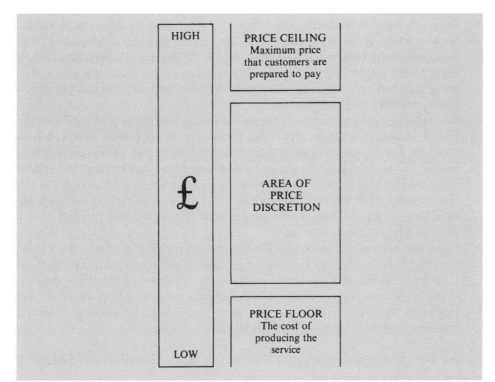

**Figure 10.1**
The key influences on price decisions

Cost information for most recent trading year:

| | |
|---|---|
| Total drivers' wage cost | £250 000 |
| Total drivers' hours worked | 45 000 |
| Cost per driver's hour | £5.55 |
| | |
| Total vehicle running costs | £100 000 |
| Total mileage operated | 250 000 |
| Vehicle operating costs per mile | £0.40 |
| | |
| Total other overhead costs | £30 000 |
| Overhead per mile operated | £0.12 |
| | |
| Required return on sales turnover | 15% |

For a price quotation based on a 200-mile journey requiring 12 hours of driver's time:

Total price =

| | |
|---|---|
| 200 miles x £0.40 | = £80.00 |
| 12 hours x £5.55 | = £66.60 |
| Overheads (based on mileage): | |
| 200 hours x £0.12 | = £24.00 |
| | |
| Total | = £170.60 |
| | |
| Add 30% margin | = £51.18 |
| | |
| TOTAL PRICE | = £221.78 |

**Figure 10.2**
'Cost plus' method of price setting for a coach operator

- Prices are easy to calculate and allow the delegation of price decisions for services which have to be tailored to the individual needs of customers. For example, every building job, vehicle repair or landscaped gardening job is likely to be unique and a price for each job can be calculated by junior staff using standard unit costs for the inputs required to complete the job and a predetermined profit margin.

- Where an agreement is made to provide a service, but the precise nature of the service which will actually be provided is unknown at the outset, a contract may stipulate that the final price will be based in some way on costs. A garage agreeing to repair a car brought in by a customer with an unidentified engine noise could not realistically give a price quotation before undertaking the job and examining the nature of the problem. In these circumstances, the customer may agree to pay an agreed amount per hour for labour, plus the cost of any parts which the garage buys in.

- Trade and professional associations often include codes of conduct which allow a service provider only to increase prices beyond those originally agreed in an estimate on the basis of the actual costs incurred. Solicitors and accountants, for example, who need to commit more resources to complete a job than was originally allowed for in their quotation are bound by their professional bodies to pass on only their reasonable additional costs.

Against these attractions, pricing services on the basis of historic costs presents a number of problems:

- In itself, cost-based pricing does not take account of the competition which a particular service faces at any given time, nor of the fact that some customers may value the same service more highly than others.

- Calculating the costs of a service can in fact be very difficult, and often more difficult than in the case of goods. One reason for this is the structure of costs facing many services businesses (discussed below).

- While it may be possible to determine costs for previous accounting periods, it can be difficult to predict what these costs will be in the future. This is a particular problem for services which are contracted to be provided at some time in the future. Unlike goods, it is not possible to produce the service at known cost levels in the current period and to store it for consumption in some future period. Historical cost information is often adjusted by an inflation factor where service delivery is to be made some time in the future, but it can be difficult to decide what is the most appropriate inflation factor to use for a specific input. Where input costs are highly volatile (e.g. aviation fuel), one solution is for a service producer to pass on part of the risk of unpredictable inflation to customers. Charter airlines frequently do this by requiring customers to pay for any increase in fuel costs beyond a specified amount.

### 10.4.1  Cost structures

The costs of producing a service can be divided into those which are variable and those which are fixed. Variable costs increase as service production increases,

**Table 10.1** Fixed and variable costs in selected service industries

| Service | Fixed costs | Variable |
|---------|-------------|----------|
| Restaurant | Building maintenance<br>Rent and rates<br>Waiters and cooks | Food |
| Bank mortgage | Staff time<br>Building maintenance<br>Corporate advertising | Sales commission<br>Paper and postage |
| Domestic air journey | Aircraft maintence and<br>  depreciation<br>Head-office administrative<br>  costs | Airport departure tax<br>In-flight meal |
| Hairdresser | Building maintenance<br>Rent and rates | Shampoos used |

whereas fixed costs remain unchanged if an additional unit of service is produced. Fixed costs therefore cannot be attributed to any particular unit of output. In between these two extremes of costs are semi-fixed costs which remain constant until a certain level of output is reached, when expenditure on additional units of productive capacity is needed. The particular problem of many services industries is that fixed costs represent a very high proportion of total costs, resulting in great difficulty in calculating the cost of any particular unit of service.

The importance of fixed costs for a number of services industries is illustrated in Table 10.1, where variable costs are defined as any cost which varies directly as a result of one extra customer consuming a service for which there is currently spare capacity. Thus, one more passenger on a domestic flight from London to Aberdeen will only result in nominal additional variable costs of an additional in-flight meal and the airport departure tax which has to be paid for each passenger. The cost of cabin crews and aircraft depreciation would not change, nor would those more remote fixed costs such as head-office administration and promotion.

It can be argued that over the long term, all costs borne by a business are variable. In the case of the airline, if the unit of analysis is a particular flight rather one individual passenger, the proportion of costs which are variable increases. So, if the airline withdrew just one return journey between the two points, it would save fuel costs, making fuel a variable cost. It would probably also save some staff costs, but may still have to incur aircraft depreciation costs and the more remote head-office administration costs. If the whole route was closed, even more costs would become variable – staff employed at the terminal could be cut, as could the flight crews. It may be possible for the airline to avoid some of its aircraft depreciation costs by reducing the size of its fleet. Even promotional costs would become variable as part of the airline's advertising would no longer need to be incurred if the service was closed completely.

High levels of fixed costs are associated with high levels of interdependency between the services which make use of the fixed cost elements. To illustrate this, the cost of maintaining a retail bank branch network is fixed over the short to medium term, yet the network provides facilities for a wide range of discrete service activities – current accounts, mortgages, business loans and foreign currency business to name but a few. Staff may be involved in handling each of these activities in the course of a working day, and it is likely that no special space is reserved exclusively for each activity. For many of these activities, the short-term direct costs are quite negligible – for example the direct cost of one order to change pounds into dollars is little more than the cost of a receipt slip. But users of this service would be expected to contribute towards the overhead costs of staff and space. There is frequently no obvious method by which these fixed costs can be attributed to specific units of output, nor even to particular types of service. The fixed costs for money exchange could, for example, be allocated on the basis of the proportion of floor space occupied, proportion of staff time used, proportion of total turnover, or some combination of these bases. Allocation bases are often the result of judgement and political infighting. They can change as a result of argument between cost centre managers who invariably feel that their product is contributing excessively to fixed costs and may put forward an argument why their pricing base is putting them at a disadvantage in the market place against competitors who have a simpler cost structure. In the end, cost allocation is a combination of scientific analysis and bargaining.

### 10.4.2 Marginal cost pricing

A special kind of cost-based pricing occurs where firms choose to ignore their fixed costs. The price which any individual customer is charged is based not on the total unit cost of producing it, but only the additional costs which will result directly from servicing that additional customer. It is used where the bulk of a company's output has been sold at a full price which recovers its fixed costs, but in order to fill remaining capacity, the company brings its prices down to a level which at least covers its variable, or avoidable costs. **Marginal cost** pricing is widely used in service industries with low short-term supply elasticity and high fixed costs. It is common in the airline industry where the perishability of a seat renders it unsaleable after departure. Rather than receive no revenue for an empty seat, an airline may prefer to get some income from a passenger, so long as the transaction provides a contribution by more than covering the cost of additional food and departure taxes. The Internet has seen the emergence of a number of companies such as Lastminute.com which specialize in selling surplus capacity at low rates.

Against the attraction of filling spare capacity and getting a contribution towards fixed costs where otherwise there would have been none, marginal cost pricing does have its problems. The biggest danger of pricing on this basis is that it can be taken too far, allowing too high a proportion of customers to be carried at marginal cost, with insufficient customers charged at full price to cover the fixed costs. Many airlines and holiday tour operators have fallen into the trap of selling holidays on this basis, only to find that their fixed costs have not been fully covered. Another problem is that it may devalue customers' perception of a service. If a service promoted for its prestige value can be sold for a fraction of its original price, it may leave potential customers wondering just what the true value of the service is. It may also cause resentment from customers who had committed themselves to a service well in advance, only to find that their fellow consumers obtained a lower price by booking later (and thereby also making marketing planning much more difficult for many service operators). Companies can try to overcome problems of marginal cost pricing by differentiating the marginally costed product from that which is purchased at full price. Holiday tour operators, for example, reduce the price of last minute standby holidays but offer no guarantee of the precise accommodation to be used – or even the precise resort – unlike the full price holiday, where this is clearly specified.

## 10.5  Demand-based pricing

The upper limit to the price of a service is determined by what customers are prepared to pay. In fact, different customers often put differing ceilings on the price which they are prepared to pay for a service. Successful demand-oriented pricing is therefore based on effective segmentation of markets to achieve the maximum price from each segment. Price discrimination, as it is often called, can be carried out on the basis of:

- discrimination between different groups of users
- discrimination between different points of use
- discrimination between different types of use.

### 10.5.1  Price discrimination between different groups of users

Effective price discrimination requires groups of consumers to be segmented in such a way that maximum value is obtained from each segment. Sometimes this can be achieved by simply offering the same service to each segment, but charging a different price. In this way, a hairdresser can offer senior citizens a haircut which is identical to the service offered to all other customer groups in all respects except price. The rationale could be that this segment is more price sensitive than other segments, and therefore additional profitable business can only be gained by sacrificing some element of margin. By performing more haircuts, even at a lower price, a hairdresser may end up having increased total revenue from this segment, while still preserving the higher prices charged to other segments.

On other occasions, the service offering is slightly differentiated and targeted to segments who are prepared to pay a price which reflects its differential advantages. This is particularly important where it is impossible or undesirable to restrict availability of a lower price to certain predefined groups. Thus airlines operating between London and New York offer a variety of fare and service combinations to suit the needs of a number of segments. One segment requires to travel at short notice and is typically travelling on business. For the employer, the cost of not being able to travel at short notice may be high, so this group is prepared to pay a relatively high price in return for ready availability. A subsegment of this market may wish to arrive refreshed ready for a day's work and be prepared to pay more for the differentiated first-class accommodation. For non-business travellers, one segment may be happy to accept a lower price in return for committing themselves to a particular flight three weeks before departure. Another segment with less income to spend on travel may be

**Figure 10.3**
Although the costs of serving different groups of individuals may not vary much, this university sports centre practises price discrimination by charging different prices for different groups of users.

## University Sports Club Annual membership

| | |
|---|---|
| Full-time Student | £ 6.00 |
| Full-time Student and Family | £19.00 |
| Part-time Student | £17.00 |
| Part-time Student and Family | £34.00 |
| Staff (Individual) | £17.00 |
| Staff and Family | £34.00 |
| Graduate (Individual) | £25.00 |
| Graduate and Family | £50.00 |
| Associate (Individual) | £40.00 |
| Associate and Family | £80.00 |
| Senior Citizen | £30.00 |
| Student (Non-University) | £17.00 |
| Associate College | £12.00 |

prepared to take the risk of obtaining a last minute standby flight in return for a lower priced ticket still.

The intangible and inseparable nature of services make the possibilities for price discrimination between different groups of users much greater than is usually the case with manufactured goods. Goods can easily be purchased by one person, stored and sold to another person. If price segmentation allowed one group to buy bread at a discounted price, it would be possible for this group to buy bread and sell it on to people in higher priced segments, thereby reducing the effectiveness of the segmentation exercise. Because services are produced at the point of consumption, it is possible to control the availability of services to different segments. Therefore, a hairdresser which offers a discounted price for the elderly segment is able to ensure that only such people are charged the lower price – the elderly person cannot go into the hairdresser to buy a haircut and sell it on to a higher price segment.

Many service sector companies have offered reduced prices for segments of senior citizens, calculating that these segments are more price sensitive than others and could usefully fill spare capacity at a profit, even at the lower prices charged. Services marketers are more fortunate than marketers of goods, where price discrimination can backfire. With services, a supplier can insist that only the senior citizen receives the benefit of the service they have paid for (for example by insisting on seeing proof of age before a train journey). But goods can be bought by a low-price segment and sold on to a relatively high price one. The pitfalls of this approach to market segmentation were learnt by a German grocery retailer which offered 20% off the price of all purchases made by senior citizens. Entrepreneurial senior citizens were then seen lining up outside the supermarket offering to do other customers' shopping for them. The 20% price saving was split between the senior citizen and the person needing the goods, saving effort for the latter and making additional income for the former, but making a mockery of the retailer's attempts at price discrimination. Had it been haircuts which were being offered at 20% discount to senior citizens, it would have been impossible for these to be sold on to other market segments.

### 10.5.2 Price discrimination between different points of consumption

Services organizations frequently charge different prices at different service locations. The inseparability of service production and consumption results in services organizations defining their price segments both on the basis of the point of consumption and the point of production. An example of this is found in chains of retail stores, who in addition to using price to target particular groups of customers, also often charge different prices at different stores. For example, Marks and Spencer charges higher prices for some of its products in its central London stores than in its stores in the provinces. For its overseas branches, it is faced with very different markets again, requiring separate price lists. Some retailers with a combination of large superstores and small convenience stores can justify charging higher prices in its convenience stores. A town centre branch of Tesco Metro is likely to attract people calling in for a few items for which they would be less prepared to shop around than if they were doing a week's shopping.

Some production locations may offer unique advantages to consumers. Unlike goods, the service offering cannot be transferred from where it is cheapest to produce to where it is most valued, hence service providers can charge higher prices at premium sites. Hotels fall into this category with high premiums charged by chains for those hotels located in 'honeypot' areas. A hotel room in the centre of StratforduponAvon offers much greater benefit to the consumer who wishes to visit the theatre without having a long drive back to their accommodation. Hotel prices for comparable standards of hotel therefore fall as distance from the town increases.

Travel services present an interesting example of price discrimination by location, as operators frequently charge different prices at each end of a route. The New York to London air travel market is quite different from the London to New York market. The state of the respective local economies, levels of competition and customers' buying behaviour may differ between the two markets, resulting in different pricing policies in each. Because of the personal nature of an airline ticket and the fact that discounted return tickets specify the outward and return dates of travel, airlines are able to avoid tickets being purchased in the low-priced area and used by passengers originating from the higher-priced area.

Within Britain, price discrimination by area is frequently used by train operators for journeys to and from London. Fares from provincial towns to London are frequently priced at a lower rate than equivalent fares from London, reflecting – among other things – the greater competitive advantage which train operators have in the London-based market.

### 10.5.3 Price discrimination by time of production

Goods produced in one period can usually be stored and consumed in subsequent periods. Charging different prices in each period could result in customers buying goods for storage when prices are low, and running down their stockpiles when prices are high. Because services are instantly perishable, much greater price discrimination by time is possible.

Services often face uneven demand which follows a daily, weekly, annual, seasonal, cyclical or random pattern. At the height of each peak, pricing is usually a reflection of:

- the greater willingness of customers to pay higher prices when demand is strong, and
- the greater cost which often results from service operators trying to cater for short peaks in demand.

The greater strength of demand which occurs at some points in a daily cycle can occur for a number of reasons. In the case of rail services into the major conurbations, workers must generally arrive at work at a specified time and may have few realistic alternative means of getting to work. A railway operator can therefore sustain a higher level of fares during the daily commuter peak period. Similarly, the higher rate charged for telephone calls during the daytime is a reflection of the greater strength of demand from the business sector during the daytime. As well as price discrimination between different periods of the day, it can also occur between different periods of the week (e.g. higher fares for using many train services on a Friday evening), or between different seasons of the year (holiday charter flights over public holiday periods).

Price discrimination by time can be effective in inducing new business at what would otherwise be a quiet period. Hotels in holiday resorts frequently lower their prices in the offpeak season to try to tempt additional custom. Many of the public utilities lower their charges during offpeak periods in a bid to stimulate demand. Lower electricity tariffs are available during the night in order to appeal to a price sensitive market which may programme washing machines to operate at night time.

In most cases of price discrimination by time, there is also some relationship to production costs. An argument of telephone operators and electricity generators is that the marginal cost of producing additional output during offpeak periods is relatively low – so long as peak demand has covered the fixed costs of providing equipment, off-peak output can be supplied on a marginal cost basis (see above).

### 10.5.4  Auctions and one-to-one pricing

Price discrimination between groups sounds fine in theory, but there can be problems in actually implementing it. Firstly, it can be very difficult to identify homogeneous segments in terms of individuals' responsiveness to price changes. Secondly, it can be very difficult to predict just what level of price will be acceptable to that group and a lot of trial and error may be necessary to establish the most appropriate price. One alternative adopted by some companies is to leave price determination to a process of individual negotiation between buyer and seller. For high-value commercial goods and services, individual negotiation of prices has been quite commonplace. But in the case of mass-market services, the existence of a published price list has simplified the process of exchange for buyer and seller who do not need to spend time negotiating a price on each occasion that a relatively low-value service is sought. Auctions have been used for some consumer sales, but mainly for high-value goods such as antiques. The emergence of Internet-based auction sites has offered new opportunities for services to set prices of relatively low-value services.

Auction sites such as Priceline.com and QXL.com essentially put the onus of pricing on the buyer by allowing customers to disclose the price at which they would be prepared to purchase. Faced with surplus aircraft seats, hotel rooms or theatre seats, service providers can make them available on a website and sell them to bidders who bid the highest amount, so long as this is above a minimum reserve price. If the system is working effectively, the service provider can be reasonably sure that it has secured the maximum achievable price for the services on offer.

While auctioning of services to the highest bidder has numerous attractions, there are also problems. An auction may be fine in the short term for clearing spare capacity, but in itself does nothing to develop strong brand values. In fact, auctions may treat a service like a commodity in which the only distinguishing feature is price. Auctions can be administratively difficult to administer, even with the use of the Internet. It can be difficult to control auction sites to ensure that bidders actually buy the service that they successfully bid for. Many consumers would prefer the certainty of fixed prices rather than take a chance with an auction where neither the availability of a specific service or its price can be guaranteed.

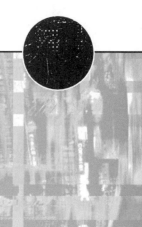

What is there in common between the haggling over prices which takes place in many Eastern markets, and modern direct marketing? At first sight the two would appear to be worlds apart, but in fact they can both be processes by which the seller seeks to establish the maximum amount that a buyer is prepared to pay. In the Eastern bazaar, the seller will learn that some buyers are more price sensitive than others, resulting in each transaction being uniquely priced. This is exactly what modern direct marketing firms often seek to achieve, except that they have a mass of information on each customer to initiate a price or a level of purchase incentive. And if this price is too high, the company might try again with a lower price or better incentive, knowing what the likely reaction of a particular market segment will be to the lower price. Credit card companies, mortgage lenders and banks have used such techniques and are becoming increasingly sophisticated in their use. Can a centralized database do a better job than one-to-one haggling in a marketplace?

### 10.5.5 Customer lifetime pricing

It will be recalled from Chapter 5 that the development of ongoing buyer–seller relationships is becoming a much more important part of business strategy. Rather than seeing each transaction in isolation, companies are trying to view each transaction with a customer in the context of those that have gone before, and those that they hope will occur in the future. Information technology is increasingly allowing companies to track individual customers and to charge a price which is appropriate to their position in the relationship life cycle.

A very low price may be needed to tempt a customer to try a supplier in the first place. An example of this is satellite television companies' offers of one-month low-price or free trials of their services. With repeated transactions, a company can build up a picture of a customer's price sensitivity with regard to different types of services. As the relationship develops, the nature of the service may become tailored to the precise needs of the customer, such that the customer will be quite happy to pay a higher price in return for the benefit received. To switch to a lower cost provider would involve the psychological cost of searching and explaining their needs to a new supplier and understanding their service production systems. A customer who has found a reliable car repair garage may come to be happy to pay a little bit over the odds if they can trust the garage to understand their needs and to satisfy them effectively.

Sometimes, there may be financial as well as psychological switching costs when a relationship develops into some form of structural tie between buyer and seller. A commercial customer may have invested heavily in a computer software system and switching to another company for service support or upgrades may be very expensive.

Sometimes, inertia sets in and a supplier may try to raise its prices in the expectation that the buyer could not be bothered to shop around. Many customers of telephone companies do not switch to cheaper alternatives because the psychological cost of doing so is seen as too great in relation to the likely financial benefits.

## 10.6  Competitor-based pricing

There are very few situations where an organization can set its prices without taking account of the activities of its competitors. Just who the competition is against which prices are to be compared needs to be carefully considered, for competition can be defined in terms of the similarity of the service offered, or merely similar in terms of the needs which a product satisfies. For example, a chain of video rental shops can see its competition purely in terms of other rental chains, or more widely to include cinema and satellite television services, or wider still to include any form of entertainment.

Having established what market it is in and who the competition is, an organization must establish what price position it seeks to adopt relative to its competitors (see Chapter 7). This position will reflect the service's wider marketing mix strategy, so if the company has invested in providing a relatively high-quality service whose benefits have been effectively promoted to target users, it can justifiably pitch its price level at a higher level than its competitors.

For services targeting similar subsegments of a market, the pricing decisions of competitors will have a direct bearing on an organization's own pricing decisions. Price in these circumstances is used as a tactical weapon to gain short-term competitive advantage over rivals. In a market where the competitors have broadly similar cost structures, price cutting can be destabilizing and result in costly price wars with no sustainable increase in sales or profitability. An example of price being used to gain short-term competitive advantage is provided by the decision of Midland Bank (now HSBC bank) to offer free banking for customers who kept their accounts in credit. While the Midland's market share increased in the short term, it was neutralized during the following year when competing banks offered free banking to match that originally offered by Midland. The market eventually stabilized with all of the main competitors offering free banking and all had lost revenue as a result of the continuance of free banking.

### 10.6.1 Going rate pricing

In some services markets which are characterized by a fairly homogeneous service offering, demand is so sensitive to price that a firm would risk losing most of its business if it charged just a small amount more than its competitors. On the other hand, charging any lower would result in immediate retaliation from competitors. An example of this situation is found in areas where a number of restaurants cluster closely together, all offering a basically similar service at a similar price. For the price sensitive diner, the 'Dish of the Day' may be set at the going rate, while more specialized dishes for which there is less direct competition are priced at a premium rate.

Where cost levels are difficult to establish, charging a going rate can avoid the problems of trying to calculate costs. As an example, it may be very difficult to calculate the cost of renting out a video film, as the figure will be very dependent upon assumptions made about the number of uses which the initial purchase cost can be spread over. It is much easier to take price decisions on the basis of the going rate among nearby competitors.

### 10.6.2 Sealed-bid pricing

Many industrial services are provided by means of a sealed-bid tendering process where interested parties are invited to submit a bid for supplying services on the basis of a predetermined specification. In the case of many government contracts, the organization inviting tenders is often legally obliged to accept the lowest priced

**Figure 10.4**
This video rental store guarantees to match the prices of its competitors. In doing so, it reduces buyers' need to shop around to compare prices, thereby reducing their perceived level of risk

tender, unless exceptional circumstances can be proved. Price therefore becomes a crucial concern for bidders, regardless of their efforts to build up long-term brand values which in other markets might have allowed them to charge a premium price. The first task of a bidding company is to establish a minimum bid price based on its costs and required rate of return, below which it would not be prepared to bid. The more difficult task is to try to put a maximum figure on what it can bid. This will be formed on expectations of what its competitors will bid, based on an analysis of their strengths and weaknesses.

In Britain, the Local Government Acts of 1980 and 1988 and the Housing and Local Government Act 1989 have required a comprehensive list of local authority services to be opened up to competitive tendering. Tendering was first required for refuse collection services and subsequently extended to include housing maintenance, grounds maintenance, the operation of leisure centres, and the provision of accounting and architectural services. The desire of many organizations to gain market share by underbidding has resulted in many financial failures part way through the operation of a contract. Although compulsory competitive tendering has been moderated by more recent 'Best Value' guidelines, tendering remains important for most new high-value government service contracts.

## 10.7 Distortions to market-led pricing decisions

Services are more likely than goods to be supplied in non-competitive environments. As an example, the high fixed costs associated with many public utility services means that it is unrealistic to expect two companies to compete. More importantly, much investment in services infrastructure is fixed and cannot be moved to where market opportunities are greatest. While a car manufacturer can quite easily redirect its new cars for sale from a declining market to an expanding one, a railway operator cannot easily transfer its track and stations from one area to another. The immobility of many services can encourage the development of local monopoly power. The nature and consequences of such market distortions, and government responses, are discussed below.

### 10.7.1 Market imperfections

In most Western countries there is a presumption that competition is necessary as a means of minimizing prices charged to consumers. However, while price competition may appear to act in the short-term interests of consumers, this normally restrains the combined profits of competitors. It is therefore common for competing organizations to seek to come to some sort of agreement (formal or informal) among themselves about prices to be charged, in order to avoid costly price competition.

Anticompetitive pricing occurs not just at a national level between large organizations, but also locally for services where the possibility of newcomers entering a market is limited by technical, economic or institutional barriers. Many local services providers have understandings – if not outright agreements – which have the effect of limiting price competition. In this way, local estate agents and building contractors have sometimes been accused of covert collusion to not engage in price competition, although obtaining evidence of such collusion can be very difficult.

To counter market imperfections, most Western governments have actively sought to eliminate anticompetitive practices. Government regulations of prices charged by private sector services providers can be divided into two broad categories:

1    Direct government controls to regulate monopoly power.
2    Government controls on price representations.

### 10.7.2  Direct government controls to regulate monopoly power

The 1998 Competition Act reformed and strengthened UK competition law by prohibiting anti-competitive behaviour. The Act introduced two basic prohibitions: a prohibition of anticompetitive agreements, based closely on Article 85 of the Treaty of Rome, and a prohibition of abuse of a dominant position in a market, based closely on Article 86 of the Treaty. The Competition Act prohibits agreements which have the aim or effect of preventing, restricting or distorting price competition. Since anticompetitive behaviour between companies may occur without a clearly delineated agreement, the prohibition covers not only agreements by associations of companies, but also covert practices.

The Competition Commission has power to investigate alleged anticompetitive pricing practices referred to it by a number of designated bodies, including the Secretary of State for Trade and Industry, the Office of Fair Trading and industry regulatory bodies. The following are examples of previous investigations by the Commission, or its predecessor body, the Monopolies and Mergers Commission (MMC):

●    In a 1994 report, the MMC found evidence of a 'complex' monopoly in private healthcare services which served to strengthen the British Medical Association's role in helping to fix consultants' fee levels. The Association had published a list detailing prices which should be charged by its members for operations, ranging from £310 for the removal of a wisdom tooth to £5825 for a liver transplant. The MMC's report concluded that the BMA's price guidelines resulted in consultants charging more than would be the case had they arrived at their own prices. The Commission recommended that the use of a standard price list should end. The government gave its full backing to the report and the price guidelines were withdrawn.

- The Competition Commission doesn't just involve itself with national organizations – it also investigates local abuse of monopoly power. Since the deregulation of the UK bus industry, the MMC has investigated several alleged anticompetitive practices by bus companies. For example, during an investigation of bus services in Darlington, the MMC found a scale monopoly that acted in favour of the Stagecoach and Go-Ahead Northern bus companies. It found that Stagecoach recruited most of the drivers of the ailing Darlington Transport Company, registered services on all its routes and then ran free services causing the sale of the municipal bus company to fall through and the company to collapse. The Director General of Fair Trading sought undertakings from Stagecoach and Go-Ahead Northern that they would maintain fares and service frequencies for three years after a competitor withdrew from a route, if their lower fares or increased frequencies had been responsible for the competitor withdrawing. The MMC eventually recommended a 12-month fares and frequencies freeze, despite protests by both companies that their behaviour had been in the public interest, pointing to their investment in new vehicles and staff training.

- A report in March 2000 accused the main UK banks of colluding through their shared 'Link' cash dispenser network to set fees for withdrawing cash at an unreasonably high level which bore no relation to actual costs incurred.

During the 1980s and 1990s, the privatization of many UK public sector utilities resulted in the creation of new private sector monopolies. To protect the users of these services from exploitation, the government's response has been twofold. Firstly, it has sought to increase competition, in the hope that this in itself will be instrumental in moderating price increases. In this way, the electricity generating industry was divided into a number of competing private suppliers (National Power, Powergen, Nuclear Electric, Scottish Power and Scottish Hydro), while conditions were made easier for new generators to enter the market. In some cases, measures to increase competition have had only limited effect, as in the very limited competition faced by the privatized water supply companies.

For many of the newly privatized monopolies, effective competition proved to be an unrealistic possibility. The result has been the creation of a series of regulatory bodies which can determine the level and structure of charges made by these utilities. Thus British Telecom, British Gas and the regional water companies are controlled by Oftel, Ofgem and Ofwat respectively. In the case of British Gas, Ofgem regulations allow the company to increase gas supply charges in line with changes in energy prices, but the price charged for ancillary services such as standing charges and repairs can only rise by the rate of inflation, less 2%. The regulatory bodies have power to prohibit any practices which allow the companies to exploit their monopoly position. In 1996, Oftel investigated complaints from rival telephone companies that BT had abused its dominant market position by offering low prices on combined telephone/satellite television packages with BSkyB. Oftel upheld the cable television companies' claims that the bulk of BT customers were cross-subsidizing those BT customers who were most vulnerable to competition from cable operators.

Americans are devoted to the idea that air travel is cheap following deregulation of the domestic market for air travel in the 1970s. But are low prices in fact a myth? And is it really a competitive market? The theory of airline deregulation in the USA was irresistible. Any airline would be allowed to operate on any route, setting its fares as it liked. New airlines soon appeared and initially held down fares through competitive pressures. However, the major carriers have since acquired such a dominant position that US air fares rose on average 20% during 1997. What went wrong? The established airlines had managed to control 'slots' at the principal hub airports, making it difficult for new entrants to obtain slots. Many of the larger airlines also resorted to predatory pricing to keep away newcomers. This involves offering low fares on routes and at times that are competitive with other airlines, but charging higher fares where it has an effective monopoly. The lesson from US airline deregulation is that price competition may be expected in theory, but there are many reasons why it doesn't happen in practice. Even anti-interventionist governments recognize the need to intervene in order to maintain the competitiveness of a market.

### 10.7.3 Government controls on price representations

In addition to controlling or influencing the actual level of prices, government regulations often specify the manner in which price information is communicated to potential customers. This is particularly important for services which are mentally intangible and for which many customers would be ill-equipped to make valid comparisons between competing suppliers. In the UK, the Competition Act 1998 requires that all prices shown should conform to a code of practice on pricing. Misleading price representations which relegate details of supplementary charges to small print or give attractive low lead in prices for services which are not in fact available are made illegal by this Act. There are other regulations which affect specific industries. The Consumer Credit Act 1974 requires that the charge made for credit must include a statement of the annual percentage rate (APR) of interest. Also within the financial services sector, the Financial Services Act 1986 has resulted in quite specific requirements in the manner in which charges for certain insurance-related services are presented to potential customers.

## 10.8 Pricing strategy

The fundamental economic, organizational and legal factors which underpin pricing decisions have now been described. This section moves on to analyse how organizations give strategic direction to pricing policy in order that organizational objectives can be met. The challenge here is to make pricing work as an effective element of the marketing mix, combining with the other mix elements to give a service provider a profitable market position. An effective strategy must identify how the role of price is to function as a service goes through different stages in its life from the launch stage through growth to maturity.

This analysis of pricing strategy will consider firstly the development of a strategy for a new service launch, and secondly price adjustments to established services. In practice, of course, it is often not easy to distinguish the two situations, as where an existing service is modified or relaunched.

## 10.9 New service pricing strategy

In developing a price strategy for a new service, two key issues need to be addressed:

1  What price position is sought for the service?
2  How novel is the service offering?

The choice of price position cannot be separated from other elements of the marketing mix – Chapter 7 analysed some of the issues involved in selecting a position for a new service. For many consumer services, the price element can itself interact with the product quality element of a positioning strategy. This can happen where consumers have difficulty in distinguishing between competing services before consumption, and the price charged is seen as an important indication of the quality of the service. Private consumers choosing a painter or decorator with no knowledge of their previous work record may be cautious about accepting the cheapest quotation on the basis that it may reflect an inexperienced decorator with a poor quality record.

The novelty of a new service offer can be analysed in terms of whether it is completely new to the market, or merely new to the company providing it, but already available from other sources. In the case of completely new innovative services, the company will have some degree of monopoly power in its early years. On the other hand, the launch of a 'me too' service to compete with established services is likely to face heavy price competition from its launch stage. The distinction between innovative services and copycat services is the basis of two distinct pricing strategies – 'price skimming' and 'saturation pricing', which are now examined in more detail.

### 10.9.1 Price skimming strategy

Most completely new product launches are aimed initially at the segment of buyers who can be labelled 'innovators'. These are buyers who have the resources and inclination to be the trend setters in purchasing new goods and services. This group includes the first people to buy innovative services such as telephone banking and mobile phone services. Following these will be a group of early adopters, followed by a larger group often described as the 'early majority'. The subsequent 'late majority' group may only take up the new service once the market itself has reached maturity. Laggards are the last group to adopt a new service and only do so when the product has become a social norm and/or its price has fallen sufficiently (a diffusion model is illustrated in Figure 11.2).

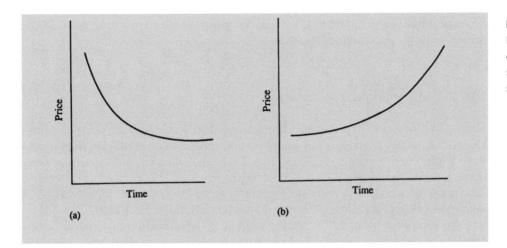

**Figure 10.5**
Pricing strategies
compared: (a) price
skimming; (b)
saturation pricing

Price skimming strategies seek to gain the highest possible price from the early adopters. When sales to this segment appear to be approaching saturation level, the price level is lowered in order to appeal to the early adopter segment which has a lower price threshold at which it is prepared to purchase the service. This process is repeated for the following adoption categories.

The art of effective pricing of innovative services is to identify who the early adopters are, how much they are prepared to pay and how long this price can be sustained before competitors come on the scene with imitation services at a lower price. A price skimming strategy works by gradually lowering prices to gain access to new segments and to protect market share against new market entrants. Pricing strategy is therefore closely related to the concept of the product life cycle and a typical price skimming strategy showing price levels through time is shown in Figure 10.5(a).

While the above analysis may be true of services bought by private consumers, is the same effect likely to be true for services bought by businesses? Business buyers are less likely to want to be a trend setter for its own sake, although individuals within an organization may gain status by being the first to have an innovative service. Sometimes, using a new service ahead of competitors can give a forward-thinking firm a cost advantage over its competitors (e.g. the first firms to use desk-based geographical location systems may gain advantages over competitors who rely on more traditional techniques which are more expensive and less accurate).

For many innovative services, the trend of falling prices may be further enhanced by falling costs. Lower costs can occur due to economies of scale (e.g. the cost per customer of providing the technical support for a home shopping service declines as fixed costs are spread over more volume of throughput) and also to the experience effect. The latter refers to the process by which costs fall as experience in production is gained. It is of particular strategic significance to service industries, since by pursuing a strategy to gain experience faster than its competitors, an organization lowers its cost base and has a greater scope for adopting an aggressive pricing strategy. The combined effects of these two factors can be seen in the UK mobile phone market where high initial prices have been brought down by the ability of network operators to spread their capital costs over increasing numbers of users. Also, operators have learnt from experience how a given level of service can be provided more efficiently, for example through adjusting transmitter locations.

### 10.9.2  Saturation pricing strategy

Many 'new' services are launched as copies of existing competitors' services. In the absence of unique features, a low initial price can be used to encourage people who show little brand loyalty to switch service suppliers. Once an initial trial has been made, a service provider would seek to develop increased loyalty from its customers, as a result of which they may be prepared to pay progressively higher prices. A saturation pricing strategy is shown diagrammatically in Figure 10.6(b).

The success of a saturation pricing strategy is dependent upon a sound understanding of the buying behaviour of the target market, in particular:

- *The level of knowledge which consumers have about prices*  For some services, such as the rate of interest charged on credit cards, consumers typically have little idea of the charge which they are currently paying, or indeed of the 'going rate' for such charges. There is now considerable research showing the effects of consumers' knowledge of prices on their buying behaviour (Dickson and Sawyer, 1990; Wakefield and Inman, 1993). Any attempt to attract new customers on the basis of a differential price advantage may prove unsuccessful if knowledge of prices is low. Other incentives (e.g. free gifts or money-off vouchers for reduced price holidays) may be more effective at inducing new business. Sometimes, companies offering a diverse range of services may offer low prices on services where price comparisons are commonly made, but charge higher prices on other related services where consumer knowledge is lower. Customers of solicitors may shop around for a standard service such as house conveyancing, but may be more reluctant to do so when faced with a non-routine purchase such as civil litigation.

- *The extent to which the service supplier can increase prices on the basis of perceived added value of the service offering*  The purpose of a low initial price is to encourage new users of a service to try a service and return later, paying progressively higher prices. If the new competitor's service is perceived to offer no better value than that of the existing supplier, the disloyalty which caused the initial switching could result in a switching back at a later date in response to tactical pricing. Worse still, a new service could be launched and experience teething troubles in its early days, doing nothing to generate a perception of added value.

- *The extent to which the service supplier can turn a casually gained relationship into a long-term committed relationship*  Incentives are frequently offered to lessen the attractiveness of switching away from the brand. This can take the form of a subscription rate for regular purchase of a service, or offering an ever-increasing range of services which together raise the cost to the consumer of transferring their business elsewhere. Banks may offer easy transfers between various savings and investment accounts and in doing so, aim to reduce the attractiveness of moving one element of the customer's business elsewhere.

To what extent do buyers of services shop around and compare prices when choosing between competing services? Do they even have any idea of a baseline price for a category of service? The BT Business Price Perception Survey suggests that even business buyers – who are sometimes thought to act with greater economic rationality than private buyers – are often wide of the mark when it comes to understanding services prices. In its 1997 survey, it found knowledge of telephone prices to be particularly bad, probably reflecting the plethora of price plans which have emerged in recent years. Respondents gave the average price of a five minute peak national call as £2.15, whereas in fact it was only 44p.

Another service sector with confusing price structures is railways. Here, respondents estimated the price of a second class return ticket from London to Edinburgh at £54, compared to the actual price of £64. By contrast to the wide variations in service price estimates, respondents were quite accurate in their assessment of the price of a pint of beer. The average estimate of £1.73 for a pint of lager was just 2p off the true average. What does this say about service companies' pricing policies? Has the process of price discrimination be taken so far that it leaves buyers confused? Is there sometimes a case for adopting an 'Everyday Low Price'

In some cases, a high initial uptake of a new service may itself add value to the service offering. This can be true where coproduction of benefits among consumers is important. A telecommunications operator offering data exchange facilities will be able to offer a more valuable service if large numbers of users are contracted to its system, offering more communications possibilities for potential new users. In the same way, airport landing slots become increasingly valuable to an airline as an airport becomes progressively busier, as each airline is able to offer a more comprehensive and valuable set of potential connections to customers. In both cases, a low initial price may be critical to gain entry to a market, while raising prices is consistent with increasing value to the users of the service.

### 10.9.3 Evaluating strategic pricing options

In practice, pricing strategies often contain elements of skimming and saturation strategies. The fact that most new services are in fact adaptations and are easy to copy often prevents a straight forward choice of strategy. Even when a price strategy has been adopted and implemented, it may run off target for a number of reasons:

- Poor market research may have misjudged potential customers' willingness to pay for a new service. As an example, National Westminster Bank sought to charge personal customers £30 for using its innovative Internet-based banking service, NatWest Online. Take-up was reported to be less than expected, with the result that the charge was abolished after less than one year. A service provider may have misjudged the effect of price competition from other services, which although different in form, satisfied the same basic needs.

- Competitors may emerge sooner or later than expected. The fact that new services can often be easily and quickly copied can result in a curtailment of the period during which an organization can expect to achieve relatively high prices. As an example, an optician opening the first eye-care centre in an expanding market town may expect to enjoy a few years of higher price levels before competitors drive down price levels, only to find another optician had a similar idea and opens a second eye-care centre shortly afterwards.
- The effects of government regulation may be to extend or shorten the period during which a company has a protected market for its new market. The announcement by the British government in 1991 that it was to license a number of new cellular telephone networks had the effect of bringing forward the time when the existing operators had to face direct competition on price.

### 10.9.4 Price leader or follower?

Many services markets are characterized by a small number of dominant suppliers and a large number of smaller ones. Perfect competition and pure monopoly are two extremes which rarely occur in practice. In markets which show some signs of interdependency among suppliers, firms can often be described as price makers or price followers. Price makers tend to be those who as a result of their size and power within a market are able to determine the levels and patterns of prices which other suppliers then follow. Within the UK insurance industry, the largest firms in the market often lead changes in rate structures. Price takers, on the other hand, tend to have a relatively low size and market share and may lack product differentiation, resources or management drive to adopt a proactive pricing strategy. Smaller estate agents in a local area may find it convenient to simply respond to pricing policies adopted by the dominant firms – to take a proactive role themselves may bring about a reaction from the dominant firms which they would be unable to defend on account of their size and standing in the market.

## 10.10 Service portfolio pricing

Multi-output service providers usually set the price of a new service in relation to the prices charged for other services within their portfolio. A number of product relationships can be identified as being important for pricing purposes:

- Optional additional services
- Captive services
- Competing services

*Optional* additional services are those which a consumer chooses whether or not to add to the core service purchase, often at the time that the core service is purchased. As a matter of strategy, an organization could seek to charge a low lead-in price for its core service, but to recoup a higher margin from the additional optional services. Simply breaking a service into core and optional components may allow for the presentation of lower price indicators, which through a process of rationalization may be more acceptable to buyers. Research may show that the price of the core service is in fact the only factor which buyers take into account when choosing between alternative services. In this way, many travel agents and tour operators cut their margins on the core holiday which they sell, but make up some of their margin by charging high mark-ups for optional extras such as travel insurance policies and car hire.

*Captive* services occur where the core service has been purchased and the provision of additional services can only be provided by the original provider of the core service. Where these are not specified at the outset of purchasing the core service, or are left up to the discretion of the service provider, the latter is in a strong position to charge a high price. Against this, the company must consider the effect which the perception of high exploitative prices charged for these captive services will have on customer loyalty when a service contract comes due for renewal. An example of captive service pricing is provided by many car insurance companies who after selling the core insurance policy can treat the sale of a 'green card' (which extends cover beyond the geographical limits defined in the policy) as a captive sale.

*Competing* services within a company's portfolio occur where a new service targets a segment of the population which overlaps the segments served by other products within the portfolio. By a process of 'cannibalization', a service provider could find that it is competing with itself. In this way, an airline offering a low-priced direct service from Glasgow to Frankfurt may find that the low price – in addition to generating completely new business – has an important side effect in abstracting traffic from its connecting services from Glasgow to London and from London to Frankfurt.

### 10.10.1 Price bundling

Price bundling is the practice of marketing two or more services in a single package for a single price. Bundling is particularly important for services on account of two of their principal characteristics. Firstly, the high ratio of fixed to variable costs which characterize many services organizations makes the allocation of costs between different services difficult and sometimes arbitrary. Secondly, there is often a high level of interdependency between different types of service output from an organization. In this way, the provision of an ATM card and cheque guarantee card becomes an interdependent part of the current bank account offering which most UK banks do not charge for separately.

Price bundling of diverse services from an organization's service portfolio is frequently used as a means of building relationships with customers. In this way, a mortgage could be bundled with a household contents insurance policy or a legal protection policy. Where the bundle of service represents ease of administration to the consumer, the service organization may be able to achieve a price for the bundle which is greater than the combined price of the bundle's components.

'Pure' bundling occurs where services are only available in a bundled form (e.g. where a tour operator includes insurance in all of its package holidays) whereas 'mixed' bundling allows customers to choose which specific elements of the service offering they wish to purchase. In a study of price bundling, Guiltinan (1987) showed that as service firms expand their range of service outputs, simple cost-based or price-follower strategies become too simplistic for two reasons. Firstly, as the number of services offered increases, the opportunities for differentiation and bundling are enhanced. Secondly, the high ratio of fixed to variable costs typical of many services industries make average costing increasingly arbitrary as fixed cost allocations change with the expansion of the service range. Bundling reduces the need to allocate fixed costs to individual services.

A service provider may feel compelled to bundle services in a way which is in accordance with consumers' expectations, leading to the development of a dominant pricing model. Sometimes, this standard pricing model is challenged by a new entrant, with the result that consumers' expectations are changed. The effect of dominant pricing models can be seen in the development of Internet Service Providers (ISPs) in the UK. Until 1998, the dominant pricing model for ISPs serving the private consumer market was a monthly fee giving entitlement to a specified number of hours online. In 1998, Freeserve challenged this pricing model by making its service free to consumers, but made up the income loss by selling advertising banner space and recouping a percentage of the amount consumers paid in telephone calls. Shortly afterwards, the majority of ISPs were forced to respond by copying Freeserve's pricing model.

Although price bundling may appear attractive to many service organizations, there are dangers that they may fall foul of competition legislation. In the UK, the Office of Fair Trading has investigated the anticompetitive effects of mortgage lenders bundling household insurance with their core offer and of travel agents bundling insurance with package holidays. In both cases, firms were held to be abusing their position to sell these additional services.

## 10.11 Tactical pricing

In practice, manoeuvrability around the central pricing strategy will be needed to allow detailed, local application of the overall strategy. This is the role of tactical pricing. The distinction between strategic and tactical pricing can sometimes be difficult to draw. In highly competitive, undifferentiated services markets, the development of tactical plans can be all important and assume much greater importance than for a service where an organization has more opportunity for developing a distinctive strategic price position. Some of the tactical uses of pricing are analysed below.

●　Tactical pricing can provide short-term competitive advantage. Periodic price reductions can be a means of inducing potential customers to try a service, whether it is new or established. The price cut can be a general across the board reduction, or it could be targeted (e.g. by the use of vouchers). The extent of the uptake will be dependent on the importance of price comparisons, the extent to which consumers of that type of service typically make casual purchases and are not tied to a relationship with another supplier (e.g. lower single bus fares may result in little additional demand if a large proportion of travellers are tied to a season ticket with another operator) and consumers' perceptions of the price offer. Economic rationality may expect that sales of a service will increase as its price is reduced. However, the price reduction may reduce the perceived value of a service, leading to a feeling that its quality has been eroded. Subsequent price increases may lead to the feeling that the service is over-priced if it could be offered previously at a lower price. There may also be significant price points at which a service is perceived as being of good value. A trans-Atlantic air ticket priced at £199 may be perceived as offering much better value than a ticket priced at £200.

Even if economic rationality is assumed on the part of consumers, it can be difficult to predict the effects of a price change. Comparison with previous occasions when price was adjusted assumes that all other factors are the same, whereas in reality, many factors, such as the availability of competitors' services and general macroenvironmental considerations require some judgement to be made about how a similar price change might perform this time around.

- Tactical pricing can be used to remove unplanned excess supply. The strategic price position sought by an organization may be incapable of achievement on account of excess supply, both within the organization and within the market generally. A temporary price cut can be used to bring demand and supply back into balance. Pricing can also be used to capitalize on excess demand relative to supply. In addition to removing discounts and increasing prices, firms can remove low margin elements from their service portfolio in order to maximize their returns from high margin lines.

- Short-term tactical pricing can be used to protect markets against new entrants. Where a new entrant threatens the existing market of an established supplier, the latter may react with short-term price reductions where price comparisons are commonly made. If the new entrant is a small, opportunist company seeking to make inroads into the larger, dominant firm's market, a low price may force the new company to respond with low prices, putting strain on its initial cash flow and possibly resulting in its withdrawal from the market, if not ceasing to trade completely. Following deregulation of bus services in the UK, many established bus companies found themselves challenged by relatively small companies. A common response was to run 'free buses' ahead of the new entrant's service. The new entrant often did not have the resources to match this pricing tactic for any length of time and often withdrew from the market after a short time.

- Discriminatory pricing with respect to time which may have been part of the strategic pricing plan can be implemented by a number of tactical programmes. Off-peak discounts are frequently used in industries such as rail travel, telecommunications and hotels. The converse of peak surcharges can also be employed, for example the supplementary charge levied by train operators for travel on certain West Country holiday trains during the busiest summer weekends. Other options include offering added value price bundles at certain periods (e.g. shopping vouchers for off-peak ferry passengers) and subtly altering a service offering and making it available only at certain times (e.g. a restaurant may slightly differentiate lunch from dinner and charge more for the latter on account of the willingness of customers to pay more for a social meal in the evening).

- Similarly, discriminatory pricing with respect to place must be translated from a strategic plan to a tactical programme. Implementing differential pricing by area is relatively easy for services on account of the difficulty in transferring service consumption. Hotels and shops – among others – often use different price lists for different locations, depending upon the local competitive position, and such lists are often adjusted at short notice to respond to local competitive pressure. Sometimes a common base price is offered at all of an organization's service outlets, and tactical objectives are achieved by means of discounts which are only available at certain locations. Reduced price vouchers offered by a national hotel chain may have their validity restricted to those locations where demand is relatively weak. In some cases, companies advertise a number of core services nationally at a fixed rate, while related services are priced according to local market conditions.

- For discriminatory pricing between different consumer segments, the problem of turning a strategy into a tactical programme hinges on the ease with which segments can be isolated and charged different prices. Because services are consumed at the point of production, it is often easy to confine price differences within small segments of a market. In this way, cinemas are able to ensure that only students are able to use reduced price student tickets by asking for identification as the service process is being undertaken. Sometimes the implementation of a highly segmented pricing programme can cause problems for services providers where compromise needs to be made between the desire for small, homogeneous segments and the need for segments which are of a worthwhile size to service. As an example, UK train operators place all elderly people in one segment which is offered a low-price Senior Citizen Railcard. However, the simplicity of this large, homogeneous segment is offset by the fact that many people in it are well off and less price sensitive, and may even be travelling on business. There is also the problem with this form of price segmentation that goodwill can be harmed where arguments develop over a customer's eligibility to a particular price offer.

- Tactical pricing programmes are used to motivate intermediaries. Where a service is provided through an intermediary, the difference between the price that a customer pays and the amount that the service principal receives represents the intermediary's margin. In some cases, price sensitivity of the final consumer is low, but awareness of margins by the intermediary high, requiring tactical pricing to be directed at maintaining intermediaries' margins relative to those offered by competitors. An example is provided by holiday insurance offered by travel agents – customers do not typically shop around for this ancillary item of a package holiday, but travel agents themselves decide which policy to recommend to their clients largely on the basis of the commission level which they can earn. Price charged to the final consumer can also affect an intermediary's motivation to sell a principal's service – if the agent perceives the selling price to be too high, they may give up trying to promote it in favour of a more realistic and attractive competitor. On the other hand, if the price is too low, intermediaries working on a percentage commission basis may consider that the reward for them is not worth their effort. The cut price airline Ryanair annoyed many Irish travel agents in 1997 when it cut agents' commission from 9% to 7.5%, at the same time as reducing fares charged to passengers.

This led to a threatened boycott of the airline by the Irish Travel Agents Association.

## 10.12 Pricing strategies for public sector services

It was noted at the beginning of this chapter that price is often a very constrained element of the marketing mix for public services where there is much less freedom to implement the strategies and tactics of pricing described above. At one extreme, some publicly provided services can operate in a market-mediated environment where pricing policies do not differ significantly from the private sector – indeed, legislation frequently requires such services to act as though they were a private sector operator. Local authority operated bus services are such an example. At the other extreme, some public services can only sensibly be distributed by centrally planned methods where price loses its role as a means of exchange of value.

The pricing of services which by their very nature require a high degree of central planning, but which are expected to exhibit some degree of marketing orientation, present particular challenges for marketers. It may be difficult or undesirable to implement a straightforward price–value relationship with individual service users for a number of reasons:

- External benefits may be generated by a service which are difficult or impossible for the service provider to appropriate from individual users. For example, road users within the UK are not generally charged directly for the benefits which they receive from the road system. At present, the only significant case where direct charges are levied occurs at toll bridges. The present methods of charging for roads reflects the technical difficulties in appropriating charges from users and the political problem that access to road space is deemed to be a 'birthright' which should not be restricted by direct charging. Nevertheless, in some countries, the technical and political environment has allowed governments to charge more directly for road space used. In France, for example, many motorways are operated by private sector organizations who charge tolls regulated by the government. In order to attract more usage of their motorways, effort is put into making them more attractive than the parallel non-toll roads, by such means as the provision of pleasant rest areas. In other cases (for example Singapore), attempts have been made to charge for the use of urban roads according to the level of congestion present.
- The benefits to society at large may be as significant as the benefits received by the individual who is the immediate recipient. An early argument for the free provision of doctors' services was that society as a whole benefited from an individual being cured of a disease, and therefore not spreading it to other members of the community. Similarly, education and training courses may be provided at an uneconomic charge in order to add to the level of skills available within an economy generally.
- Pricing can be actively used as a means of social policy. Subsidized prices are often used to favour particular groups, for example prescription charges are related to consumers' ability to pay, with exemption for the very ill and unemployed, among others. Communication programmes are often used by public

services to make the public aware of the preferential prices to which they may be eligible. Sometimes, the interests of marketing orientation and social policy can overlap. For example, reduced admission prices to museums for the unemployed may at the same time both help a disadvantaged group within society, while generating additional overall revenue through segmenting the market in terms of ability to pay.

Problems can occur in public services which have been given a largely financial, market-oriented brief, but in which social policy objectives are superimposed, possibly in conflict. Museums, leisure centres and car park charges have frequently been at the centre of debate about the relative importance of economic and social objectives. One solution which has sometimes been adopted is to split a service into two distinct components, one part being an essentially public service which is provided for the benefit of society at large, and the other part comprising those elements which are indistinguishable from commercially provided services. In this way, museums have often retained free or nominally priced admission charges for the serious, scholarly elements of their exhibits, while offering special exhibitions which match the private sector in the standard of production and the prices charged.

## 10.13 Internal market pricing

The development of matrix type organizations (discussed further in Chapter 14) can result in significant internal trading of services occurring within an organization. Services that are commonly traded internally include photocopying, cleaning, transport and catering. Very often, the price at which services are traded between a department which uses a resource and a department which produces that resource does not reflect a competitive market price – indeed, a market as such may not exist. Setting transfer prices can raise a number of issues for an organization, even where external market prices can be readily ascertained. Allowing users of resources to purchase their services from the cheapest source – internal or external – could result in the in-house supplier losing volume to a point where it ceases to be viable. This could result in the loss of an internal facility to perform specialized jobs which cannot easily be handled by outside contractors. By allowing part of its requirements to be bought in from outside, an organization may increase the loss incurred by its internal supplier, while adding to the profits of outside companies. The internal pricing of services therefore needs to reconcile the possibly conflicting requirements of the in-house production unit to make profits and maintain some capacity, against the resource users' requirements to minimize their total expenditure.

A number of possible solutions to the problem of internal pricing can be identified:

- If an external market exists, a 'shadow' price can be imputed to the transfer, reflecting what the transaction would have cost if it had been bought in from outside.
- Where no external market exists, bargaining between divisional managers can

take place, although the final outcome may be a reflection of the relative bargaining strength of each manager.

- Corporate management could instruct all divisions to trade on an agreed full cost pricing basis.
- A system of dual pricing can be adopted where selling divisions receive a market price (where this can be identified) while the buying division pays the full-cost of production. Any difference is transferred to corporate accounts.
- A proportion of the internal service producer's fixed costs can be spread over all resource users as a standing charge, regardless of whether they actually use the services of the unit. This would enable the internal supplier to compete on price relatively easily, while still allowing resource users for whom a higher standard of service is worth paying a premium to buy their requirements in from outside.

Public services which are provided free of charge to users are nevertheless often traded within the public sector on the basis of price. During the 1990s, the UK National Health Service moved from being a centrally planned organization to one which was based on negotiated contracts between hospitals who provide care services and the health authorities and fund-holding general practitioners who buy services on behalf of their patients. The fund-holding health authorities and GPs clearly wanted their funds to buy the best available care for their patients at the lowest possible price. The early days of internal trade within the National Health Service saw many of the pricing problems commonly associated with internal trading. The wide discrepancies in prices quoted by different hospitals for the same operation reflected a lack of costing information on which prices were based, and the high level of overhead costs associated with many medical facilities. The prospect emerged of whole hospitals being suddenly closed because of their lack of price competitiveness, undoing the benefits of centralized planning which had sought to balance supply and demand for specialised facilities at a regional level. The problems of effectively managing an internal price-led market for health services has subsequently resulted in greater resort to centralized planning and resource allocation through Primary Care Groups.

## Rail sector pricing adapts to new business environments

Case Study

The pricing of train fares in Britain has evolved over the past 30 years in response to changes in the operating environment of railways. As it has evolved from a centrally planned public service to a competitive private sector industry, new forms of pricing have emerged.

One constant theme in the development of railway pricing has been the proliferation of fares between any two points. For a return journey from Leicester to London, no fewer than 23 different fares are currently charged. A number of market segments have been identified and a distinctive marketing mix has been developed for each. The business traveller typically has a need for the flexibility of travelling at any time of the day and, because an employer is often picking up the bill, this segment tends to be relatively

insensitive to the price charged. Some segments of the business market demand higher standards of quality and are prepared to pay a price of £73.00 for an executive package which includes 'first-class' accommodation and additional services such as meals and car parking. Leisure segments are on the whole more price sensitive and prepared to accept a lower level of flexibility. Those who are able to book their ticket one week in advance can pay just £18.

A keen eye is kept on the competition in determining prices. Students are more likely than business travellers to accept the coach as an alternative and therefore the Leicester to London student rail fare of £15.20 is pitched against the equivalent student coach fare of £11.75, the higher rail fare being justified on the basis of a superior service offering. For the business traveller, the comparison is with the cost of running a car, parking in London and, more importantly, the cost of an employed person's time. Against these costs, the executive fare of £73.00 is often perceived as being good value. For the family market, the most serious competition is presented by the family car, so a family discount railcard allows the family as a unit to travel for the price of little more than two adults.

The underlying cost of a train journey is difficult to determine as a basis for pricing. Fixed costs have to be paid by train operating companies to Railtrack for the use of the track and terminals. In addition, trains and staff represent a fixed cost, although many companies have sought to make these more flexible. Companies recognize that trains operating in the morning and afternoon peak periods cost more to operate as fixed costs of vehicles used solely for the peak period cannot be spread over other off-peak periods. The underlying costs of running commuter trains has been publicly cited by train operating companies as the reason for increasing season ticket charges by greater than the rate of inflation during recent years, although the fact that commuters often have no realistic alternative means of transport may have also been an important consideration in raising prices.

The political environment has had an important effect on rail pricing policies. Before the 1960s, railways were seen as essentially a public service and fares were charged on a seemingly equitable basis which was related to production costs. Fares were charged strictly on a cost per mile basis, with a distinction between first and second class, and a system of cheap day returns which existed largely through tradition. From the 1960s, British Rail moved away from social objectives with the introduction of business objectives. With this came a recognition that pricing must be used to maximize revenue rather than to provide social equality. However, government intervention occasionally came into conflict with British Rail's business objectives – for example it was instructed to curtail fare increases during the 1980s as part of the government's anti-inflation policy and again in the autumn of 1991 it was instructed to reduce some proposed Inter-City fare increases on account of the poor quality of service on some routes.

The privatization of British Rail in the mid-1990s led to further developments in pricing. Recognizing the importance of maintaining an integrated passenger network, the government appointed a regulator of rail services with powers to specify fares charged for a range of types of tickets and to ensure that through tickets are still available for journeys which involve more than one rail company. However, the newly privatized companies have exploited opportunities to offer new types of tickets targeted at different segments of the population. Virgin Railways used the experience of its airline to promote book-ahead tickets which offered bargain prices to fill off-peak capacity. At the same time, signs of genuine price competition between rival rail operators began to appear. Segments of the London–Scotland market were contested by Great North Eastern Railways and Virgin, while Chiltern Railways sought to appeal to the price sensitivity of travellers from Birmingham to London.

Privatization had resulted in a huge range of new marketing initiatives, and a seemingly bewildering array of special ticket prices has appeared from each of the 26 rail franchise operators. With titles such as 'Virgin Value 7' and 'Network Stayaway', the public had become confused by the choices available. As a result, the Train Operators' Association, which represents the franchise operators, agreed to co-operate in offering just six 'families' of ticket types, based on the validity of the ticket.

## Case study review questions

**1**   Should governments intervene to regulate rail fares?

**2**   Evaluate the financial benefits to rail operators of offering reduced fares to students.

**3**   Are train fares too expensive?

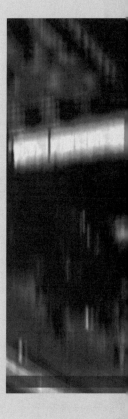

## Chapter summary and linkages to other chapters

The prices charged by an organization are the result of a range of factors, including the organization's objectives, the nature of the service and the competitiveness of the market in which it operates. Very big differences frequently exist in the price charged for two identical services. This reflects the ability of many services firms to practice price discrimination between different groups of customers and a high level of fixed costs which allows services to be charged at low marginal costs. The perishability of services further encourages wide variation in prices charged for a service.

Pricing is a crucial tool in the management of peaks and troughs in demand (**Chapter 13**). In many cases, a service offered at one time is totally different to one offered at another time (**Chapter 2**). A high-priced ticket for a commuter train may be no substitute for a lower priced ticket which is only available on off-peak trains. In circumstances where it is difficult to evaluate a service prior to consumption, customers use price as an indicator of the expected quality of a service (**Chapter 8**). Pricing is also an important part of many service organizations' relationship marketing strategies (**Chapter 5**). On the one hand, price discounts are often given to reward loyalty, but on the other hand firms would expect loyal customers to be less price sensitive. Finally, price is one aspect of the positioning of an organization and its service offers and the price position adopted must be consistent with positions adopted with respect to quality, accessibility and promotion (**Chapters 8, 9 and 11**).

## Key terms

Marginal cost 286

## Chapter review questions

1 What is the relationship between product life-cycle theory and pricing strategy?
2 Give examples to illustrate situations where price competitiveness may be largely absent in services markets.
3 Analyse the product mix of a diverse service organization and identify the pricing strategies used to increase total revenue.
4 Using examples, compare the advantages and disadvantages of cost-plus and marginal cost pricing.
5 Using a service company of your choice, analyse how price discrimination is practised between different groups of customers.
6 Examine the role which is likely to be played by pricing for a local-authority-owned leisure centre.

## Selected further reading

*For a general overview of the principles of effective pricing, the following are useful:*

Docters, R. G. (1997) 'Price Strategy: Time to Choose Your Weapons', *Journal of Business Strategy*, Vol. 18, No. 5, pp 11–15

Hanna, N. and H. R. Dodge (1995) *Pricing: Policies and Procedures*, Macmillan, Basingstoke

Trout, J. and S. Rivkin (1998) 'Prices: Simple Guidelines to Get Them Right', *Journal of Business Strategy*, Vol. 19, No. 6, pp 13–17

*The intangible nature of services and the problems which this can give rise to in consumers' pre-purchase evaluation is discussed in the following:*

Berry, L. L. and M. S. Yadav (1996) 'Capture and Communicate Value in the Pricing of Services', *Sloan Management Review*, Summer, pp 41–51

Dickson, P. R. and A. G. Sawyer (1990) 'The Price Knowledge and Search of Supermarket Shoppers', *Journal of Marketing*, Vol. 54, 42–53

Yelkur, R. and P. Herbig (1997) 'Differential Pricing for Services', *Marketing Intelligence & Planning*, Vol. 15, No. 4–5, pp 190–5

*The following paper discusses how multi-product services firms can effectively price combinations of different services rather than selling individual services in isolation:*

Guiltinan, J. P. (1987) 'The Price Bundling of Services: A Normative Framework', *Journal of Marketing*, April, Vol. 51, pp 74–85

*The impact which the Internet is likely to have on pricing is discussed in the following:*

Carr, N. G. (1999) 'Redesigning Business', *Harvard Business Review*, November–December Vol. 77, No. 6, p 19

# 11

# Promoting services

## Learning objectives

The intangible nature of services makes them difficult for buyers to evaluate prior to purchase. They are often seen as a risky purchase, and therefore a firm's promotion efforts should seek to reduce the risks associated with intangibility. The aim of this chapter is to introduce the basic principles involved in managing the promotion mix for services and to highlight the extended promotion mix for services which incorporates a firm's production processes. Methods are reviewed by which services organizations set promotional objectives, develop promotional strategies, implement programmes and monitor their effectiveness. The growing importance of the Internet as a promotional medium is discussed.

## 11.1 Introduction

Well-developed marketing strategies and tactics should have the effect of reducing reliance on promotion as a means of achieving customer take-up of a service. A well-formulated service offer, distributed through appropriate channels at a price which represents good value to potential customers places less emphasis on the promotion element of the marketing mix. Nevertheless, few services – especially those provided in competitive markets – can dispense with promotion completely. The purpose of this chapter is to examine the nature of the strategic and tactical decisions which service organizations must take in formulating this element of the marketing mix.

This chapter considers some of the basic principles of promotion decisions, but places particular emphasis on the distinctive needs of services promotion. These distinctive needs derive from the distinguishing characteristics of services, in particular:

- The intangible nature of the service offer often results in consumers perceiving a high level of risk in the buying process, which promotion must seek to overcome.
- Promotion of a service offer cannot generally be isolated from promotion of the service provider.
- Visible production processes, especially service personnel, become an important element of the promotion effort.
- The intangible nature of services and the heightened possibilities for fraud results in their promotion being generally more constrained by legal and voluntary controls than is the case with goods.

The promotion function of any service organization involves the transmission of messages to present, past and potential customers. At the very least, potential customers need to be made aware of the existence of a service. Eventually, in some way, they should be influenced towards purchase and subsequent repurchase.

It should not be forgotten that the promotion industry is a major service sector in its own right. Public relations agencies, direct mail operators and advertising agencies not only provide vital inputs to other firms' marketing efforts, but they themselves have to develop promotional plans for their own business.

## 11.2 The communication process

Promotion involves an ongoing process of communication between an organization and its target markets. The process is defined by the answers to the following questions:

- WHO is saying the message?
- To WHOM is the message addressed?
- HOW is the message communicated?
- To what EFFECT was the communication made?

The elements of this process are illustrated in Figure 11.1 and are described in more detail below.

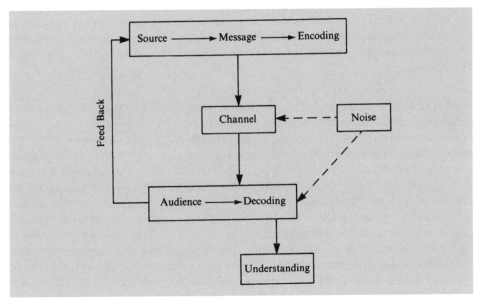

**Figure 11.1**
The communication
process

### 11.2.1 To whom is the message addressed?

The most important element of the communication process is the audience at which communication is aimed. The audience of a message determines what is to be said, when it is to be said, where it is to be said and who is to say it. The target audience of a communication must be clearly defined and this can be done in a number of ways.

- The most traditional method of defining audiences is in terms of social, economic, demographic and geographical characteristics. In this way, audiences are defined using parameters such as age, sex, social class, area of residence, etc.
- Audiences can be defined in terms of the level of involvement of potential recipients of the communication, for example a distinction can be made between those people who are merely *aware* of the existence of a service, those who are *interested* in possibly purchasing the service and those who *wish to purchase* the service.
- An audience can be defined on the basis of target customers' usage frequency (e.g. regular users of an airline are likely to respond to communications in a different way compared to occasional users).
- Similarly, audiences can differ in the benefits which they seek from a category of service. Train operators aim different messages at leisure users who may seek benefits in terms of family outings together, compared to business users for whom the benefits of speed and reliability are of greatest importance.
- In the case of services supplied to corporate buyers, audiences can be defined in terms of the type and size of business and their geographical location. More importantly, the key decision makers and influencers must be identified and

used in defining the audience (e.g. for many corporate travel services, secretaries can be important in choosing between competing services rather than the actual service user, and should therefore be included in a definition of the target audience).

Having defined its target audience, the communicator must then research a number of its important characteristics. For services, one vital aspect to explore is the audience's image of the organization and its services and the degree of image consistency among the audience. An image tends to persist over time with people continuing to see what they expect to see rather than what actually exists. The image of a service firm and its service offers can be significantly influenced by how they are delivered and therefore contact personnel play a vital role in the development of this image.

Of course, some elements of an organization's image can be derived through channels other than the formal communication process. There is a lot of evidence, for example, that when differentiating between professional services providers customers preferred to be guided by information from friends and other personal contacts rather than from the usual promotion mix (Money *et al.*, Gilly and Graham, 1998; Silverman, 1997).

A second important characteristic of the audience justifying research is its degree of perceived risk when considering the purchase of a new service. For purchases which are perceived as being highly risky, customers are likely to use more credible sources of information (e.g. word-of-mouth recommendation) and engage in a prolonged search through information sources. People differ markedly in their readiness to try new products, and a number of attempts have been made to classify the population in terms of their level of risk taking. Rogers (1962) defined a person's 'innovativeness' as the 'degree to which an individual is relatively earlier in adopting new ideas than the other members of his social system'. In each product area, there are likely to be 'consumption pioneers' and early adopters, while other individuals only adopt new products much later. This has led to a classification of markets into the following adopter categories:

- Innovators
- Early adopters
- Early majority
- Late majority
- Laggards.

The adoption process is represented as a normal distribution when plotted over time. After a slow start, an increasing number of people adopt the innovation. The number then reaches a peak before diminishing as fewer non-adopters remain. A typical adoption distribution pattern is illustrated in Figure 11.2. Innovators are venturesome in that they try new ideas at some risk. Early adopters are opinion leaders in their community (see below) and adopt new products early but carefully. The early majority adopt new ideas before the average person, taking their lead from opinion leaders. The late majority are sceptical, tending to adopt an innovation only after the majority of people have tried it. Finally, laggards are tradition bound, being suspicious of changes. They only adopt a new service when it

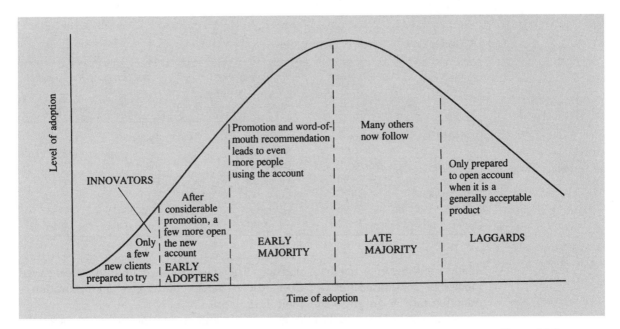

INNOVATORS

| Promotion and word-of-|
mouth recommendation |
leads to even |
more people |
using the account |

Many others
now follow

Only prepared
to open account
when it is a
generally acceptable
product

After
considerable |
promotion, a |
few more open |
Only | the new |
a few | account |

EARLY
MAJORITY

LATE
MAJORITY

LAGGARDS

new clients | EARLY
prepared to try | ADOPTERS |

Level of adoption

Time of adoption

**Figure 11.2**
Buyer adoption pattern
for a new type of bank
account

has become sufficiently widespread that it has now taken on a measure of tradition in itself.

Although adoption processes for goods and services are in principle similar, differences can result from services being perceived as riskier than goods, especially where they entail a high level of involvement by the consumer. Evaluation of quality and value before purchase is difficult and effective promotion of services must therefore start by understanding the state of mind of potential customers and the information they seek in order to reduce their exposure to risk.

## 11.2.2 Audience response

Having identified the target audience and its characteristics, the communicator must consider the type of response required from it. The required response will have an influence on the source, message and channel of communication.

In most cases, customers are seen as going through a series of stages before finally deciding to purchase a service. It is therefore critical to know these buyer-readiness stages and to assess where the target is at any given time. The communicator will be seeking any one or more of three audience responses to the communication:

- *Cognitive responses* The message should be considered and understood.
- *Affective responses* The message should lead to some change in attitude.
- *Behavioural responses* Finally, the message should achieve some change in behaviour (e.g. a purchase decision).

Many models have been developed to show how marketing communication has the effect of 'pushing' recipients of messages through a number of sequential stages,

**Table 11.1** Models of buyer states

| Domain | AIDA model | Hierarchy of effects (Lavidge and Steiner, 1961) | Innovation–adoption model (Rogers, 1962) |
|---|---|---|---|
| Cognitive | Awareness | Awareness<br>Knowledge | Awareness |
| Affective | Interest | Liking | Interest |
|  | Desire | Preference | Evaluation |
| Behavioural | Action | Conviction | Trial |
|  |  | Purchase | Adoption |

finally resulting in a purchase decision. The stages defined in three widely used models of communication – 'AIDA', the Hierarchy of Effects and Innovation – Adoption models are shown in Table 11.1.

Communication models portray a simple and steady movement through the various stages, although it should not be seen as ending when a sale is completed. It was noted in Chapter 5 that services organizations increasingly seek to build relationships with their customers, so the behavioural change (the sale) should be seen as the starting point for making customers aware of other offers available from the organization and for securing repeat business. Smooth progress through these stages is impeded by the presence of a number of 'noise' factors which are discussed below. The probabilities of success in each stage cumulatively decline due to noise and therefore the probability of the final stage achieving an actual purchase is very low.

### 11.2.3 Communication source

The source of a message – as distinct from the message itself – can influence the effectiveness of any communication. Aaker and Myers (1982) identified three major features of sources that influence communication effectiveness:

- If a source is perceived as having power, then the audience response is likely to be compliance.
- If a source is liked, then identification by the audience is a likely response. Important factors here include past experience and reputation of the service organization, in addition to the personality of the actual source of the communication. A salesperson, any contact personnel, a TV/radio personality, etc. are all very important in creating liking.
- If a source is perceived as credible then the message is more likely to be internalized by the audience. Credibility can be developed by establishing a source as important, high in status, power and prestige or by emphasizing reliability and openness.

Closely related to the notion of credibility is the 'halo effect'. Coulson-Thomas (1985) defined this as the 'tendency to impute to individuals and things, the qualities of other individuals and things with which they are associated'. The closer the perceived link between 'personality' and service, the stronger the halo effect. However, there is also a phenomenon known as the 'sleeper effect' in which the credibility of a source – and hence message retention – is built up over a period of time. The implication of this is that company and product reputation need regular reinforcement, both from formal advertising and from satisfying contacts between customers and front-line employees.

### 11.2.4 The message

A message must be able to move an individual along a path from awareness through to eventual purchase. In order for a message to be received and understood, it must gain attention, use a common language, arouse needs and suggest how these needs may be met. All of this should take place within the acceptable standards of the target audience. However, the service itself, the channel and the source of the communication also convey a message and therefore it is important that these do not conflict.

Three aspects of a communication message can be identified – content, structure and format. It is the content which is likely to arouse attention, and change attitude and intention. The appeal or theme of the message is therefore important. The formulation of the message must include some kind of benefit, motivator, identification or reason why the audience should think or do something. Appeals can be rational, emotional or moral.

Messages can be classified into a number of types, according to the dominant theme of the message. The following are common focal points for messages:

- *The nature and characteristics of the organization and the service on offer* For example, television advertisements for the airline Cathay Pacific emphasize the high quality of its in-flight service.
- *Advantages over the competition* Promotion by the airline Ryanair has emphasized the low cost of its fares compared to its competitors.
- *Adaptability to meet buyers' needs* Many insurance companies stress the extent to which their policies have been designed with the needs of particular age segments of the population in mind.
- *Experience of others* In this way, testimonials of previous, satisfied customers are used to demonstrate the benefits resulting from use and the dependability of the service provider. For example, the Prudential Assurance company has used the opinions of ordinary investors to extol the virtues of a Prudential pension plan.

Recipients of a message must see it as applying specifically to themselves and they must see some reason for being interested in it. The message must be structured according to the job it has to do. The points to be included in the message must be ordered (strongest arguments first or last) and consideration given to whether one-sided or two-sided messages should be used. The actual format of the message

**Figure 11.3**
This advert for De Montfort University gives very little specific information about educational services provided by the university. However, the university has successfully used a brand-building promotional campaign to establish a distinctive identity which differentiates De Montfort from other 'new' universities (reproduced with permission of De Montfort University)

will be very much determined by the medium used, e.g. the type of print if published material, type of voice if broadcast media is used, etc.

### 11.2.5 Noise

The creator of a message needs to encode it into some acceptable form for an audience to decode and comprehend. Unfortunately, there is likely to be interference between the stages of encoding and decoding and, although it is difficult to totally eliminate such interference in the communication process, an understanding of the various elements of this 'noise' should help to minimize its effects. The potential for 'noise' to hinder the effective communication is usually greater for

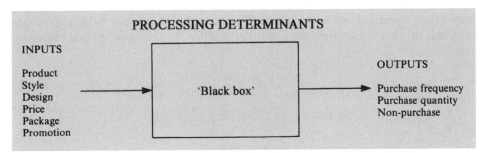

**Figure 11.4**
'Black box' model of
buyer response

services than for manufactured goods. Because of the intangible nature of services, expectations of service delivery must be created in people's minds without the help of tangible evidence which can be used to describe manufactured goods.

The nature of 'noise' factors can be examined in terms of a simple 'black box' model of buyer response (Figure 11.4). A communication of some sort (originating either from within a company or extraneously) is seen as a stimulus to some form of customer response. Response can be expressed in terms such as quantity purchased, frequency of purchase, or even non-purchase. The final response, however, is not a straightforward response to the initial stimulus. The initial stimulus is distorted within the 'black box' process, resulting in different individuals responding in different ways to a similar stimulus. The variables at work within the black box are the noise factors and can be divided into two major types:

- Those that relate to the individual, i.e. psychological factors. Both positive and negative previous experiences predispose an individual to decode messages – in a particular way. Also, the personality of specific members of an audience can significantly influence interpretation of a message – for example an extrovert may interpret a message differently to an introvert. Similarly an individual's motives can influence how a message is decoded. An individual who has just come home from work hungry and is about to eat dinner, is unlikely to be amenable to information communicated by a life assurance salesperson which may satisfy some higher order need for family security.
- Those that relate to other groups of people, i.e. sociological factors. Important sociological influences on behaviour include culture and social class. Individual members of different cultures and classes are likely to interpret messages in different ways. In this way, communications offering credit facilities may be interpreted with suspicion within certain social groups who have been conditioned to live within their means, whereas members of other social groups may welcome the opportunities represented by the message.

## 11.3  Developing the promotional mix

Having considered 'who says what to whom and with what effect', the next area of concern is 'how?'. Developing the promotional mix entails selecting and blending different channels of communication in order to achieve the promotional objectives of the marketing mix. Specifying the objectives of a communication is important if appropriate messages are to be accurately targeted through the most appropriate channels in the most cost effective manner possible. Typical promotional objectives might be:

- To develop an awareness of, and an interest in, the service organization and its service product(s).
- To communicate the benefits of purchasing a service.
- To influence eventual purchase of the service.
- To build a positive image of the service firm.
- To differentiate the service from its competitors.
- To remind people of the existence of a service and/or the service firm.

Ideally, these objectives should be quantified as far as possible, thus promotional objectives for a new type of motor insurance policy may begin with an objective to achieve awareness of the brand name by 30% of the 25–55 year-old UK insurance buying public within one year of launch.

The promotion mix refers to the combination of channels which an organization uses to communicate with its target markets. Communication is received by audiences from two principal sources – sources within an organization and external sources. The latter includes word-of-mouth recommendation from friends, editorials in the press, etc., which it has already been noted may have high credibility in the service evaluation process. Sources originating within an organization can be divided into those originating from the traditional marketing function (which can be divided into personal two-way channels such as personal selling and impersonal one-way channels such as advertising), and those originating from front-line production resources. Because services normally involve consumers in the production process, the promotion mix has to be considered more broadly than is the case with manufactured goods. Front-line operations staff and service outlets become a valuable channel of communication. The elements of the services promotion mix are illustrated in Figure 11.5.

The choice of a particular combination of communication channels will depend primarily on the characteristics of the target audience, especially its habits in terms of exposure to messages. Other important considerations include the present and potential market size for the service (advertising on television may not be appropriate for a service that has a local niche market, for example), the nature of the service itself (the more personal the service, the more effective the two-way communication channel) and, of course, the costs of the various channels.

A very important consideration is the stage that a service has reached in its life cycle (see Chapter 7). Advertising and public relations are more likely to form important channels of communication during the introductory stage of the life cycle where the major objective is often to increase overall audience awareness. Sales promotion can be used to stimulate trial and, in some instances, personal selling can be used to acquire distribution coverage. During a service's growth stage, the use of all communication channels can generally be reduced as demand during this phase tends to produce its own momentum through word-of-mouth communications. However, as the service develops into its maturity stage, there may be a call for an increase in advertising and sales promotion activity. Finally, when the service is seen as going into decline, advertising and public relations are often reduced,

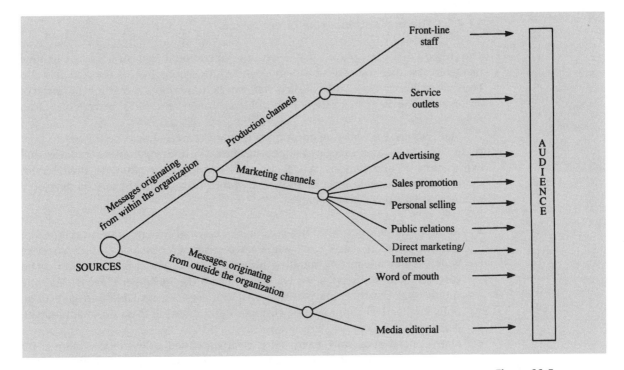

**Figure 11.5**
Extended
communication
channels for services

although sales promotion can still be quite usefully applied. Sometimes, services in decline are allowed to die quietly with very little promotion. In the case of many long-life financial services which a company would like to delete but cannot for contractual reasons, the service may be kept going with no promotional support at all.

In the following sections, each of the elements of the promotion mix through which communications can be directed is discussed. Before the traditional elements of advertising, sales promotion, personal selling and public relations are considered, attention is given to the role of production process inputs to the promotion mix of services firms.

## 11.4 The producer–customer interface of the services promotion mix

Inseparability results in consumers being involved in a series of encounters with service producers. During each of these encounters, a service organization has an opportunity to communicate with its customers. Without any effort on the part of an organization, customers will pick up messages, whether they are good or bad. With more planning, an organization can ensure that every encounter is turned into an opportunity to convey positive messages that encourage repeat business from customers and encourage them to pass on the message to others. Two important sources of non-marketer derived messages can be identified within the extended promotion mix of services – front-line employees and the physical environment of the service encounter.

### 11.4.1 The promotional role of employees

The important role played by front-line operational personnel as 'part-time marketers' has been stressed on many previous occasions in this book. It has also been noted that the activities of such staff can be important in creating an image of an organization which can live on to influence target customers' perceptions of an organization.

Staff who have front-line encounters with customers should be trained to treat these encounters as promotional opportunities. Without appropriate training and explanation of expectations, a call for such employees to promote their service more effectively can be little more than rhetoric. Training might seek to develop a number of skills in front-line staff:

- An ability to spot cross-selling possibilities can call for empathy on the part of front-line staff. A bank clerk who sees a customer repeatedly using a service which is not adequately fulfilling his or her needs could be trained to try to cross-sell another service which better meets the customer's needs. Training should make such employees aware of the services available and give them skills in effectively approaching customers and referring them on to appropriate personnel.
- Many operational staff have quite clearly defined sales responsibilities, for example restaurant waiters may be expected to encourage customers to spend more on their visit to the restaurant.
- The general manner of staff's interaction with customers is important in encouraging customers to return and to tell their friends about their good experience. Again, training should emphasize those behaviours that have a positive effect on customers' evaluation of their encounter.
- Staff can directly influence future purchases by encouraging customers to book a repeat service or by giving them literature to pass on to friends.

It can be difficult to draw a distinction between production staff and marketing staff in terms of their contribution towards the promotion of an organization. Organizational boundaries should not prevent operational staff being considered an important element of promotion mix planning.

### 11.4.2 The promotional role of service outlets

From the outside, service outlets can be seen as billboards capable of conveying messages about the services which take place within them. They are therefore powerful tools in appealing to both customers and non-customers. The general appearance of an outlet can promote the image of a service organization. A brightly coloured and clean exterior can transmit a message that the organization is fast, efficient and well run. Outlets can be used to display advertising posters which in heavily trafficked locations can result in valuable exposure. Many retailers with town centre locations consider that these opportunities are so great that they do not need to undertake more conventional promotion. Among the large UK retailers, Marks and Spencer until the 1980s paid for very little promotional activity, arguing that over half the population passed one of its stores during any week, thereby exposing them to powerful 'free' messages. Although the company's promotional mix now includes more paid-for advertising, store locations are still considered to be valuable promotional media.

Service outlets can also provide valuable opportunities to show service production processes to potential customers, something which is much more difficult to achieve through conventional media. A fast-printing shop displaying sophisticated printing equipment and a tyre retailer's large stocks and tidy appearance of employees all help to promote an organization's processes as much as its outcomes.

## 11.5  Advertising and the media

Advertising is mass, paid communication which is used to transmit information, develop attitudes and induce some form of response on the part of the audience. It seeks to bring about a response by providing information to potential customers, by trying to modify their desires and by supplying reasons why they should prefer that particular company's services.

Advertising objectives should be clearly specified in terms of target audiences and desired effects. However, in monitoring the performance of advertising, it can be extremely difficult to prove that this alone is responsible for a sales increase. Sales, after all, can be the result of many intervening variables, some of which are internal to the organization (e.g. public relations activity, pricing policy), while others are external (e.g. the state of the national economy). It is therefore too simplistic to set advertising objectives simply in terms of increasing sales by a specified amount. Given the existence of diverse adopter categories and the many stages in the communication process which were described earlier, more appropriate objectives can often be specified in terms of levels of awareness or comprehension.

### 11.5.1  Media characteristics

The choice of media is influenced by the characteristics of each medium and their ability to achieve the specified promotional objectives. The following are some of the most common types of media and their characteristics:

**Newspapers**  Daily newspapers tend to have a high degree of reader loyalty, reflecting the fact that each national title is targeted to specific segments of the population. This loyalty can lead to the printed message being perceived by readers as having a high level of credibility. Newspapers can be used for creating general awareness of a product or a brand as well as providing detailed product information. In this way, building societies use newspapers both for adverts designed to create brand awareness and liking for the organization, as well as adverts for giving specific details of savings accounts. The latter may include an invitation to action in the form of a freepost account opening coupon.

**Magazines/journals**  Within the UK, there is a wide range of magazine and journal titles available to advertisers. While some high circulation magazines appeal to broad groups of people (e.g. *Radio Times*), most titles are specialized in terms of their content and targeting. In this way, 'Which Mortgage?' can prove to be a highly specific medium for building societies to promote mortgages. Specialist trade titles allow messages to be aimed at service intermediaries – for example a tour operator seeking to promote a holiday offer may first gain the confidence and support of travel agents through such magazines as the *Travel Trade Gazette*.

Although advertising in magazines may at first seem relatively expensive compared to newspapers, they represent good value to advertisers in terms of their high number of readers per copy and highly segmented audiences.

**Outdoor advertising**  This is useful for reminder copy and can support other media activities. The effect of a television advertisement can be prolonged if recipients are exposed to a reminder poster on their way to work the following day. If strategically placed, the posters can appeal to segmented audiences – e.g. London Underground sites in the City of London are seen by large numbers of affluent business people. The sides of buses are often used to support new service facilities (e.g. new store openings) and have the ability to spread their message as the bus travels along local routes. Posters can generally only be used to convey a simple communication rather than complex details.

**Television**  This is an expensive, but very powerful medium. Although it tends to be used mainly for the long-term task of creating brand awareness, it can also be used to create a rapid sales response. The very fact that a message has been seen on television can give credibility to the message source and many smaller service companies add the phrase 'as seen on TV' to give additional credibility to their other media communications. The power of the television medium is enhanced by its ability to appeal to both the senses of sight and sound, and to use movement and colour to develop a sales message.

The major limitation of television advertising is its cost – for most local service providers, television advertising rates start at too high a level to be considered. The high starting price for television advertising reflects not only high production costs, but also the difficulty in segmenting television audiences, either socioeconomically, or in terms of narrowly defined geographical areas. Also, the question must be asked as to how many people within the target audience are actually receptive to television advertising. Is the target viewer actually in the room when an advertisement is being broadcast? If the viewer is present, is he or she receptive to the message?

**The Internet**  Most large service organizations now have their own websites which are used to disseminate messages to customers and potential customers. In addition to listing their site with search engines, companies often buy advertising space on other websites, with hotlinks provided to their own site. The Internet is good at assessing the number of visitors to a site, and advertisers can learn how visitors move around a site as they seek out information. The greatest power of the Internet is that it can become a medium for personalized messages, thereby not strictly falling within the definition of advertising given earlier. For this reason, further consideration of the Internet as part of an organization's promotion mix will be given in the later section on direct marketing.

**Cinema** Because of the captive nature of cinema audiences, this medium can potentially have a major impact. It is frequently used to promote local services such as taxi operators and food outlets whose target market broadly corresponds to the audience of most cinemas. However, without repetition, cinema advertisements have little lasting effect, but do tend to be useful for supporting press and television advertising.

**Commercial radio** Radio advertising has often be seen as the poor relation of television advertising, appealing only to the sense of sound. The threshold cost of radio advertising is much lower than for television, reflecting much more local segmentation of radio audiences and the lower production costs of radio adverts. A major advantage over other media is that the audience can be involved in other activities – particularly driving – while being exposed to an advertisement. Although there are often doubts about the extent to which an audience actually receives and understands a message, it forms a useful reminder medium when used in conjunction with other media.

## 11.5.2 Media selection criteria

In addition to the characteristics of the media themselves, a number of other important factors must be taken into account in selecting the media mix for a particular advertising campaign. These factors are:

- The characteristics of the target audience.
- The level of exposure of the target audience to the communication.
- The impact which advertising will have on the target audience.
- The extent to which the effects of a particular advertising message 'wear out' over time.
- The cost of advertising through a particular medium.

**Target audience** The media habits of the target audience must be fully understood. If a firm's target market is not in the habit of being exposed to a particular medium, much of the value of advertising through that medium will be wasted. As an example, attempts to promote premium credit cards to high-income segments by means of television commercials may lose much of their value because research suggests that the higher socioeconomic groups tend to spend a greater proportion of their viewing time watching BBC rather than commercial channels. On the other hand, they are heavy readers of Sunday newspaper magazine supplements.

Information about target audiences' media habits is obtained from a number of sources. Newspaper readership information is collated by the National Readership Survey. For each newspaper, this shows reading frequency and average issue readership (as distinct from circulation) broken down into age, class, sex, ownership of consumer durables, etc. Television viewing information is collected by the Broadcasters' Audience Research Board (BARB). This indicates the number of people watching particular channels at particular times by reference to two types of television ratings (TVRs) – one for the number of households watching a programme/advertising slot and one for the number of people watching.

**Advertising exposure** The number of advertising exposures of a particular communication is determined by two factors: cover/reach and frequency. 'Cover' or 'reach' is the percentage of a particular target audience reached by a medium or a whole campaign, while 'frequency' is the number of times a particular target audience has an 'opportunity to see/hear' (OTS/OTH) an advertising message. The combination of these two factors results in an index of advertising exposure which is usually stated in terms of 'gross rating points' (GRPs). For example, if an objective is to reach 50% of the target audience three times a year, this would be stated as a GRP of 150 (i.e. $50 \times 3$). Within a given budget, there has to be a trade-off between coverage/reach and frequency.

**Advertising impact** Impact is usually more closely related to the message than the media. If, however, the medium is the message, then advertising impact should be an important criterion for media selection. Different media vehicles can produce different levels of awareness and comprehension of an identical message. In this way, the image of McDonald's Ronald McDonald presented via television is very much more powerful compared to that presented via radio.

**Wearout** The concept of advertising exposure assumes that all advertising insertions have equal value. However, the effect of additional insertions may in fact decline, resulting in diminishing returns for each unit of expenditure. There is usually a 'threshold' level of advertising beneath which little audience response occurs. Once over this threshold, audience response tends to increase quite rapidly through a 'generation' phase until eventually a saturation point is reached. Any further advertising may lead to a negative or declining response, i.e. 'wearout'.

**Cost** The cost of using different media varies markedly, and while a medium which at first sight appears to be expensive may in fact be good value in terms of achieving promotional objectives, a sound basis for measuring cost is needed. There are generally two related cost criteria:

- *Cost per gross rating point* This is usually used for broadcast media and is the cost of a set of commercials divided by the GRP.
- *Cost per thousand* This is used for print media to calculate the cost of getting the message seen by 1000 members of the target market.

These measures can be used to make cost comparisons between different media vehicles. However, a true comparison needs to take into consideration the different degrees of effectiveness each medium has. In other words, the strength of the media vehicle needs to be considered, as does the location, duration, timing and – where relevant – size of the advertisement plus a variety of more complex factors. These are all combined to form 'media weights' which are used in comparing the effectiveness of different media. Cost effectiveness therefore, is calculated using the following formula:

$$\text{Cost effectiveness} = \frac{\text{Readers/viewers in target} \times \text{media weight}}{\text{Cost}}$$

### 11.5.3 Determining the advertising budget

Advertising expenditure could become a drain on an organization's resources if no conscious attempt is made to determine an appropriate budget and to ensure that expenditure is kept within the budget. A number of methods are commonly used to determine an advertising budget:

- *What can be afforded* This is largely a subjective assessment and pays little attention to the long-term promotional needs of a service. It regards advertising as a luxury which can be afforded in good times, to be cut back during lean times. In reality, this approach is used by many smaller service companies to whom advertising spending is seen as the first and easy short-term target for reducing expenditure in bad times.
- *Percentage of sales* By this method, advertising expenditure rises or falls to reflect changes in sales. In fact, sales are likely to be influenced by advertising rather than vice versa and this method is likely to accentuate any given situation. If sales are declining during a recession, more advertising may be required to induce sales but this method of determining the budget implies a cut in advertising expenditure.
- *Comparative parity* Advertising expenditure is determined by the amount spent by competitors. Many market sectors see periodic outbursts of promotional expenditure, often accompanying a change in some other element of firms' marketing mix. During the mid-1990s, price competition triggered an increase in advertising by ferry companies operating between the UK and France, with each ferry company responding to its competitors' increase in advertising expenditure. However, merely increasing advertising expenditure may hide the fact that it is the other elements of the marketing mix which need adjusting in order to gain a competitive market position in relation to competitors.
- *Residual* This is the least satisfactory approach and merely assigns to the advertising budget what is left after all other costs have been covered. It may bear no relationship whatever to promotional objectives.
- *Objective and task* This approach starts by defining clearly promotional objectives. Tasks are then set which relate to specific targets. In this way, advertising is seen as a necessary – even though possibly risky – investment in a brand, ranking in importance with other more obvious costs such as production and salary costs. This is the most rational approach to setting a promotional budget.

### 11.5.4 Developing the advertising campaign

An advertising campaign brings together a wide range of media related activities so that instead of being a discrete series of activities, they can act in a planned and coordinated way to achieve promotional objectives. The first stage of campaign planning is to have a clear understanding of promotional objectives (see above). Once these have been clarified, a message can be developed that is most likely to achieve these objectives. The next step is the production of the media plan. Having defined the target audience in terms of its size, location and media exposure, media must be selected which achieve desired levels of exposure/repetition with the target audience. A media plan must be formulated which specifies:

● The allocation of expenditure between the different media.
● The selection of specific media components – for example, in the case of print media, decisions need to be made regarding the type (tabloid versus broadsheet), size of advertisement, whether use of a Sunday supplement is to be made and whether there is to be national or local coverage.
● The frequency of insertions.
● The cost of reaching a particular target group for each of the media vehicles specified in the plan.

Finally, the advertising campaign must be co-ordinated with the overall promotional plan, for example by ensuring that sales promotion activities reinforce advertising messages.

While the criteria for planning a campaign for a services organization are in principle the same as would be followed by a manufacturing company, the intangible, inseparable and variable nature of services do need to be borne in mind when planning a campaign. Advertising alone is unlikely to be successful in helping customers make services purchase decisions, but their effectiveness can be increased by following a few guidelines. The following have been proposed by George and Berry (1981):

● *Use clear and unambiguous messages* The very intangibility of services can make it very difficult to communicate information defining the service offer. This is particularly true in the case of highly complex services. Here, advertising copy should emphasize the benefits of a service and how these match the benefits sought, i.e. it should have a customer orientation rather than a product/service orientation.
● *Build on word-of-mouth communication* An important influence on buyers' decision making is recommendation from others, therefore advertising should be used to enhance this. For example, advertising can be used to persuade satisfied customers to let others know of their satisfaction. Organizations can develop material that customers can pass on to non-customers or persuade noncustomers to talk to present customers. Finally, advertising campaigns can be aimed at opinion leaders who will then 'trickle down' information
● *Provide tangible cues* Organizations selling manufactured goods tend to differentiate their products from their competitors' by emphasizing intangible features such as after-sales service, guarantees, etc. Service marketers, however, tend to differentiate their services by emphasizing tangible cues or 'physical evidence'. The use of well-known personalities and objects can act as surrogates for the intangible features of a service. The use of consistent logos, catchphrases, symbols and themes can help to overcome the transitory nature of intangibility and encourage a durable company identity in the customer's mind.
● *Promise what can be delivered* The intangible nature of services results in customers holding abstract expectations about the standard of service delivery. You will recall from Chapter 8 that customers judge a service to be of poor

quality where perceived delivery does not meet up to these abstract expectations. Advertising should therefore not over-promise.

● *Aim advertising at employees too* Most services are labour intensive and advertisers need to be concerned with both the encouragement of employees to perform as well as customers to buy. Advertisements that emphasize personal service can motivate contact personnel to perform their duties more effectively as well as influencing consumer choice.

● *Remove post-purchase anxiety* Consumption of a service usually involves a high degree of customer involvement and therefore there is a greater likelihood of post-purchase dissonance occurring than is the case with most goods purchases. There is little tangible evidence to use in the post-purchase evaluation process and therefore advertising should be used to reinforce positive post-purchase feelings.

How do you strike a balance between an advertising campaign being eye-catching and accessible on the one hand, and preserving the core values of the product on the other? Retailers, banks and insurance companies have all encountered problems when their traditional mature audiences have been alienated by advertising which was aimed at increasing the number of younger customers. Wacky advertising may attract attention, but what does it say about the nature of the product on offer? Liverpool-based John Moores University used an unconventional approach to advertising its courses in 1999. Its prospectus paid relatively little attention to the details of the courses on offer, but gave great emphasis to the pubs and clubs in town. It may well be that this was based on a sound analysis of the factors that influence students' choice of university. Most prospective students have only a limited ability to distinguish between the academic credentials of competing courses, whereas nightlife is an easier point of reference. But the media picked up the story, claiming that this was further evidence of 'dumbing down' in education generally, and at John Moores University in particular. Even existing students claimed that the value of their degrees would be demeaned by advertising which made their institution appear to the outside world like a 'good time university'. But if the university went back to stuffy advertising and prospectuses, would it lose a point of difference with its nearby competitors? Would the target audience stop to read its messages?

## 11.6 Sales promotion

Sales promotion involves those activities, other than advertising, personal selling and public relations that stimulate customer purchase and the effectiveness of intermediaries. Although it can be used to create awareness, sales promotion is usually used for the later stages of the buying process, that is, to create interest, desire and, in particular, to bring about action. Sales promotion can quite successfully complement other tools within the promotion mix, for example by reinforcing a particular image or identity developed through advertising.

**Figure 11.6**

For most people, buying a mobile phone for the first time is very daunting, with countless permutations of networks, tariffs and handsets, communicated through a barrage of advertising messages. Carphone Warehouse has recognized the importance of word-of-mouth recommendation in simplifying buyers' decision processes, and offers existing customers an incentive to pass on their recommendation to friends (reproduced with permission of Carphone Warehouse)

Over the last few years there has been a rapid increase in the use of sales promotion, for a number of reasons:

- Internally, there has been a greater acceptance of the use of sales promotion by top management and more people are now qualified to use it. In addition, there is greater pressure today to obtain a quick sales response, something which sales promotion is good at achieving.
- There has been a general proliferation of brands with increased competitive pressure. As a result of this and the changing economic environment,

Find out how much you could save with The Insurance Shop. Call us now for a free quote without obligation, and we'll send you a free Parker Pen by way of a thank you.

**FREE Up to £30 worth of Marks & Spencer Gift Vouchers when you take out home insurance**

That's right, just take out a building or contents insurance policy with The Insurance Shop, and we'll send you Marks & Spencer Gift Vouchers worth £15. Or £30 if you take out both.

the insurance shop

**Figure 11.7**

In many markets where services are perceived by buyers as being basically similar, it may be necessary to offer an incentive in order to initiate a dialogue. Eager to enter buyers' choice set, many insurance companies, such as this one, provide a token gift in order to generate an initial response. Many insurance companies offer further incentives that are given following a completed purchase. Sales promotion activities of this type may be particularly important where consumers' ability to differentiate between competing products is low and an incentive offers a tangible basis for differentiation (reproduced with permission of Lloyds TSB Insurance Services Ltd)

consumers are more 'deal-oriented' and this has led to pressure from intermediaries for better incentives from manufacturers and service principals.

- It has been argued by many that advertising efficiency is declining due to increasing costs and media clutter.
- New technology in targeting has resulted in an increase in the efficiency and effectiveness of sales promotion.

The public and professional services sectors have also accepted the role of sales promotion in many areas, for example leisure centres and opticians respectively. As a promotional tool, sales promotion is likely to continue to grow in the future.

### 11.6.1   Sales promotion planning

Sales promotion contributes in a number of ways to achieving overall promotional objectives. While it can be used to merely gain attention for a service, it is more likely to be used as an incentive incorporating an offer which represents value to the target audience. It can also act as an invitation to engage in a transaction now rather than later. Sales promotion usually attracts brand switchers but is unlikely to turn them into loyal brand users without the use of other elements of the promotion mix. In fact, it is usually considered that sales promotion is used to break down brand loyalty, whereas advertising is used to build it up. Sales promotion can gain new users or encourage more frequent purchase but it cannot compensate for inadequate advertising, poor delivery or poor quality.

It is argued by many that the role of sales promotion for services is much more limited than is the case with goods. The fact that services cannot be stored may appear to limit the ability of a service firm to off-load unused services at a cheap price, something which is commonly undertaken by goods manufacturers using sales promotion. On the other hand, off-peak sales promotion activity can help to alleviate such a problem in the future. There is also a view that some promotional tools – such as the use of free samples – cannot be used for services as the sample would have to involve the whole service. However, a free first consultation by a solicitor, for example, could be thought of as an equivalent form of sales promotion.

As in the case of advertising, effective sales promotion involves an ongoing process with a number of distinct stages:

- *Establishment of objectives*  These could include the encouragement of increased usage or the building of trial among non-users or other brand users.
- *Selection of promotional tools*  These can include free samples/visits/consultations (which can be an important means of demonstrating an intangible service process); money-off price incentives (although these tend to be expensive to the service provider, as the incentive is given to customers regardless of its motivational effect on an individual customer); coupons/vouchers (which can offer targeted invitations to try a new service or to reward customer loyalty); gift offers (which can help to give tangible cues of the service company's offering as well as offering an incentive for immediate purchase); and competitions (which can add to the perceived value of a service).
- *Planning the sales promotion programme*  It is especially important to plan the timing and size of incentive to be offered.
- *Pre-testing*  This needs to be done in order to ensure that potentially expensive problems are discovered before the full launch of a promotion (e.g. false assumptions of redemption rates for an incentive may lead to the budget being exceeded, as happened in the Hoover free air tickets offer of the early 1990s).
- *Implementation*  This must specify the 'lead time' (the time necessary to bring the programme up to the point where the incentive is to be made available to the public) and the 'sell in time' (the period of time from the date of release to when approximately 90–95% of incentive material has been received by potential customers).
- *Evaluation*  With the use of customer databases, methods of evaluation are improving. However, it can be extremely difficult to separate out the effects of sales promotion activity from other promotional activity – or indeed from other marketing mix and extraneous factors.

Sales promotion activity can be aimed at intermediaries as well as the final consumers of a service. Sales promotion activity aimed at intermediaries includes: short-term increases in sales commission; competitions and gifts (useful motivators where individual sales personnel benefit directly from the incentive); point-of-sale material (e.g. tour operators who arrange a film evening for its travel agencies' clients); and co-operative advertising, where a service principal agrees to subscribe to local advertising by an intermediary, often in conjunction with a significant event, e.g. the opening of a new outlet by the intermediary. Sometimes, a service principal targets sales promotions at individual employees of its intermediaries (e.g. tour operators have given free holiday vouchers to travel agency clerks who sell a certain quota of the tour operator's holidays). This can raise ethical issues about whether employees should accept incentives when their first duty is to their employer who in turn seeks to develop the best long-term relationship with its customers.

## 11.7  Personal selling

Personal selling is a powerful two-way form of communication. It allows an interactive relationship to be developed between buyer and seller in which the latter can modify the information presented in response to the needs of the audience. Personal selling allows for the cultivation of a friendship between buyer and seller, which can be an important element of a relationship marketing strategy. It can also be powerful in creating a feeling of obligation by the customer to the salesperson, thereby helping to bring about a desired response.

Although the principles of personnel selling are basically the same for goods and services industries, services sales personnel are more likely to combine their sales duties with other functional duties, for example in the way that a travel agent – as well as being an expert on travel reservation systems – is expected to perform a selling role.

### 11.7.1  The salesperson's activities

The actual selling act is only a small part of the overall salesperson's role. In addition to their specific selling role, two further principal roles can be identified – servicing and intelligence.

The servicing element can be an important contributor to the development of long-term customer relationships where the service in question is perceived as being highly risky. Such relationships need to be regularly attended to, even if there is no short-term prospect of a sale. In a study of the life assurance sector, George and Myers (1981) found that customers viewed their purchases as being highly risky and therefore unpleasant. As a consequence, they attached particular importance to the level of support they received from a salesperson in particular, and their organization in general. There have now been many studies to identify the factors that contribute towards relationship satisfaction between buyer and seller (e.g. Crosby, Evans and Cowles, 1990).

As well as being the mouthpiece of an organization, sales personnel can also be its ears. They can be extremely useful in marketing research, for example by reporting on customers' comments or providing information about a competitor's activity. Organizations should develop systems for capturing information collected by sales personnel.

In respect of their selling role, a number of types of selling situation can be identified:

- *Trade selling* – where their role is to facilitate sales through intermediaries.
- *Technical selling* – which involve giving advice and technical assistance to customers. This type of salesperson becomes a consultant and assumes importance in many types of business-to-business service sales, e.g. business travel agencies.
- *Missionary selling* – where the salesperson is not expected to take orders but to 'prepare the ground' by building goodwill.
- *New business selling* – This involves the acquisition of new accounts and may sometimes involve 'cold calling'.

The task of selling can be broken down into a number of sequential stages:

- *Prospecting i.e. finding new customers* Sales leads can be developed in a number of ways, for example records of past customers, past enquiries and referrals from existing customers and suppliers.
- *Preparation and planning* A salesperson should attempt to gain as much information as possible about a prospect before actual contact takes place, for example in regard to their previous buying behaviour or aspirations.
- *The sales presentation* The salesperson should be recognized as a surrogate for the service – for low-contact services such as life insurance, the salesperson may be perceived as being *the* service. Appearance and demeanour are therefore very important in creating the right impression of the service offer. The sales presentation should help make tangible an intangible service. Samples of supporting goods, brochures or audio-visual aids can often give a better and more credible description of a service process than a salesperson alone. The salesperson should show a deep knowledge of their particular area, therefore the training of sales personnel in technical as well as sales skills is important. The sales presentation shouldn't offer what cannot be delivered – this applies to both goods and services but is particularly important where abstract expectations of service quality are not matched by actual performance. Customers should be given early opportunities to assess service quality, either by producing evidence of previous outcomes (e.g. previous performance of an investment fund) or by sampling the service process.
- *Handling objections* Objections to the sales presentation can be rational (e.g. objections to the price or the service itself) or irrational (e.g. objections based on resistance to change, apathy, prejudice, etc.) and need to be acknowledged, isolated and discussed.
- *Closing the sale* This is a difficult stage in that knowing how and when to close is a skill in itself.
- *Follow-up* This stage is often neglected but is essential to ensure customer satisfaction and repeat business. A letter of thanks or a phone call can help to reduce post-purchase dissonance, which is especially valuable for services where benefits are to be delivered in the distant future.

## 11.8 Direct marketing

Direct marketing has been defined by the UK Direct Marketing Association as '... *an interactive system of marketing which uses one or more media in acquiring a measurable response at a given location*'. The aim of **direct marketing** is to create and exploit a direct relationship between service producers and their customers. In recent years there has been a dramatic increase in the use of direct marketing for promoting services, largely due to the development of new technology which enables organizations to accurately target their messages. In the UK, direct marketing has been taken up in a big way by the financial services sector, particularly pensions and insurance companies. Travel companies, retailers and hotels have been more recent adopters of direct marketing methods on a large scale. While direct marketing may include personal selling, it is the other elements of direct marketing which are of interest here, including telemarketing, direct mail and directories.

The key elements of a direct marketing system are the following:

- An accurate record of the names of existing customers, ex-customers and prospective customers classified into different groups.
- A system for recording the results of communications with targets. From this, the effectiveness of particular messages, and the responsiveness of different target groups can be assessed.
- A means of measuring and recording actual purchase behaviour
- A system to follow up with continuing communication where appropriate.

Direct marketing is closely linked to firms' efforts to build long-term relationships with their customers (Chapter 5). Most critically, direct marketing allows a company to assess each of its customers' and potential customers' level of profitability and to deliver services and messages which are very closely related to their unique needs.

The two most common forms of direct marketing used by services organizations are telemarketing and direct mail. Electronic media are becoming increasingly popular.

### 11.8.1 Telemarketing

Telemarketing involves two-way communication by telephone – 'outbound' telemarketing occurs where suppliers take the initiative and 'inbound' where customers act in response to another stimulus, such as a newspaper advertisement. There has been a rapid increase in the use of inbound telemarketing using toll free 0800 numbers, particularly by the financial services sector. Inbound telemarketing is very powerful when combined with other media action and an incentive for customers to act promptly. Outbound telemarketing has sometimes been used as an alternative to personal selling, especially where some customers are seen as potentially less profitable than others and telemarketing is used for these instead of more expensive personal selling.

The effectiveness of telemarketing can be assessed in a number of ways. One possibility is to measure the cost per telephone call and from this, the cost per successful call. Alternatively effectiveness can be measured in terms of the cost per telephone hour which includes the costs incurred in managing the system. A more useful approach is to assess effectiveness in terms of benefits as well as costs. The simplest measure of benefit is the number and quality of enquiries received. Furthermore, by asking questions of enquirers, the source of particularly effective supporting advertisements can be identified. It can often be possible to measure the cost effectiveness of telemarketing in terms of the value of sales generated, especially where there is little extraneous media advertising which could itself have explained sales success.

### 11.8.2 Direct mail

Direct mail describes the way in which an organization distributes printed material aimed at specifically targeted potential customers with a view to carrying on direct interchange between the two parties. Its use is becoming increasingly popular among services industries and a number of important advantages which it has over the other promotional tools can be identified.

- It can be used very selectively to target quite specific groups of potential private or business customers.
- The sales message can be personalized to the needs of individual recipients.
- Direct mail offers a very versatile and creative medium and is flexible in the range of materials that can be used.
- It can be timed effectively to fit in with the overall marketing strategy and is quick to implement and to produce results.
- Direct mail can include tangible evidence of a highly intangible service offer (e.g. pictures of hotels).

Direct mail can be employed to achieve a number of promotional objectives, including the generation of enquiries, keeping prospects interested, keeping customers informed of new developments and improving the effectiveness of the salesperson (i.e. it can be used as a 'door opener').

Compared to advertising, the direct mail message can be more detailed. Much more space is available on a direct mailshot and this allows long and complex messages to be presented – a point which partly explains the popularity of direct mail with financial services companies whose sales messages are typically very complex. The response medium serves a variety of purposes. It can be used to obtain expressions of interest, to obtain sales orders and to measure the effect of the promotion. It is therefore extremely important to know who has responded and what the response actually is. It is also important to consider non-respondents and why they did not respond. Leaflets, inserts, pop-ups, etc. can also be included in the mail shot.

With the use of reply paid envelopes and freefone numbers, response from recipients of direct mail is facilitated. The results of individual targeted mailshots can be assessed quite easily and through further refinement of customer profiling and targeting, the cost of contact per person can be reduced to a low level.

### 11.8.3   The Internet

The Internet has emerged as a versatile element of the promotion mix which often combines a promotional function with a distribution function. At its simplest, a web page can simply give additional information about a company's services, for example many hotels have websites which give information about their location and the facilities available. The great strength of the Internet is to make the promotional message directly relevant to the user, so, for example, a train operator's website may give information relating to a specific journey that the user had enquired about. Beyond this, websites are increasingly being enabled to allow immediate fulfilment of a request, such as confirmation of a hotel booking or reservation of a plane ticket. The Internet has narrowed the gap between somebody receiving a message and being able to act upon it. The services sector has been at the leading edge of developments in electronic commerce, largely because it often does not have to cope with the problems of delivering tangible goods.

The Internet is extensively used for comparison shopping and a lot of research has gone into understanding which sites produce the best results in terms of moving an individual through the stages of purchase. A regularly updated site which contains information of direct relevance to a user and which is fast to download has become a minimum requirement for most users of the medium.

Similar to traditional promotional media, it can be difficult to make a company's website stand out in a crowded environment. With literally thousands if not millions of promotional messages seeking to find a web surfer, companies must develop a strategy for promoting their web presence. Without heavy promotion of a website address through conventional media, or paying for a 'hotlink' via a network navigator, a company's website may remain unseen in cyberspace. Many services companies have applied their website address to ancillary materials such as carrier bags, timetables and pricelists, in much the same way as they would promote their telephone number. A lot of money has been spent by companies on advertisements in the traditional media drawing attention to their website. Buying access to target customers on the Internet has become an important activity, with portals such as Yahoo! charging for the use of banner advertisements on their popular websites. A number of companies, such as Doubleclick.com exist to collect information about individuals' usage patterns with a view to improving the targeting of advertisements through paid-for websites.

E-mail has also developed rapidly as a medium for advertising messages, using very much the same principles as direct mail. An accurate database of customers' preferences is essential if e-mail messages are not to be discarded as junk messages. The prospect of m-mail to individuals' mobile phones raises the prospect of a huge amount of low-cost messages being targeted at individuals, and senders of messages must ensure that their messages stand out from competitors and have immediate relevance to the recipient.

Amidst the high expectations held by many about trade over the Internet, intangible services have rated highly in many assessments of what could be most profitably handled. The lack of tangibles reduces the problem of labour-intensive delivery systems and can allow the Internet to be used as both a promotional and distribution channel. Airlines, holiday companies and banks have been early developers of their own web sites. A report published by the UK Consumers' Association in 1997 ('Consumer Transactions On The Internet') highlighted some of the pitfalls to consumers of buying through the Internet. Despite being theoretically the most capable of promotion and delivery through the Internet, intangible services are also the most risky for consumers. What comeback have buyers got against a company which doesn't deliver what it promised when the company is based in a possibly unknown location? How can buyers ensure that advertisers of services are legitimate traders? Is a 'terrestrial' promotion campaign essential to support a 'virtual' company?

## 11.9 Public relations

Public relations is an indirect promotional tool whose role is to establish and enhance a positive image of an organization and its services among its various publics. It is defined by the Institute of Public Relations as '... the deliberate, planned and sustained effort to establish and maintain mutual understanding between an organization and its publics'. It seeks to persuade people that a company is an attractive organization with which to relate or do business, which is important for services as it has already been noted that services are evaluated very subjectively and often rely on word-of-mouth recommendation. Public relations facilitates this process of subjective evaluation and recommendation.

Because public relations is involved with more than just customer relationships, it is often handled at a corporate level rather than at the functional level of marketing management and it can be difficult to integrate public relations fully into the overall promotional plan.

As an element within the promotion mix, public relations presents a number of valuable opportunities as well as problems. Some of its more important characteristics are described below:

- *Low cost* The major advantage of public relations is that it tends to be much cheaper in terms of cost per person reached than any other type of promotion. Apart from nominal production costs, much public relations activity can be carried out at almost no cost, in marked contrast to the high cost of buying space or time in the main media.
- *Audience specificity* Public relations can be targeted to a small, specialized audience if the right media vehicle is used.
- *Believability* Much public relations communication is seen as credible because it comes from an apparently impartial and non-commercial source. Where information is presented as news, readers or viewers may be less critical of a message than if it was presented as a biased advertisement.
- *Difficult to control* A company can exercise little direct control over how its public relations activity is subsequently handled and interpreted. If successful, a press release may be printed in full, although there can be no control over

where or when it is printed. At worst, a press release can be misinterpreted and the result could be very unfavourable news coverage.

● *Competition for attention* The fact that many organizations compete for a finite amount of attention puts pressure on the public relations effort to be better than that of competitors.

### 11.9.1 The publics of public relations

Public relations can be distinguished from customer relations because its concerns go beyond the creation of mutually beneficial relationships with actual or potential customers.

The following additional audiences for public relations can be identified:

● *Intermediaries* These may share many of the same concerns as customers and need reassurance about the company's capabilities as a service principal. Service organizations can usually develop this reassurance through the use of company newsletters, trade journal articles, etc.

● *Suppliers* These may need assurances that the company is a credible one to deal with and that contractual obligations will be met. Highlighting favourable annual reports and drawing attention to major new developments can help to raise the profile and credibility of a company in the eyes of its suppliers.

● *Employees* Here, public relations overlaps with the efforts of internal marketing (see Chapter 12) and assumes great importance within the services sector where personnel become part of the service offer and it is important to develop participation and motivation among employees. In addressing its internal audiences, public relations uses such tools as in-house publications, newsletters and employee recognition activities.

● *Financial community* This includes financial institutions that have supported, are currently supporting or who may support the organization in the future. Shareholders – both private and institutional – form an important element of this community and must be reassured that the organization is going to achieve its stated objectives.

● *Government* In many cases, actions of government can significantly affect the fortunes of an organization and therefore relationships with government departments – at local, national and supranational level – need to be carefully developed. This can include lobbying of Members of Parliament, communicating the organization's views to government enquiries and civil servants and creating a favourable image for itself by sponsoring public events.

● *Local communities* It is sometimes important for an organization to be seen as a 'good neighbour' in the local community. Therefore, the organization can enhance its image through the use of charitable contributions, sponsorship of local events, being seen to support the local environment, etc.

### 11.9.2 The tools of public relations

A wide range of public relations tools are available and the suitability of each is dependent upon the promotional objectives at which they are directed. In general, the tools of public relations are best suited to creating awareness of an organization or liking for its services and tend to be less effective in directly bringing about action in the form of purchase decisions. While there can be argument as to just what constitutes public relations activity, some of the important elements which are used within the promotion mix are described below.

- *Press releases* The creation and dissemination of press releases is often referred to as 'publicity'. Kotler (1999) defines publicity as the 'activity of securing editorial space, as divorced from paid space, in all media read, viewed or heard by a company's customers or prospects, for the specific purpose of assisting in the meeting of sales goals'. Because of its important contribution towards the promotion mix, this tool is considered in more detail below.
- *Lobbying* Professional lobbyists are often employed in an effort to inform – and hence influence – key decision makers who may be critical in allowing for elements of a marketing plan to be implemented. Lobbying can take place at a local level (e.g. a bus company seeking to convince a local authority of the harm which would result to the public in general if streets in a town centre were closed to buses); at a national level (e.g. lobbying by British Telecom to reduce the constraints on its pricing); and at a supranational level (e.g. lobbying by airlines to the European Commission which took place at the time of a proposed British Airways/American Airlines alliance).
- *Education and training* In an effort to develop a better understanding – and hence liking – of an organization and its services, many services organizations aim education and training programmes at important target groups. In this way, banks frequently supply schools and colleges with educational material which will predispose recipients of the material to their brand when they come to open a bank account. Open days are another common method of educating the public by showing them the complex 'behind the scenes' production processes involved, a tactic commonly employed by theatres.
- *Exhibitions* Most companies attend exhibitions not with the intention of making an immediate sale, but to create an awareness of their organization which will result in a sale over the longer term. Exhibitions offer the chance for potential customers to talk face to face with representatives of the organization, and the physical layout of the exhibition stand can give valuable tangible evidence about the nature of the service on offer. Exhibitions are used for both consumer services and business to business services. As an example of the latter, the annual World Travel Market in London offers the chance for a wide range of tourism-related service industries to meet quite narrowly targeted customers and to display tangible cues of their service offering (e.g. brochures and staff).
- *In-house journals* Many services organizations have developed their own magazines which are given to customers or potential customers. By adopting a news-based magazine format, the message becomes more credible than if it was presented as a pure advertisement. Often, outside advertisers contribute revenue which can make such journals self-financing. This commonly happens with in-house magazines published by banks. Travel operators often publish magazines which are read by a captive travelling public.
- *Special events* In order to attract media attention, organizations sometimes arrange an event which is in itself newsworthy and will create awareness of

the organization. One example was the world's first non-stop passenger plane flight between Britain and Australia, made by a Quantas aircraft. Although Quantas had adapted the aircraft and the journey could not be made under normal operating conditions, the fact that it was a first made it newsworthy and created significant awareness of Quantas. Of course, if badly managed, a special event can turn into a public relations disaster.

● *Sponsorship* There is argument about whether this strictly forms part of the public relations portfolio of tools. It is, however, being increasingly used by services companies and is described in more detail below.

### 11.9.3  Press relations (publicity)

The aim of publicity is to create over the longer term a feeling of mutual under-standing between an organization and the media. This understanding with the media is developed by means of:

● *Press releases* This is the most frequent form of press relations activity and is commonly used to announce new service launches, new appointments or sig-nificant achievements
● *Press conferences* These are used where a major event is to be announced and an opportunity for a two-way dialogue between the organization and the media is considered desirable.
● *Availability of specialist commentators* Faced with a news story which the media wishes to report on, a newspaper or radio station may seek specialists within an industrial sector who are knowledgeable on the issues involved. For example, a local tour operator may be asked by a local newspaper to comment upon the consequences of a hurricane in an overseas resort. This helps both the reporter and the service organization in question, whose representative is fielded as an expert.

Publicity has the advantage of being a relatively inexpensive promotional tool which can reach large audiences with a high degree of credibility. Against this, a major disadvantage is the lack of control which the generator of publicity has over how the publicity is subsequently handled, in terms of appearance, timing and content (it is likely to be edited). Because of the competition from other organizations for press coverage, there can be no guarantee that any particular item will actually be used.

Service companies have begun to appreciate the PR value of the Internet as a convenient way to disseminate information quickly and widely. But against this is the realization that corporate reputations can be savaged as disgruntled customers and shareholders swap comments on the World Wide Web. Thorns in the side of PR people include the McSpotlight site (www.mcspotlight.org) which carries infor-mation critical of McDonald's Restaurants and the Lostminute.com site for dis-gruntled investors in Lastminute.com. Such sites can be created without the companies' knowledge, if the latter are not monitoring, and contributing to, the forums and chat rooms. These sites can end up disseminating a damaging mix of rumour and untruths.

Public relations agencies that have the technical expertise have set up monitoring services. One PR consultancy, Edelman, monitors the Internet, checking on 33 000 user groups and bulletin boards and regularly prepares web pages for its clients in anticipation of crises. These are then 'hidden' on the website, ready to be activated if needed.

Public relations professionals have had to face up to the new realities of the Internet. Response times need to be immediate, with no specific deadlines that are typical of conventional published media. But quite apart from the battle of technology is the fundamental question: why did a company allow itself to get into the position of exposing itself to criticism? Could this not have been foreseen? If there is little for people to campaign about, the dissident websites would probably lose much of their support.

### 11.9.4  Crisis management

An important element of public relations is avoiding negative publicity. Because services can be highly variable, there is always the possibility that the media will pick up on one bad incident and leave its audience thinking that this is the norm for that service provider. This is particularly a problem for highly visible public or quasi-public services for which readers enjoy reading bad news stories to confirm their own prejudices. External events may also lead to bad publicity, or the negative actions of similar service organizations may lead to a generally poor reputation of the sector as a whole. In all situations, an organization needs to establish contingency plans to minimize any surprise and confusion resulting from the publicity. Bad publicity is more likely to be effectively managed if an organization has invested time and effort in developing mutually supportive good relations with the media.

Service organizations, by the very nature of their operating environment, face unpredictable major crises, such as a train crash or a fire at a nightclub. At such times, the provision of timely, appropriate and honest information can help to preserve a company's image as a caring and honest organization. Services organizations therefore often prepare and practice plans to be implemented when a disaster occurs. Following a serious train crash outside London's Paddington station in 1999, the quality of communication was one bright spot in an otherwise devastating incident and showed evidence of previous rehearsal. Where a company appears to be caught on the hop and is perceived to be making things up as it goes along, the effects can cause a crisis to be remembered for even longer. The handling of a crash by a TWA aircraft on its way from New York to Paris in 1998 is cited as an example of bad crisis management.

## 11.10  Sponsorship

One way that services organizations can try to make their service tangible is to attempt to get customers to link the image of its organization or of specific services with a more tangible event or activity. While publicity can successfully perform this function, sponsorship can also have long-term value.

Sponsorship involves investment in events or causes in order that an organization can achieve objectives such as increased awareness levels, enhanced reputation, etc. Sponsorship activities include such examples as a bank sponsoring cricket matches (e.g. the NatWest Trophy) and the sponsorship of specific television programmes (such as Powergen's sponsoring of weather forecasts on commercial television).

Sponsorship is attractive to service companies as it allows the relatively known characteristics of an event or activity being sponsored to help enhance the image of an organization's own inherently intangible services. As an example, an insurance company wishing to associate itself with high quality may seek to sponsor the activities of a leading arts organization noted for the quality of its productions. A further advantage of sponsorship is that it allows a company to avoid the general media clutter usually associated with advertising. Furthermore, audiences can be segmented and a sponsorship vehicle chosen whose audience matches that of the sponsoring company, in terms of socioeconomic, demographic and geographic characteristics. In this way, a regional insurance broker might sponsor a local theatrical group operating solely in its own business area.

It is difficult to evaluate sponsorship activities because of the problem of isolating the effects of sponsorship from other elements of the promotion mix. Direct measurement is only likely to be possible if sponsorship is the predominant tool. Sponsorship should therefore be seen as a tool that complements other elements of the promotion mix.

## Promoting an 'ethical bank'

**Case Study**

The UK personal banking sector has gradually consolidated, so that by the late 1990s four major banks accounted for over three-quarters of all personal accounts. How could the much smaller Co-operative Bank promote itself as something different to the 'big four' and carve a profitable market for itself?

The origins of the Co-operative Bank go back to 1872 when it was established by the Co-operative Wholesale and Retail Societies. By the mid-1980s it had enjoyed a period of steady growth when its numbers of branches passed 100, helped by several innovative new products such as free in-credit banking, extended opening hours and interest-bearing cheque accounts. However, the bank found its market position being steadily eroded by increased competition from the major clearing banks, and particularly building societies who were able to enter the personal banking sector, following deregulation of the banking sector. As a result of increased competition following deregulation, the bank saw its market share fall from 2.7% in 1986 to 2% by 1991. Alongside this trend, the bank faced a changing customer profile. Traditionally, the bank had attracted a high proportion of its customers from the more affluent ABC1 social groups. By 1992, an increasing number of new accounts was being attracted from the C2DE social groups, while at the same time the bank was losing its core ABC1 accounts. This trend was

diluting its position as a more up-market bank and reducing its potential to cross-sell more profitable financial products.

The bank's research showed that outside its customer base, it lacked a clear image, being seen mainly as rather staid, old-fashioned and with leftwing political affinities. Furthermore, spontaneous recall of its name had steadily fallen despite extensive advertising of its innovative new products.

The bank realized that immediate action was necessary to rebuild its image and stem the loss of its ABC1 accounts. The size of the bank and its profitability meant that the advertising budget had to be modest and therefore a focused campaign with maximum effectiveness was crucial.

Advertising agency BDDH was appointed to devise a promotional campaign. The agency 'interrogated' the Co-operative Bank to identify any distinctive competencies that it could build a campaign upon. It discovered that the bank's heritage offered a unique positioning opportunity against other mainstream banks. This derived in particular from its sourcing and distribution of funds which had been governed by an unwritten ethical code, with the effect that the bank never lent money to environmentally or politically unsound organizations. BDDH set out to transform the results of its interrogation into a relevant and motivating proposition that would appeal beyond the bank's current customer base. A key strategic decision was made to target promotional activity at the growing number of 'ethical consumers' who, importantly, were found to have a more upmarket ABC1 profile.

The 'ethical bank' formed the foundation upon which BDDH built its campaign. Initially, this was tested on its existing customer base where it gained a high level of approval. The bank recognized that advertising claims must be met by actual practice and incorporated its ethical stance into its customer charter. The bank was well aware that the media enjoys making trouble for companies which claim to be ethical but in fact are caught out by undertaking unethical practices. Advertising was initially used to raise awareness of the bank's positioning. The creative work was deliberately provocative and motivating, while at the same time maintaining the bank's credentials as a high street lender. The creative images used were often simple and stark.

The key objectives of the campaign were:

1   Build customer loyalty and so stem the outflow of ABC1s.

2   Expand the customer base, targeting ABC1s.

3   Expand the corporate customer base.

National press and regional television in the bank's 'northern heartland' were the primary media used in the initial stages of the campaign. Cinema advertising was used as the campaign progressed. Continuing its theme of innovation, the bank launched an Internet banking facility called 'Smile' in 1999.

The marketing objectives were exceeded as a result of the promotional campaign. The bank established a strong and differentiated brand position which in 2000 it continued to build upon. The campaign's success can be put down to a clear understanding of the bank's customer base and its own unique competencies. The campaign was carefully targeted with the aim to achieve maximum impact which enabled the message to be delivered cost effectively. The case clearly demonstrates how effective promotional activity, linked closely to business and marketing objectives and strategy can provide a long-term sustainable competitive position in the marketplace.

(Adapted from Institute of Practitioners in Advertising (1994) *Advertising Works 8*, NTC Publications, pp 329–352.

## Case study review questions

1   How can the Co-operative Bank assess whether its promotion as an ethical bank has been effective?

2   What dangers does the Co-operative Bank face in promoting an ethical position?

3   Critically assess the promotional positioning of other banks with which you are familiar.

## Chapter summary and linkages to other chapters

This chapter has explored the role of promotion in the marketing planning of services. While many of the principles of communication for services are similar to those for goods, the promotion of services poses additional problems and opportunities. Perceived risk, caused by intangibility must be addressed by promotion, and techniques for seeking to achieve this have been discussed. The presence of consumers in the production process for services opens possibilities for promotion which are not generally available to the goods manufacturer.

Promotion has a vital role in guiding buyers through the purchase decision process (**Chapter 4**). With the development of relationship marketing strategies (**Chapter 5**), the promotional emphasis in many companies has moved from recruitment of new customers to retention of existing ones. With the development of direct marketing, promotion and accessibility strategies are becoming increasingly closely connected (**Chapter 9**). Finally, promotion strategy contributes towards the positioning strategy of a service (**Chapter 7**) and implementation requires adequate information for planning and monitoring purposes (**Chapter 6**).

## www linkages/URLs

Institute of Practitioners in Advertising, Sales & Marketing Resource Directory:
**http://salesdoctors.com/directory/dircos/3102i02.htm**

Institute of Sales Promotion:
**http://www.thebiz.co.uk/isp.htm**

The British codes of advertising and sales promotion:
**http://www.asa.org.uk/bcasp/bcasp.txt**

Institute of Direct Marketing:
**http://www.thebiz.co.uk/instdirm.htm**

Institute of Professional Sales:
**http://www.iops.co.uk/**

Institute of Public Relations:
**http://www.ipr.org.uk/**

Institute of Practitioners in Advertising:
**http://www.ipa.co.uk/contents.html**

Advertising Standards Authority:
**http://www.asa.org.uk/**

The Advertising Association (UK):
**http://www.adassoc.org.uk/**

Newspaper Readership Survey:
**http://www.inma.org/reading.html**

Independent Television Commission:
**http://www.itc.org.uk/**

Direct Marketing Association:
**http://www.the-dma.org/**

US Direct Marketing Association: Sales & Marketing Resource Directory:
**http://salesdoctors.com/directory/dircos/3101d02.htm**

## Key terms

Direct marketing  339

## Chapter review questions

1 To what extent does the intangibility of a service influence the promotional methods used by a service organization?
2 Why do you think that certain professional services still consider sales promotion to be unethical?
3 What is the link between 'internal marketing' and the promotion of services?
4 To what extent can the application of direct marketing be effective in the promotion of a university?
5 Public relations may be a more effective promotional tool for services than other communication methods. Why do you think this may be the case?
6 Identify the problems likely to be faced by an airline in evaluating the effectiveness of its promotion for a newly introduced service.

## Selected further reading

*For a fuller discussion of the general principles of promotion, the following texts are recommended:*

Brannan, T. (1998) *A Practical Guide to Integrated Marketing Communications*, Kogan Page, London
Canwell, D. and L. Maitland (1998) *Marketing Campaigns*, ITP
Fill, C. (1995) *Marketing Communications: Frameworks, Theories and Applications*, Prentice-Hall, Hemel Hempstead
Smith, P. (1998) *Marketing Comunications*, 2nd edition, Kogan Page, London
Tapp, A. (1998) *Principles of Direct and Database Marketing*, Financial Times Management, London

*During the early days of the services marketing literature, a number of articles sought to define the ways in which the promotion of services differed from that of goods:*

Firestone, S. H. (1983) 'Why Advertising a Service is Different', in L. L. Berry, G. L. Shostack and G. D. Upah (eds) *Emerging Perspectives in Services Marketing*, American Marketing Association, Chicago, IL
George, W. R. and L. L. Berry (1980) 'Guidelines for the Advertising of Services', *Business Horizons*, July–August, Vol. 24
George, W. R., J. P. Kelly and C. E. Marshall (1983) 'Personal Selling of Services', in L. L. Berry, G. L. Shostack and G. D. Upah (eds) *Emerging Perspectives in Services Marketing*, American Marketing Association, Chicago, IL

*Measuring the effectiveness of promotional spending is difficult, for both goods and services. The following article addresses problems in assessing the effectiveness of services advertising:*

Hill, D. H. and N. Gandhi (1992) 'Service Advertising: A Framework to its Effectiveness', *Journal of Services Marketing*, Vol. 6, No. 4, Fall, pp 63–77

# 12

# Internal marketing

### Learning objectives

For many service industries, the quality of service delivered to customers is very closely related to the performance of employees. The first objective of this chapter is to define the meaning of internal marketing. It then explores key issues involved in the recruitment, motivation, training and control of staff employed in the services sector, especially those involved in front-line service encounters. Issues of empowerment are related to the design of service encounters. The fact that consumers are involved as co-producers of services and that services cannot be stored makes the task of human resource management more complex for services than for goods. Marketing managers within the services sector are increasingly realizing that marketing plans cannot be seen in isolation from human resource management plans.

## 12.1 Introduction

Consider a weekend leisure break in a hotel and the things which typically are most likely to go wrong:

- The checking-in procedure is slow and unfriendly.
- Facilities in the room are not as promised and the hotel is slow to put things right.
- The promised wake-up call doesn't materialize.
- The bill is wrongly made up and it takes a lot of effort by the customer to put it right.
- The peace is disturbed by a rowdy party among fellow guests.

All of these instances illustrate the importance of people management as a means of meeting customers' quality expectations. Appropriate actions by front-line employees, and effective management of these employees could have avoided many of these problems. Of course, employees can also be responsible for particularly good service encounters, such as the hotel receptionist who spends considerable time in trying to find a Japanese-speaking babysitter for a guest who requests one.

The importance of people as a component of the service offering has been stressed on many occasions in previous chapters of this book. Most service production processes require the service organization's own personnel to provide significant inputs to the service production process, both at the front-line point of delivery and in those parts of the production process which are relatively removed from the final consumer. In the case of many one-to-one personal services, the service provider's own personnel constitute by far the most important element of the total service offering. The focus of this chapter is on personnel employed by the service organization. The management of this input, in terms of recruiting the best personnel and training, motivating, rewarding and controlling them, becomes crucial in influencing the perceived quality of service.

Services management has often been described as the bringing together of the principles of marketing, operations management and human resource management (HRM), in which it can sometimes be difficult – and – undesirable to draw distinctions between the three approaches (Figure 12.1). In this way, methods to improve the service provided by staff of a fast food restaurant can be seen as a marketing problem (e.g. the need to analyse and respond to customer needs for such items as speed and cleanliness), or an operations management problem (scheduling work in a manner which reduces bottlenecks and allows a flexible response to patterns of demand), or a human resource management problem (selecting and motivating staff in such a way that maximizes their ability to deliver a specified standard of service).

It can be almost a cliché to say that for some businesses, the employees are the business – if these are taken away, the organization is left with very few assets with which it can seek to gain competitive advantage in meeting customers' needs. While for some organizations the management of personnel can be seen as just one other asset to be managed, for others, human resource management is so central to the activities of the organization that it cannot be seen as a separate activity. Some indication of the importance attached to human resource management within any organization can be gained by examining two aspects of personnel:

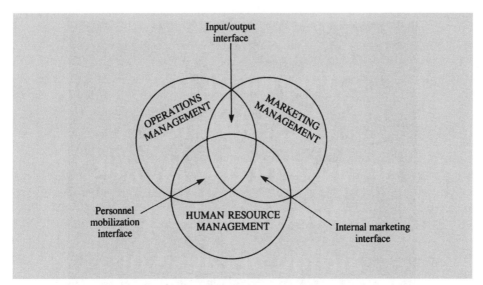

**Figure 12.1**

The interfaces between marketing management, operations management and human resource management

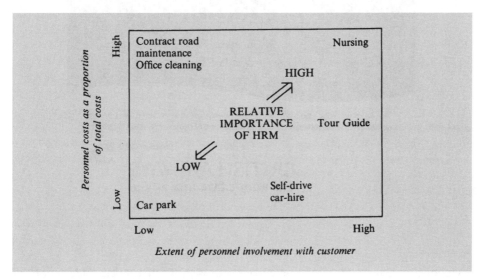

**Figure 12.2**

The importance of personnel within the service offer

1 The proportion of total costs which are represented by employee costs.
2 The importance of customer–employee encounters within the service offer.

In Figure 12.2 these two dimensions are shown in a matrix form with examples. For HRM, the most critical group of services is found where employees account for a high proportion of total costs and form an important part of the service offering perceived by the consumer. Many personal services such as hairdressing fall into this category. In other cases, employee costs may be a small proportion of total costs, but can represent key individuals who can significantly affect consumers' perceptions of a service. In this way, personnel costs are typically a relatively small proportion of the costs of a telephone service, yet the performance of key front-line staff such as

**Figure 12.3**

British Airways uses its advertising to stress the importance of good performance by its employees in delivering a high level of service to customers (Reproduced with permission of British Airways plc)

We're not the best airline because of our awards. We're the best airline because of our people.

Thanks to everyone who works for British Airways, we've been voted 'Best Airline of the Year' for the 10th year running by the readers of Business Traveller Magazine.

BRITISH AIRWAYS
The world's favourite airline

telephone operators or service engineers can significantly affect judgements of quality.

The human input to services can by its nature be highly variable, resulting in variability in perceived quality. For this reason, many service organizations have sought to replace personnel with equipment based inputs, often resulting in fewer, but more highly trained personnel being required.

The importance attached to human resource management is also a reflection of the competitiveness of the environment in which an organization operates. At one extreme, the highly competitive environment which faces most West European fast-food restaurants requires organizations to ensure that their staff meet customers' needs for speed, friendliness and accuracy more effectively than their competitors. On the other hand, organizations with relatively protected markets (for example many public sector services) can afford to be less customer-led in the manner in which their human resources are managed.

## 12.2 Defining internal marketing

The term **'internal marketing'** came to prominence during the 1980s and describes the application of marketing techniques to audiences within the organization. An early definition of internal marketing provided by Berry (1980) was:

> ... the means of applying the philosophy and practices of marketing to people who serve the external customers so that (i) the best possible people can be employed and retained and (ii) they will do the best possible work.

Internal marketing is a relatively new concept, and best practice reflects much of what has been part of organizations' HRM strategy. It may be easy to say that there should be no barriers between the marketing and HRM functions of an organization, but in practice jealousies and conflict can arise. In most organizations, HRM has its own hierarchical structure which is distinct from marketing. Even as an academic discipline, the two are usually taught as distinct subjects. This has led many people to criticize marketers' approach to internal marketing as being superficial and not being informed by the large body of knowledge on human resource management which has gone before it.

In an attempt to clarify the theory of internal marketing Varey and Lewis (1999) have conceptualized a number of its dimensions:

- *Internal marketing as a metaphor* Organization jobs and employment conditions are 'products' to be marketed and managers should think like a marketer when dealing with people. However, it is the employer who is both buyer and consumer in the employment relationship, rather than the employee.
- *Internal marketing as a philosophy* Managers may hold a conviction that HRM requires 'marketing-like' activities. However, this does not address employees' divergent needs and interests which may themselves be quite different from those of the organization. This is especially the case if the internal 'marketing' activities are actually promotional advertising and selling of management requirements. Employees may merely be seen as the manipulable subject of managerial programmes.
- *Internal marketing as a set of techniques* HRM may adopt market research, segmentation and promotional techniques in order to inform and persuade employees. But internal marketing as the manipulation of the '4Ps' imposes management's point of view on employees and cannot be said to be employee- (customer-) centred. Therefore, it is employees who must change their needs or must understand the position of the employer as they respond to the market.
- *Internal marketing as an approach* There is an explicit symbolic dimension to HRM practices, such as employee involvement and participation, and statements about the role of employees within the organization. These are used to bring about indirect control of employees. Nevertheless, the symbolism of internal marketing may reveal many contradictions. For example, individualism contradicts teamworking, and the service culture as defined by management may contradict management attitudes towards employee flexibility and

responsibility. The complexities of managing people and their actions and knowledge may be reduced to mere 'techniques' of symbolic communication.

Much debate surrounds just how internal marketing fits within traditional HRM structures and processes. Hales (1994), for example, is critical of the 'managerialist' perspective on internal marketing and of the literature on internal marketing as an approach to HRM. Viewed as an activity in isolation, internal marketing is unlikely to succeed. For that to happen, the full support of top management is required.

### 12.2.1 Employees as internal customers

Every organization can be considered to be a marketplace consisting of a diverse group of employees who engage in exchanges between each other (Foreman and Money, 1995). In order to have their needs met, employees are often dependent upon internal services provided by other departments or individuals within their organization. As in the case of external customers, these internal customers engage in numerous service encounters to satisfy the many needs they bring to the encounter. These internal encounters include relationships between customer-contact staff and the backroom staff, managers and the customer-contact staff, managers and the backroom staff, and, for large organizations, between the head office and each branch. In the most general sense, employees have been seen by some as 'consumers' of services provided by their employer, such as a pleasant working environment, provision of a pension scheme and good facilities for performing their tasks.

Increasingly, organizations are asking internal service departments, such as information technology, human resources, accounting and media services, to be more accountable. In a growing number of instances, organizations have out-sourced the services traditionally provided by such internal departments, resulting in extended 'network' or 'virtual' organizations. This has resulted in employees effectively trading services with other employees within their organization.

This view of different internal suppliers and customers, some of which deal directly within the service delivery process and some which provide support services to the service delivery process, appears to be closely related to the concept of the value chain (Porter, 1985). A modified value chain in terms of internal suppliers is shown in Figure 12.4.

This idea of a value chain and internal trading of services is closely related to the idea developed in the total quality management literature of 'next operation as a customer' (NOAC) (Denton, 1990). NOAC is based on the idea that each group within an organization should treat the recipients of their output as an internal customer and strive to provide high-quality outputs for them (e.g. Lukas and Maignan, 1996). Through this approach, quality will be built into the service delivered to the final customer.

Attempts have been made to apply external service quality dimensions to the measurement of internal service quality between employees (e.g. Reynoso and Moores, 1996; Varey, 1995). This has been justified on the basis that the interaction between the company and the customer is simply one link in a large network of relationships, many of which occur within the boundaries of the company. The

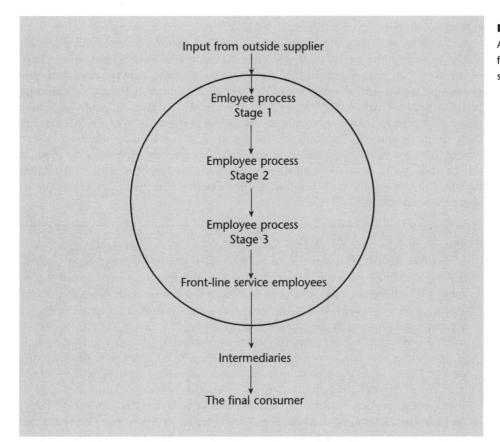

**Figure 12.4**
A modified value chain
for internally produced
services

Input from outside supplier

Emloyee process
Stage 1

Employee process
Stage 2

Employee process
Stage 3

Front-line service employees

Intermediaries

The final consumer

implication is that the principles and techniques for the creation and measurement of service quality can be transferred to the internal environment.

There are, however, problems in drawing analogies between internal and external markets for services. External customers can usually take their business elsewhere if they are not satisfied with the service provided, while internal customers may be required to use a designated service unit within their organization. Consequently, the internal customer is frequently a *captive* customer (Albrecht, 1990). Employees as customers may be tied to employment contracts with little short-term prospect of 'buying' employment elsewhere.

Many studies of internal marketing which focus on internal customers and suppliers have not differentiated between the different types of internal customers which may exist within the firm and their differing internal service expectations. This would appear to be no more marketing-oriented than a marketing plan which treats all external customers as homogeneous. There is a need to explore the service expectations of different internal customer segments within the internal market and to identify any differences between these segments. This knowledge can then be applied to the internal marketing programme to maximize its effectiveness.

There is a widely held view that if employees are not happy with their jobs, external customers will never be uppermost in their minds. Researchers have tended to agree that satisfied internal customers are a critical prerequisite to the satisfaction of external customers. From an internal marketing perspective, many researchers have argued that by satisfying the needs of their internal customers, firms enhance their ability to satisfy the needs of their external customers. Nevertheless, many have recognized that service encounters are a three-way fight between the firm, the contact personnel and the customer. The service encounter is thus a 'compromise between partially conflicting parties' (Bateson, 1989). To give an example, it may sound like a good idea to give employees longer rest breaks because this satisfies their needs as internal 'customers'. But longer rest breaks may result in greater waiting time for external customers as fewer staff are now available to serve them. A fine balance has to be drawn and there is no conclusive proof that in all situations happier employees necessarily result in happier external customers and a more profitable service operation.

Many companies have developed a philosophy of putting their employees first. This at first might sound contradictory to the marketing philosophy which puts customers at the centre of a firm's thinking, but there are many examples of companies who have made this proud claim and achieved credible results. The American South Western Airlines has frequently been cited as an advocate of this approach, and has expanded rapidly and profitably. The airline has argued that employees are such a major part of its service offer and that if they are not happy, it is unlikely that the airline's customers will be happy. Being a relatively new airline with no history of poor industrial relations undoubtedly helps employees to identify with the company's mission. Having staff incentive schemes which encourage employees to perform to their best in a highly competitive market also helps. But can this approach work in all situations? If employees do not share a company's mission, management's attempts to put employees first may not be reciprocated in the form of employees' enthusiastic contribution to the business. And if there is very little external competition to spur them on, the captive customer may come second best by a long way.

In reality, it is difficult to talk about employees coming first, if by implication customers come second. They should both be seen as part of a virtuous circle in which attention given to one reinforces attention given to the other.

## 12.3 Human resource management and its relationship to marketing

Internal marketing has much to learn from the literature on HRM. The role of marketing is to achieve organizational goals by satisfying customers' needs. HRM is concerned with achieving organizational goals. It therefore follows that HRM must itself be concerned with satisfying the needs of external customers.

At a strategic level, Boxall (1992) has identified two approaches to HRM – the 'Matching School' and the 'Harvard School'. The former, based on the work of Formbrun (1984) focuses on the importance of establishing a tight fit between HRM and business strategy, viewing HRM as something which is 'done' to employees in order to achieve predefined business goals. By contrast, the Harvard Model (Beer *et al.*, 1984) focuses on the crucial importance of getting managers involved in the dissemination of an organization's central mission to all employees. The role of employees in delivering on this mission is crucial and without this dissemination and pickup, HRM will be merely a set of specialist independent activities without a strategic business contribution. Guest (1992) identified strategic integration and improved quality as the human resource outcomes of strategic HRM. It follows that recruitment, selection, appraisal, development and participation are not considered narrowly as component parts of personnel activity but are seen as parts of corporate strategy designed to improve efficiency and profitability.

Guest (1989) identified two component parts of HRM, termed 'hard' and 'soft' HRM. Hard HRM is primarily concerned with the economic outcomes of a business, typically measured in terms of efficiency and worker productivity. Within many services organizations, the results of restructuring an organization's workforce can usually be assessed by these economic criteria. Soft HRM stresses the importance to organizations of developing paternal approaches to their employees, by emphasizing employees as essential assets to be developed and encouraged to participate within the organization. It is in this area that the generation of consent is vital in order that employees can identify with corporate goals and can see how their function contributes to these goals. Maitland (1990) discussed the relationship between internal marketing and organization theory, and suggested that the human relations approach of McGregor (1960) is most appropriate because it emphasizes prerequisites of an internal marketing culture: mutual trust, holistic supportive relationships, internal networks and self-direction, which enhance commitment, loyalty and motivation. This approach would appear to be consistent with 'soft' HRM approaches.

Human resource management can be contrasted with the more traditional personnel management which is often seen as being isolated and separate from the business aims of firms. Personnel management has frequently been oriented towards control and administrative activities rather than the alignment of human resources towards achieving strategic organizational goals. In doing so, personnel management has often become too concerned at achieving its own set of subgoals which are not necessarily related to the marketing needs of an organization. In this way, the maintenance of a uniform pay structure may have been seen as a desirable objective in its own right by personnel managers despite the fact that the marketing needs of an organization may require more flexibility in the manner in which staff are paid.

## 12.4  Controlling and empowering staff

It follows from the previous discussion of management theories that there are two basic approaches to managing people. On the one hand, staff can be supervised closely and corrective action taken where they fail to perform to standard. On the other hand, staff can be made responsible for controlling their own actions. The latter is often referred to as 'empowering' employees. The problem of control is particularly great with service industries as it is usually not possible to remove the results of poor personnel performance before their effects are felt by customers.

While the effects of a poorly performing car worker can be concealed from customers by checking his or her tangible output, the inseparability of the service production/consumption process makes quality control difficult to achieve. There is an argument that, because many services are carried out on a one-to-one basis with little possibility of management intervention, day-to-day control by management is impossible. Nevertheless, many companies which use industrialized service processes rely on control powers with varying degrees of formality.

Should employees of service organizations be closely controlled, or should they be empowered to act in the best way they see fit? It was noted in Chapter 3 that **empowerment** may be crucial for turning service failures into effective recovery, and for closely tailoring a service to individual customers' needs. The degree of empowerment given to employees, or the control exercised over them depends on the format of a service delivery system. For low contact, standardized services, employees can be controlled by mechanistic means such as rules and regulations. For high-contact, highly divergent services, high levels of empowerment may be more appropriate.

One of the underlying assumptions of those advocating empowerment is that employees' values will be in line with those of the organization. The latter must be prepared to allow employees the freedom to act and to make decisions based on their own judgement. For example, if a service employee is empowered, then that employee must be able to decide how best to deal with the needs of customers and should be accountable and responsible to deal with problems of customer complaints and operational difficulties caused.

Empowerment essentially involves giving employees discretion over the way they carry out their tasks. Kelley (1993) distinguished between three types of employee discretion: routine, creative and deviant discretion.

- Routine discretion occurs where employees are allowed to select an alternative from a prescribed list of possible actions in order to do their job (e.g. a service engineer having a choice of three subsystems to install in order to rectify a specified problem).
- Creative discretion is exercised where employees are required to develop alternative methods of performing a task (e.g. an interior design consultant may have complete freedom to choose their own designs).
- Deviant discretion is negatively regarded by the employer as it involves behaviours that are not part of the employee's formal job description and outside their area of authority.

Berry (1995, p. 208) noted that empowerment is essentially a state of mind. An employee with an empowered state of mind should experience feelings of: (1) control over how their job is performed; (2) awareness of the context in which the job is performed; (3) accountability for their work output; (4) shared responsibility for unit and organizational performance; and (5) equity in the rewards based on individual and collective performance. Discussion of empowerment frequently stresses the need to share information, so that employees understand the context in which they work.

Empowered employees need to be rewarded in a timely fashion and their initiatives, triumphs and achievements acknowledged. Empowerment also implies a culture which encourages employees to experiment with new ideas and can tolerate them making mistakes and learning from them. Such a culture would be more in line with the image of the 'Learning Organization' (Garvin, 1993).

The reasons for empowering employees can be divided into the mutually supportive dimensions of those that improve the motivation and productivity of employees and those that improve service delivery for consumers.

On the motivational side, empowerment of front-line service employees can lead to both attitudinal and behavioural changes in employees. Attitudinal changes resulting from empowerment include increased job satisfaction and reduced role stress. A consequence of increased job satisfaction is greater enthusiasm for their job which can be reflected in better interaction with customers.

Behaviourally, empowerment can lead to quicker response by employees to the needs of customers, as less time is wasted in referring customers' requests to line managers. In situations where customer needs are highly variable, empowerment can be crucial in allowing employees to customize service delivery. In the event of a service failure, empowerment can facilitate a rapid recovery (Hart *et al.*, 1990). If service failures are not rectified quickly and satisfactorily, customers may lose trust and confidence in a service provider.

Advocates of tighter control mechanisms point to the disadvantages of empowerment. One of the consequences of empowerment is that it increases the scope of employees' jobs, requiring employees to be properly trained to cope with the wider range of tasks which they are expected to undertake. It also impacts on recruitment as it is necessary to ensure that employees recruited have the requisite attitudinal characteristics and skills to cope with empowerment. Hartline and Ferrell (1996) found that while empowered employees gained confidence in their abilities, they also experienced increased frustration and ambiguity through role conflict. Additionally, because empowered workers are expected to have a broader range of skills and to perform a greater number of tasks, they are likely to be more expensive to employ because of their ability to command higher rates of pay.

Far from improving the efficiency of service delivery processes, empowerment can actually slow them down. An employee who is empowered to customize each service to individuals' specific requirements will be less efficient than one who is quite strictly controlled as to how much customization is to be carried out. Of course, it is another matter whether the empowered employee is more effective at satisfying customers' needs, but if the service blueprint is based on a no-frills, low-cost proposition, excessive empowerment and customization by employees may not be viable for a company. The company could in the short term cause delays to waiting customers who seek a standard service, and in the long term find itself delivering excessive value to customers. Customization of service could also be perceived by some customers as unfair in situations where employees are observed to be favouring some customers rather than others. It has been pointed out by Martin (1996) that employees may consciously or unconsciously discriminate to give better service to friends or people who are similar to themselves in terms of age, gender or ethnicity.

Finally, empowering employees can cost actual money in the short term, which has to be balanced against possible revenue gains in the long term. Faced with a service failure, an empowered employee may over-compensate customers, not only incurring immediate costs for the company, but raising expectations for compensation next time that a service failure occurs.

Even with highly empowered employees, some form of control systems are necessary. Control systems are closely related to reward systems in that pay can be used to control performance – e.g. bonuses forfeited in the event of performance falling below a specified standard. In addition, warnings or ultimately dismissal form part of a control system. In an ideal service organization, which has a well-developed soft HRM policy, employees' involvement in their work should lead to considerable self-control or informal control from their peer group. Where such policies are less well developed, three principal types of control are used – simple, technical and bureaucratic controls.

- Simple controls are typified by direct personal supervision of personnel – for example a head waiter can maintain a constant watch over junior waiters and directly influence performance when this deviates from standard.
- Technical controls can be built into the service production process in order to monitor individuals' performance – for example a supermarket checkout can measure the speed of individual operators and control action (e.g. training or redeployment) taken in respect of those shown to be falling below standard.
- Bureaucratic controls require employees to document their performance, for example the completion of work sheets by a service engineer of visits made and jobs completed. Control action can be initiated in respect of employees who on paper appear to be under-performing.

In addition to these internal controls, the relationship which many front-line service personnel develop with their customers allows customers to exercise a degree of informal control. College lecturers teaching to a class would in most cases wish to avoid the hostility from their class which might result from consistently delivering a poor standard of performance – in other words, the class can exercise a type of informal control.

So in what situations should a service provider decide to empower its employees, rather than to control them tightly? A number of authors have suggested a contingency approach to empowerment. Rafiq and Ahmed (1998) have built on the work of Bowen and Lawler (1992) to develop a model of five factors which influence whether a control or empowerment approach is most appropriate, namely: business strategy, tie to the customer, technology, business environment and types of employees.

- *Business strategy* Firms undertaking a differentiation business strategy, or a strategy that involves high degrees of **customization** and personalization of services should empower their employees. However, firms pursuing a low-cost high-volume strategy should use a production-line approach to controlling employees.
- *Tie to the customer* Where service delivery involves managing long-term relationships with customers rather than just performing a simple one-off transaction, empowerment is vital. This is particularly so in the case of industrial/organizational customers involving high-turnover value and long-term relationships.
- *Technology* If the technology involved in service delivery simplifies and industrializes the tasks of employees, a production line approach is more appropriate

than empowerment. However, where the technology is non-routine or complex, empowerment is more appropriate.

- *Business environment* Some environments are more variable than others, for example the operating environment of an airline is more variable than that of a fast-food restaurant. A company may make its environment more complex, for example an airline may offer to cater for special meal and accessibility requirements, or such complexity may be forced on it by generally held expectations within the market. A production line control approach is more appropriate where customer requirements are simpler and more predictable.

- *Types of employees* Bowen and Lawler (1992) recognized that empowerment and control approaches require different types of employees. Employees most likely to be effectively empowered are those who have high growth needs and who need to have their abilities tested at work. Where empowerment requires teamwork, employees should have strong social and affiliative needs and good interpersonal and group skills. Empowerment requires 'Theory Y' type managers who allow employees to work independently to the benefit of the organization and its customers. The control approach requires 'Theory X' type managers who believe in close supervision of employees (McGregor, 1960).

## 12.5 Creating involvement by employees

Strategies to empower employees to create more effective service encounters will not be effective if employees do not feel involved in their job. Motivation, consent, participation and communication form essential focal points for an organization's HRM strategy to bring about a sense of involvement which underlies empowerment. HRM stresses the individual employee and their importance to the organization and this importance cannot be made real if employees do not feel motivated to share organizational goals.

Motivation concerns the choices which employees make between alternative forms of behaviour in order that they as employees attain their own personal goals. The task of management is to equate the individual's personal goals with those of the employing organization – that is, getting employees morally involved with the service which they help to produce. This in turn requires employees to consent to the management of their work activity. Where this consent is obtained, employees can be motivated by some form of participation in the organization. Such participation gives the employee a small stake in the organization, be it financial or in the form of discretionary control over the performance of their work function.

Management seeks to get controlled performances from its employees in an effort to meet corporate and HRM goals. In the Harvard model this is facilitated by the dissemination and pick-up process, where the organization's central philosophy becomes integral to the activity of all employees. In the Matching model, the attainment of corporate goals is achieved by integrating HRM into strategic management and business policy. The challenge for HRM managers in both cases is to make HRM more market-oriented and integral by demonstrating its relevance to all employees.

### 12.5.1  Consent

The term 'consent' covers a variety of management-led initiatives and strategies which seek to give it authority without actively emphasizing its coercive power. For many services provided on a one-to-one basis, direct monitoring and supervision of employees by management may be impossible to achieve anyway. Active consent is therefore of great use to the management of services organizations.

In the UK during the 20th century, there have been various forms of employee participation and involvement designed to aid management in the generation of consent. Such initiatives include scientific management, industrial management, the human relations approach, welfare, paternalism, professionalized and procedur-alised personnel management, and more recently HRM. Each initiative has its own prescription for the generation of consent.

*Scientific management* approaches seek cooperation between employer and employee in terms of the division of labour, whereby individual employees work in predefined ways as directed by management. Advocates of scientific management saw mutual benefits for the employee and employer. For the former, specializing in one work activity would give the opportunity to earn more, especially through piece rates pay systems, while management would benefit through greater work control and higher productivity. What Taylor, the leading advocate of scientific management, did not expect was the hostility of employees to what is often described as the process of deskilling. Within the services sector, many attempts have been made to deskill jobs in accordance with the scientific management prescription. However, it is necessary to balance the benefits of specialization and improved efficiency against employees' sense of alienation from their job which occurs when they are involved in only a very small part of a service delivery process. In this way, scientific management might suggest that coach tours could be operated more efficiently by allocating different sections of a tour to different drivers who are specialists in their own area. However, a much greater sense of involvement from employees may occur if drivers are trained to be able to deliver the whole service themselves from beginning to end, although this might call for additional training.

*Paternalism* is often associated with Quaker employers such as Cadbury or Rowntree who attempted to show that they were interested in their workforce at home as well as at work. Within the services sector, many retail employers such as Marks and Spencer have taken a paternalistic attitude towards their employees by providing such benefits as on-site services or temporary accommodation for their employees. This and other benefits, such as subsidized social clubs, are designed to encourage employee identification with the company and therefore loyalty, which legitimizes managerial authority and hence consent to it.

In contrast to the economically based consent strategies of scientific management, the *human relations* approach looks at man as a social animal. Mayo in his study of General Electric in the USA argued that productivity was unrelated to work organization and economic rewards as suggested by scientific management. Mayo emphasized the importance of atmosphere and social attitudes, group feelings and the sense of identification which employees had. He suggested that the separation of employees which scientific management had created prevented them from experiencing a sense of identification and involvement which is essential for all humans. Hence one solution was to design group structures into production processes. Such processes were thought to assist in the generation of employees' loyalty to their organization via the work group. Mayo's work is similar in focus to that of Herzberg and Maslow. Maslow suggested that humans have psychological needs as well as economic needs. Only when the psychological needs have been catered for do the economic needs come into play. To Herzberg, humans have lower and higher order needs. The former are the basic economic needs of food and shelter whereas the latter are more psychologically based in terms of recognition and contribution to the group and organization.

All of the management initiatives and strategies described in this section are in part efforts to generate employee consent to management authority without management exercising its authority via coercion.

### 12.5.2  Moral involvement

Moral involvement refers to some mechanism whereby employees can identify with the corporate goals of their employer and relay their feelings about these goals back to management. Essentially employees need some institutional process through which, directly or indirectly, they can voice their concerns over decisions which affect them.

Mechanisms to develop moral involvement are closely related to policies which generate consent. Mechanisms can operate collectively, as with collective bargaining or professional recognition via professional associations. Management can generate moral involvement through joint consultation with employees on decisions made by management. Alternatively they can be individual through quality circles, team briefings, appraisals or the 'open door' policies encouraged by the human relations approach. HRM highlights the importance of the individual worker to the success of the organization and therefore stresses individual training and development.

### 12.5.3  Motivation

Motivation concerns goals and rewards. Maslow (1943) argued that motivation is based on individuals' desire to satisfy various levels of need. These levels range from the need to realize potential and self-development down to the satisfaction of basic needs such as hunger, thirst and sex. Rewards for reaching goals can be tangible, for example money, or can be intangible (e.g. commendations or awards which add to status or self-esteem). An organization has to bring about a congruence between its own goals and those of its employees. This is the basis for designing an appropriate motivation package. Within the UK tourist attractions sector, a comparison can be made between many commercial operations (e.g. Alton Towers and Warwick Castle) where financial incentives are an important motivator and the National Trust, which attracts many unpaid volunteers, motivated by a desire to share in the preservation of historic buildings.

### 12.5.4  Participation

An employee's participation in an organization may be limited to purely economic matters – payment is received in return for work performed. Alternatively, participation may manifest itself through more qualitative measures such as employee involvement in decision making through quality circles or team briefings. The process of moral involvement can take the form of a devolution of some areas of traditional personnel activity to line management in order that the employees actually doing the work and those responsible for managing particular sections feel that they are somehow involved in it together. This can apply, for example, to selecting, recruiting and appraising employees within a work group.

### 12.5.5  Communication

To many people, internal marketing is essentially about improving communication between a company and its employees. Unfortunately, many service organizations consider effective communication to be based on a one-way channel of information from managers to employees through such media as staff newsletters. This is no more a definition of internal marketing than advertising is a definition of marketing. As in the case of marketing to external customers, communication to employees needs to be based on a sound understanding of the needs of individual segments within the workforce. There should also be some facility for feedback from employees.

Communication as an element of internal marketing is most notable when it is absent. Rumours about revised working arrangements, reductions in the workforce and changes to the terms of employment often circulate around companies, breeding a feeling of distrust by employees in their management. Some managers may take a conscious decision to give employees as little information as possible, perhaps on the basis that knowledge is power. There are sometimes strategic reasons for not disseminating information to employees (for example business strategy may be a closely guarded secret in order to keep competitors guessing). However, in too many services organizations information is unnecessarily withheld from employees, creating a feeling of an underclass in terms of access to information. Such practices do not help to generate consent and moral involvement by employees.

In good-practice organizations, information can be communicated through a number of channels. The staff newsletter is a well-tried medium, but in many instances these are seen as being too little, too late and with inadequate discussion of the issues involved. Many organizations use team briefings to cascade information down through an organization and communication back upwards again. The Internet is developing new possibilities for communicating information to a company's employees and allows much greater personalization to the specific needs of individual employees. External advertising should regard the internal workforce as a secondary target market. The appearance of advertisements on television can have the effect of inspiring confidence of employees in their management and pride in their company.

### 12.5.6   Strategies to increase employees' involvement

The methods which an organization uses to encourage involvement among its employees are likely to be influenced by the type of people it employs and the extent to which their jobs present opportunities to exercise autonomy (that is, the extent to which employees are able to control their own work processes) and discretion (the degree of independent thinking they can exercise in performing their work).

This section considers various strategies to increase employees' involvement and comments on their suitability for services organizations. In practice, organizations are more likely to be concerned with securing greater employee involvement by making individual employee objectives more congruent to those of the whole organization rather than through what could be described as collective participation. This type of involvement may be available to all employees but the extent to which their participation is real and effective may well depend on where they are positioned in the employment hierarchy, that is, whether they are within the core or the peripheral groups of workers. Increased participation is brought about by a combination of consultation and communication methods, and team briefings.

- 'Open door' policies encourage employees to air their grievances and to make suggestions directly to their superiors. The aim of this approach is to make management accessible and 'employee friendly'. To be effective, the human relations approach would require employees to feel that they do in fact have a real say in managerial matters. As a consequence management must appear to be open and interested in employee relations. It is likely that this approach to managerial style and strategy will emphasize open management through some of the methods described below.
- Team briefings are a system of communication within the organization where a leader of a group provides group members (up to about 20) with management derived information. The rationale behind briefing is to encourage commitment to and identification with the organization. Team briefings are particularly useful in times of organizational change, although they can be held regularly to cover such items as competitive progress, changes in policy and points of future action. Ideally, they should result in information 'cascading' down through an organization. The difference between briefing and Quality Circles (see below) centres on their respective contents. Briefing sessions are likely to be more general and relate to the whole organization, whereas Quality Circles relate to the specific work activity of a particular group of employees. Any general points of satisfaction or dissatisfaction can be aired in briefings and then taken up in specific Quality Circles.
- Quality Circles (QCs) are small groups of employees who meet together with a supervisor or group leader in an attempt to discuss their work in terms of production quality and service delivery. QCs often work within a Total Quality Management approach (see Chapter 8). To be successful, the QC leader has to be willing to listen to and act upon issues raised by QC members. This is essential if the QC is to be sustained. Circle members must feel their participation is real and effective, therefore the communication process within the QC must be two way. If QCs appear to become only a routinized

**Figure 12.5**
In this advertisement, Burswood Resort makes clear to customers the link between employees' performance and service quality. Many successful service providers operate 'employee of the month' schemes to recognize excellent service by staff. Invariably one of the downsides of such schemes can be a feeling of disillusionment by employees who are not selected for an award but who may feel equally deserving (reproduced with permission of Burswood International Resort Pty Ltd)

## Four more reasons for our great service.

### EMPLOYEES OF THE MONTH - JUNE

**Chris**
INSPECTOR

Chris has been with Burswood since 1991. He shows commitment and dedication to his work and is always willing to do that little extra with no fuss. Chris has a commendable working attitude and gets on well with everyone.

**Jemma**
MARKETING SECRETARY

Jemma has been at Burswood since 1998. She excels in all projects she undertakes, regularly performing beyond the call of duty. Jemma never falters in her commitment to get the job done and her cheerful 'can do' approach is greatly appreciated.

**Bessie**
CAFETERIA ATTENDANT

Bessie has been with Burswood since 1994. A diligent worker she takes pride in whatever she does. Her punctuality and grooming standards are far above average. Bessie's excellent work ethic, service and communication skills have been highly commended.

**David**
NIGHT PORTER

David commenced employment at Burswood in 1998. He is dedicated to ensuring that requests made by guests are always followed through. On numerous occasions David has demonstrated his commitment by voluntarily covering extra shifts.

*Burswood*

INTERNATIONAL RESORT CASINO

♣ ♦ ♠ ♥ ♦ ♠ ♥ *Where the action is* ♦ ♠ ♥ ♣ ♦ ♠ ♥ ♣

Burswood International Resort Casino is an Investor in People organisation, recognised as setting an international standard for human resource development. www.burswood.com.au        TSG BUR2221

listening session, members may consider it to be just another form of managerial control.

• Total Quality Management (TQM) policies rest upon the generation of an organizational mission or philosophy which encourages all employees and functional areas to regard themselves as providers and customers of other departments. The central idea behind TQM is the generation among all staff of a greater awareness of customer needs, the aim of which is to improve quality and or reduce production or internal transaction costs. Employees are encouraged to act outside what they may see as a narrowly defined role, to appreciate the impact which their actions will have on the total service perceptions of the organization's customers.

- The pattern of ownership of an organization can influence the level of consent and participation. Where the workforce owns a significant share of a business, there should in principle be less cause for 'us and them' attitudes to develop between management and the workforce. For this reason, many labour-intensive service organizations have significant worker shareholders and there is evidence that such companies can out-perform more conventionally owned organizations.

Many services firms proudly promote the fact that they are owned by their employees. But do they deliver better service quality to customers? Research undertaken by Dolan and Brierley (1992) in the bus sector showed how two companies – People's Provincial of Fareham and Derbyshire-based Chesterfield Transport – had capitalized on their worker ownership to perform better than their more conventionally owned rivals.

To the employees, a financial investment in the two companies studied proved attractive. Over a period of five years, the value of employees' investments in People's Provincial more than doubled, while with Chesterfield Transport, it increased by over fourfold within two years. Like many employee buy-outs of larger government-owned organizations, takeover bids were attracted from larger predators, boosting the value of employees' shareholdings.

The research highlighted four important benefits which had resulted from worker ownership:

- Traditional hierarchies were broken down, which gave much greater operational flexibility to the companies (for example inspectors and management would accept it as normal to change their duties and drive buses when the need arose). This was particularly important as the uneven pattern of demand required great flexibility.
- Costs were held down because staff recognized that they would benefit directly from the resulting increase in profits. Similarly, staff became more willing to pass on ideas about ways in which services could be improved or costs saved.
- Absenteeism was reduced, as was the need for formal disciplinary measures to be taken. Employees could see the need for a high level of service performance and were able to share in the resulting benefits.
- All workers had access to financial information, resulting in a more constructive approach to negotiations on work schedules and pay, for example.

The authors concluded that employee ownership – by increasing the level of participation – can give companies a competitive advantage in services industries where flexibility in production and commitment to high standards of service quality are important. But the question remains why so many employee owned bus companies in the UK have sold out to larger predators. Is a one-off cash bonus to employee shareholders more important than involvement in the ownership of their company? And do customers notice any difference once a large company takes over?

## 12.6 Leadership

Many of the most successful services companies, such as Yahoo!, Federal Express and McDonald's attribute their success in part to the quality of leadership within their organizations. The results of poor leadership are evident in many failing service organizations, especially within the public sector.

The principles of human resource management need to be implemented with effective leadership. What is good leadership for one organization need not necessarily be so for another. Organizations operating in relatively stable environments may be best suited with a leadership style which places a lot of power in a hierarchical chain of command. In the UK, many banks until recently had leadership styles which have been drawn from models developed in the armed forces, evidenced by some managers having titles such as superintendent and inspector. Such rigid, hierarchical patterns of leadership may be less effective where the marketing environment is changing rapidly and a flexible response is called for (as has happened in the banking sector). The literature has developed two typologies of leadership – transactional and transformational – which broadly correspond respectively with the control and empowerment approaches described above (Stodgill, 1974; Bennis, 1989).

What makes a good leader of people? And are leaders born, or can individuals acquire the skills of leadership? On the latter point there is little doubt that development is possible, and successful companies have invested heavily in leadership development programmes. As for what makes a successful leader of people, there have been many suggestions of desirable traits, including:

- Setting clear expectations of staff.
- Recognizing excellence appropriately and facilitating staff in overcoming their weaknesses.
- Leading by example.
- Being able to empathize with employees.
- Showing adaptability to changing circumstances.

In too many companies, bad leadership is characterized by:

- 'Management by confusion' in which expectations of staff are ambiguously stated and management actions are guided by a secretive 'hidden agenda'.
- Reward systems which are not based on performance and are perceived as being unfair.
- The deliberate or inadvertent creation of an 'us and them' attitude.
- Failing to understand the aspirations of employees.
- Failing to take the initiative where environmental change calls for adaptation.

Beginning with a small shop in Dundalk in 1960, the Irish grocery retailer SuperQuinn has grown to a successful chain of 12 shops and 7 shopping centres employing over 2000 people throughout Ireland. A large part of this success has been attributed to the leadership style of the company's founder, Feargal Quinn, and the emphasis on linking employees' activities to excellence in service quality. But what makes such leadership style distinctive?

An important principle is that managers should lead by example and never lose contact with the most important person in the organization – the customer. It is the task of a leader to set the tone for customer-focused excellence. To prevent managers losing sight of customers' needs, Quinn uses every opportunity to move them closer to customers, including locating their offices not in a comfortable room upstairs, but in the middle of the sales floor. Managers regularly take part in customer panels where customers talk about their expectations and perceptions of SuperQuinn. Subcontracting this task entirely to a market research agency is seen as alien to the leadership culture of the company. The company requires its managers to spend periods doing routine front-line jobs (such as packing customers' bags), a practice which has become commonplace in many successful services organizations. This keeps managers close to the company and improves their ability to empathize with junior employees.

Does this leadership style work? Given the company's level of growth, profits and rate of repeat business, it must be doing something right, contradicting much of the scientific management theories that management is a specialist task which can be separated from routine dealings with customers and employees.

## 12.7 Recruiting, training and rewarding employees

Attention is now given to the application of a number of the important principles of HRM referred to above. Emphasis is placed on the impact of such personnel practices on the marketing activities of services organizations through the methods of recruiting, selecting, training and rewarding staff.

### 12.7.1 Recruitment and selection

Recruitment is the process by which an organization secures its human resources. Traditionally the recruitment function has been performed by personnel specialists who as functional specialists are removed from line management. Current HRM practice favours the integration of the recruitment function into the line areas where a potential employee will be working.

The focus of recruitment activity is to attract and hopefully retain the right employee for the right job within the organization. Clearly, the recruitment process is closely linked to that of selection. The process of selection (described below) concerns how potential recruits are tested in terms of the job and person specifications.

In order to recruit the right personnel, services organizations must carefully consider just what they want from particular employees. As an example, tour operators seeking to recruit representatives to work in overseas resorts recognize that academic qualifications are not in themselves an important characteristic which should be possessed by new recruits. Instead, the ability to work under pressure, to empathize with clients, to work in groups and to be able to survive for long periods without sleep may from previous experience be identified as characteristics which allow representatives to perform their tasks in a manner which meets customers' expectations.

There are five key elements of the recruitment process:

- Development of recruitment policies.
- Establishment of routine recruitment procedures.
- Establishment of job descriptions.
- Development of a person specification.
- Advertising of job vacancies.

The process of selection is concerned with identifying and hopefully employing the most suitable candidate and involves six principal tasks:

- Examining candidates CVs or application forms.
- Shortlisting candidates.
- Inviting candidates for interview.
- Interviewing and testing candidates.
- Choosing a candidate for employment.
- Offering and confirming the employment.

Traditionally all of these areas have been considered to be the preserve of the personnel department. Within an HRM approach, many of these can become the responsibility, at least in part, of line managers, largely on the grounds that these are better able to understand the needs of the organization.

### 12.7.2 Training and development

Hard HRM emphasizes labour as a factor of production to be used as effectively as any other input. This effective use of labour can be attained in a variety of ways, for example by forcing labour to become more flexible or to work more intensively. However, there is a danger that this process might cause labour to become alienated and poorly motivated. Soft HRM approaches, on the other hand, stresses the need to train and develop labour as the organization's most valuable asset. Both soft and hard HRM are concerned with the corporate aims of efficiency and profitability. The most effective organizations are those which can use elements of soft HRM in order to ensure that they do in fact get the economic benefits of hard HRM. The two dimensions of HRM are not mutually exclusive but highly integrated with soft HRM operating as the front end of hard HRM. Training and development are essential elements within the process of ensuring effective economic performance by employees.

Training refers to the acquisition of specific knowledge and skills which enable employees to perform their job effectively. The focus of staff training is the job. In contrast to this, staff development concerns activities which are directed to the future needs of the employee, which may themselves be derived from the future needs of the organization. For example, workers may need to become familiar with personal computers, electronic mail and other aspects of information technology which as yet are not elements within their own specific job requirements.

If a service organization wishes to turn all of its employees who interface with the public into 'part-time marketers', it must include such an objective within its overall corporate plan and identify the required training and development needs. This is essential if any process of change is to be actively consented to by the workforce. Initially this may be merely an awareness training programme whereby the process of change is communicated to the workforce as a precursor to the actual changes. It may involve making employees aware of the competitive market pressures which the organization faces and how the organization proposes to address them. This initial process may also involve giving employees the opportunity to make their views known and to air any concerns they might have. This can help to generate some moral involvement in the process of change and could itself be the precursor to an effective participation forum.

If marketing is to become a function which is integrated into the jobs of all employees, marketing managers cannot merely state this need at strategic HRM meetings – it is also essential that programmes are developed by which such strategies can be operationalized. In many cases, it may be possible to specify these needs in terms of the levels of competence required in performing particular tasks. For example, in the case of bank counter staff, personnel might be required to be aware of a number of specific financial services offered by the bank and be able to evaluate customers and make appropriate suggestions for service offers. Failure to develop general sales skills and to disseminate knowledge of specific services available could result in lost opportunities for the organization.

A practical problem facing many services organizations who allocate large budgets to staff training is that many other organizations in their sector may spend very little, relying on staff being poached from the company doing the training. This occurs, for example, within the banking sector where many building societies have set up cheque account operations using the skills of staff attracted from the 'big four' UK banks. The problem also occurs in many construction-related industries and in the car repair business.

While the ease with which an organization can lose trained staff may be one reason to explain UK companies' generally low level of spending on training and development, a number of policies can be adopted to maximize the benefits of such expenditure to the organization. Above all else, training and development should be linked to broader soft HRM policies which have the effect of generating longer term loyalty by employees. Judged by hard HRM policies alone, training can be seen as a short-term risky activity which adds relatively little to the long-term profitability of an organization.

Where soft HRM policies alone are insufficient to retain trained staff, an organization may seek to tie an individual to it by seeking reimbursement of any expenditure if the employee leaves the organization within a specified time period. Reimbursement is most likely to be sought in the case of expenditure aimed at developing the general abilities of an individual as opposed to their ability to perform a functional and organizational specific task. Thus an organization might seek to recover the cost of supporting an individual to undertake an Open University degree, but not a product-specific sales training course. In some instances, government initiatives exist to support staff training and development.

Where an organization is a market leader, it may have no alternative but to accept a certain level of wastage in return for maintaining a constant competitive advantage over other organizations, and hence achieving higher levels of profitability. In this way, the travel agency chain Thomas Cook provides a level of training which is considered to be one of the best in the sector. A travel clerk who is Thomas Cook trained can readily find employment with one of its competitors. Against such potential loss – which itself is offset by the soft HRM policies adopted by the company – Thomas Cook enjoys a very high reputation with the travel-buying public. This in turn has allowed it to position itself as a high-quality service provider, removing some of the need to take part in price discounting which has harmed many of its rivals.

What does it take to be a guard on a busy rail commuter service? To those who have spent many years working in the industry, an intimate knowledge of operating procedures is essential if accidents are to be avoided. Trade union representatives not surprisingly expressed shock at the Great Eastern Railway Company's plans in 1997 to recruit part-time guards for its commuter services into London's Liverpool Street station. For the company, the idea seemed to offer flexibility, given the highly peaked demand for commuter services into London. The job would suit people who live in the Essex suburbs and work in Central London, providing a paid journey to work which would supplement the modest £5.25 an hour pay. After the equivalent of a week's training, given at weekends and in the evenings, new staff would be accompanied by a trained guard for three days before taking on responsibility for a train by themselves. Was this moving towards a 'do-it-yourself railway' in which safety considerations came second to profit objectives? Or had technology, such as the use of automatic train doors and close circuit television, simplified the task of being a guard to such an extent that it could sensibly be tackled by a part-time staff?

### 12.7.3 Career development

Another mechanism which can assist an organization in its goals of recruiting and retaining staff is a clearly defined career progression pathway. Career progression refers to a mechanism which enables employees to visualize how their working life might develop within a particular organization.

Clearly defined expectations of what an individual employee should be able to achieve within an organization and clear statements of promotion criteria can assist the employee in this regard. Additionally, the creation and use of an internal labour market, for instance through counselling and the dissemination of job vacancy details, are vital. An organization can introduce vertical job ladders or age- or tenure-based remuneration and promotion programmes to assist in the retention of core employees.

During periods of scarcity among the skilled labour force, offers of defined career paths may become essential if the right calibre of staff is to be recruited and retained. As an example, many retailers which had previously operated relatively casual employment policies introduced career structures for the first time during the tight labour market of the late 1980s. Conversely, during the following period of recession it became very difficult for employers to maintain their promises with a consequent demotivational effect on staff. In this way, the demise of profitability in UK branch banking in the 1990s brought about considerable disillusionment among core bank employees who saw their career progression prospects made considerably more difficult than they had expected, despite good work performance on their part.

### 12.7.4  Rewarding staff

The process of staff recruitment and, more crucially the retention of staff, is directly influenced by the quality of reward on offer. The central purpose of a reward system is to improve the standard of staff performance by giving employees something which they consider to be of value in return for good performance. What employees consider to be good rewards is influenced by the nature of the motivators which drive each individual. For this reason, one standardized reward system is unlikely to achieve maximum motivation among a large and diverse workforce.

Rewards to employees can be divided into two categories – non-monetary and monetary. Non-monetary rewards cover a wide range of benefits, some of which will be a formal part of the reward system, for example subsidized housing or sports facilities and public recognition for work achievement (as where staff are given diplomas signifying their level of achievement). At other times, non-monetary rewards could be informal and represent something of a hidden agenda for management. In this way, a loyal, long-standing restaurant waiter may be rewarded by being given a relatively easy schedule of work, allowing unpopular Saturday nights to be removed from their duty rota.

The soft HRM approach does not recognize these non-monetary benefits as being part of a narrowly defined reward system. Instead, they are seen as going to the root of the relationship between staff and employer. Subsidized sports facilities are not merely a reward, but part of the total work environment which encourages consent, moral involvement and participation by the workforce. In the case of the hidden agenda of informal non-monetary rewards, the soft HRM approach would see these as being potentially harmful to the employment relationship by reducing the level of consent from the workforce at large.

Monetary rewards are a more direct method of improving the performance of employees and form an important element of hard HRM policy. In the absence of well-developed soft HRM policies, monetary rewards can form the principal motivator for employees. A number of methods are commonly used in the services sector to reward employees financially:

- Basic hourly wages are used to reward large numbers of secondary, or non-core, employees. These are generally rewarded according to their inputs rather than outputs. Compared to the manufactured goods sector, it is generally more difficult to measure service outcomes and to use these as a basis for payment, nevertheless, it sometimes occurs. Delivery drivers employed by a courier firm may, for instance, be paid a fixed amount for each parcel delivered. In many cases, strict payment by output could have potentially harmful effects on customers – the delivery driver may concentrate on delivering as many parcels as quickly as possible, but with little regard for courtesies when dealing with people.

- A fixed salary is more commonly paid to the core workers of an organization. Sometimes the fixed salary is related to length of service – for example many public sector service workers in the UK receive automatic annual increments not related to performance. As well as being administratively simple, a fixed salary avoids the problems of trying to assess individuals' eligibility for bonuses, which can be especially difficult where employees work in teams. A fixed salary can be useful to a firm where long-term development of relationships with customers is important and staff are evaluated qualitatively for their ability in this respect rather than quantitatively on the basis of short-term sales achievements. Many financial services companies have adopted fixed salaries to avoid possible unethical conduct by employees who may be tempted to sell commission-based services to customers whose needs have not been properly assessed.

- A fixed annual salary plus a variable commission is commonly paid to service personnel who are actively involved in selling as a direct reward for their efforts. A problem for organizations who use this approach is that a salesperson who aims to maximize his or her commission earnings is often not involved in the service production/delivery process and therefore not in a position to maximize customer satisfaction and thereby secure repeat business. Where service production employees are in fact involved in selling (e.g. many restaurant waiting staff), this form of payment can be a motivator to good service delivery as well as increasing sales.

- Performance related pay (PRP) is assuming increasing importance within the service sector. PRP systems seek to link some percentage of an employee's pay directly to their work performance. In some ways, PRP represents a movement towards the individualization of pay.

  A key element in any PRP system is the appraisal of individual employees' performance. For some workers, outputs can be quantified relatively easily – for example the level of new accounts opened forms part of most bank managers' performance related pay. More qualitative aspects of job performance are much more difficult to appraise – for example the quality of advice given by doctors or dentists. Qualitative assessment raises problems about which dimensions of job performance are to be considered important in the exercise and who is to undertake the appraisal. If appraisal is not handled sensitively, it could be viewed by employees with suspicion as a means of rewarding some individuals according to a hidden agenda. There is also the problem in many services industries that service outcomes are the result of joint activity by a number of employees and therefore the team may be a more appropriate unit for appraisal than the individual employee. Of course, appraisals should be carried out for reasons other than just determining employees' pay. Well-managed services organizations routinely appraise staff to assess their career development and training needs. Without a transparent system of assessment, suspicions can be raised within an organization about perceived favouritism which is not linked to performance.

Some form of performance related pay is generally of great use to services organizations. It can allow greater management control and enable management to quickly identify good or bad performers. If handled appropriately, it can also assist in the generation of consent and moral involvement, because employees will have a direct interest in their own performance.

Profit-sharing schemes can operate as a supplement to the basic wage or salary and can assist in the generation of employee loyalty through greater commitment. Employees can be made members of a trust fund set up by their employer where a percentage of profits are held in trust on behalf of employees, subject to agreed eligibility criteria. Profit-sharing schemes have the advantage of encouraging staff involvement in their organization. Such schemes do, however, have a major disadvantage where despite employees' most committed efforts, profits fall due to some external factor such as an economic recession. There is also debate about whether profit-sharing really does act as a motivator to better performance in large companies, or merely becomes part of basic pay expectations. In the UK, examples of profit-sharing schemes have been set up by Tescos, British Gas and Sainsbury's.

- In many services organizations, an important element of the financial reward is derived from outside the formal contract of employment. This in particular refers to the practice of tipping by customers in return for good service. The acknowledgement of tipping by employers puts greater pressure on front-line service staff to perform well and in principle puts the burden of appraisal on the consumer of a service directly. It also reduces the level of basic wage expected by employees. Against this, reliance on tipping poses a number of problems. Support personnel may be important contributors to the quality of service received by customers but may receive none of the benefits of tipping received by front-line staff. A chef may be an important element of the benefit received by a restaurant customer, but tipping systems tend to emphasize the quality of the final delivery system. Attempts to institutionalize tipping by levying service charges and sharing proceeds among all staff may, however, reduce individual motivation. A fixed service charge also reduces the ability of consumers to make charges based on perceived quality. A further problem of relying on tipping is that customers might be put off by the prospect of feeling obliged to pay a tip, and for this reason many service providers prohibit their employees from receiving tips. While customers from some countries – such as the USA – readily accept the principle of tipping, others – including the British – are more ambivalent. In the public sector, attempts at tipping are often viewed as a form of bribery.

### 12.7.5 Industrial relations

The service sector spans organizations from small family businesses to large multi-national organizations, covering external environments which range from protected and regulated to highly competitive. In reflection of this diversity, there is great variety in the manner in which managements negotiate employment conditions with their workforces. For services organizations employing large numbers of staff, much of the employment relationship has traditionally been conducted collectively between the employer and groups of employees.

The essential features of collective bargaining are threefold.

1　Firstly, a collective bargaining system recognizes trade unions with whom management negotiates on substantive issues such as pay and procedural issues, e.g. discipline and redundancy. Collective bargaining formally recognizes the presence within the organization of an outside body – the trade union.

2　Secondly, the pluralist approach to the employment relationship emphasizes a divergence of interests between the employer and employees. This divergence is considered best settled via a process of compromise and negotiation.

3　Thirdly, a recognition that industrial action of some type, for example overtime bans, 'go slows' and strikes, might be used in order to pursue employee interests. This third feature of collective bargaining is over-exaggerated by the media, some academics and politicians. As an element in collective bargaining, it only becomes a consideration if the first two elements have failed. Nevertheless, many service sectors such as railways and airlines have periodically suffered bad disruption as a result of failures in collective bargaining. Because services cannot be stored, the effects can be felt by customers immediately.

Efforts to stress a closer identification with business objectives via HRM do not sit easily with the presence of an outside body which stresses the significance of collective action. Services organizations which do not feel secure with trade unions are likely to attempt to marginalize their impact through their derecognition and the creation of organization-specific employee relations policies described below. Within the service sector, many organizations have moved on from the traditional view of industrial relations to the situation where they speak of 'employee relations'. Marchington and Parker (1990) identified three reasons for the use of the term 'employee relations'.

1　The term has become fashionable and appears to be less adversarial than industrial relations. Thus, there has been growth in the use of the term, although slippage in the use of the word occurs in some cases without any change in behaviour.

2　It is increasingly used by personnel managers to describe the part of their work which is concerned with the regulation of relations between employer and employees. The internal regulation of this relationship is seen in many organizations to supersede any external regulation, through collective bargaining and/or trade union membership. This can be the case even though trade union membership still exists in a particular organization.

3　Employee relations focuses on that aspect of managerial activity which is concerned with fostering an identification with the employing organization and its business aims. It therefore concerns itself with direct relations between employees and management – that is, independently of any collective representation by trade unions.

Employee relations may in fact become one element within a wider corporate and HRM strategy, which has already been identified as being likely to include the marketing of the services which the organization produces.

Is a mission statement a valuable guiding principle for all of a firm's employees or just more management fudge? Part of the distinctive Marks and Spencer culture which pervades all of its workers is based on its efforts at disseminating its mission statement. This is conveyed to all employees through various means – notices displayed at critical points around its stores, items in staff newsletters and training programmes among others. Soft HRM policies have worked to make employees highly receptive to its mission statement and frequent repetition in key places serves to reinforce employees' commitment. As a result, most of the organization's employees are knowledgeable about – and work towards achieving – the following mission:

- To offer customers a selective range of high-quality well-designed and attractive merchandise at reasonable prices.
- To encourage suppliers to use the most modern and efficient techniques of production and quality control dictated by the latest discoveries in science and technology.
- With the co-operation of suppliers, to ensure the highest standards of quality control.
- To plan the expansion of stores for the better display of a widening range of goods for the convenience of our customers.
- To simplify operating procedures so that business is carried on in the most efficient manner.
- To foster good human relations with customers, suppliers and staff.

If Marks and Spencer has used its mission statement effectively, the question needs to be asked why they are often ridiculed or sniggered at by employees in other companies? Are the mission statements too unrealistic? Or have these companies communicated them inappropriately and failed to get employees to share their values?

## 12.8 Reducing dependency on human resources

Employees represent an expensive and difficult asset to manage, and furthermore, the quality of output received by final consumers can often be perceived as being highly variable. Services organizations therefore frequently pursue strategies to reduce the human element of their production process. The aim of employee replacement schemes can be to increase consistency or to reduce costs. The latter could be important where an organization is pursuing a cost leadership strategy, allowing it to gain a competitive advantage. Often, humans are replaced for a combination of these reasons.

A number of strategies to reduce dependency on the organization's employees can be identified:

- At one extreme, the human element in a service production and delivery process can be completely replaced by automatic machinery. Examples include bank ATM machines, vending machines and automatic car washes. Constraints on employee replacement come from the limitations of technology (for example, completely automatic car washes can seldom achieve such high standards of cleanliness as those where an operator is present to perform some operations inaccessible to machinery); the cost of replacement machinery (it is only within the past few years that the cost of telecommunications equipment has fallen to the point where mass-market automatic telephone banking has become a possibility); and the attitudes of consumers towards automated service delivery (many segments of the population are still reluctant to use ATM machines, preferring the reassurance provided by human contact).

- Equipment can be used alongside employees to assist them in their task. This often has the effect of deskilling their task by reducing the scope they have for exercising discretion, thereby reducing the variability in quality perceived by customers. In this way, computerized accounting systems in hotels reduce the risk of front-of-house staff adding up a client's bill incorrectly. Similarly, the computer systems used by many airline reservation staff include promptings which guide their interaction with clients.

- The inseparability of the service offer means that consumers of a service are usually also involved as co-producers of the service. The involvement of the service provider's personnel can be reduced by shifting a greater part of the production process to the consumer. In this way, most petrol service stations expect customers to fill their own car with fuel, rather than have this task undertaken by its own staff. Similarly, a television repair company may require customers to bring goods to its premises for repair. In both cases, the customer has greater control over the quality of service by undertaking part of it themselves.

**Case Study**

## More managed healthcare systems use incentive pay to reward 'best doctors'

The fictional radio character Doctor Finlay would have shuddered at the thought of being paid according to how well he was liked by his patients. Doctors in Britain have largely followed a few basic principles when it comes to getting paid. They negotiate a level of fees for services to be provided, in return for which they expect to perform their duties to the best of their abilities and in accordance with their code of conduct. Doctors employed by the National Health Service (NHS), as well as self-employed general practitioners, have negotiated with the NHS by focusing on the costs of providing their services and the idea of a fair rate of pay for highly qualified staff. Performance related pay has not yet appeared to any significant extent on doctors' pay agenda in Britain, although there are pressures to introduce it. However, it is becoming increasingly common in the US, demonstrating some of the benefits – as well as problems – of evaluating performance within the personal services sector.

In the US, a large share of doctors' services are bought by Health Maintenance Organizations (HMOs) which in turn obtain their funding from employers' health insurance payments. HMOs vary in the way they pay contracting doctors, but they have traditionally been either on the basis of a fixed fee per patient per year, or a fee per visit. Doctors would typically expect to have 5000 patients on their lists – a single HMO may account for half of these. US Healthcare Inc is one of a growing number of HMOs which has introduced an incentive scheme to the way it pays its doctors. Each year, it carries out a questionnaire survey of its subscribing members to see how they like their doctors and links doctors' payments to these results, a bonus payment of 15% being typical.

Among the questions that the company uses in its questionnaire for assessing doctors' performance are:

- How easy is it to make appointments for checkups?
- How long is the waiting time in a doctor's surgery?
- How much personal concern does the doctor show?
- How readily can patients follow up test results?
- Would patients recommend their doctor to others?

In addition, the company monitors the percentage of each doctor's patients who transfer to another doctor during the course of the year.

Incentive pay schemes for doctors are gaining popularity, spurred by a belief that they may help upgrade the quality of medical care provided by HMOs and other managed care programmes. However, a number of questions have been raised about the legitimacy of this approach. Sceptics don't like the idea of basing incentives on patients' sense of 'quality', arguing that patients rely too much on fringe issues such as a receptionist's attitude or a doctor's punctuality. The sceptics would prefer to see assessment based on more sophisticated studies of illnesses, treatments and patient outcomes, something which is much more difficult to evaluate. Another problem often raised is that individual doctors' incentive payments can disrupt their ability to work together in a collegial way. The Harvard Community Health Plan typified organizations which introduced and then withdrew incentive schemes following arguments between doctors about the size of their respective bonuses. Another group of sceptics argue that where incentive payment schemes have been introduced for doctors, they have had only a short-term effect in changing doctors' behaviour.

Paying doctors partly on the basis of the quality of their service is in its early stages in the US, and many advocates of incentive payment schemes hope that current shortcomings can be remedied by more sophisticated measuring systems in the future. What happens in the US today will doubtless be observed by the UK's National Health Service as it moves towards a more competitive internal market environment.

## Case study review questions

1   What are the marketing benefits of attempting to measure the performance of doctors? If you were a marketing manager for an organization funding doctors, how would you like to see doctors appraised?

2   What part do you think ethics play in determining doctors' performance? Do you think performance assessment is really within the domain of marketing management?

3   Other professional groups, e.g. lawyers, engineers and architects, should perhaps institute performance appraisals. If you were a marketing manager of an organization representing one of these professional groups, how would you evaluate members' professional performance? What marketing benefits would you see from carrying out routine appraisals? What resistance would you expect to encounter in implementing an appraisal system?

## Chapter summary and linkages to other chapters

Human resource management is not something which should be considered as separate from marketing management. For services which involve a high level of contact between employees and customers, high levels of service quality may only be achieved with appropriate human resource management. There has been much debate about the nature of internal marketing and its relationship to human resource management theories. Control and empowerment are two important issues which have a long history of debate within the HRM literature.

The close relationship between this chapter and **Chapter 3** on the service encounter and **Chapter 8** on service quality should be evident. Issues of human resource management are central to many organizations' attempts to develop relationship marketing strategies (**Chapter 5**). Without appropriately trained staff, relationships can degenerate to little more than data stored on a computer. There is an important link between this chapter and **Chapter 14** on marketing management. At a strategic level, services organizations cannot afford to develop marketing plans in isolation from HRM plans, and much recent interest has gone into developing business processes and structures in a way that avoids these internal functional barriers.

## Key terms

Internal marketing 357        Empowerment 362
Customization 364

## Chapter review questions

1   What are the principal ways in which the management of personnel is likely to be different in a service organization, as compared with a manufacturer?
2   Discuss the ways in which a fast-food restaurant can increase the level of participation among its staff.
3   Using an industry with which you are familiar, identify methods by which the effects of variability of the personnel inputs can be minimized in order to produce a consistent standard of output.
4   What is the link between personnel and service quality?
5   What are the shortcomings of traditional personnel management for the effective marketing of services?
6   Using examples, show how human resource management policies can help to overcome the problems associated with peaked patterns of demand.

## Selected further reading

*This chapter has discussed very briefly some of the basic principles of human resource management as they apply to service organizations. For a fuller discussion of these principles, the following text is recommended:*

Beardwell, I. and L. Holden (2000) *The Human Resource Management Textbook*, Prentice-Hall, London.

*The following references provide a further insight into the role of internal marketing:*

Forman, S. K. and A. H. Money (1995) 'Internal Marketing: Concepts, Measurement and Application', *Journal of Marketing Management*, Vol. 11, No. 8, pp 755–68

Rafiq, M. and P. K. Ahmed (1993) 'The Scope of Internal Marketing: Defining the Boundary between Marketing and Human Resource Management', *Journal of Marketing Management*, Vol. 9, No. 3, pp 219–32

Rafiq, M. and P. K. Ahmed (1998) 'A Customer-oriented Framework for Empowering Service Employees', *Journal of Services Marketing*, Vol. 12, No. 5, pp 379–93

Varey, R. J. and B. R. Lewis (1999) 'A Broadened Conception of Internal Marketing', *European Journal of Marketing*, Vol. 33, No. 9–10, pp 926–45

*The marketing role of front-line employees is explored in the following three articles:*

Bitner, M., B. H. Booms and L. A. Mohr (1994) 'Critical Service Encounters: The Employee's Viewpoint', *Journal of Marketing*, October, Vol. 58, pp 95–106

Bowen, D. E. and E. E. Lawler (1992) 'The Empowerment of Service Workers: What, Why, How and Whom', *Sloan Management Review*, Spring, pp 31–39

Gummesson, E (1991) 'Marketing-orientation Revisited: The Crucial Role of the Part-time Marketer', *European Journal of Marketing*, Vol. 25, No. 2, pp 60–75

# 13

# Managing capacity

### Learning objectives

The perishability of services means that a service cannot be stored and made available during periods of peak demand. Accurately matching supply with demand therefore becomes an important task of the services marketer if delays and failed service encounters are to be avoided. This chapter builds on Chapter 3 (The service encounter) by discussing ways in which customers are fitted into the service delivery process so that the service provider can operate efficiently and the consumer does not have to wait for service. The chapter begins by discussing the nature of variable customer demand and strategies that services firms can use to try to even out patterns of demand. Making supply more flexible is an approach used where demand patterns cannot be changed. Finally, yield management techniques which allow companies to maximize their returns from variable demand for fixed capacity are discussed.

## 13.1  Introduction

Imagine a restaurant in the centre of town which is popular with tourists in summer. During the quiet winter months, the restaurant could manage with a building which is half the size it currently occupies. But during the busy summer months, it faces a very high level of demand which keeps its facilities and staff fully employed. Perishability is an important characteristic of services and the possibility of producing output during the quiet period to sell in the busy period, common among manufacturing firms, is not possible with a service such as a restaurant. Strategic marketing planning for such a seasonal service business raises a number of important questions:

- What level of demand should the business aim to cater for at its peak? It may not be viable for the company to simply invest in larger facilities if these are only going to be used for a few weeks or even days during the year.
- How should the business maximize the revenue it gets during the busy periods without alienating the core business which will be needed to sustain it during the quieter months?
- How can demand be stimulated to fill spare capacity during quiet periods?
- How are problems of congestion to be handled at times of peak demand?

Managing the relationship between supply and demand challenges the strategic and tactical skills of the services marketer. This chapter begins by gaining an understanding of the causes and consequences of fluctuating demand for services. It then looks at methods of changing patterns of demand on the one hand and changing the pattern of supply on the other. Reservation and **queuing systems** aim to reconcile differences between supply and demand at any one time. Yield management has emerged as a technique for turning fluctuating demand from a problem to an opportunity whereby service organizations can make the maximum revenue for the available level of demand.

## 13.2  The management of customer demand

Service providers face various patterns of demand, ranging from negative demand (e.g. where many people actually would have to be paid to receive dental services which are perceived as 'bad') to overfull and unwholesome demand (e.g. the queues which build up for some unique historic tourist sites during the peak tourism season). However, the pattern which causes most problems for the services sector is where demand is irregular.

Because goods manufacturers are able to separate production from consumption, they have the ability to hold stocks of goods which can be moved to even out regional imbalances in supply and demand. Stocks can also be built up in order to cater for any peaks in demand which occur. As an example, lawn-mower manufacturers can work during the winter months making lawn mowers to store in order to meet the sudden surge in demand which occurs each spring. Those lawn mowers which are not sold in that spring can be sold later in the year at a lower clearance price, or put back into stock for the following year. The perishability and inseparability of the service offer means that it is not sufficient to broadly match supply and demand over the longer term within a broadly defined geographical market. Instead, supply and demand must be matched temporally and spatially. An excess of production capacity in one time period cannot be transferred to another period when there is a shortage, nor can excess demand in one area normally be met by excess supply which is located in another area.

The fact that services cannot be stored does not generally cause a problem where demand levels are stable and predictable. However, most services experience demand which shows significant temporal variation. Peaks in demand can take a number of forms:

- Daily variation (commuter train services in the morning and evening peaks, leisure centres during evenings).
- Weekly variation (night clubs on Saturday nights, trains on Friday evenings).
- Seasonal variation (air services to the Mediterranean in summer, department stores in the run up to Christmas).
- Cyclical variation (the demand for mortgages and architectural services).
- Unpredictable variation (the demand for building repairs following storm damage).

In practice, many services experience demand patterns which follow a number of these peaks – a restaurant, for example, may have a daily peak (at midday), a weekly peak (Fridays) and a seasonal peak (e.g. December).

Financial success for organizations in competitive markets facing uneven demand comes from being able to match supply with demand at a cost which is lower than its competitors, or with a standard of service which is higher, or both. In free markets, a service organization must take a strategic view as to what level of demand it seeks to cater for. In particular, it must decide to what extent it should even attempt to meet peak demands, rather than turn business away. The precise cut-off point is influenced by a number of factors:

- Infrequently occurring peaks in demand may be very expensive to provide for where they require the organization to provide a high level of equipment or personnel which cannot be laid off or found alternative uses during slack periods. Commuter rail operators often do not stimulate peak period demand – or even try to choke it off – because they would be required to purchase and maintain additional rolling stock whose entire overhead cost would be carried by those few journeys during the peak which they operate. Similarly, enlarged platforms at terminals may be required in order to cater for just a few additional peak trains each day.
- Peaks in demand may bring in a high level of poor-quality custom. Restaurants in tourist areas may regard the once only demand brought by bank holiday day-trippers to be of less long-term value than catering for the relatively stable all-year-round trade from local residents.
- Quality of service may suffer when a service organization expands its output beyond optimal levels. For example, a bank offering a stockbroking service may suffer harm if it stimulates demand for its service at a time of peak demand, as happened during the 1980s and 1990s with share sales in privatized

**Figure 13.1**

Implications of uneven service demand relative to capacity

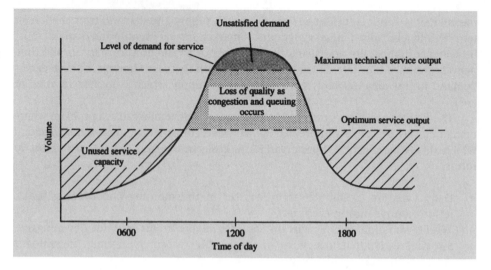

utility companies. Many UK building societies promoted their sharedealing services ahead of the 1989 electricity industry privatization, only to find that they had created queues and frustration, leading to negative attitudes which spilt over into the organization's core long-term business.

● On the other hand, some organizations may lose valuable core business if they do not cater for peaks. A bank which frequently suffers lunchtime queues for cash chequeing facilities may risk losing an entire relationship with customers if they transfer not only their cheque facility to a competing bank, but also their mortgage and insurance business.

An indication of the financial implications for organizations of uneven patterns of demand is shown in Figure 13.1, where two levels of capacity are indicated. The *optimum* capacity is notionally defined as that for which a facility was designed – any additional demand is likely to result in queues or discomfort. The *maximum* available capacity is the upper technical limit of a service to handle customers (e.g. a 70-seat railway carriage can in practice carry up to 200 people in crush conditions). At the peak, business is lost; when demand is satisfied above the optimum capacity level, customer service suffers; while in the slack period, resources are wasted.

Once a strategic decision has been made about the level of demand which it is desirable to meet, tactics must be developed to bring about a match between supply and demand for each time period. The task of marketing management can conceptually be broken down into two components:

● Managing the state of demand to even out peaks and troughs.
● Managing the supply of service to match the pattern of customer demand

### 13.2.1 Managing the pattern of customer demand

Where demand is highly peaked, an organization could simply do nothing and allow queues to develop for its service. This is bad strategy, both in harming the long-term development of relationships, and in denying short-term opportunities which peaks and troughs can present. A simple queuing strategy is most typical of services operating in non-competitive environments, for example some aspects of the National Health Service. In competitive markets, a more proactive market-oriented strategy is needed to manage the pattern of demand and the methods most commonly used are described below:

- Demand is frequently stimulated during the off-peak periods using all of the elements of the marketing mix. Prices are often reduced during slack periods in a number of tactical forms (e.g. 'off-peak' train tickets, the 'happy hour' in pubs and money-off vouchers valid only during slack periods). The product offering can itself be reformulated during an off-peak period by bundling with other services or goods (activity breaks offered at weekends in business hotels to fill spare room capacity). Distribution of a service could be made more favourable to customers during slack periods – for example during quiet times of the day or season, a takeaway restaurant may offer a free home delivery service. Promotion for many service companies is concentrated on stimulating demand during slack periods. For some services where consumption takes place in public, stimulating demand in quiet periods may be important as a means of improving the quality of the service itself. In the case of theatres, having more customers not only results in increased income, but a greater ambience for all customers who come for the atmosphere which the interaction of a live performer and audience creates.
- Similarly, demand is suppressed during peak periods using a reformulation of the marketing mix. Prices are often increased tactically, either directly (e.g. surcharges for rail travel on Friday evenings, higher package holiday prices in August), or indirectly (e.g. removing discounting during peak periods). Promotion of services associated with peak demand is often reduced (e.g. train operators in the London area concentrate most of their advertising on leisure travel rather than the highly peaked journey to work). Distribution and the product offering are often simplified at peak periods (e.g. restaurants and cafes frequently turn away low value business during peak periods).

## 13.3  Managing service capacity

There is a limit to how far it is desirable or practical to change the pattern of demand that a company faces. Where this is so, a service provider must look to managing its capacity more effectively so that it more closely follows the pattern of demand which it faces.

The output of services organizations is determined by the productive capacity of their equipment and personnel. The extent to which an organization is able to adjust its output to meet changes in demand is a reflection of the elasticity of these factor inputs. Capacity is said to be inelastic over the short term where it is impossible to produce additional capacity. It is not possible, for example, to enlarge a stately home to cater for a demand peak which occurs on summer Sunday afternoons. Capacity is said to be elastic where supply can be adjusted in response to demand. Highly elastic supply allows an organization to meet very short-term variations in demand by

**Figure 13.2**
This restaurant has a novel idea for stimulating demand during the quiet early evening period. To encourage early diners (when there is surplus capacity), it charges customers individually according to the time that their order is taken. As the evening gets busier, the price goes up.

introducing additional capacity at short notice. Sometimes, capacity can be elastic up to a certain point, but inelastic beyond that. A railway operator can provide additional trains to meet morning commuter peaks until it runs out of spare rolling stock and terminal facilities, when supply becomes very inelastic. Any discussion of the concept of elasticity of supply requires a time frame to be defined – supply may be inelastic to very sudden changes in demand, but it may be possible to supply additional capacity with sufficient advance planning.

In the area of supply management, marketing management cannot be seen in isolation from operations management and human resource management. Typical strategies which are used within services industries for making supply more responsive to demand include the following:

- Equipment and personnel can be scheduled to switch between alternative uses to reflect differing patterns of demand for different services. A hotel complex can switch a large hall from meeting a peak demand for banquets and parties – which occurs in the evenings – to meeting a peak demand for conferences which occurs during the working day. Similarly, personnel can be trained to allow different jobs to be performed at different peak periods. Tour operators often train staff to be resort representatives in Mediterranean resorts during the summer peak for beach holidays, and skiing representatives in the Alps during the winter skiing peak.

- Efforts are often made to switch resources between alternative uses at very short notice. For example, a store assistant engaged in restocking shelves can be summoned at short notice to perform much more perishable and inseparable service functions, such as giving advice on products, or reducing checkout queues.
- Capacity can be bought-in on a part-time basis specifically at periods of peak demand. This can involve both personnel resources (e.g. bar staff hired in the evenings only, tour guides hired for the summer only) and equipment (aircraft chartered for the summer season only, shops rented on short leases for the run up to Christmas).
- Operations can be organized so that as much back up work as possible is carried out during slack periods of demand. This particularly affects the tangible component of the service offering. In this way, equipment can be serviced during the quiet periods (e.g. winter overhaul programmes carried out on a holiday charter operator's fleet of aircraft) and personnel can do as much pre-paration as possible in the run up to a peak (a theatre bar taking orders for interval drinks before a performance and preparing them ready to serve during the interval).

Although it is desirable that the supply of service components should be made as elastic as possible, these components must not be looked at in isolation. The benefits of elasticity in one component can be negated if they are not matched by elasticity in other complementary components of a service. For example, a strategy which allows a holiday tour operator to increase the carrying capacity of its aircraft at short notice will be of only limited value if it cannot also increase the availability of additional hotel accommodation. A strategy to carry out routine aircraft main-tenance work during the quieter winter season may simply create an additional peak problem for the airline's maintenance facility. Capacity management must therefore identify critical bottlenecks which prevent customers' demands being satisfied.

The accountants came into a large bus company and worked out the cost of running special school buses during the peak period. Sadly, although the buses were invariably full, they were not making any profit, as they were tying-up assets with no alternative use during the day. The accountants decided that the school bus journeys should in future bear all of the fixed costs of assets used, with the result that, on paper, they then became loss making. The marketing people of the bus company were exhorted to choke-off demand for the school buses and to encourage more use of buses during the off-peak period.

The new costing base encouraged them to run more off-peak services which could make a profit with even small numbers of customers. The result? The engineers employed during the day to service the buses when they came into the depot between the morning and afternoon peaks found they had no buses to work on. Instead, they had to service the buses during the evening which involved higher overtime rates of pay. The marketing department had got rid of one peak, but had seemingly created a new maintenance peak for the engineers. This example emphasizes the importance of taking a broad view on demand management to avoid creating further bottlenecks.

### 13.3.1  Flexible employees

For many services organizations, employees are the biggest item of cost and potentially the biggest cause of bottlenecks in service delivery systems. Having the right staff in the right place at the right time can demand a lot of flexibility on the part of employees. Too often, customers are delayed because, although staff are available, they are not trained to perform the task which currently needs performing urgently. At other times, employees may go about a backroom task oblivious of the fact that delays are occurring elsewhere in the front-line delivery system. Worse still, employees could have a negative attitude towards their job which sees a customer's problem as nothing to do with them and take no interest in finding staff who may be able to help. Many services industries have been notorious in the past for rigid demarcation between jobs which were organization-focused rather than customer-focused. In Britain, train drivers and guards for a long while existed as two separate groups which were not able to stand in for each other. With privatization and increased competition for rail franchises, this mindset has been changed, so that employees who are trained in one area can substitute in the other, if required.

To improve their flexibility, many services providers have sought to develop multiple skills among their employees so that they can be switched between tasks at short notice. Within the hotel sector, for example, it is quite usual to find staff multi-skilled in reception duties, food and beverage service and room service. If staff shortages occur within one area, staff can be rapidly transferred from less urgent tasks where there may be sufficient staff coverage anyway.

An effective multi-tasking strategy must be backed up by adequate training so that employees can effectively perform all the functions that are expected of them. Transferring a poorly trained employee to a task with which they are not familiar may actually make service delivery worse, not better. Multi-skilling is closely related to the development of empowerment discussed in the previous chapter. This implies that employees become problem solvers on behalf of customers and use their initiative to resolve an issue, either by direct action themselves, or by referral to others who are capable of resolving the issue.

Flexibility in working also applies to the rostering of employees' duties. Where patterns of demand are unpredictable, it is useful to have a pool of suitably trained staff who can be called up at short notice. Many service providers therefore operate 'standby' or 'callout' rotas, where staff are expected to be available to go into work at short notice.

A flexible workforce sounds attractive in principle, but there are some drawbacks. Training in multiple skills would appear to be against the principles of scientific management (discussed in the previous chapter), wherein employees specialize in one task and perform this as efficiently as possible. Multiple skill training represents an investment for firms, and in service sectors with high turnover, such as the hospitality sector, the benefits of this training may be short-lived. Recruiting staff may become more expensive, with staff capable of performing numerous tasks able to command higher salaries than somebody whose background only allows them to perform a narrower range of tasks. Finally, there is also the problem that requiring staff to work flexible hours may make their working conditions less attractive than a job where they had certainty over the days and times that they will be working. Expecting excessive flexibility may be contrary to the principles of internal marketing discussed in the previous chapter, exacerbating problems where there is a shortage of skilled staff. Services industries must compete with other sectors for good employees and if a job is perceived as offering too much uncertainty, staff may prefer to work elsewhere where working conditions are more predictable.

As well as being able to achieve short-term flexibility, services organizations must also have the flexibility over the longer term to shift their human resources from areas in decline to those where there is a prospect of future growth. For example, in order to retain its profitability, a bank must have the ability to move personnel away from relatively static activities such as cash handling and current account chequeing towards the more profitable growth area of financial services.

Flexibility within a service organization can be achieved by segmenting the workforce into core and peripheral components. Core workers have greater job security and have defined career opportunities within an internal labour market. In return for this job security, core workers may have to accept what Atkinson (1984) terms 'functional flexibility' whereby they become responsible for a variety of job tasks. As part of a hard HRM approach, the work output of this group is intensified. In order for this to be successful, employees require effective training and motivation which in turn has to be sustained by effective participation methods.

Peripheral employees, on the other hand, have lesser job security and limited career opportunity. In terms of Atkinson's prescription they are 'numerically flexible', while financial flexibility is brought about through the process of 'distancing'. In this situation, a firm may utilize the services and skills of specialist labour but acquire it through a commercial contract as distinct from an employment contract. This process is referred to as subcontracting. The principal characteristics of the flexible firm are illustrated in Figure 13.3.

As a strategic tool, the model of the flexible firm has important implications for services organizations which experience fluctuating demand. However, critics of the concept have suggested that the strategic role attributed to the flexibility model is often illusory, with many organizations introducing 'flexibility' in very much an opportunistic manner.

The conventional wisdom is that services organizations need highly flexible employment practices so that they can effectively and efficiently meet customers' demands when and where they occur. But how far should a company go in pursuit

**Figure 13.3**

Components of the flexible firm (Adapted from J. Atkinson (1984) 'Manpower Strategies for Flexible Organization, *Personal Management*, August, pp 15–26)

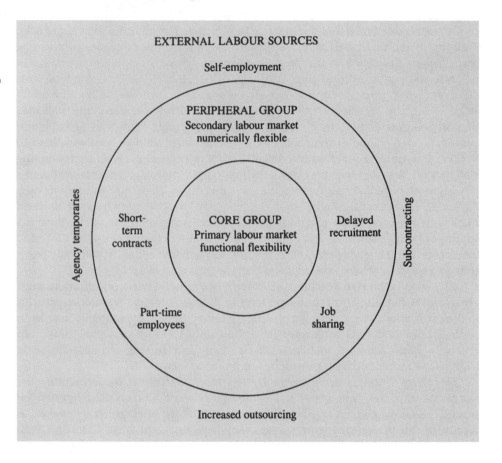

EXTERNAL LABOUR SOURCES

Self-employment

PERIPHERAL GROUP
Secondary labour market
numerically flexible

Agency temporaries

Short-term contracts

CORE GROUP
Primary labour market
functional flexibility

Delayed recruitment

Subcontracting

Part-time employees

Job sharing

Increased outsourcing

of flexibility? Stories abound of services companies who pay young people very low wages and provide very insecure employment. In the UK, the Burger King chain attracted a lot of bad publicity in 1996 when it was alleged to have paid some of its part-time staff wages which amounted to little more than £1 per hour and gave little notice of when they would be required to work. To some, this sounded like exploitation, which subsequent minimum wage legislation was designed to overcome. To others, young people were at least being given an opportunity to work and customers benefited by lower prices. But apart from the ethics of such practices is the question whether too much flexibility makes good business sense. If staff can be laid off at very short notice, will they show such concern to customers as an employee who has more secure employment? Or will the insecurity keep employees on their toes to perform well at all times? Can flexibility be applied to complex service processes, or is it realistically limited to jobs which have been highly industrialized and deskilled?

## 13.4 Queuing and reservation systems

Where demand exceeds the supply capacity of a service and demand and supply management measures have failed to match the two, some form of queuing or reservation system is often desirable. A formal queuing or reservation system is preferable to a random free-for-all for a number of reasons.

- From an operational viewpoint, advance reservation systems allow an organization to identify when peaks in demand will occur. Where there is reasonable mid- to short-term supply elasticity, supply can be adjusted to meet demand, either by bringing in additional capacity to meet an unexpected surge in demand or by laying off capacity where demand looks like falling below the expected level. In this way, advance reservations for a charter airline can help it to schedule its fleet to accommodate as many potential passengers as possible. Similarly, a low level of advance reservations could lead to some unpromising looking flights being cancelled, or 'consolidated'.
- Reservation and queuing systems allow organizations to develop a relationship with their customers from an early stage. This relationship can be formed at the simplest level by using a telephone enquiry to gain some degree of commitment from a potential customer and to offer them a service at a time when both customer and supplier can be assured of achieving their objectives. Alternatively, the relationship can be developed from the time when a potential customer walks into a service outlet and joins a queue.

Queues are an inevitable part of service delivery processes where it is not possible to manage supply or demand to bring them into line. Queues for some services which cannot easily be expanded have become legendary, for example during the summer months it is not uncommon to find queues of several hundred people waiting to get into the Tower of London. Long waits have been shown to be a major source of customer dissatisfaction (see Bitner, Booms and Tetreault, 1990). There is also evidence indicating that customers' dissatisfaction with long waits affects both their overall satisfaction with the service and their future intentions to use those providers (Taylor, 1994). There are a number of approaches to dealing with queues where these are inevitable:

- *Understand customers' expectations of waiting time* Individuals differ in their expectations of waiting time and even for a particular individual expectations may be situation-specific. A rail passenger travelling on a business journey may regard a minor delay as a failure, but be more prepared to accept a longer delay for a leisure journey. An attempt should be made to understand the psychological world of the consumer when they enter the service process. With younger people expecting instant gratification in a wide range of goods and services, their expectations of delay may be quite different to an older consumer who has long memories of waiting for goods and services.
- *Reduce actual waiting time* The most direct approach to deal with queuing is to decrease actual waiting time. Operational methods to accomplish this goal include various forecasting techniques, and the use of staffing and resource allocations models to meet the demand. If demand can be forecast accurately,

then in some instances resource allocation could be modified to deal with fluctuating demand patterns. However, it was noted above that capacity may not always be sufficiently flexible to avoid queuing situations.

- *Don't over-promise on waiting time* Organizations should be careful about the promises they make with regard to queuing time. Where expectations of a short wait are held out, any lengthening of the waiting time will be perceived as a service failure. This could have serious implications for customers' perception of subsequent stages in the service which they are about to receive. It may be better to warn customers to expect a long delay, then if the actual delay is subsequently shorter, customers will perceive this as exceeding their expectations. They will then enter the next stage of the service process with a more positive mind. Many airline customers have felt relieved when their plane departed 'only' 15 minutes late instead of the 30 minutes which was previously announced by the airline.

- *Reduce perceptions of waiting time* If the actual waiting time cannot be reduced, customers' subjective perceptions of the length of the delay might be managed. This is especially important as evidence suggests that customers tend to over-estimate the actual length of their wait time (Hornik, 1984; Katz *et al.*, 1991). By offering activities to fill up waiting time or by providing various distractions, service providers may reduce customers' perceptions of waiting time length. As an example, customers waiting to collect their car from servicing may have their mind taken off their wait by the provision of a comfortable television lounge. Waiting time will appear to pass by more quickly where the customer can perceive that progress is being made – for example by seeing that a queue is moving steadily. Uncertainty about the length of waiting time left causes anxiety and makes perceived time longer. Customers should also be able to perceive that the queue is being processed fairly. Where a delay is of uncertain duration, regular communication to customers makes time appear to pass by more quickly – the hardship caused by delay in waiting for a train can be lessened with appropriate communication to customers explaining the cause of the delay. Good communication skills by front-line employees can transform the impact of waiting time.

- *Manage the impact of waiting time* Service providers should be able to recognize where excessive waiting time has amounted to a service failure and take action to bring about an equitable resolution to the consequences of failure. Employees' actions, such as apologizing for a delay, may provide some immediate help. Other actions, such as making compensation payments may also be considered.

It should not be forgotten that a queue represents opportunities for service providers as well as problems. During the waiting process, an organization can make its customers more familiar with other services which may be of interest to them at some other time. Diners waiting for a meal may have the time and interest to read about a programme of special events which associated hotels within the chain are offering. Sometimes, the organization may be able to use a queue for one service to try to cross-sell a higher value service. In this way, a potential customer for an economy class air ticket may be persuaded to buy an upgraded class of ticket rather than wait for the next available economy class seat. Having a queue can also make a company's operations more efficient, as there is no slack time between customers. These efficiency gains may be passed on in the form of lower prices, thereby strengthening an organization's competitive position in a price sensitive market.

Ask anybody who has visited a popular theme park about their worst experience and they will probably mention the queues for the popular rides. However, researchers at Alton Towers theme park in Staffordshire, UK, found in a 1997 survey that queuing could actually enhance the enjoyment of a visit. They noted that queuing systems seemed to be so successful that visitors could wait for up to an hour for the popular Nemesis ride and hardly seemed to notice the wait. A number of tricks were used to bring this about. Queues were designed to twist in multiple directions, making it difficult for visitors to estimate their length. By exposing those in the queue to those who have just come off a ride, the level of anticipation was raised. Astonishingly, Alton Towers researchers found that on quiet days when there was very little queuing, visitors were scoring lower levels of enjoyment than on busy days. Why could this be? Could a queue actually heighten visitors' sense of anticipation and achievement? Interestingly, are there other services for which queuing might actually improve customers' perceived level of satisfaction?

## 13.5 Yield management

Many service industries struggle to match a probabilistic demand pattern to a finite set of resources in order to optimize profits. It is quite intuitive that when demand is strong, a company should seek to charge the highest price achievable for the use of its finite resources, while at less busy times it will be prepared to accept a lower price. This is the basis of **yield management** (YM) which has become an increasingly widespread management technique throughout the services sector.

Yield management has gained widespread acceptance within the airline and hotel industries. The term originated in the airline industry to mean yield per available seat mile but has since been applied to other industries by altering it to yield per available inventory unit. Simply put, YM is the process of allocating the right type of capacity or inventory unit to the right kind of customer at the right price so as to maximize revenue or yield (Kimes, 1997). Highlighting its link with marketing, YM has been defined as a revenue technique which aims to increase net yield through the predicted allocation of available (bedroom) capacity to predetermined market segments at optimum price' (Donaghy, McMahon and McDowell, 1995). In such areas as ski lifts, golf courses, theatres, museums and visitor attractions, however, the potential to use YM exists but has not yet been explored extensively (Anderson, 1996).

Yield management suits service organizations where the capacity is fixed, where the demand is unstable and where the market can be segmented (Kimes, 1989).

Analysing these features further, Kimes identified a number of preconditions for the success of YM and suggested a number of factors or ingredients that are prerequisites for the effective operation of a YM system (Kimes, 1997). Preconditions include fixed capacity; high fixed and low variable costs and variable demand through time. This means that organizations such as hotels can benefit from controlling capacity when demand is high and relaxing that control when demand is low. Utilization of reservation systems can assist in managing demand because such systems can log requests for inventory units in advance of consumption.

Managers who are familiar with their organization's booking and demand patterns will be more confident in their decision about which reservations to accept or deny. A detailed knowledge of sales and booking data is essential to help managers forecast peaks and troughs in demand, thereby allowing them to align demand with supply more effectively.

It has been noted by Kimes that 'yield management is essentially a form of price discrimination'. In reality, hotels and airlines operate YM systems that rely on opening and closing rate bands. During low periods of demand a service provider can offer discount prices. At high-demand periods discounts can be closed off. Also, by offering multiple rates, the service manager will, hopefully, profitably align price, product and buyer and increase net yield (Sieburgh, 1988). Service firms should have the ability to divide their customer base into distinct market segments, such as business and leisure, to which they can apply the principles of differential pricing. Airlines typically segment their passengers by their willingness to pay. Low fares are offered to passengers who are willing to accept restrictions on travel. Business people or time sensitive travellers are usually willing to pay higher fares to travel at peak times with no restrictions.

Over-booking is an essential aspect of YM (Lieberman, 1993). By over-booking, service firms risk not being able to accommodate customers who have made a reservation, thereby creating a service failure in the eyes of the customer. So why is deliberate over-booking an essential part of YM? In an ideal world, a company would achieve 100% utilization of its resources at all times. In some cases, the conditions of an advance booking by a customer result in the customer forfeiting payment for a service if they do not show for the service at the allotted time. However, in many markets, competitive pressures mean that customers would be deterred from making a binding commitment in advance, and therefore the market works on the basis of verbal, no-commitment reservations. This is typical, for example, within the UK car rental sector, where rental companies must presume that a certain proportion of bookings will be 'no-shows'. Where the scale of an operation is large and there is a lot of historical data to work from, a company should be able to predict the proportion of no-shows at any particular time and over-book on the assumption that this proportion of bookings will not materialize. Where there is a rapid turnaround in resources (typical of car rental businesses), the effects of an over-assumption of no-shows (i.e. more customers turn up than there is capacity) may simply be a delay (e.g. a wait while returning cars are prepared for a new customer). Sometimes, a company can overcome an over-booking situation by offering customers a free upgrade to a higher grade of facility (e.g. an over-booked airline economy cabin may be overcome if selected economy passengers are upgraded to business class). At other times, the consequences of over-booking may be difficult to handle. An airline may have over-booked a flight on a route where the next flight may not be until the following day, or even week.

Attempts are therefore made to 'buy back' a booking from customers who have turned up. Incentives such as free tickets for future use and cash bonuses are offered to try to tempt customers to wait for a later flight. Many customers are happy to accept these incentives in return for the inconvenience that has been caused. For the service provider, the cost of these incentives must be assessed against the benefits of getting closer to full utilization of resources.

At times of extreme demand (for example hotels close to major sporting events), service providers may seek non-refundable deposits. This is necessary because there may be no history of no-shows for that specific event. Also, the service provider may be much more constrained in its options for resolving an over-booked situation. Offering an incentive for a customer to come back later may be irrelevant where the whole purpose of consuming the service is to take part in a specific event.

It should also be noted that the level of over-booking is also part of a company's marketing mix positioning. A service provider may engage in less over-booking than its rivals and thereby reduce inconvenience to its customers. This should be reflected in its product mix and positioning strategy.

Over-booking occurs not just with respect to individual customer bookings, but also with respect to the utilization of components of the total service offer. Assumptions must be made in a service blueprint about how long each stage of a sequential process should take. For many service processes there will be variability in actual process times, for example the number of repair calls undertaken by an electrician or the number of journeys completed by a taxi. Service organizations are often tempted to over-book these resources, with insufficient recovery time allowed between services. So if the engineer is delayed on one job, there may be insufficient time allowed for him or her prior to the next booked job. The result is that the quality of service perceived by customers will fall. Service providers must try to balance the needs for high levels of reliable service delivery (which may imply having spare capacity in reserve) and the need for keeping costs to a minimum (which may mean reducing any unutilized capacity). In many markets, these considerations form part of companies' marketing mix with the result that different service levels are targeted at different market segments. Within the UK aircraft charter market for example, Civil Aviation Authority statistics have shown a poor reliability performance by Monarch Airlines, which can be attributed to tight scheduling of its aircraft in order to achieve lowest unit costs for a price-sensitive market segments. During 1999, one of the top operators in terms of reliability, Air 2000, was less reliant on low-cost budget travel.

### 13.5.1 The link between marketing and yield management

Using the Chartered Institute of Marketing's definition of marketing, the term 'yield management' could easily replace the word 'marketing' to define the core concept of YM. So the definition becomes 'Marketing [YM] is the management process responsible for identifying, anticipating and satisfying customer requirements profitably'. The effectiveness of a YM system is dependent upon the implementation of a number of market-focused principles and techniques:

● Identification of a customer base using a detailed segmentation process. Segmentation is identified by Cross (1997) as one of the essential steps in YM.

In relation to the hotel industry, Donaghy and McMahon (1995) and Donaghy *et al.* (1998) have proposed a yield segmentation process (YSP) which aims to determine the value of accommodation to targeted segments, thereby finding specific customers for a specific period.

- Developing an awareness among managers of the changing needs and expectations of customers.
- Estimating the price elasticity of demand for each market segment.
- Making managers responsive to changing market conditions.
- Having accurate historical demand analyses combined with a reliable forecasting method.

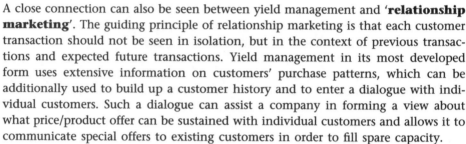 A close connection can also be seen between yield management and '**relationship marketing**'. The guiding principle of relationship marketing is that each customer transaction should not be seen in isolation, but in the context of previous transactions and expected future transactions. Yield management in its most developed form uses extensive information on customers' purchase patterns, which can be additionally used to build up a customer history and to enter a dialogue with individual customers. Such a dialogue can assist a company in forming a view about what price/product offer can be sustained with individual customers and allows it to communicate special offers to existing customers in order to fill spare capacity.

There is nothing new in the principles of YM. The process of maximizing returns on assets can be traced back to the routine bargaining for goods and services by traders in many less developed economies. Industrialization of many service processes has often had the effect of simplifying pricing structures in order that they can be administered and implemented by relatively junior employees. However, recent developments in information technology have enabled computers to do what the trader in an eastern bazaar was able to do in his head – estimate the maximum value that could be extracted from each potential customer and sell to those customers who are prepared to offer the best price.

### 13.5.2   Yield management or everyday low-cost pricing?

Many services organizations have resorted to offering standardized prices, or 'everyday low prices', instead of finely segmented prices. This would appear to be contrary to the principles of marketing and of yield management, but does appear to have a number of advantages. Firstly, the process of setting prices is simplified, resulting in less administrative effort being required by staff and less potential for confusion among customers. Secondly, there may be communication advantages of offering a single price. A price position can be readily established in the minds of potential consumers. Simple price structures may help develop trust among buyers who may otherwise feel deceived by not being able to obtain promotional prices, or by comparing the price they paid with a lower price paid by another customer for a basically similar product.

There are many recent examples of services organizations that appear to have gone against the philosophy of marketing by offering near-uniform prices for all customers. The hotel and airline sectors are among the leading advocates of YM techniques, yet Travel Inn in the former and easyJet in the latter have built a market position by offering basically standard prices for each similar unit of output sold. Is this position sustainable? There is some evidence that organizations that have initially adopted uniform prices subsequently revert to more sophisticated pricing systems based on the price sensitivity of individual segments for a basically similar product. As an example, the hotel chain Travel Inn initially promoted one single price, but has since made promotional voucher offers to fill spare capacity during off-peak times.

The co-existence of 'everyday low pricing' and YM techniques raises a number of interesting questions. Are companies who offer uniform prices going against the fundamental philosophy of marketing by not taking account of individual customers' differing needs and expectations? Is uniform pricing a stable solution or is there always the opportunity for competitors to exploit subsegments of a company's market with differentiated product offers and prices? And, finally, is it possible to define types of products and markets for which each approach (uniform pricing or yield management) is particularly appropriate?

## Cultural change needed to manage hotel yields more effectively

**Case Study**

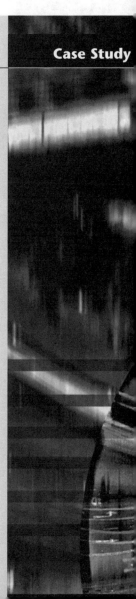

Yield management is increasingly used by hotels, but its introduction can often be far from smooth. Although interest in yield management is often focused on information technology, the critical element to success can be the people behind the system. An analysis by Huyton and Peters of a large 180 bedroom hotel in Warwick illustrated some of the problems that can occur in implementation.

Prior to introducing a YM system, the hotel had used the Champs management information system, which provided a good method for providing occupancy reports and statistics, but had only a limited use for forecasting, which is a fundamental part of yield management. It was essentially retrospective and was not able to provide meaningful forecasts about the future. Forecasting of demand is crucial to give rooms managers the confidence to 'hang out' for the highest possible rate. This idea of 'hanging out' for a higher rate, rather than taking the first available customer that comes along, is an essential part of yield management. One implication is that the volume of business for a hotel may remain constant, but through effective yield management, the amount of profit yielded by each customer may increase. Knowing when to 'hang out' for a higher rate is a management skill, helped by reliable data and forecasting methods. In addition to the forecasting system, an effective yield management system calls for a computerized decision support system, such as Fidelio, which was used in the case study hotel, and effective communications within the hotel.

Perhaps the biggest challenge facing management was to change the attitudes of front desk staff who had previously been happy to register anybody who came along. Now they had to learn to 'hang out' by saying no. As one of them commented following introduction of the new yield management system: 'The reservation staff sit there and say to prospective clients "we're terribly sorry, we are fully booked" but in actual fact we have got fifteen to twenty rooms to sell (but because of the rate offered by the client we won't take it)'. Sales staff had been used to a culture in which rewards are given according to the volume of sales, rather than the profit they yield. An early part of the

training programme for reservation staff was to teach them to say no. In practice, this proved to be quite difficult, so the rooms manager resorted to going into the system and blocking off rooms so that reservations staff could see that there was no availability. Reservations staff had to learn not to be afraid of quoting the full 'rack rate' to an enquirer. It is much easier to subsequently offer a discounted price than to try to recover margin from a customer who has been sold a room at a low price. Management has the confidence to hold out for a higher rate because they know, on the basis of probability, that they will get someone else who will pay the full or second highest 'rack rate'. Staff incentives, which were previously based on the volume of sales made, were changed to reflect the number of sales made at higher rates.

The hotel formed a forecasting team which involved a number of departmental managers:

- General manager
- Rooms manager
- Food and beverage manager
- Financial controller

The authors were surprised to note that the sales manager was not included in this forecasting team, although the results of each meeting were communicated to them in the form of sales targets.

The forecasting team met once a month to discuss forecasts for the coming months. The YM ethos helped to identify trends in demand, and in particular shifts in the balance between the main market segments of corporate, leisure and conferences.

Regular meetings, armed with appropriate information allowed the hotel to see ahead. For example, during the previous year the hotel had found itself with a very quiet Friday and Saturday in June. There had just been two bank holidays and everybody that wanted to come to Warwick for the weekend has been and gone, so there was not much more that the rooms manager could do at the time to stimulate demand. But with a yield management system, the forecasting team could have been more proactive earlier in the year when it should have been able to spot, on the basis of previous experience, the potential quiet spot in June. Back in January or February, the hotel would have had enough time to book in a relatively low-yielding coach group for that weekend – some revenue would have been better than no revenue.

Another issue which arose was the need to manage the yield of the hotel as a whole, rather than of individual elements within it. As an example, food and beverage sales may suffer as a result of the hotel holding out for a higher proportion of corporate customers paying a high rate, because business people are more likely to eat out in the evening, thereby depriving the restaurant of revenue. On the other hand, a conference may yield less per room, but this could be made up by high spending on catering and beverages.

The hotel persevered with implementation of its YM system. Was it all worth the effort? Within the first year of implementing the system, the hotel noticed an average improvement in yield per room of £5 per night, ahead of the general change in prices within the sector, and very credible given the competitive nature of the industry.

(Adapted from J. H. Huyton and S. D. Peters (1997) 'Application of Yield Management to the Hotel Industry', in I. Yeoman and A. Ingold (eds), *Strategies for the Service Industries*, Cassell, London)

## Case study review questions

1 Summarize the issues which are likely to detract from an organization-wide pursuit of maximum yields.

2 What techniques can be used to improve a hotel's accuracy in forecasting demand?

3 To what extent do you think that fluctuating prices, which are associated with YM systems, may undermine customers' trust in a hotel brand?

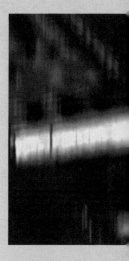

## Chapter summary and linkages to other chapters

Marketing in the service sector is made more complex by the perishability and inseparability of the service offer, with the consequence that supply and demand must be closely matched by time and place. Service offers cannot generally be transferred between time and place. This demands close integration of marketing and operations management functions. Fluctuating patterns of demand is often seen as a problem within the services sector, but it can also be seen as an opportunity which YM practices address.

Capacity management is closely related to study of the service encounter (**Chapter 3**). This chapter has taken a broader management overview to supplement the previous discussion of service design (**Chapter 2**). A critical aspect of making a service organization more flexible lies in the flexibility of its employment practices, discussed in **Chapter 12**. The need for appropriate information about demand patterns was raised in **Chapter 6**. Capacity management, and the way in which customers are processed, can contribute towards a service provider's positioning strategy (**Chapter 7**). The handling of customers during queuing processes can be a major contributor to customers' perceptions of service quality, discussed in **Chapter 8** in the context of service encounters. Finally, effective capacity management should be supported by appropriate management structures and processes (**Chapter 14**).

## www linkages/URLs

Yield management discussion group:
http://www.mailbase.ac.uk/lists/yield.management

## Key terms

Queuing systems 388          Yield management 399
Relationship marketing 402

## Chapter review questions

1  Why is a fluctuating demand pattern much more of a problem in the services sector than it is for manufacturing firms?

2  What is the difference between short- and long-term inelasticity of supply? In what ways can an airline make its services more elastic in the short term?

3  Consider a queue for service which you have been involved in recently. Critically assess the methods used for handling the queue. How could these have been improved?

4  To what extent can a city-centre sandwich bar change the pattern of demand which it faces? What methods might it use to achieve this?

5  Choose a capacity-constrained service industry and identify the options which are available to increase its elasticity of supply.

6  Which service industries is the practice of yield management particularly appropriate to? Can you identify sectors where its use may be inappropriate?

## Selected further reading

*Some of the basic principles of matching service capacity to demand through the techniques of yield management are discussed in the following:*

Donaghy, K., U. McMahon-Beattie, I. Yeoman and A. Ingold (1998) 'The Realism of Yield Management', *Progress in Tourism and Hospitality Research*, No. 4, pp 187–195

Ingold, A., U. McMahon-Beattie and I. Yeoman (2000) *Yield Management, Strategies for the Service Industries*, Continuum Books, London

*Methods of handling queuing situations are discussed in the following:*

Sarel, D. and H. Marmorstein (1999) 'Managing the Delayed Service Encounter: The Role of Employee Action and Customer Prior Experience', *International Journal of Bank Marketing*, Vol. 17, Issue 6, pp 286–94

*The role of flexible employees can be critical to matching capacity with demand and is discussed further in the following:*

Atkinson, J. (1984) 'Manpower Strategies for Flexible Organizations', *Personnel Management*, August, pp 15–26

Bitner, M., B. H. Booms and L. A. Mohr (1994) 'Critical Service Encounters: The Employee's Viewpoint', *Journal of Marketing*, October, Vol. 58, pp 95–106

# 14

# Managing the marketing effort

## Learning objectives

Services management and services marketing are seen by many as inseparable. With customers actively taking part in service production processes, the management of these processes becomes critical to their successful marketing. Previous chapters have studied management at the micro level of the service encounter. The aim of this chapter is to gain an understanding of the broader management issues which ensure that a service organization achieves and sustains a competitive position in its marketplace. A good strategy is necessary but not sufficient for a firm to gain a competitive advantage. It must also have management structures and processes to ensure that marketing strategy is consistent with corporate strategy and is effectively implemented.

## 14.1  Introduction to the marketing management process

For market-oriented services organizations, strategic marketing management is an ongoing process. Organizations which confine their planning activity to a short period surrounding the production of the annual marketing plan cannot be described as genuinely market-oriented. A number of stages within the strategic marketing planning process can be identified, although the extent to which these are carried out within a formally defined marketing department – rather than at corporate level – will vary from one organization to another. Five key elements of marketing planning within this ongoing process are:

1  *Analysing the current market position of the organization ('Where are we now?')*  In asking where the organization is at the present time, a foundation is laid on which future decisions can be based. Such issues as the organization's current market share, the size and nature of its customer base, customer perceptions of the organization's output and the internal strengths and weaknesses of the organization in terms of production, personnel and financial resources need to be addressed in both a quantitative and qualitative manner.

2  *Setting objectives for the organization and its marketing effort ('Where do we want to be?')*  Management is about using the resources of an organization to achieve some form of objectives, which can range from basic survival through to quantified financial objectives or qualitative level of service objectives. Without clearly specified objectives, marketing management can drift aimlessly.

3  *Identifying and evaluating strategic alternatives ('How can we get there?')*  The same ultimate objectives can usually be met by pursuing a number of alternative plans of action. Identifying the strategic alternatives open to an organization relies on interpreting data and evaluating a number of possible future scenarios. Within this evaluation, factors such as the likelihood of success, the level of downside risk and the amount of resources required to implement a strategy need to be taken into consideration.

4  *Implementing the chosen strategy ('What will we do?')*  Having chosen a strategic route by which to achieve objectives, this must be translated into an operational programme, specifying – among other things – detailed promotional and pricing plans which operationalize the promotional and pricing strategies.

5  *Monitoring and controlling ('Did we get there?')*  Marketing plans are of little value if they are only to be implemented half-heartedly. An ongoing part of the marketing process is therefore to monitor the implementation of the plan and to seek explanation of any deviation from plan – and where appropriate – take corrective action.

The elements of the strategic marketing management process can be summarized as analysis, planning, implementing and controlling and are shown diagrammatically in Figure 14.1.

## 14.2  The contribution of marketing planning to corporate planning

The process of marketing management can be seen as just one component of the

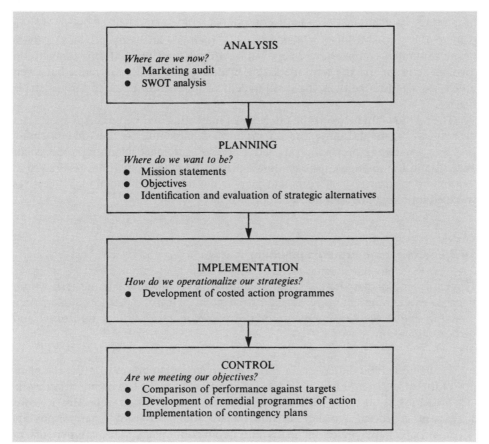

**Figure 14.1**
The analysis, planning,
implementation and
control process

overall management process within an organization. Strategic management within commercial organizations can be seen as operating at three levels:

- The corporate level which is concerned with the allocation of resources between the various business units which make up an organization.
- The strategic business unit level which is concerned with internal planning for the unit.
- The functional level which is concerned with the planning of specific functions within organizations – for example marketing, personnel and production planning.

There can be argument about the relationship between corporate planning and marketing planning. At one extreme, the two are seen as synonymous. If an organization stands or falls primarily on its ability to satisfy customer needs, then it can be argued that marketing planning is so central to the organization's activities that it becomes corporate planning. The alternative view is that marketing is just one of the functions of an organization which affects its performance. Marketing takes its goals from corporate plans in just the same way as the personnel or production functions of the organization. Clearly, in some service sectors where consumers have relatively little choice and production capacity is limited, the significance of the marketing plan to the corporate plan is somewhat less than for an easily produced service facing unlimited competition. Many public utilities face little, if any competition for their services, and the term marketing planning may be used in name but given much less significance than the development of production plans to serve a stable market.

The relationship between the processes of marketing and corporate planning can be two-way, again reflecting the importance of marketing to the total planning process. Marketing information is fed into the corporate planning process for analysis and formulation of the corporate plan in a process sometimes referred to as 'bottom-up planning'. The corporate plan is developed and functional objectives specified for marketing in a 'top-down' process.

### 14.2.1 Corporate strategic planning

The basic idea of corporate strategic planning is to provide a framework within which a whole range of more detailed strategic plans can be developed. Corporate planning embraces other elements of the planning process in a horizontal and vertical dimension.

- In the horizontal dimension, a corporate strategic plan brings together the plans of the specialized functions which are necessary to make the organization work. Marketing is just one function of an organization which generates its own planning process – other functional plans found in most organizations are financial plans, personnel plans and production plans. The components of these functional plans must recognize interdependencies if they are to be effective, for example a bank's marketing strategic plan which anticipates a 50% growth in sales of mortgages over a five-year planning period should be reflected in a strategic production plan which allows for the necessary processing capacity to be developed and a financial plan which identifies strategies for raising the required level of finance over the same time period.
- In the vertical dimension, the corporate planning process provides the framework for strategic decisions to be made at different levels of the corporate hierarchy. Objectives can be specified in progressively more detail from the global objectives of the corporate plan, to the greater detail required to operationalize them at the level of individual operational units and – in turn – for individual services.

The precise nature of the corporate planning process varies between organizations – it has been described as an essentially *ad hoc* process, pragmatically adapted by a combination of logical and irrational processes to meet the changing needs of an organization. Some organizations put a lot of detail into a corporate plan which the managers of each strategic business unit are expected to follow closely. Others may view the corporate plan as no more than a general statement of aims which strategic business unit managers achieve in a manner which they consider most appropriate. Similarly the distinction between corporate planning and marketing planning can be

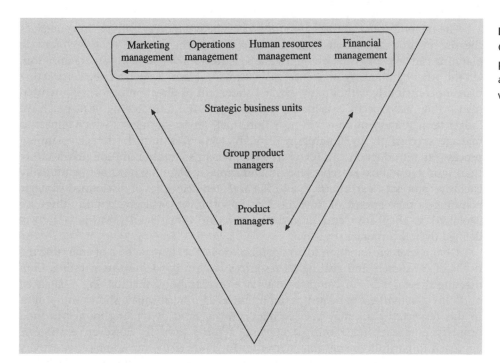

Marketing management — Operations management — Human resources management — Financial management

Strategic business units

Group product managers

Product managers

**Figure 14.2**
Corporate strategic planning as a horizontal and vertical integrator within an organization

very imprecise. Essentially, it doesn't matter who undertakes marketing planning, so long as it gets done.

## 14.3 The rationale for strategic planning

Strategic marketing planning is the process of ensuring a long-term good fit between the requirements of an organization's environment and the capabilities which it possesses. The process has been defined by Kotler (1999) as:

> ... the managerial process of developing and maintaining a viable fit between an organization's objectives, skills and resources, and its changing market opportunities. The aim of strategic planning is to shape and re-shape the company's business and products so that they yield target profits and growth.

The idea that services organizations should need to plan strategically over the medium to long term was often not recognized in the comparatively stable markets which many service industries faced before the 1970s. Banks, for example, could survive and prosper on the basis of short-term operational planning because change in their marketing environments was very gradual. During the 1980s, the effects of deregulation of financial markets and the quickening pace of technological change forced banks to pay much more attention to the direction in which they sought to move their business. Faced with competition on a large number of fronts, they had to make choices about which fronts they would use their limited financial and managerial effort to attack and which would be allowed to fade away.

The importance of strategic planning varies between organizations. In general, as the size of an organization increases, so too does the scale of its risks. Strategic planning can be seen as an attempt to manage the level of risk facing an organization. On the other hand, many smaller service businesses often develop strategic marketing plans unconsciously without any explicit statement of direction or formally written plan – they may specify a tactical programme for the forthcoming year, but leave longer term strategy unstated. Even within small service businesses which appear to manage successfully by 'muddling through' without a formal strategic planning process, its introduction can focus an entrepreneur's attention on long-term rather than short-term aims. Entrepreneurism and strategic planning need not be mutually exclusive processes – an alternative to the accepted principles of disciplined strategic planning is the concept of 'freewheeling opportunism' whereby opportunities are exploited as they arise and judged on their individual merits within a loosely defined overall corporate strategy.

Giving strategic direction to an organization is not simply a case of analysing the needs of consumers and gearing its resources to earn good short-term profits from meeting these needs. For commercial service organizations, maintaining a balanced portfolio of activities can be just as important as earning adequate short-term profits. In this respect, a bank may be meeting a proven need by lending money to fund property purchase and earning acceptable returns from it. However, a strategic approach to portfolio management may lead it to diversify into some other activity with a counterbalancing level of cash flow and risk, turning away business which may seem attractive in the short term.

## 14.4 The marketing planning process – position analysis

Many organizations begin the process of marketing planning by undertaking a marketing audit. This seeks to identify the particular strengths and weaknesses of the organization in the context of the threats and opportunities present in its environment. But what information should be collected? A company's mission statement can provide a company's employees with guidance about what is relevant and irrelevant in analysing its current position.

How much analysis of the current situation should a company undertake? While it is nearly always true that a sound analysis of the current situation is an essential prerequisite to developing a marketing plan for the future, excessive preoccupation with the current situation can have its costs. Analysis on its own will not provide management decisions which are necessary for defining the future marketing plan. A 'paralysis by analysis' can occur in organizations which avoid making hard decisions about the future by continually seeking more information about the present. A plateau is usually reached at which little additional information becomes available which will improve the quality of marketing plan decisions. Worse still, in markets which are fast changing, excessive analysis of the current position can put a firm at a competitive disadvantage to firms who are more willing to take a risk and exploit a market ahead of its competitors.

### 14.4.1 The situation analysis

Auditing systems have been used for some time as a means of gathering information in order to assess the efficiency and effectiveness of a number of functions of organizations. The financial audit is probably the most widely used, and in its widest sense is used to assess the financial health of an organization. Personnel and production audits are similarly used to establish the personnel and production strengths and weaknesses of an organization respectively, and the nature of the environments in which these functions operate. Together, these contribute towards the corporate audit – an assessment of the overall strengths and weaknesses which an organization possesses relative to its environment. The elements of a corporate audit are diagrammatically represented in Figure 14.3.

A marketing audit is a relatively recent concept and has been defined by McDonald (1995) as:

> . . . a systematical, critical and unbiased review and appraisal of the environment and of the company's operations. A marketing audit is part of the larger management audit and is concerned with the marketing environment and marketing operations.

Although many of the elements of a marketing audit overlap those of the more traditional functional audits, it contributes towards the corporate audit by addressing three major issues:

- The nature of the environmental threats and opportunities facing the organization.
- The strengths and weaknesses of the organization in terms of its ability to cope with threats and opportunities presented by its environment.
- The organization's current market position.

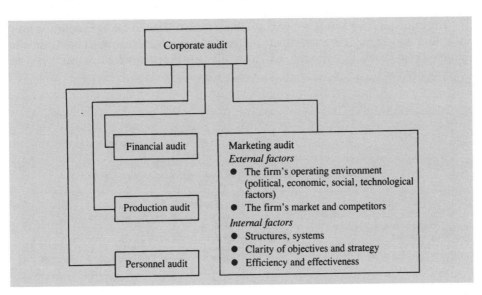

**Figure 14.3**
The corporate audit

To be effective, a marketing audit needs to be comprehensive, systematic, independent and periodic. A comprehensive audit implies that it covers all of the major elements of an organization's activities, including those that are apparently performing well, rather than concentrating solely on problem areas. A systematic audit implies that the audit has a coherent structure and is followed by the development and implementation of plans which are based on the outcome of the audit. The greater the independence of a person undertaking an audit, the more useful it is likely to be through objectivity which may be inhibited where vested interests are at stake.

There are arguments about how frequently marketing audits should be undertaken. At one extreme, it has been argued that marketing audits should be conducted on a continuous but selective basis, but against this, if the process is conducted too frequently, the process itself will demoralize marketing personnel.

### 14.4.2   SWOT analysis

A framework widely used in marketing audits is a grid which plots internal strengths and weaknesses in one half of the grid and external opportunities and threats in the other half. The terms opportunities and threats should not be viewed as 'absolutes', for as Johnson and Scholes (1988, p 77) pointed out, what might appear at first sight to be an opportunity may not be so when examined against an organization's resources and the feasibility of implementing a strategy.

A SWOT analysis summarizes the main environmental issues in the form of opportunities and threats (O&T) facing an organization. With this technique, these are specifically listed alongside the strengths and weaknesses of the organization (S&W). The strengths and weaknesses are internal to the organization and the technique is used to put realism into the opportunities and threats. In this way, the environment may be assessed as giving rise to a number of possible opportunities, but if the organization is not capable of exploiting these because of internal weaknesses then they should perhaps be left alone.

The principles of a SWOT analysis are illustrated in Figure 14.4 by examining how an airline which has an established reputation as a charter carrier could use the framework in assessing whether to enter the scheduled service market between London and Paris.

**Figure 14.4**

SWOT analysis for a hypothetical airline considering entry to the scheduled London–Paris air travel market

| STRENGTHS<br>Strong financial position<br>Good reputation with existing customers<br>Has aircraft which can service the market | WEAKNESSES<br>Has no allocated take-off or landing 'slots'<br>at main airport<br>Poor network of ticket agents<br>Aircraft are old and expensive to operate |
|---|---|
| OPPORTUNITIES<br>Market for business and leisure travel is growing<br>Deregulation of air licensing allows new<br>opportunities<br>Costs of operating aircraft are falling | THREATS<br>Channel Tunnel may capture a large share<br>of market<br>Deregulation will result in new competitors<br>appearing<br>Growth in air travel will lead to more congestion |

## 14.5 Defining corporate and marketing objectives

Having identified the current position of the organization and its environment, the next stage in the planning process is to give it direction for the future. In this section, the sense of giving direction is examined at a number of levels, starting at the general level of setting corporate goals, then working through a hierarchy of aims to the formulation of specific marketing objectives.

### 14.5.1 Defining the corporate mission

A corporate mission statement is a means of reminding everybody within the organization of its essential purpose. For services industries involving high levels of customer contact, this sharing of a common mission can significantly impact on the quality of service encounters. Drucker (1973) identified a number of basic questions which management should ask when it perceives itself drifting along with no clear purpose, and which form the basis of a corporate mission statement:

- What is our business?
- Who is the customer?
- What is value to the customer?
- What will our business be?
- What should our business be?

By forcing management to focus on the essential nature of the business which they are in and the nature of customer needs which they seek to satisfy, the problem of 'marketing myopia' advanced by Levitt (1960) can be avoided. Levitt argued that in order to avoid a narrow, shortsighted view of its business, managers should define their business in terms of the needs that they fulfil rather than the products they produce. In the classic example, railway operators had lost their way because they defined their service output in terms of the technology of tracked vehicles, rather than in terms of the core benefit of movement which they provided. Accountants learnt the lesson of this myopic example by redefining their central purpose away from a narrow preoccupation with providing 'accounting services' to a much broader mission statement which spoke about providing 'business solutions'. More recently, many freight transport companies have defined their mission in terms of managing customers' complete logistical needs.

In the services sector, where the interface between the consumer and production personnel is often critical, communication of the values contained within the mission statement assumes great importance. The statement is frequently repeated by organizations in staff newsletters and in notices at their place of work. An example of a mission statement which is widely communicated to the workforce – as well as to customers – is provided by British Gas (see Figure 14.5).

The nature of an organization's mission statement is a reflection of a number of factors:

- The organization's ownership, which can lead to marked contrasts in the mission statements of public sector, private sector and charity organizations.

Statement of Purpose
We aim to be ...
  a world class energy company and the leading international gas business
by ...
▶ running a professional gas business providing safe, secure and reliable supplies
▶ actively developing an international business in exploration and production of oil and
  gas
▶ making strategic investments in other energy-related projects and business world
  wide
▶ satisfying our customers' wishes for excellent quality of service and outstanding value
▶ constantly and energetically seeking to improve quality and productivity in all we do
▶ caring for the environment
▶ maintaining a high quality workforce with equal opportunities for all
▶ cultivating good relations with customers, employees, suppliers, shareholders and the
  communities we serve and thereby improving returns to our shareholders

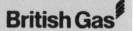

- The previous history of the organization, in particular any distinct competencies which it has acquired or images which it has created in the eyes of potential customers.
- Environmental factors, in particular the major opportunities and threats which are likely to face the organization in the foreseeable future.
- Resources available – without resources available for their accomplishment, a mission statement has little meaning.

Missions define in general terms the direction in which an organization seeks to move. They contain no quantifiable information which allows them to be operationalized. For this to happen, objectives need to be set.

## 14.6 Setting objectives

Having carried out a situation analysis and defined its corporate mission, the vital task of setting objectives can begin. Objectives have a number of functions within an organization:

- They add to the sense of purpose within an organization, without which there would be little focus for managers' efforts.
- They help to achieve consistency between decisions made at different points within the organization – for example it would be inconsistent if an operations manager used a production objective which was unrelated to the marketing manager's sales objective.
- Objectives are used as motivational devices and can be used in a variety of formal and informal ways to stimulate increased performance by employees.
- Objectives allow for more effective control within an organization. Unless clear

objectives have been set at the outset, it is very difficult to know whether the organization has achieved what it set out to achieve, and to take any corrective action if its efforts seem to be going adrift during the plan period.

To have most value to marketing management, objectives should possess a number of important characteristics:

- They should be quantified. In the private services sector, the most important objectives can usually be expressed in terms of profitability, sales or market share. Within some public services, these terms may have little meaning, but objectives should nevertheless be quantifiable – for example libraries may set objectives in terms of the number of books borrowed, or museums the number of people visiting their exhibitions.
- Objectives must specify the time period to which they relate. In the case of a new service launch, an objective may be to recover 80% of costs during the first year of operation, breaking even by year 2 and achieving a 20% return on capital invested by year 3.
- To be effective, objectives must be capable of realistic achievement and accepted as such by the people responsible for acting on them. If objectives are set unattainably high, the whole process of planning could be brought into disrepute by staff in an organization. Where objectives are devolved to a manager, these should reflect factors over which the manager has some degree of control. As an example, a product manager for mortgages should have some control over the volume of funds available for lending, otherwise any restriction may make a nonsense of an objective to achieve a specified sales target.
- There must be consistency between objectives. Inconsistency may, for example, occur where a sales objective can only be achieved by reducing selling prices, thereby making it impossible to achieve a profitability objective. Furthermore, objectives must be ranked in order of priority. Managers of a restaurant chain presented with a list of five 'key objectives', such as contribution to fixed costs, total sales revenue, number of visits by customers, average spend per visit and average customer waiting time, may struggle with apparently conflicting objectives. This can be resolved by ranking them in order of importance.

Organizations set a variety of objectives which are acted upon by their staff. The nature of these objectives can be classified into a number of categories:

- The ultimate goal of most private sector service providers is to produce an acceptable level of profits to its owners, hence it is profit objectives that feature prominently in the hierarchy of objectives which are communicated vertically through the planning hierarchy.
- Growth objectives may be important to organizations operating in rapidly expanding market sectors where a slow rate of growth effectively means that the organization is falling behind its competitors. In some industries, growth may be an essential objective in order to achieve a critical mass at which significant economies of scale occur.
- Technical objectives are set by organizations where technology is an important element in gaining competitive advantage over competitors.

- Quality of service objectives are frequently set for line managers within the private services sector – for example, one of many objectives set for branch bank managers relates to the length of waiting time for customers at their branch. Quality of service objectives often assume overriding importance for public services where financial objectives act more as constraints. Time taken to process passport applications by the Passport Agency and the length of waiting time for a health authority are typical bases for setting quality objectives.

- Sales and market share objectives are set by most private sector organizations. At the corporate level, it can be argued that these represent strategies rather than objectives. Thus to an airline, a specified profit objective could be achieved either by a low-volume, high-price strategy, or by a strategy which seeks a greater market share, but at the expense of lower prices. However, once the strategy is determined at corporate level, this is subsequently translated into specific objectives for line managers.

As an example of the diversity of objectives set by firms, a study of 28 professional services firms by Moutinho (1989) found that most firms had defined their primary goals in terms of sales volume (fee income) and profitability. Following these criteria, in order of use were the firm's image goals, return on investment and market share.

Having studied its operating environment, an organization will come to a view as to what objectives it should set itself for the planning period. A common starting point for goal setting is to look at previous performance and project past trends forwards to see what the organization would be capable of achieving if all other factors were held constant. Where the actual objectives set are greater than the position projected from previous trends, the result is a 'planning gap', illustrated in Figure 14.6. The planning process aims to close this gap. This can be done either by reducing downward the original objective to a level that is more realistic, given the

**Figure 14.6**

The planning gap

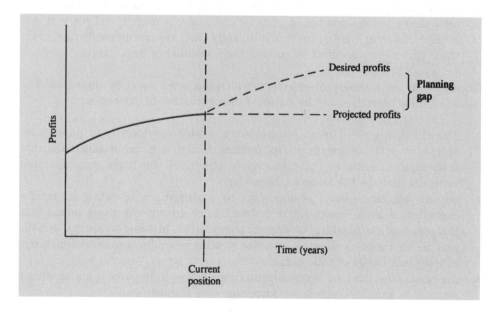

historical pattern or, alternatively, action can be taken to accelerate the trend rate from its historical pattern to a higher level by means of marketing strategy. In practice, the planning gap is reduced by a combination of revising objectives and amending marketing strategies. In the case of totally new service offerings, it can be difficult to identify the historical trend line.

## 14.7 Identifying strategic alternatives

The relationship between the corporate planning and marketing planning processes is neither clear-cut nor uni-directional. It was noted earlier that the importance of the marketing plan to the corporate plan varies from one organization to another. Furthermore, the process of planning is iterative. Corporate plans require information to be fed upwards from the functional areas of an organization, synthesized into a corporate plan and fed back to these functional areas in the form of specific objectives. The process of finalizing the corporate plan could involve a number of iterations until optimization is achieved between all areas.

Having established the objectives which it is to work to, marketing management can set about the task of developing plans to achieve these objectives. Plans are produced at three levels – strategic, tactical and contingency.

### 14.7.1 Strategic, tactical and contingency planning

The strategic element of a marketing plan focuses on the overriding direction which an organization's efforts will take in order to meet its objectives. The tactical element is more concerned with plans for implementing the detail of the strategic plan. The division between the strategic and tactical elements of a marketing plan can sometimes be difficult to define. Typically, a strategic marketing plan is concerned with mapping out direction over a five-year planning period, whereas a tactical marketing plan is concerned with implementation during the next twelve months. Naturally, many services industries view their strategic planning periods very differently. The marketing of large-scale infrastructure projects, such as airports or underground railways requires a much longer strategic planning period to allow for the time delays in developing new capacity and the fact that when capacity does become available, it will have a very long life with few alternative uses. The time taken to build a new airport terminal from the proposal stage to full opening is typically in excess of 5–10 years. Not only does the technology of airports require a long strategic planning period, the nature of the competitive environment allows an airport operator to take a longer term view, with little likelihood of unexpected competitors coming on to the scene during its planning period. On the other hand, some service industries operate to much shorter strategic planning periods where new productive capacity can be produced quickly and where the environment is turbulent. During the late 1990s, the market for Internet access services grew very rapidly, spurred by changes in technology and growing household ownership of computers. At the same time, new market entrants appeared from a number of directions, including supermarkets, telephone companies and computer manufacturers. In this environment, strategic planning periods became very short and an organization's strategic marketing plan could give only a very general statement of direction beyond a two- or three-year planning period.

A third element of the marketing plan involves the development of contingency plans. These seek to identify scenarios where the assumptions of the position analysis on which strategic decisions were based turn out to be false. For example, the planning of a new airport might have assumed that fuel prices would rise by no more than 10% during the plan period. A contingency plan would be useful to provide an alternative strategic route if, halfway through the plan period, fuel prices suddenly doubled and looked like remaining at the higher level for the foreseeable future, causing a fall in the total market for air travel. A contingency plan would identify options for the airport to react to such events, such as increasing its promotional expenditure to preserve its share of a diminishing market, or identifying alternative sources of revenue – such as the development of industrial estates and business centres on airport land – which are not directly related to the level of demand for air travel.

## 14.8   Strategy formulation

Having analysed its business environment and formed a view of the future, organizations must then identify the strategic alternatives which would allow them to achieve their objectives. From these alternatives, a strategy will be selected and implemented.

Competitors within any one industry may each pursue very different strategies, but all may be capable of achievement, given that each organization may be pursuing quite different objectives, and may possess differing strengths and weaknesses. Analysts have developed numerous methodologies for classifying the diversity of marketing strategies. While there is no definitive basis for categorizing the strategic alternatives open to an organization, three focal points for strategy development will be considered here:

- Strategies which focus on gaining competitive advantage.
- Strategies which focus on growth options.
- Strategies which focus on the development of product portfolios.

It should be noted that this does not represent a strategy typology, but just a useful classification device for considering the literature. In practice, strategy development will bear some relation to each of these three focal points.

## 14.9   Strategies for competitive advantage

Firms must be aware of who their competitors are and of their relative strengths and weaknesses. In all markets which are competitive in nature, the strategic decisions made by an organization are frequently a response to actions – or possible future actions – of competing organizations. One method of identifying and selecting strategies is to identify those activities for which an organization has a competitive advantage over its competitors. Porter (1980) has reduced competitive advantage-based strategies to three generic types:

**Overall cost leadership**   Here, the organization puts a lot of effort into lowering its production and distribution costs so that it can win competitive advantage by charging lower prices. Organizations pursuing this strategy need to be efficient at production.

Cost leadership can result from being able to achieve economies of scale. In services which use high technology or which require highly trained labour skills, a learning curve effect may be apparent (also called a cost experience curve). By operating at a larger scale than its competitors, a firm can benefit more from the learning curve and thereby achieve lower unit costs. While this may be true of some service industries, others face only a very low critical output at which significant economies of scale occur – niche retailing and hairdressing for example. For organizations in these sectors, cost leadership would be a difficult strategy as many rival firms would also be able to achieve maximum cost efficiency. A cost leadership strategy is more likely to be effective where a high level of output relative to market size is necessary in order to achieve economies of scale, as is the case with the operation of a national car breakdown and recovery service which requires a high minimum level of investment in infrastructure. This prevents small local operators competing on the basis of lower overhead costs, leaving the major competitors to cut costs and hence offer a lower price for a basically generic service.

**Differentiation**   Organizations seek to achieve superior performance of a service, adding value to the offering which is reflected in the higher price which a customer is prepared to pay. One way in which firms seek to gain advantage over their competitors is by offering greater quality relative to price than their competitors. Added value can also be provided by offering completely new services which are not yet available from competitors, by modifying existing services, or by making them more easily available in order to give them a competitive advantage. In this way, a bank could seek superior performance in areas such as the greatest number of branches, the highest rates of interest, the greatest number of cash machines or the most convenient home banking service. An organization can realistically aim to be leader in one of these areas, but not in all at the same time. It therefore develops those strengths which will give it a differential performance advantage in one of these benefit areas. A bank which has the most comprehensive branch network may build upon this by seeking to ensure that they are open at times when customers wish to visit them; that there is no excessive waiting time and that they present a bright and inviting image to customers.

A problem of a differentiation strategy for services is that a service can easily be copied and a company seeking to differentiate by innovation may soon find its innovatory service copied by competitors.

**Focus**   An organization may focus on one or more small market segments rather than aiming for the whole market. The organization becomes familiar with the needs of these segments and gains competitive advantage by cost leadership or differentiation within its chosen segment, or both.

A cost focus strategy requires an organization to segment its market and to specialize in products for that market. By concentrating on a narrow geographical segment, or producing specialized services for a very small segment, the organization can gain economies of scale in production. In this way a holiday tour operator could focus on disabled travellers living in the south-east of England. By building up volume of specialized holidays, it may achieve operating economies – e.g. the ability to spread the capital cost of specialized vehicles over a large number of customers. By focusing on the south-east market, it can reduce the costs which may result from attempting to arrange transport connections from geographically remote market segments.

A focus strategy may be appropriate for a company which is seeking to enter a market for the first time. Mortgage lenders seeking to enter a new national market may seek to focus on small segments by providing specialized products such as foreign currency mortgages or special mortgages for second holiday homes.

Despite the advantages of a focus strategy described above, there are also dangers. The segments which form the focus may be too small to be economical in themselves. Moreover, an over-reliance on narrow segments could leave an organization dangerously exposed if these segments go into decline. Overseas financial institutions who focused on segments of the UK mortgage market faced great difficulty when the UK housing market went into decline from 1988 onwards and many of them were forced to abandon the UK market completely.

For firms pursuing a similar strategy aimed at similar market segments, Porter contends that the one which pursues that strategy most effectively will meet its objectives most effectively. Of all the car hire companies pursuing a cost leadership strategy, the one which actually achieves the lowest level of costs will be the most successful. Firms which do not pursue a clear strategy are the least effective. Although they try to succeed in all three strategic alternatives, they end up showing no cost leadership, no differential advantage and no clear focus on one customer group. Like many models, Porter's model has been challenged. Critics have pointed to successful firms who have managed to pursue multiple strategies simultaneously.

### 14.9.1 The dynamics of competition

It is all too easy to portray competition within a market as a static concept. In reality, market attractiveness is a dynamic measure and, for evaluation purposes, a prime consideration for firms considering entering a market is how attractive the market will appear at the time when a proposed strategy is implemented. If a market appears attractive to one organization, then it probably appears equally attractive to others as well. These may possess equal competitive advantage in addressing the market. If all such firms decide to enter the market, over-supply results, profit margins become squeezed and the market becomes relatively unattractive. Services which are easy to copy can be designed and introduced to the market relatively quickly and can result in unstable markets. An example is the UK video rental market which in the mid-1980s looked highly attractive, given the rapid growth in ownership of video cassette recorders and good margins earned by those operators in the market. This was the signal for many companies to enter it, with some chains such as Ritz and Blockbuster being built up very rapidly. The result was that by the mid-1990s the market – which had ceased to grow on account of the rising proportion of videos which were sold rather than rented – had become very unattractive, with poor returns and a number of business failures.

## 14.10 Growth strategies

Most private sector service organizations pursue growth in one form or another, whether this is an explicit aim of the organization or an implicit aim of its managers. The thrust for growth can be channelled into one of a number of directions and it would therefore be useful to develop frameworks for analysing the growth strategies open to organizations.

### 14.10.1 Product–market growth strategies

An organization's growth can conceptually be analysed in terms of two key development dimensions – markets and products. This conceptualization forms the basis of the Product/Market Expansion Grid proposed by Ansoff (1957). Products and markets are each analysed in terms of their degree of novelty to an organization and growth strategies identified in terms of these two dimensions. In this way, four possible growth strategies can be identified. An illustration of the framework, with reference to the specific options open to a seaside holiday hotel is shown in Figure 14.7.

The four growth options are associated with differing sets of problems and opportunities for organizations. These relate to the level of resources required to implement a particular strategy, and the level of risk associated with each. It follows, therefore, that what might be a feasible growth strategy for one organization may not be for another. The characteristics of the four strategies are described below.

1   *Market penetration strategies*   This type of strategy focuses growth on the existing product range by encouraging higher levels of take-up of a service among the existing target markets. In this way a specialist tour operator in a growing sector of the holiday market could – all other things being equal – grow naturally, simply by maintaining its current marketing strategy. If it wanted to accelerate

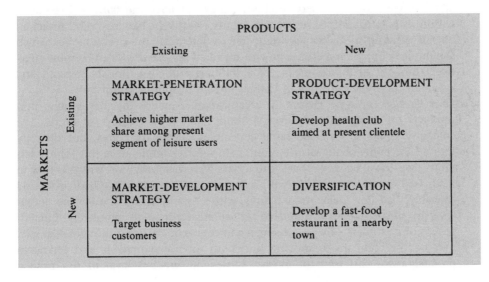

**Figure 14.7**

An application of Ansoff's growth matrix to a hotel operator this growth, it could do this firstly by seeking to sell more holidays to its existing customer base and secondly by attracting customers from its direct competitors. If the market was in fact in decline, the company could only grow by attracting customers from its competitors through more aggressive marketing policies and/or cost reduction programmes. This strategy offers the least level of risk to an organization – it is familiar with both its products and its customers.

2   *Market development strategies*   This type of strategy builds upon the existing product range which an organization has established, but seeks to find new groups of customers for them. In this way a specialist regional ski tour operator which had saturated its current market might seek to expand its sales to new geographical regions or aim its marketing effort at attracting custom from groups beyond its current age/income groups. While the organization may be familiar with the operational aspects of the service which it is providing, it faces risks resulting from possibly poor knowledge of different buyer behaviour patterns in the markets which it seeks to enter. As an example of the potential problems associated with this strategy, many UK retailers have sought to offer their UK shop formats in overseas markets only to find that those features which attracted customers in the UK failed to do so overseas.

3   *Product development strategy*   As an alternative to selling existing products into new markets, an organization may choose to develop new products for its existing markets. A ski tour operator may have built up a good understanding of the holiday needs of a particular market segment – perhaps the 18–35-year-old affluent aspiring segment – and seeks to offer a wider range of services to them than simply skiing holidays. It might offer summer activity holidays in addition. While the company minimizes the risk associated with the uncertainty of new markets, it faces risk resulting from lack of knowledge about its new product area. Often a feature of this growth strategy is collaboration with a product specialist who helps the organization produce the service, leaving it free to market it effectively to its customers. A department store wishing to add a coffee shop to its service offering may not have the skills and resources within its organization to run such a facility effectively, but may subcontract an outside catering specialist, leaving it free to determine the overall policy which should be adopted. Sometimes growth into new service areas can be most effectively brought about by means of a joint venture (e.g. British Telecom and Securicor jointly set up the UK Cellnet mobile telephone company).

4   *Diversification strategy*   Here, an organization expands by developing new products for new markets. Diversification can take a number of forms. The company could stay in the same general product/market area, but diversify into a new point of the distribution chain – for example an airline which sets up its own travel agency moves into a type of service provision which is new to it, as well as dealing directly with a segment of the market it had previously probably had few sales transactions with. Alternatively, the airline might diversify into completely unrelated service areas aimed at completely different groups of customers – by purchasing a golf course or car dealership, for example. Because the company is moving into both unknown markets and unknown product areas, this form of growth carries the greatest level of risk from a

marketing management perspective. Diversification may, however, help to manage the long-term risk of the organization by reducing dependency on a narrow product/market area.

In practice, most growth that occurs is a combination of product development and market development. In very competitive markets, the service supplier would probably have to slightly adapt its product if it was to become attractive to a new market segment. For the leisure hotel seeking to capture new business customers, it may not be enough to simply promote existing facilities. In order to meet business people's needs, it might have to offer refurbished facilities to make them more acceptable to business customers and offer new services – e.g. the facility for visitors to pay by account.

### 14.10.2   Organic growth versus growth by acquisition

There are two basic means by which an organization can grow – through organic growth and by acquisition, although many organizations grow by a combination of the two processes. The manner of growth has important marketing implications, for instance in the speed with which an organization is allowed to expand into new market opportunities. The basis of the two types of growth is analysed below.

**Organic growth**   Organic growth is considered to be the more 'natural' pattern of growth for an organization. The initial investment by the organization results in profits, an established customer base and a well-established technical, personnel and financial structure. This provides a foundation for future growth. In this sense, success breeds success for the rate of the organization's growth is influenced by the extent to which it has succeeded in building up internally the means for future expansion.

In terms of marketing, an organization may grow organically by tackling one segment at a time, using the resources, knowledge and market awareness it has gained in order to tackle further segments. A firm may grow organically into new segments in a number of ways.

Many retail chains have grown organically by developing one region before moving on to another. In the UK, Sainsbury's grew organically from its southern base towards the northern regions, while Asda grew organically during the 1970s and early 1980s from its northern base towards the south. Other organizations have grown organically by offering additional services to its established customer base, as Marks and Spencer has done in offering a growing range of financial services to its established retail customers.

There is evidence that service firms may find organic growth difficult where new market opportunities suddenly arise. Within the financial services sector, a study by Ennew, Wong and Wright (1992) found that many of the assets of companies – such as specialized staff and distribution networks – were quite specific to their existing markets and couldn't easily be adapted to exploit new markets. Growth by acquisition was in many cases considered to be a better method of expansion.

**Growth by acquisition** The rate of organic growth is constrained by a number of factors, including the rate at which a firm's market is itself growing. An organization seeking to grow organically in a slowly developing sector such as household insurance will find organic growth more difficult than an organization serving a rapidly growing sector such as Internet service provision. Growth by acquisition may appear attractive to organizations where organic growth is difficult. In some cases it may be almost essential in order to achieve a critical mass which is necessary for survival. The DIY retail sector in the UK is one where chains have needed to achieve a critical mass in order to pass on lower prices resulting from economies in buying, distribution and promotion. Small chains have not been able to grow organically at a sufficient rate to achieve this size, resulting in their takeover or merger to form larger chains. The market leader – B & Q – has seen mainly organic growth, while the Homebase chain grew significantly with the acquisition of the rival Texas chain.

Growth by acquisition may occur where an organization sees its existing market sector contracting and it seeks to diversify into other areas. The time and risk associated with starting a new venture in an alien market sector may be considered too great. Acquiring an established business could be less risky, allowing access to an established client base and technical skills. A takeover can be mutually beneficial where one company has a sound customer base but lacks the financial resources to achieve a critical mass while the other has the finance but needs a larger customer base.

A major problem for firms seeking to grow within the service sector by acquisition lies in the fact that often the main assets being acquired are the skills and knowledge of the organization's employees. Unlike physical assets, key personnel may disappear following the acquisition, reducing the earning ability of the business. Worse still, key staff could defect to the acquiring company's competitors. There is evidence that much of the investment of financial institutions in acquiring estate agencies during the late 1980s was lost when key personnel left with their list of contacts to set up rival agencies.

## 14.11 Portfolio planning

Service providers operating in a market environment face increasingly turbulent patterns of demand. For a company to put all of its efforts into supplying a very limited range of services to a narrow market segment is potentially dangerous. Over-reliance on this one segment can make the survival of the organization dependent upon the fortunes of this one segment and its liking for its product. In any event, the fact that most markets change to some extent over time would imply that its products will eventually move out of line with customers' requirements. Also, with the development of relationship marketing strategies, firms are increasingly keen to develop opportunities for offering customers a broad range of products which attract a higher share of their total expenditure. For all of these reasons, organizations seek to manage their growth in a manner that maintains a desired portfolio of activities (discussed in Chapter 7).

Risk spreading is an important element of **portfolio management** which goes beyond marketing planning. Some service providers deliberately provide a range of services which – quite apart from their potential for cross-selling – act in contrasting manners during the business cycle. For this reason, accountancy firms have become potentially more stable units as they have amalgamated, by allowing pro-cyclical activities such as management buy-out expertise and venture capital investment to be counterbalanced by contra-cyclical activities such as insolvency work. Service organizations often take on a base load of relatively unattractive but predictable work to counterbalance highly cyclical work. Solicitors may undertake criminal defence work to cushion themselves against over-reliance on relatively lucrative but cyclical property conveyancing work. Sometimes, statutory requirements may require a balanced portfolio of output. The Bank of England's regulation of the UK banking system, for example, imposes constraints on banks' freedom to be market-led in the pattern of their lending decisions.

## 14.12 Implementing and controlling the marketing plan

Marketing plans are of little value if they are not effectively implemented. Previous chapters have discussed how elements of the marketing plan may be implemented, for example in respect of pricing and promotion decisions. The extent to which management structures and processes help or hinder the implementation of the marketing plan is considered in subsequent sections of this chapter. In this section, general issues about management control over the implementation of the marketing plan are considered.

Management control is the process by which managers influence other members of the organization to implement the organization's strategies. Effective control systems demand timely, accurate and relevant information about an organization's operations and environment. Sources of information used for control purposes were discussed in Chapter 6. It was noted there that control systems require three underlying components to be in place:

- The setting of targets or standards of expected performance.
- The measurement and evaluation of actual performance.
- Taking corrective action where necessary.

Conflict can arise in the process of setting targets where trade-offs are necessary between short-term and long-term targets. Very often, in order to improve short-term goal attainment, control action may be taken at the expense of long-term targets. Similarly, controls in respect of long-term objectives might call for short-term sacrifices. Very often managers are under pressure to achieve good short-term results, on the basis of which they may gain promotion. This can continue up the management hierarchy, with managers being rewarded for meeting short-term targets, even if these may damage long-term organizational prospects in the process.

Many control systems fail because employees within an organization have been given inappropriate or unrealistic targets. Even where targets are set, and appropriate data is collected, control systems may still fail because of a failure by management to act on the information available. Control information should identify variances from target and should be able to indicate whether the variance is within or beyond the control of the person responsible for meeting the target. If it is beyond their control, the issue should become one of revising the target so that it becomes once more achievable. If the variance is the result of factors which are subject to a manager's control, a number of measures can be taken to try to revise their behaviour:

- Bureaucratic controls can be used where instructions are sent to subordinates, failing which disciplinary action is taken.
- Incentive schemes can be used as a control mechanism. Incentives are often linked directly to performance – performance-related pay and sales commission for example.
- The allocation of resources (including personnel) offers an important form of organizational control as this has the effect of facilitating some actions and inhibiting others (for example a branch manager of a bank which has missed its targets may be denied an increase in staff levels).
- Informal controls can often be exercised by an employees' peer group in an attempt to bring about conformity.

## 14.13 Managing the marketing function

Developing marketing plans is one thing – actually implementing them can be quite a different challenge. In businesses generally, there have been too many cases of marketing planners developing a marketing plan for which the operational implications have not been fully thought through and which therefore fails to deliver value to customers and profits to the company. In the services sector, where production takes place in front of customers, the problem of integrating marketing planning with operations management and human resource management issues can be particularly acute.

The following sections begin by reviewing the range of possibilities for organizing marketing departments within services organizations. The activities of the marketing department will then be considered in the context of the other functional departments of an organization, and how these can work together better in order to improve profitable service delivery.

## 14.14 Organizing the marketing department

Should a service organization actually have a marketing department? The idea is becoming increasingly popular that the existence of a marketing department in an organization may in fact be a barrier to the development of a true customer-centred marketing orientation. By placing all marketing activity in a marketing department, non-marketing staff may consider themselves to be absolved of responsibility for the development of customer relationships. In service industries where production personnel are in frequent contact with the consumers of their service, a narrow definition of marketing responsibility can be potentially very harmful. On the other hand, a marketing department is usually required in order to coordinate and implement those functions which cannot sensibly be delegated to operational personnel – advertising, sales management and pricing decisions for example. The importance that a marketing department assumes within any organization is a reflection on the nature of its operating environment. An organization operating in a fiercely competitive environment would typically attach great importance to its marketing department as a means of producing a focused marketing mix strategy by which it can gain competitive advantage over its rivals. By contrast, an organization operating in a relatively stable environment is more likely to allow strategic decisions to be taken by personnel who are not marketing strategists – for example pricing decisions may be taken by accountants with less need to understand the marketing implications of price decisions.

Responsibilities given to marketing departments within service organizations vary from one organization to another, reflecting the competitive nature of their business environments and also their traditions and organizational inertia. Within marketing departments, four basic approaches to allocating these responsibilities are identified here, although in practice, most marketing departments show more than one approach. The four approaches allocate marketing responsibilities by:

- Functions performed.
- Geographical area covered.
- Products or groups of products managed.
- Market segments managed.

**Organization based on functional responsibilities**  A traditional and common basis of organizing a marketing department is to divide responsibilities into identifiable marketing functions. Typically, these functions may be advertising, sales, research and development, marketing research, customer services, etc. The precise division of the functional responsibilities will depend upon the nature of an organization. Buying and merchandising are likely to be an important feature in a retailing organization, while research and development will be important for technology-based services such as telecommunications.

The main advantage of a functional organization lies in its administrative simplicity. Against this, there can be a tendency for policy responsibility on specific services or markets to become lost between numerous functional specialists. There is also the possibility of destructive rivalry between functional specialists for their share of marketing budgets – for example rivalry between an advertising manager and a sales manager for a larger share of the promotional budget.

**Organization based on geographical responsibilities**  Organizations providing a service nationwide frequently organize many marketing functions on a geographical basis. This particularly applies to the sales function, although it could also include geographically designated responsibilities for service development (e.g. opening new outlets) and some local responsibility for promotion. For service organizations operating at an international level, there is usually some geographical basis to organization in the manner in which marketing activities are organized in individual national markets.

**Management by product type**  Multi-output organizations frequently appoint a product manager to manage a particular service or group of services. This form of organization does not replace the functional one, but provides an additional layer of management which co-ordinates the functions' activities. The product manager's role includes a number of key tasks:

- Developing a long-range and competitive strategy for a product or group of products.
- Preparing a budgeted annual plan.
- Working with internal and external functional specialists to develop and implement marketing programmes, for example in relation to advertising and sales promotion.
- Monitoring the product's performance and changes occurring in its business environment.
- Identifying new opportunities and initiating product improvements to meet changing market needs.

A product management organization structure offers a number of advantages for service providers:

- The company's service offer benefits from an integrated cost-effective approach to planning. This particularly benefits minor products which might otherwise be neglected.
- The product manager can in theory react more quickly to changes in the product's marketing environment than would be the case if no one had specific responsibility for the product. Within a bank, a mortgage manager is able to devote a lot of time and expertise to monitoring trends in the mortgage market and can become a focal point for initiating and seeing through change when this is required because of environmental change.
- Control within this type of organization can be exercised by linking divisional managers' salaries to performance.

Against this, product management structures are associated with a number of problems.

- The most serious problem occurs in the common situation where a product manager is given a lot of responsibility for ensuring that objectives are met but relatively little control over resource inputs which they have at their disposal. Product managers typically must rely on persuasion to get the co-operation of advertising, sales and other functional specialist departments. Sometimes this can result in conflict, for example where a product manager seeks to position a service in one direction, while the advertising manager seeks to position it in another in order to meet broader promotional objectives.
- Confusion can arise in the minds of staff within an organization as to whom they are accountable to for their day-to-day actions. Staff involved in selling insurance policies in a branch bank may become confused at possibly conflicting messages from an operations manager and a product marketing manager.
- Product marketing management structures can lead to larger numbers of people being employed, resulting in a higher cost structure which may put the organization at a competitive disadvantage in price-sensitive markets.
- Research has suggested that the existence of the optimal product management form is rare and that it is typically associated with an unwillingness of senior management to delegate authority to product managers. Furthermore, research in the service industries (for example Ingham, 1991) suggests that the

interdependencies within many service industries makes product management structures difficult to implement and control. Research by Ingham into the UK insurance industry found a high level of intra-organization transactions and a lack of profit centre status enjoyed by divisions, associated with inappropriate internal transfer pricing and poor incentive and control systems. While the product management form may be appropriate for a diversified conglomerate, it was shown to be inappropriate for insurance businesses where many functions are closely interdependent, allowing very little freedom of action for individual product managers. Within the insurance industry, a hybrid structure was observed which reflected the need for some degree of centralization.

The conventional wisdom is that product managers in service firms should work together to put their customers' needs above internal management demarcations. But could there sometimes be an ethical case against too much sharing of information by product managers?

Consider the case of merchant banks which offer investment management and capital raising services. In a proposed takeover bid, it is often necessary for those involved in raising the capital required by a client to work very discreetly for fear of prematurely raising the share price of the target company. If this information was available to those staff working in investment management, it would give them an unfair advantage over the market generally, allowing them to build up a share-holding in the target company ahead of the announcement of a takeover bid. Merchant banks have sought to build 'Chinese walls' around their operations where this risk is present and the adoption of a functional marketing management structure allows greater effective separation of functions. Numerous other service industries can be identified where similar ethical problems can be lessened by the adoption of a product management structure – accountants selling both auditing services and management consultancy services to a company may be tempted to gain business in the latter area at the expense of integrity in the former. How do large diversified services firms convince their customers that information given in confidence to one section of the organization will not be used against them in another section?

**Market management organization** Many organizations provide services to a diverse range of customers who have widely varying needs. As an example, a cross-channel ferry operator provides a basically similar service of transport for private car drivers, coach operators and freight operators, among others. However, the specific needs of each group of users vary significantly. A coach operator is likely to attach different importance to a road haulier to service attributes such as flexibility, ease of reservations, the type of accommodation provided, etc. In such situations, market managers can be appointed to oversee the development of particular markets, in much the same way as a product manager oversees particular products. Instead of being given specific financial targets for their products, market managers are usually given growth or market share targets. The main advantage of this form of organization is that it allows marketing activity to be focused on meeting the needs of

**Figure 14.8**

Alternative forms of
marketing department
organization structure
showing typical
applications to a ferry
operator

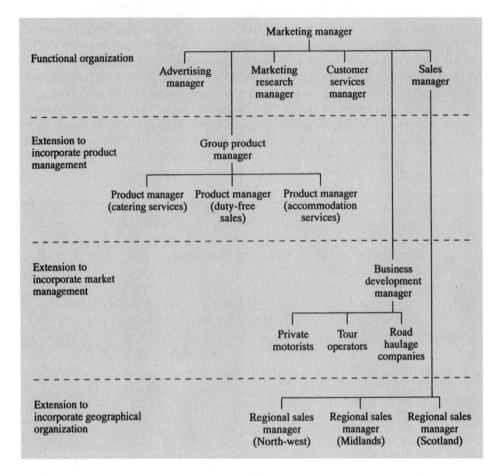

distinct and identified groups of customers – something which should be at the heart
of all truly marketing-oriented organization. It is also likely that new innovative
services are more likely to emerge within this structure than where an organization's
response is confined within traditional product management boundaries – for
example a market manager specifically responsible for developing coach tour
traffic might be in an advantageous position to develop innovative group package
holidays aimed at coach operators. Market management structures are also arguably
more conducive to the important task of developing relationships with customers,
especially for business to business services. Where an organization has a number of
very important customers, it is common to find the appointment of key account
managers to handle relationships with those clients in order to exploit marketing
opportunities which are of mutual benefit to both.

Many of the disadvantages of the product management organization are also
shared by market-based structures. There can again be a conflict between responsibility and authority and this form of structure can also become expensive to operate.

The differences in organizational structures described above, and their typical application to a car ferry operator are shown in Figure 14.8. The great diversity of

organizational structures highlights the fact that there is not one unique structure which is appropriate to all firms, even within the same service sector. Overall, the organization of a marketing department must allow for a flexible and adaptable response to customers' needs within a changing environment, while aiming to reduce the level of confusion, ambiguity and cost inherent in some structures.

## 14.15 The relationship between marketing and other organizational functions

In a truly marketing-oriented service organization, marketing responsibilities cannot be confined to something called a marketing department. In the words of Drucker (1973):

> Marketing is so basic that it cannot be considered to be a separate function. It is the whole business seen from the point of view of its final result, that is, from the customer's point of view.

In marketing-oriented organizations, the customer is at the centre of all of the organization's activities. The customer is not simply the concern of the marketing department, but also all of the production and administrative personnel whose actions may directly or indirectly impinge upon the customers' enjoyment of the service. In a typical service organization, the activities of a number of functional departments impinge on the service outcome received by customers:

- Personnel plans can have a crucial bearing on marketing plans. The selection, training motivation and control of staff cannot be considered in isolation from marketing objectives and strategies. Possible conflict between the personnel and marketing functions may arise where, for example, marketing demands highly trained and motivated front-line staff, but the personnel function pursues a policy which places cost reduction above all else.
- Production managers may have a different outlook compared to marketing managers. A marketing manager may seek to respond as closely as possible to customers' needs, only to find opposition from production managers who argue that a service of the required standard cannot be achieved. A marketing manager of a railway operating company may seek to segment markets with fares tailored to meet the needs of small groups of customers, only to encounter hostility from operations managers who are responsible for actually issuing and checking travel tickets on a day-to-day basis and who may have misgivings about the confusion which finely segmented fares might cause.
- The actions of finance managers frequently have direct or indirect impact on marketing plans. Ultimately, finance managers assume responsibility for the allocation of funds which are needed to implement a marketing plan. At a more operational level, finance managers' actions in respect of the level of credit offered to customers, or towards stockholdings where these are an important element of the service offering can also significantly affect the quality of service and the volume of customers which the organization is able to serve.

Marketing requires all of these departments to 'think customer' and to work together to satisfy customer needs and expectations. There is argument as to what authority the traditional marketing department should have in bringing about this customer orientation. In a truly mature marketing-oriented service company, marketing is an implicit part of everybody's job. In such a scenario, marketing becomes responsible for a narrow range of specialist functions such as advertising and marketing research. Responsibility for the relationship between the organization and its customers is spread more diffusely throughout the organization. Gummesson (1999) uses the term 'part-time marketer' to describe staff working in service organizations who may not have any direct line-management responsibility for marketing, but whose activities may indirectly impinge on the quality of service received by customers.

It can be argued that the introduction of a traditional marketing department – as described above – to a service organization can bring problems as well as benefits. In a survey of 219 executives representing public and private sector services organizations in Sweden, Gronroos (1982) tested the idea that a separate marketing department may widen the gap between marketing and operations staff. This idea was put to a sample drawn from marketing as well as other functional positions using a Likert-type scale with five points ranging from agreeing strongly to disagreeing strongly. The results indicated that respondents in a wide range of service organizations considered there to be dangers in the creation of a marketing department – an average of 66% agreed with the notion, with higher than average agreement being found among non-marketing executives, and those working in the hotel, restaurant, professional services and insurance sectors.

The problem of how to bring people together in an organization to act collectively, while also being able to place responsibility on an individual is one which continues to generate considerable discussion. Two recent developments in this debate are noted here: matrix organization structures and the idea of business process reengineering.

**Matrix approach to management**  Organizations which produce many different products for many different markets may experience difficulties if they adopt a purely product- or market-based structure. If a product management structure is adopted, product managers would require detailed knowledge of very diverse markets. Likewise, in a market management structure, market managers would require detailed knowledge of possibly very diverse product ranges. The essence of a matrix type of organization is to allow individuals to concentrate on a functional, product or market specialization and to bring them together in taskforce teams to solve problems taking an organizational view rather than their own narrow specialist view. Product managers can concentrate on excellence in production, while market managers focus on meeting consumer needs without any preference for a particular product (see Figure 14.9). An example of matrix structures can be found in many vehicle distributors where market managers can be appointed to identify and formulate a market strategy in respect of the distinct needs of private customers and contract hire customers among others, as well as being appointed to manage key customers. Market managers work alongside product managers who can develop specialized activities such as servicing, bodywork repairs and vehicle hire which are made available to final customers through the market managers.

The most important advantages of matrix structures are that they can allow

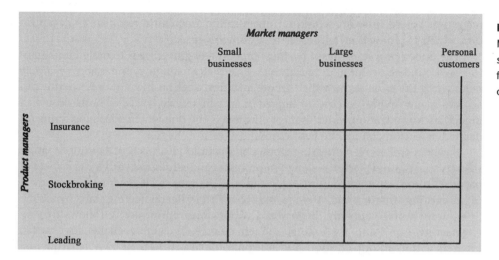

**Figure 14.9**
Matrix organization
structure applied to a
financial services
organization

organizations to respond rapidly to environmental change. Short-term project teams can be assembled and disbanded at short notice to meet changed needs. Project teams can bring together a wide variety of disciplines and can be used to evaluate new services before full-scale development is undertaken. A bank exploring the possibility of developing a banking system linked to personal customers' home computers might establish a team drawn from staff involved in marketing to personal customers and staff responsible for technology-based research and development. The former may include market researchers and the latter computer development engineers.

The flexibility of matrix structures can be increased by bringing temporary workers into the structure on a contract basis as and when needed. During the 1990s, there was a trend for many services organizations to lay off significant numbers of workers – including management – and to buy these back when needed. As well as cutting fixed costs, such 'modular' organizations have the potential to respond very rapidly to environmental change.

Where matrix structures exist, great motivation can be present in effectively managed teams. Against this, matrix-type structures can be associated with problems. Most serious is the confused lines of authority which may result. Staff may not be clear about which superior he or she is responsible to for a particular aspect of their duties, resulting in possible stress and demotivation. Where a matrix structure is introduced into an organization with a history and culture of functional specialization, it can be very difficult to implement effectively. Staff may be reluctant to act outside a role which they have traditionally defined narrowly and guarded jealously. Finally, matrix structures invariably result in more managers being employed within an organization. At best, this can result in a costly addition to the salary bill. At worst, the existence of additional managers can also slow down decision-making processes where the managers show a reluctance to act outside a narrow functional role.

**Business process reengineering** Most management change within organizations occurs incrementally. The result of this is often a compromised organization structure which is unduly influenced by historic factors which are of no continuing relevance. Vested interests within an organization frequently result in an organization which is production- rather than customer-focused.

The underlying principle of business process reengineering is to design an organization around key value adding activities. Essentially, reengineering is about *radically* redesigning the *processes* by which an organization does business in order that it can achieve major savings in cost, or improvements in service levels, or both. Seen as a model, the organization which is most effective is the one which adds most value (as defined by customers) for the least cost.

Business process reengineering focuses on operational aspects of a business, rather than its strategy and starts the design of processes and structures with a clean sheet of paper. This is in contrast to most organizational change which starts with an analysis of the existing structure and attempts to tinker with it. Reengineering starts by asking: 'If we were a new company, how would we organize ourselves?' It follows that reengineering can stand for a total sudden change, inevitably challenging vested interests within an organization that are comfortable within their own departmental boundary.

To be effective, reengineering needs to be led by strong individuals who have authority to oversee implementation from beginning to end. They will need a lot of clout because fear, resistance and cynicism will inevitably slow the task down. At first sight though, this approach to reorganization would appear to be in conflict with the principles of Total Quality Management and other participative schemes that stress employee involvement in change. In fact, reengineering only works effectively if it takes place in an environment of continuous improvement based on TQM principles. Successful companies therefore seek to involve their employees in the detail of implementation, even if the radical nature of the agenda is not negotiable.

The activities of the American telecommunications company GTE provide a model for business process reengineering which have been copied by many companies within the sector throughout Europe. The starting point was the company's belief that its customers wanted one central point of contact who could be responsible for seeing an enquiry through, whether the enquiry was to fix a faulty phone, question a bill, sign up for additional services or any combination of services offered by the company. The company wanted to avoid the all too common situation where customers were bounced from one office to another, and sometimes disappeared in cracks which were on the boundary between departmental responsibilities.

An early change involved examining the work of repair clerks, who had traditionally taken down information from a customer, filled out a report card and sent it on to other employees who would check out the problem and fix it. GTE wanted the whole process to happen while the customer was still on the line – something that was currently happening just once for every 200 calls. The first step in reengineering was to move testing and switching equipment to the desks of the repair clerks who were renamed 'front-end technicians'. The aim was to increase the proportion of calls that the clerks could pass on without further referral.

The second step was to link the repair service with sales and billing. To do this,

GTE gave its telephone operators new computer software linked to databases that allowed them to handle almost any problem a customer may have.

The results of this reengineering? After two years, the company claimed to have raised its customer satisfaction levels and improved productivity by 20–30%, although the costs in terms of staff training and redundancies were high. Sceptics of business process reengineering were more doubtful. Hadn't telecommunications firms been doing this kind of internal change for a long time, and wasn't the current change merely a result of new technology and increasingly competitive markets?

## 14.16 Improving organizational effectiveness for marketing

Numerous studies have sought to identify those factors within organizations which result in an organization being able to address its markets most effectively. The McKinsey 7S framework developed by Peters and Waterman (1982) identified seven essential elements for a successful business, based on a study of the most successful American companies. The elements are broken down into the hardware (Strategy, Structure and Systems) and the software (Skills, Staff, Styles and Shared Values). Formalized strategies, structures and systems on their own were not considered to be sufficient to bring about success – these could only be operationalized with appropriate intangible 'software'.

At a strategic level, a number of methods can be used to develop a more responsive marketing orientation within an organization:

- The appointment of senior management who have a good understanding of the philosophies and practices of marketing.
- The introduction of in-house educational programmes which aim to train non-marketing employees to empathize with customers' expectations.
- The introduction of outside consultants who can apply their previous experience of introducing a marketing culture to an organization from an impartial perspective.
- A commonly used method of making management think in marketing terms is to install a formal market-oriented planning system. This can have the effect of forcing managers to work through a list of market-related headings, such as an analysis of the competitive environment and identification of market opportunities when developing their annual plans.

Key to the change from a production-oriented to a marketing-oriented organization is the development of a customer-focused culture. Organizational culture can be defined as 'some underlying structure of meaning that persists over time, constraining people's perception, interpretation and behaviour' (Jelinek, Smirich and Hirsch, 1983). Within many parts of the service sector, it has proved difficult to change cultural attitudes when the nature of an organization's operating environment has significantly changed, rendering the established culture a liability in terms of strategic marketing management. As an example, the cultural values of UK clearing banks have for a long time continued to be dominated by prudence and caution when in some product areas, such as insurance sales, a more aggressive approach to marketing management is called for.

As service organizations develop, it is essential that the dominant culture adapts. While a small business may quite successfully embrace a centralized power culture, continued growth may cause this culture to become a liability. Similarly, the privatization of public utilities calls for a transformation from a bureaucratic role culture to a task-oriented culture (see Handy, 1989).

There has been debate on the relationship between marketing strategy and the organizational structure within which such strategy is developed and implemented. The traditional view is that structures adapt to fit the chosen strategy, although more recent thought has focused on the idea that strategy is very much dependent upon the structure adopted by an organization. An approach suggested by Giles (1988) is a 'structured iterative marketing planning process' which works by creating a cross-functional team of managers for the purpose of designing a marketing plan for a market or market segment selected by top management for attention. The managers' initial view of their target market is challenged and refined through a focused marketing audit which requires continual iteration, forcing participants to go backwards and forwards through the process. The resulting marketing plan is likely to represent a high degree of commitment and ownership by those involved in creating it. The attraction of this type of approach is that it challenges managers to design better ways of addressing their markets by allowing things to be said which in a conventional planning process may be politically unacceptable. The marketing problem defines the agenda, rather than having it determined by the structure and political ideology of the organization. The process is designed to bring about marketing-led strategic change within the organization (Piercy, 1998).

## 14.17 Introducing strategic marketing management within the public sector

Marketing management is increasingly being introduced to the public sector. However, attempts to introduce marketing management structures must recognize the great diversity of public sector marketing tasks. While some parts of the public sector function in competitive markets just like any private sector organization, others provide very complex services which by their nature can only be distributed by centrally planned allocation. To assess the appropriateness of marketing management structures within the public sector, public services can be classified using a framework analysing two aspects of the service in question:

1   The complexity of the service which is provided.
2   The nature of the environment in which the service is provided.

Public services can be described as complex where they involve diverse interdepartmental relationships in production. The operation of a youth service may involve considerable liaison between the education, social services, police and recreation sections of local authorities. At the other end of the scale, services can be described as simple where a relatively narrow range of functional specialists are

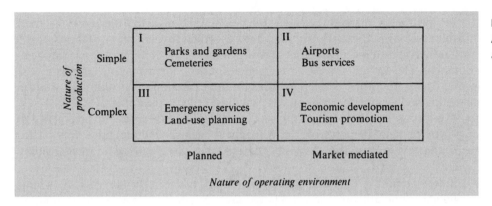

**Figure 14.10**
A classification of local
authority services

involved in their production. The operation of a local authority parks department, for example, is less likely to involve much interaction with specialists from other departments.

The second dimension of this analysis concerns the nature of the operating environment of a service. This can range from a totally planned environment where the existence of external benefits and costs (and often legislation) make market-mediated exchanges very difficult to achieve (for example land-use planning and emergency services), to a market-mediated environment which is for practical purposes indistinguishable from that facing a private sector company. These two scales are shown in Figure 14.10, where four quadrants are identified with reference to local authority services.

The most straightforward task for marketing management is found in quadrant 2 (a simple service in a market-mediated environment), where marketing has gained a ready acceptance. Local authority bus services and airports can easily be isolated into separate operating units and can develop their own marketing culture to respond to the challenges of their environment. The task of marketing management is essentially similar to that of a private sector organization

In Quadrant 3 (a complex service in a planned environment) marketing philosophies can have little meaning where the presence of external costs and benefits require significant centralized methods of distributing costs and benefits. Examples include emergency services and land-use planning. Here, strategic decisions are based on social/political criteria and any attempt to introduce marketing management can only allow for some relatively superficial marketing practices (such as client care programmes).

In quadrant 1 (simple services in a planned environment), services have often been simplified further with a distinction made between those parts of the service which yield too many external costs and benefits to allow market mediated distribution and those parts where market forces represent a desirable distribution mechanism. As an example, some activities of a museum – such as assessing the scholarly significance of an object – cannot sensibly be left to market forces, whereas other activities (e.g. refreshment facilities) are capable of competing with other private and public sector facilities. In this quadrant, there is frequently ambiguity over the expectations of marketing management – for example the refreshment manager's profit objectives may be constrained by the wider needs of the museum service.

In quadrant 4 marketing management within local authorities faces its most difficult challenge. These are complex services which involve many sections of the local authority in their production, and which are subject to a market-mediated environment. The authority must develop an authority-wide marketing culture, or risk losing clients to other competing organizations. Examples include the tourism marketing and economic development functions of local authorities.

A growing feature of the public sector during the 1990s was the emergence of single service, 'arm's length' agencies which have been given duties previously carried out within government itself. A number of reasons can be identified for their creation:

- A desire to bridge the cultural gap which exists between the bureaucracy of large public sector structures and the potential dynamism of small semi-autonomous quasi-private sector organizations.
- With many private and public sector organizations responsible for marketing overlapping services, it may be possible to reduce duplication by pooling these efforts in a semi-autonomous organization.
- By creating a semi-autonomous body at arm's length, it is sometimes possible for the body to gain access to additional funds from the private sector (although in many cases government continues to set an external financing limit).

While these new single service agencies may be more dynamic in the manner in which they address their users, Barnes and Campbell (1988) contrasted the benefits of escape from a bureaucratic planning culture against the potential problems associated with a market-based culture. Their study of quasi-autonomous Economic Development Companies showed that the creation of these organizations had resulted in them losing sight of their original values. They found that many had become more conservative by dismissing financially marginal but socially valuable projects.

**Case Study**

## Marketing inward tourism – an organizational challenge for local authorities

Tourism is rapidly developing as one of the world's biggest service industries, and was expected to account for 11.5% of global gross domestic product by the year 2000 (WTTC, 1996). Because of its vital role in local economic regeneration, many local authorities in the UK have developed strategies to attract tourists to their areas. But how do local authorities manage the marketing of their areas as tourism destinations, when they have very limited promotional budgets at their disposal, and they are dependent on the activities of firms in the industry for success? Furthermore, local authorities are not noted for their culture of entrepreneurship, something which was becoming vital with the increasingly competitive market for tourists' spending.

The tourism destination product being marketed is a combination of elements from both the private and public sectors. The private sector is responsible for tourist attractions operating to narrow commercial criteria, while the public sector has responsibility for infrastructure and planning policies which affect tourism. In view of the external benefits inherent in area tourism promotion, local authorities play a large role in promoting the benefits of their areas.

Tourism marketing management poses a number of problems for local authorities. Many of the facilities which impinge on tourists' enjoyment of an area – such as car parking, cleanliness, planning and conservation policies – have traditionally operated in a bureaucratic planning culture rather than a marketing culture. In marketing an area, local authorities are constrained by a bureaucratic culture and political pressure to meet the needs of its own residents as well as those of potential visitors. But against this, the visitors the local authority is seeking to attract are becoming increasingly selective in the face of competition from many areas – in short, local authorities have had to become very customer-centred in their attempts to attract visitors.

In an effort to combine the need for centrally administered marketing of an area with the dynamism of the private sector, local collaborative marketing ventures have become common in this field. Various forms of public–private sector partnerships have emerged, such as visitor and convention bureaux in which public and private sector organizations own shares in a specially created limited company.

In many areas of England, local tourism development companies have been created as an initiative of the English Tourist Board and typically involve partnerships between district and county councils, urban development corporations, local land owners, hotel owners and operators of tourism attractions. Each partner would contribute funds to support items of expenditure which in their own right might not yield a return, but result in more tourist spending across the area as a whole. The creation of an arm's-length tourism development company provides an organizational structure which is separately accountable and is attractive to private sector partners.

The creation of collaborative tourism marketing associations has brought the dynamism of the private sector to bear on strategic marketing decisions and action programmes. This marketing management culture has been found to filter back to the local authority in the way in which it provides public sector facilities to satisfy tourists' needs. Examples of successful collaboration include the development of conference centres which bring together private sector conference and hotel developers, transport operators and local authorities. The latter can achieve diverse objectives (such as creating employment or eliminating eyesores) more effectively by delivering its services – such as signposting, car park provision and land-use planning – within the framework of a marketing strategy developed jointly with the private sector. But while there are many acknowledged successes (such as the Greater Glasgow Tourist Board and Convention Bureau), others have failed to develop any momentum, often through ambiguity over members' roles or the lack of an energetic driving force. Paradoxically, there is a suggestion that the effectiveness of collaborative marketing in less popular tourism destinations is more effective than in tourism 'hotspots', probably indicating the danger of complacency.

## Case study review questions

1   Contrast the objectives of public and private sector organizations that are involved in tourism.

2   Summarize the benefits of collaboration between public and private sector organizations in the tourism sector.

3   Identify the main problems of collective marketing of a tourism destination, compared to the marketing of an individual hotel.

## Chapter summary and linkages to other chapters

This chapter has taken a broad and strategic approach to the management of services organizations. As services markets become increasingly competitive, strategic marketing management has become more important. It has been emphasized that in the services sector where production processes take place in the presence of customers, marketing management cannot be separated from operations management and human resource management. Implementing marketing plans gives similar rise to concerns about artificial boundaries between the main functions of a business. Numerous approaches to improving the effectiveness of a service firm's marketing implementation have been discussed and the importance stressed of focusing around key processes which create customer value. Within the public sector, the constraints on implementing a marketing orientation tend to be greater, but change is evident in the way that many public services have been restructured as profit centres.

This chapter brings together many aspects of previous chapters. Indeed, it is the task of management to bring these aspects together in a coherent and imaginative way, better than is achieved by competitors. So **Chapter 2** discussed service products, but the range of services offered needs to be constantly monitored and updated by management. The quality of service encounters (**Chapters 3 and 8**) can be greatly influenced by the quality of high level management interaction and the leadership given to employees. Relationship marketing programmes (**Chapter 5**) can fail badly where management within a company has not sorted out its internal relationships, or where employment practices are not conducive to relationship development (**Chapter 12**). The distribution, pricing and promotion of services (**Chapters 9, 10 and 11**) all need to be managed in order to give a company a sustainable competitive position (**Chapter 7**). Information is becoming increasingly important to the task of managing most organizations (**Chapter 6**). Management of any service organization faces major challenges when it seeks to expand overseas (**Chapter 15**). Finally, this chapter builds on the internal marketing issues discussed in **Chapter 12**. That chapter emphasized the need for top management commitment to the principles of internal marketing.

## www linkages/URLs

Chartered Institute of Marketing:
**http://www.cim.co.uk/**

British Institute of Management:
**http://www.inst-mgt.org.uk**

Institute of Management and Administration (US source of business and management information):
**http://www.ioma.com/**

Inc. magazine Small Business Resource Index:
**http://www.inc.com/idx/idx_t_Sb.html**

Strategy & Business Articles, book reviews and special features for business leaders (sponsored by Booz Allen and Hamilton:
**http://www.strategy-business.com/**

Business information sources on the net:
**http://www.atlantic.net/~bdarl/business.html**

## Key terms

Portfolio management  426

## Chapter review questions

1   Giving examples, in what ways does the setting of marketing objectives differ between the private and public services sectors?
2   Examine the strategic alternatives open to a restaurant chain seeking to expand and suggest a framework within which strategic alternatives may be evaluated.
3   What is the value of contingency planning within the service sector? Identify one sector where the production of contingency plans is likely to be important, and the factors which need to be taken into account.
4   What factors should be taken into consideration by a travel agency in seeking to position its chain of outlets?

**5** Do you agree with the notion that a marketing department can actually be a barrier to the successful development of a marketing orientation within services organizations? Give examples.

**6** What are the main differences in implementing a market-oriented management structure within the public as opposed to the private service sector?

## Selected further reading

*For a discussion of the general principles of marketing management, the following references provide a useful introduction:*

Baker, M. J. (1999) *Marketing Strategy and Management*, 3rd edition, Macmillan, Basingstoke

Fifield, P. (1998) *Marketing Strategy*, 2nd edition, Butterworth-Heinemann, Oxford

Gilligan, C. and Wilson, R. (1997) *Strategic Marketing Management*, 2nd edition, Butterworth-Heinemann, Oxford

Kotler, P. (1999) *Marketing Management: Analysis, Planning, Implementation and Control*, 10th edition, 1999, Prentice-Hall, New York

Piercy, N. (1998) *Market-led Strategic Change*, 2nd edition, Butterworth-Heinemann, Oxford

*The following references discuss how the distinctive characteristics of services call for adaptations of the general principles of marketing strategy:*

Gronroos, C. (1984) *Strategic Management and Marketing in the Service Sector*, Chartwell-Bratt, Bromley

Thomas, D. R. E. (1978) 'Strategy is Different in Service Businesses', *Harvard Business Review*, July–August, pp 158–65

*The ways in which marketing strategy can give a firm a competitive advantage are discussed in the following three articles:*

Peters, T. J. and R. H. Waterman (1982) *In Search of Excellence: Lessons from America's Best Run Companies*, Harper & Row, New York

*(A classic article which emphasized the importance of excellence in service among America's leading companies.)*

Gronroos, C. (1994) 'From Scientific Management to Service Management: A Management Perspective for the Age of Service Competition', *Journal of Service Industry Management*, Vol. 5, No. 1, pp 5–20

*(Discusses how the concept of service management emerged, what it is and what contributions it offers to management research and practice. Contains an extensive literature review.)*

Bharadwaj, S. G., P. Rajan and J. Fahy (1993) 'Sustainable Competitive Advantage in Service Industries: A Conceptual Model and Research Propositions', *Journal of Marketing*, October, Vol. 57, pp 83–99

*(Provides an overview of the concept of sustainable competitive advantage and develops a contingency model of the concept which is relevant to service industries. Explores the moderating effects of services, service industries and firms within an industry on potential sources of sustainable competitive advantage.)*

*The following references offer a general insight into internal organizational structure and its relation to organizational effectiveness:*

Handy, C. (1994) *Understanding Organizations*, 4th edition, Penguin, London

Hogg, G., S. Carter and A. Dunne (1998) 'Investing in People: Internal Marketing and Corporate Culture', *Journal of Marketing Management*, Vol. 14, pp 879–95

Simkin, L. (1996) 'Addressing Organisational Prerequisites in Marketing Planning Programmes, *Marketing Intelligence and Planning*, Vol. 14, No. 5, pp 39–47

*For more discussion on the appropriateness of marketing management processes and structures for the services sector, the following references are useful:*

Bowen, D. E. and B. Schneider (1988) 'Services Marketing Management: Implications for Organisational Behaviour', *Research in Organisational Behaviour*, Vol. 10, pp 43–80

Ennew, C., P. Wong and M. Wright (1992) 'Organisational Structures and the Boundaries of the Firm: Acquisitions and Divestments in Financial Services', *The Services Industries Journal*, Vol. 14, No. 4, pp 478–97

Gummesson, E. (1990) 'Organizing for Marketing and Marketing Organizations', in C. A. Congram and M. L. Friedman (eds), *Handbook of Services Marketing*, AMACON, New York

# 15

# International marketing of services

**Learning objectives**

Markets for services are becoming increasingly global. When firms see their domestic markets reaching saturation, they often try to recreate their domestic success in overseas markets. The first aim of this chapter is to examine the nature of international trade in services and reasons for its development. The concept of exporting intangible and inseparable services is quite different to that involving manufactured goods and the problems and opportunities which this gives rise to are discussed. The initial stages of a firm's overseas expansion involve assessing the attractiveness of overseas opportunities and methods of market evaluation are discussed. From this, marketing strategies are developed which should be sympathetic to local market needs. An important element of an overseas market development plan is the identification of market entry strategies, often involving joint venture partners.

## 15.1 Introduction

At some point, many services organizations recognize that their growth can only continue if they exploit overseas markets. However, entering overseas markets can be an extremely risky business for services companies as evidenced by examples of recent failures where companies failed to forsee all of the problems involved:

- British Airways failed in its attempts to enter the North American market through its investment in the ailing airline USAir. BA had difficulties in overcoming trade union objections to changes in working practices among other things, which led the company to eventually pull out of its involvement with USAir.
- The British retailer Laura Ashley failed to adapt its US stores to meet local conditions and in 1999 effectively abandoned the investment it had made in the US market.
- Even the fast-food retailer McDonald's initially failed to make profits when it entered the UK market in the 1970s, and had to rapidly adjust its service offer in order to achieve viability.

Nevertheless, a company which has successfully developed its marketing strategy should be well placed to extend this development into overseas markets. There are many examples of companies who have successfully developed overseas markets, including the following:

- The retailer Tesco successfully reduced its dependence on the saturated UK grocery market by developing outlets in Ireland, the Far East and eastern Europe.
- The bus and rail operator Stagecoach has achieved success in its domestic UK market. However, much of its activities at home are regulated by government agencies, and it has successfully diversified by acquiring bus operators in Africa.
- The Irish airline Ryanair started life with a route network which focused on Ireland. With successful expansion of its route network, most of its services now do not call at its Irish base.

Many of the fundamental principles of marketing management which have been applied to a firm's domestic market will be of relevance in an international setting. The processes of identifying market opportunities, selecting strategies, implementing those strategies and monitoring performance involve fundamentally similar principles as those which apply within the domestic market. One study found that foreign operations in service firms are driven by a similar set of variables to those of manufacturing companies, but that the intensity and direction of some key relationships require modification and adaptation (Shoham and Kropp, 1998). The major challenge to services companies seeking to expand overseas lies in sensitively adapting marketing strategies which have worked at home to the needs of overseas markets whose environments may be totally different to anything previously experienced.

The purpose of this chapter is to identify the main differences facing the task of marketing management when services are provided in an international rather than a purely domestic environment. Some of the key differences between trade in goods and trade in services are emphasized, in particular the diverse nature of buyer–seller interaction which causes international trade in services to take a number of forms.

## 15.2 The importance of international trade in services

International trade in services is becoming increasingly important, representing not only opportunities for domestic service producers to earn revenue from overseas, but also a threat to domestic producers from overseas competition. Some indication of the importance of international trade in services for Britain can be seen in the trade statistics. In 1997, the UK earned £18.8 billion from 'exporting' services overseas (£173 billion was earned from exporting goods). More importantly, the UK had a small surplus (£8.7 billion) in services, compared with a deficit in goods (£16.1 billion). A closer examination of trade statistics indicates the relative importance of the main service sectors. The most important in terms of overseas sales continues to be financial services, with credits ('exports') exceeding debits ('imports'). Travel-related sectors were the next most significant group recorded by national statistics, although, here, the UK is a now a net importer of services as UK tourists' spending overseas exceeds that of foreigners visiting the UK.

Many national economies have come to rely heavily on foreign currency earnings generated by their services industries. Notable examples include the Bahamas and Malta whose financial services and tourism sector earnings offset the countries' need to import many manufactured goods and agricultural products. Developing countries often find that they need to buy in specialist services in order to develop their economies further (e.g. banking and consulting engineering), but eventually aim to achieve self-sufficiency (or even export earnings) in these sectors. India is a good example of a developing economy which has deliberately sought to reduce its reliance on imported services.

The EU as a whole has in recent years managed a small surplus in its trade in services with non-EU countries. Net earners included banking, air transport, tourism and business services. There is a net deficit in insurance, sea transport and communications.

## 15.3 Defining international trade in services

Conceptual difficulties can occur in attempting to analyse international trade in services. While trade in manufactured goods can be represented by stocks of goods moving in one direction, and payment (in cash or in goods) in the other, the intangible nature of most services makes it difficult to measure a physical flow. Trade statistics, for example, cannot rely on records of goods passing through Customs. Any analysis of international trade in services is complicated by the diverse nature of producer/supplier interaction, stemming from the inseparability of service production/consumption processes.

International trade statistics for services hide the fact that trade can take a number of forms. Sometimes, credits are earned by customers from overseas travelling to an organization's domestic market in order to consume a service (for example an overseas tourist visiting the UK). On other occasions, credits are earned by domestic producers

**Figure 15.1**

Patterns of producer/consumer interaction in overseas trade for services

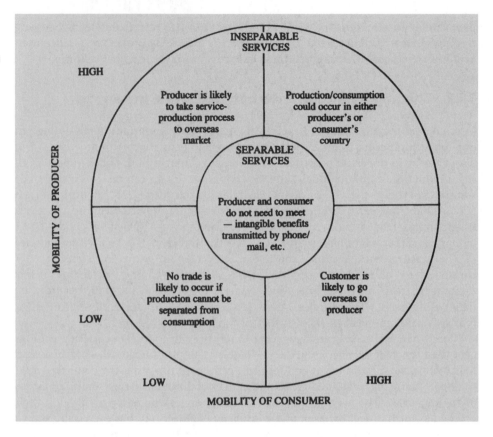

INSEPARABLE SERVICES

HIGH

Producer is likely to take service-production process to overseas market

Production/consumption could occur in either producer's or consumer's country

SEPARABLE SERVICES

Producer and consumer do not need to meet — intangible benefits transmitted by phone/mail, etc.

MOBILITY OF PRODUCER

No trade is likely to occur if production cannot be separated from consumption

Customer is likely to go overseas to producer

LOW

LOW                    HIGH

MOBILITY OF CONSUMER

taking their production processes to customers in overseas markets. A further category of services can be identified which allow production and consumption to be separated – for these services, producers and consumers do not need to meet in order for international trade to occur. The form that international trade takes is dependent on the mobility of both producer and consumer and the separability of the production/consumption process (see Figure 15.1).

Immobility in service production processes occurs where it is either not possible or sensible to produce a service in an overseas market – customers in these markets must travel if they are to receive the service. This is typical of many tourism related services which are based on a unique historic site. In other cases, it is customers who are inflexible, requiring the production process to be taken overseas to wherever customers are located (e.g. building contractors must travel to a building requiring renovation).

Because of the diverse ways in which international trade takes place, estimates of the total value of international trade in services are much more unreliable than for manufactured goods, and frequently subject to subsequent revision.

From the diversity of producer/consumer interaction, three important patterns of trade can be identified:

1   **Production of a service in one country for consumption in another country**   While manufactured goods are commonly traded on this basis, this

can only occur for services where production and consumption can be separated. This has often been achieved using postal and telephone communications. In this way, an insurance policy for a ship can be produced at Lloyds in London but the benefits of the policy relayed to the policyholder at the point of their choice. Similarly, many information services can be traded between countries by modern telecommunications. It can be difficult for official statistics to accurately record both the outward flow of services and the inward flow of money for this type of trade. The development of the Internet has opened up new possibilities for many highly intangible services, such as data analysis and information services, and the subject of global e-commerce is considered later in a separate section of this chapter.

2   **Production of a service by a domestic company in an overseas market for overseas consumption**   Where the problem of inseparability cannot be overcome, a domestic service producer may only be able to access an overseas market by setting up production facilities in that market. Examples of services in this category include catering and cleaning services which must deliver a tangible outcome at a point of the customer's choice. The various methods by which a company can set up overseas service outlets are discussed in more detail later in this chapter. While this type of international trade can be of great importance to services organizations, it only appears in a country's balance of payments in the form of capital movements, remitted profits and trade in the tangible components of a service offer.

3   **Production of a service at home for sale to overseas customers for consumption in the domestic market**   It is often expensive or impossible to take a service production process to overseas customers, therefore customers must travel to consume the service. This can occur for a number of reasons:

- Demand for a highly specialized service may be very thinly dispersed, making it uneconomic to take highly specialized staff and equipment to the market. As an example, it is common for patients to travel long distances to visit specialist doctors in London's Harley Street.
- The laws of an overseas country may make the provision of a service in that market illegal, forcing those seeking the service to travel overseas. Countries which forbid abortion operations often do so to the benefit of abortion clinics in countries such as Britain where a more liberal regime applies.
- Production costs may be lower in an organization's own country, making it attractive for overseas customers to travel in order to obtain a service. As an example, the lower price of labour in many less developed countries makes it attractive for shipowners to send their ships away for major overhaul work to be undertaken.
- A country may possess unique geographical features which form an important element of a service offer, and in order to receive the benefits of related services, customers must travel to that country. This is particularly important in the case of tourism-related industries, where the benefits of services associated with heritage sites or climatic differences cannot be taken to consumers. If American citizens wish to visit the Tower of London, they must travel to London. Similarly, if British holiday makers want to purchase a holiday with guaranteed sunshine, they must travel overseas.

## 15.4 Reasons for international trade in services occurring

However it is measured, international trade in services has been increasing. From the perspective of national economies, a number of reasons can be identified for its increasing importance:

- Services are traded between economies in order to exploit the concept of comparative cost advantage. This holds that an economy will export those goods and services that it is particularly well suited to producing, and import those for which another country has an advantage. Although the concept of comparative cost advantage was developed to explain the benefits to total world wealth resulting from each country exploiting its comparative cost advantages with regard to access to raw materials and energy supplies, it can also have application to the services sector. In this way, a favourable climate or outstanding scenery can give a country an advantage in selling tourism services to overseas customers, a point which has not been lost to tourism operators in the Canary Islands and Switzerland respectively. Another basis for comparative cost advantage can be found in the availability of low-cost or highly trained personnel (cheap labour for the shipping industry and trained computer software experts for computer consultancy respectively). Sometimes the government of a country can itself directly create comparative cost advantages for a service sector, as where it reduces regulations and controls on an industry, allowing that industry to produce services for export at a lower cost than its more regulated competitors (for example many 'offshore' financial services centres impose lower taxation and standards of regulation than their mainstream competitors).
- The removal of many restrictions on international trade in services (such as the creation of the Single European Market) has allowed countries to exploit their comparative cost advantages. Nevertheless, restrictions on trade in services generally remain more significant than those on manufactured goods.
- Increasing disposable household incomes result in greater consumption of those categories of services which can only be provided by overseas suppliers, especially overseas travel and tourism. Against this, economic development within an economy can result in many specialized services which were previously bought in from overseas being provided by local suppliers – many developing countries, for example, seek to reduce their dependence on overseas banking and insurance organizations.
- Cultural convergence which has resulted from improved communications and increasing levels of overseas travel has led to a homogenization of international market segments. Combined with the decline in trade barriers, convergence of cultural attitudes towards services allows many service providers to regard parts of their overseas markets as though they are part of their domestic market.

For an individual company, development of overseas markets can be attractive for a number of reasons. These can be analysed in terms of 'pull' factors which derive from the attractiveness of a potential overseas market and 'push' factors which make an organization's domestic market appear less attractive.

- For firms seeking growth, overseas markets represent new market segments which they may be able to serve with their existing range of products. In this way, a company can stick to producing services that it is good at. Finding new overseas markets for existing or slightly modified services does not expose a company to the risks of expanding both its product range and its market coverage simultaneously.

- Saturation of its domestic market can force a service organization to seek overseas markets. Saturation can come about where a service reaches the maturity stage of its life cycle in the domestic market, while being at a much earlier stage of the cycle in less developed overseas markets. While the market for fast-food restaurants may be approaching saturation in a number of Western markets – especially the USA – they represent a new service opportunity in the early stages of development in many Eastern European countries.

- Environmental factors may make it difficult for a company to fully exploit its service concept in its domestic market, forcing it to look overseas for opportunities. As an example, restrictions on new out-of-town retail developments in the UK during the 1990s led many retailers to seek expansion of their format in overseas markets such as Ireland and Eastern Europe.

- As part of its portfolio management, an organization may wish to reduce its dependence upon one geographical market. The attractiveness of individual national markets can change in a manner which is unrelated to other national markets. For example, costly competition can develop in one national market but not others, world economic cycles show lagged effects between different economies, and government policies – through specific regulation or general economic management – can have counter-balancing effects on market prospects.

- The nature of a service may require an organization to become active in an overseas market. This particularly affects transport-related services such as scheduled airline services and courier services. A UK scheduled airline flying between London and Paris would most likely become involved in exploiting an overseas market at the Paris end of its route.

- Industrial companies operating in a number of overseas countries may require their services suppliers to be able to cater for their needs across national boundaries. A company may wish to engage accountants who are able to provide auditing and management accounting services in its overseas subsidiaries. To achieve this, the firm of accountants would probably need to have created an operational base overseas. Similarly, firms selling in a number of overseas markets may wish to engage an advertising agency which can organize a global campaign in a number of overseas markets.

- There are also many cases where private consumers demand a service that is internationally available. An example is the car hire business where customers frequently need to be able to book a hire car in one country for collection and use in another. To succeed in attracting these customers, car hire companies need to operate internationally.

- Some services are highly specialized and the domestic market is too small to allow economies of scale to be exploited. Overseas markets must be exploited in order to achieve a critical mass which allows a competitive price to be reached.

Specialized aircraft engineering services and oil exploration services fall into this category.

● Economies of scale also result from extending the use of service brands in overseas markets. Expenditure by a fast-food company on promoting its brand image to UK residents is wasted when those citizens travel abroad and cannot find the brand which it has come to value. Newly created overseas outlets will enjoy the benefit of promotion to overseas visitors at little additional cost.

## 15.5 Analysing opportunities for overseas development of services

Overseas markets can represent very different opportunities and threats compared to those which an organization has been used to in its domestic market. Before a detailed market analysis is undertaken, an organization should consider in general terms whether the environment of a market is likely to be attractive. By considering in general terms such matters as political stability or cultural attitudes, an organization may screen out potential markets for which it considers further analysis cannot be justified by the likelihood of success. Where an exploratory analysis of an overseas marketing environment appears to indicate some opportunities, a more thorough analysis might suggest important modifications to a service format which would need to be made before the service could be successfully offered to the market.

This section firstly identifies some general questions which need to be asked in assessing the marketing environment of overseas countries and then considers specific aspects of researching such markets.

The story is told of two representatives from a tour operator who were sent abroad to investigate the possibilities for offering package holidays in the format which had worked well at home. The main finding was that very few people in that market bought package holidays. But what did this mean? One representative sent back a message saying that the current level of sales indicated a lack of interest in the product and the market should therefore be best avoided in favour of other possible markets. But to the other this was the sign of huge potential – 'Just wait until these people discover the advantages of buying package holidays!' This simple example emphasizes that any analysis of overseas market potential can only be based on a combination of factual analysis and judgement.

## 15.6 The overseas marketing environment

The combination of environmental factors that contributed to success within an organization's domestic market may be absent in an overseas market, resulting in the failure of attempts to export a service format. In this section, questions to be asked in analysing an overseas marketing environment are examined under the overlapping headings of the political, economic, social, demographic and techno-logical environments.

### 15.6.1 The political environment

Government and quasi-government organizations influence the legislative and economic frameworks within which businesses operate. Although the most important political influences originate from national governments, intergovern-ment agreements can also be important in shaping a national market.

**National government framework**   At a national level, individual governments can influence trade in services in a number of ways:

- At the most general level, the stability of the political system affects the attrac-tiveness of a particular national market. While radical change rarely results from political upheaval in most Western countries, the instability of many Eastern European governments leads to uncertainty about the economic and legislative framework in which services will be provided.
- Licensing systems may be applied by governments in an attempt to protect domestic producers. Licences can be used to restrict individuals practising a particular profession (e.g. licensing requirements for accountants or solicitors may not recognize experience and licences obtained overseas) or licences can be used to restrict foreign owners setting up a service operation (e.g. the US government does not allow non-US investors to own more than 25% of the shares in its domestic scheduled airlines).
- Regulations governing service standards may require expensive reconfiguration of the service offer to meet local regulations, or may prohibit its provision com-pletely – gambling-related and medical services often fall into this category.
- Import controls can be used to restrict the supply of goods which form an integral part of a service. A restaurant seeking overseas outlets may be forced to source its materials locally, leading to possible problems in maintaining con-sistent quality standards and also possibly losing economies of scale.
- Service production possibilities can be influenced by government policies. Minimum wage levels and conditions of service can be important in determin-ing the viability of a service. For example, many countries restrict the manner in which temporary seasonal staff can be employed – this could make the operation of a seasonal holiday hotel inflexible and uneconomic.
- Restrictions on currency movements may make it difficult to repatriate profits earned from an overseas service operation.
- Governments are major procurers of services and may formally or informally give preference in awarding contracts to locally owned services organizations.
- Legislation protecting trademarks varies between companies – in some countries, such as Greece, the owner may find it relatively hard to legally protect itself from imitators.

Beyond the nation state, international institutions can have important consequences for the international marketing of services. Some of the more important are described below:

**The European Union**  Although the EU was conceived as a vehicle for reducing trade barriers, this has so far benefited mainly trade in raw materials and manufactured goods. Many non-tariff barriers have existed to restrict the amount of services trade which takes place between EU member states. However, the Single European Act 1987 has sought to remove many of these barriers. Most importantly, licensing arrangements are being harmonized so that a company seeking to set up in another member state does not need to go through a lengthy approval process in that country. Licences of one state are increasingly being accepted as valid for companies seeking to operate in other member states. This can potentially benefit a wide range of services organizations such as insurance companies and banks which are heavily regulated and can increasingly regard Europe as one large domestic market, free of national borders.

As an example, national licensing regulations have previously restricted the ability of airlines and road haulage companies located in one EU member state to offer domestic services within other member states. The result has been large differences in prices charged by these industries within different EU member states. The effective removal of trade barriers will create a more competitive market in which prices for road haulage and airline services should become harmonized throughout the EU. Already a number of low-cost airlines, such as Ryanair and easyJet have exploited Europe-wide opportunities beyond their own domestic markets. Services organizations are also increasingly affected by the requirement that large public service contracts should be put out to EU-wide tendering – this has resulted in cross-border competition for highway building and maintenance contracts.

Probable 'gainers' in the UK from greater liberalization of trade are likely to include the insurance and airline industries. These are industries in which UK companies appear to have a comparative cost advantage and/or where trade barriers are high. The disappearance of such barriers is likely to benefit these sectors and will provide an incentive for firms to take advantage of their relative strength by expanding into Europe, in some cases through acquisition or merger.

Nevertheless, uncertainties still remain for UK firms seeking expansion within the EU. The UK's non-membership of the single European currency means that companies earning money overseas can never be sure how much this will translate to in sterling, a particular problem where income is in one currency and expenditure in another. The cost alone of exchanging money can put non-domestic companies at a competitive disadvantage. Despite talk of a single market in services, many ingrained differences in consumer behaviour and language barriers will continue to pose a challenge for UK marketers.

**Other trading blocs**  The EU is an example of a trading bloc which seeks to create favourable trading conditions for companies located within the bloc, regardless of the existence of national borders within the bloc. The development of the EU has been paralleled by the development of a number of other regional trading blocs, most notably the ASEAN group of South-East Asian countries and the NAFTA grouping of the USA, Canada and Mexico.

For services organizations seeking to develop within one of those countries, the creation of trading blocs creates problems and opportunities. The problems occasionally arise where tariffs or other restrictions are placed on goods and services imported from outside the bloc. The biggest opportunity is that once an exporter is inside one member country, the process of expansion to other bloc member countries can be made very much easier through the harmonization of standards and dismantling of internal borders.

**The World Trade Organization (WTO)** The World Trade Organization has its origins in the postwar General Agreement on Tariffs and Trade. Members of the World Trade Organization seek greater international economic prosperity by exploiting fully the comparative cost advantages of nations by reducing the barriers which inhibit international trade. Members agree not to increase tariffs or quotas on imports, except in permitted circumstances.

The World Trade Organization has proceeded to reduce tariffs and quotas through several rounds of negotiations. However, success in respect of services has been relatively slow compared to goods. Because of the multilateral nature of WTO negotiations, attempts to liberalize trade in services can be impeded by arguments in completely unrelated areas of trade. For example, attempts to liberalize trade in financial services have been linked to demands for action to reduce agricultural subsidies given by some countries. The signing of the General Agreement on Trade in Services in 1995 by member countries occurred only after a lot of such bargaining, and there are signs that implementing it is a slower process than in the case of manufactured goods.

**Other international agreements and institutions** A wide range of other agreements and institutions affect service organizations. At their simplest, they include bilateral agreements between two countries, for example the Bermuda agreement which governs the allocation of transatlantic air rights between Britain and the USA, although even here, change can be slow when there are many items on a hidden agenda. More complex multi-lateral agreements between governments can create policies and institutions which directly affect the marketing environment of firms – examples include the International Civil Aviation Organization and the Universal Postal Union.

### 15.6.2 The economic environment

A generally accepted measure of the economic attractiveness of an overseas market is the level of GDP per capita. The demand for most services increases as this figure increases. However, organizations seeking to sell services overseas should also consider the distribution of income within a country which may identify valuable niche markets. As an example, the relatively low GDP per head of South Korea still allows a small and relatively affluent group to create a market for high value overseas holidays (see Figure 15.2).

An organization assessing an overseas market should place great emphasis on future economic performance and the stage which a country has reached in its economic development. While many Western developed economies face saturated

**Figure 15.2**

This graph shows, for selected European countries, the tendency for GDP per capita to be closely correlated with per capita expenditure on leisure services (based on National Statistical Offices/Keynote data for 1998 or the most recent year available)

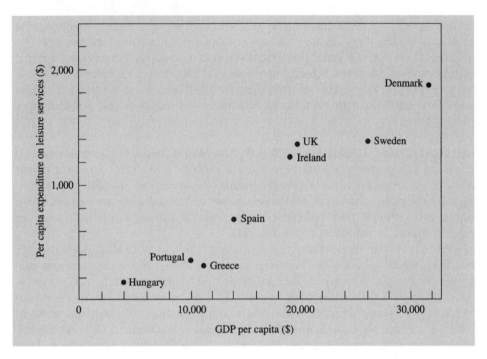

markets for a number of services, less developed economies may be just moving on to that part of their growth curve where services begin to appeal to large groups of people.

A crucial part of the analysis of an overseas market focuses on the level of competition within that market. This can be related to the level of economic development achieved within a country – in general, as an economy develops, its markets become more saturated. This is true of the market for household insurance which is mature and highly competitive in North America and most western European countries, but relatively new and less competitive in many developing economies of the Pacific Rim, allowing better margins to be achieved.

The level of competitive pressure within a market is also a reflection of government policy towards the regulation of monopolies and the ease with which it allows new entrants to enter a market. The government of a country can significantly affect the competitive pressure within a market by legislation aimed at reducing anti-competitive practices.

### 15.6.3 The social and cultural environment

Together, the social and cultural environments represent the values of a society. An understanding of culture and, in particular, an appreciation of cultural differences is clearly important for marketers. Individuals from different cultures not only buy different services, but may also respond in different ways to the same service. Examples of differing cultural attitudes and their effects on international trade in services include the following:

- Buying processes vary between different cultures – for example the role of women in selecting a service may differ in an overseas market compared to the domestic market, thereby possibly requiring a different approach to service design and promotion.
- Some categories of services may be rendered obsolete by certain types of social structure. As an example, extended family structures common in some countries have the ability to produce a wide range of services within the family unit, including caring for children and elderly members. Extended families also often reduce the need for bought-in financial services by recirculating funds within a very close system.
- A service which is taken for granted in the domestic market may be seen as socially unacceptable in an overseas market – interest charged on bank loans may be regarded as a form of usury in some Muslim cultures, for example.
- Attitudes towards promotional programmes differ between cultures – the choice of colours in advertising or sales outlets needs to be made with care because of symbolic associations (e.g. the colour associated with mourning/bereavement varies across cultures).
- What is deemed to be an acceptable activity in procuring sales varies between cultures. In Middle Eastern markets, for example, a bribe to a public official may be considered essential, whereas it is unacceptable in most Western countries.

In short, culture not only conditions an individual's response to products and influences the nature of the purchase process, but it also exercises considerable influence on the structure of consumption within a given society. It should also be remembered that no society is totally homogeneous. Every culture contains smaller subcultures, or groups of people with shared value systems which are based on common experiences and situations. These identifiable subgroups may be distinguished by race, nationality, religion, age, geographical location or some other factor, and share attitudes and behaviour which reflect subcultural influences.

### 15.6.4  The demographic environment

An analysis of the population of an overseas market will reveal first of all whether it is increasing in terms of the total number of people available to purchase services. Overall, the population of EU countries increased at a natural rate of 1.0 per 1000 population in 1998 (that is, for every 1000 deaths, there were 1001 births). However, this hides a number of differences, with rates of increase ranging from 6.0 per 1000 in Ireland to −0.9 in Germany (Eurostat, 1999). Much faster population growth has occurred outside Europe. Between 1960 and 1994, the population of Africa rose by 150 % and Latin America by 100 %, compared to just 17 % in EU countries. Of most importance is the projected population growth rate during the planning period.

Within these population totals, structures can differ significantly. For example, there are significant differences within the EU in the proportion of the population which is either young or elderly, with consequent implications for demand for age-related services. As an example, the proportion of the population aged 60–79 ranges from 9 % in the Irish Republic to 13 % in Spain. By contrast, the Irish Republic has the greatest proportion of under 20s (23%), compared to Germany which has the lowest (16%) (Eurostat, 1999).

In addition, the geographical distribution of the population and structure of household units may be significantly different to that which had brought about success in the domestic market. For example, EU statistics show a number of interesting contrasts in geo-demographic characteristics between member states which could have implications for the marketing of a service:

● Very significant differences occur in home ownership patterns, with implications for demand for a wide range of home-related services. The proportion of households living in rented accommodation ranges from 21% in Spain to 53% in Germany, while the proportion with a mortgage ranges from 8% in Spain to 44% in the UK.
● The proportion of the population living within metropolitan areas varies from 13% in Italy to 44% in France. The resulting differences in lifestyles can have implications for services as diverse as car repair services, entertainment and retailing.
● The proportion of self-employed people ranges from 45% in the Netherlands to 17% in Italy, with implications for the sale of personal pension schemes, etc.
● Average household size ranges from a low of 2.26 in Denmark to a high of 4.16 people in Ireland, having implications for the types and quantities of services bought by household units.

### 15.6.5 The technological environment

An analysis of the technological environment is important for services organizations who require the use of a well-developed technical infrastructure and a workforce which is able to use technology. Communications are an important element of the technological infrastructure – poorly developed telephone and postal communications may inhibit attempts to make credit cards more widely available, for instance.

## 15.7 Sources of information on overseas markets

The methods used to research a potential overseas market are in principle similar to those which would be used to research a domestic market. Companies would normally begin by using secondary data about a potential overseas market which is available to them at home. Sources which are readily available through specialized libraries, on-line services, government organizations and specialist research organizations include Department of Trade and Industry information for exporters, reports of international agencies such as the Organization for Economic Co-operation and Development (OECD), chambers of commerce and private sources of information such as that provided by banks. Details of some specific sources are shown in Table 15.1.

Initial desk research at home will identify those markets which show greatest potential for development. A company will then often follow this up with further

---

**Table 15.1** Sources of secondary information on overseas markets

Government agencies
    Department of Trade and Industry market reports
    Overseas governments – e.g. US Department of Commerce
    Overseas national and local development agencies
International agencies
    European Community (Eurostat, etc.)
    Organization for Economic Co-operation and Development (OECD)
    World Trade Organization (WTO)
    United Nations (UN)
    International Monetary Fund (IMF)
    Universal Postal Union
    World Health Organization (WHO)
Research organizations
    Economist Intelligence Unit
    Dun and Bradstreet International
    Mintel Online
    Market research firms
Publications
    *Financial Times* country surveys/ft.com
    *Business International*
    *International Trade Reporter*
    Banks' export reviews
Trade associations
    Chambers of commerce
    Industry specific associations – e.g. International Air Transport Association

---

desk research of materials available locally within the shortlisted markets, often carried out by appointing a local research agency. This may include a review of reports published by the target market's own government and specialist locally based market research agencies.

Just as in home markets, secondary data has limitations in assessing market attractiveness. Problems in overseas markets are compounded by the greater difficulty in gaining access to data, although the development of online information services has helped in this respect. There may also be language differences and problems of definition which may differ from those with which an organization is familiar. In the case of services which are a new concept in an overseas market, information on current usage and attitudes to the service may be completely lacking. For this reason, it would be difficult to use secondary data to try to assess the likely response from consumers to large out-of-town superstores in many eastern European countries. Despite these problems, the World Wide Web is allowing companies to undertake a lot of preliminary assessment of an overseas market from their office-based computer.

Primary research is used to overcome shortcomings in secondary data. Its most important use is to identify cultural factors which may require a service format to be modified or abandoned altogether. A company seeking to undertake primary research in a proposed overseas market would almost certainly use a local specialist research agency. Apart from overcoming possible language barriers, a local agency would better understand attitudes towards privacy and the level of literacy that might affect response rates for different forms of research. However, the problem of comparability between markets remains. For example, when a Japanese respondent claims to 'like' a product, the result may be comparable to a German consumer who claims to 'quite like' the product. It would be wrong to assume on the basis of this research that the product is better liked by Japanese consumers than German consumers.

Primary research is generally undertaken overseas when a company has become happy about the general potential of a market, but is unsure of a number of factors which would be critical for success, for example whether intermediaries would be willing and able to handle their new service or whether traditional cultural attitudes will present an insurmountable obstacle for a service not previously available in that market. Prior to commissioning its own specific research, a company may go for the lower cost, but less specific route of undertaking research through an omnibus survey. These are surveys regularly undertaken among a panel of consumers in overseas markets (for example the Gallup European Omnibus) which carry questions on behalf of a number of organizations.

## 15.8 International services marketing management

Having decided to enter a new overseas market, a company must consider the most effective way of managing its marketing effort in that market. The process of defining the organization's mission, analysing opportunities, setting quantifiable goals, implementing and monitoring results is just as important in overseas operations, if not more so.

Objectives must be clearly stated for each overseas market, preferably in a quantified form. Objectives must be set with due regard to local conditions by being achievable. A global return on investment objective may be inappropriate in locally competitive markets where a service firm wants a presence in order to secure international coverage and thereby develop wide-ranging relationships with its profitable customers. For this reason, a hotel chain might develop in a popular area to satisfy the needs of its regular users and retain their international loyalty, even though the hotel will not be able to achieve its normal profit objective.

Like any new venture, objectives are essential if performance is to be monitored and any corrective action taken. Because overseas markets are generally much less certain than domestic markets, it is important that any variance from target is rapidly analysed and corrective action taken. There must be a clearly defined process by which failing services can be assessed for their prospects of long-term viability or withdrawn from an overseas market. It may be, for instance, that assumptions on which a market entry decision were based have proved to be false and that no amount of local reformulation of a service will allow it to break even.

A major issue in the international management of services marketing concerns the extent to which an organization's headquarters should intervene in the management of overseas subsidiaries. A commonly heard complaint from marketing managers of the latter is that they are given insufficient freedom to respond to local market conditions. Against this is the argument that intervention from headquarters is vital in order to secure the development of a consistent standard of service output in a planned way. Where a service is quite specialized to a national market and international brand building relatively unimportant (e.g. municipal contract cleaning services), there is strong argument for delegation of management responsibilities on a geographical basis. On the other hand, where the service appeals to an international audience, there is a stronger case for introducing product or market management structures to which overseas managers are answerable.

## 15.9 Refining the marketing programme for overseas markets

A crucial task of overseas marketing management is the design of a marketing programme which is sensitive to local needs. The following sections examine the extent to which adaptation of the marketing mix to local needs is either desirable or possible. In particular, should a company seek to develop one globally uniform service offer, or make it different in each of the overseas markets which it serves?

The process of globalizing a service offer can be quite different than is the case with tangible goods, on account of the greater variability of services. In addition to being highly variable, services can be extremely flexible – they are more likely than goods to be designed around the specific requirements of small groups of consumers using a basically common formula. Whether services firms choose to standardize their products globally or to adapt them to the needs of local markets is dependent on the nature of the services which they offer. Some fast-food restaurants, for example, have adapted their menus, architectural designs and staff training methods to suit local needs, while retaining a common process formula worldwide. Services can often enjoy the best of both worlds, retaining their competitive advantage by remaining true to their basic managerial approach, while changing their product to meet local needs.

One approach to globalizing services is the process of 'industrializing' the service through the replacement of people with machines and through a systems approach to management. Levitt (1976) found an explanation of the worldwide success of McDonald's restaurants in the 'same systematic modes of analysis, design, organization and control that are commonplace in manufacturing'. This process has occurred not just within the restaurant sector, but also in the construction, hotel, professional and technical service sectors. Standardization is often accompanied by a high degree of centralization, sometimes creating further management problems when local managers are instructed to sacrifice their local autonomy in order to benefit the organization globally.

### 15.9.1 Product and promotion decisions

At the heart of international marketing mix strategy are product and promotion decisions. Five generic strategies can be identified, based on the extent to which the configuration of the service offer and the promotional effort differ from a global norm:

1 **Maintain a uniform product and promotion worldwide** This approach effectively develops a global marketing strategy as though the world was a single

entity. The benefits of this approach are numerous. Customers travelling from one market to another can immediately recognize a service provider and the values which its global brand stands for. If, on the other hand, the service formulation was different in an overseas market, a traveller visiting an overseas outlet may come away confused about the qualities of the brand. As an example, a car rental company with an established position in its home market as the operator of a very modern fleet of cars, could harm its domestic image if it pursued a strategy of operating older cars in an overseas market. Standardization of the service offer can also yield benefits of economies of scale which include economies in market research and the design of buildings and uniforms, etc., although the greater adaptability of services often renders these benefits less than in the case of manufactured goods. The use of a common brand name in overseas markets for either the service provider or for specific services also benefits from economies of scale. Travellers to overseas markets will already be familiar with the brand's values as a result of promotion in the domestic market. However, care must be taken in selecting a brand name which will have no unfortunate connotations in overseas markets – the 'Big Mac', for example, translates in French as 'the big pimp'. There can also be problems where legislation prevents an international slogan being used. In France, for example, law no 75-1349 of 1975 makes the use of the French language compulsory in all advertising for services – this also applies to associated packaging and instructions, etc.

In the case of transport services which operate between different markets, it may not be feasible to adapt the service offering to each of the local markets served, and either a compromise must be reached or the needs of the most important market given precedence. Airlines flying between two countries may find the pricing of in-flight services, the decor of the aircraft and catering having to satisfy very different market needs at either end of the route.

2  **Retain a uniform service formulation but adapt promotion** This strategy produces an essentially uniform global service but adapts promotional effort to meet the sensitivities of local markets. The manner in which brand values are communicated in advertisements is a reflection of the cultural values of a society. For this reason, an airline may use a straightforward, brash, hard-sell approach in its American market, a humorous approach in its British market and a seductive approach in its French market, even though the service offer is identical in each market. Similarly, certain objects and symbols used to promote a service might have the opposite effect to that which might be expected at home. Animals, which are often used in Britain to promote a range of home-based goods and services present a caring and comfortable image, but in some markets such as Japan, animals are seen as unclean, disgusting objects.

How do you promote the image of a holiday destination in foreign markets? The destination itself cannot be adapted to suit the needs of individual markets. The Tower of London will always be the same for tourists whether they are from Manchester, Madras or Melbourne. But the promotional message can be fine tuned to stress aspects which different markets place high value on. Take the

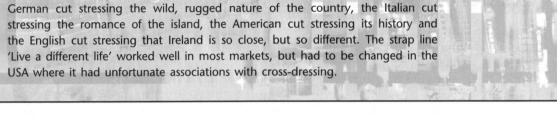

case of the Brand Ireland campaign, a joint effort by the Northern Ireland Tourist Board and Bord Failte to increase the number of visitors to Ireland, north and south. A 30-second television commercial was recut several times, with the German cut stressing the wild, rugged nature of the country, the Italian cut stressing the romance of the island, the American cut stressing its history and the English cut stressing that Ireland is so close, but so different. The strap line 'Live a different life' worked well in most markets, but had to be changed in the USA where it had unfortunate associations with cross-dressing.

3 **Adapt the service offering only** This may be done in order to meet specific local needs or legislation, while retaining the benefits of a global image. For this reason, a car rental company may offer a range of predominantly compact cars in areas where average journeys are short (e.g. the Channel Islands), while offering jeeps and vans in areas such as the USA where motoring costs are lower and distances generally much greater.

How does a large American hotel chain adapt its service offer to the Japanese market? Hotels operated by Hilton International in the USA have bedrooms which to many visitors from overseas are surprisingly large. But what would an American think of a typical Japanese hotel? Land prices in America are generally fairly low outside of the main metropolitan areas, hence the relatively spacious facilities offered. But in Japan, space is at a premium and has given rise to all sorts of miniaturized hotel formats, aimed at keeping prices at an affordable level. How could Hilton International remain affordable yet retain its generic brand values? Following extensive research, the company developed a hotel format which was appropriate to the Japanese market. To avoid the problem of visitors from America being shocked by the relatively cramped hotels, Hilton International developed and applied a separate brand format, 'Wa No Kutsurogi', providing comfort and service the Japanese way.

4 **Adapt both product and promotion** In practice, a combination of slight service and promotion modification is needed in order to meet both differing local needs and differences in local sensitivity to advertising.
5 **Develop new services** Markets may emerge overseas for which a domestic company has no product offering which can be easily adapted. In the field of financial services, the absence in some overseas countries of state provision for certain key welfare services may create a market for insurance related products (e.g. dental health insurance cover) which is largely absent in the domestic UK market where the welfare state is relatively comprehensive. Similarly, the social and economic structure of a country can result in quite different products being required. For example, the pattern of property ownership in Malaysia has given rise to a novel two-generation property mortgage not generally found in western European markets.

### 15.9.2 Pricing decisions

The issue of whether to globalize or localize the service offer arises again in respect of pricing decisions. On the one hand, it might be attractive for an organization to be able to offer a standard charge for a service regardless of where in the world the service is consumed – consumers will immediately have an idea of how much a service will cost and this helps to develop a long-term relationship between client and company. However, the reality is that a variety of factors cause global service operators to charge different prices in the different markets in which they operate. There is usually no reason to assume that the pricing policies adopted in the domestic market will prove to be equally effective in an overseas market. Furthermore, for those overseas produced services which are consumed mainly by the local population, it may be of no great importance that comparability between different markets is maintained.

There are a number of factors which affect price decisions overseas:

● Competitive pressure varies between markets, reflecting the stage of market development that a service has reached and the impact of regulations against anti-competitive practices.

● The cost of producing a service may be significantly different in overseas markets. For services which use people intensive production methods, variations in wage levels between countries will have a significant effect on total costs. Personnel costs may also be affected by differences in welfare provisions which employers are required to pay for. Other significant cost elements which often vary between markets include the level of property prices or rental costs – the cost of acquiring space for a service outlet in Britain, for example, is usually significantly more than in southern or eastern Europe.

● Taxes vary between different markets – for example the rate of value added tax (or its equivalent sales tax) can be as high as 38 % in Italy compared to 17.5 % in the UK. There are also differences between markets in the manner in which sales taxes are expressed – in many markets, these are fully incorporated into price schedules, although on other occasions (such as in the USA) it is more usual to price a service exclusive of taxes (Figure 15.3).

● Local customs influence buyers' expectations of the way in which they are charged for a service. While customers in the domestic market might expect to pay for bundles of services, in an overseas market consumers might expect to pay a separate price for each component of the bundle, or vice versa. Also, in some countries, it is customary to expect customers to pay a tip to the front-line person providing a service, whereas other cultures expect to pay an all-inclusive price without the need to subsequently add a tip. Formal price lists for a service may be expected in some markets, but in others, the prevalence of bartering may put an operator which sticks to a fixed price list at a competitive disadvantage.

● Government regulations can limit price freedom in overseas markets. In addition to controls over prices charged by public utilities, many governments require 'fair' prices to be charged in a wide range of services – e.g. tourism-related services – and for the prices charged to be clearly publicized.

● For a category of service which is already established in an overseas market, a newcomer might only be able to gain market share by offering significant price incentives. In the early stages, discounting may have to be used to establish trial of the service until the brand is sufficiently strongly established that the company can charge a premium price. As an example of this, international airlines often charge premium prices at the domestic end of a route (where their brand is well known), compared to the overseas end (where the brand is relatively unknown).

It is worth noting that service organizations are generally much better able to sustain **discriminatory pricing** policies between countries compared to exporters of manufactured goods. If wide differences in the pretax price of goods emerge between countries, it is open to entrepreneurs to buy goods in the lower priced market and sell them in the higher priced market (evidenced by the large volumes of cigarettes and alcohol which are imported from the low-price French market to the high-price UK market). The inseparability of production and consumption generally prevents this happening with services – a low-priced hotel room cannot be taken from the relatively cheap Spanish market and offered for sale in the London market.

### 15.9.3  Accessibility decisions

Where a service organization is launching a service into a new overseas market, intermediaries can have a vital role in making the service available to consumers. The selection of intermediaries to facilitate the introduction of a service to a new overseas market is considered in more detail below. Consideration is given briefly here to the place and manner in which a service will be made available.

The analysis of location decisions presented in Chapter 9 can be applied equally to overseas markets. However, a service provider must avoid assuming that a locational strategy that has worked in one market will work just as effectively in an overseas market. A revised strategy may be required on account of differences in the geography of the overseas market, differences in consumer expectations, differences in current methods of making that type of service available and differences in legislative constraints.

- Geographical differences can be important where land-use patterns differ greatly in the target overseas market. As an example, the extensive nature of many urban areas within the USA results in there being a series of suburban commercial areas rather than a clearly defined central business district. A European retail bank with a city-centre service format which had worked well in its domestic market may only be able to succeed by developing out-of-town formats of its branches for a proposed expansion in the USA.
- Consumer behaviour may differ significantly in overseas markets. What is a widely accepted outlet in one country may be regarded with suspicion in another. The idea of taking refreshments in a snack bar located within a clothing store may appear quite ordinary within the UK, but may encounter resistance in more traditional markets. Also, the extensiveness of outlet networks will be influenced by customers' expectations about ease of access, for example in relation to the availability of car parking facilities or the distance that they are prepared to travel.

**Figure 15.3**
National Car Rental has sought to simplify its pricing structure and strengthen its brand position by offering one price throughout Europe. Inevitably there is some risk inherent in this approach, as taxes and competitive pressures differ throughout Europe. In non-Euro countries, there is also the potential problem of currency fluctuations. To try to limit these risks, the company has restricted the single price offer according to the type of car and type of customer (reproduced with permission of National Car Rental)

- Differences in the social, economic and technical environments of a market can be manifested in the existence of different patterns of intermediaries. As an example, the interrelatedness of wholesalers and retailers in Japan can make it much more difficult for an overseas retailer to get into that market compared to other overseas opportunities. In some markets, there may be no direct equivalent of a type of intermediary found in the domestic market – estate agents on the UK model are often not found in many markets where the work of transferring property is handled entirely by a solicitor. The technological environment can also affect accessibility decisions – the relatively underdeveloped postal and telecommunications services of many eastern European countries makes direct availability of services to consumers relatively difficult.

- What is a legal method of distributing a service in the domestic market may be against the law of an overseas country. Countries may restrict the sale of financial services, holidays and gambling services – among others – to a much narrower set of possible intermediaries than is the case in the domestic market.

### 15.9.4 People decisions

It has already been noted that the people element of the marketing mix is more important for services than for goods, therefore it is important that this element is appropriately formulated for an overseas market. Where overseas service delivery involves direct producer–consumer interaction, a decision must be made on whether to employ local or expatriate staff. The latter may be preferable where a service is highly specialized and may be useful in adding to the global uniformity of the service offering. In some circumstances, the presence of front-line expatriate serving staff can add to the appeal of a service, for example a chain of traditional Irish pubs established in mainland Europe may add to their appeal by employing authentic Irish staff.

For relatively straightforward services, a large proportion of staff would be recruited locally, leaving just senior management posts filled by expatriates. Sometimes, an extensive staff development programme may be required to ensure that locally recruited staff perform in a manner which is consistent with the company's global image. This can in some circumstances be quite a difficult task – a fast-food operator may have difficulty developing values of speed and efficiency among its staff in countries where the pace of life is relatively slow.

Where staff are recruited locally, employment legislation can affect the short- and long-term flexibility of service provision. This can affect the ease with which staff can be laid off or dismissed should demand fall – for example, in Germany, the Dismissals Protection Law (Kundigungsschutzgesetz) gives considerable protection to salaried staff who have been in their job for more than six months, allowing dismissal only for a 'socially justified' reason. There are also differences between countries in the extent to which an employer can prevent an employee with valuable trade secrets leaving their employment to work for a competitor. In Germany, a 'non-competition' clause can be expressly agreed for a maximum of two years after termination of employment, but only under a number of conditions.

### 15.10 Market-entry strategies

A new overseas market represents both a potential opportunity and a risk to an organization. A company's market-entry strategy should aim to balance these two elements. The least risky method of developing an overseas service market is to supply that market from a domestic base, something which can be a possibility in the case of separable service offerings. A wide variety of financial and information services can be provided to overseas markets by post or telephone, avoiding the cost and risk of setting up local service outlets.

Where inseparability of service production and consumption occurs and the producer must go to the consumer, local outlets must be established. Risk can be minimized by gradually committing more resources to a market, based on experience to date. Temporary facilities could be established which have low start-up and close-down costs and where the principal physical and human assets can be transferred to another location. A good example of risk reduction through the use of temporary facilities is found in the pattern of retail development in East Germany following reunification. West German retailers who initially entered East Germany in large numbers were reluctant to commit themselves to building stores in specific locations in a part of the country which was still economically unstable and where patterns of land use were rapidly changing. The solution adopted by many retailers was to offer branches of their chain in temporary marquees or from mobile vehicles. These could move in response to the changing pattern of demand. While the location of retail outlets remained risky, this did not prevent retailers from establishing their networks of distribution warehouses which were considered to be more flexible in the manner in which they could respond to changing consumer spending patterns.

Market-entry risk reduction strategies also have a time dimension. While there may be long-term benefits arising from being the first company to develop a new category of service in an overseas market, there are also risks. If development is hurried and launched before service quality can be guaranteed to live up to an organization's international standards, the company's long-term image can be damaged, both in the new overseas market and in its wider world market. In the turbulent marketing environment of eastern Europe in the late 1980s, two of the world's principal fast-food retailers – McDonalds and Burger King – pursued quite different strategies. The former waited until political, economic, social and technological conditions were capable of allowing it to launch a restaurant which met its global standards. In the case of Burger King, its desire to be first in the market led it to offer a very substandard service giving it an image which it subsequently struggled to recover from.

Where the inseparability of a service offer makes it impossible for an organization to supply the service to an overseas market from its home base, an assessment of risk is required in deciding whether an organization should enter an overseas market on its own, or in association with another organization. The former maximizes the strategic and operational control which the organization has over its overseas operations, but it exposes it to the greatest risk where the overseas market is relatively poorly understood. A range of entry possibilities are considered below.

### 15.10.1  Direct investment in overseas subsidiary

This option gives a service organization maximum control over its overseas operations, but can expose it to a high level of risk on account of the poor understanding which it may have of the overseas market. A company can either set up its own overseas subsidiary from scratch (as many UK hotel companies have done to develop hotels in overseas markets), or it can acquire control of a company which is already trading (such as the acquisition by Stagecoach of Coach USA).

Where the nature of the service offer differs relatively little between national markets, or where it appeals to an international market (e.g. hotels), the risks from creating a new subsidiary are reduced. Where there are barriers to entry and the service is aimed at an essentially local market with a different culture to the domestic market, the acquisition of an established subsidiary may be the preferred course of action. Even the latter course of action is not risk free, as was illustrated by the problems encountered by British Airways following its acquisition of a substantial share in the American airline USAir, which it eventually sold in 1997 following operating losses.

Direct investment in an overseas subsidiary may also be made difficult by legislation restricting ownership of certain services by foreigners – civil aviation is a good example where many countries prevent foreign companies owning a controlling interest in a domestic airline.

### 15.10.2  Management contracting

Rather than setting up its own service organization overseas, a company with a proven track record in a service area may pursue the option of running other companies' businesses for them. For a fee, an overseas organization which seeks to develop a new service would contract a team to set up and run the facility. In some cases, the intention may be that the management team should get the project started, and gradually hand over the running of the facility to a local management. This type of arrangement is useful for an expanding overseas organization where the required management and technical skills are difficult to obtain locally. In countries where the educational infrastructure offers less opportunity for management and technical training, a company (or in many cases, overseas governments) can buy in state of the art management skills.

For the company supplying management skills under such contracts, the benefits are numerous. Risks are kept to a minimum as the company generally does not need to invest its own capital in the project. The company gathers overseas market knowledge which it may be able to use to its own advantage if it plans similar ventures of its own in other countries. For staff employed by the company, the challenge of working on an overseas project can offer career opportunities outside the mainstream domestic management route.

**Management contracting** has found many applications in the service sector. For UK companies, the demise of the British empire resulted in most newly independent colonies seeking to establish their own service organizations, for which they were ill-equipped to manage themselves. Most countries immediately set up their own airline, making use of management expertise bought in from BOAC – the forerunner of British Airways. More recently, developments in eastern Europe have resulted in many opportunities for UK-based service companies, including the management of hotels, airlines and educational establishments.

### 15.10.3  Licensing/franchising

Rather than setting up its own operations in an overseas market, a company can license a local company to provide a service. At its simplest, a licence allows an overseas company to sell a service on behalf of the principal. In the service sector, it can be difficult to define when a licence becomes a franchise. Licensing is more commonly associated with manufactured goods where the identity of the overseas licensee who manufactures the goods is not usually important to the customer, so long as quality control is adequate. The inseparability of service offers makes service producers an integral part of a service, requiring greater control over the whole process by which an overseas business operates. Therefore, while exporters of manufactured goods frequently license an overseas producer to manufacture and sell their products, a company developing a service overseas is more likely to establish a franchise relationship with its overseas producers.

Franchising in an overseas market can take a number of forms. At one extreme, the organization seeking to develop overseas could enter into a direct franchising relationship with each individual franchisee. The problem of this approach is the difficulty in monitoring and controlling a possibly large number of franchisees in a country far from home. To alleviate some of these problems, the franchisor would normally establish its own subsidiary in the overseas territory which would negotiate and monitor franchisees locally or, alternatively, grant a master franchise for an area to a franchisee where the latter effectively becomes the franchisor in the overseas country. In between these options are a number of permutations of strategy – for example a subsidiary could be set up as a joint venture with a local company in order to develop a franchise network.

As with the development of a domestic franchise service network, franchising can allow an organization to expand rapidly overseas with relatively low capital requirements. While a clearly defined business format and method of conducting business is critical to the success of an overseas franchise, things can still go wrong for a number of reasons.

The service format could be poorly proven in the home market, making overseas expansion particularly difficult. Unrealistic expectations may be held about the amount of human and financial resources which need to be devoted to the operation of an overseas franchise. Problems in interpreting the spirit and letter of contractual agreements between the franchisor and franchisee can result in acrimonious misunderstanding. These problems were evident in 1997 when the UK retailer The Body Shop decided to take back control of its French outlets from its French master franchisor, following the latter's poor performance.

### 15.10.4 Joint ventures

An international joint venture is a partnership between a domestic company and an overseas company or government. A joint venture can take a number of forms and is particularly attractive to a domestic firm seeking entry to an overseas market in the following circumstances:

● The initial capital requirement threshold is high, resulting in a high level of risk for an overseas investor. A joint venture can spread this risk.
● Where overseas governments restrict the rights of foreign companies to set up business on their account, a partnership with a local company – possibly involving a minority shareholding – may be the only means of entering the market.

- There may be significant barriers to entry which a company already based in the overseas market could help to overcome. For services, an important barrier is often posed by the availability of intermediaries. As an example, the UK mortgage market is dominated by banks and building societies, largely selling their own mortgages, and a number of foreign banks have taken the view that their best market-entry strategy would be to work in partnership with a smaller building society, providing them with funds and allowing them to sell the mortgages under their own name through their established network of branches.
- There may be reluctance of consumers to deal with what appears to be a foreign company. A joint venture can allow the operation to be fronted by a domestic producer with whom customers can be familiar, while allowing the overseas partner to provide capital and management expertise.
- A good understanding of local market conditions is essential for success in an overseas market. A joint venture with an organization already based in the proposed overseas market makes the task of collecting information about a market, and responding sensitively to it, relatively easy.
- Taxation of company profits may favour a joint venture rather than owning an overseas subsidiary outright.

A distinction can be made between equity and non-equity joint ventures. The former involves two or more organizations joining together to invest in a 'child' organization which has its own separate identity. A non-equity joint venture involves agreement between partners on such matters as marketing research, new service development, promotion and distribution, without any agreement to jointly provide capital for a new organization.

Joint ventures are an important feature of many services sectors where the benefits listed above can be achieved. They have assumed particular importance in the hotels, airline and financial services sectors some recent examples in the latter are shown in Table 15.2.

Strategic alliances – whether or not involving joint equity – are becoming increasingly important within the service sector. These are agreements between two or more organizations where each partner seeks to add to its competencies by combining its resources with those of a partner. A strategic alliance generally involves co-operation between partners rather than joint ownership of a subsidiary set up for a specific purpose, although it may include agreement for collaborators to purchase shares in the businesses of other members of the alliance.

Strategic alliances can be very powerful within the service sector. They are frequently used to allow individual companies to build upon the relationship which they have developed with their clients by allowing them to sell on services which they do not produce themselves, but are produced by another member of the alliance. This arrangement is reciprocated between members of the alliance. Strategic alliances have assumed great importance within the airline industry, where operators share their route networks through 'code-sharing', thereby increasing the range of origin–destination opportunities which can be provided with a through ticket (Figure 15.4).

International strategic alliances can involve a principal nominating a supplier in related service fields as a preferred supplier at its outlets worldwide. This strategy has been used by car rental companies to secure a tie-in with other transport principals, to offer what the latter sees as a value added service. An example is the agreement

**Table 15.2** Examples of UK financial service organizations' involvement in overseas joint ventures

| Venture partners | Holding (%) | Subsidiary/purpose |
|---|---|---|
| *Equity joint ventures* | | |
| British Telecom | 50 | Development of Telfort mobile |
| NS Dutch Railways | 50 | telephone service in the Netherlands |
| Prudential | 50 | Creation of Prudential Assicurazione |
| Inholding (Italy) | 50 | to provide insurance services in Italy |
| Abbey National | 92 | Creation of Abbey National Mutui to |
| Diners Club (Italy) | 0 | offer mortgages in Italy |
| Winterthur (Switzerland) | 8 | |
| British Energy | 50 | Creation of new company Amergen |
| PECO Energy | 50 | to acquire nuclear power stations in USA |
| *Non-equity joint ventures* | | |
| Commercial Union | | Agreement for CI to sell and distribute |
| Credito Italiano (Italy) | | CU's life and non-life insurance policies in Italy |
| Hambros Merchant Bank | | Co-operation agreement in cross-frontier |
| Bayerische Vereinsbank (Germany) | | merger and acquisition finance |
| Barclays Bank | | Agreement gave Barclays Bank a banking |
| Tokyo Trust (Japan) | | licence to operate in Japan to provide trust management and securities handling in collaboration with its partner |

whereby Hertz Car Rental was appointed by British Airways as preferred supplier worldwide. Under the arrangement, passengers could reserve a Hertz car at the same time as their air ticket and in some instances (e.g. shuttle passengers), Hertz guaranteed that a car would be waiting for passengers at their destination airport even if no prior reservation had been made. Hertz gained additional custom for its car rental business, while British Airways was able to add value to its service offer.

### 15.10.5 Global e-commerce

The development of the Internet has offered new opportunities for the providers of services which are essentially intangible and which can overcome the problems of inseparability. At the business-to-business level, a lot of back-room service processing, such as invoicing, data entry and software development can now be carried out in parts of the world where there is a plentiful supply of low cost, skilled workers,

An introduction to **one**world
The alliance that revolves around you

AmericanAirlines

BRITISH AIRWAYS

Canadian Airlines

CATHAY PACIFIC

QANTAS

**Figure 15.4**
'With the globalization of markets, strategic alliances are becoming increasingly crucial in order to facilitate overseas growth. In the airline sector, an alliance such as the One World Alliance allows one airline's services to be marketed by all other alliance members. For customers, British Airways is able to offer 'seamless' travel around the globe on services of fellow alliance members. For the company, there are opportunities to rationalize its operations in foreign countries (reproduced with permission of One World Alliance)

and the results sent back to the customer by a data link (see case study). At the consumer level, many service providers now promote themselves to global audiences through the Internet. A consumer in the UK, for example, could find a hotel in Australia and book a room on line without the hotel needing to use an intermediary. The costs to service providers of reaching global audiences in this way can be low.

The service sector has been at the leading edge of developments in **e-commerce**, helped by the fact that there is often very little, if any, tangible content which must be physically delivered to the customer. Travel-related services and financial services have seen major developments in e-commerce (discussed in Chapter 10). However, the limitations of the Internet in gaining access to overseas markets should be recognized. For private consumers, purchasing through the Internet is often perceived as being very risky, and this riskiness is likely to increase when the supplier is based overseas. In the case of Internet banking services offered in the UK from overseas, customers may find themselves not protected by legislation which protects customers of UK-based banks. Some services providers are reluctant to make their services available globally through the Internet in order to preserve price discrimination. It will be recalled that providers of inseparable services are able to charge different groups different prices, without the fear of a low-price segment selling on the service to high-price segments. For this reason, airlines often restrict sales of tickets through the Internet to local national markets, to prevent customers buying in the cheapest global market.

Finally, it should be remembered that the Internet is becoming increasingly cluttered with websites, and it is not sufficient for a service 'exporter' to simply have a website. It must also ensure that the site is brought to the attention of a global audience. Many small service providers realize that the most cost-effective means of doing this is by paying various types of information intermediaries (such as online hotel booking agencies) to do this for them.

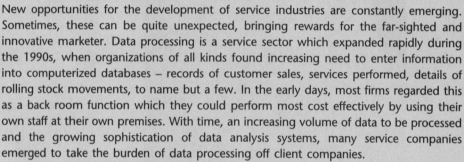

**Case Study**

## Philippines gets a share of emerging world trade in data

New opportunities for the development of service industries are constantly emerging. Sometimes, these can be quite unexpected, bringing rewards for the far-sighted and innovative marketer. Data processing is a service sector which expanded rapidly during the 1990s, when organizations of all kinds found increasing need to enter information into computerized databases – records of customer sales, services performed, details of rolling stock movements, to name but a few. In the early days, most firms regarded this as a back room function which they could perform most cost effectively by using their own staff at their own premises. With time, an increasing volume of data to be processed and the growing sophistication of data analysis systems, many service companies emerged to take the burden of data processing off client companies.

At first, most data-processing companies operated close to their clients. However, by the late 1980s, large volumes of data began entering international trade to be processed by companies in overseas countries where costs were lower, working regulations more relaxed and trade unions often non-existent. An important factor accounting for this development in international trade was the rapid pace of technological developments. Processed data could now be transmitted back to a client company very quickly using satellites or fibre optic links.

Data processing has established a firm foothold as an exportable service in areas such as the Caribbean, the Philippines and to some extent the Irish Republic. Each of these countries is characterized by relatively low wage rates with skills which are at least as good as those of workers in more developed countries.

The development of the Kansas, US-based Saztec company illustrates the way in which international trade can be developed. Saztec has won data-processing contracts from major organizations throughout the world, including a number of UK government departments, such as the Home Office and Treasury. Yet these services are generally produced far away from either the company's or the client's base. The company employs over 800 people in the Philippines, who earn an average of £75 per month – much less than the salary paid to its staff in Kansas. Staff turnover at less than 1% is much lower than the 35% annual rate in Kansas. Furthermore, the company is able to obtain a higher quality of output by the military style organization and control of its staff – something which would not be accepted in the USA.

The Philippines has become an important exporter of data processing services by exploiting its comparative cost advantage in labour inputs – something that is useful in capturing high-volume, basic data input where accuracy and cost are paramount. Another country which has developed this service sector in a big way is Jamaica, which in addition to exploiting its low labour costs offers the advantages of a sophisticated infrastructure – such as satellite links – and generous tax incentives. Ireland by contrast has exploited the fact that it has a relatively highly educated and

English-speaking workforce who have earned less than their counterparts would earn in the UK or USA. A number of computer companies, such as AOL and Dell have set up customer telephone support services in Ireland to handle customer enquiries. For a caller from the UK, only the accent may indicate that their call is being answered overseas.

The Philippines, like most developing countries, has a long way to go before it becomes a predominantly service-based, rather than an agriculture- or manufacturing-based economy. In the case of data processing, new communications technologies have allowed production to take place in a totally different location to the customer, thereby overcoming the problem of inseparability. There are clearly limits on developing countries' abilities to export services, but marketers in these countries will be looking for new opportunities to separate production and consumption and export the benefits to relatively wealthy Western clients. Meanwhile, the development of these countries' domestic economies will doubtless lead to growing demand for producer services from the growing business sector and for consumer services from the emerging middle classes.

## Case study review questions

**1**  Why has data processing emerged as a major new service industry in world trade?

**2**  What other service sectors have emerged during the past two decades? What factors explain their emergence?

**3**  What are the advantages to the Philippines economy of developing its data-processing industry? Are there any disadvantages?

## Chapter summary and linkages to other chapters

This chapter has highlighted the increasingly competitive and global nature of services markets. The inseparable nature of services is reflected in quite different challenges for the development of overseas markets, compared to goods. Very often, a services organization can only develop an overseas market by locating there. Understanding an overseas market is crucial and firms have available to them a variety of techniques for assessing the cultural, economic and political acceptability of a service in a foreign market. Sensitive adaptation of a service formula is crucial to success and many services which have been successful at home have failed because of false assumptions about the needs of a proposed overseas market. The involvement of a joint venture partner can lessen the risk of entering an unknown market, but this has to be balanced against a loss of control.

All of the principles of services marketing which have been discussed in previous chapters in the context of the domestic market apply also to overseas markets. However, their application may differ. So the nature of the service offer and the processes involved in service encounters may need to be adapted (**Chapters 2 and 3**). Buyers may evaluate a service offer quite differently and be more or less amenable to the concept of relationship marketing (**Chapters 4 and 5**). Managing people in an overseas operation can be quite different, and inhibit the development of universal brands and standards of service (**Chapters 7 and 12**). Issues of accessibility, pricing and promotion need be sensitively managed (**Chapters 9, 10 and 11**). Management processes and structures face new strains when stretched to foreign markets and information for planning and control purposes becomes more difficult to obtain, analyse and disseminate (**Chapters 6, 12 and 13**).

## www linkages/URLs

EmuNet: The online gateway to Europe:
**http://www.euro-emu.co.uk**

*Financial Times* archive, including country reports:
**http://www.ft.com**

International Business Resources on the WWW: Statistical Data and Information Resources:
**http://www.ciber.msu.edu/busres/statinfo.htm**

OECD International Trade – Statistics on international transactions:
**http://www.oecd.org/std/serint.htm**

UK overseas trade statistics:
**http://www.ons.gov.uk**

University of Massachusetts database of international business periodicals, economic surveys, country factbooks, export/import information, statistical complications and guides to government contacts and trade associations:
**http://www.lib.umb.edu/reference/int_buss.html**

US International Trade Statistics:
**http://www.census.gov/ftp/pub/foreign-trade/www/**

## Key terms

Discriminatory pricing 467          E-commerce 475
Management contracting 471

## Chapter review questions

1 Examine the reasons why a UK based general insurance company should seek to expand into continental Europe.
2 What cultural differences might cause problems for a hotel chain developing a location in India?
3 How might a bank go about researching market potential for business development loans in an overseas country?
4 In what circumstances is a global rather than a localized marketing strategy likely to be successful?
5 Suggest methods by which a firm of consulting engineers can minimize the risk of proposed overseas expansion.
6 What is meant by a strategic alliance and why are they of importance to the services sector? Give examples of strategic alliances.

## Selected further reading

*The following references offer a general review of the factors that influence firms' overseas expansion decisions:*

Cateora, G. and P. Ghauri (1999) *International Marketing*, European edition, McGraw-Hill, Maidenhead
Chee, H. and R. Harris (1998) *Global Marketing Strategy*, Pitman, London
Paliwoda, S. J. (1998) *International Marketing*, 3rd edition, Butterworth-Heinemann, Oxford

*There is relatively little literature which specifically relates to service organizations' overseas market-entry decisions. The following are useful:*

Cicic, M., P. G. Patterson and A. Shoham (1999) 'A Conceptual Model of the Internationalization of Services Firms', *Journal of Global Marketing*, Vol. 12, No. 3, pp 81–106
Erramilli, M. K. and C. P. Rao (1993) 'Service Firms' International Entry-mode Choice: A Modified Transactional Cost Analysis Approach', *Journal of Marketing*, July, Vol. 57, pp 19–38

*The homogenization of world markets and the development of global brands is covered in the following:*

Ritzer, G. (1995) *The MacDonaldization of Society*, Pine Forge Press
Samiee, S. and K. Roth (1992) 'The Influence of Global Marketing on Performance', *Journal of Marketing*, Vol. 56, No. 2, pp 1–17

*For a general overview of trends in international business, consult the following:*

Czinkota, M. R. and M. Kotabe (1997) *Trends in International Business*, Blackwell, Oxford
World Trade Organization, *Annual Report*, published annually
*Economic Trends:* A monthly publication of the UK Office for National Statistics which includes statistics relating to international trade performance

# 16

# Integrative case study Circular Distributors Marketing Services

Few people would have imagined 50 years ago that large amounts of consumer profile data would be bought and sold by companies. But today the collection, analysis and dissemination of marketing information has led to the emergence of a whole new service sector. Services organizations have been both major consumers of information services and producers of increasingly sophisticated services. Information has become ever more crucial to firms in their attempts to target new customers and to track existing ones. The 'information age' and firms' desire to target customers individually rather than *en masse* have given rise to new opportunities for services suppliers. A seemingly bewildering array of organizations has developed a previously unimaginable range of information services which help client companies to get their message more cost effectively to customers than those of their competitors.

One company that has ridden the crest of the information wave is Circular Distributors Ltd. It has been in business for over half a century as a supplier of targeted messages, acting on behalf of numerous goods and services suppliers. Like most companies in the services sector, it has found its marketing environment changing at an increasingly rapid rate. The company has been deeply affected by technological developments which affect the way it operates, the expectations of its customers and the activities of its competitors. An analysis of its recent marketing activities shows how services organizations must constantly monitor their marketing environment and respond to change.

The company is essentially in the business of supplying direct marketing services. As a proportion of all firms' promotional expenditure, direct marketing has been increasing its share during the 1990s, giving rise to exciting opportunities for companies who had developed a sound knowledge of techniques for dealing with customers on a one-to-one basis. Some indication in the shift of promotional expenditure is shown in Figure 16.1. When the direct mail component of this expenditure is examined more closely, it is evident that the business-to-consumer element was expanding more rapidly during the 1990s than the business-to-business element (Figure 16.2).

Circular Distributors was founded over 50 years ago as a very low-tech distributor of leaflets from door-to-door. In its early years it delivered 10 million free samples for

**Figure 16.1**

Advertising expenditure
by medium (adapted
from Advertising
Association data)

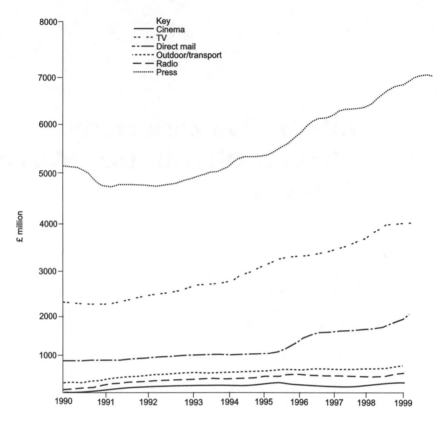

**Figure 16.2**

Composition of direct
mail volume 1990–99
(adapted from Royal
Mail data)

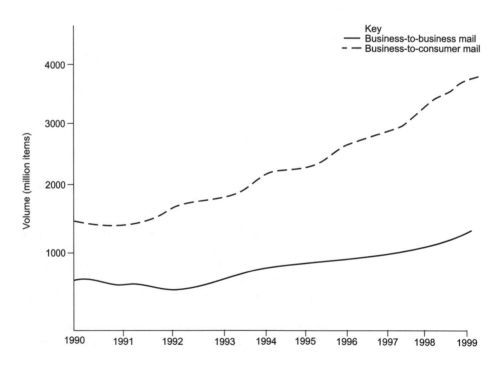

Lever Brothers in the first ever door-to-door distribution of its kind. From a scatter-gun approach to distribution, the company had gradually refined its techniques to deliver promotional leaflets and sample offers of products which typically included shampoo, tea bags and soap. Fifty years ago, many manufacturers of fast-moving consumer goods (fmcg) would have been more than happy with the company's approach which by today's standards would be considered quite simplistic. It was essentially putting a fairly generic product into the hands of a fairly homogeneous market to encourage trial and, hopefully, a subsequent purchase. Over time, markets have become more fragmented as distinctive lifestyle groups have emerged. In response to this, companies have sought to differentiate their products to appeal to ever smaller niche segments. The fairly generic, low value added service which Circular Distributors was selling had become too blunt an instrument for fmcg companies, who now had an exciting range of value added marketing services available to them to target customers more cost effectively.

Circular Distributors' present management team, headed by Nick Wells and three fellow directors, had taken control of the company in a £1.1 million management buyout in 1991. An important part of the new management's business development plan during the 1990s was based on a publication called *Emma's Diary*, launched in 1992 and produced in association with the Royal College of General Practitioners. The 132-page booklet is a week-by-week guide to pregnancy and is given out by GPs and midwives to women when their pregnancy is confirmed. Research has shown that it is read by 78% of expectant mothers and 81% of first-time mothers-to-be. This gives *Emma's Diary* higher readership than all of the competing 13 parenting magazines combined.

Advertising in the biannual publication by producers of baby-related products has accounted for almost a third of *Emma's Diary*'s revenue. A further third of revenue comes from companies paying for the distribution of product samples in the mother's gift pack, which is distributed free to readers through Superdrug shops. The mother's gift pack is an effective marketing medium, collected in 1999 by 400 000 of the total of 720 000 expectant mothers. The remaining one-third of revenue comes from sales of consumer information, which is gathered when expectant mothers register to qualify for the mother's pack.

The success of *Emma's Diary* prompted a spin-off publication in 1997. Operating under the same *Emma's Diary* brand name, the *One Step Ahead* publication is distributed by registrars when a baby's birth is registered. The editorial content concentrates on child-accident prevention. Some 84% of new parents receive the booklet and more than half go on to collect a baby gift pack from Boots stores.

By 1999 the company appeared to be moving along at a very pedestrian pace. In the information age, too much of its energies appeared to be directed at stuffing envelopes, and too little to the collection, analysis and sale of marketing information. The third of revenue for *Emma's Diary* which came from data sales had highlighted the possibilities for the company, but it seemed to be moving at a much slower pace than other companies such as Claritis and Experian who were growing rapidly through the sale of consumer information. In June 1999, the *Sunday Times* ran an article on the company and the expert commentators consulted were not over impressed. Ray Perry of the Chartered Institute of Marketing described Circular Distributors as 'a flat and stagnant company' that needed 'a new lease of life and a new identity'. John Eggleston of KPMG said its managers 'need to take action quickly, accept that growth demands some risk and develop firm and practical plans' to seize opportunities for growth. Managers were criticized for focusing too much on internal issues and lacking the drive to respond to market changes. The article concluded: 'If Circular Distributors is to maintain its profits, it needs to provide door-to-door services of a higher value. It must change its image from a letter-box-stuffing operation to a distributor of marketing materials and services. Ultimately it may need to change its name to attract the right clients.'

The criticism implicit in the *Sunday Times* article goaded the company into a more adventurous approach to its business. For a start, the company changed its name from Circular Distributors to CD Marketing Services and developed Lifestyle Marketing as a brand in its own right to distinguish it from the relatively low-value letter-box distribution service. The Circular Distributors name was retained for the door-to-door distribution service. This part of the business was still very large and in 1999 delivered a total of more than one and a half billion items throughout the UK. Within its portfolio of services, the sale of consumer information may have been the star or growth service, but door-to-door distribution was in danger of going from being a cash cow to a dog.

During 1999, the company invested heavily in new technologies aimed at giving it a competitive advantage in the growing field of data analysis. The immediate effect of this investment was to reduce profits by about £400 000, but this expenditure contributed to an increase in sales to £33 million and profits to £2.4 million. CD invested heavily in developing more sophisticated services than stuffing promotional material and product samples through letter boxes.

Meanwhile, CD developed two further publications that followed a similar formula to the original *Emma's Diary*. In April 2000, CD began to publish *Emma's Diary Pre-School Guide*, aimed at mothers of children aged 3–5 and distributed through doctors' surgeries when youngsters are brought in for their MMR inoculation booster. A further publication called *Married Life . . . The Small Print* was planned for launch in August 2000. This would contain relevant editorial material and sample packs, and would be distributed to couples when they visit vicars and registrars to make wedding arrangements. Both publications generate revenue through advertising and sample packs. However, even greater emphasis was placed on data collection for subsequent sale. Both publications included reader survey forms which generated a 21% response rate during a pilot in November 1999 – high by market research industry standards.

In developing these more specifically targeted products, the company had subtly changed its core business. The emphasis was now as much on collecting information about consumers as on distributing product samples. The focus of the company's service offer had shifted from distribution to information management.

The most important role of the company's new publications was to collect data on consumers at key stages in their life cycles. By 1999, CD already had a database of 3.5 million families, with 1.1 million having been collected in the past two years. It was now collecting data on 600 000 families each year, with 100 000 being 'cleansed' to remove those that change address. The aim was to build Britain's largest database of families with young children.

What was the nature of the service being offered by the company's Lifecycle Marketing division? Segmented lists of consumers created by the company could be rented by organizations for one-off use. The company also sold licences by which other organizations could include CD's data in their own databases. As a further service, CD offered its clients the chance to include specific questions in its publications, for which the client would have exclusive rights to use the data generated. Given the growing difficulty of getting consumers to respond to question-naires, and the high response rates achieved by CD's targeted publications, this service was highly valuable in its own right.

Who were the customers for CD's information services? The two most important groups of customers were financial services and home-shopping businesses, which each accounted for about 30% of data sales. Remaining sales were spread between suppliers of baby products, children's book clubs and various other types of business. All of these clients were attracted by the fact that readers of the company's publications were going through some form of life change, such as becoming a parent or getting married, or having a child starting at school. Each of these life changes is typically associated with new spending priorities and in the absence of previous knowledge about these new types of purchases, mailshots may be particularly welcomed by individuals. Client companies particularly valued the high coverage of the target segments, and the low wastage rate within the lists.

In 1999, the company expected that within three years the revenue of its Lifecycle Marketing division would grow almost threefold, generating sales of £3 million from the publications and gift packs, and more significantly, £4 million from information sales. This was a much faster growth rate than that of the core door-to-door distribu-tion business, which had continued to show modest growth. But did a dash into information services spell dangers as well as opportunities for the company?

The company knew the door-to-door business inside out and had carved a valuable niche for itself where it could offer unrivalled coverage, flexibility and economies of scale. But now that it was moving into the supply of information services it was competing on territory already staked out by much larger competitors. Companies such as Claritas, ICD and Experian had already built up massive databases of consumer information. ICD, for example, claimed to have an average of 72 pieces of information about every household in the country. They could also offer services in many of the overseas markets which their clients operated in. It was not good enough for CD to claim that it had superior knowledge of a small number of niche market segments, because its larger competitors had been steadily building up ever more sophisticated databases of consumer niches. The company saw a major problem in convincing clients to defect from its larger competitors to use its own information services. Would CD always be seen as a low-value letter-box stuffer? Or could it use its long-standing relationships with many fmcg companies to add information services to its service offer? The company needed to build trust and confidence among clients that had never used its services or only perceived the company as a provider of lower value door-to-door distribution.

At the same time, the company was aware that it should not lose sight of its core letterbox market which was still profitable. A number of initiatives to raise the value of services offered to clients were attempted, for example offering a weekend distribution service. The company had previously only operated a weekday distribution service, but had identified that clients' messages could be more effective if they were delivered to a target customer on the day when they have most time to read it. New types of clients appeared for the door-to-door service, such as Internet Service Providers who sought distribution of free CD ROMs to targeted households. The company also extended its gift pack concept by delivering it door to door, without the need to collect it from a designated retail outlet. During 2000, a trial took place to distribute children's school packs door to door. Each pack consisted of a plastic bag containing a back-to-school calendar (carrying advertising messages), a CD-ROM from an Internet service provider; and samples of products aimed at children aged between 5 and 14. A response card sought to increase the volume of information that the company could sell on to its clients.

CD also sought to expand into mainland Europe. It formed strategic alliances with a number of companies who are members of the European Letterbox Marketing Association, so that it is now able to offer its UK clients a 'one-stop shop' distribution service to 140 million homes in France, Germany, Spain and Italy. As evidence that it was taking European expansion seriously, it recruited three multilingual sales staff to handle European sales. By having the ability to offer Europe-wide distribution, the company hoped that it would be able to cater for clients such as L'Oréal, Kimberley-Clark and Gillette who have pan-European marketing operations. Europe-wide distribution was expected to generate £2.5 to £3 million in additional business during 2001.

The company has moved into areas of expertise which were previously unknown to it and thereby has taken big risks. But in the rapidly changing market for information services it could not afford to stand still. New methods of distributing information to target customers are appearing all of the time, with recent examples being the Internet, digital television and WAP mobile phones. How widely should CD spread its resources? Which new media are worth investing in, and which ones may disappear as quickly as they appeared? How far can the company's brand be stretched? There is a great danger that any investment in emerging media may be too little to be effective. It could simply end up having some representation with all media, but being effective in none. The company has made tentative steps into the Internet by setting up a website for *Emma's Diary*, and has gained some information about visitors to the site. It has also earned some revenue from 'click throughs' to advertisers on the site. But to be in this business seriously, the company needs to devote serious amounts of time and resources to it. With an ever-increasing number of Internet Service Providers offering portals which seek users and advertisers, CD is just one of many minnows in a crowded market place.

Circular Distributors has moved from providing a low-value service in a slowly growing market to providing higher value services in rapidly expanding markets. Although the information age has produced many opportunities, it has also produced many casualties among companies that have expanded too fast and failed to deliver a credible value proposition to their customers. During early 2000, 'dot.com' fever appeared to reach a peak with large amounts of money being poured into new ventures seeking to gain more information about consumers. Should CD have taken a bolder approach, or was caution more appropriate? And what about door-to-door distribution, the bread and butter of CD's business – shouldn't the company focus on what it knows best? For the future, one of the main problems facing the company is knowing just where the next threat to its business will come from. What, for instance, will the effect of third generation mobile phones be on consumer information services? Which new technologies should the company invest in? What new services should it seek to offer? Where does the traditional service of door-to-door distribution fit into its portfolio?

(Based on the following: Circular Distributors Ltd website (http://www.cdltd.co.uk) and http://www.Emmasdiary.co.uk); Direct Mail Information Service (http://www.dmis/keystats/html); Sunday Times Enterprise Network 21 May 2000 p(3) 17.)

## Case study review questions

**1**  What business is CD Marketing Services in? What business should it be in?

**2**  Draw a product/market expansion matrix identifying the growth options for CD Marketing Services. How would you assess the riskiness of each identified growth option?

**3**  On what bases can CD position itself relative to its competitors? What position would you recommend that it adopts? What do you consider to be the most important sources of sustainable competitive advantage for CD?

**4**  What methods should the company use to scan its environment for new opportunities/threats? How should they be assessed?

**5**  There is a view that information technology will increasingly allow CD's clients to do much of the data analysis that they currently buy in from CD. In such a scenario, how can CD add value to its service offer?

**6**  Critically assess CD's opportunities for overseas expansion. What factors should influence the company's overseas expansion strategy?

# Glossary

**Benchmarking** Setting performance standards by reference to best practice elsewhere.

**Blueprint** A method of visually portraying the processes and participants involved in the production of a service.

**Branding** The process of creating a distinctive identity for a service or service organization.

**Competitive advantage** A firm has a marketing mix that the target market sees as meeting its needs better than the competitors' marketing mix.

**Consumer services** Services that are finally used up in consumption by individuals and give rise to no further economic benefits.

**Co-production of service** A service benefit can be realized only if more than one party contributes to its production, e.g. customer–producer co-production implies that customers take a role in producing service benefits.

**Core service** The essential nature of a service, expressed in terms of the underlying need which it is designed to satisfy.

**Critical incidents** Encounters between customers and service producers that can be especially satisfying or dissatisfying.

**Culture** The whole set of beliefs, attitudes and customs common to a group of people.

**Customer charter** A statement by a service organization to its customers of the standards of service which it pledges to achieve.

**Customer expectations** The standard of service against which actual service delivery is assessed.

**Customer needs** The underlying forces that drive an individual to make a purchase and thereby satisfy his or her needs.

**Customization** The deliberate and planned adaptation of a service to meet the special requirements of individual customers.

**Direct marketing** Direct communication between a seller and individual customers using a method of promotion other than face-to-face selling.

**Discriminatory pricing** Selling a service at two or more prices, where the difference in prices is not based on the differences in costs.

**Disintermediation** Simplifying a channel of distribution by reducing the role of intermediaries.

**E-commerce** Trading activities which are facilitated by computer-mediated exchange

**Empowerment**  Giving employees authority to act using their own initiative, without reference to senior management.

**Ethics**  A set of principles based on moral judgement.

**Extended marketing mix**  An extension of the '4Ps' marketing mix framework to make it relevant to services. Usually includes people, processes and physical evidence.

**External benefits**  Service benefits for which the producer cannot appropriate value from recipients.

**Franchise**  An agreement where a franchisor develops a good service format and marketing strategy and sells the rights for other individuals or organizations ('franchisees') to use that format.

**Functional quality**  Customers' subjective judgements of the quality of service delivery.

**High-contact services**  Services in which the production process involves a high level of contact between an organization's employees and its customers.

**Human–computer interaction**  The study of how people use computers.

**Industrialization of services**  The process of de-skilling and simplifying service production processes with the aim of reducing variability in outcomes and processes.

**Informediaries**  Intermediaries whose main resource is information, collected and distributed using information technology.

**Inseparability**  The production of most services cannot be spatially or temporally seperated from their consumption.

**Intangibility**  Pure services present no tangible cues which allow them to be assessed by the senses of sight, smell, sound, taste or touch.

**Intermediary**  An individual or organization involved in transferring service benefits from the producer to the final consumer. For services, this usually requires the intermediary to become a co-producer of the service.

**Internal marketing**  The application of the principles and practices of marketing to an organization's dealings with its employees.

**Just-in-time (JIT)**  Reliably getting products to the customer just before the customer needs them. An essential aspect of perishable service production processes.

**Key clients**  Customers who are particularly important to an organization.

**Knowledge management**  The collection and analysis of relevant information for the benefit of the organization as a whole.

**Management contracting**  Selling an organization's management expertise to manage another organization's facility on its behalf.

**Marginal cost**  The addition to total cost resulting from the production of one additional unit of output.

**Market**  A group of potential customers with similar needs who are willing to exchange something of value with sellers offering products that satisfy their needs.

**Market segmentation**  A process of identifying groups of customers within a broad product market who share similar needs and respond similarly to a given marketing mix formulation.

**Marketing**  The management process which identifies, anticipates and supplies customer requirements efficiently and profitably.

**Marketing information system**   Structured systems and processes for collecting, analysing and disseminating marketing information.

**Marketing mix**   The aspects of marketing strategy and tactics that marketing management use to gain a competitive advantage over its competitors. A conceptual framework which – for services – usually includes elements labelled the 'product offer', 'price', 'promotion', 'accessibility', 'people', 'physical evidence' and processes'.

**Mission statement**   A means of reminding everyone within an organization of the essential purpose of the organization.

**Multiplier effect**   The addition to total income and expenditure within an area resulting from an initial injection of expenditure.

**Mystery shopper**   A person employed by an organization to systematically record the standard of its service delivery.

**New service**   An additional service offered by a company, ranging from a completely new service which is unlike anything previously offered in the market, to minor modification of existing services.

**Organizational image**   The way consumers see the organization providing a service, based on the consumers' set of beliefs and previous exposure to the organization.

**Perishability**   Describes the way in which service capacity cannot be stored for sale in a future period – if capacity is not sold when it is produced, the chance to sell it is lost forever.

**Portfolio management**   Managing a range of services to ensure long-term stable profitability.

**Positioning**   Developing a marketing mix which gives an organization a competitive advantage with its chosen target market.

**Postmodern marketing**   An alternative to the traditional scientific, rules-based approach to marketing.

**Producer services**   Services that are sold to other businesses in order to assist them in producing something else of value. Often referred to as 'business-to-business services'.

**Product life cycle**   A hypothetical description of the stages that a product passes through between its development and deletion.

**Product line**   A range of service offers that are related to each other.

**Product mix**   The total range of services offered by an organization.

**Productivity**   The efficiency with which inputs are turned into outputs. Difficult to measure for services as inseparability means that changes in production inputs often affect consumers' perceptions of the value of service outcomes.

**Pure services**   Services which have none of the characteristics associated with goods, i.e. are intangible, inseparable, instantly perishable and incapable of ownership.

**Quality of service**   The standard of service delivery, expressed in terms of the extent to which the customers' expectations are met.

**Quality circles**   Groups of employees formed to discuss methods of better meeting customers' expectations of quality.

**Queuing system**   A system for handling temporal excesses of demand relative to capacity.

**Reintermediation**  Increasing the role played by intermediaries in a channel of distribution.

**Relationship marketing**  A means by which an organization seeks to maintain an ongoing relationship between itself and its customers, based on continuous patterns of service delivery, rather than isolated and discrete transactions.

**Roles**  Behaviour of an individual which is a result of his or her social conditioning, as distinct from innate predispositions.

**Scripting**  Pursuing a pattern of behaviour that is tightly specified by another party.

**Services**  Products which are essentially intangible, inseparable, perishable, and cannot be owned.

**Service agents**  Intermediaries who assist a service principal in making service benefits available to consumers. An agent is usually a co-producer of a service and acts on behalf of the service principal, with whom customers enter into legal relations.

**Service encounter**  The period during which an organization's human and physical resources interact with a customer in order to create service benefits.

**Service failure**  Failure to meet customers' expectations about the standard of service delivery.

**Service image**  The way consumers picture a service offer, based on their set of beliefs and previous experience of the service.

**Services multiplier**  The addition to total expenditure resulting from an initial investment.

**Service offer**  The complexity of tangible and intangible benefits that make up the total functional, psychological and social benefits of a service.

**Service principal**  A relational term describing an organization which produces a service, but which makes some or all of the benefits available through intermediaries.

**Service process**  The activities involved in producing a service which can be specified in the form of a blueprint.

**Service recovery**  Processes used by a company to recover from a service failure.

**Servicescapes**  A description of the environment in which service delivery takes place.

**SERVQUAL**  A method of researching service quality and the gaps betwen the expectations of customers and the perceptions of actual service delivery.

**Servuction**  A description of the producer–consumer service production system.

**Substantive service**  The essential function of a service.

**Tangible cues**  Physical elements of the service offer, brochures and adverts which provide tangible stimuli in the buying decision-making process.

**Technical quality**  Objective measures of quality, not necessarily the measures that consumers consider to be important.

**Variability**  The extent to which service processes or outcomes vary from a norm.

**Yield management**  Methods used to maximize revenue from each unit of finite and perishable capacity.

# References

Aaker, D. A. and J. G. Myers (1982), *Advertising Management*, Prentice-Hall, Englewood Cliffs, NJ

Abell, D. F. and J. S. Hammond (1979) *Strategic Market Planning: Problems and Analytical Approaches*, Prentice-Hall, Englewood Cliffs, NJ

Ackoff, R. L. (1970) *A Concept of Corporate Planning*, Wiley-Interscience, New York

'Advertising', *International Journal of Advertising*, Vol. 4, No. 3, pp 241–6

Albrecht, K. (1990) *Service Within*, Dow Jones-Irwin, Homewood, IL

Anderson, A. (1996) 'Yield Management in Small to Medium Sized Enterprises in the Tourism Industry', European Commission, *DGXXIII*, Tourism Unit

Anderson, E. W. and C. Fornell (1994) 'A Customer Satisfaction Research Prospectus', in R. T. Rust and R. L. Oliver (eds), *Service Quality: New Directions in Theory and Practice*, Sage Publications, Thousand Oaks, CA, pp 241–68

Anderson, E. W., C. Fornell and D. R. Lehmann (1994) 'Customer Satisfaction, Market Share and Profitability', *Journal of Marketing*, Vol. 58, No. 3, pp 53–66

Anderson, P. (1982) 'Marketing, Strategic Planning and Theory', *Journal of Marketing*, Spring, pp 15–26

Ansoff, I. H. (1957) 'Strategies for Diversification', *Harvard Business Review*, September–October, pp 113–24

Anthony, R. N. (1988) *Planning and Control Systems: A Framework for Analysis*, Harvard University Press, Cambridge, MA

Asubonteng, P., K. McCleary and J. Swan (1996) 'SERVQUAL revisited', *Journal of Services Marketing*, Vol. 10, No. 6, pp 62–81

Atkinson, J. (1984) 'Manpower Strategies for Flexible Organizations', *Personnel Management*, August, pp 15–26

Bagozzi, R. P. (1995) 'Reflections on Relationship Marketing in Consumer Markets', *Journal of the Academy of Marketing Science*, Vol. 23, No. 4, pp 272–77

Baker, W. E. (1994) *Networking Smart: How to Build Relationships For Personal And Organizational Success*, McGraw-Hill, New York

Barnes, I. and J. Campbell (1988) 'From Planners to Entrepreneurs: The Privatisation of Local Economic Assistance?' *Public Policy and Administration*, Vol. 3, No. 3

Barnes, J. G. (1994) 'Close to the Customer: But Is It Really a Relationship?' *Journal of Marketing Management*, Vol. 10, No. 7, pp 561–70

Barry, H., M. K. Bacon and K. L. Child (1957) 'A Cross Cultural Survey of Some Sex Differences in Socialization', *Journal of Abnormal and Social Psychology*, Vol. 55, pp 327–32

Barwise, P. and T. Roberston (1992) 'Brand Portfolios', *Europe Management Journal*, Vol. 10, No. 3 (September), pp 277–85

Bateson, J. (1977) 'Do We Need Service Marketing?' in *Marketing Consumer Services: New Insights*, Report 77-115, Marketing Science Institute, Boston, MA

Bateson, J. E. G. (1989) *Managing Services Marketing – Text and Readings*, 2nd edn, Dryden Press, Forth Worth

Bebko, A. (2000) 'Service Intangibility and Its Impact on Consumer Expectations of Service Quality', *Journal of Services Marketing*, Vol. 14, No. 1, pp 9–26

Becker, L. C. (1990) *Reciprocity*, University of Chicago Press, Chicago

Beer, M. *et al.* (1984) *Managing Human Assets*, Free Press, New York

Bennis, W. G. (1989) 'Managing the Dream: Leadership in the 21st Century', *Journal of Organisational Change Management*, Vol. 2, No. 1, pp 6–10

Berger, P. L. and T. Luckmann (1966) *The Social Construction of Reality*, Doubleday, Garden City, NY

Berry, L. L. (1980) 'Services Marketing is Different', *Business*, May–June, Vol. 30, No. 3, pp 24–9

Berry, L. L. (1995) 'Relationship Marketing of Services – Growing Interest, Emerging Perspectives', *Journal of the Academy of Marketing Science*, Vol. 23, No. 4, pp 236–45

Bhutta, K. S. and F. Huq (1999) 'Benchmarking Best Practices: An Integrated Approach', *Benchmarking: An International Journal*, Vol. 6, No. 3, pp 256–70

Bickert, J. (1992 'Database Marketing: An Overview', in Edward L. Nash (ed), *The Direct Marketing Handbook*, McGraw-Hill, New York

Bitner, M. (1990) 'Evaluating Service Encounters: The Effects of Physical Surroundings and Employee Responses', *Journal of Marketing*, April, Vol. 51, pp 69–82

Bitner, M. J., B. H. Booms and M. S. Tetreault (1990) 'The Service Encounter: Diagnosing Favorable and Unfavorable Incidents', *Journal of Marketing*, January, Vol. 54, pp 71–84

Bolton, R. and J. Drew (1991) 'A Multistage Model of Customers' Assessments of Service Quality and Value', *Journal of Consumer Research*, March, Vol. 17, pp 375–84

Bolton, R. N. and K. N. Lemon (1999) 'A Dynamic Model of Customers' Usage of Services: Usage as an Antecedent and Consequence of Satisfaction', *Journal of Marketing Research*, Vol. 36, No. 2, pp 171–86

Booms, B. H. and M. J. Bitner (1981) 'Marketing Strategies and Organisation Structures for Service Firms', in J. Donnelly and W. R. George (eds), *Marketing of Services*, Chicago, IL, pp 51–67

Borden, N. H. (1965) 'The Concept of the Marketing Mix', in G. Schwartz (ed), *Science in Marketing*, Wiley, New York, pp 386–97

Boshoff, C. (1997) 'An Experimental Study of Service Recovery Options', *International Journal of Service Industry Management*, Vol. 8, No. 2, pp 11–130

Boulding, W., A. Kalra, R. Staelin and V. A. Zeithaml (1993) 'A Dynamic Process Model of Service Quality: From Expectations to Behavioral Intentions', *Journal of Marketing Research*, February, Vol. 30, pp 7–27

Bowden, D. E. and B. Scheider (1988) 'Services Marketing Management: Implications for Organisational Behaviour', *Research in Organisational Behaviour*, Vol. 10, pp 43–80

Bowen, D. E. and E. E. Lawler, III (1992) 'The Empowerment of Service Workers: What, Why, How, and When', *Sloan Management Review*, Vol. 33, No. 3, pp 31–9

Boxall, P. (1992) 'Strategic HRM: Beginnings of a New Theoretical Direction', *Human Resource Management Journal*, Vol. 2, No. 3, pp 59–73

Boyle, B., F. R. Dwyer, R. Robicheaux and J. T. Simpson (1992) 'Influence Strategies in Marketing Channels: Measures and Use in Different Relationship Structures', *Journal of Marketing Research*, Vol. 29, No. 4, pp 462–73

Brady, J. and I. Davis (1993) 'Marketing's Mid-Life Crisis', *The McKinsey Quarterly*, Vol. 2, pp 17–28

Brookes, R. (1988) *The New Marketing*, Gower Press, Aldershot

Brown, S. W., P. G. Churchill and J. P. Peter (1993) 'Research Note: Improving the Measurement of Service Quality, *Journal of Retailing*, Spring, Vol. 69, pp 127–39

Brown, S. (1995) *Postmodern Marketing*, Routledge, London

Burt, R. (1992) *Structural Holes: The Social Structure Of Competition*, Harvard University Press, Cambridge, MA

Carlzon, J., 1987: *Moments of Truth*, Ballinger Books, Cambridge, MA

Carman, J. M. (1990) 'Consumer Perceptions of Service Quality: An Assessment of the SERVQUAL Dimensions', *Journal of Retailing*, Vol. 66, No. 1, pp 33–55

Carman, J. M. and E. Langeard (1979) 'Growth Strategies for Service Firms', *Proceedings of the 8th Annual Meeting of the European Academy for Advanced Research in Marketing*, Gröningen

Channon, D. F. (1978) *The Service Industries*, Macmillan, London

Chase, R. B. (1978) 'Where Does the Customer Fit in a Service Operation?' *Harvard Business Review*, November–December, pp 137–42

Christopher, M., A. Payne and M. Ballantyne (1991) *Relationship Marketing*, Butterworth-Heinemann, London

Cole, G. (1988) *Personnel Management*, DP Publications, London

Copulsky J. R. and M. J. Wolf (1990) 'Relationship Marketing: Positioning for the Future', *Journal of Business Strategy*, July–August, pp 16–20

Coulson-Thomas, C. T. (1985) *Marketing Communications*, Butterworth-Heinemann, London

Cowell, D. (1984) *The Marketing of Services*, Butterworth-Heinemann, London

Cowell, D. (1988) 'New Service Development', *Journal of Marketing Management*, Vol. 3, No. 3, pp 142–57

Cronin, J. J. and S. A. Taylor (1992) 'Measuring Service Quality: A Re-examination and Extension', *Journal of Marketing*, July, Vol. 56, pp 55–68

Cronin, J. J. and S. A. Taylor (1994) 'SERVPERF versus SERVQUAL: Reconciling Performance-based and Perceptions-minus-Expectations Measurement of Service Quality, *Journal of Marketing*, Vol. 58, No. 1, pp 125–31

Crosby, Philip B. (1984) *Quality Without Tears*, New American Library, New York

Crosby, L. A., K. R. Evans and D. Cowles (1990) 'Relationship Quality in Services Selling: An Interpersonal Influence Perspective', *Journal of Marketing*, July, Vol. 54, pp 68–81

Cross, R. (1997) *Revenue Management*, Broadway Books, New York

Cunningham, M. T. and P. W. Turnbull (1982) 'Inter-organizational Personal Contact Patterns', in H. Hakansson (ed), *International Marketing and Purchasing of Industrial Goods*, Wiley, New York

Cutts, Robert L. (1992) 'Capitalism in Japan: Cartels and Keiretsu', *Harvard Business Review*, July–August, Vol. 70, pp 48–55

Cyert, R. M. and J. G. March (1963) *A Behavioural Theory of the Firm*, Prentice-Hall, Englewood Cliffs, NJ

Dabholkar, P.A., D. I. Thorpe and J. O. Rentz. (1996) 'A Measure of Service Quality for Retail Stores: Scale Development and Validation', *Journal of the Academy of Marketing Science*, Vol. 24, No. 1, pp 3–16

Davies, B., S. Baron, T. Gear and M. Read (1999) 'Measuring and Managing Service Quality', *Marketing Intelligence & Planning*, Vol. 17, No. 1, pp 33–40

Davis, D. L., J. P. Guiltinan and W. H. Jones (1979) 'Service Characteristics, Consumer Search and the Classification of Retail Services', *Journal of Retailing*, Vol. 55, No. 3

Day, G. S. (1995) 'Advantageous Alliances', *Journal of the Academy of Marketing Science*, Vol. 23, No. 4, pp 297–300

Day, G. S. and R. Wensley (1983) 'Marketing Theory with a Strategic Orientation', *Journal of Marketing*, Fall, Vol. 47, pp 79–89

De Chernatony, L. and G. McWilliam (1990) 'Appreciating Brands as Assets Through Using a Two-Dimensional Model', *International Journal of Advertising*, Vol. 9, No. 2, pp 111–19

Demski, J. S. (1980) 'Economically Optimal Performance Evaluation and Control Systems', *Journal of Accounting Research*, Vol. 18, pp 184–220

Denton, D. K. (1990) 'Customer Focused Management', *HR Magazine*, August, pp 62–7

Department of Transport (1996) *Transport Statistics*, HMSO, London

Dibb, S., L. Simkin, W. M. Pride and O. C. Ferrell (1994) *Marketing: Concepts and Strategies*, 2nd European edition, Houghton-Mifflin, London

Dick, Alan S. and K. Basu (1994) 'Customer Loyalty: Toward an Integrated Conceptual Framework', *Journal of the Academy of Marketing Science*, Vol. 22, No. 2, pp 99–113

Dickson, P. R. and A. G. Sawyer (1990) 'The Price Knowledge and Search of Supermarket Shoppers', *Journal of Marketing*, Vol. 54, pp 42–53

Diffenbach, J. (1983) 'Corporate Environmental Analysis in US Corporations', *Long Range Planning*, Vol. 16, No. 3, pp 107–16

Dolan, P. and I. Brierley (1992) *A Tale of Two Bus Companies*, Partnership Research, London

Donaghy, K. and U. McMahon (1995) 'Managing Yield: A Marketing Perspective', *Journal of Vacation Marketing*, Vol. 2, No. 1, pp 655–62

Donaghy, K., U. McMahon and D. McDowell (1995) 'Yield Management: An Overview', *International Journal of Hospitality Management*, Vol. 14, No. 2, pp. 139–50

Donaghy, K., U. McMahon-Beattie, I. Yeoman and A. Ingold (1998) 'The Realism of Yield Management', *Progress in Tourism and Hospitality Research*, No. 4, pp 187–95

Dretske, F. (1981) *Knowledge and the Flow of Information*, MIT Press, Cambridge, MA

Drucker, P. F. (1973) *Management: Tasks, Responsibilities and Practices*, Harper & Row, New York

Drucker, P. F. (1993) *Post-capitalist Society*, Butterworth-Heinemann, Oxford

Drucker, P. (1999) *Management Challenges for the 21st Century*, Harper & Row, New York

Dwyer, F. R., P. H. Schurr and S. Oh (1987) 'Developing Buyer and Seller Relationships', *Journal of Marketing*, April, Vol. 51, pp 11–27

Easingwood, C. J. (1986) 'New Product Development For Service Companies', *Journal of Product Innovation Management*, No. 4, pp 207–18

Eccles, R. G. (1983) 'Control with Fairness in Transfer Pricing', *Harvard Business Review*, November–December, pp 149–56

Edvardsson, B. and T. Strandvik (2000) 'Is a Critical Incident Critical for a Customer Relationship?' *Managing Service Quality*, Vol. 10, No. 2, pp 82–91

Edvardsson, B., B. Thomasson and J. Ovretveit (1994) *Quality of Service: Making it Really Work*, Maidenhead, McGraw-Hill

Eiglier, P. and E. Langeard (1977) 'A New Approach To Service Marketing', in *Marketing Consumer Services: New Insights*, Report 77-115, Marketing Science Institute, Boston, MA

Ennew, C., P. Wong and M. Wright (1992) 'Organisational Structures and the Boundaries of the Firm: Acquisitions and Divestments in Financial Services', *The Services Industries Journal*, Vol. 12, No. 4, pp 478–97

Eurostat (1995) *Europe in Figures*, 4th edition, Office for Official Publications of the European Communities, Luxembourg

Firestone, S. H. (1983) 'Why Advertising a Service is Different', in L. L. Berry, G. L. Shostack and G. D. Upah (eds), *Emerging Perspectives in Services Marketing*, American Marketing Association, Chicago, IL

Fishbein, M. (1967) *Readings in Attitude Theory and Measurement*, Wiley, New York

Fisk, R. P. (1981) 'Toward a Consumption/Evaluation Process Model for Services', in J. H. Donnelly and W. R. George (eds), *Marketing of Services*, American Marketing Association, Chicago, IL

Fisk, R. P., S. W. Brown and M. J. Bitner (1993) 'Tracking the Evolution of the Services Marketing Literature', *Journal of Retailing*, Vol. 69, No. 1, pp 61–103

Ford, D. (1981) 'The Development of Buyer–Seller Relationships in Industrial Markets', *European Journal of Marketing*, Vol. 14, pp 339–53

Foreman, S. and A. Money (1995) 'Internal Marketing: Concepts, Measurement and Application', *Journal of Marketing Management*, Vol. 11, No. 8, pp 755–68

Formbrun, C. (1984) *Strategic Human Resource Management*, Wiley, New York

Fornell, C., M. D. Johnson, E. W. Anderson, J. Cha and B. E. Bryant (1996) 'The American Customer Satisfaction Index: Nature, Purpose and Findings', *Journal of Marketing*, October, Vol. 60, pp 7–18

Fox, A. (1988) *Man Mismanagement*, IRRU, Warwick

Fuchs, V. (1968) *The Service Economy*, National Bureau of Economic Research, Columbia University Press, New York

Gabbie, O. and M. O'Neill (1997) 'SERVQUAL and the Northern Ireland Hotel Sector: A Comparative Study', *Managing Service Quality*, Vol. 7, No. 1, pp 43–9

Galloway, L. (1999) 'Hysteresis: A Model of Consumer Behaviour?' *Managing Service Quality*, Vol. 9, No. 5, pp 360–70

Gardner, B. and S. Levy (1955) 'The Product and the Brand', *Harvard Business Review*, March–April, Vol. 33, pp 33–9

Garvin, D. A. (1993) 'Building a learning organization', *Harvard Business Review*, July–August, pp 78–91

George, W. R. and L. L. Berry (1981) 'Guidelines for the Advertising of Services', *Business Horizons*, July–August, Vol. 24, pp 43–9

George, W. R. and T. A. Myers (1981) 'Life Underwriters' Perceptions of Differences in Selling Goods and Services', *CLU Journal*, April

Gershuny, J. (1978) 'After Industrial Society? The Emerging Self-Service Economy', Macmillan, London

Getty, J. M. and K. N. Thompson (1994) 'The Relationship Between Quality, Satisfaction and Recommending Behaviour in Lodging Decisions', *Journal of Hospitality and Leisure Marketing*, Vol. 2, No. 3, pp 3–22

Gilbert, D. C. and V. Karabeyekian (1995) 'The frequent flyer mess – a comparison of programmes in the USA and Europe', *Journal of Vacation Marketing*, Vol. 1, No. 3, pp 248–56

Giles, W. (1988) 'Marketing Planning for Maximum Growth', in M. J. Thomas (ed.) *The Marketing Handbook*, Gower Press, Aldershot

Goodwin, Cathy (1996) 'Moving the Drama into the Factory: The Contribution of Metaphors to Services Research, *European Journal of Marketing*, Vol. 30, No. 9, pp 13–36

Goodwin, C. and I. Ross (1992) 'Consumer Responses to Service Failures: Influence of Procedural and Interactional Fairness Perceptions', *Journal of Business Research*, September, Vol. 25, pp 149–63

Goodwin, F. (1998), 'Simplicity Ends Confusion', *Marketing*, June, Vol. 11, p 15

Grant, J. (1999), *The New Marketing Manifesto: The 12 Rules for Building Successful Brands in the 21st Century*, Orion Business, London

Grant, L. (1998) 'Your Customers Are Telling the Truth', *Fortune*, 16 February, pp 164–6

Gronroos, C. (1978) 'A Service Orientated Approach to the Marketing of Services', *European Journal of Marketing*, Vol. 12, No. 8, pp 588–601

Gronroos, C. (1982) *Strategic Management and Marketing in the Service Sector*, Swedish School of Economics and Business Administration, Helsingfors

Gronroos, C. (1984) 'A Service Quality Model and its Marketing Implications', *European Journal of Marketing*, Vol. 18, No. 4, pp 36–43

Gronroos, C. (1984b) *Strategic Management and Marketing in the Service Sector*, Chartwell Bratt, Kent

Gronroos, C. (1989) 'Defining Marketing: A Market-Oriented Approach', *European Journal of Marketing*, Vol. 23, No. 1, pp 52–60

Gronroos, C. (1990) 'Relationship Approach to Marketing in Service Contexts: The Marketing and Organisational Interface', *Journal of Business Research*, Vol. 20, pp 3–11

Gronroos, C. (1994) 'From Marketing Mix to Relationship Marketing', *Management Decision*, Vol. 32, No. 1, pp 4–20

Gronroos, C. (1997) 'From Marketing Mix to Relationship Marketing: Towards a Paradigm Shift in Marketing', *Management Decision*, March–April, Vol. 35, No. 3, pp 322–40

Guest, D. (1989) 'HRM and Personnel Management: Can You Spot the Difference?' *Personnel Management*, January

Guest, D. (1992) 'HRM Current Trends and Future Prospects'. Unpublished paper for the LSE industrial relations trade union seminar

Guiltinan, J. P. (1987) 'The Price Bundling of Services: A Normative Framework', *Journal of Marketing*, April, Vol. 51, pp 74–85

Gummesson, E. (1991) 'Marketing-orientation Revisited: The Crucial Role of the Part-time Marketer', *European Journal of Marketing*, Vol. 25, No. 2, pp 60–75

Gummesson, E. (1993) 'Relationship Marketing – A New Way of Doing Business', *European Business Report*, 3Q, Autumn, pp 52–56

Gummesson, E. (1997) 'Relationship Marketing as a Paradigm Shift: Some Conclusions from the 30R Approach', *Management Decision*, March–April, Vol. 35, No. 3-4, pp 267–73

Gummesson, E. (1999) *Total Relationship Marketing*, Butterworth-Heinemann, London

Gwynne, A. L., J. Devlin and C. T. Ennew (1998) 'Service Quality and Customer Satisfaction: A Longitudinal Analysis', The British Academy of Marketing Annual Conference, Sheffield Hallam University, 8–10 July 1998, pp 186–91

Hakansson, H. (ed.) (1982) *International Marketing and Purchasing of Industrial Goods*, IMP Group, Wiley, New York

Hales, C. (1994) 'Internal Marketing as an Approach to Human Resource Management: A New Perspective or a Metaphor Too Far?' *Human Resource Management Journal*, Vol. 5, No. 1, pp 50–71

Halstead D., C. Drogue and M. B. Cooper (1993) 'Product Warranties and Post Purchase Service: A Model of Consumer Satisfaction without Complaint Resolution', *Journal of Services Marketing*, Vol. 7, No. 1, pp 33–40

Hamel, Gary (1991) 'Competition for Competence and Inter-Partner Learning Within International Strategic Alliances', *Strategic Management Journal*, January–February, Vol. 12, pp 83–103

Hamel, G., Y. Doz and C. K. Prahalad (1989) 'Collaborate With Your Competitors – And Win', *Harvard Business Review*, January–February, Vol. 67, pp 133–9

Han, S. L., D. T. Wilson and S. P. Dant (1993) 'Buyer–Supplier Relationships Today', *Industrial Marketing Management*, Vol. 22, 331–8

Handy, Charles B. (1989) *The Age of Unreason*, Harvard Business School Press, Boston, MA

Hart, Christopher W. L., W. E. Sasser Jr and James L. Heskett (1990) 'The Profitable Art of Service Recovery', *Harvard Business Review*, July–August, pp 148–56

Hart, S. (1989) 'Product Deletion and the Effects of Strategy', *Journal of Marketing*, Vol. 23, No. 10, pp 6–17

Hartline, M. D. and O. C. Ferrell (1996) 'The Management of Customer Contact Service Employees: An Empirical Investigation', *Journal of Marketing*, October, Vol. 60, pp 52–70

Heide, J. B. (1994) 'Interorganizational Governance in Marketing Channels', *Journal of Marketing*, January, Vol. 58, pp 71–85

Hendry, C. and A. Pettigrew (1986) 'The Practice of Strategic HRM', *Personnel Review*, Vol. 15, No. 5, pp 406–17

Hendry, C. and A. Pettigrew (1990) 'An Agenda for the 1990's', *International Journal of HRM*, Vol. 1, No. 1

Henley Centre (1995) 'The Loyalty Paradox', report for Christian Brann, London, The Henley Centre

Henry, H. (1971) 'Corporate Strategy, Marketing and Diversification, in Perspectives on Management Marketing and Research', Crosby Lockwood, London

Heskett, J. L., W. E. Sasser and L. A. Schlesinger (1998) 'The Service Profit Chain: How Leading Companies Link Profit and Growth to Loyalty, Satisfaction and Value', *International Journal of Service Industry Management*, Vol. 9, No. 3, pp 145–76

Hill, C. W. L and J. F. Pickering (1986) 'Divisionalisation, Decentralisation and Performance of Large United Kingdom Companies', *Journal of Management Studies*, January, Vol. 23, pp 26–50

Hise, R. T. (1977) *Product/Service Strategy*, Petrocelli/Charter, New York

HMI (1991) 'Higher Education in Further Education Colleges', HMI report, ref 228/91/NS, Department of Education and Science, London

Hoffer, C. W. and D. E. Schendel (1978) *Strategy Formulation: Analytical Concepts*, West, New York

Hoffman, K. D. and S. W. Kelley (2000) 'Perceived Justice Needs and Recovery Evaluation: A Contingency Approach', *European Journal of Marketing*, Vol. 34, No. 3/4, pp 296–304

Hoffman, K. D., S. W. Kelley and H. M. Rotalsky (1995) 'Tracking Service Failures and Employee Recovery Efforts', *Journal of Services Marketing*, Vol. 2, pp 49–61

Hope, C. and A. Muhlemann (1997) *Service Operations*, Prentice-Hall, Englewood Cliffs, NJ

Hornik, J. (1984) 'Subjective versus Objective Time Measures: A Note on the Perception of Time in Consumer Behavior', *Journal of Consumer Behavior*, Vol. 32, pp 44–53

Howard, J. A. and J. N. Sheth (1969) *The Theory of Buyer Behavior*, Wiley, New York

Hudson, S. and G. W. H. Shephard (1998) 'Measuring Service Quality at Tourist Destinations: An Application of Importance–Performance Analysis to an Alpine Ski Resort', *Journal of Travel and Tourism Marketing*, Vol. 7, No. 3, pp 61–77

Huff, D. L., (1966) 'A Programmed Solution for Approximating an Optimal Retail Location, *Land Economics*, Vol. 42, pp 293–303

Iacobucci, D., K. A. Grayson and O. L. Omstrom (1994) 'The Calculus of Service Quality and Customer Satisfaction: Theoretical and Empirical Differentiation and Integration', in T. A. Swartz, D. E. Bowen, and S. W. Brown (eds), *Advances in Services Marketing and Management*, Vol. 3, JAI Press, Greenwich, CT, pp 1–68

Iacobucci, D., A. Ostrom and K. Grayson (1995) 'Distinguishing Service Quality and Customer Satisfaction: The Voice of the Consumer', *Journal of Consumer Psychology*, Vol. 4, No. 3, pp 277–303

Ingham, H. (1991) 'Organisational Structure and Internal Control in the UK Insurance Industry', *The Services Industries Journal*, October, Vol. 11, No. 4, pp 425–38

*Inside Research* (1998) February, Vol. 107

International Labour Office (1996) *Year Book of Labour Statistics*, International Labour Office, Geneva

Jackson, B. B. (1985) 'Build Customer Relationships that Last', *Harvard Business Review*, November–December

Jaworski, B. J. (1988) 'Toward a Theory of Marketing Control: Environmental Context, Control Types and Consequences', *Journal of Marketing*, Vol. 52, No. 3, pp 23–39

Jelinek, M., L. Smirich and P. Hirsch (1983) 'Introduction: A Code of Many Colours', *Administrative Science Quarterly*, Vol. 28, p 337

Johnson, G. and K. Scholes (1988) *Exploring Corporate Strategy*, 2nd edition, Prentice-Hall, London

Johnston, B. (1995) 'The Determinants of Service Quality: Satisfiers and Dissatisfiers', *International Journal of Service Industry Management*, Vol. 6, No. 5, pp 128–41

Jones, G. (1992) 'Setting Measurable Standards in Customer Service'. Paper presented at BEM seminar on the measurement of customer service. London, June 1992.

Jones, K. G. and D. R. Mock (1984) 'Evaluating Retail Trading Performance', in R. L. Davies and D. S. Rogers (eds), *Store Location and Store Assessment Research*, Wiley, London

Juran, J. M. (1982) *Upper Management and Quality*, Juran Institute, New York

Kahil, O. and T. Harcar (1995) 'Relationship Marketing and Data Quality Management', *SAM Advanced Management Journal*, Spring, Vol. 64, No. 2, pp 26–33

Kahneman, D. and D. T. Miller (1986) 'Norm Theory: Comparing Reality to its Alternatives', *Psychological Review*, Vol. 93, pp 136–53

Kanter, R. M. (1994) 'Collaborative Advantage', *Harvard Business Review*, July–August, Vol. 72, pp 96–108

Katz, K. L., B. M. Larson and R. C. Larson (1991) 'Prescription for the Waiting-in-Line-Blues: Entertain, Enlighten, and Engage', *Sloan Management Review*, Winter, Vol. 32, pp 44–53

Kaufmann, C. F. and L. W. Stern (1992) 'Relational Exchange, Contracting Norms and Conflict in Industrial Exchange', in G. L. Frazier (ed), *Advances in Distribution Channel Research*, Vol. 1, 135–59

Keegan, W. J. (1995) *Global Marketing Management*, Prentice-Hall, Englewood Cliffs, NJ

Kelley, S. W. (1993) 'Discretion and the Service Employee', *Journal of Retailing*, Spring, Vol. 69, No. 1, pp 104–26

Kelley, S. W. and M. A. Davis (1994) 'Antecedents to Customer Expectations for Service Recovery', *Journal of the Academy of Marketing Science*, Vol. 22, No. 1, pp 52–61

Kelly, D. and C. Storey (2000) 'New Service Development: Initiation Strategies', *International Journal of Service Industry Management*, Vol. 11, No. 1, pp 45–65

Kent, R. A. (1986) 'Faith in the Four Ps: An Alternative', *Journal of Marketing Management*, Vol. 2, No. 2, pp 145–54

Kimes, S. (1989) 'The Basics of Yield Management', *Cornell Hotel and Restaurant Administration Quarterly*, Vol. 30, No. 3, pp 14–19

Kimes, S. (1997) 'Yield Management: An Overview', in I. Yeoman and A. Ingold (eds), Yield Management, Strategies for the Service Industries. Cassell, London, pp 3–11

King, S. (1991) 'Brand Building in the 1990s', *Journal of Marketing Management*, Vol. 7, No. 1, pp 3–13

Kingman-Brundage, J. (1989) 'The ABCs of service system blueprinting', in M. J. Bitner and L. A. Crosby (eds), *Designing a Winning Service Strategy*, American Marketing Association, Chicago, IL

Knox, S. (1998) 'Loyal to the Core', *Campaign*, 3 July, pp 30–2

Kohli, A. K. and B. J. Jaworski (1990) 'Market Orientation: The Construct, Research Propositions and Management Implications', *Journal of Marketing*, April, Vol. 54, pp 1–18

Kotler, P. (1991) *Marketing Management: Analysis, Planning, Implementation and Control*, Prentice-Hall, Englewood Cliffs, NJ

Kotler, P. (1999) *Marketing Management: Analysis, Planning, Implementation and Control*, 10th edition, Prentice Hall, Englewood Cliffs, NJ

Kotler, P. and A. Andreasen (1991) *Strategic Marketing for Non-Profit Organizations*, Prentice-Hall, Englewood Cliffs, NJ

Kotler, P., G. Armstrong, J. Saunders and V. Wong (1999) *Principles of Marketing*, European edition, Prentice-Hall, Hemel Hempstead

Lancaster, G. and I. Waddelow (1998) 'An Empirical Investigation into the Process of Strategic Marketing Planning in SME's: Its Attendant Problems and Proposals Towards a New Practical Paradigm', *Journal of Marketing Management*, Vol. 14, pp 835–78

Lavidge, R. J. and G. A. Steiner (1961) 'A Model for Predictive Measurements of Advertising Effectiveness', *Journal of Marketing*, October, Vol. 25, pp 61–5

Levitt, T. (1960) 'Marketing Myopia', *Harvard Business Review*, July–August, pp 45–56

Levitt, T. (1972) 'Production Line Approach to Service', *Harvard Business Review*, September–October, pp 41–52

Levitt, T. (1976) 'Addendum on Marketing and the Post-industrial Society', *The Public Interest*, Summer, No. 44, pp 69–103

Levitt, T. (1981) 'Marketing Intangible Products and Product Tangibles', *Harvard Business Review*, May–June, Vol. 59, 95–102

Lewis, B. R. (1991) 'Bank Service Quality', *Journal of Marketing Management*, Vol. 7, No. 1, pp 47–62

Lewis, R. (1981) 'Restaurant Advertising: Appeals and Consumers' Intentions', *Journal of Advertising Research*, Vol. 21, No. 5, pp 69–74

Lieberman, W. H. (1993) 'Debunking the Myths of Yield Management', *Cornell Hotel and Restaurant Administration Quarterly*, Vol. 34, No. 1, pp 34–44

Liljander, V. and T. Strandvik (1995) 'The Nature of Customer Relationships in Services', in T. A. Swartz, D. E. Bowen and S. W. Brown (eds), *Advances in Services Marketing and Management*, Vol. 4, JAI Press, London

Lovelock, C. (1981) 'Why Marketing Needs To Be Different for Services', in J. H. Donnelly and W. R. George (eds), *Marketing of Services*, American Marketing Association, Chicago, IL

Lovelock, C. H. (1983) 'Classifying Services to Gain Strategic Marketing Insight', *Journal of Marketing*, Summer, Vol. 47, pp 9–20

Lovelock, C. H. (1984) 'Developing and Implementing New Services', in *Developing New Services*, American Marketing Association, Chicago, IL

Lovelock, C. H. and R. F. Young (1979) 'Look to Consumers to Increase Productivity', *Harvard Business Review*, May–June, pp 168–78

Lukas, B. A. and I. Maignan (1996) 'Striving for Quality: The Key Role of Internal and External Customers', *Journal of Market Focused Management*, Vol. 1, pp 175–97

Lunn, T. (1986) 'Segmenting and Constructing Markets', in R. Worcester and J. Downham (eds), *Consumer Market Research Handbook*, ESOMAR/McGraw-Hill, New York

MacKay, S. and A. Conway (1992) 'A Network Approach to New Service Development', Working Paper for the Marketing Education Group Conference, Salford University, Salford

Macneil, I. R. (1980) *The New Social Contract: An Inquiry into Modern Contractual Relations*, Yale University Press, New Haven, CT

Main, J. (1990) 'Making Global Alliances Work', *Fortune*, 17 December, pp 123–6

Marchington, M. and P. Parker (1990) *Changing Patterns of Employee Relations*, Harvester Wheatsheaf, London

*Marketing* (1994) 'Heinz Picks Duo for £22m Push', *Marketing*, 16 June, p 1, Haymarket Publishing, London

*Marketing* (1994) 'Marketing is Something Else', 8 December, p 31, Haymarket Publishing, London

Martin, C. L. (1996) 'Editorial: How Powerful Is Empowerment?' *Journal of Services Marketing*, Vol. 10, No. 6, pp 4–5

Maslow, A. (1943) 'A Theory of Human Motivation', *Psychological Review*, Vol. 50, No. 4, pp 370–96

Mayo, E. J. and L. P. Jarvis (1981) *The Psychology of Leisure Travel*, CBI Publishing, Boston, MA

McAlexander, J. H., D. O. Kaldenberg and H. Koenig (1994) 'Service Quality Measurement', *Journal of Health Care Marketing*, Fall, Vol. 14, No. 3, pp 34–9

McDonald, M. H. B. (1995) *Marketing Plans: How to Prepare Them, How to Use Them*, 3rd edition, London, Butterworth-Heinemann

McGregor, D. (1960) *The Human Side of Enterprise*, McGraw-Hill, New York

McNair, M. P. (1958) 'Significant Trends and Developments in the Post-War Period', in A. B. Smith (ed.), *Competitive Distribution in a Free High Level Economy and its Implications for the University*, University of Pittsburgh Press, Pittsburgh, pp 1–25

McNerney, D. J. (1996) 'Compensation: The Link to Customer Satisfaction', *HR Focus*, September, Vol. 9, p 1

Mels, G., C. Boshoff and N. Deon (1997) 'The Dimensions of Service Quality: The Original European Perspective Revisited', *The Service Industries Journal*, January, Vol. 17, pp 173–89

Meyers-Levy, J. and B. Sternthal (1991) 'Gender Differences in the Use of Message Cues and Judgements', *Journal of Marketing Research*, February, Vol. 28, pp 84–96

Miniard, P. W. and J. E. Cohen (1983) 'Modeling Personal and Normative Influences on Behavior', *Journal of Consumer Research*, September, Vol. 10, pp 169–80

Mitchell, A. (1998) 'Concentrate on How to Serve Your Existing Customers Better', *Management Today*, January, pp 84–6

Money, R. B., M. C. Gilly and J. L. Graham (1998) 'Explorations of National Culture and Word-of-Mouth Referral Behavior in the Purchase of Industrial Services in the United States and Japan, *Journal of Marketing*, October, Vol. 62, No. 4, pp 76–87

Moorman, C., G. Zaltman and R. Deshpande (1992) 'Relationships Between Providers and Users of Market Research: The Dynamics of Trust Within and Between Organisations', *Journal of Marketing Research*, August, Vol. 29, 314–28

Mortished, C. (1999) 'BA Fined £4m Over Illegal Sweeteners', *The Times*, 15 July, p 2

Moschis, G. P. (1976) 'Social Comparison and Informal Group Influence', *Journal of Marketing Research*, August, Vol. 13, pp 237–44

Moutinho, L. (1989) 'Goal Setting Process and Typologies: The Case of Professional Services', *Journal of Professional Services Marketing*, Vol. 4, No. 2, pp 83–100

Moutinho, L. and M. Evans (1992) *Applied Marketing Research*, Addison Wesley, Reading, MA

Mowlana, H. and G. Smith (1993) 'Tourism in a Global Context: The Case of Frequent Traveller Programmes', *Journal of Travel Research*, Winter, pp 20–27

Munson, J. M. and W. A. Spivey (1981) 'Products and Brand Users Stereotypes Among Social Classes', in K. Munroe (ed.), *Advances in Consumer Research*, ACR, Ann Arbor

Murphy, C. (1998) 'Tesco Customer Numbers Rocket', *Marketing*, 29 October, p 6

Murray, J. A. and A. O'Driscoll (1997) 'Messianic Eschatology: Some Redemptive Reflections on Marketing and the Benefits of a Process Approach', *European Journal of Marketing*, September–October, Vol. 31, No. 9–10, pp 706–20

Narver, J. C. and S. F. Slater (1990) 'The Effect of a Market Orientation on Business Profitability', *Journal of Marketing*, October, pp 20–35

Nonaka, I. (1991) 'The Knowledge-Creating Company', *Harvard Business Review*, Vol. 69, No. 6, pp 96–104

Nyer, P. U. (2000) 'An Investigation into Whether Complaining Can Cause Increased Consumer Satisfaction', *Journal of Consumer Marketing*, Vol. 17, No. 1, pp 9–19

O'Brien, L. and C. Jones (1995) 'Do Rewards Really Create Loyalty?', *Harvard Business Review*, May–June, pp 75–82

Ohmae, K. (1989) 'The Global Logic of Strategic Alliances', *Harvard Business Review*, March–April, Vol. 67, No. 2, 143–54

Oliver, R. L. (1980) 'A Cognitive Model of the Antecedants and Consequences of Satisfaction Decisions', *Journal of Marketing Research*, November, Vol. 17, pp 460–69

Oliver, R. (1996) 'Equity: How Consumers Interpret Fairness', in R. Oliver (ed.), *Satisfaction: A Behavioral Perspective on the Consumer*, McGraw Hill Series in Marketing, McGraw-Hill, New York, pp 193–215

Oliver, R. (1997) *Satisfaction: A Behavioral Perspective of the Consumer*, McGraw-Hill, New York

O'Neill, M., A. Palmer and R. Beggs (1998) 'The Effects of Survey Timing on Perceptions of Service Quality', *Managing Service Quality*, Vol. 8, No. 2, pp 126–32

Palmer, A., R. Beggs and C. McMullan (2000) 'Equity and Repurchase Intention Following Service Failure', *Journal of Services Marketing*, Vol. 14, No. 6

Palmer, A. and D. Bejou (1994) 'Buyer–Seller Relationships: A Conceptual Model and Empirical Investigation', *Journal of Marketing Management*, Summer, Vol. 6, No. 10, pp 495–512

Palmer, A. and D. Bejou (1995) 'The Role of Gender in the Development of Buyer–Seller Relationships', *International Journal of Bank Marketing*, Vol. 13, No. 3, pp 18–27

Parasuraman, A. (1991) *Marketing Research*, Addison Wesley, Reading, MA

Parasuraman, A., V. A. Zeithaml and L. Berry (1985) 'A Conceptual Model of Service Quality and its Implications for Future Research', *Journal of Marketing*, Fall, Vol. 49, pp 41–50

Parasuraman, A., V. A. Zeithaml and L. L. Berry (1988) 'SERVQUAL: A Multiple Item Scale for Measuring Consumer Perceptions of Service Quality', *Journal of Retailing*, Vol. 64, pp 12–37

Passikoff, R. (1997) 'The Limits of Customer Satisfaction', *Brandweek*, Vol. 38, No. 9, p 17

Paterson, P., L. Johnson and R. Spreng (1997) 'Modelling the Determinants of Customer Satisfaction for Business to Business Professional Services', *Journal of the Academy of Marketing Science*, Winter, Vol. 25, pp 4–17

Peppers, D. and M. Rodgers (1995) 'A New Marketing Paradigm: Share of Customer Not Market Share', *Planning Review*, Vol. 23, No. 2, p 14

Perrien, J., P. Filiatrault and L. Ricard (1992) 'Relationship Marketing and Commercial Banking: A Critical Analysis', *International Journal of Bank Marketing*, Vol. 10, No. 7, pp 25–9

Peters, T. J. and R. H. Waterman (1982) *In Search of Excellence: Lessons from America's Best Run Companies*, Harper & Row, New York

Pfeffer, J. and G. R. Salanick (1978) *The External Control of Organizations*, Harper & Row, New York

Piercy, N. (1985) *Marketing Organisation: An Analysis of Information Processing, Power and Politics*, Allen and Unwin, London

Piercy, N. (1990) 'Marketing Concepts and Actions: Implementing Marketing-led Strategic Change', *European Journal of Marketing*, Vol. 24, No. 2, pp 24–39

Piercy, N. (1997) *Market-led Strategic Change*, Butterworth-Heinemann, Oxford

Piercy, N. and M. Evans (1983) *Managing Marketing Information*, Croom Helm, London

Pitcher, A. (1985) 'The Role of Branding in International Advertising', *International Journal of Advertising*, Vol. 4, No. 3, pp 241–6

Porter, M. E. (1980) *Competitive Strategy: Techniques for Analyzing Industries and Competitors*, Free Press, New York

Porter, M. E. (1985) *Competitive Advantage*, Free Press, New York

Porter, M. and V. Millar (1985) 'How Information Gives You Competitive Advantage', *Harvard Business Review*, July–August, Vol. 85, pp 149–60

Quinn, J. B. (1992) *Intelligent Enterprise: A Knowledge and Service Based Paradigm for Industry*, Free Press, New York

Rafiq, M. and P. K. Ahmed (1998) 'A Customer-oriented Framework for Empowering Service Employees', *Journal of Services Marketing*, Vol. 12, No. 5, pp 379–93

Ramaswamy, R. (1996) *Design and Management of Service Processes: Keeping Customers for Life*, Addison-Wesley, Reading, MA, pp 362–3

Rathmell, J. M. (1974) *Marketing in the Service Sector*, Winthrop, Cambridge, MA

Reichheld, F. (1993) 'Loyalty Based Management', *Harvard Business Review*, Vol. 71, No. 2, pp 64–73

Reichheld, F. F. and W. E. J. Sasser (1990) 'Zero Defections', *Harvard Business Review*, Vol. 68, No. 5, pp 105–11

Reynoso, J. F. and B. Moores (1996) 'Internal Relationships', in F. Buttle (ed.), *Relationship Marketing: Theory and Practice*, Paul Chapman, London, pp 55–73

Ries, A. and J. Trout (1981) *Positioning*, McGraw-Hill, New York

Rogers, E. M. (1962) *Diffusion of Innovation*, Free Press, New York

Rushton, A. M. and D. J. Carson (1985) 'The Marketing of Services: Managing the Intangibles', *European Journal of Marketing*, Vol. 19, No. 3, pp 19–41

Sasser, W. E., R. P. Olsen and D. D. Wyckoff (1978) *Management of Service Operations: Texts, Cases, Readings*, Allyn and Bacon, Boston, MA

Schriver, S. (1997) 'Customer Loyalty: Going, Going …', *American Demographics*, Vol. 19, No. 9, pp 20–3

Shaw, K., J. Fenwick and A. Foreman (1993) 'Client and Contractor Roles in Local Government: Some Observations in Managing the Split', *Local Government Policy Making*, Vol. 20, No. 2, pp 22–7

Sheth, J. (1995) 'Searching For a New Definition of Relationship Marketing'. Paper presented to the 3rd International Colloquium in Relationship Marketing, July, Melbourne

Sheth, J. N. and A. Parvatiyar (1995) 'Relationship Marketing in Consumer Markets: Antecedents and Consequences', *Journal of the Academy of Marketing Science*, Vol. 23, No. 4, pp 255–71

Shoham, A. and F. Kropp (1998) 'Explaining International Performance: Marketing Mix, Planning and Their Interaction', *Marketing Intelligence and Planning*, Vol. 16, No. 2, pp 114–23

Shostack, G. L. (1977) 'Breaking Free From Product Marketing', *Journal of Marketing*, April, Vol. 41

Shostack, G. L. (1984) 'Designing Services that Deliver', *Harvard Business Review*, January–February, pp 133–9

Shostack G. L. (1985) 'Planning the Service Encounter', in J. A. Czepiel, M. R. Solomon and C. F. Suprenant (eds), *The Service Encounter*, Lexington Books, Lexington, MA, pp 243–54

Shostack, G. L. (1987) 'Service Positioning Through Structural Change', *Journal of Marketing*, Vol. 51, pp 34–43

Shrimp, T. A. and W. O. Bearden (1982) 'Warranty and Other Extrinsic Cue Effects on Consumers' Risk Perceptions', *Journal of Consumer Research*, June, Vol. 9, pp 38–46

Sieburgh, J. A. (1988) 'Yield Management at Work in the Royal Sonesta', *Lodging Hospitality*, October, pp 235–7

Silverman, G. (1997) 'How to Harness the Awesome Power of Word of Mouth', *Direct Marketing*, November, Vol. 60, No. 7, pp 32–6

Simon, H. (1996) 'You Don't Have to be German to be a "Hidden Champion"', *Business Strategy Review*, Vol. 7, No. 2, pp 1–12

Sisson, K. (1990) *Personnel Management in Britain*, Blackwell, Oxford

Smith, A. (1977) *The Wealth of Nations*, Penguin, Middlesex (first publication 1776)

Solomon, M. (1983) 'The Role of Products in Social Stimuli: A Symbolic Interactionism Perspective', *Journal of Consumer Research*, December, Vol. 10, pp 319–29

Solomon, M. and B. Buchanan (1991) 'A Role Theoretic Approach to Product Symbolism: Mapping of Consumption Constellation', *Journal of Business Research*, Vol. 22, No. 2, pp 95–109

Solomon, M. R. and S. J. Gould (1991) 'Benefitting from Structural Similarities among Personal Services', *Journal of Services Marketing*, Spring, Vol. 5, No. 2, pp 23–32

Solomon, M. R., C. Surprenant, J. A. Czepiel and E. G. Gutman (1985) 'A Role Theory Perspective on Dyadic Interactions: The Service Encounter', *Journal of Marketing*, Winter, Vol. 49, pp 99–111

Spreng, R. A., G. D. Harrell and R. D. Mackoy (1995) 'Service Recovery: Impact on Satisfaction and Intentions', *Journal of Services Marketing*, Vol. 9, No. 1, pp 15–23

Stanton, W. J. (1981) *Fundamentals of Marketing*, McGraw-Hill, New York

Stanworth, J. and C. Gray (eds) (1991) *Bolton 20 Years On: The Small Firm in the 1990's*, Paul Chapman Publishing, London

Staus, B. and B. Weinlich (1995) 'Process Oriented Measurement of Service Quality by Applying the Sequential Incident Method', Proceedings of the Workshop on Quality Management, Tilburg

Stodgill, R. M. (1974) *Handbook of Leadership: A Survey of Theory and Research*, Free Press, New York

Swan, J. E. and L. J. Combs (1976) 'Product Performance and Consumer Satisfaction: A New Concept', *Journal of Marketing*, Vol. 40 (April), pp 25–33

Taylor, S. (1994) 'Waiting for Service: The Relationship between Delays and Evaluation of Service', *Journal of Marketing*, Vol. 58, April, pp 56–69

Thomas, D. R. E. (1978) 'Strategy is Different in Service Businesses', *Harvard Business Review*, July–August, pp 158–65

*Times, The* (1999), 'Ryanair Shareholders Reduce Their Stakes Through Public Offerings', 29 May, p 26

Treacy, M. and F. Wiersema (1993) 'Customer Intimacy and Other Value Disciplines', *Harvard Business Review*, Vol. 71, No. 1, 84–93

Turnbull, P. W. and D. T. Wilson (1989) 'Developing and Protecting Profitable Customer Relationships', *Industrial Marketing Management*, Vol. 18, 233–8

US Department of Transportation (1990) 'Airline Marketing Practices: Travel Agencies, Frequent Flier Programmes and Computer Reservation Systems', February

Vandermerwe, S. and S. Birley (1997) 'The Corporate Entrepreneur: Leading Organisational Transformation', *Long Range Planning*, Vol. 30, No. 3, pp 345–52

Varey, R. (1995) 'A Model of Internal Marketing for Building and Sustaining a Competitive Service Advantage', *Journal of Marketing Management*, Vol. 11, No. 1–3, pp 41–54

Varey, R. J. and B. R. Lewis (1999) 'A Broadened Conception of Internal Marketing, *European Journal of Marketing*, Vol. 33, No. 9/10, pp 926–44

Wakefield, K. L. and J. J. Inman (1993) 'Who Are the Price Vigilantes? An Investigation of Differentiating Characteristics Influencing Price Information Processing', *Journal of Retailing*, Vol. 69, pp. 216–33

Walsh, K. (1991) 'Competitive Tendering for Local Authority Services – Initial Experiences', Department of the Environment, HMSO, London

Warnaby, G. and B. J. J. Davies (1997) 'Cities as Service Factories? Using the Servuction System for Marketing Cities as Shopping Destinations', *International Journal of Retail & Distribution Management*, Vol. 25 No. 6–7, pp. 204–10

Webster, F. E. (1992) 'The Changing Role of Marketing in the Corporation', *Journal of Marketing*, October, Vol. 56, pp 1–17

Williamson, O. (1975) 'Markets and Hierarchies: Analysis and Antitrust Implications', Free Press, New York

Williamson, O. (1993) 'Calculativeness, Trust, And Economic Organisation', *Journal of Law and Economics*, Vol. 34, pp 453–500

Williamson, O. E. (1985) *The Economic Institutions of Capitalism*, Free Press, New York

Wilson, R. and C. Gilligan (1997) *Strategic Marketing Management*, Butterworth-Heinemann, London

Wind, Y. J. (1982) *Product Policy: Concepts, Methods and Strategy*, Addison-Wesley, Reading, MA

Wind, Y. J. (1986) 'Models for Marketing Planning and Decision Making', in V. P. Buell (ed.), *Handbook of Modern Marketing*, 2nd edition, McGraw-Hill, New York pp 49.1–49.12

Witt, C. and A. Muhlemann (1955) 'Service Quality in Airlines', *Tourism Economics*, Vol. 1, No. 1, pp 33–49

Wood, P. A. (1987) 'Producer Services and Economic Change, Some Canadian Evidence', in K. Chapman and G. Humphreys (eds), *Technological Change and Economic Policy*, London, Blackwell

Woodruff, R. B., E. R. Cadotte and R. L. Jenkins (1983) 'Modelling Consumer Satisfaction Processes Using Experience Based Norms', *Journal of Marketing Research*, August, Vol. 20, pp 296–304

WTTC (1996) *Progress and Priorities 1996*, World Travel and Tourism Council, Brussels

Wyckham, R. G. *et al* (1975) 'Marketing of Services: An Evaluation of the Theory', *European Journal of Marketing*, Vol. 9, No. 1, pp 59–67

Zeithaml, V. A. (1981) 'How the Consumers' Evaluation Processes Differ between Goods and Services', in J. H. Donnelly and W. R. George (eds), *Marketing of Services*, American Marketing Association, Chicago, IL

Zeithaml, V. A., L. L. Berry and A. Parasuraman (1993) 'The Nature and Determinants of Customer Expectations of Service', *Journal of the Academy of Marketing Science*, Vol. 21, No. 1, pp 1–12

Zeithaml, V. A., L. L. Berry and A. Parasuraman (1996) 'The Behavioral Consequences of Service Quality', *Journal of Marketing*, Vol. 60, pp 31–46

Zeithaml, V. A., A. Parasuraman and L. L. Berry (1985) 'Problems and Strategies in Services Marketing', *Journal of Marketing*, Spring, Vol. 49, pp 33–46

Zeithaml, V. A., A. Parasuraman and L. L. Berry (1990) *Delivering Quality Service*, Free Press, New York

Zeithaml, V. A., A. Parasuraman and L. L. Berry (1990) 'Delivering Service Quality: Balancing Customer Perceptions and Expectations', Free Press, New York

# Index of companies and brands

# Index of authors cited

# Index of subjects